D1132862

A BIBLIOGRAPHY OF
THE WRITINGS OF NOAH WEBSTER

A BIBLIOGRAPHY OF THE WRITINGS OF

NOAH WEBSTER

Compiled by

EMILY ELLSWORTH FORD SKEEL

Edited by

EDWIN H. CARPENTER, JR.

NEW YORK

The New York Public Library

1958

Library of Congress Catalog Card Number 57–10131

Printed in the United States of America

TO THE MEMORY OF ROSWELL SKEEL, JR.

They, who one another keep

Alive, ne'er parted be.

JOHN DONNE

TABLE OF CONTENTS

LIST OF ILLUSTRATIONS xiii

COMPILER'S PREFACE xv

EDITOR'S PREFACE xix

CHRONOLOGY OF NOAH WEBSTER xxv

IDENTIFICATION OF NEWSPAPERS CITED xxvii

IDENTIFICATION OF BIBLIOGRAPHICAL CITATIONS xxxi

IDENTIFICATION OF LOCATION SYMBOLS xxxiii

ADDITIONS AND CORRECTIONS xxxviii

Section One: THE GRAMMATICAL INSTITUTE

PART ONE: SPELLER

A. *The Original Text*, 1783–1787 5
B. *The American Spelling Book*, 1787–1804 10
C. *The American Spelling Book, Revised*, 1804–1832 36
D. *Versions of the American Spelling Book after Expiration of the 1818 Copyright*, 1833–1843 78
E. *The Elementary Spelling Book*, 1829–1845 85
F. *Adapted and Translated Spellers*, 1847–1887 129
G. *Primers Derivative from the Speller*, 1786–1843 135

PART TWO: GRAMMAR

A. *The Original Text*, 1784–1785 141
B. *The First Revision*, 1787 143
C. *The Second Revision*, 1787–1806 144
D. *Philosophical and Practical Grammar*, 1807–1822 151
E. *Improved Grammar*, 1831–1843 154
F. *Derivative Grammars*, 1788–1831 156

Table of Contents

PART THREE: READER

- A. *The Original Text*, 1785–1786 — 161
- B. *An American Selection*, 1787–1804 — 163
- C. *An American Selection, Revised*, 1804–1816 — 185
- D. *Instructive and Entertaining Lessons*, 1835 — 190
- E. *Derivative Readers*, 1790–1836 — 191

Section Two: OTHER TEXT BOOKS

PART ONE: ELEMENTS OF USEFUL KNOWLEDGE, 1802–1815 — 199

PART TWO: LETTERS TO A YOUNG GENTLEMAN, 1823 — 207

PART THREE: BIOGRAPHY FOR THE USE OF SCHOOLS, 1830 — 209

PART FOUR: HISTORY OF THE UNITED STATES, 1832–1841 — 210

PART FIVE: THE TEACHER, 1836–1839 — 218

PART SIX: MANUAL OF USEFUL STUDIES, 1839–1842 — 220

Section Three: DICTIONARIES

GENERAL NOTE ON THE DICTIONARIES — 225

PART ONE: COMPENDIOUS DICTIONARY, 1806 — 227

PART TWO: COMMON SCHOOL DICTIONARY, 1807 — 229

PART THREE: AMERICAN DICTIONARY, UNABRIDGED

- A. *Prospectuses and Preliminaries*, 1806–1826 — 231
- B. *The First Edition*, 1828 — 233
- C. *Prospectuses and Preliminaries for a Second Edition*, 1838–1841 — 235
- D. *The Second Edition*, 1841 — 237
- E. *Later Editions*, 1844–1845 — 238

PART FOUR: DICTIONARY OF THE ENGLISH LANGUAGE, 1830 — 240

PART FIVE: AMERICAN DICTIONARY, ABRIDGED

- A. *Webster's Abridgment*, 1829–1845 — 244
- B. *Worcester's Abridgment*, 1829–1841 — 249
- C. *Worcester's Abridgment, Revised*, 1841–1846 — 254

PART SIX: PRIMARY SCHOOL DICTIONARY, 1833–1845 256

PART SEVEN: RELATED DICTIONARIES AND POSTHUMOUS ABRIDGMENTS
A. *The Elementary Dictionary*, 1844? 260
B. *Hawaiian Translation*, 1845 261
C. *Abridgments Published by Huntington and Savage*, 1845–1846 262

Section Four: PHILOLOGICAL, DIDACTIC, AND RELIGIOUS WORKS

PART ONE: DISSERTATIONS ON THE ENGLISH LANGUAGE, 1789 267

PART TWO: THE PROMPTER, 1791–1839 271

PART THREE: LETTER TO THE GOVERNORS, 1798 291

PART FOUR: LETTER TO DR. RAMSAY, 1807 292

PART FIVE: PECULIAR DOCTRINES OF THE GOSPEL, 1809–1811 293

PART SIX: LETTER TO JOHN PICKERING, 1817 297

PART SEVEN: VALUE OF THE BIBLE, 1834 298

PART EIGHT: BRIEF VIEW, 1834? 299

PART NINE: MISTAKES AND CORRECTIONS, 1837 301

PART TEN: OBSERVATIONS ON LANGUAGE AND COMMERCE, 1839 302

Section Five: POLITICAL WORKS

PART ONE: SKETCHES OF AMERICAN POLICY, 1785 305

PART TWO: EXAMINATION OF THE CONSTITUTION, 1787 308

PART THREE: ATTENTION, OR NEW THOUGHTS, 1789 309

PART FOUR: EFFECTS OF SLAVERY, 1793 310

PART FIVE: REVOLUTION IN FRANCE CONSIDERED, 1794 311

PART SIX: TEN LETTERS TO PRIESTLEY, 1800 313

PART SEVEN: A ROD FOR THE FOOL'S BACK, 1800 314

PART EIGHT: LETTER TO GENERAL HAMILTON, 1800 316

Table of Contents

PART NINE: MISCELLANEOUS PAPERS, 1802 319

PART TEN: ADDRESS TO THE CITIZENS OF CONNECTICUT, 1803 321

PART ELEVEN: LETTER TO DANIEL WEBSTER, 1837 322

PART TWELVE: APPEAL TO AMERICANS—VOICE OF WISDOM, 1838? 323

Section Six: PUBLISHED SPEECHES

PART ONE: ORATIONS AND LECTURES, 1776–1786 327

PART TWO: FOURTH OF JULY ORATIONS, 1798–1814 328

PART THREE: AGRICULTURAL SOCIETY ADDRESS, 1818 330

PART FOUR: AMHERST CORNERSTONE ADDRESS, 1820 331

Section Seven: MISCELLANEOUS WORKS

PART ONE: TWO CARRIER'S ADDRESSES, 1790 335

PART TWO: COLLECTION OF ESSAYS, 1790 337

PART THREE: TWO UNFINISHED PROJECTS, 1798, 1801 343

PART FOUR: EPIDEMIC AND PESTILENTIAL DISEASES, 1799–1800 345

PART FIVE: WEBSTER GENEALOGY, 1836–1876 350

PART SIX: COLLECTION OF PAPERS, 1843 352

PART SEVEN: ADVERTISEMENTS, RECOMMENDATIONS, AND DEFENSES OF WEBSTER'S PUBLICATIONS

A. *Education of Youth*, 1807 355

B. *Series of Books*, 1830?–1832? 356

C. *Attacks on Lyman Cobb*, 1831–1835 357

D. *To the Friends of Literature*, 1836 359

E. *Commendations*, 1841? 360

PART EIGHT: POSTHUMOUS PUBLICATIONS, 1881–1954 362

Section Eight: WORKS EDITED BY WEBSTER

PART ONE: THE NEW ENGLAND PRIMER, 1787–1818 367

PART TWO: WINTHROP'S JOURNAL, 1790 371

Table of Contents

PART THREE : COLLECTION OF PAPERS ON BILIOUS FEVERS, 1795–1796 373

PART FOUR : THE HOLY BIBLE (AND NEW TESTAMENT), 1833–1841 377

Section Nine: PERIODICALS

GENERAL NOTE ON PERIODICALS 385

PART ONE : PERIODICALS EDITED BY WEBSTER

A. *American Magazine*, 1787–1788 387
B. *The Minerva and the Herald*, 1793–1797 398
C. *The Commercial Advertiser and the Spectator*, 1797–1803 413

PART TWO : WEBSTER'S CONTRIBUTIONS TO PROCEEDINGS OF LEARNED SOCIETIES, 1793–1810 430

PART THREE : WEBSTER'S CONTRIBUTIONS TO OTHER PERIODICALS, 1771–1843 433

PART FOUR : NEWSPAPER CONTROVERSIES INVOLVING WEBSTER

A. *"Dilworth's Ghost" Controversy*, 1784–1785 483
B. *Philadelphia Controversies*, 1787 485
C. *"Argus"-Thomas Greenleaf Controversy*, 1794 490
D. *Controversies over the Jay Treaty*, 1794–1795 491
E. *Philadelphia vs. New York Controversy*, 1795 495
F. *"Calm Observer" Controversy*, 1795 496
G. *"Harrington" Controversy*, 1796 496
H. *Controversy about Joshua Coit*, 1798 498
I. *Controversy over British Atrocities*, 1798 499
J. *Controversies with Lyman Cobb*, 1827–1841 500
K. *Attack on Worcester's Dictionary*, 1834–1835 509
L. *Reactions to "A Voice of Wisdom,"* 1837–1838 510
M. *"Americanus"-Chapin Controversy*, 1841–1842 516

APPENDIX A : CORPORATE WRITINGS BY OR PROBABLY BY WEBSTER 521

APPENDIX B : WEBSTER'S LECTURES AND SPEECHES 531

APPENDIX C : PUBLISHED PERSONAL LETTERS OF WEBSTER 540

APPENDIX D : UNFINISHED AND UNPUBLISHED WORKS 558

APPENDIX E : DUBIOUS AND ERRONEOUS ASCRIPTIONS TO WEBSTER 562

Table of Contents

APPENDIX F: WORKS RELATED TO THE SPELLER, PLAGIARISMS, ETC. 565

APPENDIX G: WEBSTER'S PUBLIC SERVICE 575

APPENDIX H: ANNE ROYALL AND NOAH WEBSTER 586

APPENDIX I: PORTRAITS AND STATUES OF NOAH WEBSTER 588

APPENDIX J: SELECTED REFERENCES ON THE LIFE AND WRITINGS OF NOAH WEBSTER 594

APPENDIX K: GEOGRAPHICAL DIRECTORY OF PRINTERS, PUBLISHERS, BOOKSELLERS, STEREOTYPERS, ETC. 601

Illustrations (following page 616)

INDEX 621

LIST OF ILLUSTRATIONS

(following page 616)

ILLUSTRATIONS FOR THE SPELLER

PLATE I

The "porcupine portrait" (Title 16 and later)

PLATE II

Young and M'Culloch's set of fable cuts (Title 7 and later)

PLATE III

Thomas and Andrews' set (Title 16 and later)

PLATE IV

Hudson and Goodwin's first set (Title 17 and later)

PLATE V

Hudson and Goodwin's second set, by Asa W. Lay (Title 26 and later)

PLATE VI

Samuel Campbell's set, by Isaac Sanford (Title 28)

PLATE VII

Samuel Campbell's frontispiece, by Alexander Anderson (Title 28)

PLATE VIII

Bonsal and Niles' frontispiece (Title 69 and later)

PLATE IX

Hudson and Goodwin's third set, by Zadoc Howe and William Wadsworth (Title 55 and later)

PLATE X

Hudson and Goodwin's fourth set, by Abner Reed (Title 62 and later)

PLATE XI

Bonsal and Niles' set (Title 69 and later)

PLATE XII

Martin and Ogden's set (Title 79)

PLATE XIII
First set by Alexander Anderson (Title 89 and later)

PLATE XIV
Fessenden, Holbrook, and Porter's set (Title 119 and later)

PLATE XV
Second set by Alexander Anderson (Title 178 and later)

PLATE XVI
Hudson and Company's set, by John W. Barber (Title 200 and later)

PLATE XVII
Cuts for the *Elementary Spelling Book* (Title 273 and later)

PLATE XVIII
First frontispiece by Alexander Anderson (Title 178 and later)

TITLE-PAGES

PLATE XIX
First edition of the speller, 1783 (Title 1)

PLATE XX
First known edition entitled *American Spelling Book*, 1788 (Title 11)

PLATE XXI
The model copy of the *American Spelling Book*, revised, 1804 (Title 89)

PLATE XXII
First edition of the *Elementary Spelling Book*, 1829 (Title 261)

PLATE XXIII
First edition of the reader entitled *American Selection*, 1787 (Title 452)

PLATE XXIV
Webster's first dictionary, 1806 (Title 577)

PLATE XXV
First edition of the unabridged dictionary, 1828 (Title 583)

PLATE XXVI
Mastheads of newspapers edited by Webster (Titles 789, 791–793)

COMPILER'S PREFACE

THIS WORK, *begun before the publication in 1912 of my Mother's appreciation of my great-grandfather,* Notes on the Life of Noah Webster, *was originally aimed to supply an inclusive list of Webster's writings either in books or newspapers. Seeking all light possible on the editions, often undated and elusive, of his Blue Back Speller, it was found that letters to or from him would sometimes throw light on a hazy issue's provenance or actuality. So it came about that much of his correspondence was gradually incorporated into notes, which it is hoped may be helpful in proving or invalidating the findings entered here. Finally, it seemed to the compiler that, in view of the kindness of many who, though strangers, were yet generous givers of their manuscript or printed material, a nearly complete inclusion of such might be expedient. For Erwin S. Shoemaker's scholarly book on Webster's works and Harry R. Warfel's genial biography of the man, taken together, having covered the ground very thoroughly, it is not likely that Webster will again claim attention as well as space on modern diminishing bookshelves, where the Merriam successors to his original octavo of 1806 already occupy an ample ducal estate which their vast usefulness alone justifies.*

Webster himself seemed to suggest inclusiveness. Any man who began to write for the press in 1782 and in a disillusioned moment belonging to ardent youth recorded the futility of such activity and his intention to desist thereafter, yet who went on expressing himself on every imaginable topic till within a few days of his death in 1843, can hardly have his works listed in a bibliography without some attention being given to the background of his so widely expressed opinions. For no matter how greatly his own ideas changed (a thing he never hid from the public eye) —whether it was from leaning on English grammarians to complete self-assertion of his validities, or from an early faith in political liberalism through a firm yet middle course of Federalism ending in unpredictable conservatisms; or, again, from a religious latitudinarianism finding anchorage in the strictest Calvinistic belief—the fabric of all his works was woven of definite threads constantly reappearing. However often and cogently he was called to account for inconsistencies between his dictionaries and his spellers, he himself ever emphasized his "system" as fundamental to his life purpose, first, to develop a national spirit in language, education, literature, and public polity, and, second, to encourage the nascent American, that "new man," to independence from foreign leading strings. As early as May 25, 1786, he had written to Timothy Pickering: "A national language is a national tie, and what country wants it more than America?"

It is a curious fact that he blazed a new trail in several directions: he worked to obtain copyright earlier than any other individual before 1790 and resurrected the question in Congress in the 1830's, materially bettering the terms; he made a semi-weekly newspaper for country circulation out of his daily by transferring matter en bloc; he first issued a simple manual of citizenship to be read or learned by children. The patriotic orations of Americans were placed in his reader side by side with the oratorical wheelhorses of Rome. He early counseled good roads and strong bridges for commercial growth and prosperity. During his service in the Massachusetts legislature he urged public accountings to ensure against dishonest practices. He proclaimed the dangers inherent in party spirit more wholly and far more persistently than any other publicist or politician. "Noah Webster may not have been a great man in his generation," Horace E. Scudder *wrote of him, "but he had a singular faculty of being the first in time in many departments of literary industry, and constantly to have anticipated other people."*

It were unmannerly for a descendant of no achievement to appraise a forebear of considerable, the more so as this book in no wise springs from ancestor worship. But in viewing Noah Webster's long life of energy, toil and enterprise, I cannot avoid seeing his little attendant shade,

Rebecca Greenleaf Webster, nor making my obeisance to that tiny mercurial one of my great-grandmothers. Coming from an opulent and vivacious milieu in Boston, she became the chief ministrant to her laborious husband, living harmoniously, effectively, and lovingly with a mate of no humor, finding an escape in old age through novel reading, once abhorred and condemned in his writings as a temptation of the evil one. Not in vain did she spring from Gallic blood tempered by that of the serious Huguenots. Had she quailed at her post Webster's life and career must have been quite other than they proved.

In taking leave of her husband as a daily companion I am glad to state, without fear or favor, that my opinion of him as a man, a worker, a thinker, a planner, and a doer has risen year by year. His integrity was well nigh unimpeachable, and on that rock, as well as his earnest desire to serve his country and his time, is based my revering admiration.

No compilation of Webster's work could boast of finer sponsors than this. First instigated by the late Wilberforce Eames—generous sower of seeds in lesser minds—his inspiring power and quiet generosity can be likened only to a great dynamo whose diurnal force is transmitted far and wide by the pressure of a great river; that my small cylinders and wheels should have yielded without demur to such a thrust is not surprising, even though they were to take me into forgotten regions. Forgotten but not altogether unvisited, for with the close companionship through childhood of my chum brother Paul, and impelled by his never-failing eagerness to share, I had, as amanuensis, skirted and drifted along the coasts of small bibliographical islands in the shape of check-lists, as gifts to our Father, before we either of us were well into our teens. Through the later years, while camping alone in a tiny field and working it intensively, untrained in the infinite and delicate precisions of modern bibliography, I received unstinted help and encouragement from many librarians and their staffs. No hint, by so much as a lifted eyebrow or a dropped lid, was ever conveyed to me that anyone questioned "que diable allait-elle faire dans cette galère?" so I pursued the game with only inner misgivings of my skill in gunning. To those Chiefs of greater and lesser book collections and to their lieutenants I owe and feel gratitude for such forbearance.

Above all, to three Brahmins of bibliography whom I am blest in counting as friends and advisers do I gladly make a salaam: Harry M. Lydenberg, Lawrence C. Wroth, and Robert W. G. Vail, who, glancing over my edifice, have by their candor, as rare as their knowledge, advised the removal of redundancies, excrescences, and superfluities; as well as to its one and only godmother, Margaret Bingham Stillwell, whose own works set an example of purism modified by delicate humor and grace. To Harry R. Warfel I owe the generous gift of transcripts of many letters exhumed by his patience and resourcefulness. To my assistants Helen Mouat, Effie Anne Lindley, and Hester Meigs my special appreciation is tendered.

It is a keen satisfaction to avow how much there is due to the skillful and ever-recurring helpfulness of others. The New York Public Library, the Library of Congress, the American Antiquarian Society, and Yale University Library have, through their Chiefs and their staffs, proven staves indeed to the pilgrim-quester for nearly fifty years. Other librarians and collectors have alike given lavishly of their lore and ladings. If a few are singled out for acknowledgement it is only because a special sense of gratitude is felt toward them. But there is a host of others, institutions and individuals, to whom an immeasurable debt is owing, far exceeding any power to acknowledge.

If, paraphrasing Shakespeare, this is a book whereon the wild time grows, it has been throughout its long span a source of unending pleasure to the compiler. As was wittily said of Browning's poetry, it shows her best foot and her worst foot and the tag end of her (prosaic) dreams.

EMILY ELLSWORTH FORD SKEEL

EDITOR'S PREFACE

THE COMPILER has already mentioned, in quoting from his first biographer, that Noah Webster holds a pioneer position in several aspects of American intellectual endeavor—epidemiology and statistics, for example, to name but two in the non-academic realm. Interesting as it is to find Webster in the van in so many different activities, his chief significance is that he is a pervasive element in the life of every user of American English, whether or not he realizes it. The effect of Webster's dictionaries has been incalculable, beginning with those he compiled single-handed and coming down to those of today, prepared by large staffs of specialists. The fact that even dictionaries compiled "from scratch" assume the name of Webster is ample evidence of its potency, and better critics than the compiler and editor have made clear the almost incredible influence of this one man on the spelling, definition, and pronunciation of American English.

Working alongside the dictionaries in exerting this wide-spread influence was the spelling book, the success of which gave Webster the income that enabled him to devote years to lexicographical work. Again, critics and literary historians have often pointed out the major role of this textbook in American elementary education. Different methods and approaches prevail today, but many successive student generations learned their spelling and other lessons from it. The work is still in print, though its present sale arises mostly from nostalgia, for those who learned from it have not yet all left this world, by any means.

In his biography of Webster Harry R. Warfel estimates that "more than fifty impressions, some of them of 25,000 copies each, appeared before 1800, one hundred by 1814, and one hundred fifty by 1829." This is put forth as a conservative estimate, and the user of the present list will observe that the compiler's researches have markedly raised these figures. Warfel goes on to suggest that some twenty million copies had been sold by the last-named date, though the estimates of other writers sometimes do not reach that figure until about the time of Webster's death, in 1843. At any rate, by Webster's death (the point at which recording of the spellers is broken off herein) the various versions of the work had sold many, many millions, and there is fairly general agreement that before its course was run it achieved a sale of about a hundred million. Thus bulk as well as quality gives the speller a position in American history which cannot be ignored.

Despite the stupendous number of spelling books printed, the copies located herein for any given edition are not many. It is a commonplace in book collecting and bibliography that books much read by children, whether from love or duty, are worn out and disappear. Because of their cheapness the speller, grammar, and reader were often discarded when they became worn or old, and this is only to a small degree offset by the sentiment which prompted some individuals to keep the family's old school books. Less wear, continued usefulness, bulk, and relatively high price, however, kept dictionaries from being freely discarded, and it is striking how many copies are to be found of the first edition of the unabridged dictionary. This is not to say, though, that some of the dictionaries have not become rare. Doubtless there are many additional copies of Webster's writings, especially the spellers and dictionaries, in attics, private collections, and small libraries, probably including examples of some editions listed hypothetically herein, or not listed at all.

The New York Public Library is the most important repository of Websteriana, both in bulk and in significance of copies—that is, copies which were Webster's own or have other association values. Possession of the major portion of Webster's personal and business papers makes this collection outstanding. The library of Yale—Webster's Alma Mater—also has many association copies and manuscripts among its strong Webster holdings, and has the second-ranking collection. Not by relative rank but geographically these further libraries are cited as strong in this field: the Boston Public, Harvard, the American Antiquarian Society, the G. and C. Merriam Company, Amherst, the Connecticut State Library, the Watkinson Library (Trinity College), the Connecticut Historical Society, the New Haven Colony Historical Society, Columbia University, the Library of Congress, and the Henry Ford Museum at Dearborn. Of these, the Connecticut Historical Society particularly owns significant manuscript material. Several other libraries are strong in Webster titles which fall within specialized holdings limited by date, subject, or place of printing.

As indicated in the compiler's preface, the inception of the present work goes back to a checklist which she and her brother Paul compiled in 1882 as a Christmas present for their father. Twenty years later she edited her mother's book on Noah Webster, and the compilation of the checklist therein and a suggestion from Wilberforce Eames crystallized her determination to assemble as complete a bibliography as humanly possible. The omission of large numbers of later editions from the Sabin bibliography in expectation of the publication of the present work gave her a sense of responsibility for its completion.

Mrs. Skeel had at first no conception of the size of the task she was undertaking. The number of editions of Webster's works which she found, particularly of the speller, and the number of his known or surmised contributions to periodicals multiplied hugely, and the bulk of her notes grew accordingly. At the time she did most of her research there was no good biography of Webster, and she felt it wise to incorporate as annotations long excerpts from his unpublished letters, with the idea of making the information available to scholars and the general public. This and certain other material which she included became less needed after the appearance of two good modern biographies and various monographs and articles about Webster, but these passages were not removed by her from the manuscript, partly because time and energy were devoted to further research and partly because Mrs. Skeel took the view, as in her work on Mason Locke Weems, that she was constructing and filling a storehouse from which scholars and non-scholars alike could draw what they wanted.

In 1940 the compiler had the work nearly ready to print, but the dislocations resulting from the war and the weak spots which were disclosed in putting the manuscript in final form delayed publication. She then thought in terms of reducing the work to a mere skeletal list of editions and of leaving unpublished the material on Webster's journalistic activities, placing the files thereon in The New York Public Library. The first serious health problem in a long and active life, however, caused her to abandon this plan; eventually the Library accepted the whole body of her notes and manuscript, under an arrangement for the editing and publication of the material, and the undersigned was engaged to discharge the task. This was felt appropriate because of the Library's preeminent Webster holdings and because of its long and intimate association with the Ford family, from whom came most of its Websteriana.

Because of the availability of the other works on Webster which have been mentioned and because of printing costs, the editor has effected the excisions which the compiler planned to make. The result, of course, is not precisely what she would have produced had she finished the work herself, for unless the two have worked closely together (which is not the case here) it is impossible for one person to complete a task begun by another in the exact form the originator intended.

The great length of time involved in the compilation and the shift, without communication, from the compiler to the editor make it difficult to insure that adequate acknowledgment is made of help received. It has seemed best not to attempt to add to the names given in the compiler's preface, relying on the understanding of the scores of librarians, collectors, book dealers, professors, and others who have cheerfully given assistance to the compiler and the editor but are not mentioned by name. Obviously, the libraries named above have all been drawn upon heavily, with constant help from their staffs. They have also been generous in allowing quotation from letters and other documents in their possession. The editor wishes to echo the compiler's gratitude to Miss Helen Mouat, who served as the connecting link between the two, and to add his thanks to the several officers and staff members of The New York Public Library who directed and assisted his work.

The editor has followed closely the arrangement of material projected by the compiler, though, at the risk of inconsistency, he has created one subdivision (Published Speeches) which is defined by form rather than by content. The following information about the mechanics of presentation may assist the user:

Criteria for establishment of entries: Copies of the same text are recorded as different editions if on the title-page there is a difference in the year, the city, the publisher, or the printer, or if there is a difference in pagination or other evidence of a resetting of type or recasting of all or part of stereotype plates. Versions with lesser differences in collation or title-page differences consisting only of a change in a firm name or an added phrase are given as a subdivision of the prime entry. Differences which could occur in binding or rebinding are recorded in annotations.

Title entry. Line endings, different sizes and faces of type, and rules or ornaments are not indicated, unless necessary to distinguish between identical wordings. Although it does not represent the compiler's preference, it has proved necessary to adopt for the title entry the Library of Congress system of minimum capitalization. In the imprint advertising phrases, street addresses, and added vendors' names are normally omitted. Swash brackets are used to indicate square brackets which are found in the original. Successive entries are recorded with a dash to represent repetition of title, author's name, etc.

Description. The compiler did not record the true collation of each book, either by signature marks or by folding. It has not seemed feasible to retrace her steps to fill in this information, since the vast majority of the works listed were stereotyped, both literally and figuratively, and since they are of a period recent enough that the signaturing does not have the significance that it did in earlier centuries. The dimension given is the page height, to the nearest centimeter; it has not been possible to work back over the compiler's course to ascertain if each measurement is that of the largest known copy. Where two dimensions are given, as for broadsides, the first is the height.

For pagination the editor has, in the few cases in which the situation occurs, followed the modern practice of not recording initial roman pagination if it is part of the same numerical sequence as the arabic pagination. Pages recorded in parentheses bear letter press but are not numbered. Terminal blank pages are not recorded, and no attempt is made to distinguish binder's end papers from those which are an integral part of the book. Bibliographical purists to the contrary, in describing the contents of a book a formula such as [1]–100 has been used to indicate that the first page is unnumbered, the numbering beginning on the second.

The most serious lack in the description of the books is that of an indication of the original binding. Fortunately a general statement will take care of most of them, especially the speller, the grammar, and the reader, which constitute the majority of the entries. The standard publisher's binding for these—and for many of Webster's other works—was paper-covered boards with a leather or cloth spine, unstamped. During the earlier part of the period concerned binders' "boards" really were boards: thin pieces of wood rather than pasteboard or other composite material. They were covered with paper, usually the blue kind known as "cartridge paper," for which reason the major work came to be known as "the blue-back speller." At first the covers were blank, but later they came to bear letter press. Where it is known that publishers offered other forms of binding these have been mentioned, either as a separate annotation or under the advertisements cited.

Location of copies. These are fuller and, subject to the margin allowed human error, more accurate than locations recorded in the National Union Catalog, Evans' *American Bibliography*, and other sources. Familiarity with the vast number of almost-identical title-pages of Webster's works (and a few which *are* identical in title-page but not in content) has enabled the compiler and editor to uncover many errors in the locations of copies given in other reference tools. In locating copies a special collection in the institution has not been mentioned unless its holdings are not recorded in the general card catalogue (e.g., the Sinclair Hamilton collection at Princeton). Some copies located were seen by the editor but may not yet be found in the institution's card catalogue; this is particularly true of Columbia and Rutgers universities. Locations in the Mercantile Library, Philadelphia, recorded by Mrs. Skeel many years ago, have not been verified because the collection was not available at the time of editing. Copies owned by individuals are listed only if unique.

Except for one or two which have been created by analogy, the location symbols used are those given in the fifth edition (1953) of *Symbols used in the National Union Catalog of the Library of Congress.* Identification of the symbols used here will be found on pages xxxiii-xxxvii. The word "imperfect" in the location of copies is used in its bibliographical sense: that is, one or more leaves of the book as printed are missing—copies not described as imperfect may in fact be mutilated or in poor condition.

Bibliographical citations. References to Evans, Sabin, and other standard bibliographies are by entry number unless preceded by "p." Identification of the surnames and catch titles used will be found on pages xxxi-xxxii.

References to Webster's personal papers. Footnotes have not been made for each reference to an entry in Webster's diaries, account books, or memoranda; all of these are in the Manuscript Division, New York Public Library, unless otherwise described. The diaries are printed in Emily E. Ford's *Notes on the Life of Noah Webster,* which is cited herein as Ford's *Notes.*

EDWIN H. CARPENTER, JR.

CHRONOLOGY OF NOAH WEBSTER

1758, October 16	Born in West Hartford, Connecticut.
1774, September	Entered Yale; graduated September, 1778.
1779–1780	Taught school in Hartford and West Hartford.
1780–1781	Read law in Litchfield, Connecticut; admitted to bar, April, 1781.
1781, July–October	Conducted school in Sharon, Connecticut.
September	Received M.A., Yale.
1782–1783	Conducted school in Goshen, New York; compiled speller.
1783, spring	Returned to Hartford; practiced law and wrote.
October	Published Part I of the *Grammatical Institute*.
1784, March	Published Part II.
1785, February	Published Part III.
March	Published *Sketches of American Policy*.
1785–1786	Traveled to further copyright legislation; lectured.
1786, December	Moved to Philadelphia; taught and wrote.
1787, November	Moved to New York; published the *American Magazine*.
1789, May	Published *Dissertations on the English Language*; moved to Hartford; practiced law and wrote; served on city council.
October 26	Married Rebecca Greenleaf (seven children who survived infancy).
1790, July	Published *Collection of Essays and Fugitiv Writings*.

Chronology of Webster

1791, October	Published *The Prompter*, anonymously.
1793, August	Moved to New York; edited Federalist newspapers.
1798, April	Moved to New Haven; wrote and did research; served on city council and in state legislature.
1799, December	Published *Brief History of Epidemic and Pestilential Diseases.*
1800	Began lexicographical work.
1803, November	Disposed of interest in New York newspapers.
1806, February	Published *Compendious Dictionary.*
1812, September	Moved to Amherst; farmed and worked on dictionaries; served in state legislature; helped found Amherst College.
1822, summer	Moved to New Haven; worked on dictionaries.
1823, September	Received LL.D., Yale (and from Middlebury College, 1830).
1824–1825	Research trip to France and England.
1825, January	Completed unabridged dictionary, Cambridge, England.
1827, July	Series of controversies with Lyman Cobb began.
1828, November	Published unabridged dictionary.
1830, December	Visited Washington to support copyright legislation.
1832, August	Published *History of the United States.*
1833, September	Published revision of Holy Bible.
1841, March	Published second edition of unabridged dictionary.
1843, May	Published *Collection of Papers.*
May 28	Died in New Haven.

IDENTIFICATION OF NEWSPAPERS CITED

This list includes only titles that do not indicate the place of publication, or which are not identified when mentioned.

American Apollo	Boston
American Citizen	New York
American Daily Advertiser	Philadelphia
American Farmer	Baltimore
American Mercury	Hartford
American Minerva	New York
American Traveller	Boston
Argus	New York
Aurora	Philadelphia
Carey and Markland's Daily Advertiser	Philadelphia
Chelsea Courier	Norwich, Conn.
Christian Advocate and Journal	New York
Christian Watchman	Boston
Chronicle of the Church	New Haven
Columbia Republican	Hudson, N. Y.
Columbian Centinel	Boston
Columbian Chronicle	Georgetown, D.C.
Columbian Herald	Charleston
Columbian Mirror	Alexandria, Va.
Columbian Museum	Savannah
Columbian Register	New Haven
Commercial Advertiser	New York
Congregational Observer	Hartford and New Haven
Connecticut Courant	Hartford
Connecticut Gazette	New London
Connecticut Herald	New Haven
Connecticut Journal	New Haven
Connecticut Mirror	Hartford
Connecticut Observer	Hartford
Country Porcupine	Philadelphia
Daily National Intelligencer	Washington
Dunlap's American Daily Advertiser	Philadelphia
Essex Journal	Newburyport, Mass.

Newspapers Cited

Exchange Advertiser	Boston
Farmer's Journal	Danbury, Conn.
Farmer's Weekly Museum	Walpole, N. H.
Farmer's Oracle	Lansingburg, N. Y.
Federal Intelligencer	Baltimore
Federal Orrery	Boston
Franklin Herald	Greenfield, Mass.
Free Elector	Hartford
Freeman's Chronicle	Hartford
Freeman's Journal	Philadelphia
Gazette of the United States	Philadelphia
General Advertiser	Philadelphia
Genesee Farmer	Rochester, N. Y.
Georgia Journal	Savannah
Hampshire Chronicle	Springfield, Mass.
Hampshire Gazette	Northampton, Mass.
Herald	New York
Impartial Gazetteer	New York
Impartial Register	Salem
Independent Chronicle	Boston
Independent Gazette	New York
Independent Gazetteer	Philadelphia
Indiana Democrat	Indianapolis
Journal of Commerce	New York
Kentucky Gazette	Lexington
Log Cabin	New York
Maryland Gazette	Baltimore
Maryland Herald	Easton
Maryland Journal	Baltimore
Massachusetts Centinel	Boston
Massachusetts Eagle	Lenox
Massachusetts Gazette	Springfield
Massachusetts Mercury	Boston
Massachusetts Spy	Worcester
Mercantile Advertiser	New York
Merchant's Daily Advertiser	Philadelphia
Mercury and New England Palladium	Boston
Middlesex Gazette	Middletown, Conn.
Minerva	New York
Mirror of the Times	Wilmington, Del.
National Aegis	Worcester

Newspapers Cited

National Intelligencer	Washington
New England Advocate	Middletown, Conn.
New England Palladium	Boston
New England Puritan	Boston
New England Weekly Review	Hartford
New Era	New York
New Hampshire Gazette	Portsmouth
New Hampshire Journal	Walpole
New Hampshire Mercury	Portsmouth
New Hampshire Patriot	Concord
New-Jersey Journal	Elizabethtown
New Jersey State Gazette	Trenton
Niles' Weekly Register	Baltimore
Norfolk Repository	Dedham, Mass.
North Carolina Journal	Halifax
Oracle of the Day	Portsmouth, N. H.
Palladium-Republican	New Haven
Pellet	Boston
Pennsylvania Evening Herald	Philadelphia
Pennsylvania Gazette	Philadelphia
Pennsylvania Herald	York
Pennsylvania Journal	Philadelphia
Pennsylvania Mercury	Philadelphia
Pennsylvania Packet	Philadelphia
People's Press and Addison County Democrat	Middlebury, Vt.
Political Repository	Dover, N. H.
Porcupine's Gazette	Philadelphia
Poulson's American Daily Advertiser	Philadelphia
Practical Christian and Church Chronicle	New Haven
Religious Intelligencer	New Haven
Republican Farmer	Bridgeport, Conn.
Republican Watch-Tower	New York
Russell's Gazette	Boston
Sentinel of Freedom	Newark, N. J.
South Carolina State Gazette	Charleston
Southern Centinel	Augusta, Ga.
Spectator	New York
State Gazette of South Carolina	Charleston
Time Piece	New York
United States Chronicle	Providence

Newspapers Cited

United States Gazette	Philadelphia
Universal Gazette	Washington
Vermont Chronicle	Windsor
Vermont Gazette	Bennington
Vermont Telegraph	Brandon
Virginia Patriot	Richmond
Washington Spy	Elizabethtown, N. J.
Western Presbyterian Herald	Louisville
Western Star	Stockbridge, Mass.

IDENTIFICATION OF BIBLIOGRAPHICAL CITATIONS

Alden	Alden, John E.: *Rhode Island Imprints, 1727–1800* (New York, 1949)
Crandall	Crandall, Marjorie L.: *Confederate Imprints* (2 vols., Boston, 1955)
Evans	Evans, Charles: *American Bibliography...to...1820* (13 vols., Chicago and Worcester, 1903–1955)
Gilmore	Gilmore, Barbara: *A Puritan Town and its Imprints, Northampton, 1786–1845* (Northampton, 1942)
Heartman	Heartman, Charles F.: *The New England Primer Issued prior to 1830* (3d ed., New York, 1934)
Hill and Collins	Hill, Frank P., and Varnum L. Collins: *Books... printed at Newark, New Jersey, 1776–1900* ([Newark], 1902)
McMurtrie, Albany	McMurtrie, Douglas C.: *A Check List of Eighteenth Century Albany Imprints* (University of the State of New York, *Bulletin* No. 1155, Albany, 1939)
McMurtrie, Canandaigua	McMurtrie, Douglas C.: "A Bibliography of Books ...printed at Canandaigua, New York, 1799–1850," *Grosvenor Library Bulletin*, Vol. 21, pp. 61–107 (Buffalo, 1939)
McMurtrie, Oregon	McMurtrie, Douglas C.: *Oregon Imprints*, 1847–1870 (Eugene, Ore., 1950)
Noyes	Noyes, Reginald Webb: *A Bibliography of Maine Imprints to 1820* (Stonington, Me., 1930)
O'Callaghan	O'Callaghan, Edmund B.: *A List of Editions of the Holy Scriptures...printed in America previous to 1860* (Albany, 1861)
Ohio Imprints	*A Check List of Ohio Imprints, 1796–1820* (American Imprints Inventory, No. 17, Columbus, 1941)
Rosenbach	Rosenbach, Abraham S. W.: *Early American Children's Books* (Portland, Me., 1933)
Sabin	Sabin, Joseph: *A Dictionary of Books relating to America* (29 vols., New York, 1868–1936)

Sealock	Sealock, Richard B.: "Publishing in Pennsylvania, 1785–1790," M.S. thesis, Columbia University, 1935 (photostat in The New York Public Library)
Spargo	Spargo, John: *Anthony Haswell* (Rutland, Vt., 1925)
Utica Imprints	*A Check List of Utica Imprints, 1799–1830* (American Imprints Inventory, No. 36, Chicago, 1932)
Waters	Waters, Willard O., comp.: *American Imprints... in the Huntington Library, supplementing Evans* [San Marino, Calif., 1933]
Weeks	Weeks, Stephen B.: "Confederate Text-books," *Report* of the United States Commissioner of Education for 1898/99, pp. 1139–1155 (Washington, 1900)
Williams	Williams, John C.: *An Oneida County Printer, William Williams* (New York, 1906)

IDENTIFICATION OF LOCATION SYMBOLS

California

C	California State Library, Sacramento
C-S	Sutro Branch, San Francisco
CL	Los Angeles Public Library
CLU	University of California, Los Angeles
CLU-C	——William Andrews Clark Memorial Library
CMC	Mills College, Oakland
CSf	San Francisco Public Library
CSmH	Henry E. Huntington Library and Art Gallery, San Marino
CSt	Stanford University, Palo Alto
CU	University of California, Berkeley

Connecticut

Ct	Connecticut State Library, Hartford
CtFHi	Fairfield Historical Society
CtH	Hartford Public Library
CtHT	Trinity College, Hartford
CtHT-W	——Watkinson Library
CtHi	Connecticut Historical Society, Hartford
CtNhHi	New Haven Colony Historical Society, New Haven
CtSoP	Pequot Library Association, Southport
CtY	Yale University, New Haven

District of Columbia

DAFM	United States Armed Forces Medical Library
DFSA	United States Federal Security Agency, Central Library*
DFo	Folger Shakespeare Library
DLC	Library of Congress

Georgia

GEU	Emory University, Decatur

*Earlier called United States Office of Education and later Department of Health, Education, and Welfare.

Location Symbols

Illinois

IC	Chicago Public Library
ICHi	Chicago Historical Society
ICJ	John Crerar Library, Chicago
ICN	Newberry Library, Chicago
ICU	University of Chicago
IHi	Illinois State Historical Society, Springfield
IU	University of Illinois, Urbana

Massachusetts

MA	Amherst College, Amherst
MAJ	Jones Library, Amherst
MB	Boston Public Library
MBAt	Boston Athenaeum
MCM	Massachusetts Institute of Technology, Cambridge
MFHi	Fall River Historical Society
MH	Harvard University, Cambridge
MHi	Massachusetts Historical Society, Boston
MLeo	Leominster Public Library
MNF	Forbes Library, Northampton
MSaE	Essex Institute, Salem
MWA	American Antiquarian Society, Worcester
MWiW	Williams College, Williamstown
MWiW-C	——Chapin Library

Maryland

MdBE	Enoch Pratt Library, Baltimore
MdHi	Maryland Historical Society, Baltimore

Maine

MeHi	Maine Historical Society, Portland

Michigan

Mi	Michigan State Library, Lansing
MiD-B	Burton Historical Collection, Detroit Public Library
MiDeaEd	Henry Ford Museum, Dearborn
MiU	University of Michigan, Ann Arbor
MiU-C	——William L. Clements Library

Minnesota

MnU	University of Minnesota, Minneapolis

Location Symbols

Missouri

MoSHi	Missouri Historical Society, St. Louis

New York

N	New York State Library, Albany
NBLiHi	Long Island Historical Society, Brooklyn
NBuG	Grosvenor Library, Buffalo
NBuHi	Buffalo Historical Society
NBuT	New York State Teachers College, Buffalo
NCanHi	Ontario County Historical Society, Canandaigua
NHi	New-York Historical Society, New York
NN	New York Public Library
NNC	Columbia University, New York
NNC-T	——Teachers College
NNG	General Theological Seminary, New York
NNNAM	New York Academy of Medicine, New York
NNP	Pierpont Morgan Library, New York
NNS	New York Society Library, New York
NNU	New York University, New York
NNU-W	——Washington Square Library
NNUT	Union Theological Seminary, New York
NRHi	Rochester Historical Society
NRU	University of Rochester
NUt	Utica Public Library

North Carolina

NcD	Duke University, Durham
NcU	University of North Carolina, Chapel Hill

New Hampshire

Nh	New Hampshire State Library, Concord
NhD	Dartmouth College, Hanover
NhHi	New Hampshire Historical Society, Concord

New Jersey

NjHi	New Jersey Historical Society, Newark
NjN	Newark Public Library
NjP	Princeton University, Princeton
NjR	Rutgers University, New Brunswick

Ohio

O	Ohio State Library, Columbus
OC	Cincinnati Public Library
OCHP	Historical and Philosophical Society of Ohio, Cincinnati
OClW	Western Reserve University, Cleveland
OClWHi	Western Reserve Historical Society, Cleveland
OHi	Ohio Historical Society, Columbus
OO	Oberlin College, Oberlin
OOxM	Miami University, Oxford
OU	Ohio State University, Columbus

Oregon

OrHi	Oregon Historical Society, Portland

Pennsylvania

P	Pennsylvania State Library, Harrisburg
PHC	Haverford College, Haverford
PHi	Historical Society of Pennsylvania, Philadelphia
PMA	Alleghany College, Meadville
PP	Free Library of Philadelphia
PPAmP	American Philosophical Society, Philadelphia
PPCP	College of Physicians of Philadelphia
PPFrankI	Franklin Institute, Philadelphia
PPL	Library Company of Philadelphia
PPM	Mercantile Library Branch, Free Library of Philadelphia
PPPM	Philadelphia Museum of Art
PPPrHi	Presbyterian Historical Society, Philadelphia
PPeSchw	Schwenkfelder Historical Library, Pennsburg
PU	University of Pennsylvania, Philadelphia

Rhode Island

RHi	Rhode Island Historical Society, Providence
RNHi	Newport Historical Society
RPB	Brown University, Providence
RPJCB	John Carter Brown Library, Providence

Texas

TxComT	East Texas State Teachers College, Commerce

Virginia

Vi	Virginia State Library, Richmond

Location Symbols

ViU	University of Virginia, Charlottesville
ViW	College of William and Mary, Williamsburg

Vermont

VtBrat	Brattleboro Public Library
VtHi	Vermont Historical Society, Montpelier
VtMidbC	Middlebury College, Middlebury
VtMidbS	Sheldon Art Museum, Middlebury
VtU	University of Vermont, Burlington

Washington

WaU	University of Washington, Seattle

West Virginia

Wv-Ar	West Virginia Department of Archives and History, Charleston

Canada

An-C-M	Montreal Civic Library

*Private Collections**

Field	Mrs. Howard B. Field, Durham Center, Connecticut
Greenwood	Mrs. Arthur M. Greenwood, Marlborough, Mass.
Merriam	G. and C. Merriam Company, Springfield, Mass.
Mott	Dr. Frank Luther Mott, Columbia, Missouri
Munroe	Mr. Robert C. Munroe, Springfield, Massachusetts
Stark	Mr. Lewis M. Stark, New York, New York

* During the editing of this work the compiler's niece, Gillian Barr Bailey, presented to The New York Public Library the unique or especially rare Webster items in her collection. They have been incorporated in the record of that Library's holdings.

ADDITIONS AND CORRECTIONS

Page 12, Title 8

This edition has been found in the form of a title-page only, inserted in copy No. 1 of *Websteriana* in the Yale library:

———The eighth edition, with additional lessons. Philadelphia: Printed, by W. Young. . . . M,DCC,LXXXVIII.

Page 15, Title 16

The cross-reference in the fifth line of note 1 should read "Appendix I."

Page 15, Title 17

The phrase "With the privilege of copy-right" should be added after the date in the imprint. The same correction applies to Titles 26, 27, 39, 42, 48, 55, 59, 65, 68, 75, 76, and 77.

Page 21, Title 31

Delete annotation and insert above this title:

30 *bis*

———Thomas & Andrews's seventh edition. . . . Printed at Boston. . . . MDCCXCIII.

144 pp., incl. frontis., illus. 17 cm.

CtY.

Page 45, Title 119

Add "imperfect" to NN symbol.

Page 57, Title 169

Add "imperfect" to NNC symbol.

Page 78, introductory note to rubric D

The editor is informed by a lawyer interested in copyright history that the reason Webster did not claim the protection of this renewal in 1831 is probably that it was not granted him; at that time, through careless wording of the law, there was no provision for an author himself to secure a renewal beyond twenty-eight years.

Page 119, Title 359

In the imprint "Sons" should be followed by a period and "Stereotyped by J. S. Redfield, New York."

Page 138, Title 401

Delete symbol for NNC and add it to Title 402.

Additions and Corrections

Page 147, Title 417
Add "imperfect" to PP symbol.

Page 163, Title 452
After "two lines of quotation" in title, add "from Mirabeau."

Page 212, Title 558
Mr. Ben Grauer of New York owns a copy of this edition in which there is an inserted slip reading, "Notice to the Reader. In the hurry of stereotyping this edition of the History, several errors have occurred in the orthography; such as *honour* for *honor* . . . for which neither the author nor the publishers are responsible, but which deserve notice here, as they lay the author open to the charge of inconsistency. A part of the edition was sold before the errors were detected. These errors will all be corrected in future editions."

Page 245, Title 592
In the imprint the firm name Towar should read Tower [sic]; add MB to list of symbols.

Page 245, Title 592a
The Free Library of Philadelphia has a copy consisting of 532 pages, but the title-page is missing, so it is not possible to say if it is 592 or 592a.

Page 245, Title 593
Add MH to list of symbols.

Pages 250, Title 609
Add as Note 3: Ayres was a publisher in Philadelphia, not New York.

Pages 254, Title 626.
There should be a hyphen in "New York" in the imprint.

Page 255, Title 628
There should be a period instead of a comma after "Sanderson" in the imprint.

Page 337, Title 745
Yale now also has Webster's own copy.

Page 381, Title 786
Yale now also has a copy inscribed to another grandchild, Emily Ellsworth Fowler (later Mrs. Ford).

A BIBLIOGRAPHY OF THE WRITINGS OF NOAH WEBSTER

Section One

THE GRAMMATICAL INSTITUTE

PART ONE: SPELLER

A. *The Original Text*[1]

1

A grammatical institute, of the English language, comprising, an easy, concise, and systematic method of education, designed for the use of English schools in America. In three parts. Part I. Containing, a new and accurate standard of pronunciation. By Noah Webster, A.M. *Usus est norma loquendi.* CICERO. Hartford: Printed by Hudson & Goodwin, for the author. [1783.]

119, (1) pp. 16 cm. P. [1], title-page. P. [2],"Advertisement," inviting criticisms, and warning that the work is protected by copyright. Pp. [3]–15, "Introduction," describing Webster's aim of making an "American" language; censuring the neglect of the study of English grammar in the schools and the frequent use of the Bible therein; and lamenting the custom of procuring patrons, to which he yields partially in securing testimonials. Pp. [16]–119, text, including (pp. 90–99) lists of geographical data, emphasizing Connecticut, and (pp. 118–119) "A Chronological Account of remarkable Events in America," 1492–January 20, 1783. P. [120], errata.

CT (imperfect), CTHT–W, DLC (Batchelder Collection), MH (gift of the author, December 6, 1783), MWA, NN (imperfect), NNC.

Evans 18297, Sabin 102355.

[1]Although the following list is broken down bv the four major versions of the speller (1783, 1787, 1804, and 1829), it should be borne in mind that—at least until the introduction of stereotype plates—there were minor corrections, additions, deletions, and alterations in almost every printing, sometimes effected by the printers without reference to Webster.

For the first few years of publication of the speller the final number in the section "Of Numbers" was almost always the same as the title-page date in the dated editions, so it has been taken as a strong indication of the year for undated editions.

NOTES

1. Entered for Connecticut copyright at Hartford, August 14, 1783. The edition was 5,000. Price, fourteen pence or ten shillings a dozen. On May 15, 1784, Webster told an unidentified correspondent that the whole edition had been sold.[2]

2. Announced in the *Connecticut Courant*, September 16, 1783, and advertised therein October 7 and later and in the *Freeman's Chronicle*, October 6 and later. The former's advertisement of October 14 contains a recommendation signed by nine persons, the first appearance of a device of which Webster made much use. He apparently wrote many of the advertisements himself, and even the recommendations, which others then signed. Although he secured testimonials and recommendations from many scholars and important persons, Webster never managed to get any from the two biggest "names" he approached, Benjamin Franklin and George Washington.

3. In a contract in June, 1783, Hudson and Goodwin accepted Webster's note for the printing bill, in return for sole printing rights "for a term of years."[3] Joel Barlow lent Webster $500 toward the cost of printing, and John Trumbull lent a smaller amount.

4. Webster planned to call the work "The American Instructor," but adopted the more ponderous title on the advice of President Ezra Stiles of Yale.

5. This book and other later works by Webster include many Biblical precepts, but he felt that extensive use of the Bible in schools tended to cause irreverence through too much use of sacred names. Despite the reverent basis of this view, it was strongly attacked by the orthodox, and in subsequent editions Webster modified his position, though his belief seems to have remained unchanged.

6. The geographical tables, listing the countries of Europe, the West Indian islands, the United States, British North American "Provinces not in Union," and the counties and county seats of the states, were an early example of providing this sort of information in a textbook. The fullest details were given for Connecticut, for the towns of which population figures were provided, from the census of 1774, though some errors were made in transcribing the figures. In the introduction Webster apologizes for the imperfect condition of the geographical portion, and promises to try to improve it.

[2]Rhode Island Historical Society MSS.

[3]Advertisement, *Connecticut Courant*, June 1, 1784.

7. The chronology, though omitted in subsequent editions, was the germ of similar tabulations in other of Webster's works, especially the "Outline of American History" in the 1806 edition of Volume I of his *Elements of Useful Knowledge* (Title 538).

8. Despite Webster's sensitiveness to plagiarisms and borrowings from him, in this work he draws freely, without acknowledgment, from Thomas Dilworth's *New Guide to the English Tongue* (London, 1740 etc.), even while excoriating it. His caustic remarks on this work and on Daniel Fenning's *Universal Spelling Book* (London, 1756 etc.) drew a good portion of the flood of hostile criticism this work evoked. Webster was also ridiculed for using "A.M." on the title-page, as he was later for the use of "Esquire."

2

——— The second edition, corrected and improved.... Hartford: Printed by Hudson and Goodwin, M,DCC,LXXXIV. With the privilege of copy-right.

123, (1) pp. 15 cm.
PHC.
Evans 18298, entered incorrectly under 1783.

NOTES

1. The contents are the same as the preceding, except: P. [ii], "Advertisement," expressing obligation for the favorable reception of the first edition, and thanks for criticisms, of which he requests more. P. [iii], dedication, to Ezra Stiles. P. [iv], recommendation, signed by twelve persons, who are all given full honorifics, perhaps to support Webster's use of "A.M." and "Esq." Pp. [v]–viii, new preface, criticizing the defects and omissions of other compilers, criticizing earlier methods of dividing syllables, and acknowledging help from friends and from "Mr. Perry's Dictionary" and "Mr. Sheridan's Rhetorical Grammar," which he had not earlier seen.[4] In this preface Webster first announces his aim of creating "a comprehensive system of education." The emphasis on Connecticut, the expressed disapproval of the use of the Bible in schools, and the chronology are deleted. The text is expanded by new matter, "Moral Sentiments," on pp. 120–123; the errata are on p. [124].

[4] Probably William Perry, *Royal Standard English Dictionary* (Edinburgh, 1775) and Thomas Sheridan, *General Dictionary*...[and] *Rhetorical Grammar* (2 vols., London, 1780).

2. Announced in the *Connecticut Courant*, June 1, and advertised therein June 8 and later.

3. Beginning with this edition, Webster's name is followed by "Jun. Esq.," instead of "A.M."

4. The first edition received ridicule and severe criticism, some of which Webster took into consideration in revising the work. One of the features which drew much adverse comment was the syllabification, in which Webster modified older practices, without knowing that others were experimenting along the same lines. In justification, he wrote that he had been encouraged in his attempted improvements by "the most eminent scholar[s] in America," particularly some of those at Princeton and the University of Pennsylvania.[5]

3

——— The third edition. . . . Hartford, Printed by Hudson & Goodwin, M,DCC,LXXXIV. With the privilege of copy-right.

138 pp. (the last misnumbered 137). 16 cm.
MH (gift of the author, June 11, 1785).
Evans 18870.

NOTES

1. There are some minor changes in the prefatory matter and a few in the text.

2. As late as December 1, 1784, in an advertisement in the *Connecticut Courant*, Hudson and Goodwin referred to this edition as being in press. Thomas and Andrews of Boston advertised it on December 9 in the *Massachusetts Spy*, but Hudson and Goodwin did not advertise it for sale until January 4, 1785. Since the printers would probably be the first to publicize the work, Thomas and Andrews may have been jumping the gun. Despite the title-page date, there is an internal date of 1785 (the last figure in the table "Of Numbers"), and the compiler believes that this edition did not actually appear until 1785.

3. With this edition extensive newspaper advertising began, scores of advertisements having been located by the compiler.

4. "Pronounciation" is thus misspelled on the title-page, and with this edition the quotation from Cicero disappears.

5. A copy of this edition was carried by Webster on a trip to the South,

[5] *New York Journal*, September 23, 1784.

and was the text entered for copyright in Philadelphia, May 11, 1785, and Charleston, June 30.

6. A mock advertisement for the *Grammatical Institute*, ridiculing Webster's claims for his speller, signed "N. W. Secundus," appeared in the *Essex Journal*, April 20, 1785.

4

——— The fourth edition.... Hartford, Printed by Hudson & Goodwin, M,DCC,LXXXV. With the privilege of copy-right.

138 pp. (the last misnumbered 137). 16 cm.

RPJCB.

Evans 19361, with slight discrepancies.

Minor changes in content. Poorly printed, with many mistakes. Probably Webster did not see this edition until after it was printed, for he was in the South at the time.

5

——— Boston, Printed by Peter Ed[es.] With the privilege of copy-right. [1786?]

134+pp. 15 cm. P. [1], title-page. P. [2], dedication. Pp. [3–4], two recommendations and the beginning of a third. Pp. [5–8] missing in the only located copy; the contents were probably a continuation of the recommendation on p. [5] and a preface on [6–8]. Pp. 9 +, text, all after p. 134 missing; the final page was probably 138.

NN (imperfect).

NOTES

1. Advertised in the *Exchange Advertiser*, November 16 and 23, 1786.

2. The date 1786 is almost certainly correct in view of (a) the advertisements cited, (b) that year's being the last entry in the table "Of Numbers," and (c) an ownership inscription on the inside front cover, dated 1786. This inscription gives the price paid as 1*s* 1*d*.

3. Because of his dissatisfaction with the quality of the fourth edition and with what he considered inadequate distribution, Webster sought other publishers than Hudson and Goodwin, turning first to Boston. He corresponded with Peter Edes during 1786, and this edition is doubtless the upshot, though on October 30 of that year Webster and Hudson and

Goodwin renegotiated their contract, renewing the firm's monopoly in New England. Webster made other arrangements in New York and Philadelphia (Titles 7–10).

4. No Hudson and Goodwin fifth edition has been located, so it is likely that they counted this Edes edition as the fifth and omitted that number in their sequence.

5. The title-page of the copy located is frayed in the lower right hand corner, so it is not certain if "Esq." followed "Noah Webster, Jun.," but it probably did.

6

——— The sixth edition. . . . Hartford, Printed by Hudson & Goodwin, M,DCC,LXXXVII. With the privilege of copy-right.

136 pp. 15 cm.

NN, NNC.

Evans 20863, but this is an error, confused with 20868, which should be Part I, not Part II, of the *Grammatical Institute.*

NOTES

1. Advertised in the *Connecticut Courant,* December 10, 1787, and later.

2. There are many minor changes in content.

3. Apparently not published until December, so it may actually follow rather than precede the following entry.

B. *The American Spelling Book*

7

[The American spelling book, or First part of the Grammatical institute of the English language. By Noah Webster, Jun. Esq. The seventh edition. Philadelphia, Young & M'Culloch, 1787.]

[Frontis.?], 140 pp., illus. 17 cm. Pp. [i] and [ii] were doubtless the title-page and dedication. Pp. [iii]–v, recommendations, partly the same as earlier ones, partly new. Pp. [vi]–viii, new preface, promising geographical material in the forthcoming Part III of the *Grammatical Institute* and stressing the importance of correct orthography in place names. Pp. 9–140, text.

NNS (lacking all before p. [iii]).

Evans 20864, Sabin 102337, note.

NOTES

1. A thorough revision, some of the changes reflecting the influence of the criticisms of the earlier editions and of Part II. For the first time there is an "Introduction to Grammar," a brief summary of Part II (pp. [127]–140). This is the first edition to be illustrated. From contemporary references there appears to have been a frontispiece, a portrait of George Washington. Throughout the text are eight cuts, signed "I.S." or "I. Sanford" (Plate II), to accompany the fables, which are also a new feature. Some of the fables are derived from Aesop, some from La Fontaine, and some from earlier textbooks, such as Daniel Fenning's *Universal Spelling Book* (London, 1756 etc.).

2. Advertised in the *Neue Unparteyische Lancaster Zeitung*, supplement to September 5, 1787 (in German), *Pennsylvania Herald* and *Pennsylvania Gazette*, October 31, and elsewhere.

3. Although the eleventh edition (Title 11) is sometimes said to have been the first to bear the shortened title "The American Spelling Book," Evans seems to be correct in hypothecating such wording for this edition, since the German advertisement uses the phrase as the main title.

4. At first Webster objected to the use of a portrait of Washington on the grounds of disrespect, but later he considered using this frontispiece in other editions, for on June 24, 1788, he wrote one of his other printers that he had "sent to Philadelphia to know on what terms I can procure a Plate of Genl Washington's Portrait, which Mr Young has prefixed to the works & which is pretty well executed. I intend that all future impressions shall be alike; & . . . I shall expect that you get a plate, for it will certainly assist the sale."[6]

5. On October 24, 1787, Webster signed a contract (copy in the Webster Papers) by which William Young of Philadelphia received the exclusive right to print and sell all three parts of the *Grammatical Institute* in Pennsylvania, Delaware, Maryland, and Virginia for a period of three years.

6. The copy located, since it lacks the title-page, could just as well be

[6] *American Historical Record*, Vol. I (1872), p. 374. The addressee is unknown, and the letter begins "Gentlemen." The magazine suggests Thomas and Andrews as the firm addressed, but the compiler thinks Hudson and Goodwin more likely.

Title 8, 9, or 10, but has been described as the seventh edition because it is bound with a Philadelphia, 1787, edition of Webster's grammar.

8

[—— Eighth edition. Philadelphia: William Young, 1788.]

Although no copy has been located, it is adequately documented that William Young published an eighth edition in Philadelphia early in 1788. The *Pennsylvania Herald* of February 5 and later contains an advertisement which says, "In the press, and will speedily be published by said Young.—the American Spelling-Book; the Eighth Edition. . . . the price will be reduced to two French crowns per dozen, bound in leather, and 14s. when half bound. . . . the types will be kept standing solely for this work, both to render the book correct and to . . . supply any order on short notice. . . ." The advertisements refer to the work's having been enlarged, and also to a portrait of Washington as a frontispiece. The book, however, seems to have contained many errors, for on June 23 Webster wrote Young, "I have this day purchased one of your last edition of the Spelling Book & find it full of errors,"[7] and on the following day he wrote on the same subject to an unidentified addressee, probably Hudson and Goodwin.[8]

9

[—— Ninth edition. New York: Samuel Campbell, 1788.]

No copy of a ninth edition has been located, but such an edition in New York is documented. On April 25, 1788, Samuel Campbell advertised in the New York *Morning Post* that he had "just published" an edition of Webster's speller, and on July 1, in the same paper, he refers to it as "a neat and accurate Edition (being the ninth) . . . With Plates and other Improvements." The existence of this edition is further demonstrated by Noah Webster's reference to "Mr Campbell's ninth" (which he did *not* consider "neat and accurate") in a letter in the *Connecticut Courant* of November 12, 1792. That this edition, based on Young's eighth, was printed for Campbell by Hudson and Goodwin in Hartford is shown by a letter from him to them, May 21, 1788, discussing business details.[9] Webster's signing a five year contract with Campbell is recorded in his diary on October 31, 1787.

[7]Yale University Library.
[8]See footnote 6 above.
[9]Connecticut Historical Society.

10

[—— Tenth edition. Philadelphia: William Young, 1788.]

A tenth edition was advertised by William Young of Philadelphia in the *Pennsylvania Packet*, September 27, 1788, and later, and elsewhere.
Evans 21584.
No copy located.

11

The American spelling book: Containing, an easy standard of pronunciation. Being the first part of a Grammatical institute of the English language. In three parts. By Noah Webster, Jun'r. Esquire. The eleventh edition. Hartford: Printed by Hudson and Goodwin. [1788?]

153 pp., illus. 17 cm.
RPJCB.
Sabin 102337.

NOTES

1. Assigned to 1788 because that is the last figure in the table "Of Numbers."
2. Evans (21585) lists an eleventh edition by Young in Philadelphia in 1788, but the compiler has been unable to locate the Young advertisement given as authority, and the other advertisement cited could just as well apply to Hudson and Goodwin's eleventh edition.
3. The cuts are the same as those in Title 7.

12 & 13

[—— Bennington: Haswell and Russell, 1788.]

Haswell and Russell in Bennington, Vermont, appear to have published two editions there in 1788, though it seems likely that the books were printed in Philadelphia or New York. The existence of an edition before June is suggested by a letter from Webster to Hudson and Goodwin, June 22, in which he says, "I have just returned from Vermont.... 2000 Spellers have been sold... and the printers say they could have sold

5000 more."[1] An edition in August is indicated by the firm's advertisement in the *Vermont Gazette* of August 4 and later: "This day published ...." On September 7 Webster wrote the Vermont firm from New York complaining of their having published one edition "without my knowledge, and another without any notice," but offering to legitimatize the waifs by making a formal agreement.[2] He records an agreement with them in his diary on September 20, 1790. To jibe with later numbering, these may be considered the first and second Vermont editions.

14

[——— Boston: John Folsom, 1788.]

On May 28 Webster wrote Hudson and Goodwin that John Folsom of Boston had written him inquiring about printing an edition, and that he had referred him to them.[3] That an edition eventuated is suggested by another letter from Webster to the same firm, written from Boston on August 16: "I find Mr. Folsom has begun the Spelling Book, but he intended to print it without cuts. This I object to, for all the future editions must be alike. At his request therefore I write for your plates—please to forward them by the next stage," adding, "he will give you your price for them, and you can get new ones of Sanford" (who had made the cuts Hudson and Goodwin were using).[4]

Webster hoped to have all editions numbered in correct sequence, but at about this point the situation got out of hand. From here on, no attempt is made to present the editions in chronological order within the year; they are listed alphabetically by place of publication.

15

[——— Bennington: Haswell and Russell, 1789.]

On February 23, 1789, Haswell and Russell of Bennington, Vermont, advertised in the *Vermont Gazette* an edition of the speller, "this day published, And in a few days will be bound, ready for sale."[5] This must be considered the third Vermont edition in order to make the later numbering of editions correct.

[1] Webster Papers, New York Public Library. [2] Ibid. [3] Ibid. [4] Ibid.
[5] This wording should be taken as a warning against accepting the words "this

16

——— Thomas and Andrews's first edition. With additional lessons, corrected by the author. Printed at Boston, by Isaiah Thomas and Ebenezer T. Andrews . . . , MDCCLXXXIX.

144 pp., incl. frontis., illus. 17 cm.
MHi, MWA.
Evans 22257.

NOTES

1. There are slight changes in the contents. The cuts are different from those found earlier (Plate III). This is the first edition found with a frontispiece of Webster, a miserable likeness which has been called "the porcupine portrait," because of the spiky appearance of the hair (Plate I). There is no support for its attribution to Paul Revere (see Appendix H). The Thomas and Andrews editions continued, until their twenty-fifth, to use this frontispiece, with the number of the edition printed thereon.

2. Advertised in the *Massachusetts Magazine* for October-November, 1789, and as "this day published" in the *Massachusetts Spy*, November 12.

3. "In three parts" is dropped from the title-page, and "Author of 'Dissertations on the English Language' " added after Webster's name. Thomas and Andrews were printing Webster's *Dissertations* (Title 651) when they undertook this edition of the speller.

4. The firm issued its successive editions as page-for-page reprints, probably from standing type.

17

——— The eighth Connecticut edition. . . . Hartford: Printed by Hudson and Goodwin. . . . [1789.]

153 pp., illus. 17 cm.
NN.
Evans' first Connecticut edition of 1790 (23051) is probably this edition.

day" in an advertisement as indicating definitely that a book was placed on sale on that date. Further, an advertisement reading "this day" was often repeated without change in subsequent issues of a newspaper.

NOTES

1. The cuts differ from those in Title 11; perhaps, as suggested in Title 14, Hudson and Goodwin sent their Sanford cuts to Folsom and did not get them back, thus having to order new ones. This set is obviously based on the original Sanford cuts, though each is reversed (Plate IV).

2. Advertised to be published "next week" in the *Hampshire Chronicle*, August 26, 1789, and later.

3. Dated from the advertisement and the fact that 1789 is the last figure in "Of Numbers."

4. This is the first effort to keep the editions straight by numbering those of each state; the present printing, however, is the eighth in Connecticut only if the Boston fifth edition is counted in the sequence (see Note 4 to Title 5).

18

[——— Twelfth edition. New York: Samuel Campbell, 1789.]

Campbell advertised a twelfth edition in the New York *Daily Advertiser*, May 8, 1789, and later, and also in a 1789 broadside catalogue of his publications. He continued to advertise this edition for at least three years. Its actuality is demonstrated by Webster's referring to a copy of it in the *Connecticut Courant*, November 12, 1792. For a possible copy, see Note 4 to Title 28.

19

[——— Twelfth edition. Philadelphia: William Young(?), 1789.]

A twelfth edition, Philadelphia, 1789, is cited by William S. Baker in *The Engraved Portraits of Washington* (Philadelphia, 1880), No. 38. A frontispiece of Washington seems also to have been used by Young in Philadelphia in 1787 and 1788 (Titles 7-8), but no copy of any of Young's editions has been located still retaining its frontispiece.

20

——— The twelfth edition, with additional lessons. Providence: Printed by John Carter, M,DCC,LXXXIX. [With the privilege of copy-right.]

146 + pp., illus. 17 cm.
MWA (lacking all after p. 146).
Alden 1190.

NOTES

1. The contents follow those of Title 11, so the last page was probably 153.
2. Announced in the *Providence Gazette*, October 18, 1788, and advertised as ready January 3, 1789, and later.

21

——— The fourth Vermont edition.... Bennington, by Anthony Haswell .... [1790?]

96 + pp., illus. 16 cm.
MWA (imperfect).
Spargo 201.
The only located copy is unbound and untrimmed and lacks all pages after 96, as well as some others. Spargo assigns the edition to 1796, but because an eighth Vermont edition appeared in 1794 and for other reasons the compiler believes this to have been published about 1790–1791.

22

——— Thomas and Andrews's second edition.... Printed at Boston.... MDCCXC.

144 pp., incl. frontis., illus. 17 cm.
DLC.
Evans 23052.

NOTES

1. Advertised in the *Massachusetts Spy*, January 13, 1791, and later as "this day published," so perhaps the edition was not published until 1791 despite the 1790 title-page date.
2. This is the first edition located which contains a notice of Federal copyright. The entry, in the Massachusetts District, was dated October 7, 1790, and was recorded in the *Massachusetts Spy*, October 28 and later.

23

[——— Hartford: Hudson and Goodwin, 1790.]

On October 14, 1790, Webster wrote to Secretary of State Thomas Jefferson regarding deposit of a copy under the new Federal copyright law; he refers to the fact that he had entered the *Grammatical Institute* in the Connecticut District on June 22[6] and that he will submit a copy "as soon as an improved edition, now in the press, shall be finished." Writing again on December 12, he sends a copy, saying that he would like to replace it later with one "more correct."[7] Thomas and Andrews' second edition may possibly have been printed in time to be the one which Webster sent, or it may have been a now-lost Connecticut printing. Ninth and tenth Connecticut editions are called for to make later Hudson and Goodwin edition numbers correct.

24

——— Thomas and Andrews's third edition.... Printed at Boston .... MDCCXCI.

144 pp., incl. frontis., illus. 16 cm.
MH.
Evans 23965.
Advertised in the *Columbian Centinel*, April 9, 1791, and later.

25

——— Thomas and Andrews's fourth edition.... Printed at Boston..., MDCCXCII.

144 pp., incl. frontis., illus. 17 cm.
MSaE (imperfect), British Museum.
Evans 24999.

26

——— The eleventh Connecticut edition. Hartford: Printed by Hudson and Goodwin.... [1792?]

6 Announcement of this entry appeared in the *American Mercury*, July 19 and later.
7 Jefferson Papers, Manuscripts Division, Library of Congress.

153 pp., illus. 16 cm.
CST.

NOTES

1. The last figure in "Of Numbers" is 1792.
2. A new set of cuts, three signed by Asa W. Lay (Plate V); these continue in Hudson and Goodwin editions through the eighteenth Connecticut edition.

27

——— The twelfth Connecttcut [sic] edition. Hartford: Printed by Hudson and Goodwin. . . . [1792?]

153 pp., illus. 16 cm.
CT, NN (imperfect).
Evans 26446, under 1793.
The last figure in "Of Numbers" is 1792.

28

——— The fourteenth edition, with the author's last corrections. New York: Printed for, and sold by Samuel Campbell . . . : Who has the privilege of copy-right, for the states of New-York, New-Jersey, North-Carolina, South-Carolina, and Georgia. M,DCC,XCII.

144 pp., incl. frontis., illus. 17 cm. P. [i], blank. P. [ii], frontispiece (see below). P. [iii], title-page. P. [iv], dedication to Stiles. Pp. [v]–vi, recommendations. Pp. [vii]–ix, preface, unsigned and undated. Pp. [10]–144, text, part of last page containing a publisher's advertisement.
CT (imperfect).
Evans 25000.

NOTES

1. The last page contains an item found only in Campbell's editions, a "Jewish Story concerning Abraham," which is a garbled version of Benjamin Franklin's *Parable against Persecution.*
2. The frontispiece is a portrait of George Washington, one of the earliest works of Alexander Anderson (Plate VII).[8] The cuts (Plate VI)

[8]No. 2 in William S. Baker: *Engraved Portraits of Washington* (Philadelphia, 1880); see also [Benson J. Lossing?]: "Wood Engraving in America," *American Historical Record,* Vol. I (1872), pp. 152-153.

are very similar to the original set by Isaac Sanford (Plate II), except that the first six are reversed; the seventh and eighth are signed by Sanford.

3. Webster was displeased with this edition because of its many errors, and published in the *Connecticut Courant*, September 17, 1792, and later an advertisement disclaiming it and the corrections which Campbell claimed were Webster's. When this was reprinted in the New York *Daily Advertiser*, September 22, Campbell claimed this was injurious to his license for that state, and protested in a letter in the *American Mercury*, November 5. Webster replied to this in the *Connecticut Courant* of November 12, denying responsibility for the New York republication of the notice. In the course of this letter, Webster refers to Campbell's ninth and twelfth, as well as to his fourteenth edition. The exchange closed with a letter from each man in the *American Mercury*, December 31.

4. The Massachusetts Historical Society has a Campbell edition of which all before p. 11 is lacking. The final page is [136] (the page number being torn off), containing the "Jewish Story" and Campbell advertising. Because of the pagination this is not his fourteenth edition, but it may be his twelfth (Title 19) or fifteenth (Title 33).

29

—— Thomas & Andrews's fifth edition.... Printed at Boston .... MDCCXCIII.

144 pp., incl. frontis., illus. 17 cm.
ICHi, PP.

30

—— Thomas & Andrews's sixth edition.... Printed at Boston .... MDCCXCIII.

144 pp., incl. frontis., illus. 17 cm.
MWA, NN.

31

—— Thomas & Andrews's eighth edition.... Printed at Boston .... MDCCXCIII.

144 pp., incl. frontis., illus. 17 cm.
NN.
No trace has been located of a Thomas and Andrews seventh edition.

32

[——— Thirteenth Connecticut edition. Hartford: Hudson and Goodwin, 1793.]

Evans 28044.
No copy located.

33

[——— Fifteenth edition. New York: Samuel Campbell, 1793.]

In a letter to Webster, dated September 22, 1792, published in the *American Mercury* on December 31, Samuel Campbell of New York refers to his fifteenth edition's being in preparation. He also lists it in a 1794 catalogue of his publications. For a possible copy, see Note 4 to Title 28.

34

[——— Albany: Charles R. and George Webster, 1794.]

Evans 28042.
Although no copy has been located, such an edition seems to be verifiable. The Websters (twin brothers, Noah Webster's second cousins once removed) advertised an edition, including the "Federal Catechism" (see Title 36) as "this day printed" in the *Albany Gazette* of November 3, 1794, and later.

35

——— The eighth Vermont edition. Bennington: Printed by Anthony Haswell.... 1794.

156 pp., illus. 17 cm.
OCLWHi (lacking all before p. [v]).
P. [v] is the title-page. The contents are similar to the Hartford edition of the same year, but not identical. No fifth, sixth, or seventh Vermont editions located.

36

——— To which is now first added, an appendix, containing A moral catechism and A Federal catechism.... Thomas & Andrews' ninth edition.... Printed at Boston.... MDCCXCIV.

156 pp., incl. frontis., illus. 17 cm.
CT, CTY (imperfect), MH (imperfect), MWA, NN, NJR, RPJCB.
Evans 28043.

NOTES

1. Pp. [145]–153 contain the new "Moral Catechism" (see below) and pp. 154–156 are a further addition, "A Federal Catechism," reprinted with changes from Webster's *Rudiments of English Grammar*, 1790 (Title 445).
2. At this point the firm shortened "Andrews's" to "Andrews'."
3. It is not certain which 1794 edition first appeared with the "Moral Catechism," but the compiler believes it was that of New York. Webster referred to preparing such a section as early as 1791.[9]

37

[——— Thomas and Andrews' tenth edition. Boston, 1794?]

Evans 29852 (dated 1794, listed under 1795).
No copy located.

38

[——— Fourteenth Connecticut edition. Hartford: Hudson and Goodwin, 1794.]

Evans 28044.
No copy located.

39

——— The fifteenth Connecticut edition. Hartford: Printed by Hudson and Goodwin. [1794?]

[9] Letters to Timothy Pickering of October 10 and December 18, Massachusetts Historical Society *Proceedings*, Vol. 43 (1909), pp. 133–135.

164 pp., illus. 16 cm.
CT, CTHI (imperfect), ICN.
Evans 28045.

NOTES

1. Contains the new "Moral Catechism," pp. 154–164.
2. Although the last figure in "Of Numbers" is 1793, the compiler feels that this edition is of 1794, since Webster apparently did not prepare the "Moral Catechism" until early in that year.

40

[—— New York: George Bunce, 1794.]

Evans 28046.
Although no copy has been located, there seems adequate evidence for the edition. It was sponsored by Webster, who was dissatisfied with the business methods of the various licensees who were printing his works. He made an agreement of some sort with Bunce, writing Timothy Pickering on January 8, 1794, "My principal view in forming my present plan of business was to print my own books, correctly, and take the benefit of them. We shall have out an edition early in the Spring."[1] To Mathew Carey he wrote on February 19, 1794, "We shall soon have an impression of Spelling books for sale—in sheets."[2] In the *American Minerva* of February 25 and later Bunce advertised as in press and soon ready "A New and Improved Edition, printed under the inspection of the author"; it was advertised as ready in the issues of March 24 and later.

Because this edition was done under Webster's direct supervision and because he hoped to make it superior to those already on the market, the compiler feels that it was probably the first to contain the "Moral Catechism."

41

[—— Thomas and Andrews' eleventh edition. Boston, 1795.]

Evans 29853.
No copy located.

[1]Massachusetts Historical Society, *Proceedings*, Vol. 43 (1909), p. 138.
[2]Lea and Febiger Papers, Historical Society of Pennsylvania.

42

—— The sixteenth Connecticut edition. Hartford: Printed by Hudson & Goodwin.... [1795?]

164 pp., illus. 16 cm.
DLC, NHi, NN, RPJCB.
Evans 29850.

NOTES

1. The last figure in "Of Numbers" is 1795.

2. Although Evans says the cuts were made by Alexander Anderson, this does not seem to be the case; no Anderson cuts (except for the frontispiece of Title 28) have been identified by the compiler until 1804 (Title 89). The cuts in this edition are the regular Hudson and Goodwin set of this period (see Title 26).

43

—— The seventeenth Connecticut edition. Hartford: Printed by Hudson & Goodwin. [With the privilege of copy right.] [1795?]

164 pp., illus. 16 cm.
CtHT, MiDeaEd.
Evans 29851.
The last figure in "Of Numbers" is 1795.

44

—— The IXth Vermont edition. Bennington: Printed by Anthony Haswell. (With the privilege of copy-right.).... M,DCC,XCVI.

167 pp., incl. frontis., illus. 16 cm.
VtMidbS.
Not seen; data supplied by library.

45

—— Thomas & Andrews' twelfth edition.... Printed at Boston .... 1796.

156 pp., incl. frontis., illus. 17 cm.
MB (imperfect), MH (imperfect).
Evans 29854, under 1795, with slight differences.

NOTES

1. From this point on, Thomas and Andrews editions repeat 1796 as the last figure in "Of Numbers," regardless of the title-page date.

2. Earlier Thomas and Andrews editions listed only their Boston and Worcester shops, sometimes with the addition of the phrase "and by the Booksellers in Town and Country"; this edition adds to the Boston and Worcester outlets "Thomas, Andrews & Butler, in Baltimore; and . . . Thomas, Andrews & Penniman, in Albany."

46

[—— Thomas and Andrews' thirteenth edition. Boston, 1796.]

Evans 31590.
No copy located (see Title 47).

47

[—— Thomas and Andrews' fourteenth edition. Boston, 1796.]

Evans 31591.
No copy located. There is in the Boston Public Library a Webster speller of which the title-page and many other pages are missing; it may be a copy of this or the preceding item, since it differs from all earlier Thomas and Andrews editions seen. However, it could equally well be an example of their unlocated fifteenth or sixteenth editions.

48

—— The eighteenth Connecticut edition. Hartford: Printed by Hudson & Goodwin. . . . [1796?]

165, (1) pp., illus. 16 cm.
NN.
Evans 31592.
The last figure in "Of Numbers" is 1796.

49

[—— Thomas and Andrews' fifteenth edition. Boston, 1797.]

Evans 33180.
No copy located. See note on Title 47.

50

[—— Thomas and Andrews' sixteenth edition. Boston, 1797.]

Evans 33181.
No copy located. See note on Title 47.

51

[—— Nineteenth edition. New-York: Printed by W. A. Davis . . . for T. Allen, E. Duyckinck, & Co.[,] N. Judah, P. S. [sic, for A.] Mesier, and D. Dunham. 1797.]

Evans 33183.

Although he does not locate a copy, Evans apparently examined one, for he gives the imprint specifically as above. At the end of an article on another bookseller,[3] R. W. G. Vail cites a New York, 1797, edition as in the American Antiquarian Society, but the Society was unable to locate it in searches made in 1942 and 1955.[4]

Presumably the printer or group of booksellers listed in the preceding entry had bought the license to publish at a public auction of the "exclusive right and license to print One hundred & fifty thousand copies of... Part First" in New York or Philadelphia, held March 30, 1796, advertised in the American Minerva, *March 23 and later. In later years Webster opposed this method of procuring publication, but at this time he seems to have needed ready money. A split impended between him and George Bunce, and the plan to publish his books himself (see Title 40) was apparently not working out. This is the first instance found by the compiler of an auction of a license to print a Webster work.*

[3]"A Curtain Call for Benjamin Gomez," *The Colophon*, Pt. 9 (1932), pp. [79-90].
[4]Letters, C. S. Brigham, Director, to the editor, September 23 and October 13, 1955.

52

—— Thomas & Andrews' seventeenth edition.... Printed at Boston.... 1798.

156 pp., incl. frontis., illus. 17 cm.
MWA, MiDeaEd, NNC-T, RPB.
Evans 34976.

53

—— Thomas & Andrews' eighteenth edition.... Printed at Boston.... 1798.

156 pp., incl. frontis., illus. 17 cm.
CtY, MH, MWA.
Evans 34977.

54

[—— Thomas and Andrews' nineteenth edition. Boston, 1798.]

Evans 34978.
No copy located.

55

—— The nineteenth Connecticut edition. Hartford: Printed by Hudson & Goodwin.... [1798?]

[165, (1)] pp., illus. 16 cm.
CtHT-W (imperfect), MWA (imperfect).
Evans 33182, under 1797.

NOTES

1. The final figure in "Of Numbers" is 1798.
2. Both copies located lack the terminal pages, but the text follows Title 48, so the collation was probably the same.
3. This edition has cuts which differ from the earlier Hudson and Goodwin editions; four are signed by Z. Howe and two by W. Wadsworth (Plate IX).
4. Mrs. Howard B. Field has a speller which has the title-page of this edition but the contents of about 1803.

56

[—— Twentieth Connecticut edition. Hartford: Hudson and Goodwin, 1798(?).]

Evans 34979.
No copy located. The Watkinson Library has a fragmentary Webster speller of which the last figure in "Of Numbers" is 1798, but which differs slightly from the preceding; it may be this edition.

57

—— Thomas & Andrews' twentieth edition.... Printed at Boston.... 1799.

156 pp., incl. frontis., illus. 17 cm.
MWA.
Evans 36684.

58

[—— Thomas and Andrews' twenty-first edition. Boston, 1799.]

Evans 36685.
No copy located.

59

—— The twenty-first Connecticut edition. Hartford: Printed by Hudson & Goodwin.... [1799?]

165, (1) pp., illus. 16 cm.
CT, NBLIHI, NHI, NN, NJP.
Evans 36686.
The last figure in "Of Numbers" is 1799.

60

—— The third Albany edition. Albany: Printed by Charles R. and George Webster.... 1800. With privilege of copy-right.

168 pp., illus. 17 cm.

NN (imperfect).
Evans 39041.
There was another third Albany edition in 1803; no trace has been found of a second Albany.

61

——— Thomas & Andrews' twentysecond [sic] edition.... Printed at Boston.... 1800.

156 pp., incl. frontis., illus. 17 cm.
MWA, NhD.
Evans 39040.

62

——— The twenty-second Connecticut edition. Hartford: Printed by Hudson & Goodwin.... [1800?]

165, (1) pp., illus. 16 cm.
NN.
Evans 39042.

NOTES

1. The last figure in "Of Numbers" is 1800.
2. Contains a new set of cuts, by Abner Reed, one signed "A Reed" (Plate X).

62 *bis*

——— Thomas & Andrews' twenty-third edition.... Printed at Boston.... 1801.

156 pp., incl. frontis., illus. 17 cm.
MiDeaEd.

63

——— Thomas & Andrews' twenty-fourth edition.... Printed at Boston.... 1801.

156 pp., incl. frontis., illus. 17 cm.
MWA, MiDeaEd, NRU.
Note that this firm issued another twenty-fourth edition in 1802.

64

——— The twenty-third Connecticut edition. Hartford: Printed by Hudson & Goodwin. [With the privilege of copy right.] [1801?]

165, (1) pp., illus. 18 cm.
CT (imperfect), MIDEAED.
The last figure in "Of Numbers" is 1801.

65

——— The twenty-fourth Connecticut edition. Hartford: Printed by Hudson & Goodwin.... [1801?]

165, (1) pp., illus. 16 cm.
CTHI, CTY, NN.
The last figure in "Of Numbers" is 1801.

66

——— Thomas & Andrews' twenty-fourth edition.... Printed at Boston.... 1802.

156 pp., [incl. frontis.], illus. 17 cm.
CTY, DLC, MIDEAED, NN, PU (all lacking frontispiece).

NOTES

1. The title-page is reproduced in George E. Littlefield, *Early Schools and School-Books of New England* (Boston, 1904), p. 133.
2. Note that this firm had already issued a twenty-fourth edition in 1801.

67

——— Correctly printed from the best Hartford edition. [Brooklyn,] Printed by Thomas Kirk. 1802.

168 pp., illus. 16 cm.
NN.
Thomas Kirk was a printer and publisher in Brooklyn from 1799 to 1813; see Oscar Wegelin, "The Brooklyn, New York, Press, 1799–1820,"

Bulletin of the Bibliographical Society of America, Vol. IV (1912), pp. 34–47, and Douglas C. McMurtrie, *Issues of the Brooklyn Press* (Brooklyn, 1936), though neither lists this title.

68

——— The twenty-fifth Connecticut edition. Hartford: Printed by Hudson & Goodwin.... [1802?]

165, (1) pp., illus. 17 cm.
CtHT-W, MWA, MiDeaEd, NN.
The last figure in "Of Numbers" is 1802.

69

——— Tenth Wilmington edition. Wilmington: Printed and sold by Bonsal & Niles. 1802.

151 pp., incl. frontis., illus. 17 cm.
NN.

NOTES

1. The frontispiece resembles that used by Thomas and Andrews, but is cruder (Plate VIII). On its recto (p. [i]) is the printed statement, "Copy Right secured according to Law." The cuts have also been redone, based on earlier sets (Plate XI).
2. No trace has been found of any first to ninth Wilmington editions.

70

——— Eleventh Wilmington edition. Wilmington: Printed and sold by Bonsal & Niles. 1802.

150 pp., incl. frontis., illus. 17 cm.
MWA (imperfect).

71

——— Windsor, Vermont. Printed by Nahum Mower. [With the privilege of copy-right.] [1802?]

165, (1) pp., illus. 14 cm.
NNC.
The last figure in "Of Numbers" is 1802.

72

—— The third Albany edition. Albany: Printed by Charles R. and George Webster.... 1803. With privilege of copy-right.

168 pp., illus. 16 cm.
N, British Museum.
Note that there had already been a third Albany edition in 1800.

73

—— Thomas & Andrews' twenty-fifth edition.... Printed at Boston.... 1803.

156 pp., incl. frontis., illus. 17 cm.
CT, MWA, NHD.

NOTES

1. This is the last of the Thomas and Andrews editions to contain the "porcupine portrait" as a frontispiece.
2. Thomas, Andrews, and Penniman of Albany drop out of the imprint with this edition.

74

—— Thomas & Andrews' twenty-sixth edition.... Printed at Boston.... 1803.

156 pp., illus. 17 cm.
MIU, PU.
Note that the firm issued another twenty-sixth edition in 1804.

75

—— The twenty-sixth Connecticut edition. Hartford: Printed by Hudson & Goodwin.... [1803?]

165, (1) pp., illus. 16 cm.
CT, CTHT-W, CTY (imperfect), MIDEAED, NN, NJHI.

NOTES

1. The last figure in "Of Numbers" is 1803.
2. A different setting of type from the twenty-fifth Connecticut, though the same cuts, by now badly worn, are employed.

76

——— The twenty-seventh Connecticut edition. Hartford: Printed by Hudson & Goodwin.... [1803?]

165, (1) pp., illus. 17 cm.
DFSA, NN, British Museum (imperfect).
The last figure in "Of Numbers" is 1803.

77

——— The twenty-eighth Connecticut edition. Hartford: Printed by Hudson & Goodwin.... [1803?]

165, (1) pp., illus. 17 cm.
CTHI (imperfect), British Museum.
The last figure in "Of Numbers" is 1803.

78

——— New York: Printed by William W. Vermilye, Jun. for E. Duyckinck, T. and J. Swords, P. A. Mesier, and I. Collins. 1803.

156 pp., illus. 17 cm.
CT.

79

——— Corrrectly printed from the last New York edition. Newbern: Martin & Ogden. 1803.

156 pp., illus. 16 cm.
NHI.

NOTES

1. The cuts are different from those of any other edition seen (Plate XII).

2. Despite the title-page date, the last figure in "Of Numbers" is 1804.

3. Webster wrote to Jacob Johnson, December 6, 1804: ". . . I am afraid also that Martin & Ogden of North Carolina have printed, under a license for 25,000, given 18 months ago, a much larger number."[5]

80

—— Windsor, Vermont. Printed by Nahum Mower. [With the privilege of copy-right.] [1803?]

165 pp., illus. 16 cm.
ICU.
The last figure in "Of Numbers" is 1803.

81

—— Thomas & Andrews' twenty-sixth edition.... Printed at Boston..., 1804.

156 pp., illus. 18 cm.
CtHT-W, MWA (imperfect).

NOTES

1. With this edition, Thomas and Andrews revert to listing in the imprint as vendors only their Boston and Worcester shops.

2. Note that the firm had already issued a twenty-sixth edition in 1803.

82

—— Thomas & Andrews' twenty-eighth edition.... Printed at Boston..., 1804.

156 pp., illus. 17 cm.
MWA.
No Thomas and Andrews twenty-seventh edition has been located.

[5]In the possession of Mrs. Theodore L. Bailey.

83

—— Thomas & Andrews' twenty ninth edition.... Printed at Boston..., 1804.

156 pp., illus. 17 cm.
MWA.

In a manuscript catalogue of his publications, now in the American Antiquarian Society, Isaiah Thomas recorded that his firm printed thirty editions of the speller, and that in 1804 they printed five. This suggests the actuality of the editions not located in their sequence up to this point, and possibly of a thirtieth edition.

84

[—— Brookfield, Mass.: E. Merriam and Co., 1804.]

On August 9 Ebenezer Andrews wrote to Isaiah Thomas, "I mentioned to Mr. West what you wrote about the Merriams printing Webster's Spell'g Book. Can you ascertain whether they are really printing it?"[6] On December 21 Webster wrote to John West, "I directed a prosecution of the Merriams, which bro^{t} them to a settlement—& upon their paying me a considerable sum in damiges [sic], I acquitted them, on condition they send the books out of N England."[7]

It is ironic that the first publishing of Webster's work by a Merriam should have been unauthorized, for other members of the family in the course of time became the publishers who have kept his name green.

85

[—— New Bern, N. C.: Franklin and Garrow, 1804.]

This advertisement, dated July 27, appeared half a dozen times between August 10 and December 21 in the *North Carolina Circular and Newbern Weekly Advertiser*: "WEBSTER'S SPELLING BOOKS. The printers of this paper [Franklin and Garrow] have lately struck off a very large edition of the above work and will supply...any quantity at seventeen shillings and six-pence, per dozen."

[6]American Antiquarian Society.
[7]Personal Papers Miscellaneous, Manuscripts Division, Library of Congress.

86

—— New-York: Printed for and sold by G. & R. Waite..., 1804.

156 pp., illus. 16 cm.
NN.
From various hints in correspondence of the time, the compiler thinks that the Waites may well have issued an edition earlier, perhaps in 1803. They were advertising the book for sale as early as January 18, 1804, in the *Commercial Advertiser*.

87

[—— Troy, N. Y.: Thomas Collier, 1804.]

Collier advertised an edition in press in the *Troy Gazette*, March 20, 1804, and later. No copy has been located; the compiler believes that if this edition existed it was the old version rather than the 1804 revision.

88

—— Thirteenth Wilmington edition. Wilmington: Printed by Bonsal & Niles, for James Wilson. 1804.

144 pp., incl. frontis., illus. 16 cm.
DLC.
No trace of a twelfth Wilmington edition has been found.

c. *The American Spelling Book, Revised*

With the approaching expiration of the first copyright under the Federal law —it had been taken out in 1790—and apparently dissatisfied with the general pattern of publishing the earlier editions of the speller, Webster revised it thoroughly, took out a new copyright, and realigned the licensees. For the new version these were initially Charles R. and George Webster of Albany, John West of Boston, Hudson and Goodwin of Hartford, and Jacob Johnson of Philadelphia; later others were added.

Application for copyright was made in the Connecticut District on November 1, 1803, *and Webster records in his diary that "In Novr. & December I was in Philadelphia procuring types for the revised Spelling Book." On December* 28 *he signed a contract with Jacob Johnson and delivered to him a sample copy. Since Johnson's seems to have been the first printing, his editions are listed first in this year.*

Hereafter, 1804 *was almost always the last figure in "Of Numbers," regardless of the year of publication. With this revision Webster dropped "Junior" from his name on the title-page, although his father lived until* 1813.

During the period of this copyright Webster kept a careful account of numbers printed by the licensees. He recorded these figures as running from one June to the next; when quoted below, they are applied to the earlier year.

89

The American spelling book; containing, the rudiments of the English language, for the use of schools in the United States. By Noah Webster, Esq. The first revised impression. [Philadelphia? 1804?]

168 pp., illus. 17 cm. P. [i], title-page. P. [ii], notice of copyright application, November 1, [1803]. Pp. [iii]–vi, new preface, signed "N.W. New Haven, 1803." Pp. [7]–168, text.
MWA.

NOTES

1. The text includes such new material as four poems (pp. 77–80), of which the compiler attributes the first two, "The Rose" and "The Lamb," to Webster; "Precepts concerning the social relations" (pp. 81–82); the 1800 census figures (p. 114); and "Additional Lessons" (pp. 151–154). There is a new set of cuts for the fables, executed – though not signed – by Alexander Anderson (Plate XIII).[8] There are minor differences in the execution of the engravings in the Boston, Hartford, and Philadelphia editions.

2. In this doubtless unique copy Webster wrote on the front flyleaf, "Sample copy delivered to Jacob Johnson, in pursuance of the Contract dated Decr. 28, 1803," and, as shown in the reproduction, he changed "The" to "Johnson's" on the title-page. No copies with "Johnson's" printed have been found, but there seems to have been such an edition.

[8]Identified by their presence in No. 7 of Anderson's personal scrapbooks in The New York Public Library.

Johnson advertised the new speller in *The Library, or Philadelphia Literary Reporter* on June 18 as "this day . . . published."

3. Because of the words "delivered to Jacob Johnson," the compiler originally thought that this book must have been printed elsewhere, but the type and format suggest that it was printed by Benjamin Johnson, who did much of Jacob Johnson's printing. It is likely that only the title-page was specially prepared, and that "delivered" is to be taken in a legalistic sense.

90

——— Johnson's second revised impression. Philadelphia: Published by Jacob Johnson & Co.... 1804.

168 pp., illus. 16 cm.
DLC.

NOTES

1. Advertised in *The Library, or Philadelphia Literary Reporter*, September 8, 1804.

2. The notice of application for copyright on the verso of the title-page has been replaced by the official entry, March 14, 1804.

91

——— Johnson's third revised impression. Philadelphia, Published by Jacob Johnson & Co.... 1804.

168 pp., illus. 17 cm.
MWA (imperfect).
Account books: "June 1805...24,500," which probably applies to all three Johnson printings of 1804.

92

[——— Albany: Charles R. and George Webster, 1804.]

Account books: "June, 1805 11,800." There is also a letter of February 18, 1804, from him to them, referring to their intention of printing an edition.[9]

[9] Webster Papers, New York Public Library.

93

——— Revised copy—West's first edition. Printed at Boston, for John West. . . . 1804. David Carlisle, printer. . . .

168 pp., illus. 17 cm.
MH.
Account books: "To June 1805 29,150."
Other booksellers listed in the imprint are West and Greenleaf, Ebenezer Larkin, and Thomas and Andrews, all in Boston.

94

——— The first revised impression. Hartford: Printed by Hudson & Goodwin, 1804.

168 pp., illus. 17 cm.
CtNhHi, CtY, RPB, Merriam.
Announced in the *Connecticut Courant*, June 6, 1804, and elsewhere, and advertised therein December 26 and later.

95

[——— Albany: Charles R. and George Webster, 1805.]

Account books: "June 1806 28,650."
Part of the Utica edition of 1805 seems either to have been printed in Albany or to have had an Albany imprint; see below, Title 99.

96

——— Revised copy—West's edition. Printed at Boston, for John West, proprietor of the copy right. 1805. David Carlisle, printer . . . .

168 pp., illus. 16 cm.
CtHT-W, MHi, MWA.
Account books: "To June 1806 40,900."
Thomas and Whipple, Newburyport, and Charles Pierce, Portsmouth, are added to the booksellers in the imprint, and also "all other Booksellers in the United States."

97

[—— Hartford: Hudson and Goodwin, 1805.]

Webster's account with Hudson and Goodwin calls for 50,000 copies from June, 1805, to June, 1806. The compiler's notes record a Hartford, 1805, edition seen in the possession of a private collector, but in 1956 the book could not be found for verification by the editor.

98

—— Johnson's fourth revised impression. Philadelphia, Published by Jacob Johnson.... 1805.

168 pp., illus. 16 cm.
MWA (imperfect).
Account books: "June 1806...22,500."

99

[—— First revised impression(?). Utica: Merrell and Seward, 1805.]

Utica Imprints 21; Williams p. 22.
No copy located. In 1804 Webster assigned a right to print "in territory Westward of Albany" to his nephew Ebenezer Belden; on February 4, 1805, Belden sold the right to print in Utica to Asahel Seward. Webster's account with Seward records, "June 1806...5000—& 2000 at Albany 7000." Williams says the work was advertised in the Utica *Patriot*, June 10, 1805.

100

—— Revised copy—West's edition. Printed at Boston, for John West.... 1806. David Carlisle, printer....

168 pp., illus. 17 cm.
MB, MWA.
Account books: "To June 30th 1807 85,150."

101

—— The revised impression. Hartford: Printed by Hudson & Goodwin. 1806.

168 pp., illus. 16 cm.
CtHT-W, MiDeaEd.
Account books: "June 1806 to June 1807 35,000."

102

[—— Lexington, Ky.: Joseph Charless, 1806.]

Charless advertised an edition, "page for page and letter for letter with Johnson's," in the *Kentucky Gazette,* September 22, 1806. Webster engaged Henry Clay to handle his contract with Charless, and Clay wrote him on November 18, 1806, that "the types...are now received & the contract is executed. He has struck 5000 copies of the book."[1]

103

[—— Philadelphia: Jacob Johnson, 1806.]

Account books: "June 1807...52,715."

104

—— The second revised impression. Utica: Printed by Asahel Seward. 1806.

168 pp., illus. 17 cm.
NRU.
Not seen; data provided by the library.

105

—— The first revised impression Albany Printed by Websters and Skinner. 1807.

168 pp., illus. 17 cm.
NBuHi (imperfect).
Account books: "June 1808...43,000." Since there is no entry in the accounts for 1807 to cover the 1806 output, this figure may actually represent an edition in 1806 as well as one in 1807.

[1] Ibid.

106

—— Bennington, Vt. Printed by Wright, Goodenow, & Stockwell, and sold by them . . . at the Rensselaer Book-Store, Troy, N.Y. Also, by Thomas & Thomas, Walpole, N.H. 1807.

168 pp., illus. 16 cm.
NN, VtHi.
Account books: "March 8, 1809. 27,500. This contract assigned to Holbrook, Fessenden & Porter of Brattleborough, 1808."

NOTES

1. This contains a new set of cuts which are based on, but cruder than, Alexander Anderson's first set (Plate XIII).
2. Since the firm was located at Troy, they advertised in the *Albany Gazette* and other New York state papers. See also the advertisement quoted under Title 119.

107

——Revised copy—West's edition. Printed at Boston, for John West . . . 1807. David Carlisle, printer. . . .

168 pp., illus. 16 cm.
DLC, MH, MWA, NN.
Account books: "To June 30 1808 62,800."
"One thousand copies . . . printed at Boston," *Commercial Advertiser*, May 13, 1807, and later.

108

——The revised impression. Hartford: Printed by Hudson & Goodwin. 1807.

168 pp., illus. 16 cm.
NN.
Account books: "June 1807 to June 1808 40,000."

109

[——Philadelphia: Jacob Johnson, 1807.]

Account books: "June 1808 . . . 47,349."

110

[—— Third revised impression(?). Utica: Asahel Seward, 1807.]

Account books: "In 1807, 220 quires & April 1807 66 quires, copies, 18,000."

111

——The first revised impression. Albany: Printed by Websters and Skinner. 1808.

168 pp., illus. 16 cm.
N, NN, NHD, OCLWHI.
Account books: "April 1810...23,000." Since there is no entry in 1809, this may cover editions in both 1808 and 1809.

112

—— Revised copy—West's edition. Printed at Boston, for John West, proprietor of the copy right, 1808.... E. G. House, printer ....

168 pp., illus. 17 cm.
OHI.
Account books: "To June 30 1809 54,300."

112a

—— Revised copy—West's edition. Printed at Boston, for John West and Co., proprietors of the copy right, 1808.... E. G. House, printer....

DLC, MA, PHC, RPB, Merriam.

113

[—— Brattleboro: Holbrook, Fessenden, and Porter, 1808.]

Account books: "June 1809...28,600."

114

—— The revised impression. Hartford: Printed by Hudson & Goodwin. 1808.

168 pp., illus. 16 cm.
MH.
Account books: "June 1808 to June 1809 35,000."

115

[—— Lexington, Ky.: Maccoun, Tilford, and Co., 1808.]

Account books (as "Assignees of Joseph Charless"): "Jany 24 1809 —7300," followed by "No returns—& the house failed." There are entries for three small payments which came in during 1809, 1810, and 1813, partly through the agency of Henry Clay.

116

[—— Philadelphia: Jacob Johnson, 1808.]

Account books: "June 1809...32,600."

117

—— The fourth revised impression. Utica: Printed by Seward and Williams.... 1808.

168 pp., illus. 17 cm.
N.
Utica Imprints 54.
Account books: "April, 1809...29,000."

118

—— Revised copy—West's edition. Printed at Boston, for John West and Co.... 1809. E. G. House, printer....

168 pp., illus. 17 cm.

MWA.

Account books: "To June 30 1810 54,300."

The booksellers listed in the imprint are now John West and Co., David West, Ebenezer Larkin, and Thomas and Andrews, Boston; Thomas and Whipple and William Sawyer and Co. in Newburyport; and Charles Pierce and Charles Tappan in Portsmouth.

119

—— Printed by William Fessenden, for Fessenden, Holbrook & Porter. Brattleborough, (Vermont) 1809.

168 pp., illus. (incl. cut on title-page). 17 cm.

ICU, NN, NJR, Merriam.

Account books: "June 1810 . . . 107,700."

NOTES

1. Contains a new set of cuts (Plate XIV). In the University of Chicago copy the cut for the eighth fable does not belong to the new set, but is the old one from the Bennington, 1807, edition, so it is likely that in addition to buying the copyright from Wright, Goodenow, and Stockwell (see Title 106), the Brattleboro firm also bought their cuts. The title-page cut is an oval scene showing a ship in a river or bay with fields on one side and buildings on the other, surrounded by the legend, "By agriculture we live. By commerce we thrive."

2. "William Fessenden, & Holbrook & Porter, have lately purchased of Messrs. Wright, Goodenow & Stockwell, for a very valuable consideration, the copy right . . . for the State of Vermont. They are determined, their copy shall not be inferior to any published in the Union. . . . Dec. 10, 1808." Brattleboro *Reporter*, February 20, 1809, and later.

3. In the New York Public Library copy the date in the imprint has been altered by hand to make it appear to be 1800.

120

—— The revised impression. Hartford: Printed by Hudson & Goodwin. 1809.

168 pp., illus. 17 cm.

MH, MWA, NRU, OClWHi.

Account books: "June 1809 to June 1810 55,000."

121

——— Thirtieth revised impression. Philadelphia: Published by Johnson & Warner.... Also sold by Peter Brynberg, Wilmington, Delaware. 1809.

168 pp., illus. 16 cm.
ICN, MiDeaEd, NN, PHi.
Account books: "June 1810...53,269."

NOTES

1. Despite the title-page date, this edition contains the 1810 census figures. Since these figures were not available until 1812 there is something suspect about this printing, but it has been put under 1809, since that is clearly the date in the imprint.

2. The numbering of this edition cannot be accounted for, even if "thirteenth" is meant. Johnson and Warner were given to erratic numbering of editions; cf. Title 165.

3. Webster records in his account book that on October 31, 1808, he renegotiated the Jacob Johnson contract, the balance of the term being taken over by Johnson and Warner.

122

——— The fifth revised impression. Utica: Printed by Seward and Williams. 1809.

168 pp., illus. 17 cm.
NBuT.
Utica Imprints [65], from which the entry is taken; not seen by the compiler.
Account books: "Sept 1 1810...20,000."

A fragment of a letter, in the possession of Mrs. Theodore L. Bailey, which the compiler identifies as Webster to Jacob Johnson, about 1809, *gives a suggestion of editions in the South, otherwise unrecorded: "I have additional information that this book has been printed in Edenton, N. Carolina, in large numbers. Will you be kind enough to ask Binney [sic] & Ronaldson whether they have sold the types which were composed for Collier and Hill & if so, to whom?" Collier and Hill being a Savannah firm, this is a hint of at least a projected edition there also.*

123

[—— Albany: Charles R. and George Webster, 1810.]

Account books: "May 1811 13,000."

124

—— Revised copy—West's edition. Printed at Boston, for John West and Co.... 1810. E. G. House, printer....

168 pp., illus. 17 cm.
MH, MWA (imperfect), MiDeaEd, NNC.
Account books: "To June 30 1811 45,800."
The list of vendors in this imprint has again changed slightly, David West becoming West and Blake, O. C. Greenleaf being added in Boston, and E. Little and Co. replacing William Sawyer and Co. in Newburyport.

125

[—— Brattleboro: Holbrook, Fessenden, and Porter, 1810.]

Account books: "May 10, 1811...67,000."

126

—— The revised impression. Hartford: Printed by Hudson & Goodwin. 1810.

168 pp., illus. 17 cm.
CtY.
Account books: "June 18 1810 to June 15 1811 40,000."

127

[—— Philadelphia: Johnson and Warner, 1810.]

Account books: "June 30, 1811...56,873."

128

[—— Albany: Charles R. and George Webster, 1811.]

Account books: "March, 1814 printed in 1811, 1812 & 1813... 48,560."

129

—— Revised copy—West's edition. Printed at Boston, by E. G. House..., for John West and Co.... 1811.

168 pp., illus. 16 cm.
MH, MWA, MiDeaEd, MiU-C, RPB.
Account books: "To July 22 1812 40,000."

130

—— Brattleborough, Vt. Printed by William Fessenden. 1811.

168 pp., illus. (incl. cut on title-page). 17 cm.
MH (imperfect).
The text up to page 11 has been condensed to make room for two additional cuts (children at play and a school in session); the cuts for the fables are the same as those in the University of Chicago copy of Title 119.

131

—— The revised impression. Hartford: Printed by Hudson & Goodwin. 1811.

168 pp., illus. 16 cm.
MWA, NHi.
Account books: "June 15, 1811 to June 9, 1812 30,000."

132

[—— Philadelphia: Johnson and Warner, 1811.]

Account books: "July 5, 1812...56,873."

133

[—— Utica: Asahel Seward, 1811.]

Account books: "June 5, 1812...20,000."

134

[—— Albany: Charles R. and George Webster, 1812.]

Account books: "March, 1814 printed in 1811, 1812 & 1813... 48,560."

135

—— Revised copy—West's edition. Printed at Boston, by E. G. House..., for John West and Co.... 1812.

168 pp., illus. 17 cm.
CtHi (imperfect), MH (imperfect), MiDeaEd, NNC.
Account books: "To July 6, 1813 31,500."
Contains the 1810 census figures.

136

[—— Brattleborough, Vt. Printed by William Fessenden. 1812.]

168 pp., illus. approx. 17 cm.
A copy was offered for sale by Rosenbach and Co. of Philadelphia in 1943, in their catalogue "For Librarians, Collectors and Scholars" (item 417), from which the imprint and collation have been completed by analogy with other Fessenden editions.
Account books: "June 1813...88,636."

137

—— The revised impression. Hartford, Printed by Hudson & Goodwin. 1812.

168 pp., illus. 16 cm.
Ct, CtHT-W, MH.
Account books: "June 9, 1812 to June 24, 1813 50,000."

The Harvard copy has only the 1800 census figures (p. 114), while the other copies have the figures for both 1800 and 1810.

138

[—— Philadelphia: Johnson and Warner, 1812.]

Account books: "July 22, 1814 for two years...75,000."

139

[—— Utica: Asahel Seward, 1812.]

Account books: "June 1, 1813...11,950."

140

—— The first revised impression. Albany: Printed by Websters and Skinners, 1813.

168 pp., illus. 16 cm.
NjR.
Note that Skinner of the firm name has now become plural, as well as the Webster. Noah Webster had to write them more than once to chide them for not reporting their editions annually, as they were supposed to do. See his account book entry under Title 128.

141

[—— Boston: John West, 1813.]

Account books: "To June 1, 1814 41,000."

142

—— Brattleborough, Vt. Printed by William Fessenden. 1813.

168 pp., illus. (incl. cut on title-page). 16 cm.
MH, MiDeaEd, NRU, VtBrat.
Account books: "June 1, 1814...126,000."

143

—— The revised impression. Hartford, Printed by Hudson & Goodwin. 1813.

168 pp., illus. 17 cm.
CT, CTHT-W (imperfect).
Account books: "June 1813 to June 29, 1814 45,000."

144

[—— Philadelphia: Johnson and Warner, 1813.]

Account books: "July 22, 1814 for two years...75,000."

145

[—— Utica: Asahel Seward, 1813.]

Account books: "June 1 1814...13,000."

146 & 147

On November 20, 1815, *Webster wrote a memorandum in which he discusses the printing and sales of the speller under the* 1804 *copyright. In this he indicates the existence of two otherwise unknown editions: "To this number may be added two small impressions in Ohio & New Orleans printed within two years, equal to* 6000 *copies...."*[2]

148

—— Revised copy—West's edition. Printed at Boston, by E. G. House..., for West & Richardson.... 1814.

168 pp., illus. 17 cm.
MIDEAED.
Account books: "To May 13, 1815 51,475."

[2]Webster Papers, New York Public Library.

149

—— Brattleborough, Vt. Printed by William Fessenden. 1814.

168 pp., illus. (incl. cut on title-page). 17 cm.
MH, MWA, Merriam.
The American Antiquarian Society has two copies, one a variant, the cut on p. 83 differing in shape.

150

——The revised impression. Brattleborough, Vt. Published by William Fessenden. 1814.

168 pp., illus. 17 cm.
MWA.
Account books: "May 22, 1815 . . . 118,600."
Differs from the preceding in the wording of the title and imprint, in not having a cut on the title-page, and in the cuts in the text, which are closer to those used in the Philadelphia editions than to the earlier Brattleboro editions. The text up to page 12 has been spaced out to replace the cuts added in 1811 but now dropped (see Title 130).

151

[—— Hartford: Hudson and Goodwin, 1814.]

Account books: "[July 1814 to] Augt. 15 1814 10,000" and "June 26, 1815 30,000."

152

[—— Philadelphia: Johnson and Warner, 1814.]

Account books: "June 30, 1815 . . . 66,000."

153

[—— Utica: Asahel Seward, 1814.]

Account books: "Augt 1, 1815 . . . 13,000."

154

—— Revised copy—stereotype edition. Charleston, S.C. Printed for Bradford & Read, Boston, 1815. P.W. Johnston, printer.

168 pp., illus. 16 cm.
Munroe.

NOTES

1. The title-page is reproduced in *The House that Merriam-Webster Built* (Springfield, Massachusetts, 1940), p. 5.

2. According to the memorandum quoted under Titles 146–147, Bradford and Read had a license to print 100,000 copies in "the three Southern States."

3. This is an early example of American stereotyping, for the process was introduced in the United States only in 1813.

155

[—— Boston: John West, 1815.]

Account books: "To June 1, 1816 51,473."

156

—— The revised impression. Brattleborough Vt. Published by William Fessenden. 1815.

168 pp., illus. 17 cm.
CtNhHi, MFHi, MWA (imperfect), MiDeaEd, Merriam.
Account books: "April 6, 1816. . . 128,160."

157

—— The revised impression. Hartford, Printed by Hudson & Goodwin. 1815.

168 pp., illus. 16 cm.
DLC.
Account books: "June 30, 1816. . . 60,000."

158

[—— Philadelphia: Johnson and Warner, 1815.]

Account books: "June 1816...86,950." The initial digit may be a three; it has to be read as an eight to make the total of the column correct, but this could be a case of Webster's having misread the digit in figuring the total. Either number is within the usual range of the edition size.

159

—— The ninth revised impression. Utica: Printed by Seward and Williams. 1815.

168 pp., illus. 17 cm.
DFSA (fragmentary).
Utica Imprints 162.

160

—— The first revised impression. Albany: Printed by Websters and Skinners. 1816.

168 pp., illus. 17 cm.
Not seen by the compiler. A copy was formerly in the possession of Mr. Harlow Lindley, who provided a description. The present location of this copy is unknown.

161

—— Revised copy—West's edition. Printed at Boston, by T. W. White..., for West & Richardson.... 1816.

168 pp., illus. 17 cm.
CT, MH, NBuHi, NNC (imperfect).
Account books: "To June 18, 1817 68,810."
Again the list of outlying booksellers is slightly changed, the Portsmouth dealers now reading "J. F. Shores and Tappan and Foster."

162

—— The revised impression. Brattleborough, Vt. Published by William Fessenden. 1816.

168 pp., illus. 16 cm.
DFSA, VtBrat.
Account books: "March 31, 1817. . .91,250."

Fessenden died in 1815 and apparently his rights were taken over by his father-in-law, John Holbrook (see following entry). Holbrook later formed a partnership with Fessenden's brother Joseph, and the imprint "Holbrook and Fessenden" occurs. (Mary R. Cabot, *Annals of Brattleboro, 1681–1895*, [2 vols., Brattleboro, 1921–1922].)

163

—— The revised impression. Brattleborough, Vt. Published by John Holbrook. 1816.

168 pp., illus. 16 cm.
MWA, NN, VtBrat.

164

—— The revised impression. Hartford, Printed by Hudson & Co. 1816.

168 pp., illus. 17 cm.
CtFHi.
Account books: "June 10, 1817. . .40,000."

165

—— Nintieth [sic] revised impression. Philadelphia: Published by Johnson and Warner. . . . 1816.

168 pp., illus. 17 cm.
CtY, MWA (imperfect), NN, PPeSchw.
Account books: "[June] 1817. . .64,000."

NOTES

1. Perhaps "nineteenth" is meant, but neither number can be exactly arrived at. The Schwenkfelder Library copy reads "thirtieth" instead of "ninetieth"; cf. Title 121.

2. An added bookseller in the imprint is Robert Porter, Wilmington, Delaware.

166

—— The tenth revised impression. Utica: Printed by Seward and Williams. 1816.

168 pp., illus. 16 cm.
NN.
Utica Imprints 183.
Account books: "June 1, 1817 . . . 13,360."

167

—— The twelfth revised impression. Utica: Printed by Seward and Williams. . . . 1816.

168 pp., illus. 16 cm.
NN.
Utica Imprints 182.

NOTES

1. It seems reasonable to assume a Seward and Williams eleventh edition in the same year, though a total of only slightly over 13,000 (as cited in the preceding entry) is a small number for three printings, especially since, as Webster specifically states in his account book, this firm was wont to exceed its annual allotment of 10,000.

2. The compiler's notes show that at one time she saw a copy with a front cover reading, "Spelling-Book. Sold by H. & E. Phinney . . . Cooperstown."

For later editions which are sometimes erroneously assigned to 1817, *see the introductory note to* 1818.

168

—— Revised copy—West's edition. Printed at Boston, for West & Richardson. . . . 1817.

168 pp., illus. 16 cm.
DLC, MWA, MiDeaEd, NN, NNC, NjR.
Account books: "March 14 1818 43,378."

168a

—— Revised copy—West's edition. Printed at Boston by T. W. White..., for West & Richardson.... 1817.

MWA.

169

—— The revised impression. Brattleborough, Vt. Published by John Holbrook. 1817.

168 pp., illus. 16 cm.
CT, MWA, MIDEAED, N, NN, NNC, OO.
Account books: "March 14, 1818...113,500."

170

—— The revised impression. Hartford, Printed by Hudson & Co. 1817.

168 pp., illus. 16 cm.
CTHI (imperfect), MWA, NN.
Account books: "March 14, 1818...40,000."

171

[—— Philadelphia: Johnson and Warner, 1817.]

Account books: "March 1818...50,000."

172

—— The thirteenth revised impression. Utica. Printed by William Williams.... 1817.

168 pp., illus. 17 cm.
CTHT-W, MIDEAED, NN (imperfect).
Utica Imprints 210.

The 1804 *copyright expired in* 1818. *Webster made slight changes in the content of the work and applied in the Massachusetts District on September* 15, 1817, *for a renewal to go into effect March* 14, 1818. *The application was published in the* Connecticut Courant, *September* 23, 1817, *and later.*

It should be noted that after the renewal expired, in 1832, *various unauthorized editions were published which contain as their only date the* 1817 *copyright application. Care has to be taken not to ascribe these printings to* 1817, *as has sometimes been done in library catalogues. Danger signals which indicate later printings include the phrase "with the Latest Corrections" in the title and pages numbering* 144 *rather than* 168.

The Brattleboro and the first-listed Hartford edition of this year still bear the old copyright date, 1804; *the other Hartford edition contains the* 1818 *copyright, and so do all printings of the* American *speller through* 1832, *unless otherwise stated.*

173

——— The revised impression. Brattleborough, Vt. Published by John Holbrook. 1818.

168 pp., illus. 16 cm.
MiDeaEd, RPB (imperfect), VtMidbS.

There are occasional references (e.g., *in the* 1889 *printed catalogue of the California State Library*) *to an* 1818 *edition in Concord, New Hampshire. This appears to be a ghost, being probably one of the Concord editions of* [1834–1835?] *or later.*

174

——— The revised impression. Hartford: Printed by Hudson & Co. 1818.

168 pp., illus. 16 cm.
CtHT-W.
The cuts are Alexander Anderson's set from the Philadelphia editions (Plate XIII), rather than the earlier Hartford set.

175

——— The revised impression, with the latest corrections. Hartford: Printed by Hudson and Co. 1818.

168 pp., illus. 16 cm.
PHi.
Contains the Alexander Anderson set of cuts, as in the preceding entry.

175a

[Identical title-page.]

Contains the Brattleboro set of cuts (Plate XIV).
MWA, MiDeaEd.

176

—— The revised impression, with the latest corrections. Albany Printed by Websters and Skinners. 1819.

168 pp., illus. 17 cm.
Merriam.

177

—— The revised impression, with the latest corrections. Boston: Printed by J. H. A. Frost, for West, Richardson and Lord. . . . 1819.

168 pp., illus. 17 cm.
Ct, MWA, MiDeaEd.

178

—— The revised impression, with the latest corrections. Brattleborough, Vt. Published by John Holbrook. 1819.

168 pp., incl. frontis., illus. 16 cm.
CtHT-W, CtY, DLC, MH, MiDeaEd, NN, NRU, NjR, OClWHi (imperfect).

NOTES

1. The eight cuts are new ones by Alexander Anderson, though not signed (Plate XV), and for the first time his frontispiece—signed "A"—appears, although it docs not become standard until the *Elementary Spelling Book* of 1829 (Plate XVIII). It seems to be based upon Francis Hayman's frontispiece to Volume I of the London, 1758, edition of Robert

Dodsley's *The Preceptor.*[3] The four lines of verse below the picture have not been found elsewhere despite search and inquiry; Webster may have written them himself.

2. The Rutgers copy is a variant, in which the imprint reads "Brattleborough, Vt. Printed by John Holbrook for Abijah Burbank, on paper of his own manufacture, by special contract. 1819."

179

[Identical title-page.]

Fables I to VI and Tables 32 to 39 are in slightly different order on pp. 83–95. In this, Tables 32–34 precede rather than follow Fable I.

MB, MWA, VtU.

180

—— The revised impression, with the latest corrections. Hartford: Printed by Hudson and Co. 1819.

168 pp., illus. 16 cm.
CT, CTHI, CTHT-W, NNC.

181

—— The revised impression, with the latest corrections. Albany: Printed by Websters and Skinners. 1820.

168 pp., illus. 17 cm.
TxComT (imperfect).
Not seen; data provided by the library.

182

—— The revised impression, with the latest corrections. Boston: Printed by J. H. A. Frost, for West, Richardson and Lord.... 1820.

[3] And in turn to have been the inspiration for the seal of the University of Michigan. See Frank E. Robbins, "Where Did Minerva Seal Come From?", *The Michigan Alumnus*, October 2, 1927 (Vol. XLIV, pp. 5–6); the author errs in placing the first appearance of the Anderson frontispiece in 1829.

168 pp., illus. 17 cm.
CtNhHi (imperfect).

183

—— The revised impression, with the latest corrections. Brattleborough, Vt. Published by John Holbrook. 1820.

168 pp., incl. frontis., illus. 16 cm.
VtU.
Not seen; data provided by the library.

183a

—— The revised impression, with the latest corrections. Brattleborough, Vt. Published by Holbrook & Fessenden. 1820.

CtY, MA, MH, MWA, MiDeaEd, MiU-C, NN, RPB.

184

—— The revised impression Stereotyped by E. & J. White, New-York. Canandaigua: Published by Bemis & Ward. 1820.

168 pp., illus. 16 cm.
Not seen by the compiler. A copy was formerly in the possession of Mr. Harlow Lindley, who provided a description. The present location of this copy is unknown.

185

—— The revised impression, with the latest corrections. Hartford: Printed by Hudson and Co. 1820.

168 pp., illus. 16 cm.
CtHT-W, MWA.

186

—— The latest edition, revised and corrected by the author. Lexington, Ky.: Published by James W. Palmer, bookseller and stationer, (Sign of the Bible). 1820.

168 pp., illus. 15 cm.
Ct.

187

——— The revised impression, with the latest corrections. Albany: Printed by Websters and Skinners. 1821.

168 pp., illus. 16 cm.
CT, ICHI, MIDEAED, NN, NRU.

188

——— The revised impression, with the latest corrections. Boston: Printed by J. H. A. Frost, for West, Richardson and Lord.... 1821.

168 pp., illus. 17 cm.
MWA.

189

——— The revised impression, with the latest corrections. Stereotyped by E. White, New-York. Brattleborough, Vt. Published by Holbrook and Fessenden. 1821.

168 pp., incl. frontis., illus. 17 cm.
CSMH (imperfect), DFSA (imperfect), MWA, VTHI, VTMIDBS.

NOTES

1. On page 14 there is an added alphabet, headed by a new cut, a mother teaching her children. There is a blank column in the census tables, headed "1820."

2. From 1809 through 1820 Brattleboro editions used 1804 as the last figure in "Of Numbers." With this edition they change to 1821; in the roman form the final "XXI" is squeezed into what should be blank space.

190

——— Revised copy. Stereotyped by B. & I. [?] Collins. Cincinnati, Ohio. Published for John P. Foote. 1821.

168 pp., illus. 16 cm.
OOXM.
Contains only the 1804 copyright entry.

191

—— The revised impression, with the latest corrections. Hartford: Printed by Hudson and Co. 1821.

168 pp., illus. 16 cm.
MiDeaEd, NN, OU.

192

—— The revised impression. Stereotyped by E. & J. White, New-York Albany: Printed by Websters and Skinners. 1822.

168 pp., illus. 17 cm.
Ct, CtHT-W, DFSA, MH, MWA, MiDeaEd, N, NN, ViW, VtMidbS, Merriam.

193

—— The revised impression, with the latest corrections. Stereotyped by G. Bruce, New-York. Albany: Printed by Websters and Skinners. 1822.

168 pp., illus. 16 cm.
MWA, MiDeaEd.

194

—— The revised impression, with the latest corrections. Boston: Printed by J. H. A. Frost, for West, Richardson and Lord.... 1822.

168 pp., illus. 17 cm.
Ct, CtY.

195

—— The revised impression, with the latest corrections. Stereotyped by E. White, New-York. Brattleborough, Vt. Printed by Holbrook and Fessenden. [1822?]

168 pp., incl. frontis., illus. 17 cm.
DFSA, MWA, MiDeaEd, NN, Merriam.

NOTES

1. Attributed to 1822 by the compiler because it is virtually identical with Title 189 and because 1822 is the only gap in a series of Brattleboro dated editions appearing annually.

2. A blank column is provided for the 1820 census figures, as in Title 189.

196

—— The revised impression. Stereotyped by E. & J. White, New-York Cincinnati: Published by J. P. Foote, and Morgan, Lodge and Co. 1822.

168 pp., illus. 17 cm.
IHi (imperfect).
Not seen; data provided by the library.

197

—— The revised impression, with the latest corrections. Hartford: Printed by Hudson and Co. 1822.

168 pp., illus. 16 cm.
Ct, CtHT-W, CtY, ICN, IU, NN, NjR.

198

—— The revised impression, with the latest corrections. Boston: Printed by J. H. A. Frost for West, Richardson and Lord. . . . 1823.

168 pp., illus. 16 cm.
CtHT-W, CtY, NNC.

199

—— The revised impression, with the latest corrections. Stereotyped by E. White, New-York. Brattleborough, Vt. Published by Holbrook and Fessenden. 1823.

168 pp., incl. frontis., illus. 17 cm.
CSmH, Ct, CtHi, MWA, MiDeaEd, NN.

200

—— The revised impression, with the latest corrections. Hartford: Printed for Hudson and Co. By W. Hudson and L. Skinner. 1823.

168 pp., illus. 16 cm.
CtY, NN.

At this point Hudson introduced a new set of cuts, of which the first is signed by, and the second and sixth initialled by, John W. Barber (Plate XVI).

201

—— The revised impression. Stereotyped by E. & J. White, New York. Lexington, Kentucky: Printed by W. W. Worsley. . . . 1823.

168 pp., illus. 16 cm.
NN.

NOTES

1. At head of title: "Worsley's stereotype impression."
2. In addition to Worsley's Lexington store, the imprint lists as an additional vendor Worsley and Collins, Louisville.

202

Roscoe M. Pierson's Preliminary Checklist of Lexington, Ky., Imprints. . . *records (No. 488) an 1823 edition "with the latest corrections," stereotyped by C. N. Baldwin instead of E. and J. White. He lists copies at the American Antiquarian Society and the Library of Congress, and there is a printed Library of Congress catalogue card for such an edition. Yale and the Henry Ford Museum also have copies which have been described as 1823. All four institutions, however, report that the imprint date is blurred, and is more likely 1826. All these copies agree in small points with others in which the blurred date has been read as 1826, and there are internal factors favoring the later date, so all are here described as the same printing (Title 217).*

203

——— Revised copy—stereotype edition Boston. Printed by J. H. A. Frost, for Richardson & Lord.... 1824.

168 pp., illus. 17 cm.
MH, MWA, MiDeaEd.

NOTES

1. Does not contain the 1818 copyright.
2. Amherst College has an imperfect copy in which "Spelling Book" and "English Language" on the title-page are in open letter rather than roman.

204

——— The revised impression, with the latest corrections. Stereotyped by E. White, New-York. Brattleborough, Vt. Published by Holbrook and Fessenden. 1824.

168 pp., illus. 17 cm.
CtY, DLC (imperfect), MH, MHi, MWA, MiDeaEd, MiU (imperfect), NjR.

205

——— The revised impression. Stereotyped by E. & J. White, New-York Cincinnati: Published by John P. Foote and Morgan and Lodge. 1824.

168 pp., illus. 16 cm.
OCHP (imperfect).

206

——— The revised impression, with the latest corrections. Hartford: Printed for Hudson and Co. By W. Hudson and L. Skinner. 1824.

168 pp., illus. 17 cm.
CtHT-W, MA, MiDeaEd, MiU.

207

—— The revised impression. Stereotyped by E. & J. White, New York Lexington, Kentucky: Printed by W. W. Worsley.... 1824.

[168] pp., illus. 16 cm.
ICU (imperfect).

NOTES

1. At head of title: "Worsley's stereotype impression."
2. The copy located is incomplete, but since the text is standard there were no doubt 168 pages in a complete copy.

208

—— The revised impression, with the latest corrections. Stereotyped by J. Howe—Philadelphia. Philadelphia: Published by Kimber and Sharpless.... 1824.

168 pp., illus. 17 cm.
DLC (imperfect).

209

—— The revised impression, with the latest corrections. Stereotyped by C. N. Baldwin, New-York. Baltimore: Published by Cushing and Jewett.... 1825.

168 pp., illus. 16 cm.
MdHi, NHi, Merriam.
Webster's annotations on a letter to Henry Hudson, September 14, 1831, include, in a list of sales by Hudson of licenses to print, "Cushing & Sons. June 25, 1825, for 280,000 copies."[4]

210

—— The revised impression, with the latest corrections. Stereotyped by E. White, New-York. Brattleborough, Vt. Published by Holbrook and Fessenden. 1825.

[4] Webster Papers, New York Public Library.

168 pp., illus. 17 cm.
CtNhHi, ICU, MB, MH, MiDeaEd, NN.

211

—— The revised impression.... Canandaigua: Printed by J. D. Bemis and Co., 1825.

168 pp., illus. 17 cm.
OClWHi.
Not seen by the compiler; data provided by the library. The information was taken from a catalogue card, the book being unavailable at the time. On the basis of the 1827 Canandaigua edition the title probably did not contain the phrase "with the latest corrections." The missing words may be "Stereotyped by E. White, New-York."

211 *bis*

—— The revised impression. Stereotyped by E. & J. White, New-York Cincinnati: Published and sold by N. & G. Guilford.... Anson [?] N. Deming, printer. 1825.

168 pp., illus. 16 cm.
MiDeaEd.
The Guilfords later appear as adapters of Webster, verging on plagiarism; see Appendix F, Nos. 7–10.

212

—— The revised impression, with the latest corrections. Hartford: Printed for H. Hudson, by W. Hudson and L. Skinner. 1825.

168 pp., illus. 17 cm.
CMC (imperfect), Ct, MiDeaEd, OO.

213

—— The revised impression. Stereotyped by E. & J. White, New York Lexington, Ky. Printeby [sic] W. W. Worsley.... 1825.

168 pp., illus. 16 cm.
CtHT-W.
At head of title: "Stereotype edition."

214

—— The revised impression, with the latest corrections. Stereotyped by J. Howe—Philadelphia. Philadelphia: Published by Kimber and Sharpless.... 1825.

168 pp., illus. 16 cm.
MWA, MiDeaEd, NNC, OClW.

215

—— The revised impression, with the latest corrections. Stereotyped by E. White, New-York. Brattleborough, Vt. Published by Holbrook and Fessenden. 1826.

168 pp., illus. 17 cm.
Ct, CtHT-W, NN.

216

—— The revised impression, with the latest corrections. Hartford: Printed for H. Hudson, by W. Hudson. 1826.

168 pp., illus. 16 cm.
Ct, MH, OCHP.
Although Henry Hudson's license ran until 1832, this was apparently the last edition published by him; he and Webster had a difference of opinion over the latter's desire to suppress the *American Spelling Book* before the end of its copyright term (see introductory note to 1829).

217

—— The revised impression, with the latest corrections, Stereotyped by C. N. Baldwin, New-York. Lexington, Ky. Published by W. W. Worsley. 1826.

168 pp., illus. 16 cm.
CtY, DFSA, DLC, MWA, MiDeaEd, NBuG, NN.

NOTES

1. The place and publisher lines of the imprint are not aligned with the rest of the title-page; perhaps they are a later insert.

2. In 1940 the Midland Rare Book Company offered for sale (*Midland Notes*, No. 11, item 153) a Lexington, 1826, edition in which, according to their description, the imprint read "Printed by W. W. Worsley and sold at his book-store, Jordan's Row, and at the book store of John P. Morton, Louisville."

218

—— The revised impression, with the latest corrections. Stereotyped by C. N. Baldwin, New-York. Baltimore: Published by Cushing and Jewett.... 1827.

168 pp., illus. 16 cm.
MdHi, MiDeaEd, NNC (imperfect).

219

—— The revised impression, with the latest corrections. Stereotyped by E. White, New-York. Brattleborough, Vt. Published by Holbrook and Fessenden. 1827.

168 pp., incl. frontis., illus. 17 cm.
CtHT-W, MWA, MiDeaEd, RPJCB, VtBrat, Merriam.

Something seems to have happened to Holbrook and Fessenden's stereotype plates in this year, for in this dated edition they revert to the plates used in their 1821 edition, and their undated edition attributed to 1827 (see following entry) differs in content from their usual editions. Reversion to the 1821 content meant dropping the 1820 census figures, though this firm was usually one of the most prompt in adding new census returns as they became available. (The 1820 figures had been added by them in 1823; by 1827 about half the editions contain them, the others still giving the 1810 figures.)

220

—— The revised impression, with the latest corrections. Brattleborough, Vt. Printed and published by Holbrook and Fessenden. [1827?]

168 pp., illus. 15 cm.
CtY, MH, MiDeaEd, NN, NNC, OClWHi (imperfect), VtMidbC.
Undated, and different in make-up from other Holbrook and Fessenden editions. Placed in 1827 because that is the last figure in "Of Numbers." This edition resembles most closely that of Middletown, 1829.

221

—— The revised impression Stereotyped by E. & J. White, New-York. Canandaigua: Printed by Bemis, Morse & Ward. 1827.

168 pp., illus. 17 cm.
MiU, NCanHi.
McMurtrie, Canandaigua, 103.

222

—— The revised impression, with the latest corrections. Cincinnati: Published by N. & G. Guilford Stereotyped by J. Howe. Philadelphia. 1827. W. M. & O. Farnsworth, Jun. printers.

168 pp., illus. 16 cm.
MiDeaEd.

223

—— The revised impression. Stereotyped by E. & J. White, New-York Cincinnati: Published by Morgan, Fisher and L'Hommedieu. 1827.

168 pp., [illus.] 17 cm.
OC.
Not seen by compiler; data provided by the library.

223*bis*

—— The revised impression, with the latest corrections. Concord, N.H. Published by Manahan, Hoag & Co. 1827.

168 pp., illus. 17 cm.
MiDeaEd.

224

—— The revised impression, with the latest corrections. Concord, N.H. Published by Manahan, Hoag & Co. [1827?]

168 pp., illus. 16 cm.
MH, NNC.
The preface is that of 1803 but is dated 1823, as are certain later (?) Concord editions (Titles 250–252). This is assigned to 1827 by the Harvard University Library, largely on the basis of the firm name, which by 1829 had changed to C. Hoag and M. G. Atwood.

225

—— The revised impression, with the latest corrections. Middletown, Conn. Published by William H. Niles. Stereotyped by A. Chandler. 1827.

168 pp., illus. 16 cm.
CT, CTHT-W, CTHI, CTNHHI, CTY, MH, MIDEAED, NHI, NN.

226

—— The revised impression, with the latest corrections. Philadelphia: Published by Kimber and Sharpless. . . . 1827.

168 pp., illus. 17 cm.
CTHI, MIDEAED, NNC.

227

—— The revised impression. Stereotyped by E. & J. White, New-York. Canandaigua: Printed by Bemis, Morse and Ward. 1828.

168 pp., illus. 16 cm.
NBUG.
McMurtrie, Canandaigua, 109. (His location of a copy in the Pennsylvania State Library is an error, their copy being Title 236.)

228

—— The revised impression, with the latest corrections. Cincinnati: Published by Morgan & Sanxay. Stereotyped by J. Howe. Philadelphia 1828.

168 pp., illus. 16 cm.
MiDeaEd, OHi.

229

—— The revised impression, with the latest corrections. Concord, N.H. Published by Manahan, Hoag & Co. 1828.

168 pp., illus. 16 cm.
MWA, NNC.

230

—— The revised impression, with the latest corrections. Concord, N.H. Published by Horatio Hill & Co. 1828.

168 pp., illus. 16 cm.
MH, MSaE, MiDeaEd, NhD, NhHi.

231

—— The revised impression, with the latest corrections. Middletown, Conn. Published by William H. Niles. Stereotyped by A. Chandler. 1828.

168 pp., illus. 16 cm.
CSmH, Ct, CtHT-W, CtNhHi, CtY, MB, MH, MWA, NN, NNC.

232

[—— Montreal, 1828.]

The 1870-71 and 1889 printed catalogues of the California State Library list an edition of Montreal in 1828, no longer to be found in the library, and of which no other trace has been found. There are occasional references in Webster's correspondence showing that his spellers were used in Canada, and editions were printed there at later dates.

233

——— The revised impression, with the latest corrections. New-Brunswick, N.J. Published by Terhune & Letson. 1828.

168 pp., illus. 16 cm.
CtY (imperfect), MiDeaEd, OClWHi (imperfect).

234

——— The revised impression, with the latest corrections. Philadelphia: Published by Robert H. Sherburne. South Street. Stereotyped by J. Howe. 1828.

168 pp., illus. 17 cm.
DFSA, MH, MWA, MiDeaEd, NN, OClWHi (imperfect), RPB, VtMidbS, VtU, Merriam.
There is a short blank space between "South" and "Street," which may mark a deletion.

The 1818 *copyright* (1817 *entry*) *ran until early in* 1832, *but about* 1828 *Webster, because the orthography of the* American Spelling Book *was not consistent with that of his* 1828 *dictionary, and for other reasons, decided to produce an entirely new speller. This he did, copyrighting and publishing it in* 1829 *as the* Elementary Spelling Book. *He wished it to replace entirely the earlier version, asking the holders of licenses which were to run until* 1832 *to give them up and make arrangements for the new work. Most of the licensees had paid for stereotyped plates, and naturally were not willing to give up their investment, so they continued to publish the* American *speller. Until the expiration of the* 1818 *copyright and of their licenses, this was legal, and Webster could do nothing about it. For the situation after* 1832 *see rubric D below.*

235

——— The revised impression, with the latest corrections. Stereotyped by C. N. Baldwin, New-York. Baltimore: Published by Cushing and Jewett, No. 6 North-Howard-Street. 1829.

168 pp., illus. 16 cm.
NN.

235a

—— The revised impression, with the latest corrections. Stereotyped by C. N. Baldwin, New-York. Baltimore: Published by Joseph Jewett, No. 229 Market Street. 1829.

MdBE (imperfect), NN, PHi.

236

—— The revised impression. Stereotyped by E. & J. White, New York. Canandaigua: Printed by Bemis and Ward. 1829.

168 pp., illus. 16 cm.
NRHi, P.
There are slight typographical differences between the two copies. In both the final digit of the date is blurred; it seems most likely a 9, though the Pennsylvania State Library copy is catalogued as 1828. When the copy now in the Rochester Historical Society was last sold (Swann Auction Galleries, New York, June 11, 1948) it was catalogued as 1823. That 1829 is the correct reading is supported by the fact that in McMurtrie's checklist of Canandaigua imprints the firm name "Bemis, Morse and Ward" occurs from 1826 through 1828 and "Bemis and Ward" from 1829 through 1831.

237

—— The revised impression, with the latest corrections. Middletown, Conn. Published by William H. Niles. Stereotyped by A. Chandler. 1829.

168 pp., illus. 15 cm.
Ct, CtHi, CtNhHi, CtY, ICHi, ICU, MWA, MiDeaEd, NN, PPM, RPB, Merriam.

238

—— The revised impression, with the latest corrections. New-Brunswick, N.J. Published by Terhune & Letson. 1829.

168 pp., illus. 16 cm.
Ct, MH, NN, OClWHi.

239

—— The revised impression, with the latest corrections. Philadelphia: Published by Kimber & Sharpless.... Stereotyped by J. Howe. 1829.

168 pp., illus. 17 cm.
MiU, NN.

240

The American Antiquarian Society possesses a copy of this spelling book of which the first ten pages are missing. The text and cuts do not agree exactly with any identified edition, and it has not been possible to establish a place and date; the compiler's inclination is to place the edition about 1829–1831, *during the rush to print this version of the speller while licenses under the* 1818 *copyright were still in effect.*

241

—— The revised impression, with the latest corrections. Concord, N.H. Published by Horatio Hill & Co. 1830.

168 pp., illus. 17 cm.
MH.

242

—— The revised impression, with the latest corrections. Louisville, (Ken.) Published by W. W. Worsley. Stereotyped by L. Johnson, Phil'a. 1830.

168 pp., illus. 15 cm.
CtY.
At head of title: "Stereotype edition."

In 1831 *there appeared in Cincinnati an edition of Webster's* American Spelling Book *with his name on the title-page, but also with "Revised and im-*

proved by Nathan Guilford"—in larger type. It does not contain a copyright notice. This edition and its cognates are listed in Appendix F.

243

—— The revised impression, with the latest corrections. Middletown, Conn. Published by William H. Niles. 1831.

168 pp., illus. 17 cm.

CT, CTY, DFSA, MWA (imperfect), MIDEAED, NN, NNC-T.

That no further Middletown editions of this version of the speller have been found bears out Niles' assertion that he did not print any after the expiration of his license, as he was suspected of having done. N. and J. White wrote Webster on August 26, 1835:"Since we wrote Prof: G[oodrich] about Niles, we have seen him and charged him with printing the Old Book, which he flatly denied."[5]

244

—— The revised impression, with the latest corrections. New-Brunswick, N.J. Published by Terhune & Letson. 1831....

168 pp., illus. 16 cm.

MWA, NNUT, NJP.

The copy of the American Spelling Book *lacking a title-page described below (introductory note to rubric D) is catalogued by the Library of Congress as New Haven,* 1831, *but the compiler has found no evidence that there was such an edition.*

245

—— The revised impression, with the latest corrections. Philadelphia: Published by Kimber & Sharpless.... Stereotyped by J. Howe. [1831?]

168 pp., illus. 17 cm.

MH, MWA.

Ascribed to 1831 by Harvard University Library.

[5]Ellsworth Papers, Connecticut Historical Society.

246

[—— Baltimore: Cushing and Sons, 1832.]

Account books: "Jany 1833 . . . both [*American* and *Elementary*] 9848."

D. *Versions of the American Spelling Book after Expiration of the* 1818 *Copyright*

As pointed out in the introductory note to 1829, *the publication of the* Elementary Spelling Book *and the expiration of the* 1818 *copyright on the* American *did not terminate the issuance of editions of the latter. Except for two possible Baltimore editions, published by a firm which appears in Webster's accounts (Titles* 249 *and* 253), *these printings were at best unauthorized and at worst pirated. Large numbers of the old editions were thrown onto the market en bloc,*[6] *and even the old stereotype plates were openly sold.*[7]

To capitalize on the established value of the name "American Spelling Book," Webster tried the system of concurrent editions under both the old and new names (Titles 247–248), *but this did not work out. To combat the unauthorized publication of the old text he took various legal steps, which will be discussed under* 1834 *below. Webster's position would have been strengthened had he renewed the copyright on the old speller. That he at least started to do so is shown by a copy (lacking a title-page, but agreeing in format and content with the editions of* 1829–1831) *in the Library of Congress, inside the front cover of which is written, "District of Connecticut. District Clerk's Office. Sept.* 26, 1831. *Deposited by the Author. Charles Ingersoll, Clerk." Apparently, however, in his attempts to take action against unauthorized printings Webster did not claim such a copyright.*

247

The new American spelling book for the use of primary schools in the United States. By Noah Webster, LL.D. New Haven: Published by Durrie & Peck, and by S. Babcock, for the author. Stereotyped by A. Chandler, New York. 1833.

[6] E.g., *Sixteenth New York Trade Sale*, August 27, 1833, p. 58.
[7] *Gurley's Second New-York Trade Sale*, October 22, 1833, p. 42.

108 pp., illus. 14 cm. P. [i], title-page. P. [ii], notice of copyright entry on June 26, 1833, with no holder's name given. Pp. [iii]–iv, new preface, dated June, 1833, stating that the old *American* speller has many faults, that some editions are counterfeit, and that some, though genuine, are "miserably printed," and that therefore Webster wishes it were withdrawn from circulation. Pp. 5–108, text, based on the old speller, but with seventeen new cuts. Seven of these illustrate the fables; of the ten portraying animals, three are the same as those used in the *Elementary* speller after 1831.

MB.

248

——— New Haven: Press of Whitmore & Minor. [1833?]

108 pp., illus. 14 cm.

DLC, MiDeaEd, NN.

The same as the preceding, except that the preface is set in five paragraphs instead of six. The compiler has at times been inclined to date this edition as late as 1836, but there is no evidence inconsistent with 1833, the date assigned by the Library of Congress and The New York Public Library.

249

[American spelling book. . . . Baltimore: Cushing and Sons, 1834.]

Account books: "Feby 1835 . . . American 9000."

On January 30, 1835, N. and J. White wrote to Webster, "We have just recd a letter from Moses G. Atwood of Concord [New Hampshire] in which he says that 100,000 of the Old Sp Book have been printed since Jany 1, 1834 in Concord & that a binder there now has a contract for 15,000 and then 20,000."[8] Because of the large number thus attributed to Concord in 1834 and from the letters quoted below it would seem that 1834 or 1835 was the most likely time of publication of three undated Concord editions which present a problem in chronological placement. They have sometimes been catalogued by libraries as 1823, which is their latest internal date; it has been substituted for 1803 on the preface, though the text thereof has not been changed. All three contain the 1817 copyright application, which was meaningless after 1832.

N. and J. White wrote Webster on March 11, 1835, that they had noted

[8]Ellsworth Papers, Connecticut Historical Society.

in a catalogue of a Philadelphia Trade Sale "more than 10,000 Old Spellers & 5,000 in the N York Sale the succeeding week. If some decisive measures are not taken to stop the sale of this Book we shall have serious difficulty. We doubt not but most if not all of them come from the Concord Press[.] *If they are to be sold in this public manner . . . without a strenuous effort to stop them, it will be generally understood that anyone can print & sell them. We urge you to take* strong ground immediately.*Have a suitable paper drawn up by some Lawyer in New Haven. . . ."*[9] *Webster took some such step, for ten days later the firm wrote him that "one of our Young Men has just returned from Phil<u>da</u> He called upon M<u>r</u>. Chauncey, who served your notice upon the auctioneers. But they sold the Books. . . ."*[1]

In addition to legal attacks on the point of distribution, Webster also took steps to attack at the point of origin. N. and J. White informed him on August 26, 1835, "We are gratified to learn that you have commenced a suit against the 'pirates' in N Hampshire,"[2] *and on October 8 of the same year Webster wrote his son that he had "directed the piratical printers of my old books in Concord to be prosecuted."*[3] *He did not succeed, however, in making any progress along this line, as he explained in a letter to E. W. and C. Skinner of Albany, January 4, 1836: "I visited Concord last summer; but I found that the* American *is printed by men of no responsibility; the real owners of the plates & publishers not being easily discovered. I have had thoughts of prosecuting the men—but the difficulty of finding the real trespassers, & of getting evidence together with the distance & the expenses & delay of law suits & the uncertainty of the issue, have deterred me from the attempt."*[4] *He told the Skinners that he had decided the best defense was to advertise the incorrect nature of the continuing editions of the old speller.*

250

—— The revised impression, with the latest corrections. Concord, N.H. Published by Horatio Hill & Co. [1834–5?]

168 pp., illus. 16 cm.
MWA.

251

—— The revised impression, with the latest corrections. Stereotyped by Chase & Dunlap, Concord, N.H. Concord, N.H. Horatio Hill and Company. [1834–5?]

[9]Ibid. [1]Ibid. [2]Ibid. [3]Pierpont Morgan Library.
[4]Webster Papers, New York Public Library.

168 pp., illus. 15 cm.
MH, NNC-T, NHD, RPB.

252

—— The revised impression, with the latest corrections. Stereotyped by Jacob Perkins, Concord, N.H. Concord, N.H. [1834–5?]

168 pp., illus. 16 cm.
CU, CTHT-W, CTY, IU, MH, MWA, MEHI, NN, NNC, NJR, OC, British Museum.

253

[—— Baltimore: Cushing and Sons, 1835.]

Account books: "Jany 1836...American 6000."

254

—— The revised impression, with the latest corrections. Stereotyped by the publisher. Sandbornton, N.H. Samuel Gerrish Hayes. 1835.

144 pp., illus. 15 cm.
MSAE (imperfect), NHHI.

NOTES

1. Contains the 1817 copyright application, though it was no longer applicable. The 1803 preface is omitted.
2. The plates were later used by another publisher; see Title 256.

254a

—— The revised impression, with the latest corrections. Stereotyped by the publisher. Sandbornton Power Press. 1835.

NN, RPB.

254*bis*

—— The revised impression, with the latest corrections. Montreal, Printed and sold by H. H. Cunningham.... 1836.

168 pp., illus. 16 cm.
MIDEAED.

255

——— The revised impression, with the latest corrections. Stereotyped by the publisher, Samuel G. Hayes: Sandbornton Power Press. 1836.

144 pp., illus. 15 cm.
NRU.

NOTES

1. Not seen; data provided by the library.
2. Contains the 1817 copyright application.

256

Webster's old spelling book; containing the rudiments of the English language, for the use of schools in the United States. The revised impression, with the latest corrections. Sandbornton, N.H. Published by Charles Lane. 1836.

144 pp., illus. 15 cm.
NBuHi.

NOTES

1. Not seen; data provided by the library.
2. Contains the 1817 copyright application.
3. This is an attempt to capitalize on the tradition of Webster's spellers. Lane apparently wanted to publish both the old and the new versions, for he asked Webster for a license to publish the *Elementary*, in addition to acquiring Samuel G. Hayes' stereotype plates of the 144-page version of the *American* (Titles 254, 255). Webster wrote to Samuel Fletcher of Concord, October 6, 1840, referring to Lane: "since I have discovered that he has printed great numbers of my old Sp. Book, or rather a deformed work calling it *mine*, I have utterly declined to give him a license as I had intended and as I promised to do, before I made this discovery. I have written to him, that his conduct has impaired my confidence in him, & that had I known the facts, I should not have given him encouragement of a license to print the Elementary. I find he has *new plates* of the old book—& I suppose he intends to use them. . . ."[5]

[5]Teachers College Library, Columbia University.

One or both of the following variants may date as late as 1840, as suggested in Webster's letter, but the New York Public Library copy is certainly not from new plates—it is printed from Samuel G. Hayes' plates, badly worn.

256a

——— Sandbornton, N.H. Published by Charles Lane.

MH, MWA, MiDeaEd, NN, OClW, RPB.

256b

——— Sandbornton, N.H. Published by Charles Lane. D. D. Fiske, printer, Power Press.

DFSA.
Fiske was located in Concord, N. H., not Sanbornton.

257

The American spelling book. . . . New York: Published by Collins, Keese & Co. . . ., 1839.

156 pp., illus. 16 cm.
NjR.

NOTES

1. The contents are similar to the editions under the 1804 copyright, somewhat compressed. There is no copyright notice. The 1803 preface is used, with a footnote dated 1818. There is no "revised impression" or "with the latest corrections" phrase in the title.

2. On verso of title-page: "Geo. A. & J. Curtis, New England Type and Stereotype Foundry, Boston."

257*bis*

——— The revised impression, with the latest corrections. Concord, N.H. Published by John F. Brown. 1841. Stereotyped by J. Howe.

168 pp., illus. 16 cm.
MiDeaEd.

258

—— Franklin, N.H. Peabody & Daniell. 1842.

156 pp., illus. 17 cm.
TxCoмT.

NOTES

1. Not seen; data provided by the library.
2. Has the same stereotype notice as Title 257.

259

—— The revised impression, with the latest corrections. Boston: Published by R. H. Sherburne, proprietor of the revised edition. 1843.

168 pp., illus. 17 cm.
NN, NjR (imperfect).

NOTES

1. At head of title: "The last revised edition."
2. Copyright by Sherburne, 1843. Includes the census figures for 1840.
3. Note that Sherburne had published an edition in Philadelphia in 1828.
4. In 1844 the owners of the rights to the *Elementary* speller, the Cooledges in New York, issued a circular warning purchasers against the 1843 Boston and Wells River editions of the *American*.

260

—— The revised impression, with the latest corrections. Wells River, Vt. Published by Ira White. Proprietor of the revised edition. 1843.

168 pp., incl. frontis., illus. 16 cm.
CtY, DFSA, MH, MWA, MiDeaEd, NN, NNC, ViW, VtHi, VtMidbS, Merriam.

NOTES

1. At head of title: "The last revised edition."
2. This seems to be printed from the same plates as the preceding

entry; it contains the Sherburne copyright. The frontispiece is a poor impression of the Anderson Minerva frontispiece, without the quatrain. On the verso of the title-page there is a cut of a stag.

3. The Henry Ford Museum and Yale copies are a variant, in which there is no frontispiece and on the verso of the title-page there is an American eagle in addition to the stag. The Federal Security Agency has a copy of each form.

E. *The Elementary Spelling Book*

As mentioned in the introductory note to the American *speller, 1829, in that year Webster introduced a new speller, intended to be consistent with his 1828 dictionary and to replace the* American. *Such an intention had long been in his mind, references to it being found in his correspondence with Henry Hudson as early as 1820. In 1828, when the matter was being actively pushed, Hudson raised objections to the issuance of a new work while the copyright and licenses to print for the old one still had some time to run. He was willing, however, to serve as sole agent for the rights in the new work, but Webster decided to keep control in his hands.*[6]

Because he was engrossed in his lexicographical work, Webster engaged another person to do the labor of revision:"It is agreed by & between Noah Webster of New Haven & Aaron Ely of New York, that the said Ely shall take the materials for a spelling book prepared by said Webster, & with these & such materials as the said Ely has prepared, & may hereafter prepare shall as soon as may be compile a spelling book for said Webster, submitting the same to revision of said Webster—for which labor & services the said Webster . . . shall be held to pay to the said Ely . . . in . . . March . . . 1832, one thousand dollars. . . . New Haven this fifteenth day of December 1828."[7] *Ely did the work, and his wife was paid for it; he had died on September 28, 1829, thus escaping the acrimonious debate, in newspapers and pamphlets, in which rival publishers accused Webster of not writing his own books (see Section Nine, Part Four, rubric J).*

In the spring of 1829 Webster went to New York to oversee the stereotyping of the new work, to begin a campaign to have it introduced in the schools, and to work on other books. The progress of the speller is shown in references in a series of letters to a son-in-law, W. C. Fowler: April 24, "I expect to go to

[6]Webster to Hudson, March 19, 1829, Webster Papers, New York Public Library. In 1831 he made other arrangements; see introductory note to that year.

[7]Webster Papers, New York Public Library.

N York in a day or so, where I shall remain probably till I have procured the new Sp. Book to be stereotyped. . . ." May 7, "I have been here nearly a fortnight, completing my new Sp. Book & preparing the way for its reception." June 30, "My new Spelling Book will be finished next week, & I shall then see how it is to be received."[8] *(The New York edition is listed first in this year only.)*

The work was entered for copyright in the Connecticut District on May 22, 1829, and the notice was published in the Connecticut Herald, *July 21 and later.*

Although the compiler has been unable to locate a copy, it seems clear that Webster issued a circular, dated November 12, 1828, setting forth terms for licenses to print the forthcoming speller. Such a circular is mentioned in various letters and memoranda of the time, e.g., Webster to Richardson and Lord of Boston, June 15, 1829, in which he says he wants "to know whether you intend to be the publishers of it, as proposed to you in the circular, last fall. . . ."[9] *Whether the circular was printed or in manuscript form is not known.*

Early advertisements for the work appeared in the New York Atlas, *July 25, 1829, the* New Haven Daily Advertiser, *December 8 and later, the* Connecticut Herald *and the* Connecticut Courant, *December 15 and later, and the* Advertiser *again, with testimonials, on January 1, 1830.*

261

The elementary spelling book; being an improvement on the American spelling book. By Noah Webster, LL.D. New-York. Published by J. P. Haven and R. Lockwood. Stereotyped by A. Chandler. 1829.

168 pp., incl. frontis. 17 cm. P. [1], blank. P. [2], frontispiece by Anderson, a re-engraving of the same scene occasionally used earlier, now signed in full "Anderson" (cf. Plate XVIII). Here the quatrain is not used. P. [3], title-page. P. [4], copyright notice. Pp. [5]–7, preface, undated. Pp. 8–168, text.

CtHT-W, DLC, MH.

In the main the contents are those of the *American* speller rewritten; the fables, the "Moral Catechism," and certain other elements are omitted.

[8]Letters in the possession of Mrs. Howard B. Field; transcripts by courtesy of Prof. Harry R. Warfel.

[9]Middlebury College Library.

262

—— Albany: Published by Webster and Skinners. Stereotyped by A. Chandler. 1829.

168 pp., incl. frontis. 17 cm.
MH, MWA, N, NNC (imperfect).

NOTES

1. Note that "Webster" in the firm name has become singular.
2. The edition was apparently 9,000; see the letter quoted in the introductory note to 1832.

263

[—— Baltimore: Cushing and Sons(?), 1829.]

Listed in the 1870–71 and 1889 printed catalogues of the California State Library but not now to be found there, and not otherwise recorded.

264

—— Boston: Published by Richardson & Lord. Stereotyped by A. Chandler. 1829.

168 pp., incl. frontis. 17 cm.
MH.
Webster wrote the firm from New York on June 15, 1829, asking them if they wished to publish the work and to order a set of plates while Chandler was making some.[1]

265

—— Brattleborough, Vt. Published by Holbrook & Fessenden. Stereotyped by A. Chandler. 1829.

168 pp., incl. frontis. 18 cm.
CtY, MWA, N, NBuHi, NN.

NOTES

1. In this edition the copyright notice is on p. [1] and p. [4] is blank.

[1]Ibid.

2. The edition may have been as large as 36,000; see the letter quoted in the introductory note to 1832. This figure may, however, include an unlocated edition in 1830 or Title 273 or both.

266

——— Middletown, Conn. Published by W. H. Niles. Stereotyped by A. Chandler. 1829.

168 pp., incl. frontis. 17 cm.
CtHT-W, CtNhHi, CtY (imperfect), MH, NN (imperfect).

267

——— New-Brunswick, N.J. Published by Terhune & Letson. Stereotyped by A. Chandler. 1829.

168 pp., incl. frontis. 17 cm.
Ct, NjP.

268

——— Philadelphia: Published by Kimber and Sharpless.... Stereotyped by A. Chandler. 1829.

168 pp., incl. frontis. 17 cm.
NN (imperfect), OClWHi.

269

——— Boston: Richardson Lord & Holbrook.... Stereotyped by A. Chandler. 1830.

168 pp., [incl. frontis.?]. 20 cm.
MWA (imperfect).
The copy located is uncut and unbound. The missing first leaf doubtless contained the frontispiece, as in the Boston edition of the preceding year.

270

——— Philadelphia: Published by Kimber & Sharpless.... Stereotyped by A. Chandler. 1830.

168 pp., incl. frontis. 17 cm.

CT, MWA, MIDEAED, NN, RPB, VTMIDBS.

The edition was apparently 5,000; see the letter quoted in the introductory note to 1832.

In 1831 Webster gave up personal control of the publishing of the Elementary *speller. On June 7, 1831, he made the following agreement:*

"This instrument witnesseth: that whereas Noah Webster of New Haven in Connecticut hath by a letter of attorney and agency bearing even date with these presents constituted Elihu White, William Gallaher & Norman White Booksellers in New York trading under the firm of White, Gallaher & White, his sole agents for managing the concerns of his Elementary Spelling Book in the United States for thirteen years from this date.[2]

"Now it is covenanted by and between the said parties that the premium for copyright to be demanded of purchasers, shall be seven mills for each copy of said book which shall be permitted to be printed: neither more nor less—and the said White, Gallaher & White shall pay to the said Webster . . . five sevenths of said premium which they may receive, all accounts to be adjusted and the money paid semi annually.

"It is further covenanted that all copies of said Spelling Book shall be printed on Stereotyped plates cast by Adoniram Chandler of New York or on plates taken from said Chandler's plates. . . .

"It is further covenanted that if William G. Webster son of said Noah Webster shall enter into partnership with any person or persons for the purpose of carrying on the business of Printing or Bookselling[3] *then the said White, Gallaher & White shall grant to said Wm. G. Webster & Co. a license to print annually a number of copies of the said book not less than thirty thousand. . . ."*[4]

The firm advertised the speller, among other of Webster's works, in the New York Observer, *August 27, 1831, and later. The compiler has not found their imprint on the work, although they appear as an added vendor in the New Haven edition of 1831. Apparently they did not grant any licenses in New York City, for there are no editions there until after they surrendered the sole management of the work.*

[2] The firm, however, surrendered their privilege late in 1839, before the full term of this agreement.

[3] Which he did with Durrie and Peck of New Haven in 1832.

[4] Webster Papers, New York Public Library.

271

—— Baltimore: Published by Cushing and Sons.... Stereotyped by A. Chandler. 1831.

168 pp., incl. frontis. 16 cm.
MdBE, MdHi (imperfect).
Account books: "April, 1832...12,000."

272

—— Boston: Richardson Lord & Holbrook.... Stereotyped by A. Chandler. 1831.

168 pp., incl. frontis. 18 cm.
MWA.

273

—— Brattleborough, Vt. Published by Holbrook & Fessenden. Stereotyped by A. Chandler. [1831?]

168 pp., incl. frontis., illus. 17 cm.
CtHT-W, MH, MiDeaEd, NNC-T (imperfect).

NOTES

1. The Harvard copy has the copyright entry on page [1] and page [4] blank, instead of the reverse, as in the other copies.

2. Four of the eight fables of the *American* speller are restored to the text. Each has a new illustration, based on but not the same as the earlier cuts. Three additional illustrations are a dog, a stag, and a squirrel, which often occur in later editions of the *Elementary* speller (Plate XVII).

3. Dated 1829 by Harvard, but since there was a dated 1829 Holbrook and Fessenden edition the compiler is inclined to place this slightly later. It has been put in 1831 because that is the year in which the added fables and cuts first appear in a dated edition.

274

—— Burlington, Vt. Published by Chauncey Goodrich. 1831.

168 pp., incl. frontis. 17 cm.
NNUT (imperfect), VtMidbS.

NOTES

1. This edition contains, on the verso of the title-page, a series of commendations of Webster's dictionaries and spellers. Goodrich was one of Webster's sons-in-law.

2. The edition was 3,500; see the letter quoted in the introductory note to 1832.

275

——— Middletown, Conn. Published by W. H. Niles. Stereotyped by A. Chandler. 1831.

168 pp., incl. frontis. 17 cm.
CT, CTHT-W, MH, MWA, MIDEAED.
Contains the commendations mentioned in the preceding entry.

276

——— New-Brunswick, N.J. Published by Terhune & Letson. Stereotyped by A. Chandler. 1831.

168 pp., incl. frontis. 17 cm.
MIDEAED, NJR, PPESCHW.
The edition was 8,000; see the letter quoted in the introductory note to 1832.

277

——— New Haven, Ct Published by Durrie and Peck. Sold also by White, Gallagher [sic, for Gallaher] and White, New-York. 1831.

168 pp., incl. frontis., illus. 17 cm.
CTHT-W, CTHI, MWA (imperfect).

NOTES

1. Contains the restored fables and new cuts described for Title 273.

2. P. [1] bears a Durrie and Peck advertisement dated August 1, 1834, which the compiler suggests was added to copies still on hand in sheets in that year.

278

—— White & Wilcox, Wells River, Vt. 1831.

168 pp., incl. frontis. 18 cm.
MH, MWA, NN, VtHi (imperfect), Merriam.

NOTES

1. The edition was 9,000; see the letter quoted in the introductory note to 1832.

2. The New York Public Library copy has on the recto of the frontispiece two extraneous cuts—a girl picking roses, and four men mowing—and a quatrain celebrating the beauties of summer.

Some time in the first half of 1832 exclusive rights to print and to sell printing rights in this text passed to N. & J. White of New York, presumably the result of a reorganization of the firm of White, Gallaher, and White. In the process of the negotiations, Webster wrote them, March 17, 1832, a letter in which he discussed the progress of the new version to date, and gave these figures: "Terhune & Letson have printed 8000 of the New Book. . . . Kimber & Sharpless have printed 5000. . . . Wilcox has printed 9000. Webster & Skinner 9000. Goodrich, 3,500. Fessenden 36,000 (under the old contract). I have no return from Niles."[5]

In Webster's account book is found a list of the licenses to print issued by N. and J. White under their right. Those in 1832 are:

J. Fessenden, Brattleboro	20,000
H. C. Frisbee, [Fredonia, N. Y.], "sold to O G Steele, Buffaloe"	50,000
Chauncey Goodrich, Burlington, Vt.	20,000
Bemis, Hoyt, Porter & Co., Canandaigua	40,000[6]
Corey & Fairbanks[sic], Cincinnati	20,000
Moses G. Atwood, Concord, N. H.	10,000
William H. Niles, Middletown	100,000
Terhune & Letson, New Brunswick	75,000
Kimber & Sharpless, Philadelphia	100,000
White & Wilcox, Wells River, Vt.	50,000

and "1832 or 3,"

Madison Kell[e]y, Cleveland	10,000

[5]New-York Historical Society.

[6]Here Webster seems to be telescoping two firms, Bemis and Ward of Canandaigua and Hoyt, Porter, and Co. of Rochester.

Licenses granted in later years will be entered under the appropriate date. Unless there is other evidence for the actuality of an edition, a license has not been taken as a basis for imputing editions, since the rights may not have been used in each case. As previously, however, a royalty entry is taken as proof of an edition, since a printer would hardly pay royalties on books he had not issued.

279

[—— Baltimore: Cushing and Sons, 1832.]

Account books: "Jany 1833...9000."

280

—— Boston: Carter, Hendee & Co. Brattleboro' Power Press Office. 1832.

168 pp., incl. frontis. 17 cm.
NN, NNC.

On December 26, 1842, Melville Lord of Boston wrote Webster, "In answer to your inquiry regarding the set of plates for the Elementary Spelling Book which the firm of Richardson & Lord once owned, I would state that they were sold about ten years ago to Carter & Hendee of this city, who kept them on hand, unused, until two or three years since...."[7]

281

—— Buffalo: Printed and Published by Steele & Faxon....1832.

168 pp., incl. frontis. 17 cm.
N (imperfect).

282

—— Burlington, Vt. Published by Chauncey Goodrich. 1832.

168 pp., incl. frontis. 17 cm.
NN, VtU.

283

[—— Canandaigua: Bemis and Ward, 1832.]

[7]Ellsworth Papers, Connecticut Historical Society. For the later history of this set of plates, see Title 385.

On January 16, 1833, this firm wrote Webster: "In regard to your Elementary, we are gratified to say, that it is fast taking the place of other Spelling books, through this region. The publishers of the book, at Rochester, Buffalo, and ourselves, have not at all times been able to supply the demand, thus far. But hereafter, it is hoped, more ample editions will be printed—at any rate we intend it shall be so here."[8]

284

—— Concord, N.H Published by Moses G. Atwood. Sold also by N. and J. White.... New-York 1832.

168 pp., incl. frontis. 17 cm.

Ct, CtHT-W, MH, MiDeaEd, Nh, NhHi, RPB.

The American Antiquarian Society has a copy in which the imposition of the title-page is so poor that the line with the date does not show. The book is probably this edition, but it could be Atwood's unlocated printing of 1834 (Title 295).

284a

—— Concord, N.H Published by Atwood & Sanborn. Sold also by N. and J. White.... New-York 1832.

Stark.

285

—— Rochester: Published by Hoyt, Porter & Co. 1832.

168 pp., incl. frontis. 17 cm.

MH.

Licenses granted by N. and J. White in 1833 were:

Melville Lord, Boston	20,000
Chauncey Goodrich, Burlington, Vt.	15,000[9]
Bemis, Hoyt, Porter & Co., Canandaigua	15,000[1]

[8] Webster Papers, New York Public Library.

[9] "Plates sold to Smith & Harrison [sic, for Harrington]" is entered after this name between 1833 and 1835.

[1] See footnote 6, introductory note to 1832.

S. H. Henry, Cazenovia, N. Y.	20,000
Corey & Fairbank, Cincinnati	30,000
Jenkins & Glover, [*Columbus, Ohio*]	25,000
Moses G. Atwood, Concord, N. H.	20,000
Wilcox, Dickerman, & Co., Louisville	25,000
"*To N. W. for his Son & Durrie & Peck,*" *New Haven*	90,000
Knowlton & Rice, Watertown, N. Y.	10,000
J. Fisher & Son, Wheeling, Va.	20,000

286

[——— Baltimore: Cushing and Sons, 1833.]

Account books: "Jany 1834...both [*Elementary* and *American*] 9,848."

287

——— Columbus, Ohio: Jenkins & Glover. Stereotyped by A. Chandler. 1833.

168 pp., incl. frontis. 17 cm.
Not seen by the compiler; description provided by Mr. Harlow Lindley about 1938 from an imperfect copy then in private hands.

288

——— Watertown, N.Y. Published by Knowlton and Rice. Sold also by N. & J. White, New-York. 1833.

168 pp., incl. frontis., illus. 18 cm.
MWA, NN.
In addition to the regular Anderson frontispiece of Minerva, this edition has on the recto of the frontispiece a full-page cut, signed "C. Rice Des^{r}" and "J. W(?). Hall, S^{c}," an allegorical scene of Athena, the printing press, books for children, etc.

289

——— White & Homan, Wells River, Vt. 1833.

168 pp., incl. frontis., illus. 17 cm.

CtY, MiDeaEd, NNC.

This edition has the two extraneous cuts on the recto of the frontispiece, as described under Title 278, and also has an added cut—an elephant—on p. 7.

290

[—— Wheeling, W. Va.: J. Fisher and Son, 1833.]

In his *Recollections of Life in Ohio from* 1813 *to* 1840 (Cincinnati, 1895), William Cooper Howells (father of William Dean Howells) relates that about 1833 "wc moved to Wheeling.... I got a situation as pressman in a printing establishment, where I worked on 'Webster's Spelling Book'—stereotype plates. The press had a rolling attachment, so that I worked the press alone, making $1.50 a day" (p. 179).

Licenses granted by N. and J. White in 1834 were:

Webster & Skinner, Albany	100,000
J. Fessenden, Brattleboro	10,000
E. and L. Merriam, Brookfield, Mass.	10,000
Corey & Fairbank, Cincinnati	50,000
Knowlton & Rice, Watertown	20,000, 10,000, and 15,000

291

[—— Baltimore: Cushing and Sons, 1834.]

Account books: "Feby 1835...6000."

292

[—— Brookfield, Mass.: E. and L. Merriam, 1834.]

Webster recorded payment of a premium from this firm in his notes on a letter from N. and J. White to him, January 22, 1835.[2]

293

—— Buffalo: Printed and published by Oliver G. Steele.... 1834.

[2]Ellsworth Papers, Connecticut Historical Society.

168 pp., incl. frontis. 17 cm.
MH, NRU.

293*bis*

—— Cazenovia, N.Y. Published by S. H. Henry & Co. Stereotyped by A. Chandler. 1834.

168 pp., incl. frontis., illus. 17 cm.
MiDeaEd.

294

—— Cincinnati: Published by Corey & Fairbank.... 1834.

168 pp., incl. frontis. 17 cm.
NjR.

NOTES

1. P. [i] contains a publisher's advertisement. The book was printed, according to a notice on p. [iv], by the Students' Typographical Association of Lane Seminary. The color of the paper is not uniform throughout the volume, but it is all bluish.

2. N. and J. White wrote Webster, January 26, 1835: "We received a letter from Corey & Fairbanks [sic] this morning stating that they had printed much to their own surprise 81,700 copies of the Spelling Book over former licences," and that they asked for a renewal for 20,000 more, "making the whole number which they have printed from the commencement including the licence now granted 311,700 copies."[3]

295

[—— Concord, N.H.: Moses G. Atwood, 1834.]

Account books: "overprinted in 1834 27,000."
See note on Title 284.

296

—— William H. Niles, Middletown, Conn. 1834.

[3]Ibid.

168 pp., incl. frontis. 17 cm.
Ct, CtHT-W, NcU, OO.

297

——— Rochester: Published by Hoyt, Porter & Co. 1834.

168 pp., incl. frontis. 16 cm.
MiDeaEd.

Licenses granted by N. and J. White in 1835 were:

Holbrook & Co., Brattleboro	50,000
E. and L. Merriam, Brookfield, Mass.	19,000
Smith & Harrison [i.e., Harrington], Burlington, Vt.	10,000
Morse & Harvey, Canandaigua, N. Y.	10,000 and 10,000
S. H. Henry, Cazenovia, N. Y.	20,000
Corey & Fairbank, Cincinnati	50,000, 30,000, 101,700, and 30,000
Corey & Webster, Cincinnati	30,000[4]
Moses G. Atwood, Concord, N. H.	20,000
Terhune & Letson, New Brunswick	75,000
R. and G. Wood, New York[5]	
Knowlton & Rice, Watertown, N. Y.	20,000 and 20,000
White & Wilcox, Wells River, Vt.	20,000

Attacks by compilers of rival spellers, such as Lyman Cobb, goaded Webster into further efforts to improve his speller and increase its consistency with his dictionaries. Beginning about August, 1835, he tried to get the printers to incorporate some changes, which was not always done because of the trouble and cost of altering stereotype plates. In writing to W. C. Fowler on September 3, 1836, Webster said, ". . . last winter, I made a list of the mistakes, & sent

[4]In 1835 William G. Webster went to Cincinnati to help further the use of his father's books, and joined A. W. Corey in this new firm, which failed within a few months.

[5]The Whites wrote Webster on August 26, 1835, that they had agreed to let this firm have a license, but on April 26, 1836, they said, ". . . as we have heard nothing from them, we do not know what they intend to do." Ellsworth Papers, Connecticut Historical Society.

[it] to stereotype founders, with direction to every publisher to send the plates to them for correction. This direction has been complied with by most of the publishers. . . . The original plates from which all future sets are to be struck, are also corrected."[6]

298

[——— Baltimore: Cushing and Sons, 1835.]

Account books: "Jany 1836 Elementary 12,000."

299

——— Brookfield: Published by E. and L. Merriam. 1835.

168 pp., incl. frontis. 18 cm.
DFSA, MH, Merriam.

300

——— Burlington, Vt. Smith and Harrington. 1835.

168 pp., incl. frontis., illus. 17 cm.
NN.
Poorly printed. Contains most of the corrections desired by Webster.

301

——— Canandaigua, N.Y. Published by Morse and Harvey. Stereotyped by A. Chandler. 1835.

168 pp., incl. frontis., illus. 17 cm.
CT (imperfect), N, NN.

302

[——— Cincinnati: Corey and Fairbank(?), 1835.]

Both Corey and Fairbank and Corey and Webster advertised the speller extensively during 1835, and N. and J. White drew upon the

[6]In the possession of Mrs. Howard B. Field, transcript by courtesy of Prof. Harry R. Warfel. In the Webster Papers are three MS lists of corrections to be made, dated August, 1835, January 25, 1836, and April, 1836.

former firm for the premium due for the license,[7] so at least part of the numbers licensed must have been printed.

303

——— Concord, N.H. Published by Moses G. Atwood. Stereotyped by A. Chandler. 1835.

168 pp., incl. frontis. 16 cm.
MEHI, NHD.

N. and J. White wrote Webster, August 26, 1835, "We duly notified Atwood that he could have the new plates with the cuts—but as he has never ordered them from us we supposed he did not want them."[8]

304

——— Pittsburg. Johnston and Stockton. Stereotyped by A. Chandler, New-York. 1835.

168 pp., incl. frontis. 17 cm.
OCLWHI.

NOTES

1. Contains some of the corrections desired by Webster.
2. Following the entry for the 1833 license to Wilcox, Dickerman & Co., Louisville, the account book reads, "plates sold to Stockton and Joh[n]ston, Pittsburg, who purchased the right of printing 50,000 of Kimber & Sharpless." Since no Wilcox, Dickerman edition has been found, that firm may never have used these plates.

305

——— Ira White, Wells River, Vt. 1835.

168 pp., incl. frontis., illus. 17 cm.
CSMH, CTHI, CTNHHI, MWA, VTMIDBC.

NOTES

1. Contains some of the corrections desired by Webster.

[7] N. and J. White to Webster, August 26, 1835, Ellsworth Papers, Connecticut Historical Society.
[8] Ibid.

2. N. and J. White wrote Webster, August 26, 1835, "We wrote Ira White about printing so badly[;] he replied stating that the Book which we saw so badly printed, was done by Homans [Title 289?], that he was now printing a good Ed: a sheet of which he sent us."[9]

306

Webster published, about 1835, *a circular denying the rumor that he himself had not made the revisions in the current speller. The compiler has been unable to locate a copy, but its existence is shown in a letter from William G. Webster to his father, Cincinnati, November* 18, 1835, *in which he says, "I find that the impression is very general that you are not the author of the Elementary Sp. Bk; your circular contradicting the report did not get out here...."*[1]

307

In 1836 Webster issued another circular bearing on the speller, in the form of an open letter to some rival textbook compilers, charging them with substantial plagiarisms from the speller:

> Circular. To Messrs. A. Picket and J. W. Picket. Gentlemen, I trust.... N. Webster, New Haven, November, 1836.

Two leaves, printed only on the first (both sides). 26 cm.
NN.

William G. Webster wrote to his father on January 22, 1837, "Pres^d McGuffey told me last eve^g that he spoke to the Picketts about your letter, & that there were some things of importance in it. The Picketts pretend not to have seen it & requested of Mr McGuffey a copy which he sent them."[2]

[9] Ibid.

[1] Webster Papers, New York Public Library; quoted in the compiler's "Not Quite *Spurlos Versunkt*," in *Bookmen's Holiday* (New York, 1943), pp. 84–85. An example of the claims that Webster did not compile the *Elementary Spelling Book* is a detailed review by "Senex" in the *Indiana Democrat* (Indianapolis), March 16, 1837.

[2] Webster Papers, New York Public Library.

The 1836 and later editions incorporated most of the corrections desired by Webster, unless otherwise stated.

On May 23, 1836, N. and J. White wrote Webster that they had received a letter from "Mr. Emory" [Josiah Emery] of Wellsboro, Pennsylvania, asking for a license to publish the speller there. They told Webster they did not want to issue him a license, on the basis that the town and its region were so thinly populated that publication there would do little good in combating Cobb, and that they had told Emery that Kimber and Sharpless' license in Philadelphia covered the area, so that he should do business with that firm.[3]

308

[Elementary spelling book.... Baltimore: Cushing and Sons, 1836.]

Account books: "Feby. 1837...21,000."

309

—— Cazenovia, N.Y. Published by S. H. Henry, & Co. Stereotyped by A. Chandler. 1836.

168 pp., incl. frontis., illus. 17 cm.
OCLWHI (imperfect).

310

[—— Cincinnati: Burgess and Morgan(?), 1836.]

"A Citizen," writing in the *Cincinnati Daily Gazette* of October 8, 1836, refers to "a series of school books, now in the course of publication, by the firm of Webster Burgess & Morgan...in this city...particularly the 'Elementary Spelling Book...,'" and there are other indications of a Cincinnati edition of 1836. However, William G. Webster's association with the firm was so short (August 12 to October 11) that it is probable that the imprint was Burgess and Morgan (see Title 561). The younger Webster wrote his father on February 1, 1837, "I have heard some complaint made that their spellers are not well bound—the covers are too thin...."[4] N. and J. White wrote Webster on February

[3] Ellsworth Papers, Connecticut Historical Society.
[4] Webster Papers, New York Public Library.

8, "...the licence to Burgess & Morgan was made with the usual stipulation to renew for 30,000 copies more, and we stipulated to grant no other licence in Cincinnati...."[5] On May 1, 1837, William Webster wrote, "I have also promised them a renewal...for 30,000 copies, of which they have already printed 8000 copies over their former licence...."[6]

311

——— Cleaveland, Ohio: Published by Sanford & Lott, printers, bookbinders [&] booksellers. 1836.

168 pp., incl. frontis. 17 cm.

MiDeaEd.

The compiler suggests an ampersand in the space where a tear makes an illegible spot.

312

——— Concord, N.H. Published by Atwood and Brown. Stereotyped by A. Chandler. 1836.

168 pp., incl. frontis. 17 cm.

MH (imperfect).

This edition does not incorporate the corrections desired by Webster. The frontispiece differs from any other found; it shows a teacher and his pupils, in classical garb.

313

——— William H. Niles, Middletown, Conn. 1836.

168 pp., incl. frontis., illus. 17 cm.

CtNhHi.

314

——— New Brunswick, N.J.: Published by Terhune & Letson. Stereotyped by Redfield and Lindsay, New York. 1836.

[5] Ellsworth Papers, Connecticut Historical Society.
[6] Webster Papers, New York Public Library.

168 pp., incl. frontis., illus. 17 cm.

CT, CLU, MIU (imperfect), MIDEAED, NN (imperfect), NJR (imperfect), OHI (imperfect).

N. and J. White wrote Webster, January 7, 1836,"... we have enquired of Redfield and Lindsey [sic] whether they will buy the plates of Chandler, and they have informed us that on *their* part they have concluded to make the purchase. . . . They have recd the cuts."[7]

315

[—— Baltimore: Cushing and Sons, 1837.]

Account books: "Jany 1838...15,000."

316

—— Cincinnati: Burgess & Crane. [1837?]

168 pp., incl. frontis., illus. 16 cm.

CTY.

The firm of Burgess and Crane was formed about May 1, 1837, and secured a license for the *Elementary* speller. On September 26, William Webster wrote his father,"They have published nearly 30,000 copies, they say, since May, & will want another license soon,"and on November 7 he wrote that they had taken one for 30,000.[8] There is no indication of the year in which this undated edition appeared; it has been placed in 1837 as a year of large output by the firm, but it might belong in 1838 or later.

317

—— Concord, N.H. Brown's Edition. 1837.

168 pp., incl. frontis., illus. 17 cm.

MH.

318

—— Concord, N.H. Roby, Kimball, and Merrill. 1837.

[7]Ellsworth Papers, Connecticut Historical Society.

[8]Webster Papers, New York Public Library.

168 pp., incl. frontis., illus. 17 cm.

CtHT-W, CtY, MWA (imperfect), MiDeaEd, MiU, NHi, NN, Nh, NhHi.

Apparently in 1837 the firm of Morton and Smith of Louisville applied to the Whites for a license, but at the end of the year had not yet printed any books, not having suitable equipment.[9]

319

——— New Haven: Published by S. Babcock. 1837.

168 pp., incl. frontis., illus. 18 cm.

CtY.

Babcock advertised the speller for sale, among other of Webster's works, in the New Haven *Daily Herald*, October 19, 1836, and later, though he is not credited with an edition in 1836.

B. B. Mussey, 29 Cornhill, Boston, wrote Webster on November 3, 1838, asking for a license to publish the speller in Boston, saying, "I wish to make a little Better Book than is now in the market."[1] *Apparently nothing came of this. Mussey later appears as an added vendor on one of Webster's dictionaries.*

On December 27, 1838, Webster wrote his son William, "I have just recd a letter from J S & S A Bagg, the State printers at Detroit, requesting license to print my Elementary. I shall give them the terms & let them apply to you. They ought however to give you satisfactory evidence of their responsibility. I have heard that the old house of Bagg, Barnes & Co failed, but I do not know the truth of the report. I believe it is best that they should get the plates & furniture in Cincinnati, that the books may correspond in the size of the page with the copy of Burgess. Burgess has got new plates & of a smaller size than the New York copy, & this without my permission. I regret this; but since it is done, Mess Bagg may get the same plate[s]."[2] *No Detroit edition has been found, nor a license to the Baggs in the records, so this proposal probably fell through; nor has a markedly smaller Burgess edition been found.*

[9]Morton and Smith to Webster, January 1, 1838, Ellsworth Papers, Connecticut Historical Society.

[1]Ellsworth Papers, Connecticut Historical Society.

[2]Lee Kohns Memorial Collection, Manuscript Division, New York Public Library.

320

—— Cushing & Sons,... Jno. Cushing & Co...., Baltimore. [1838?]

168 pp., incl. frontis., illus. 16 cm.
NN.

The front cover reads "Cushing & Brother" instead of "Cushing & Sons," and on the rear cover are notices of the dissolution of the one firm and the establishment of the other, as of January 1, 1839. This would suggest that the body of this edition was printed in 1838 and the covers in 1839. The final entry in Webster's account with Cushing and Sons is "Jany. 1839 12,000." This makes a total for the firm of 111,848 copies, including both the *American* and *Elementary* spellers from 1831. The new firm took out a license in December, 1839, and in 1841 paid Webster royalties on 64,000 copies, but none has been found with their imprint on the title-page.

321

—— Cazenovia, N.Y. Published by S. H. Henry, & Co. Stereotyped by A. Chandler. 1838.

168 pp., incl. frontis., illus. 17 cm.
NN (imperfect).

322

[—— Cleveland: Sanford and Lott, 1838.]

On December 11, 1837, William Webster wrote his father that since March, 1836, Sanford and Lott had printed 7,000 copies.[3] These may all be accounted for by their 1836 edition, but on December 7 he had told his father, "I have an application for a new license from Sanford & Lott ...for 10,000 copies,"[4] and in the other letter cited said that the firm intended to publish all 10,000 in one winter.

323

—— Columbus (O.) I. N. Whiting. Stereotyped by J. S. Redfield, New York, 1838.

[3]Webster Papers, New York Public Library. [4]Ibid.

168pp., incl. frontis., illus. 17 cm.
OClWHi, PPM.
Not seen by the compiler.

324

—— Concord, N.H. Roby, Kimball, and Merrill 1838.

168 pp., incl. frontis., illus. 17 cm.
MiDeaEd, NN, Nh, NhD.

325

—— New Haven: Published by S. Babcock. [1838?]

168 pp., incl. frontis., illus. 17 cm.
MiDeaEd, NRU.
On p. [i] there is a publisher's advertisement dated June, 1838.

326

—— Wells River, Vt.: Published by Ira White. 1838.

168 pp., incl. frontis., illus. 17 cm.
Ct, MH, MWA, MiDeaEd, NN, NjP, VtU.
In the Henry Ford Museum copy the frontispiece is printed on both sides.

In the Webster papers is a sheet recording licenses granted in 1839. It contains three lists, one headed June, one December, and one not headed. Each of the lists is totalled—one incorrectly—and a grand total is run, against which is written "Copies of Elemy. Sp. Book licensed in 1839." The following is a consolidation of the lists, the locations of the firms being supplied:

	June	December	undated
Knowlton & Rice, Watertown, N. Y.	15,000	17,640	
	20,000	20,000	
	15,000		
Henry & Co., Cazenovia, N. Y.	20,000	20,000	

Terhune, New Brunswick, N. J.[5]	25,000		
C[larendon] Morse, Rochester	10,000		
Roby & Co., Concord, N. H.	55,000	160,000	
Sanborn, Portland, Me.	20,000	20,000	
Ira White, Wells River, Vt.		22,000	
Cushing & Brothers, Baltimore		30,000	
J. Letson, New Brunswick, N. J.[5]		45,000	
Th[omas,] Cowperthwaite [sic] & Co., Philadelphia		50,000	
Walton & Co., Montpelier, Vt.		10,000	
Brown & Parsons, Hartford		10,000	
Patterson, (Pittsburgh?)			12,000
Fisher, Wheeling, Va.			80,000
Kimber & Sh[arpless], Philadelphia			30,000
E. Morgan, Cincinnati			30,000
Morg[a]n & An[thon]y, Lawrenceburg, Ind.[6]			20,000
Harvey, Canandaigua, N. Y.			20,000
S. Babcock, New Haven			23,000
Glover, Portsmouth, Ohio			10,000

The correct grand total is 809,640.

Another list of licenses headed "Nov. 4, 1839," which applies to 1840–1842, will be discussed in the introductory note to 1840.

As in earlier cases, a license is not taken as evidence of an edition without some other indication of actuality.

[5]Terhune and Letson were a partnership earlier, but here seem to be independent.

[6]In a letter of August 4, 1841, Ephraim Morgan partially explained to Webster the ramifications of these firms, and the organization prevailing then had doubtless been virtually the same in 1839. "Our firm is composed of Ephraim Morgan, William Phillips, Sacket[t] Reynolds and James T. Morgan—the business here [Cincinnati] is done in the name of *E. Morgan & Co.* We have a house at St. Louis which is managed by my son, James T. Morgan, and the business is done in the name of *James T. Morgan & Co.* About the time I received authority to act as thy agent, our firm sold to my Brother, *Jas. Augustus Morgan*, the *plates &c.* for thy Elementary Spelling Book, on condition that the *printing* should be done by us, on our Power presses. He does the Binding and is considered the publisher of the Spelling Book. I have not given him a license for any Specific number but require him to settle for all printed every six months, and I consider myself responsible for all printed on our presses." (Ellsworth Papers, Connecticut Historical Society.)

James A. Morgan is probably the firm that appears in the list as Morgan and Anthony, though the imprint in the spellers located is either James A. Morgan and Co. or J. A. Morgan. Ephraim Morgan was the man represented in the earlier Cincinnati imprints of Morgan, Lodge and Co., 1822, Morgan and Lodge, 1824, Morgan, Fisher, and L'Hommedieu, 1827, and Morgan and Sanxay, 1828; his son, James T., was the partner in Burgess and Morgan, 1836.

327

——— Brookfield: Published by E. and L. Merriam. 1839.

168 pp., incl. frontis., illus. 17 cm.
MWA, MiDeaEd.
The firm wrote Webster on January 2, 1838, that the sales of the speller were increasing, but that so many copies had been sold at low prices that "we have about come to the conclusion not to print any more, without we can realize more for them." They said they did not want to reduce the quality of their editions, but if they did not do so, they could not price competitively. On June 11, 1842, they wrote, "We have long since ceased to publish your Spelling Books; for the obvious reason that we could not make them well and sell them as low as others sold them. When we made them we made the best Book there was in [the] Market, that is the best executed, but they Cost us more than others sold them for."[7]

327*bis*

——— Erie, Pa. Published by Henry L. Harvey. 1839.

168 pp., illus. 17 cm.
MiDeaEd.
The copy located contains, after the Webster text, four leaves of unrelated material of an almanac nature, the last pasted down to the back cover.

328

——— Lawrenceburgh, Ia. [Indiana] James A Morgan and Co. Stereotyped by J. A. James, Cincinnati. 1839.

168 pp., incl. frontis., illus. 15 cm.
NjR.

NOTES

1. The frontispiece, while basically that of Anderson, is unsigned; it has been reworked, and differs in detail from Anderson's.
2. "Jas. A. Morgan & Co. . . . are now publishing about Four Thou-

[7]Both in Ellsworth Papers, Connecticut Historical Society.

sand copies weekly . . . ," *Political Beacon* (Lawrenceburg, Ind.), May 18, 1839, and later.

3. The publisher bought the book in sheets from his brother, Ephraim Morgan of Cincinnati; see the letter quoted as a footnote to the introductory note of this year.

329

——— Montpelier, Vt. Published by E. P. Walton & Son, 1839.

168 pp., incl. frontis., illus. 17 cm.

CtHT-W, CtHi, MWA, MiDeaEd, VtHi.

The Vermont Historical Society copy has printed on the front cover, "Webster's Elementary Spelling-Book 1842."

330

——— Portland, (Me.): Published by O. L. Sanborn. Stereotyped by J. S. Redfield, New York. 1839.

168 pp., incl. frontis., illus. 17 cm.

MH, MiDeaEd, NBuG, NN, NNC-T, RPB.

Ira White of Wells River, Vt., wrote Webster on January 2, 1841, that the market had been oversupplied because Sanborn and Roby, Kimball, and Merrill of Concord, N. H. were selling at too low a price.[8]

331

——— Watertown, N.Y. Published by Knowlton and Rice. Sold also by N. & J. White, New-York. 1839.

168 pp., incl. frontis., illus. 17 cm.

Ct (imperfect), MiDeaEd.

Contains, on the recto of the frontispiece, the added allegorical cut described under Title 288.

332

[——— Wells River, Vt.: Ira White, 1839.]

[8]Ibid.

A letter from Ira White to Webster, February 19, 1840, begins with a certificate to the effect that he had printed 15,000 copies from January, 1839, to January, 1840.[9]

333

—— Wheeling, (Va.) Published by A. & R. Fisher, Stereotyped by A. Chandler. 1839 [?].

160 + pp., incl. frontis., illus. 17 cm.

Wv-Ar (imperfect).

Not seen by the compiler. Listed on p. 20 of "West Virginia Imprints (1797 to 1863) . . . ," pp. 13–27 of *Report, Department of Archives and History, West Virginia*, 1950–1952 ([Charleston, W. Va., 1952]). The date is queried, since the final figure is blurred; it might be a 7. All after p. 160 is lacking, but the final page was probably 168.

334

Circular. Messrs. N. & J. White.... N. Webster. New Haven, November [blank] 1839.

Broadside, 25 x 20 cm. (Probably originally two leaves, printed only on the recto of the first.)

NN.

Announces that Webster had resumed from N. and J. White the agency for the licensing of his speller, and gives the terms on which licenses could be obtained. On September 1, 1840, Webster explained the situation to Samuel Fletcher: "Mr. N[orman] White of New York was my agent for granting licenses for several years; but at the close of last year, I purchased back his agency for the benefit of my son, who is now here [New Haven] & will hereafter conduct the business." In the same letter he refers to his licenses as dating from January 13, 1840.[1]

Various records relating to the licensing of spellers during 1840, 1841, and 1842 are found in the Ellsworth Papers in the Connecticut Historical Society. One page is headed "Licenses for Spellers Nov. 4, 1839," though the total

[9] Ibid.

[1] In the possession of Prof. Harry R. Warfel, who kindly provided a transcript.

figure is marked "Two years from Jan'y 1, 1840 to Oct. 20, 1842." The figures for each firm in this list tally fairly well with another sheet on which lists of numbers licensed and premiums paid during the same three-year period are recorded, though some names do not occur in both lists. The comparative totals are given below; the exact entries from the more detailed list will be cited under the separate editions.

Payment of a premium is taken as evidence of the existence of an edition. In earlier accounting the premium paid in a given year seems to represent the printings in the previous year, and attributions were made on this basis. Here, however, such entries seem to represent printings in the current year, and have been so entered.

	List of Nov. 4	*Other list*
Cushing & Brothers, Baltimore	64,000	64,000
Henry & Co./Henry, Hitchcock & Co. Cazenovia, N. Y.	20,000	20,000
Morgan, Cincinnati	140,000	
Sanford & Lott, Cleveland	20,000	10,000
Whiting, Columbus, Ohio	20,000	
Roby & Co./Roby, Kimball & Merrill, Concord, N. H.	218,000	279,150
Oliver Spafford, Erie, Pa.	10,000	10,000
Brown & Parsons, Hartford	10,000	20,000
E. P. Walton & Sons, Montpelier, Vt.	33,000	33,000
Terhune, New Brunswick, N. J.	58,000	58,000
G. F. Cooledge, New York	160,000	160,000
Kimber & Sharpless, Philadelphia	50,000	50,000
Sherborn/Robert H. Sherburne, Portland	40,000	20,550*
Sanborn/Sanborn & Carter, Portland	20,000	20,000
Loomis & Co./Loomis & Brayton, Pulaski, N. Y.	22,000	22,000
Morse, Rochester, N. Y.	10,000	
Knowlton & Rice, Watertown, N. Y.	83,000	107,082*
I. White, Wells River, Vt.	20,000	20,000
	998,000†	893,782

** Includes overprintings not recorded by number in the original, but calculated from the premium paid.*

† In the original this total has been adjusted by deducting 15,000 and adding 20,000, making the final figure 1,003,100.

335

—— Cleaveland, Ohio. Published by Sanford & Lott [1840?]

168 pp., incl. frontis. 17 cm.

A copy was offered for sale by the Midland Rare Book Company in 1942 (*Midland Notes*, No. 11, item 151), from which the entry is taken.

In 1841, 1842, and 1843 there are frequent references in the Webster correspondence to difficulties with Sanford and Lott, both in failure to account for numbers printed and in overprinting. The firm appears under 1840 with an entry of $60, which represents 10,000 copies.

336

—— Concord, N.H. Roby, Kimball & Merrill. Stereotyped by J. S. Redfield, New York. 1840.

168 pp., incl. frontis., illus. 17 cm.

CtH, CtY (imperfect), MBAt, MH, MWA (imperfect), MiDeaEd, N, NN, Nh, NhHi, RPB, British Museum.

Account books: "1840 Jan. 13.–June 8 . . . 68,430 479.00."

There are several Webster letters in 1840–1841 concerning the poor workmanship, inadequate accounting, and dubious stability of this firm.

337

[—— Montpelier, Vt.: E. P. Walton and Sons, 1840.]

The firm wrote Webster, December 12, 1840, that the demand for the speller was increasing, and that they would have published more had they not had to rebuild a paper mill, which gave the printers of the Concord, N.H., and Wells River, Vt., editions an opportunity to sell in their market. They continue, "We have completed and paid [White] for the first 10,000; since which we have published . . . 5000; and have just commenced upon a new edition of . . . 5000 more, which, when completed will make the sum total *of all we have published* 20,000. . . . We have now a new and good paper-mill in operation, with one of Adam's new power presses, propelled by water-power; and . . . we hope to publish in 1841, at least 20,000; and shall make an effort to do More."[2] There is an entry for this firm in the accounts for $60 for 10,000 copies, apparently under 1840.

[2]Ellsworth Papers, Connecticut Historical Society.

338

—— New Brunswick, N.J. Published by John Terhune.... Stereotyped by J. S. Redfield, New York. 1840.

168 pp., incl. frontis., illus. 17 cm.
MH.

339

—— New Haven. Published by S. Babcock. Stereotyped by J. S. Redfield, New York. 1840.

168 pp., incl. frontis., illus. 17 cm.
NN.
On p. [1] there is a publisher's advertisement referring to the use of stereotype plates.

340

—— New York: Published by George F. Cooledge.... Stereotyped by J. S. Redfield, New York. [1840?]

(1), 168 pp., incl. frontis., illus. 17 cm.
DLC, ICN, NN, PP.
Account books: "[1840] Nov. 26...20,000 120.00."

NOTES

1. Although Cooledge was at 374 Pearl Street, the address given in the imprint, from 1834 on, this edition has been placed in 1840 because he first appears as a licensee in Webster's accounts on November 4, 1839. These might, however, be examples of Cooledge's edition of 1841.

2. The paste-down leaf inside the front cover bears Cooledge advertising matter.

3. On January 12, 1842, Webster wrote to a Mr. Harris, "Mr Cooledge of New York now prints more of my books than any other publisher, & he makes good books."[3] After Webster's death the Cooledge firm became the sole proprietor of the speller (see below, p. 126).

[3]Pierpont Morgan Library.

341

—— Pulaski, N.Y. Published by C. D. Loomis & Co. Stereotyped by J. S. Redfield, New York. 1840.

168 pp., incl. frontis., illus. 17 cm.
MH, MiDeaEd.

342

[—— Rochester: Hoyt, Porter, and Co., 1840.]

343

[—— Rochester: Clarendon Morse, 1840.]

Morse wrote Webster, November 23, 1840, sending a remittance for $28.00, "Eighteen of it from Mr Hoyt for Spell[er]s published this past summer before selling the plates to me...." On September 11 Morse had written to Webster applying for a license and saying he had paper ready; apparently he got out an edition of his own during the year.[4]

344

[—— Watertown, N.Y.: Knowlton and Rice, 1840.]

Account books: "Nov. 4, 1839 to Oct. 27, 1840...68,000 420.80."

345

[—— Wells River, Vt.: Ira White, 1840.]

In a letter to Webster, January 2, 1841, White certified that in 1840 he printed 7,000 copies beyond his license, including 2,000 to replace imperfect copies.[5]

346

[—— Wheeling, W. Va.: Stephens and Garwood, 1840.]

[4]Both in Ellsworth Papers, Connecticut Historical Society.
[5]Ellsworth Papers, Connecticut Historical Society.

On August 19, 1840, Ephraim Morgan of Cincinnati wrote Webster: "Canst thou inform me how many Books Stephens & Garwood of Wheeling, Va. have a right to print [?] A friend of mine who resides in Wheeling, informs me a few days since that they told him they had about 40,000 to print. If their license was only for 50,000, which I understand was the case, I think it very *strange* as I am satisfied they have sold considerably more than 10,000 in this city. This market is pretty well stocked with their books which are a very poor article..., and I understand it is the case at Louisville and St. Louis.... The friend alluded to informs me that they were not only printing themselves but employed others to print for them. Those engaged in printing other Spelling Books keep a supply of the Wheeling Edition, many of which are so badly printed that they cannot be read."[6] Stephens and Garwood do not appear in the lists of 1839 or 1840 licensees; they may have purchased all or part of the 1839 license for 80,000 to the Fisher firm in Wheeling.

347

[—— Baltimore: Cushing and Brother, 1841.]

Account books: "1841 Aug. 7...44,000 246.94" and "20,000 120.00."

348

—— Published by the Brattleboro' Typographic Company, Brattleboro', Vt. 1841.

168 pp., incl. frontis., illus. 17 cm.
CtH, CtHT-W (imperfect), MWA, NNC-T, Merriam.

349

—— Cazenovia: Published by Henry, Hitchcock, & Co. Stereotyped by J. S. Redfield, New York. 1841.

168 pp., incl. frontis., illus. 17 cm.
MiDeaEd, Merriam.
Account books: "1841 June 18...20,000 120.00."

[6]Ibid.

350

[—— Cincinnati: E. Morgan and Co., 1841.]

For 1841 Morgan reported to Webster: "To 40,000 copies published by self & co. 200.00; 1841 July 1 To 50,000 copies published by self & co. 250.00."[7]

351

—— Cleveland, Ohio. Published by M. C. Younglove. Stereotyped by J. S. Redfield, New York. 1841.

168 pp., incl. frontis., illus. 17 cm.
MiDeaEd, NjR, NN.

Ephraim Morgan wrote Webster, August 14, 1841: "I shall comply with thy request and grant a license to [Moses C.] Younglove in place of Sandford [sic] & Lot [sic]. . . ." Younglove wrote Webster on October 4 that he had paper on hand and was daily expecting plates from Redfield. In Morgan's account with Webster for 1841 there is the entry, "1842 Jan. 1 To 50,000 copies published by self & Younglove 250."[8]

352

[—— Cleveland: Sanford and Co., 1841.]

Before the substitution of Younglove for Sanford and Lott mentioned in the letter quoted in the preceding entry, the latter firm paid a premium for 1841; Morgan's account records: "To license granted to Sanford & Co. of Cleaveland 10,000 copies 50.00." Writing to Webster on March 14, 1842, Younglove reported that Sanford and Lott had continued to print up to December 20.[9]

353

[—— Columbus: I. N. Whiting, 1841.]

Ephraim Morgan's accounting for 1841: "License to I. N. Whiting 20,000 copies 100.00."[1]

[7]Ibid.
[8]All three in Ellsworth Papers, Connecticut Historical Society.
[9]Both ibid. [1]Ibid.

354

[—— Concord, N.H.: Roby, Kimball, and Merrill, 1841.]

Account books: "1841 Jan 4, Apr. 20...50,000 300.00."

355

—— Erie, Pa. Published by Oliver Spafford. 1841.

168 pp., incl. frontis., illus. 17 cm.
Mott.
Account books: "10,000 70.00," apparently 1841.

356

—— Hartford: Published by Brown & Parsons. Stereotyped by J. S. Redfield, New York. 1841.

168 pp., incl. frontis., illus. 18 cm.
CtHT-W.
Account books: "1841 Feb. 10...10,000 60.00."

357

—— Lawrenceburgh, Ia. [Indiana] James A. Morgan and Co. Stereotyped by J. A. James, Cincinnati. 1841.

168 pp., incl. frontis., illus. 15 cm.
Greenwood.
On July 17, 1841, Ephraim Morgan of Cincinnati wrote Webster,"I herewith forward a check for Copy Right of 50,000 Elementary Spellers, printed at the Office by E Morgan & Co. for Jas. Augustus Morgan, during the last six months."[2] Since two entries occur under "self & co." in his 1841 accounting (quoted above under Title 350), the second may represent this lot, which he printed but did not publish.

358

—— Medina, Ohio: Printed by O. W. M'Kinney. [1841?]

[2]Ibid.

168 pp., incl. frontis. 17 cm.
OHi.

NOTES

1. Placed in 1841 by the compiler on the basis of the letter quoted below and an 1842 ownership inscription in the copy located.

2. Moses C. Younglove wrote Webster from Cleveland, March 14, 1842, complaining that Sanford and Lott, the former licensees there, had either sold or loaned their plates to McKinney, "who has been printing them constantly up to the present time," and that McKinney had contracted to furnish Sanford and Lott 40,000 copies in sheets, 2000 of which had already been delivered and were being bound.[3]

359

—— Montpelier, Vt. Published by E. P. Walton & Sons, 1841.

168 pp., incl. frontis., illus. 17 cm.
MH.
The firm, writing to Webster on May 17, 1842, stated that they had printed 23,000 copies since December 23, 1840, but had sold only 3,000 of them.[4] They appear in his accounts with "1842 June 28 . . . 23,000 141.00."

360

[—— New York: George F. Cooledge, 1841.]

Account books: "1841 March 10-November 15 . . . 100,000 600.00."
See Note 1 to Title 340.

361

[—— Philadelphia: Kimber and Sharpless, 1841.]

Account books: "1841 May 26 . . . 50,000 300.00."

362

—— Portland, (Me.): Sanborn, Sherburne & Co. Stereotyped by J. S. Redfield, New York. 1841.

[3]Ibid. [4]Ibid.

168 pp., incl. frontis., illus. 17 cm.
CtHT-W (imperfect), NN, NjR.

362a

——— Portland, (Me.): Sherburne & Co. Stereotyped by J. S. Redfield, New York. 1841.

DFSA.

Account books: "1841 Sept. 16 Robert H. Sherburne 20,000 120.00" and "overprint [5,500] 33.00."

The line consisting of the firm name is misaligned with the others, as if separately printed. Sherburne is an erratic element in the history of Webster imprints. He published one speller in Philadelphia in 1828 and this one in Portland in 1841, and appears as an added vendor on another in Boston in 1843.

363

[——— Pulaski, N.Y.: Loomis and Brayton, 1841.]

Account books: "1841 Oct. 1 . . . 12,000 84.00" and, apparently also under 1841, "Sept. 5 . . . 10,000 70.00."

364

[——— Watertown, N.Y.: Knowlton and Rice, 1841.]

Account books: "1841 March 5 . . . 15,000 90.00" and "overprint [5,823] 34.94."

365

——— Wells River, Vt. Published by Ira White. Stereotyped by J. S. Redfield[,] New York. 1841.

168 pp., incl. frontis., illus. 17 cm.
CtHT-W, CtHi, MWA, MiDeaEd, PU, VtHi, WaU.

White wrote Webster, April 5, 1841, that he had just received a new set of plates, stereotyped by Redfield, and asked for a license for 20,000 more copies.[5]

[5]Ibid.

366

[—— Wheeling, W. Va.: Robb and Stephenson, 1841(?).]

Ephraim Morgan wrote Webster on April 7, 1842, that he had been informed that Robb and Stephenson in Wheeling had been printing spellers without a license.[6]

367

[—— One or more editions in Tennessee, 1841.]

On July 17, 1841, Ephraim Morgan of Cincinnati wrote Webster that he had received a request for a license from Pryor and Whiteman in Tennessee, and on August 4 that "J. A. James [a Cincinnati stereotyper] informed me that he furnished Pryor & Whiteman with the small plates on which they have commenced printing." Neither of these surnames appears in the checklists of Tennessee imprints compiled by the American Imprints Inventory; the only appearance of either name in Tennessee printing history found by the compiler is in the firm of Moseley, Finnie, and Pryor in Memphis a dozen years later (1853).

Morgan's accounts under date of July 1, 1842, show "30,000 copies published by self & in Tenn. 152.50," and in December, 1842, he sent Webster fifty dollars which he had collected for spellers printed without license in Tennessee, saying that there was no chance of collecting from a firm which had printed a considerable number, since it had gone bankrupt.[7] Unfortunately he does not mention firm names. These references may be to Pryor and Whiteman, or perhaps to James Williams who was printing in Knoxville in 1841 and 1842, and whose name appears in an undated list of publishers of the *Elementary* speller in the Webster Papers.

368

—— Cincinnati: J. A. Morgan 1842.

168 pp., [incl. frontis.], illus. 14 cm.
NjR (lacking frontis.).

NOTES

1. The title-page is very poorly aligned.

[6]Ibid. [7]Ibid.

2. On February 10, 1842, Ephraim Morgan wrote Webster, "My brother will probably print about 50 thousand Spellers the next six months," and on December 2 he remitted the premium for 20,000 printed by J. A. Morgan.[8]

369

[—— Claremont, N.H.: Claremont Manufacturing Co.(?), 1842.]

In 1841 Simeon Ide of Claremont made a contract with Webster to take over the sole publishing rights for the speller and the dictionaries. He was connected with the Claremont Manufacturing Company, which was experiencing severe financial difficulties, so he surrendered the contract;[9] the dictionary portion went to the Merriams and the spellers to the Cooledges. The Claremont Manufacturing Company survived, and printed an edition of the speller about 1849. That they also printed one in 1842 is suggested by references in a letter of E. P. Walton of Montpelier, Vt., to Webster, February 11, 1843, referring to the financial difficulties of the Claremont firm, and saying in a postscript that Mr. Ide's sons were responsible for the printing of a large edition of the speller without having paid for the right in advance.[1]

370

[—— Cleveland: Moses C. Younglove, 1842.]

In a letter of January 25, 1843, Younglove admitted to Webster that he had printed 10,000 copies beyond his license, and that he had another edition partly completed. In the same letter he tells Webster that Sanford and Lott are still causing trouble, having printed between ten and twenty thousand spellers since their right expired, though they pretend to have sold their plates to a man in Michigan.[2] (See the references to copies supplied to them in sheets in 1842 by McKinney in Medina, Ohio, under Title 358.)

371

—— Concord, N.H. Luther Roby. 1842.

[8] Ibid.
[9] Louis W. Flanders, *Simeon Ide*... (Rutland, Vt., The Tuttle Co., 1931), p. 89.
[1] Ellsworth Papers, Connecticut Historical Society. [2] Ibid.

168 pp., incl. frontis., illus. 17 cm.
CtY, NN, NhHi.
Account books: "1842 Jan.–Dec. 29... 160,720 714.32."

372

——— Lawrenceburgh, Ia. [Indiana] James A. Morgan and Co. Stereotyped by J. A. James, Cincinnati. 1842.

168 pp., incl. frontis., illus. 16 cm.
CSmH (imperfect), O.

373

——— New Brunswick, N.J. Published by John Terhune.... Stereotyped by Redfield & Savage, New-York. 1842.

168 pp., incl. frontis., illus. 17 cm.
MiDeaEd, NjP, NjR.

Account books: "1842 Feb. 1	8,000	56.00
1842 Feb. 1, new license	20,000	140.00";
"[1842?] Feb.– Oct. 30	25,000	175.00
overprint	5,000	35.00."

374

[——— New Haven: Brown and Parsons, 1842.]

Account books: "1842 Dec. 15... 10,000 60.00."

375

——— New York: Published by George F. Cooledge,... Stereotyped by Redfield & Savage, New York. Applegate's Steam Presses..., New York. [1842?]

(1), 163 pp., incl. frontis., illus. 18 cm.
MWA.
Account books: "1842 Mar. 10, Oct. 13... 40,000 240.00."

NOTES

1. The contents are somewhat differently arranged than usual; the table "Of Numbers" falls on p. 163, which is pasted down to the back

cover. The front paste-down contains publisher's advertising matter and Applegate's imprint.

2. The date of this edition can be narrowed down to 1842 or early 1843. It is before Cooledge instituted the "authorized" title-page in mid-1843; but it was not until the 1842/1843 New York city directory that the firm of J. S. Redfield became Redfield and Savage or William Applegate added "steam presses" to his listing.

376

—— Portland, (Me.): Sanborn & Carter. Stereotyped by J. S. Redfield, New York. 1842.

168 pp., incl. frontis., illus. 17 cm.
MA, MH, MWA, NjR, OClWHi.
Account books: "1842 Mar. 26...20,000 120.00."

377

[—— Rochester: Clarendon Morse, 1842.]

Morse wrote Webster, December 28, 1842, "The 10,000 Spellers authorized by my license have been printed & sold."[3]

378

—— Utica: Bennett, Backus & Hawley. Stereotyped by J. S. Redfield, New-York. 1842.

168 pp., [incl. frontis.,] illus. 17 cm.
NNC (lacking frontis.).

379

[—— Watertown, N.Y.: Knowlton and Rice, 1842.]

Account books: "1842 March 1...overprint 7,816 46.90."

380

[—— Cincinnati, 1843.]

[3]Ibid.

168 pp., "12mo."

Offered for sale by the Smith Book Company of Cincinnati in October, 1939, but the compiler's efforts to trace the copy or get fuller information were not successful.

381

——— Cleveland, Ohio. Published by M. C. Younglove. Stereotyped by J. S. Redfield, New York. 1843.

168 pp., incl. frontis., illus. 17 cm.

DLC.

382

——— Columbus, Ohio: Published by I. N. Whiting and Huntington. Stereotyped by Redfield & Savage, New York. [1843?]

168 pp., incl. frontis., illus. 18 cm.

NN (imperfect).

Assigned to 1829 by The New York Public Library, probably on the basis of the copyright date, but since it contains commendations which are not earlier than 1830 it cannot antedate that year. Because of the firm name of the stereotypers (see Note 2 to Title 375), this has been placed as late as 1843.

383

——— Concord, N.H.: Published by Luther Roby. Sold by R. H. Sherburne,... Boston. 1843.

168 pp., incl. frontis., illus. 17 cm.

MWA, NhHi.

384

——— Hartford: Published by Brown & Parsons. Stereotyped by J. S. Redfield, New York. 1843.

168 pp., incl. frontis., illus. 17 cm.

DLC, MWA.

The Library of Congress copy is one which was used at a later date for copyright entry, having a MS slip pasted in with an 1857 entry.

385

—— Montreal: Armour & Ramsay; Kingston: Ramsay, Armour & Co.; Hamilton: A. H. Armour & Co. 1843.

168, (3) pp., incl. frontis. 18 cm.
AN-C-M.

NOTES

1. Not seen by the compiler; information supplied by the library.

2. On p. [4], the verso of the title-page, is "Stereotype Edition" and "Printed by Armour & Ramsay Montreal." The three unnumbered pages at the end contain publisher's advertisements.

3. Melville Lord of Boston wrote Webster on December 26, 1842, "In answer to your inquiry regarding the set of plates for the Elementary Spelling Book which the firm of Richardson & Lord once owned, I would state that they were sold about ten years ago to Carter & Hendee of this city, who kept them on hand, unused [?—see Title 280], until two or three years since, when they were sold to Messrs. Armour & Ramsay, an honourable and well known firm of Montreal, and were carried to that place, there to be worked and the books used in Canada. Mr A. was at that time in this city on his way to England, to obtain a set of plates for a Spelling Book and some other School books, and accidentally hearing of this set of plates, he bought them. . . ."[4]

After Webster's death in 1843 his family signed a contract with George F. Cooledge and Brother of New York, by which this firm became the proprietors of the speller, subject to adjustment of certain rights held by Sanborn and Carter of Portland, Maine. In order to make authorized editions readily recognizable, the Cooledges adopted an elaborate engraved title-page with a statement in a cartouche at the bottom: "All genuine authorized editions of the Spelling Book, published after August 4th, 1843, by the permission of the proprietors, contain this Engraved Title-page." The contents followed substantially the editions after Webster's revisions of 1835–1836.

Few of the editions issued by the Cooledges and their licensees and successors are dated, and these editions are difficult to arrange in sequence. The firm "devoted the whole capacity of the fastest steam press in the United States to the printing" of the speller, producing over 5,000 a day,[5] *so the bibliographical*

[4]Ellsworth Papers, Connecticut Historical Society.

[5]Henry L. Mencken, *The American Language*... (4th ed., New York, 1936), p. 385.

complexity of the editions after 1843 can readily be imagined. A further complication is found in the constantly shifting advertising matter on the flyleaves and frontispiece.

Because these vast printings of the mid- and late nineteenth century have so tenuous a connection with Webster's own work, the compiler has omitted the authorized editions. Below are listed continued instances of publication of the pre-1843 speller without Cooledge authorization, and in rubric F will be found derivative and translated spellers which are of bibliographical interest. At the end of this section are some criteria to assist owners of post-1843 authorized editions to place them chronologically.

386

—— Cincinnati: Published by E. Morgan & Co.... [1843-4?]

168 pp., incl. frontis., illus. 17 cm.
OHi (imperfect).

NOTES

1. The copy located lacks the title-page; the imprint is taken from the front cover.
2. Contains a new set of cuts; in that for Fable I the boy is, for the first time, thumbing his nose at the farmer.
3. Not later than 1844, because of the firm's address (131 Main St.).

387

—— Montpelier, Vt. Published by E. P. Walton & Sons, 1844.

168 pp., incl. frontis., illus. 17 cm.
VtHi.

388

—— Montreal—Armour & Ramsay. Kingston—Ramsay, Armour & Co. Hamilton—Ramsay & M'Kendrick. 1845.

168 pp., incl. frontis. 18 cm.
CtY.

There are two pages of publisher's advertisements at the end; this leaf is smaller than the rest, and is probably not part of the book as printed.

Note

Criteria for dating authorized spellers after 1843

As mentioned above, on August 4, 1843, the firm of George F. Cooledge and Brother of New York became the authorized publishers of the *Elementary*, and almost all editions after that date stem from them or their successors, D. Appleton and the American Book Company, though by arrangement other firm names often appear in the imprints, especially on the front covers. The title-pages are seldom dated, though the cover sometimes bears a date when the title-page does not. Although the compiler has not listed the authorized editions after Webster's death, it has seemed desirable to record certain points which she determined as criteria for dating these editions, at least relatively.

Generally speaking, the less advertising matter on the flyleaves and frontispiece, the earlier the edition. "Last Revised Edition" was added at the head of the title-page about 1845. Copies which do not have this legend and contain no advertising probably date from 1843–1844. Copies which lack the legend but advertise a "Pictorial Edition" as to be published January 1, 1845, are doubtless 1844 printings. (The "Pictorial" was the regular edition with some 150 added cuts; the text was identical, page for page.) Some printings also advertised a *Sequel* to the speller, published in mid-1844.[6]

Later the frontispiece came to be surrounded with advertising matter. In the earlier years there is at most a statement above the picture claiming an annual sale of 500,000 or 1,000,000 copies; the smaller figure would presumably represent an earlier edition, but this does not seem to be a consistent indicator.

Beginning with 1848 there is a series of dated references which help place a given edition within a fairly narrow range. A new "Advertisement," dated May, 1848, was added on p. [4]. Copies with the 1829 copyright and 1848 "Advertisement" date from 1848 to 1857, and those of 1848–1849 can be distinguished by the fact that the name of the stereotypers changed in 1849 from Redfield and Savage to Charles C. Savage.

In 1855 an edition appeared with added arithmetical material. This has a pagination of 217 rather than 168, and bears an 1855 copyright entry on the added matter. The compiler has noted only one printing of this version. About this time the Cooledges also issued a *National Pic-*

[6]This is really a dictionary, and is listed below (Section Three, Part Seven, rubric A).

torial Primer of 48 pages; the contents do not seem to be related to Webster's spellers or primers, though the flyleaf advertising is mostly for Webster's various works. This advertising matter closely parallels that found in Cooledge spellers of 1855–1857.

In 1857 the rights to the speller were taken over by the G. and C. Merriam Company, though they did not publish the work over their own imprint; instead, they contracted with D. Appleton for publication. In this year there are three new features: a copyright notice in the name of the Webster heirs, one in the name of the Merriams, and a new "Advertisement," dated May, 1857. These features distinguish editions from 1857 to 1866, and the period can be subdivided by the change, in 1860, from 346–348 Broadway to 443–445 Broadway as the Appletons' address.

In 1866 there is a new copyright to the Merriams and a new preface. These distinguishing features set off editions from 1866 to 1880, and the dating can be further narrowed by changes in the Appletons' address: 443–445 Broadway until 1869, 90–94 Grand St. from 1869 to 1871, and 549–551 Broadway to 1880. In 1880 there is still another copyright to the Merriams, and a "Preface to the Latest Edition" is added to the 1866 preface. Originally this new preface was dated March, 1880, but some later printings do not include the date line. The 1880 copyright and the new preface distinguish editions up to 1908.

In 1890 the American Book Company took over publication on behalf of the Merriams, but printings occur with the Appletons' name on the title-page and the American Book Company's on the front cover, and vice-versa. In 1908 there appeared a new Merriam copyright, which is the latest date indicated in the printing on sale in the 1950's.

F. *Adapted and Translated Spellers*

For Nathan Guilford's various adaptations of the speller in 1831, see Appendix F.

389

Abridged edition of The elementary spelling book; being an improvement on the American spelling book. By Noah Webster, LL.D. Oregon City: Printed and published by the Oregon Printing Association. 1847.

96 pp. 18 cm.
CtY (fragmentary), OrHi (imperfect).
McMurtrie, Oregon, 5.

NOTES

1. "ELEMENTARY SPELLING BOOK.—The [Oregon Printing] Association's edition of Webster's Elementary Spelling Book, will be ready for all who may be in want thereof, by the first of next month. It is excellently well gotten up, and we think will prove highly satisfactory. Stitched copies may be obtained for twenty five cents, and bound ones for the additional tax of the binding, which is certainly very cheap, as the volume will comprise ninety six pages of actual matter." *Oregon Spectator* (Oregon City), January 21, 1847. A similar paragraph in the issue of February 4 confirms the publication of the book on the first of that month, and gives the price of bound copies as thirty-seven and a half cents.

2. The minutes of the Board of Directors of the Association, in the Oregon Historical Society, record the plans and estimates for the publication of the book. The estimate for 1000 copies was $176, including about $35 needed for equipment in the pressroom; a second thousand was estimated at $65.20. On November 16, 1846, the directors voted to order two thousand copies, though McMurtrie says the edition printed was eight hundred. The Association records indicate that five hundred were bound.

3. This was the first book printed in English west of the Rockies, being preceded only by works printed in Indian languages at the Lapwai Mission, in what is now Idaho, and works in Spanish printed in California.

390

The revised elementary spelling book. The elementary spelling book, revised and adapted to the youth of the Southern Confederacy, interspersed with Bible readings on domestic slavery. By Rev. Robert Fleming. Atlanta, Georgia: Franklin Steam Printing House, J. J. Toon, & Co.... 1863.

168 pp. 17 cm. P. [1], title-page. P. [2], dedication, to parents and children, teachers and pupils, and "all the Lovers of Learning and Bible Truth in the Confederate States of America"; copyright notice, Southern District of Georgia, 1863, to Fleming. Pp. [3]–5, preface (see below), signed by Fleming, Thomasville, Ga. Pp. 5–7, abridged version of Web-

ster's preface. Pp. 7–168, text. Publisher's advertisements on front and back covers. There are no illustrations except for a portrait of Washington on the front cover and a cut of an open Bible on the title-page.

DLC, GEU.

Crandall 4054.

In his preface, Fleming says that "no better Spelling-book than Dr. Webster's has ever been presented to the American people," and that it has long been almost the only one in use in the South. Cut off from the publisher and "driven from [the Union] never to return, we ask, what must now be done to meet the needs of our schools?" He says that when it occurred to him to prepare a speller he felt he could not improve on Webster's, and that it could be adapted to his purpose. He has retained Webster's orthography and most of his pronunciation. He promises that as soon as possible the work will be stereotyped, and closes by referring to the question of slavery, saying that "the people of these Confederate States of America will not henceforth withhold from their school-books, the teachings of the Scriptures on this subject." The text in general follows the Cooledge editions of the late 1840's, with omissions (including the fables) and the addition of Biblical verses, lists of the Confederate and United States, a thumbnail biography of General Thomas J. Jackson, and new recommendations.

390a

[—— Twenty-ninth thousand. Atlanta, Georgia: J. J. Toon & Co., publishers. Franklin Steam Printing House. Edition] 1863. [40,000.]

Weeks, p. 1141.

Weeks locates a copy in the library of the United States Office of Education (later Federal Security Agency), but the compiler did not find it there.

390b

—— Thirty-fourth thousand. Atlanta, Georgia: J. J. Toon & Co., publishers. Franklin Steam Printing House. Edition] 1863. [40,000.

DLC, ICU.

Crandall 4055.

Crandall locates a copy at Duke University, but its imprint is missing, so it could be 390, 390a, or yet another variant.

391

The elementary [s]pelling book, being an improvement on ["] The American spelling book," by Noah Webster, LL.D. [The] cheapest, the best, and the most extensively used spelling book ever published. Macon, Ga.: Burke, Boykin & Co.'s Steam Presses. 1863.

156 pp. 16 cm. P. [1], title-page. P. [2], publisher's preface. Pp. [3]–5, Webster's preface. Pp. 6–156, text.

GEU.

Crandall 4114.

NOTES

1. At head of title, "Southern edition."

2. Not seen; data provided by the library. Mending tape has obliterated the beginning of three lines on the title-page.

3. The contents follow the Appleton authorized edition fairly closely, though the printers had to omit the cuts and certain portions requiring the use of accented letters, which they did not have. The first four fables are included.

392

—— Macon, Ga.: Burke, Boykin & Co.'s Steam Presses. 1863.

140 pp. 18 cm. P. [1], blank, pasted down to front cover. P. [2], publisher's advertisements. P. [3], title-page. P. [4], publisher's preface. P. [5], preface. Pp. 6–140, text.

OClWHi (imperfect), MiDeaEd (imperfect?).

NOTES

1. At head of title: "Second Southern edition."

2. The same contents as the preceding, though in fewer pages. Webster's preface is reduced to two paragraphs. There was almost certainly a leaf (advertising?) following p. 140; the signaturing calls for one, and there are traces of it in the Western Reserve Historical Society copy. The Henry Ford Museum copy breaks off at the end of p. 122, but since this leaf is conjugate with the paste-down inside the back cover, the book was apparently issued in this form by the publisher.

393

The elementary spelling-book, revised from Webster, and adapted to Southern schools, by the publishers. Raleigh: Bronson, Farrar & Co., publishers. Hillsboro Street. [1863.]

x, 152 pp. 17 cm. P. [i], title-page. P. [ii], copyright notice and imprint (see below). P. [iii], publisher's preface. Pp. iv–x, 1–152, text.
CtY (imperfect), NcU.

NOTES

1. This edition follows the Cooledge editions of the late 1840's more closely than does Title 390, though there are some changes; it does not include Webster's preface.
2. On the verso of the title-page there is the imprint, "Biblical Recorder Print," and the perhaps deliberately vague notice, "Copy Right Secured According to Law."
3. On the front cover the date is added to the imprint, and the publisher's address is given as 12 Fayetteville Street.
4. This firm also published, in 1864, a "Dixie Speller," by Mrs. M. B. Moore; it is not related to Webster's work.

394

The elementary spelling book, being an improvement on "The American spelling book".... Macon, Ga.: Burke, Boykin and Company. 1865.

137, 7 pp. 18 cm. P. [1], title-page. P. [2], publisher's preface and advertising. P. [3], preface. Pp. 4–137, text. Pp. 1–7, publisher's advertisements. (Of this numbering, p. 1 is the verso of p. 137; thus p. 7 is a verso also.)
GEU, MBAt, NHi.
Crandall 4115.

NOTES

1. At head of title, "Third Southern edition."
2. Similar to Title 391, though in fewer pages. On the front cover the firm name is given as J. W. Burke and Company.

395

Soyaku tsuzuriji-sho. Translated by Yoyu Shisui. Tokyo, Bensei Kyosho, 1871.

(58) pp. 18 cm. P. [1], title-page in Japanese, with "Spelling Book" in English, pasted down to front wrapper. Pp. [2–3], preface. Pp. [4–7], alphabets. Pp. [8–9], arabic and roman numerals (the highest being 1820). P. [10], ligatures. Pp. [11–15], discussion of English letters and articles. Pp. [16–17], pronunciation of English. Pp. [18–57], twenty-four numbered lessons, consisting of syllables and simple sentences. P. [58], colophon, pasted down to back wrapper.
NN.

NOTES

1. That the work is derived from Webster is stated on the title-page.
2. This book is printed from neither movable type nor stereotype plates; each page—including both Japanese and English text, the latter in script form—is from a woodblock cut by hand.

396

The elementary Noah Webster, L.L.D. New edition Spelling book [Osaka, 1887.]

(4), 24, (4), [25]–123, (1) pp., illus. 18 cm.
MH.

Cover title only. The pagination is erratic, running [i–iv], 1-24, "24 of 1" to "24 of 4," 52 [sic], 26–84, [85], 86–123, [124]. P. [i] is a crude cut of Webster, after the Morse portrait. P. [ii], Japanese alphabet. P. [iii], figures for manual sign language. P. [iv], English script alphabet. Pp. 1–[25], equivalents of English letters, alphabets, etc. (p. "24 of 2" is blank). Pp. 26–121, text. Pp. 122–[124], punctuation, etc. On pages 10 and 12–20 are cuts showing positions of the lips and vocal chords. On p. [124] (translation): "Copyrighted May 31, 1887, July, 1887 Translator. . . Chojiro Ogasawara Publisher Masajiro Kashiwabara Osaka."

In addition to being translated into Japanese, Webster's spelling book circulated in Japan in its standard form. The Henry Ford Museum possesses a copy of the D. Appleton edition of the Elementary *speller current in the*

1880's; it is printed from Occidental type or stereotype plates, but the illustrations are by a Japanese artist, based on the American originals. Inside the back cover is a paste-down colophon in Japanese stating that the book was "submitted for reprint March 26, 1887" and issued in May of the same year, published by Jironosuke Kansaki and printed by the Shoundo Kappan-sho, both of Tokyo.

G. *Primers Derivative from the Speller*[7]

1. *Abridgment of the original Speller*

397

[The First part of the Grammatical institute of the English language, abridged; for the use of small children who are beginning to learn the letters. By Noah Webster Jun. Philadelphia: Printed for Thomas Dobson, at the New Book-Store.... 1786.]

Evans 20128.

No copy located, but the edition is documented.

"It is often observed by parents and masters, that children wear out two or three spelling books, in learning a few of the first tables; of course two thirds of the expence of those books is lost. To prevent this waste of money, is the design of this little collection of easy words."[8] Timothy Pickering once made this point in a letter to Webster, who replied (October 28, 1785), "Your idea of dividing the first part strikes me favorably."[9]

The work was entered for copyright in Maryland on January 7, 1786,[1] and on February 20 of that year Webster wrote to Hudson and Goodwin from Philadelphia, "May I [i.e., I may] have an Abridgement of the first

[7] Webster's editions of the *New England Primer* are entered in Section Eight, Works edited by Webster. The related *Western Primer* of 1833–1837 is listed in Appendix F. *The Teacher* (1836) is called "a Supplement to the Elementary Spelling Book," but it is actually more than that, and is entered in Section Two, Other Text Books. The *Sequel to Webster's Elementary Spelling Book* (1844?) is really a dictionary, and is entered in Section Three, Part Seven.

[8] From an advertisement for this work, *Hudson* (N.Y.) *Weekly Gazette*, August 3, 1786, and later.

[9] Pickering MSS, Massachusetts Historical Society; both letters are printed in the Society's *Proceedings*, Vol. 43 (1909), pp. 122–124, and in Ford's *Notes*, Vol. I, pp. 97–101.

[1] Liber T.B.H., No. 1, folio 532, Maryland Record Office.

part, or Primer published in Philadelphia & shall want it published in Connecticut this spring."[2] In his correspondence with Pickering during 1786 there are references to passing back and forth a manuscript for suggestions and correction. The work was advertised as "This Day... Published" in the *Pennsylvania Gazette* of July 26, 1786, and later, and in other papers.

2. *The Elementary Primer*

398

[First lessons for children(?). New Haven? 1829?]

In the *Connecticut Herald* of July 21, 1829, and later, there is notice of a copyright taken out on July 1 for "First Lessons for Children," and the December, 1829, issue of the *Quarterly Christian Spectator* (Ser. 3, Vol. I, No. 4) has on a flyleaf an advertisement for Webster's *Elementary* speller which continues "A small book of FIRST LESSONS, to be sold at six cents, intended for beginners, is compiled as an introduction to the Spelling Book...." No further trace of such a work has been found; if it existed it must have been the fore-runner of the following entry.

399

The elementary primer, or First lessons for children; being an introduction to The elementary spelling book. By Noah Webster, L.L.D. New-York: Published by M'Elrath and Bangs...and L. D. Dewey.... 1831.

34 pp., illus. 14 cm. P. [1], title-page. P. [2], copyright entry in Connecticut District to Noah Webster, 1831, and "John T. West & Co., Printers." Pp. [3]–34, text, including alphabets, one and two syllable words, diphthongs, etc., interspersed with cuts of animals.

DLC, MiDeaEd.

NOTES

1. Reviewed in the *New York Whig*, November 16, 1831.
2. The price was six and one-quarter cents.
3. On the front cover Morton and Smith of Louisville are added as

[2]American Antiquarian Society.

publishers of the work, and the following are listed as vendors: New York, Collins and Hannay; White, Gallaher and White; E. Bliss. Philadelphia, John Grigg; U. Hunt; Towar and Hogan; Key and Mielke. Boston, Carter and Hendee. Hartford, D. F. Robinson and Co. Albany, O. Steele; Little and Cummings. Buffalo, Steele and Faxon. Rochester, Hoyt, Porter and Co. Baltimore, Cushing and Sons; M'Dowell and Son; Plaskitt and Co. Charleston, O. A. Roorbach. The back cover contains M'Elrath and Bangs advertisements.

4. On November 6, 1833, M'Elrath and Bangs wrote Webster that the edition they printed "about two years ago...has all been disposed of. We sold a set of plates to a Bookseller at the East also [John Wilcox? See following three entries], but have never recd any account of his sales.... We have 2 sets of plates, one of which was designed for the West, but we have never been able to find a purchaser, altho' we advertised."[3]

400

[Identical title-page.]

36 pp., illus. 14 cm.
CtHi, CtY, NN, British Museum.

NOTES

1. The title-page is identical with the preceding, but it does not have the printer's imprint on the verso. There is an added leaf (pp. 35–36), which contains three poems.

2. The front cover of the British Museum copy has the imprint, "Wells River, Vt. John Wilcox. 1832." On the other copies it has "New Haven: Printed and published by S. Babcock..., 1835," and the back cover contains Babcock advertising matter dated April, 1835.

3. Webster's accounts for May, 1835, record shipments by Babcock and Durrie and Peck, also of New Haven, of lots of fifty primers to various dealers in Massachusetts, Connecticut, and New York state. One of the recipients was Sylvester Galpin, Litchfield, Conn.; he advertised the book as "just received" in the *Litchfield Enquirer* on May 25.

401

[Identical title-page except that the imprint has been removed.]

[3]Webster Papers, New York Public Library.

36 pp., illus. 14 cm.
CtSoP (at CtY), MB, MBAt, MWA, NNC, NNC-T, Nh.

NOTES

1. The title-page seems to be from the same type or plates as the preceding; it even preserves the row of dots which was above the date. There is no printer's imprint on the verso.

2. On all copies on which the covers survive there is a cover imprint, "Newport, N.H. John Wilcox. 1834."

402

—— Newport, N.H. John Wilcox. 1834.

36 pp., illus. 15 cm.
DLC, Nh.
This still seems to be the same setting of type, though the line of dots has disappeared; no printer's imprint on verso.

The compiler's notes indicate that over forty years ago she saw a copy with the imprint "Brookfield, Mass. Published by E. and L. Merriam . . . , 1835." She was unable later to find such a version; since this firm published other primers in 1835, this may be a ghost.

403

—— New Haven. Published by S. Babcock. . . . 1841.

36 pp., illus. 14 cm.
MH.
On the back cover there is an Alexander Anderson woodcut of a family in a summer house.

404

The elementary primer, being an introduction to The elementary spelling book. By Noah Webster, LL.D. Concord, N.H. Published by Rufus Merrill 1843.

36 pp., illus. 15 cm.
MH (imperfect), NhHi.

The front cover has an elaborate pictorial border within which the title-page is repeated except for the omission of the words "published by." On the Harvard copy this border contains the heading "Museum of Natural History"; on the New Hampshire Historical Society copy it does not. The rear cover has publisher's advertising, in which the work is referred to as "Webster's First Book," and the price is given as six cents.

404a

——— Concord, N.H. Rufus Merrill 1843.

NH.

In this both the front cover and the title-page have the pictorial border, with the "Museum of Natural History" heading.

PART TWO: GRAMMAR

A. *The Original Text*

405

A grammatical institute of the English language, comprising, an easy, concise, and systematic method of education, designed for the use of English schools in America. In three parts. Part II. Containing, a plain and comprehensive grammar. . . and an essay towards investigating the rules of English verse. By Noah Webster, Jun. Esq. *Usus est norma loquendi.* Hartford: Printed by Hudson & Goodwin, for the author, M,DCC,LXXXIV. Under protection of the statute.

139 pp. 15 cm. P. [1], title-page. P. [2], blank. Pp. [3]–6, preface, unsigned and undated (see below). Pp. [7]–139, text, including (pp. 119–132) "Prosody," which was largely written by John Trumbull, though not so acknowledged,[4] and (pp. 132–139) "Punctuation. Abridged from Dr. Lowth."

CtHi, CtY, DLC, MB, MH (gift of the author, 1785), MHi, MWA, MWiW, NN, OCHP, RPJCB (imperfect), British Museum.

Evans 18871, Sabin 102356.

NOTES

1. Announced in the *Connecticut Courant*, September 16 and 23, 1783, and as "now publishing" on March 2, 1784, and later. Advertised in the same paper on March 23 and later, and in many other papers.

2. In the preface Webster both praises and censures Dilworth's grammar (then the one most widely used) and says, "We are apt to be sur-

[4]Acknowledgment of the authorship of this section was later made by Webster in his *Philosophical and Practical Grammar* of 1807 (Title 433).

prised, that men who made the languages their principal study, and during their whole lives, were employed in teaching youth, should not discover that the grammar of one language would not answer for another; but our wonder will cease when we reflect, that the English nation at large have, till very lately, entertained the idea that our language was incapable of being reduced to a system of rules; and that even now many men of much classical learning warmly contend that the only way of acquiring a grammatical knowledge of the *English Tongue* is first to learn a *Latin Grammar*. That such a stupid opinion should ever have prevailed in the English nation—that it should still have advocates—nay that it should still be carried into practice, can be resolved into no cause but the amazing influence of habit upon the human mind." Commenting upon the grammars of Lowth, Buchanan, and Ash, he adds that "in the short treatise here presented I have endeavoured to throw the principles of our language into a style and method suited to the most ordinary capacities," but that he has been forced to use a variety of distinctions and terms not used in earlier grammars.

3. The "–our" spelling is retained throughout.

4. In a footnote on pp. 19–20 Webster denies the existence of a passive mood in English, for which he was severely censured by "Philomathes" in the *Salem Gazette*, July 12, 1785.

5. The New York Public Library copy was Webster's own, and has corrections in his hand. It used to bear his signature on a flyleaf, but this has been destroyed by the Library's binder. Webster wrote "Horace" after the quotation on the title-page, but this is an error; the attribution appears correctly (Cicero) in the second edition, after which the quotation is dropped.

6. On February 23, 1784, Webster wrote Isaiah Thomas, "The second part or Grammar will be published in about two weeks. I will sell the sheets at 8/. I shall sell them at 12/ pr dozen bound as the first part—& neatly bound in leather at 18/. But I must expect cash in hand for all I sell—as otherwise I cannot carry on the business."[5]

406

——— Hartford: Printed by Barlow & Babcock, M,DCC,LXXXV. Under protection of the statute.

139 pp. 15 cm.

[5]Isaiah Thomas Papers, American Antiquarian Society.

CT, CTHI, CTNHHI, MH, MWA, MWIW-C, MIDEAED, N, NBUG, NN.

Evans 19363 (queried as third edition).

NOTES

1. The contents are the same as the first edition except that a reference in a footnote to the forthcoming second edition of Part I has been deleted, and the preface has been expanded. It has, however, been set in smaller type, so that p. [6] is blank.

2. From wording of advertisements and other evidence, partly negative, the compiler believes that this edition did not come out until about December, 1785. One or another edition continued to be advertised extensively in 1785 and 1786, e.g., in the New York *Daily Advertiser*, April 4, 1786, and later, offering for sale Parts I and II. This advertisement is accompanied by an essay on the work, possibly written by Webster.

407

[—— Second edition. Hartford: Hudson and Goodwin, 1785.]

Evans 19362.

Evans locates a copy in the American Antiquarian Society, but no such edition can now be found there, and this is probably a ghost. Another possible 1785 edition is indicated by an entry in Webster's diary for May 2, 1785: "Contract with Mr Fitch [in New Haven] to print an edition of the 2^d^ part of the Institute," but no trace of such a printing has been found. Webster's reference in his diary, February 1, 1787, to the following entry as the third edition, as well as the wording of the title-page, are strong indications that Titles 405 and 406 were the only two earlier editions.

B. *The First Revision*

408

—— The third edition, revised and amended. Philadelphia: Printed and sold by Young and M'Culloch.... M.DCC.LXXX.VII.

132 pp. 17 cm. P. [1], title-page. P. [2], Pennsylvania copyright entry, May 11, 1785. Pp. [3]–5, new preface, dated New York, January,

1787, discussing the revisions. P. [6], "Advertisement." Pp. [7]–132, text, with many deletions, additions, revisions, etc. Trumbull's section on prosody is omitted.

CtY, ICN, MWA, MiDeaEd, N (imperfect), NHi, NN, NNS, NNU-W, PPL, PU, RPJCB, British Museum.

Evans 20869.

NOTES

1. Announced in the *Pennsylvania Herald*, March 10, 1787, and later and in other papers, as ready in about three weeks; advertised at 2/6, in the same, March 31 and later, and elsewhere.

2. Webster, writing to Hudson and Goodwin from Philadelphia, January 30, 1787, told them that he was going to have Parts I and II printed there, and said that "the second part will be much improved by the assistance of some books which Dr. Franklin has furnished me."[6] On February 1 he recorded in his diary, "My Grammar 3d edition goes to press, in Philadelphia."

3. The revisions in this edition were no doubt the result of criticisms, private and public, of the first two editions; this edition too came in for adverse comment (see Section Nine, Part Four, rubric B).

4. Young advertised in the *Pennsylvania Herald*, February 5, 1788, that he was about to issue a fourth edition, but no such edition has been found.

C. *The Second Revision*

409

——— The fourth edition, revised and amended. Hartford: Printed and sold by Hudson and Goodwin, [With the privilege of copy-right for the New England states.] [1787?]

129 pp. 17 cm. P. [i], title-page. P. [ii], "Advertisement," virtually identical with the third edition. Pp. [iii]–iv, preface, the same as the third edition, with one slight change. Pp. [5]–129, text, with extensive changes.

Ct, CtHi (imperfect), CtY, DFo, MB, MBAt, MH, MHi, MWA, NN, NNC (imperfect), Nh, NjR, OClWHi, RPJCB, Merriam.

This edition seems to have been issued in 1787, for the Massachusetts Historical Society copy has an ownership inscription of that year. The

[6] American Antiquarian Society.

work, probably in this edition, was advertised extensviely in the Connecticut papers of late 1787 and early 1788. Later an advertisement appeared announcing that "the instructors of Yale College have also determined to use the... Grammar, as a classical book. The last edition of this part is greatly improved, and in this the objections to the first editions are removed." (*Connecticut Courant*, October 6, 1788, and elsewhere.)

410

[——— Fifth edition. Hartford: Hudson and Goodwin, 1787.]

Evans 20867.

411

[——— Sixth edition. Hartford: Hudson and Goodwin, 1787.]

Evans 20868.

Evans locates a copy of the sixth edition in The New York Public Library, an error. It is likely that both 410 and 411 are ghosts, perhaps arising from confusion with the fifth and sixth Connecticut editions of 1796 and 1800.

412

[——— Philadelphia: William Young, 1789.]

Evans 22260.

Also mentioned in other references, such as the Brinley catalogue, under 7222, but this edition too appears to be a ghost. It may arise from confusion with Young's imputed edition of the speller in 1789 (Title 19) or with his *Plain and Comprehensive Grammar* of the same year (Title 444). The latter is catalogued by some libraries as an edition of Part II, but it has been listed here as a derivative grammar, since the amendments and additions were not made by Webster.

413

——— Thomas and Andrews's first edition. With many corrections and improvements, by the author. Printed at Boston, by Isaiah Thomas and Ebenezer T. Andrews.... Sold... by said Thomas at his bookstore in Worcester, and by booksellers in town and country. MDCCXC.

125 pp., incl. frontis. 17 cm. P. [1], blank. P. [2], frontispiece, the same portrait of Webster used in this firm's editions of the speller. P. [3], title-page. P. [4], "Advertisement," same as the fourth edition, and Massachusetts District copyright entry, October 7, 1790. Pp. [5]–6, preface, as in the fourth edition, but dated Hartford, August 28, 1790. Pp. [7]–125, text, with some changes.

CtHT-W, CtY, DFo, DLC, MH, MWA, NN (lacking frontis.), NNC, NjP, NjR, RPB.

Evans 23054.

Advertised in the *Massachusetts Spy*, January 13, 1791, and later, and elsewhere; also in Thomas and Andrews' editions of the speller.

414

[—— First Connecticut edition. Hartford: Hudson and Goodwin, 1790.]

Evans 23055.

415

[—— Second Connecticut edition. Hartford: Hudson and Goodwin, 1791.]

Evans 23966.

The compiler has found no evidence for the existence of 414 and 415.

416

—— Thomas and Andrews's second edition.... Boston..., MDCCXCII.

120 pp., incl. frontis. 17 cm.

CLU, CSmH, CtY, DFo, DLC, MB, MH, MWA, MiDeaEd, NHi, NN, NNC, NNC-T, NjR, PU, RPB, RPJCB, VtMidbC, Merriam, British Museum.

Evans 25001.

NOTES

1. The contents are the same as the firm's first edition; the smaller number of pages is accounted for by a resetting in smaller type.

2. The frontispiece is labelled "Thomas & Andrew's [sic] Second

Edition." The number was changed in each subsequent edition to match the title-page, as had been done with their editions of the speller.

3. At this point the form "Andrews's" changes to "Andrews'."

417

——— The third Connecticut edition. Printed at Hartford, by Hudson and Goodwin. MDCCXCII.

131 pp. 16 cm.

CtY, DLC, NN, NRU, PP, RPB, Merriam.

Evans 25002.

Similar, though not identical, in content to the fourth edition (Title 409).

418

——— Thomas and Andrews' third edition.... Boston..., MDCCXCIV.

116 pp., incl. frontis. 16 cm.

Ct, CtHT-W, CtY, DLC, MH, MiDeaEd, MWA, NBuG, NN, NNC, NcD, NhD, RPJCB, Merriam, British Museum (imperfect).

Evans 28047.

419

——— The fourth Connecticut edition. Hartford: Printed by Hudson and Goodwin. [With the privilege of copy-right.] [1794?]

129 pp. 16 cm.

CtHT (imperfect), CtHi, CtNhHi, MWA, NN.

Evans 28048.

Dated 1794 by Evans, which is probably correct; it would place this edition halfway between the third and fifth Connecticut editions.

420

[Identical title-page.]

131 pp. 16 cm.

DLC.

The material on pages 25–26 and 107–110 is differently arranged, with the result that the text runs to page 131 instead of 129.

421

—— Albany: Printed by Charles R. & George Webster.... 1796. [With the privilege of copy-right for the first, second and third parts of Webster's Grammatical institute.]

115 pp. 17 cm.
CtHT-W, DLC, N, NN.
Evans 31594 (the copy which he locates in the New-York Historical Society cannot now be found there); McMurtrie, Albany, 140.
Similar in content to the third Connecticut edition.

422

—— Thomas and Andrews' fourth edition.... Boston..., Nov. 1796.

116 pp., incl. frontis. 16 cm.
CtHi, MH, MWA, MiDeaEd, NN.
Evans 31595.
Similar in pagination and content to the firm's third edition. Thomas, Andrews, and Butler in Baltimore and Thomas, Andrews, and Penniman in Albany are now added to the imprint as vendors.

423

—— The fifth Connecticut edition. Hartford: Printed by Hudson & Goodwin. 1796.

136 pp. 16 cm.
Ct, CtHT-W, CtHi, CtY, DLC, ICN, MWA, NHi, NN, NNC, RPJCB.
Evans 31596.

NOTES

1. The contents are similar to earlier Hudson and Goodwin editions, though the "Advertisement" on the verso of the title-page has been rewritten.

2. The Watkinson Library copy is a variant, having after the date on the title-page, "With Privilege of Copy-Right for the *First, Second* and *Third* Parts of Webster's Grammatical Institute."

3. Webster wrote the firm from New York, March 30, 1796, "An edition of the Grammar is wanted here, and it seems hardly worth while to print it here and at Hartford too. Unless I can sell the right of printing a few thousands to some bookseller here, I should wish you to take the copy—print it—and supply me. I would advance the one half of the expense of 4 or 5000, and take the books in sheets at prime Cost.... I am determined to have nothing to do with selling in small quantities. I am selling off the stock on hand...and I intend only to supply Booksellers in sheets, or sell the right of printing the books."[7]

424

—— Thomas and Andrews' fifth edition.... Boston..., July, 1797.

116 pp., incl. frontis. 17 cm.
DLC, MH, MWA, NNC, NjR, OClW, OU.
Evans 33184.

425

—— New-York: Printed by Robert Wilson, for Evert Duyckinck, & Co. booksellers and stationers. 1798.

119, (1) pp. 17 cm.
CLU, Ct, CtNhHi, DLC, MHi, MWA, MiDeaEd, N, NN, NNC.
Evans 34980.
Similar in content to the fifth Connecticut edition. The final page consists of a publisher's advertisement.

In the third Albany edition of An American Selection, 1800, *Charles R. and George Webster advertised the grammar, as they also did in the fourth Albany,* 1802. *Despite the wording "just printed" in* 1802, *these may represent advertising for their* 1796 *edition of the grammar. No other indication of any Albany edition between* 1796 *and* 1803 *has been found.*

426

—— Thomas & Andrews' sixth edition.... Boston..., June, 1800.

[7]Webster Papers, New York Public Library.

116 pp., incl. frontis. 17 cm.
CT, DFO, MWA, NCANHI, NN.
Evans 39044.

427

—— The sixth Connecticut edition. Hartford: Printed by Hudson and Goodwin. 1800.

131 pp. 17 cm.
CT, CTHT-W, CTHI, CTNHHI, CTY, ICU, MB, MH, MWA (imperfect), MIDEAED, N (imperfect), NHI, NN, OCLWHI, OO, RPB, RPJCB.
Evans 39043.

428

—— Copy-right secured. New-York: Printed by L. Nichols, & Co. for E. Duyckinck..., 1801.

119 pp. 17 cm.
DFO, DLC, MWA, MIDEAED, NJR.

429

—— Albany: Printed by Charles R. and George Webster.... 1803. [With the privilege of copy-right for the several parts of the Grammatical institute.]

106, (2) pp. 16 cm.
CTHI, MWA, N, NHI, NN (imperfect).
The unpaged leaf at the end contains publisher's advertisements.

430

—— Thomas & Andrews' seventh edition.... Boston..., Feb. 1803.

116 pp., incl. frontis. 16 cm.
CTHT-W (imperfect), CTY, MH, MWA, MIDEAED, NN, NNC, NNC-T, NCU.

On November 22, 1803, the firm wrote to Webster suggesting that they receive rights under a new copyright without charge, since the grammar "was so little used and the small demand...[is] on the decrease," and on February 13, 1804, they wrote him, "The 2^{d} part we have not standing and it is not likely we shall ever find it worth our while again to print it."[8] Instead of taking out a new copyright, Webster prepared a new text, rubric D below.

431

—— Copy-right secured. New York: Printed for E. Duyckinck, by L. Nichols. 1804.

119, (1) pp. 17 cm.

CT, CTHT-W, CTHI, CTY, ICN, MWA, NBUG, NHI, NN, NNC, NNU, PU, Merriam.

P. [120] contains publisher's advertising.

432

—— Albany: Printed by Websters and Skinner.... 1806. With privilege of copy-right.

112, (4) pp. 17 cm.

MWA.

P. 112 and the two unpaged leaves contain publisher's advertisements.

D. *Philosophical and Practical Grammar*

The grammar did not meet with anything like the success that the speller did, and had much more competition. When, on May 20, 1805, Mathew Carey wrote to ask permission to print an edition, Webster replied that he preferred him not to do so, on the grounds that the work was not worthwhile, saying that "I am compiling a Grammar upon what appear to be the true idioms & fundamental principles of the Language—which I hope to have ready for the press within a year— & if agreeable to you, it shall be at your service on as low terms as I give to ot[hers.]" With his usual eye for publicity, he added,

[8] Ibid.

"From the information contained in this letter, you are at liberty to frame a paragraph of literary intelligence for the public prints, if you see proper. It may be useful to booksellers as well as to me."[9]

433

A philosophical and practical grammar of the English language. By Noah Webster, Esq. [*six lines of quotations.*] New-Haven: Printed by Oliver Steele & Co. For Brisban & Brannan, booksellers, New-York. 1807.

250 pp. 18 cm. P. [1], title-page. P. [2], copyright entry, Connecticut District, March 12, 1807. Pp. [3]–10, preface, unsigned and undated, giving Webster's views on reform of the parts of speech, criticizing earlier grammars, and acknowledging great indebtedness to John Horne Tooke's *Diversions of Purley* (London, 1786 etc.). Pp. [11]–250, text, including (pp. 220–227) the section on "Prosody" from the first edition of the original grammar, here duly credited to John Trumbull.

CLU, CSmH, CSt, Ct, CtHT-W, CtHi, CtNhHi, CtY, DLC, ICN, ICU, IU, MA, MB, MBAt, MH, MNF, MWA, MiDeaEd, MiU, MnU, N, NBLiHi, NBuG, NHi, NN, NNC, NNC-T, NjP, NjR, OO, OOxM, OU, PHi, PPL, PPM, RPB, VtMidbC, Merriam, British Museum.

Sabin 102375.

NOTES

1. Announced in the *Panoplist*, March, 1807, and advertised in the *Commercial Advertiser*, May 13, 1807, and later, and elsewhere.

2. Reviewed: *Medical Repository*, 2nd Hexade, Vol. V, [No. 1], (May-July, 1807), pp. 72–74 (favorable). *Panoplist*, Vol. III, No. 5 (October, 1807), pp. 215–217 (temperate; by Jeremiah Evarts?). *Monthly Anthology*, Vol. V, No. 5 (May, 1808), pp. 267–277 (hostile; almost certainly by James Savage).

3. Webster wrote to Joel Barlow, October 19, 1807, "My Grammar had its run, but has been superseded by Murray's. Both are wrong. I have lately published one on Horne Tooke's plan, which President Smith, of Princeton, pronounces the best analysis of the language ever published."[1]

[9]Lea and Febiger Papers, Historical Society of Pennsylvania.

[1]Ford's *Notes*, Vol. II, p. 30 (location of original not given).

4. As he had promised in the letter quoted in the introductory note to this title, Webster offered the first printing to Mathew Carey, August 18, 1806: "I have a copy of a grammar now ready for the press, & agreeable to my promise, give you the offer of it for publication. I have other applications, but yours has the prior claim. My price for the entire copy right is $750 dollars [sic]. It will make from 200 to 250 pages, duodecimo in Long Primer, with brevier notes. It would please me to have the first impression printed here [New Haven], that I might inspect the proofs, but this is not indispensable."[2]

5. The text was later used by Webster in the introductory matter of his *American Dictionary* of 1828; it was also used in the English editions thereof.

6. Apparently Webster tried to arrange for an English edition, to appear anonymously, but nothing came of this.[3]

7. Twenty years later Webster had this to say of the work, in writing to Lemuel Shattuck, November 18, 1829: "My 'Philosophical and Practical Grammar' was first published in 1807, and a second edition in 1822. This work has been but little used; but, except for my quarto Dictionary, I consider it as altogether the most valuable work I have ever published...."[4]

434

—— The second edition.... New-Haven: Published by Howe & Spalding. Printed by S. Converse. 1822.

223 pp. 18 cm.
MA, MH, MWiW, MiDeaEd, NN.

NOTES

1. Copyright October 7, [1822]. The text is that of the 1807 edition somewhat amended, and with the preface omitted.

2. In a letter of March 27, 1824,[5] Webster refers to the wholesale price of his grammar as forty cents in sheets.

[2]Historical Society of Pennsylvania; Ford's *Notes*, Vol. II, pp. 433–434.

[3]Ford's *Notes*, Vol. I, pp. 549–552; the letters from Benjamin Silliman there quoted are in the Webster Papers, New York Public Library. Webster seldom sought anonymity, but in this case he apparently thought the book would receive a fairer hearing in England without his name on it.

[4]Published in the *New England Magazine*, Vol. II, No. 12 (June, 1832), and elsewhere.

[5]To Lucius Boltwood; Webster Papers, New York Public Library.

E. *Improved Grammar*

435

An improved grammar of the English language. By Noah Webster, LL.D. New Haven: Published and sold by Hezekiah Howe. Sold also by A. H. Maltby, Durrie and Peck, S. Babcock and S. Wadsworth, New Haven: and White, Gallaher and White, New York. 1831.

180 pp. 18 cm. P. [1], title-page. P. [2], copyright notice, Connecticut District, 1831, and "Printed by Hezekiah Howe." Pp. [3]–4, preface, unsigned and undated. Pp. [5]–180, text, in general like the 1822 edition of the *Philosophical and Practical Grammar*.

CSmH, Ct, CtHT-W, CtNhHi, CtY, DLC, IC, IU, MB, MH, MWA, MiU, NN, NNC, NRU, NjP, OClW, OClWHi, OOxM, PU, ViU, Merriam.

NOTES

1. Advertised in the *Connecticut Journal*, June 21, 1831, and elsewhere.
2. Reviewed in the *Connecticut Journal*, June 24, 1831.
3. Webster wrote W. C. Fowler, October 23, 1832, "Notwithstanding the colleges do not use my grammar, the teachers of academies are beginning to use it & the demand for it increases."[6]

436

——— New Haven: Published by Durrie and Peck. 1833.

180 pp. 18 cm.

Ct, CtNhHi, CtY, MH, MiU, NNC, NNC-T.

NOTES

1. The text is the same as the preceding entry, the preface being somewhat expanded.
2. Advertised in the *Connecticut Journal*, October 15, 1833, and later.

[6]In the possession of Mrs. Howard B. Field, transcript provided by Prof. Harry R. Warfel.

437

[Identical title-page.]

192 pp. 18 cm.
CU, CtY, NN.

NOTES

1. The cover title adds "New Haven: Published by S. Babcock. 1835."
2. Contains the same material as the preceding, with added pp. [181]–192, with sections on declension of nouns, false syntax, parsing, etc. These pages appear in subsequent editions.

438

——— Cincinnati: Published by Corey and Webster. 1836.

192 pp. 18 cm.
MH, MWA, British Museum.

NOTES

1. The text is substantially the same as that of the preceding item.
2. Advertised in the *Cincinnati Daily Gazette*, February 15, 1836, and later, and elsewhere.

Webster wrote W. C. Fowler, December 14, 1837, "A company of booksellers in Detroit have written for a license to publish my Grammar, which I have granted;"[7] *but no trace of a Detroit edition has been found. The work was an approved text at the University of Michigan, as announced in an article—very likely by Webster—in the* New Haven Record, *January 25, 1840, reprinted in part in the New York* Evangelist *and the* Connecticut Observer, *February 8.*

439

——— New Haven: Published by Sidney Babcock. 1839.

192 pp. 18 cm.
CtHt, CtNhHi, CtY, MBAt, MH, NN, NRU, OO.

[7]Ibid.

NOTES

1. Advertised in the *New Haven Record*, January 18, 1840, and elsewhere.

2. On some copies (e.g., Yale) the printed cover is dated 1842.

440

——— New Haven: Published by Sidney Babcock. 1842.

192 pp. 17 cm.

MB, MiDeaEd, NhD, OClWHi.

441

——— New Haven: Published by Sidney Babcock. 1843.

192 pp. 17 cm.

NN, RPB, Merriam.

442

——— New York: Webster & Clark.... 1843.

192 pp. 19 cm.

NN, NNC, PU.

From a letter from Noah Webster to Webster and Clark, May 5, 1843, in the Pierpont Morgan Library, it appears that copies were printed for the firm by Babcock in New Haven, and possibly by B. L. Hamlen.

F. *Derivative Grammars*

443

An introduction to English grammar; being an abridgement of the second part of The grammatical institute. By Noah Webster, Jun. Esq. Philadelphia: Printed by W. Young.... M,DCC,LXXXVIII.

36 pp. 14 cm. P. [1], title-page. P. [2], blank. Pp. [3]–36, text, consisting of simplified extracts from the basic grammar.

CSmH, DLC, MWA, PHi, PPL.

Sabin 102359, Waters 554, Sealock 182.

Webster wrote to Young from New York, March 14, 1788, "Your several letters have been duly received. There is no article which requires a particular answer, but your proposal for abridgeing the Grammar. At your request I shall set about it immediately, & endeavor to execute it to public satisfaction. As soon as finished it shall be forwarded to you. I perceive some person has made a little abridgment which was lately printed[8]—it is too small to be of any real utility, except to save expense of buying a larger Grammar, for learning the elements. As an introduction it may be of some use."[9]

444

A plain and comprehensive grammar of the English language: being the second part of Mr. Webster's Grammatical institute. With amendments and additions. *Grammar is the guardian of language.* SANCTIUS. Philadelphia: Printed for W. Young,... 1789.

220 pp. (5–8 omitted). 14 cm. P. [1], title-page. P. [2], "Advertisement," unsigned and undated, stating that "some alteration has been made in the manner of exhibiting the modes and tenses of Verbs.... These, together with a few verbal alterations, are liberties, which, in the absence of Mr. Webster, were hazarded by the Editor, and for which... he alone is responsible." Pp. 3–4, table of contents. Pp. [9]–220, text, including (pp. 132–168) "An Essay on Punctuation, Lately Published in London." The pagination jumps from 4 to [9], but the catchword reads correctly, and the text is continuous.

CTY, MHI (imperfect), MWA, N, NN, NRU.

Evans 22260 (as if it were the regular grammar).

NOTES

1. The first few pages are similar to but not identical with the preceding item. The essay on punctuation, although described in the "Advertisement" as an added feature, had been included in the basic grammar in 1787.

[8]Perhaps the work advertised by John M'Culloch in the *Freeman's Journal*, January 30, 1788, and later: "The Elements of English Grammar. Designed for Youth, and as an Introduction to larger Treatises on the Subject." At this point a later writer has footnoted the original letter, "A severe stroke on Mr. Es. Abridgement of the Elements of Grammar. C. C.W."

[9]Henry Ford Museum.

2. A series of articles by "Grammaticaster" critically examining this edition appeared in the *Independent Gazetteer*, August 25 and 28 and September 7 and 10, 1789.

445

Rudiments of English grammar; being an introduction to the second part of The grammatical institute of the English language; compiled at the desire of the committee of the grammar school in Hartford. By Noah Webster, Jun. Esq. Published according to statute. Hartford: Printed by Elisha Babcock. M,DCC,XC.

80 pp. 13 cm. P. [1], title-page. P. [2], blank. P. [3], preface, unsigned, dated Hartford, February 5, 1790, stressing the desirability of children's learning to speak correctly by ear and practice rather than by rules. P. [4], blank. Pp. [5]–51, first section of text, similar to earlier abridged grammars, but adding (pp. 44–51) "A Collection of Improper and vulgar expressions, found in various authors and heard in conversation." Pp. [52]–69, "A Federal Catechizm; containing A short explanation of the Constitution of the United States...," Webster's first use of this feature, which later appeared in other of his works. Pp. 69–77, "Principles of Government and Commerce," reprinted, with changes, from Webster's *American Magazine* (December, 1787, pp. 9–12). Pp. [78]–80, "On a Reform of Spelling," reprinted in part from his *Dissertations on the English Language*, 1789.

DFo, DLC, MWA (imperfect), NBuG, NN, NNC, British Museum.
Evans 23057, Sabin 102367.

NOTES

1. Announced in the *American Mercury*, February 15, 1790, and advertised therein March 8 and later, and elsewhere.

2. The "Federal Catechizm" was the first introduction of "civics" into the American curriculum. Nathaniel W. Appleton wrote Webster from Boston, January 24, 1790, "It is certainly a truly republican principle to instruct our Children in the principles of our Constitution to teach them, as you say, that their Happiness here, depends upon enjoying Liberty with Law."[1] In 1788 John M'Culloch had published in Philadelphia a *Federal Catechism... By a Friend to Religion*, but it was purely religious in content.

[1]Webster Papers, New York Public Library.

3. In the New York Public Library copy the "Federal Catechizm" is marked in Webster's hand with changes for a new printing.

4. The Library of Congress copy has bound in added pages [129]–141, containing "The Farmer's Catechizm," but these pages properly belong to the second edition of the *Little Reader's Assistant*, 1791.

446

[—— Albany: Charles R. and George Webster, 1790.]

Evans 23058.

No copy located. Advertised by the Websters as "this day published" in the *Albany Gazette*, March 22, 1790.

447

[—— Boston: Benjamin Guild, 1790(?).]

Evans 23059.

The compiler believes this to be a ghost. In Webster's account books there is an entry dated March 20, 1790, which reads, "D[r] Benjamin Guild of Boston...To 112 Rudiments on Commission @ 6 £ 2 16 0."

From this point, the sub-title of the Rudiments *changed, depending on the title of the main grammar in print at the time; however, the text of the* Rudiments *had its own continuity, and the successive editions are not truly abridgments of the respective grammars.*

448

Rudiments of English grammar; being an abridgement of The philosophical and practical grammar of the English language. By Noah Webster, Jun. Esq. New-York: Published by Isaac Riley. 1811.

87 pp. 14 cm. P. [i], title-page. P. [ii], copyright entry, Connecticut District, September 23, [1811]. Pp. [iii]–iv, "Advertisement," unsigned and undated, discussing his earlier grammars. Pp. [5]–87, text, not specifically based on the *Philosophical and Practical Grammar* except in certain technical passages which did not admit of much abbreviation.

CtHT-W, DLC, MA, MB, MWA, MiDeaEd, NBLiHi, NHi, NN,

PPL, PPM, PU, ViW, Merriam.
Sabin 102375.
Advertised in the *Connecticut Herald*, August 11, 1811, and later. The price was twenty cents.

449

Rudiments of English grammar; being an abridgment of The improved grammar of the English language. By Noah Webster, LL.D. New-Haven: Published by Durrie & Peck. 1831.

87 pp. 15 cm. P. [1], title-page. P. [2], copyright entry, Connecticut District, 1831, and "Baldwin and Treadway, Printers." Pp. [3]–4, preface, unsigned and undated. Pp. [5]–87, text, with some slight alterations from the preceding entry.
CtHT-W, CtNhHi, MH, NN, NNC.
Sabin, under 102375.

PART THREE: READER

A. *The Original Text*

450

A grammatical institute of the English language; comprising an easy, concise and systematic method of education; designed for the use of schools in America. In three parts. Part III. Containing the necessary rules of reading and speaking, and a variety of essays.... By Noah Webster, Jun. Esq. Hartford: Printed by Barlow & Babcock, for the author, M,DCC,LXXXV. With the privilege of copyright.

186 pp. 17 cm. P. [1], title-page. P. [2], blank. Pp. 3–5, preface, unsigned, dated Hartford, January, 1785 (see below). P. [6], blank. Pp. [7]–186, text (see below).

CtHi, CtY, DLC, ICU, MH (imperfect), MWA (imperfect), MWiW, MiDeaEd, N, NN, RPJCB (imperfect), Merriam, British Museum.

Evans 19364, Sabin 102357.

NOTES

1. Announced in the *Connecticut Courant*, September 16, 1783, and later, and elsewhere; advertised in the *American Mercury*, February 7, 1785, and later, and elsewhere.

2. In the preface, Webster mentions the various excellent textbooks on reading and speaking available, but says they are too large and expensive; gives his objections to the use of the Bible as a reading book (small type, archaic style, vulgarization of holy things); says that some of his selections are from fugitive American sources, some from MSS of friends, some from his own pen; and concludes that his aim is "to refine and establish our language, to facilitate the acquisition of grammatical knowledge, and diffuse the principles of virtue and patriotism..., and whether

the success should equal my wishes or not, I shall still have the satisfaction of reflecting that I have made a laudable effort to advance the happiness of my country."

3. Following a set of rules for reading and speaking (pp. 7–11) and eleven chapters of "Select Sentences" from Swift, Shakespeare, Johnson, etc. (pp. 12–44), the readings are:

pp. 45–49, "Agathocles and Calista," anonymous.
pp. 49–67, "Story of La Roche," from the [Edinburgh] *Mirror*, [June 19, 22, and 26, 1779]; by Henry McKenzie?
pp. 67–80, "Story of Sir Edward and Louisa," from the same, [May 20 and 23, 1780].
pp. 80–84, "Emelius, or Domestic Happiness." } not identified,
pp. 84–89, "Emelia, or the Happiness of Retirement." } but written by
pp. 89–94, "Character of Juliana." } Webster himself
pp. 94–101, "From the Vision of Columbus, A Poem, *not yet published*," unattributed; by Joel Barlow.
pp. 101–106, "From the Conquest of Canaan. A Poem, *not yet published*," unattributed; by Timothy Dwight.
pp. 106–113, "Burlesque. *The opening of the Town meeting M'Fingal.* Canto 2," unattributed; by John Trumbull.
pp. 113–114, "Queen Mab," by Shakespeare.
pp. 115–153, "Dialogues," including examples from Shakespeare, Otway, Swift, Addison, and others.
pp. 153–165, "Address of Congress to the People of Great Britain... 1774."
pp. 165–175, "Address of Congress to the Inhabitants of the Province of Quebec." Four pages of this are set in smaller type.
pp. 175–176, "Extract from the American Crisis No. V... by Thomas Payne [sic], Esq."
pp. 177–186, "Fragment of an original Letter on the slavery of the Negroes; written in... 1776, by Thomas Day, Esq...."

4. The "-our" spelling is retained throughout.

5. This work was entered for copyright in Pennsylvania on May 11, 1785, in South Carolina on June 30, 1785, and in Maryland on January 7, 1786.

6. Webster's diary from October, 1784, through March, 1785, contains frequent references to the reading and writing he did in preparing this work. On November 18, 1829, he wrote to Lemuel Shattuck, "This was, I believe, the first collection for reading published in this country."[2]

[2] *New England Magazine*, Vol. II, No. 12 (June 1, 1832), p. 475.

451

——— The second edition. By Noah Webster, Jun. Esq. Hartford: Printed by Hudson and Goodwin. With the privilege of copy-right. [1786.]

188 pp. 17 cm.

CtHT-W, CtY, DFo, MH, MNF, MWA, NBLiHi, NN, NjR, RPJCB.

Evans 19365 (with slightly different wording).

NOTES

1. The contents are the same as the first edition with very slight changes. A new setting of type accounts for the added leaf.

2. Advertisements for Part III, which began appearing in February, 1785, appear at more or less regular intervals until February, 1786, with one isolated one in April. They begin again in August, which suggests that the first edition went out of print about February, 1786, and that this edition appeared about August. This is further suggested by the fact that Webster wrote Hudson and Goodwin from Philadelphia, February 20, 1786, "If another edition of the third part is wanted, print it. I designed to vary my plan a little before another impression; but it is not material. . . . You may do an edition of 2 or 3000. . . ."[3]

B. *An American Selection*

452

An American selection of lessons in reading and speaking. Calculated to improve the minds and refine the taste of youth. . . . Being the third part of A grammatical institute of the English language. By Noah Webster, jun. Esq. The third edition, greatly enlarged. [*two lines of quotation.*] Philadelphia: Printed and sold by Young and M'Culloch. . . . M.DCC.LXXXVII.

372 pp. 17 cm. P. [1], title-page. P. [2], Pennsylvania copyright notice, May 11, 1785. P. [3], dedication "To the Rev. John Andrews, D.D. Principal of the Academy of the Protestant [Episcopal] Church in

[3] American Antiquarian Society.

Philadelphia...." P. [4], blank. Pp. [5]–6, preface, unsigned, dated October, 1787, shortened from the earlier editions, especially in the omission of Webster's views on the use of the Bible. Pp. [7]–12, table of contents, giving the authorship of many of the selections. Pp. 13–372, text, revised and expanded. On p. 372 there is an errata list.

CU (imperfect), CtY, DLC, MB, MWA, NN, NNS, NH, NjR, P (imperfect), PHi, PU, RPB (imperfect), Merriam.

Evans 20862, Sabin 102336.

NOTES

1. Pp. 16–24 contain new matter on elocution, with prose and verse selections from Henry Home, Nicholas Rowe, Ambrose Phillips, Shakespeare, James Thomson, Thomas Otway, Pope, and others. Other added selections include:

"Rules for Behavior," mostly from Lord Chesterfield.
"The Way to Wealth," by Benjamin Franklin.
"Advice to a Young Tradesman," by Franklin.
"Family Disagreements the frequent Cause of Immoral Conduct," unattributed.
"Self-Tormenting," by Nathaniel Hooker.
"History of Columbus," the introduction to Joel Barlow's *Vision of Columbus*, with minor changes.
"Discovery and Settlement of North America," by Webster.[4]
"Geography...," by Webster.
"Geography of the United States," by Webster.
"A Sketch of the History of the late War in America," by Webster.[4]
"An Account of the most remarkable battles fought in America during the late War," consisting largely of letters, probably compiled by Webster.
"General Washington's farewel [sic] Orders to the Armies... 1783."
"General Washington's Circular Letter... 1783."
"Remarks on the Manners, Government, Laws and Domestic Debt of America," by Webster.[5]

[4]Reprinted as "The History of the United States," *Old South Leaflets*, No. 198 (Boston, 1908). A few paragraphs were incorporated into Webster's longer historical sketch in Jedidiah Morse's *American Geography*, 1789, which was in turn reprinted in Webster's *Essays*, 1790 (Title 745). He also wrote similar but differently organized sketches for Volume II of his *Elements of Useful Knowledge*, 1804, and his *History of the United States*, 1832.

[5]Reprinted, with considerable alterations, from the *Pennsylvania Packet* of February 15, 17, 19, and 21, 1787, and the *Pennsylvania Herald* of February 21, 24, and 28, 1787. Later used in Webster's *Essays*, 1790.

These are followed by a section of "Lessons in Speaking," which includes several Revolutionary and early Federal orations and documents, among them an abridged version of Joel Barlow's Fourth of July oration delivered in Hartford in 1787. There is then a section of dialogues, similar to earlier editions, and a final section of poetry, mingling with Pope and Shakespeare such American poets as Freneau, Livingston, Barlow, and Dwight.

2. George E. Littlefield, in his *Early Schools and School-Books of New England* (Boston, 1904, pp. 154–156) describes and reproduces a portrait of Washington as being a frontispiece from this edition of Webster's reader. Such a frontispiece is recorded, from a later edition, as No. 38 in William S. Baker, *Engraved Portraits of Washington* (Philadelphia, 1880). Because of the once widespread fad of collecting portraits of Washington such a frontispiece may well have been removed from books which contained it; however, since none of the copies of this edition located contains it, and it is not called for by the signaturing, it must be considered a ghost until its existence can be proved.

3. The "-our" spelling is altered to "-or" in some words but not in others.

4. Webster's diary for December, 1786, and January, 1787, records various work done in preparation of this revision. He took advantage of his presence in Philadelphia to show at least part of the MS to Benjamin Franklin, as evidenced by a note to the latter, [January 4, 1787]: "Mr Webster presents his respects to his Excellency President Franklin & begs him to peruse the enclosed papers & correct any mistakes in the principles. It is designed to collect some American pieces upon the discovery, history, wars, geography, economy, commerce, government &c. of this country & add them to the third part of the Institute, in order to call the minds of our youths from ancient fables & modern foreign events, & fix them upon objects immediately interesting, in this country. A Selection for this purpose should be judicious & the compiler feels his need of assistance in the undertaking...."[6] Webster's correspondence during 1787 contains several letters to Hudson and Goodwin and others about the progress of the work, and future editions.

5. This is the only edition in which the dedication to Andrews appears. Webster taught during 1787 at the academy of which Dr. Andrews was the principal. The relations between the two were friendly but Webster's appointment drew forth a scurrilous newspaper debate which made his sojourn in Philadelphia unpleasant (see Section Nine, Part Four, rubric

[6]Franklin Papers, American Philosophical Society.

B). The paragraph about the Academy in the geographical section of this book is deleted in Thomas and Andrews' first edition (1790) and thereafter disappears.

6. Directly connected with this edition is a separate work whose place in the Webster canon is difficult to determine:

453

Introduction to the history of America. [*twenty-four lines, summarizing contents.*] Philadelphia: Printed and sold by Young and M'Culloch.... M.DCC.LXXX.VII.

207, (1) pp. 19 cm. P. [1], title-page. P. [2], copyright notice, August 10, 1787, in the name of Young and M'Culloch. Pp. [3]–207, text, consisting of historical, geographical, and political information about the United States. P. [208], table of contents.

CtHT-W, DLC, MH, PHi.

Evans 20471, Sabin 34949.

NOTES

1. This work appears to have been put together with scissors and paste, large portions being taken directly from Webster's reader. In fact, pp. [3]–114 and 129–157 are—except for the page numbers—from the same setting of type as pp. 103–214, 241–265, and 271–275 of the third edition. The volume also contains a "Chronology of Remarkable Events in America," but it differs markedly from the chronology in the reader.

The Historical Society of Pennsylvania has in addition a variant copy which is obviously an earlier printing, since the portion after p. 188 (the text of the proposed Constitution) has its own title-page and pagination, and is on different paper. That it was intended to be part of the work, however, is shown by the catchword "Constitution" at the foot of p. 188.

2. Evans suggests that M'Culloch was the compiler of this volume. The present compiler does not feel that this is a downright piracy, though she has found nothing in correspondence, contracts, newspaper controversies, etc. to indicate that Webster had a hand in the compilation. She suggests that since Webster left Philadelphia for New York late in 1787, and that as he needed money for his various projects, he may have accepted payment from Young and M'Culloch for the use of his material. Relations between him and Young—and indirectly M'Culloch—were not very harmonious, and they published none of his works as such after

1787. For John M'Culloch as a compiler and publisher, see Alice W. Spieseke, *The First Textbooks in American History* (New York, 1938. Teacher's College, Columbia University, Contributions to Education, No. 744).

454

[The art of speaking, being an American selection.... Albany: Charles R. and George Webster, 1788.]

Evans 21583, giving the title as above.

The compiler believes this to be a ghost. The Websters advertised such a title in the *Albany Argus* of December 8, 1788, but this may well refer to one of the known editions, under a garbled title.

455

An American selection....The fourth edition.... Hartford: Printed and sold by Hudson and Goodwin.... M.DCC.LXXXVIII.

204 pp. 17 cm.

CT, CTHT-W, CTHI, ICU, MWA, NHI, NN.

Evans 21582.

NOTES

1. The contents are substantially the same as the third edition.

2. The American Antiquarian Society copy served as printer's copy for Title 457, and includes a MS note, "To the printer. Spell honor &c. without *u* public &c without *k* luster theater &c *e* before *r*." The MS corrections in the text appear in the fifth and sixth editions.

3. Webster was in Boston early in 1789, and wrote Hudson and Goodwin on February 10, "I do not know your price for the 3d part Instt in sheets. You sold me some half bound at 1/. I presume therefore your price cannot be more than /9 in sheets. I can dispose of a few, part of them for money, which I will send you, if you see fit to send me a hundred by the next stage...." In a postscript he added, "I have just called on some of the Booksellers & made a sale of about 200 of the third part, most [of] them at /11 & some of them for cash. If you will send me 250 in sheets at /9, I will send you one half the money on receipt. If you send any to Mr Hall or others, you may set them at /11, as they fetch that partly in money & partly in barter. But if I take any trouble in the business, I must have a small profit. But this need not be known to the

booksellers here, as they do not expect the books at less than /11. The sale seems to be increasing & they will always command that price. . . ."[7]

456

——— The fifth edition. . . . Hartford: Printed and sold by Hudson & Goodwin. [With the privilege of copy-right.] M.DCC.LXXXIX.

302 pp. 16 cm.

CtHi, DLC, MH, MWA (imperfect), NN, NNC, NjP.

Evans 22255.

The contents are substantially the same as the fourth edition, incorporating the corrections marked in the printer's copy at the American Antiquarian Society (see notes on preceding entry).

457

——— The sixth edition. . . . Newport (Rhode-Island) Printed by Peter Edes for the author. M,DCC,LXXXIX.

204, 12 pp. 17 cm.

CLU, CSmH, DLC, MWA, MiDeaEd, NN, Nh, RHi, RNHi. The CLU, MWA, NN, and RHi copies have the twelve added pages.

Evans 22256, Alden 1189, Waters 572.

NOTES

1. The contents are like the fourth edition, with the corrections. Added pp. [1]–6, "An Address to the Ladies," abridged from Webster's *American Magazine*, March, 1788, and pp. [7]–12, "An Address to Young Gentlemen," dated Hartford, January, 1790. Both were used in Webster's *Essays*, 1790. The copies which contain these added pages are doubtless the later ones.

2. Nathaniel W. Appleton, a brother-in-law of Webster's wife, wrote him from Boston on June 14, 1790, "I am glad to learn that you do not think so badly of the Newport Edition as I do. The day after I wrote my last, [I] was at M[r. Caleb] Bingham's school, when he observed to me that some of his Scholars had the Newport new edition of your 3d part;

[7] Webster Papers, New York Public Library.

& remarked that it was very badly printed, was very incorrect & very bad paper, that he was very sorry to observe it—that in his opinion the two additional Addresses were not calculated for such Children as generally attend School, that they were very good & very proper for young Gentlemen & Ladies of 18 or 20—he was in expectation that in this Edition, certain expressions, which were indelicate & improper to be read, especially by Misses, would have been left out."[8]

3. In 1790 Webster presented twelve copies of this work annually to be distributed as prizes in the Boston schools; this is referred to in the letter above quoted, in other letters from Appleton, and in the *Gazette of the United States*, September 8, 1790. The New York Public Library copy of this edition was one of the copies so presented; it contains a "Mr. Webster's Donation" bookplate with the name of the recipient in manuscript.

458

[——— Albany: Charles R. and George Webster, 1790.]

Evans 23058.

The Websters advertised an edition as "this day published" in the *Albany Gazette* of March 22, 1790, but the compiler has found no copy.

459

——— Thomas and Andrews's first edition. With many corrections and improvements, by the author.... Printed at Boston, by Isaiah Thomas and Ebenezer T. Andrews.... MDCCXC.

239, (1) pp., incl. frontis. 18 cm. P. [1], blank. P. [2], frontispiece (see below). P. [3], title-page. P. [4], publisher's advertisement, mentioning the adoption of the work by the Boston public schools, and copyright notice, October 7, 1790. Pp. [5]-6, preface. Pp. [7]-239, text, similar to the fifth edition, incorporating the "Address to the Ladies" and "Address to Young Gentlemen" from the Newport sixth edition. P. [240], table of contents.

CT, CTY (lacks frontis.), DLC, ICU, MB (imperfect), MBAT, MWA, MIDEAED, NBUG, NN (imperfect), NNC, NNC-T.

Evans 23050.

[8]Ibid.

NOTES

1. Announced in the *Massachusetts Spy*, January 13, 1791, and later, and advertised in various Boston papers in April.

2. The frontispiece is the crude cut of Webster used by this firm in their editions of the speller and the grammar. As in those works, it bears a caption in which the number of their edition is given.

3. Thomas and Andrews editions add on the title-page after Webster's name "Author of 'Dissertations on the English Language,' 'Collection of Essays and Fugitive [sic] Writings,' &c."

4. The imprint includes Thomas' bookstore in Worcester as an added vendor.

460

——— The sixth edition. . . . Hartford: Printed and sold by Hudson and Goodwin. With the privilege of copy-right. M.DCC.XC.

202 pp. 17 cm.

CT, CTHT-W (imperfect), CTHI, CTNHHI, NN.

Similar in format and content to the fifth edition.

461

——— Thomas and Andrews's second edition. With many corrections and improvements, by the author. . . . Printed at Boston by Isaiah Thomas and Ebenezer T. Andrews. . . . MDCCXCII.

239, (1) pp., incl. frontis. 17 cm.

CTHT-W, MB, MH, MWA, MIU-C, NN, Merriam, British Museum.

Evans 24997.

NOTES

1. The American Antiquarian Society has a series of letters between Thomas and Andrews and Hudson and Goodwin in the first quarter of 1792 relating to the printing of this edition, of which 5,000 were produced. Thomas ran out of his first edition before his second was ready, and had to buy copies in sheets from Hudson and Goodwin for his retail store.

2. The title-page and frontispiece are reproduced in Alice Morse Earle, *Child Life in Colonial Days* (New York and London, 1899), p. 144 and facing p. 142.

462

——— The seventh Connecticut edition.... Hartford: Printed and sold by Hudson and Goodwin. [With the privilege of copy-right.] M.DCC.XCII.

252 pp. 17 cm.
CSmH, MWA, NBuG, NN, Merriam.
Evans 24998.

The text follows the first Boston edition, with slight changes and some additions, including several excerpts from Addison's *Spectator* and some passages from Fanny Burney's *Cecilia*, rewritten into dialogue form.

463

——— Thomas and Andrews's third edition.... Boston.... MDCCXCIII.

239, (1) pp., incl. frontis. 17 cm.
CtY, DLC, MA, MHi, MWA, PP.
Evans 26443.

464

——— Thomas and Andrews' fourth edition.... Boston.... MDCCXCIII.

239, (1) pp., incl. frontis. 17 cm.
CtY, MB, MH, MWA, MeHi, NN, OC, OClWHi, RPJCB.
Evans 26444.

NOTES

1. Some changes in contents, and the frontispiece reworked.

2. Note the change in the form of the possessive of Andrews' name, which was made in the speller and the grammar in 1794.

3. Andrews wrote to Thomas, August 1, 1793, "Have just begun an edition of 10,000.... We finished an edition of 5000 in March last, and have only 1000 left...."[9]

[9] American Antiquarian Society.

465

—— The eighth Connecticut edition.... Hartford: Printed and sold by Hudson and Goodwin. [With the privilege of copy-right.] M.DCC.XCIII.

252 pp. 16 cm.

CT, CTHT-W, CTHI, CTNHHI, CTY, MWA, MID-B, MIDEAED, NN, RPJCB (imperfect), British Museum.

Evans 26445.

466

[—— Albany: Charles R. and George Webster, 1794.]

Evans 28042.

The compiler believes this to be a ghost.

467

—— Thomas and Andrews' fifth edition.... Boston.... MDCC-XCIV.

239, (1) pp., incl. frontis. 17 cm.

CST, CTHT-W (imperfect), CTY, MH, MHI, MNF, MWA, MIDEAED, MIU-C, NN, NNC, NNC-T, NJN, OO, RPB, RPJCB, Merriam.

Evans 28041.

NOTES

1. The frontispiece is reproduced in George E. Littlefield, *Early Schools and School-Books in New England* (Boston, 1904), p. 134.

2. The New York Public Library has also a variant copy, in which signature T is from Thomas and Andrews' fourth edition; this results in p. 227's ending with "The Virtuous," an eight-line poem, rather than the thirteen-line "Prologue" which replaced it in this edition.

468

—— The ninth Connecticut edition.... Hartford: Printed and sold by Hudson and Goodwin, With the privilege of copy-right. M,DCC,XCIV.

252 pp. 17 cm.

Ct, CtHT-W (imperfect), CtHi, CtY (imperfect), IC, ICN, ICU, MH, MWA, MiDeaEd, MiU, MnU, NBuG, NN, NNC, NNC-T, NRU, NjR, OClWHi, OO, ViW, Merriam.

Evans 28039.

After this edition Hudson and Goodwin dropped "Connecticut" in their title, but continued the numbering. They also discontinued dating their printings, which makes placement difficult, and libraries vary widely in the conjectural dating of some of them. Since the sequence had been appearing at the rate of about one edition a year, this pattern has been followed in placing undated editions, with the exception of the Hudson and Goodwin tenth edition, which documentary evidence shows did not appear until the second year after their ninth.

469

——— The first edition by George Bunce & Co.... New-York: Printed by George Bunce & Co.... [With the privilege of copy-right.] M,DCC,XCIV.

239 pp. 16 cm.

MWA, MiD-B, MiDeaEd, N (imperfect), NN, NNC, NjP.

Evans 28040.

The contents are like the eighth Connecticut edition. Most copies have an inverted "t" in "Grammatical" on the title-page. The New York Public Library copy has corrections in Webster's hand.

470

——— The first Albany edition.... Albany: Printed by Charles R. and George Webster,... M,DCC,XCV. With privilege of copy-right....

237, (3) pp. 17 cm.

MH, MWA (imperfect), N, NN.

Evans 29847; McMurtrie, Albany, 123.

NOTES

1. The three unnumbered pages at the end contain publisher's advertisements.

2. The wording of the title certainly suggests that this firm had not published any earlier editions; cf. Titles 454, 458, and 466.

471

——— Second edition by George Bunce & Co. New-York: Printed and sold...by George Bunce & Co.... MDCCXCV. [With the privilege of copy right.]

[239] pp. (see below). 17 cm.
CT, CTHI, CTNHHI, NN.
Evans 29849.

NOTES

1. Rather than following Bunce's first edition in content, this follows the Thomas and Andrews fifth. The pagination is irregular at the end, 236 being misnumbered 240, and 237 misnumbered 239; these are followed by [238–239], the table of contents, in which for the first time Webster's authorship of several of the selections is indicated.

2. With this edition the quotation from Mirabeau disappears from the title-page of most of the editions.

3. "Collection" is misspelled "Colleclion" on the title-page.

4. The edition was probably 4,000, of which initially 1,000 were bound; Webster to Hudson and Goodwin, April 10 and May 25, 1796.[1]

472

——— The second Albany edition. Printed by Charles R. & George Webster, [With the privilege of copy-right]..., Albany; 1796.

239, (1) pp. 16 cm.
MWA (imperfect), N.
Evans 31584; McMurtrie, Albany, 139.

The format and contents follow the first Albany edition. P. 239 and the unnumbered page contain commendations for the *American Spelling Book* and publisher's advertising.

[1]Pierpont Morgan Library and Webster Papers, New York Public Library, respectively.

473

——— Thomas and Andrews' sixth edition.... Boston.... Jan. 1796.

239, (1) pp., incl. frontis. 17 cm.
CtY, DFSA, MWA, NN, OOxM, RPB.
Evans 31585.
With this edition Thomas, Andrews, and Butler in Baltimore are added to the imprint as vendors.

474

——— Thomas and Andrews' seventh edition.... Boston.... June, 1796.

240 pp., incl. frontis. 17 cm.
MA, MH, MWA, NjR, RPJCB, Merriam.
Evans 31586.

475

———Thomas and Andrews' eighth edition.... Boston.... June, 1796.

240 pp., incl. frontis. 17 cm.
CtY, MBAt, MH, MWA (pages misbound).
Evans 31587.

476

——— Thomas and Andrews' ninth edition.... Boston.... Dec. 1796.

240 pp., incl. frontis. 17 cm.
DLC, MH, MWA, MiDeaEd.
Evans 31588, ascribing a copy to the John Carter Brown Library, but theirs is the 1797 Thomas and Andrews ninth edition.

NOTES

1. Thomas' bookstore in Worcester here becomes Thomas, Son, and Thomas; and Thomas, Andrews, and Penniman in Albany are added to the imprint.
2. Note that the firm issued another ninth edition in 1797.

477

——— The tenth edition with great improvements. Printed by Hudson & Goodwin, Hartford. [With the privilege of copy right.] [1796?]

261, (2) pp. 17 cm. P. [1], title-page. P. [2], "Advertisement to the Tenth Edition," mentioning substitution of further readings for the geographical portions, since good geography texts are now available. P. [3], preface, following Webster's revisions in the New York Public Library copy of Title 469. P. [4], blank. Pp. [5]–261, text, which in general follows the ninth Connecticut edition, with several selections omitted and others added, from John Burgoyne, David Humphreys, Thomas Dawes, Jeremy Belknap, Andrew Ellicott, Franklin, the Marquis de Chastellux, Fisher Ames, and others. Pp. [262–263], table of contents, the first time this firm had provided one; Webster had suggested it to them in a postscript to a letter of September 2, 1796.[2]

CtHT-W, CtHi, CtNhHi, CtY, DLC, MWA, NN (imperfect), NNC-T (imperfect), OClWHi.

Evans 29848, under 1795.

NOTES

1. A series of letters to the firm from Webster during 1796, in the Pierpont Morgan Library and the Webster Papers, New York Public Library, shows that this edition did not appear until late in 1796. Webster did not want this revision to appear until he had sold the copies he had on hand (Title 471).

2. One of the added readings is "Logan's Speech," taken ultimately from Jefferson's *Notes on Virginia*, though the text here is derived from the 1794 edition of Caleb Bingham's *American Preceptor*. Webster had used this as early as 1790 in his *Little Reader's Assistant*, but Albert Mordell is mistaken in saying (*Saturday Review of Literature*, August 27, 1927) that this piece had been in the reader from the beginning.

478

——— The eleventh edition. Hartford: Printed by Hudson & Goodwin. [With the privilege of copy right.] [1796?]

[2] *Vineland Historical Magazine*, January, 1929 (Vol. 14, No. 1), pp. 102–103.

261, (2) pp. 17 cm.
CtHi, MH (imperfect), MiDeaEd, MiU-C, NN, OO.
Evans 31589.

NOTES

1. Assigned to 1796 by Evans and the Harvard University Library.
2. P. [2] is blank, there being no "Advertisement" in this edition.

479

——— The third Albany edition. Printed by Charles R. and George Webster, [With privilege of copy-right]..., Albany, 1797....

236, (4) pp. 16 cm.
MWA, N, NjR, Merriam.
Evans 33174 (listing copies at the Boston Athenaeum and the John Carter Brown Library, at neither of which can a copy now be located); McMurtrie, Albany, 162.

NOTES

1. Following the table of contents, pp. [237–238], is a leaf of publisher's advertisements.
2. Note that this firm issued another third Albany edition in 1800.

480

——— Thomas and Andrews' ninth edition.... Boston.... Dec. 1797.

240 pp., incl. frontis. 17 cm.
MH, MSaE, MWA, NN.
Evans 33175.
Note that the firm had already published a ninth edition in 1796.

480a

——— Thomas and Andrews' ninth edition.... Boston.... 1797.

Ct, CtY, MHi, MiDeaEd, RPJCB.

481

——— Thomas and Andrews' tenth edition.... Boston.... Sold ...at their bookstore; by Thomas Son & Thomas, in Worcester; by Thomas, Andrews & Butler, in Baltimore; and by Thomas, Andrews & Penniman, in Albany. 1797.

240 pp., incl. frontis. 18 cm.
MWA (imperfect), NjP.
Evans 33177.

481a

——— Thomas and Andrews' tenth edition.... Boston.... Sold ...at their bookstore; by said Thomas, in Worcester; by Thomas, Andrews & Penniman, in Albany; and by Thomas, Andrews & Butler, in Baltimore. 1797.

DLC, MWA (imperfect), N, NBuG, NN, VtMidbC.
Evans 33176.

NOTES

1. Despite Evans' order, this variant has been placed second because "Thomas Son & Thomas" follows the firm's ninth editions, while "Thomas" alone agrees with the firm's eleventh and later editions.

2. Harvard University Library has a copy of this edition but it is not possible to say which variant it is, since the title-page is damaged at the imprint.

482

——— Thomas and Andrews' eleventh edition.... Boston.... 1797.

240 pp., incl. frontis. 17 cm.
DLC, MB, MH, MWA (imperfect), RPJCB.
Evans 33178, listing a copy in the Rhode Island Historical Society, where it cannot now be found.
Note that this firm issued two other eleventh editions, in 1799 and 1800.

483

—— The twelfth edition. Hartford: Printed by Hudson & Goodwin. [With the privilege of copy right.] [1797?]

261, (2) pp. 16 cm.
CT, CTHT-W, CTHI, MH (imperfect), MWA, NBUG, NN, OU.
Evans 33179.
See note on Title 468.

484

—— The thirteenth edition. Hartford: Printed by Hudson & Goodwin. [With the privilege of copy right.] [1798?]

240 pp. 17 cm.
CT, CTHI, CTNHHI, CTY, DLC, MWA, NN, OC, RPB, RPJCB.
Evans 34975.
See note on Title 468.

485

—— Thomas and Andrews' eleventh edition.... Boston.... 1799.

240 pp., incl. frontis. 18 cm.
MH, MWA, NN, NNC, NH.
Evans 36682.
Note that the firm published two other eleventh editions, in 1797 and 1800.

486

—— The fourteenth edition. Hartford: Printed by Hudson and Goodwin. With the privilege of copy right. [1799?]

240 pp. 16 cm.
CT, CTHT, CTHT-W, CTHI, CTNHHI, CTY (imperfect), DLC, ICN, MB, MWA, MID-B, MIDEAED, MIU-C, NN, OCLWHI, PPESCHW, PU, RPJCB.
Evans 36683.
See note on Title 468.

487

—— The twelvth [sic] edition. New-York: Printed for E. Duyckinck, R. Magill, N. Judah, P. A. Mesier, C. Davis, J. Harrisson, and B. Gomez. 1799.

261, (2) pp. 17 cm.
CT, N.

NOTES

1. The contents are the same as Title 477, except that there is no "Advertisement" on p. [2], which is blank.

2. The Connecticut State Library copy has no date on the title-page, but this appears to be an erasure rather than a variant imprint.

488

—— The third Albany edition. Albany: Printed by Charles R. and George Webster. [With privilege of copy right].... M,DCCC, [sic]

236, (2) pp. 17 cm.
NN (imperfect).
Evans 39038; McMurtrie, Albany, 270 (who errs in locating a copy in the Huntington Library).
Note that this firm had already issued a third edition in 1797.

489

—— The fourth Albany edition. Albany: Printed by Charles R. and George Webster, [With privilege of copy right].... MDCCC.

236, (2) pp. 17 cm.
CSmH, OOxM.
Evans 39039.
Note that this firm published another fourth Albany edition in 1802.

490

—— Thomas and Andrews' eleventh edition.... Boston.... 1800.

240 pp., incl. frontis. 17 cm.

MB, MH, MWA, NBuG, NHi, NN, NNC-T, PU, British Museum.

Evans 39036.

Note that this firm had already issued two eleventh editions, in 1797 and 1799.

491

——— Thomas and Andrews' twelfth edition.... Boston.... 1800.

240 pp., incl. frontis. 17 cm.

CtNhHi, CtY, ICHi, MA, MH, MWA, MiDeaEd (imperfect), NN, NjR, RPJCB (lacking frontispiece), VtMidbS.

Evans 39037.

Note that the firm published another twelfth edition in 1802.

Chapters I-VIII of one or the other Boston 1800 *edition were reprinted, with added text of a personal nature, in San Diego, California, in* 1925, *by Arthur and Helen-May Johnson, as a combined Christmas and wedding anniversary keepsake. (Copy in The New York Public Library.)*

492

——— The fifteenth edition. Hartford: Printed by Hudson and Goodwin. With the privilege of copy right. [1800?]

240 pp. 16 cm.

Ct, CtHT-W (imperfect), MWA (imperfect).

See notes on Titles 468 and 507.

493

——— New-York: Printed by G. and R. Waite, for Evert Duyckinck. 1800.

261, (3) pp. 17 cm. P. [1], title-page. P. [2], blank. P. [3], preface. P. [4], blank. Pp. [5]–261, text. Pp. [262–264], table of contents. The text and preface are like the Hartford tenth edition, 1796. There are small cuts as tailpieces on pp. 188, 261, and [264].

CtY, MH, MWA, NN, NhD.

494

—— The sixteenth edition. Hartford: Printed by Hudson and Goodwin. With the privilege of copy right. [1801 ?]

240 pp. 17 cm.
CT, CTHI, CTY, MH, MWA, MIDEAED, NN, PPM.
See note on Title 468.

495

—— New-York: Printed by G. and R. Waite, . . .for C. Davis, . . . 1801.

261, (3) pp. 16 cm.
MWA, NN.
Similar in form and content to Title 493.

496

—— New York: Printed for and sold by T. B. Jansen and Co. . . . and G. Jansen and Co. . . . 1801.

264 pp. 19 cm.
DLC.

497

[American lessons in reading and speaking. Cushing and Appleton's edition. Salem, 1801.]

Henry Stevens, *Bibliotheca Historica* (Boston, 1870), from which the title is taken (No. 2339). The compiler has found no other trace of such an edition.

498

—— The fourth Albany edition. Albany: Printed by Charles R. and George Webster, [With privilege of copy right]. . ., 1802.

245, (7) pp. 18 cm.
NBLIHI (imperfect), NN, NRU, NJR.

NOTES

1. The contents are similar to their earlier editions, the larger number of pages being due to larger type. More chapters have been created by redivision of the material. Pp. 245–[247] are the table of contents; the bottom of [247] has the start of publisher's advertising, which continues on five unnumbered end pages.

2. Note that this firm had already published a fourth Albany edition in 1800.

499

——— Thomas and Andrews' twelfth edition.... Boston.... 1802.

240 pp., incl. frontis. 18 cm.
CT, DLC, MWA, NN, NNC-T, Merriam.
Note that this firm had already published a twelfth edition in 1800.

500

——— The seventeenth edition. Hartford: Printed by Hudson and Goodwin. With the privilege of copy right. [1802?]

240 pp. 17 cm.
CT, CTHI, CTY, MWA, MIDEAED, NJR (imperfect), OCLWHI, PP, Merriam.
See note on Title 468.

501

——— New-York: Printed by G. & R. Waite, for N. Judah.... 1802.

261, (3) pp. 16 cm.
MH, MWA, N, NN.

502

——— Elizabeth-Town: Printed by John Woods, for Evert Duyckinck, New-York—1802.

236, (3) pp. 17 cm.
CTY, MWA, NN, OOXM.
The contents are similar to the Hartford tenth edition, 1796.

503

—— Thomas & Andrews' thirteenth edition.... Boston.... 1803.

240 pp., incl. frontis. 18 cm.

MB, MH, MWA, MiDeaEd, NN, NNC-T, NcD, NcU, NjR, British Museum.

504

[—— Windsor, Vt.: Nahum Mower, 1803.]

Suggested in a letter from Webster to Stephen Jacob of that place, October 3, 1803, in which he says, "I have heard nothing from Mr. [Nahum] Mower since last winter, but have been informed by Mr. Miller, that Mr. Mower had printed and disposed of 3000 copies of selections which he had permission to publish. This he wrote me last May. Mr. Mower should have advised me of the *time* & the *number of copies* printed...."[3] There is a known edition by Mower in Windsor in 1805.

505

—— The fifth Albany edition. Albany: Printed by Charles R. and George Webster, With privilege of copy right..., 1804.

245, (7) pp. 17 cm.

DLC, MWA.

Concludes with five unnumbered pages of publisher's advertisements, like the fourth Albany edition, 1802.

506

—— Thomas & Andrews' fourteenth edition.... Boston.... 1804.

240 pp. 17 cm.

MH, MHi, MWA, MiDeaEd.

Apparently issued without the usual frontispiece of this firm. 1803 was the year in which they discontinued its use in the speller.

[3]Boston Public Library.

507

——— Thomas & Andrews' fifteenth edition.... Boston.... 1804.

240 pp. 18 cm.
NN, RPB.

NOTES

1. Does not have the frontispiece.
2. The American Antiquarian Society has a mongrel copy which is made up partly of pages of this edition and partly of those of the Hartford fifteenth edition, 1800.

508

——— New-York: Published by Evert Duyckinck.... W. W. Vermilye, printer. 1804.

236, (3) pp. 17 cm.
CLU, NN, NNC.

509

[——— Utica: Merrell and Seward, 1804.]

Williams, p. 21.
Williams cites an advertisement in a local newspaper of August 16. The compiler has found no other trace of such an edition. If it existed, it was probably the old text, since the preface to the new (see the next section) is dated September.

C. *An American Selection, Revised*

510

——— A new edition. From Sidney's Press, New-Haven, for I. Beers & Co. and I. Cooke & Co. 1804.

225 pp. 17 cm. P. [1], title-page. P. [2], "Advertisement to the Revised Edition," unsigned, dated New Haven, September, 1804, stating that although the book has been widely used, it has been "thought susceptible of improvement," and that certain alterations and omissions of

"some pieces...believed to be less adapted to interest young minds" have been effected; copyright notice, Connecticut District, January 30, 1804. Pp. [3]–225, text.

CT, CTHT-W, CTY, MH, MWA, MIDEAED, NHI, NN, NJR, Merriam.

NOTES

1. The text is in general like the Hartford tenth edition, 1796, with various deletions and substitutions; the latter include several extracts from the travel books of Sir John Chardin and William Coxe, and from Garcilaso de la Vega's *Royal Commentaries of Peru.*

2. The edition was 3,000.

511

—— Hogan's second improved edition. Philadelphia, Printed for and sold by David Hogan.... 1805.

230, (2) pp. 18 cm. Pp. [i–iv], blank. P. [v], title-page. P. [vi], the same advertisement as in the preceding edition, and copyright notice. Pp. [vii]–xii, introduction. Pp. [13]–230, text, with the imprint "Thomas Irwin, Printer. 1805" on 230. Pp. [231–232], table of contents.

MoSHI, PHI.

NOTES

1. Advertised in *The Library, or Philadelphia Literary Reporter,* March 30, 1805.

2. The compiler has found no evidence of a Hogan "first improved edition"; this may be numbered to follow the New Haven first edition.

512

—— Cushing and Appleton's edition. Salem: Printed by Joshua Cushing, for Cushing and Appleton, proprietors of the copy right for Massachusetts and Newhampshire. 1805.

260, (4) pp. 17 cm.

MH, MWA, MIDEAED, MIU, NNC, PU, British Museum.

Similar in content to the New Haven first edition, but requiring more pages because of larger type. Following the text are two leaves of publisher's advertisements.

513

—— [Copied from the last revised edition.] Windsor, (Vt.) Printed by Nahum Mower. 1805.

226 pp. 16 cm.
MH, MWA, MiDeaEd, NhD (imperfect), OClWHi (imperfect), VtHi.

514

—— A new edition. Utica: Printed by Asahel Seward, for Charles R. and George Webster, Albany. 1806.

226, (2) pp. 17 cm.
MWA, MiDeaEd.

515

—— A new edition.... Printed at Boston, by Isaiah Thomas and Ebenezer T. Andrews.... 1807.

240 pp. 18 cm.
Ct, MH, MWA (imperfect), MiDeaEd, N, NN.

NOTES

1. Despite the phrase "new edition" on the title-page and the 1804 copyright entry on p. [iii], this is the old text, similar in content and format to the firm's earlier editions.
2. Cushing and Appleton, Salem, are added in the imprint as vendors.

516

—— Hogan's third improved edition. Philadelphia, Printed and sold by David Hogan.... 1807.

230, (2) pp. 18 cm.
Ct, ICU, MH, MWA, NNC-T (imperfect), PHi.

517

—— Second edition. Utica: Printed by Asahel Seward.... 1807.

226, (2) pp. 17 cm.
CtHi, MiDeaEd, NN.

518

—— Third edition. Utica: Printed by Seward and Williams.... 1808.

226, (2) pp. 17 cm.
CtHi, NNC (imperfect), NUt.
William Williams had gone into partnership with Asahel Seward in mid-1807, according to an advertisement in the Utica *Patriot*, July 27, 1807, quoted by John C. Williams in *An Oneida County Printer, William Williams* (New York, 1906), p. 24.

519

—— Exeter: Printed by Charles Norris & Co. for Edward Little & Co. proprietors of the copy right for Massachusetts and New-Hampshire..., Newburyport.—1809.

240 pp. 17 cm.
MH, MWA, Nh, NhD, NjR, OClW.
Despite the 1804 copyright on p. [2], this is the old text, similar to the editions of about 1796.

520

—— Hogan's fourth improved edition. Philadelphia: Published and sold by David Hogan.... 1809.

230, (2) pp. 18 cm.
CtHT-W, ICN, MWA, MiDeaEd, NN, NNC-T (imperfect), NjR, PPM.

521

—— Fourth edition. Utica: Printed by Seward and Williams. 1809.

226, (2) pp. 17 cm.
CSmH, CtNhHi, CtY, MH, MWA, NBuG, NHi, NN, NNC.

522

——— Hogan's fifth improved edition. Philadelphia: Published and sold by David Hogan.... Stiles, printer. 1810.

230, (2) pp. 18 cm.

CT, CTY, DLC, MWA, MIDEAED, NN, PU, VIU.

Duyckinck's *Cyclopaedia of American Literature* (2 vols., New York, 1855) is in error in stating (Vol. I, p. 475) that this edition contains Franklin's "Whistle" and "Logan's Speech."

523

——— Fifth edition. Utica: Printed by Seward and Williams. 1810.

226, (2) pp. 17 cm.

MWA, N, NCANHI, PU.

524

——— Newburyport: Published by Edward Little & Co. proprietors of the copy right for Massachusetts and New-Hampshire .... C. Norris & Co. printers. Exeter. 1811.

240 pp. 17 cm.

MH, MWA, MIDEAED, NN, NH, NHHI, NJR, OOXM.

Like the Newburyport edition of 1809, this is the old text of the mid-1790's, despite the 1804 copyright notice.

525

——— Sixth edition. Utica: Printed by Seward and Williams. 1813.

226, (2) pp. 17 cm.

CSF, CSMH, DLC, ICU, MWA, MID-B, MIDEAED, N, NN, NUT, OCLWHI (imperfect).

In 1813 Seward and Williams printed the second Utica edition of Lindley Murray's reader, and they published other editions in 1816 and 1817 (John C. Williams, *An Oneida County Printer, William Williams* [New York, 1906], p. 58); apparently with this edition they ceased printing Webster's reader, though he wrote to Erastus Clark on September 26, 1815, "Please to inform me whether Messrs. S. & W. printed an edition of my Selections last winter, as they wrote me they expected to do."[4]

526

——— Hogan's seventh improved edition, carefully corrected. Philadelphia: Published and sold by David Hogan.... Thomas T. Stiles, printer. 1814.

230, (2) pp. 18 cm.
MH, NN, PP, Merriam.
The compiler has been unable to locate a Hogan sixth edition. Note that Hogan published another seventh edition, in 1816.

527

——— Hogan's seventh improved edition, carefully corrected. Philadelphia: Published and sold by David Hogan.... 1816.

230, (2) pp. 18 cm.
CU, DLC (imperfect), ICN, MiDeaEd, NNC, PP, PU.
Note that Hogan had already issued one seventh edition, in 1814.

On September 15, 1817, *Webster applied for a new copyright on the* American Selection, *though he seems not to have done anything about a new edition until* 1835. *This application was published in the* Connecticut Courant, *September* 23, 1817, *and later.*

D. *Instructive and Entertaining Lessons*

528

Instructive and entertaining lessons for youth; with rules for reading with propriety, illustrated by examples: designed for use in schools and families. By Noah Webster, LL.D. New-Haven: Published by S. Babcock and Durrie & Peck: and sold by booksellers in general. 1835.

[4]In the possession of Mr. R. C. McNamara, Chicago.

252 pp., incl. frontis., illus. 18 cm. Pp. [1–2], publisher's advertisements. P. [3], blank. P. [4], frontispiece, consisting of two cuts, "Agriculture" and "Commerce and Manufactures," by J. W. Barber. P. [5], title-page. P. [6], copyright notice, Connecticut District, 1835, and "Printed by J. Peck." Pp. [7]–10, preface, unsigned, dated New Haven, May, 1835, stating that Webster had been requested "through the medium of the press" to republish his *American Selection*. Pp. [11]–12, table of contents. Pp. [13]–252, text.

CT, CTHT-W, CTHI, CTNHHI, CTY, DLC, MH, MWA, MIDEAED, NN, NNC, OCLW, Merriam.

NOTES

1. The text is in large part the same as the older reader, with some of the pieces reworked. Some of the new material is by Webster (e.g., Chapters IV–V, "Of the Materials of Clothing . . .") and some by others, such as William Wirt, Daniel Drake, William Ellery Channing, Baron von Humboldt, and Lyman Beecher.

2. Advertised in the *Litchfield* (Conn.) *Enquirer*, May 28, 1835, and later, and elsewhere.

3. Reviewed in the *Massachusetts Eagle*, September 24, 1835.

4. The price was fifty cents, with a twenty-five percent discount by the dozen (*Commercial Advertiser*, July 9).

5. The edition did not sell very well, and Webster's correspondence and accounts record many copies given away for publicity purposes. Soon after the publication of this reader the field was taken over by William H. McGuffey.

6. The same frontispiece was used in Webster's *Teacher* (Title 569), and portions of the new material were used in one of the 1837 editions thereof.

E. *Derivative Readers*

1. *The Little Reader's Assistant*

529

The little reader's assistant; containing I. A number of stories, mostly taken from the history of America, and adorned with cuts. II. Rudiments of English grammar. III. A Federal catechism, being a short and easy explanation of the Constitution of the United States. IV. General principles of government and commerce. All adapted to the capacities of children. By Noah Webster, Jun. Attorney at law. Hartford: Printed by Elisha Babcock. M,DCC,XC.

48, 80, 13 pp., illus. 12 cm. P. [1], title-page. P. [2], "Advertisement," stating that "it is hoped these few stories will serve as a step by which children will rise with more ease to the *American Selection*. . . ." Pp. [3]–48, Part I, consisting of stories, mostly from American history, including (pp. 28–29), "Story and Speech of Logan, a Mingo Chief." P. [1], separate title-page for Part II, identical with the 1790 separate edition of *Rudiments of English Grammar* (Title 445). Pp. [2]–80 follow that edition, including the "Federal Catechizm" and "Principles of Government and Commerce," which are entered on the title-page of this work as Parts III and IV. This is all from the same setting of type as the separate edition. Pp. [1]–13, "The Farmer's Catechizm. . ." (caption title). The verso of p. 13 is blank. As indicated on the title-page, all the cuts are in Part I.

NN, NHD.

Evans 23056, though his location of copies in the American Antiquarian Society and the British Museum is in error.

NOTES

1. Announced in the *American Mercury*, October 18, 1790, and later, and advertised therein December 20 and later.

2. In a letter of December 12, 1790, sending a copy of this work to Secretary of State Thomas Jefferson for copyright entry, Webster said, "As a school book, it is getting into use, & tho it may never be so generally used as the Institute, yet it may diffuse some useful truths; which is my primary object in all my publications. The farmers catechizm at the end, I design to improve in a future impression."[5] No evidence has been found that Webster carried out this intention.

530

——— The second edition. . . . Hartford: Printed by Elisha Babcock. M,DCC,XCI. Published according to act of Congress.

[5]Jefferson Papers, Manuscripts Division, Library of Congress.

48, 80, [129]–141 (*or* 141) pp., illus. (see below). 13 cm.
CtHi, CtY, DLC with disjointed pagination; Ct, CtHT-W, CtHi, MWA, NHi with continuous pagination.
Evans 23967, Sabin 102367.

NOTES

1. The contents are the same as the first edition. The earlier copies follow its pagination except that pp. [1]–13 of the "Farmer's Catechizm" are renumbered [129]–141, leaving a gap between pages 80 and [129]. In later copies the pagination is redone in one continuous series. The cuts are similar to, but not identical with, those in the first edition.
2. Advertised in the *Connecticut Gazette*, February 11, 1791, and elsewhere.
3. The title-page is reproduced in Alice Morse Earle, *Child Life in Colonial Days* (New York, 1899), facing p. 144.
4. The Library of Congress has a copy of the final section, pp. [129]–141, bound into the first edition of the *Rudiments of English Grammar*, 1790.

531

——— The third edition.... Northampton: Re-printed by William Butler. M,DCC,XCI. [Published according to act of Congress.]

138 pp. (the last misnumbered 137), illus. 12 cm.
MB (Part I only), MNF (imperfect), MWA (imperfect), NN (imperfect).
Evans 23968, Sabin under 102367, Gilmore 16.

NOTES

1. The contents are the same as the preceding editions, but reset in fewer pages. The cuts are similar but not identical.
2. In the New York Public Library copy pp. 39–42 have been supplied from the 1798 edition.

532

[——— Hartford: Elisha Babcock, 1793.]

Evans 26449.
The compiler has found no trace of this. There is an advertisement

for this title as "just published" in the *American Mercury*, December 23, 1793, but, as previously noted, the phrase "just published" was used loosely in newspapers of that time.

533

There is in the American Antiquarian Society a photograph of a title-page of an edition of A Farmer's Catechism *with the imprint "Canaan: Prnited [sic] and sold, by Elihu Phinney.* 1795," *of which the wording is identical, except for an added verse, with the caption title of Webster's section of this name in the* Little Reader's Assistant. *Evans* (29855) *attributes this work to Webster and describes it as if it were a copy of the book rather than only a reproduction of the title-page. He gives the collation as eight pages; the version in the* Little Reader's Assistant *occupies thirteen, but a different setting of type could account for the difference. Sabin* 102353.

534

[—— Hartford: Elisha Babcock, 1798.]

Evans 34982.
No copy located, or evidence of its existence.

535

—— The fourth edition.... Printed at Northampton (Massachusetts) by William Butler. M,DCC,XCVIII. Published according to act of Congress.

138 pp., illus. 12 cm.
CT, DLC, MNF, MWA (imperfect), NN (title-page fragmentary), Merriam.
Evans 34983, Sabin under 102367, Gilmore 49.
The contents and cuts are the same as the third edition; the misnumbering of p. 138 has been corrected.

2. *The Little Franklin*

536

The little Franklin: teaching children to read what they daily speak, and to learn what they ought to know. By Noah Webster, LL.D. New Haven: Published by S. Babcock. 1836.

72 pp., incl. frontis., illus. 14 cm. P. [1], blank. P. [2], frontispiece, a portrait of Franklin. P. [3], title-page. P. [4], copyright entry to Webster, 1836. P. [5], preface, unsigned and undated. P. [6], blank. Pp. [7]–72, text, consisting of short lessons and anecdotes, including Franklin's "The Whistle."

CU, CtHi, CtY, MB, MWA, Mi, MiDeaEd, NN.

The period 1835–1836 *marks the end of publication of Webster's various readers. An* Elementary Reader *"to accompany Webster's Spelling Book" was published in* 1835 *and* 1837; *it is described in Appendix F. About twenty years later Ward and Lock published in London* The Illustrated Webster Reader, Series I, *dated* 1856 *by the British Museum, which has a copy. The only connection with Webster's reader is the use of his name in the title and his picture (after the Morse portrait) as the frontispiece. The same firm published a "new edition" of this work in* 1858 *or* 1859.

In 1867 *and* 1868 *D. Appleton Company of New York published, in conjunction with firms in other cities, two editions of* The Webster Elementary Reader. *This work too is related to Webster's only in the use of his name in the title.*

Section Two

OTHER TEXT BOOKS

PART ONE: ELEMENTS OF USEFUL KNOWLEDGE

A. *Volume I*

537

Elements of useful knowledge. Volume I. Containing a historical and geographical account of the United States: for the use of schools. By Noah Webster, Jun. [*six lines of quotation.*] Hartford: Printed and sold by Hudson & Goodwin. 1802.

206 pp. 17 cm. Pp. [1–4], blank. P. [5], title-page. P. [6], "Registered according to Law" and errata list. Pp. [7–11], preface, unsigned and undated, outlining Webster's plan for a system of education. P. [12], table of contents. Pp. [13]–206, text.

CT, CTHT-W, CTNHHI, CTY, IC, IU, MA, MH, MWA (imperfect), NHI, NN, NNC, NRU, NCU, NJHI, NJR, PU, Merriam.

Sabin 102350.

NOTES

1. The text is in thirteen numbered sections: Solar System; Geography; Rivers of the United States; Origins of Man, and of the Americans; Discovery of America by Europeans; Discovery and Settlement of North America; Indian Wars; Political and Ecclesiastical Affairs, Commerce, Arts, Customs, Education; Military Events; Bills of Credit; Piracy; Diseases and Remarkable Events; and Controversies and their Effects.

2. Advertised in the *Connecticut Journal*, August 19 and 26, 1802, as "just published," containing quotations from the preface; *Commercial Advertiser*, September 2, 1802, and later; and elsewhere.

3. The edition was 2,500.

4. In his *Brief View*, 1834(?), Webster claimed that Joseph Worcester plagiarized from this work in his *Elements of History* (1826, 1833, and later). Webster himself used portions in other works.

538

—— Hartford: Printed for O. D. Cooke, by Hudson & Goodwin. 1806.

(12), 208 pp. 17 cm.

CLU, Ct, CtHT-W, CtNhHi, CtY, DFSA, DLC, ICU, IU, MH, MNF, MWA (imperfect), Mi, MiDeaEd, NN, NNC, NNC-T, NNUT, NcD, OClWHi, PHi, ViU, Merriam, British Museum.

NOTES

1. The twelve unnumbered pages correspond to pp. [1–12] of the first edition, and the text is paged [1]–208. It is substantially the same as the first edition, with the addition (pp. [195]–208) of "A Chronological Table of the Most Remarkable Events . . . of American History." This table had been used in the first edition of the speller (Title 1), and also appears in the *Compendious Dictionary* of 1806 (Title 577).

2. The edition was 5,000.

3. The copyright notice, on p. [vi], is dated July 21, 1802.

4. The New Haven Colony Historical Society copy is bound with the first edition of Volume II; the New York Public Library copy has parts of Volume II bound in, and is marked by Webster for a new printing.

539

—— Third edition. New-London: Printed for O. D. Cooke, by Ebenezer P. Cady. 1807.

(12), 208 pp. 17 cm.

CSt, Ct, CtHT-W, CtHi, CtY, MA, MH, MWA, MiD-B, MiDeaEd, MiU-C, N, NHi, NN, NNC-T, NhD, OClWHi, PP, PU, Merriam.

NOTES

1. The edition was 5,000.

2. A. S. W. Rosenbach, as No. 359 in his *Early American Children's Books* (Portland, Me., 1933), describes a copy of this edition and Cooke's third edition of Volume II bound together, apparently as issued. This is the copy now in the Free Library of Philadelphia.

540

——— Fourth edition. Hartford: Printed by Hudson & Goodwin. 1809.

(12), 208 pp. 16 cm.

CT, CTHT-W, CTHI, CTY, DLC, MH, MWA (imperfect), MID-B (imperfect), MIDEAED, MIU-C, NBUG, NN, NJR, OO, RHI, RPB, Merriam, British Museum.

Thomas Dawes, Mrs. Webster's brother-in-law, writing Webster from Boston on August 1, 1809, about insertion of a communication from the latter in a newspaper there, said, "I have seized the occasion to mention your Elements of U.K. with, I hope, sufficient tho' qualified praise. I have told the *truth* about it, viz that there is no better book, and that it would have been in every school boy's hands had its author sacrificed such trifles to the common notions of people as to retain the *a* in breadth, &c, about which, however, I say that scholars differ, and that so valuable a book ought not to be condemned for an objection of doubtful foundation. If I can get people to talk about it, I may be able to help it up to the notice it deserves."[6]

541

——— Fifth edition. New-York: Published by Evert Duyckinck .... G. Bunce, print. 1810.

viii, 207, (1) pp. 16 cm.

CTY, MBAT, MH, MWA, MIDEAED, N, NN, OOXM, RPB (imperfect), Merriam.

NOTES

1. The contents are the same as the second edition, but the make-up of the volume is different, being: P. [i], title-page; p. [ii], copyright notice; pp. [iii]–viii, preface; pp. [1]–207, text; p. [208], table of contents.

2. On June 25, 1810, Webster mentioned in a letter to Hudson and Goodwin, "I am in hopes of getting the work published in Philad. & one more attempt made to introduce it Westward."[7]

[6] Webster Papers, New York Public Library; Ford's *Notes*, Vol. II, pp. 71–72.
[7] Webster Papers, New York Public Library.

542

—— Fifth edition. Hartford: Printed by Hudson and Goodwin. 1812.

(8), 208 pp. 17 cm.

Ct, CtHT-W, CtHi, CtY, MA, MH, MWA, MiDeaEd, NN, NjR, OO, Merriam.

In this and the following edition none of the preliminary pages are numbered, and the table of contents has been placed on p. [viii], after the preface.

543

—— Sixth edition. Hartford: Printed by Hudson and Goodwin 1815.

(8), 206 pp. 17 cm.

Ct, CtH, CtHT-W, CtY, DLC, MA, MH, MWA, MiDeaEd, NN, NNC, NUt, NjR, OClW, PMA, Merriam.

The chronological table occupies fewer pages than in preceding editions.

B. *Volume II*

544

Elements of useful knowledge. Volume II. Containing a historical and geographical account of the United States: for the use of schools. By Noah Webster, Jun. [*eight lines of quotation.*] From Sidney's Press, New-Haven, for the author, and sold by the booksellers. 1804.

206, (1) pp. 17 cm. P. [1], title-page. P. [2], copyright notice, March 3, [1804]. Pp. [3–4], preface, unsigned, dated New Haven, 1804, suggesting that Volumes I and II be used together. Pp. [5]–206, text (see below). P. [207], table of contents.

CtHT-W, CtNhHi, CtY, DLC, IC, IU, MH, MHi, MWA, MiDeaEd, NN, NNC, NcU, RPB.

Sabin under 102350.

NOTES

1. The text is in eight sections, the first seven numbered fourteen to twenty, to follow Volume I: History of the Revolution in America...; General Description of the United States, and the Climate; Vegetable Productions; Animals...; Mines, Minerals and Mineral Springs; Present condition of the several states...; Constitution of the United States; and Conclusion, General Views of the Inhabitants of the United States.

2. The edition was 1,500.

3. Josiah Meigs, a college classmate of Webster's and president of the University of Georgia, wrote him on November 22, 1804, acknowledging receipt of Volumes I and II and saying, "I am much pleased with your manner of describing our North America. You have risen from the briars and brambles of detail and given us a luminous and comprehensive view of a *whole*. I shall use my influence to introduce it into our schools & all Seminaries of learning for which it is designed."[8]

4. The copyright notice was published in the *Connecticut Post & New Haven Visitor*, March 22, 1804, and later.

545

——— Second edition. From Sidney's Press, New-Haven, for Increase Cooke & Co. 1806.

224,(1) pp. 16 cm.

CU, CLU, CT, CTH, CTHT-W, CTHI, CTY, DLC, MH, MNF, MWA, NN, NNC, NNC-T, NCD, NJR, OCLWHI, OO, PU, VIU, Merriam, British Museum.

NOTES

1. The text is similar to the first edition, with the addition (pp. 207–224) of Washington's Farewell Address. P. [225], table of contents.

2. The edition was 5,000.

3. Webster wrote to Websters and Skinner of Albany, November 6, 1807, "I have sent to your care for sale 100 copies of the first & 100. do of the second volume of 'Elements of Useful Knowledge.' Please to offer them for sale at 37 cents single—& 30 cents by the doz^{n}—Inclosed is a recommendation which I will thank you to insert in your paper, under an advertisement of the work—two or three times."[9]

[8] Webster Papers, New York Public Library; Ford's *Notes*, Vol. II, pp. 513–514, where the letter is misdated 1801.

[9] Webster Papers, New York Public Library.

546

—— Third edition. From Sidney's Press, New-Haven, for Increase Cooke & Co. 1808.

224, (4) pp. 17 cm.
CSt, Ct, CtHT-W, CtNhHi, CtY, ICU, MBAt, MH, MWA, MiD-B, MiDeaEd, NHi, NN, NNC-T, NjR, OOxM, PP, PU.

NOTES

1. At the end are three pages of publisher's advertisements.
2. The edition was 5,000.
3. See Note 2 to Title 539.

547

—— Third edition. [Hartford:] Printed for Hudson & Goodwin, by T. Dunning. 1809.

224, (1) pp. 16 cm.
CSt, Ct, CtHT-W, CtHi, CtY, DLC, MB, MH, MWA, MiDeaEd, N, NBuG, NN, NNC, NjR, OClWHi, OO, PHi, PU, Merriam.
Like the preceding editions except that the preface is undated. The place of publication was Hartford, but the printer was located in Middletown, Conn.

548

—— Fourth edition. Hartford: Printed by Hudson and Goodwin. 1813.

224, (1) pp. 17 cm.
Ct, CtHT-W, MH, MWA, MiD-B, NHi, NN, NNC, PU, RPB, Merriam.

c. *Volume III*

549

Elements of useful knowledge. Vol. III. Containing a historical and geographical account of the empires and states in Europe, Asia and

Africa, with their colonies. To which is added, a brief description of New Holland, and the principal islands in the Pacific and Indian oceans. For the use of schools. By Noah Webster, Esq. New-Haven, (Connecticut) Published by Bronson, Walter & Co. O. Steele & Co. printers. 1806.

294, (2) pp. 17 cm. P. [1], title-page. P. [2], copyright notice, July 23, [1806]. Pp. [3–4], "Advertisement," dated New Haven, July, 1806, explaining Webster's theories of orthography. Pp. [5]–294, text, consisting of about sixty sections on the subjects mentioned in the title. P. [295], note explaining the absence of maps. P. [296], table of contents.

CSmH, Ct, CtHT-W, CtNhHi, CtY, ICN, MA, MBAt, MH, MWA, MiDeaEd, NBuG, NN, NNC, NNC-T, NjR, OClWHi, PU, RPB, Merriam, British Museum.

Sabin under 102350.

The edition was 2,500.

550

——— Hartford, Printed by Hudson and Goodwin. 1812.

287, (1) pp. 16 cm.

Ct, CtHT-W, CtY, IC, IU, MA, MH, MWA, N, NN, NNC, OClWHi, RPB.

Except for the omission of a table of contents, this edition is the same in content as the first; the difference in pagination is accounted for by a different setting of type.

D. *Volume IV*

551

History of animals; being the fourth volume of Elements of useful knowledge. For the use of schools, and young persons of both sexes. By Noah Webster, Jun. Esq. New-Haven, Published and sold by Howe & Deforest, and Walter & Steele. Walter & Steele, printers. 1812.

247 pp. 17 cm. P. [1], title-page. P. [2], copyright entry, June 26, [1812]. P. [3], preface, dated New Haven, June, 1812, stating that the "descriptions here given are interspersed with some amusing anecdotes; and with occasional moral and religious reflections, calculated to lead the young mind to contemplate the character, and to admire the wisdom, power and goodness of the divine author of all life...," and referring readers to the *Compendious Dictionary*. P. [4], blank. Pp. [5]–247, text, an organized narrative presentation of zoology.

CT, CTHT-W, CTNHHI, CTY, ICU, MA, MBAT, MH, MWA, MIDEAED, N, NN, NNC, NNC-T, NHD, NHHI, NJR, OCLWHI, PU.

Sabin under 102350.

Years later Webster summarized the history of his *Elements of Useful Knowledge* as follows: "The first volume...was published in 1802—the second volume in 1804. These contain the geography and history of the United States. The third volume, containing the geography and history of the Eastern continent, was published in 1806; and the fourth volume containing a history of animals, in 1812. These books were for several years extensively used in Connecticut; and, when the predilection for English books shall subside, it is not improbable they may be again used."[1]

552

History of animals; designed for the instruction and amusement of persons of both sexes, by Noah Webster, Jun. Esq. New-Haven, Published and sold by Howe & Deforest, and Walter & Steele. Walter & Steele, printers. 1812.

247 pp. 17 cm. P. [1], title-page. P. [2], copyright entry, July 2, [1812]. Pp. [3]–247, same as the preceding entry.

CU, CTHT, CTY, DLC, ICJ, MA, MB, NHI, NN, NNC, NJR, OCLWHI, PU, RPB, VTMIDBC, Merriam.

[1] Webster to Lemuel Shattuck, November 18, 1829, quoted in the *New England Magazine*, June, 1832 (Vol. II, p. 476).

PART TWO: LETTERS TO A YOUNG GENTLEMAN

553

Letters to a young gentleman commencing his education: to which is subjoined a brief history of the United States. By Noah Webster, Esq. New-Haven: Sold by Howe & Spalding. S. Converse, printer. 1823.

335 pp. 23 cm. P. [1], title-page. P. [2], copyright notice, June 11, [1823]. Pp. [3]–4, table of contents. Pp. [5]–335, text, consisting of nine "letters" and ten "sections" of material on the United States (see below).

CSmH, Ct, CtH, CtHT-W, CtNhHi, CtY, DLC, IC, IChi, ICN, ICU, M, MA, MB, MH, MWA, MiDeaEd, N, NBuG, NHi, NN, NNC, NNC-T, NhD, NjN, NjR, OClW, OU, PU, RPB, RPJCB, ViU, VtMidbC, VtU, Merriam, British Museum.

Sabin 102365.

NOTES

1. The "sections" are a reprint of the last nine chapters of Volume I and the first of Volume II of the *Elements of Useful Knowledge*. The "letters" are: I, "Instructions respecting Moral and Political Conduct...." II, III, and IV, "Respecting accuracy in speaking and writing the English language—Low state of Philology, illustrated by examples from the best authors." V, "On conjectures and theories in Philosophy...." VI, "On the question whether Moses was the writer of...the Pentateuch." VII, "On the divinity of Christ, and the nature of the Atonement." VIII, "A brief History of our Ancestors...exhibiting a concise view of the Japhetic settlements...and the migration of our ancestors from Asia, to their establishment in West of Europe." IX, "General view of the character, manners and religion of our ancestors...."

2. Letter I is reprinted in Webster's *Collection of Papers*, 1843. Extracts from the book were published in the*Hampshire Gazette*, December 29, 1824, and the *Connecticut Herald*, July 24, 1827.

3. At the end of the table of contents is this statement: "This History is adapted to the use of families and schools—and forms a convenient Manuel [sic] for travellers and seamen."

4. The retail price was $1.75, ninety cents in sheets; Webster offered dealers bound copies at $1.29 and copies in sheets at eighty cents in amounts of one hundred or more.

5. Thomas Dawes wrote Webster on February 14, 1824, "As to that Book, I was much instructed and pleased, as indeed I always have been by your publications. I have no fault to find with your *Seventh* letter.... No writer could have treated the *mysterious* subject better than you have done. But as Christians have differed so much about it, I wish you could have reserved your creed for some work, other than a *school* book." He suggested that some school districts might boggle at adopting the text because of the amount of controversial religious matter in it.[2]

[2] Webster Papers, New York Public Library; Ford's *Notes*, Vol. II, pp. 194–195.

PART THREE: BIOGRAPHY FOR THE USE OF SCHOOLS

554

Biography for the use of schools. By N. Webster, LL.D. New Haven: Printed by Hezekiah Howe, and sold by the booksellers. 1830.

214 pp., incl. frontis., illus. 14 cm. P. [1], blank. P. [2], frontispiece by Alexander Anderson, "View of the U.S. Capitol at Washington." P. [3], title-page. P. [4], copyright notice, May 8, [1830]. P. [5], table of contents. P. [6], blank. Pp. [7]–202, text. Pp. 203–214, "A Moral Catechism" (see Title 36).

CtNhHi, DLC, MB, MiDeaEd, NN, NNC (imperfect), British Museum.

Sabin 102340.

NOTES

1. The text consists of short biographical sketches of classical authors, Biblical figures, European writers and scholars, and American pioneers and statesmen. The illustrations include unsigned portraits of Franklin and Washington and an Anderson woodcut of Goliath going forth to battle.

2. Perhaps actually issued in 1829, since it was advertised as being on sale in the *Connecticut Courant* on October 12 and later in that year. An advertisement in the September 21, 1830, *Connecticut Journal* gives the price as twenty-five cents.

3. The same frontispiece was used in Webster's *History of the United States*.

PART FOUR: HISTORY OF THE UNITED STATES

555

History of the United States; to which is prefixed a brief historical account of our English ancestors, from the dispersion of Babel, to their migration to America; and of the conquest of South America, by the Spaniards. By Noah Webster, LL.D. New-Haven, Published by Durrie & Peck. Baldwin and Treadway, print. 1832.

356 [i.e., 358] pp., incl. frontis., illus. 14 cm. P. [1], blank. P. [2], frontispiece by Alexander Anderson, the same as in the preceding work. P. [3], title-page. P. [4], copyright notice, 1832. Pp. [5]–8, preface, unsigned, dated New Haven, 1832. P. [9], table of contents. P. [10], blank. Pp. [11]–356, text, in numbered paragraphs, divided into twenty sections, with questions following each section except the last two (see below). Twenty-two cuts in the text, some signed J. W. Barber or J. W. B., and one E. L. B. Page numbers 287 and 288 are repeated, which makes the actual total 358; there are other errors in pagination which do not affect the total.

CT, CTH, CTHT-W, CTHI, CTNHHI, CTY, IC, ICN, ICU, MA, MBAT, MH, MWA, MIDEAED, NBUG, NHI, NN, NNC, NRU, NH, OOXM, VTMIDBC.

Sabin 102358.

NOTES

1. Most of the text is material already used by Webster in his *Elements of Useful Knowledge*. The table of contents differs widely from the actual contents, which are, with their misnumberings: I, Origin of the Human Race. II, Teutonic and Gothic Nations. III, Saxons. III, After the Norman Conquest. IV, America. V, Discovery of America. VI, Discovery and Settlement of North America. VII, Indian Wars. VIII, Political Events. X, Government and Laws. X, Military Events. XI, Bills of Credit. XII, Piracy. XIII, Diseases and Remarkable Events. XIV, War of the Revolution. Constitution of the United States [including material

on the Puritans, general description of the country, climate, etc.]. XVI, Vegetable Productions. XVII, Animals of the United States. Advice to the Young. The Farewell Address of George Washington.

2. Reviewed: New Haven *Palladium-Republican*, August 4, 1832; *Middlesex Gazette*, August 8, 1832, by "T.M.," identified by Webster on a clipping as Dr. Thomas Miner; *New York Observer*, October 6, 1832; *New York Evangelist*, October 20, 1832; *American Monthly Review*, November, 1832 (Vol. II, pp. 381–383). Dr. Miner predicted that the book would be in use a century later. The *American Monthly Review* thought the "Advice to the Young" good, but out of place in a United States history.

3. The printed covers of the New-York Historical Society and Watkinson copies add to the imprint N. and J. White of New York and seventeen other distributors in different parts of the country. These covers and those seen on the New York Public Library copies before they were rebound each bear one of the cuts from the book, though a different one in each case.

4. Webster wrote Durrie and Peck on March 12, 1832, "If you print an edition of my History of the United States of 2000 copies, you may do it without paying me any premium, except an hundred copies of the books [sic], chiefly for donations, to make it known. And if the work should succeed, you may have the exclusive publication of it, for three cents a copy."[3] Advertisements for the second edition show that the first was actually 3,000 copies.

556

——— New Haven: Published by Durrie & Peck. Louisville, Ky.: Wilcox, Dickerman, & Co. 1832.

324 pp., incl. frontis., illus. 14 cm.

CSmH, Ct, CtHT-W, CtNhHi, DLC, ICN, IU, MH, MWA, MWiW, MiDeaEd, NN, NNC, OClWHi, ViU, Merriam.

NOTES

1. The same as the first edition with the following exceptions: "English" on the title-page is enclosed in brackets (which continues in all later editions); the legend on the frontispiece reads "View of the United States' Capitol at Washington"; the preliminary pagination is in roman

[3]Webster Papers, New York Public Library.

instead of arabic numerals; and the divisions are called chapters and are numbered correctly from I to XX. The table of contents, though more nearly correct than in the first edition, is still not a correct list of the actual contents.

2. On the back printed cover is a publisher's advertisement, "In presenting this second edition of the History to the public, the publishers would remark, that no essential alteration has been made from the first, except in the enlargment [sic] of the pages, and as it is now stereotyped, all further editions will be uniform with this. So unprecedented has been the demand for this work, that the first edition (3000) was all disposed of in three months . . .," followed by recommendations.

3. The printed covers add a long list of other vendors. Some of the covers have "Second Edition" and the date 1833, while others have "Third Edition" and 1833.

557

——— New Haven: Published by Durrie & Peck. Louisville, Ky.: Wilcox, Dickerman, & Co. 1833.

324 pp., incl. frontis., illus. 14 cm.

CtHT-W, CtY, DLC, MdBE, MH, MHi, MWA, MiDeaEd, N, NHi, NN, NNC, NNC-T, OCHP, OClWHi, PU.

The contents are the same as the second edition. The copies vary slightly in the legend on the frontispiece; some have "Third Edition" on the front cover.

558

——— Cincinnati: Published by Corey, Fairbank & Webster. 1835.

318 pp., illus. 15 cm.

MB, MH, MiDeaEd, NN, OC, OClWHi.

NOTES

1. The preface has been somewhat altered, and the last four sections, which were not historical in nature, have been replaced by a new Chapter XVII (pp. 283–318), "Continuation of the History of the United States, from 1789 to 1815." The frontispiece and one illustration have been omitted, but four illustrations added in the new chapter.

2. The printed cover on the Western Reserve Historical Society copy reads "Fourth Edition," while some of the others say "Fifth Edition."

3. William G. Webster wrote his father, July 22, 1835, "The plates for the History arrived last week, & we have already put an edition of 1500 copies in press...," and on September 14 he wrote, "Our edition of 1000 Hist'y is out & we are beginning to sell...."[4]

559

——— New Haven: Published by Durrie & Peck. 1835.

322 pp., incl. frontis., illus. 15 cm.

CT, CTHT-W, CTNHHI, CTY, MA, MWA, MIDEAED, NN, OCLWHI, OO.

NOTES

1. The contents have the same changes as the Cincinnati edition of the same year. The "Continuation" is on pp. 283–322; it is not quite identical with that in the Cincinnati edition.
2. The cover imprint adds "Sixth Edition."
3. The New York Public Library copy was Webster's, and has been marked for corrections. All the marks occur in the new chapter, the heading of which is changed by hand to "Appendix."

560

[——— Cincinnati: Corey, Fairbank & Webster, 1836(?).]

On January 12, 1836, William G. Webster wrote his father, "...of the History, we are receiving from the press the third edition. The 1st and 2d 1000 copies each & the 3d 2000...."[5] His "first" and "second" are no doubt the Cincinnati "fourth" and "fifth" editions (Title 558); no other evidence of his "third" (possibly labelled "sixth"?) has been found, for the following entry probably did not appear earlier than late 1836.

The possibility of other western editions is indicated in an advertisement of Corey & Webster in the *Cincinnati Whig*, October 23, 1835, which asserts that ten editions of the history had been published in less than two years.

[4] Webster Papers, New York Public Library.
[5] Ibid.

561

——— Cincinnati: Burgess and Morgan. [1836?]

318 pp., illus. 15 cm.
MA, MiDeaEd.

NOTES

1. There is a blank space at the beginning of the line of imprint which consists of the firm name, a space just about the size to contain the word "Webster." The firm name was Webster, Burgess and Morgan from August to October, 1836, which suggests that this edition appeared soon after young Webster's leaving the partnership, and that his name was cut out of the stereotyped plates.

2. The younger Webster wrote his father on February 1, 1837, referring to Burgess and Morgan, "They do little with the History & I wish it were in other hands. . . . They now say they have printed but 1000. . .," and on February 22 he wrote, "I asked Burgess & M. about your a/c with them. There is not much due you. They published 928 Hist^{y}—at 4^{c}—37.12."[6]

562

——— New Haven: Published by S. Babcock. 1836.

324 pp., incl. frontis., illus. 15 cm.
OClWHi (imperfect), Field.

NOTES

1. Not seen; description provided by Prof. Harry R. Warfel.

2. The contents have reverted to those of the first three editions, omitting the "Continuation." The frontispiece is a view of the capitol, but is by R. N. White instead of Alexander Anderson. On the verso of the title, stereotype notice of Redfield and Lindsay, New York.

3. On the back cover are publisher's advertisements dated November, 1836.

4. By error pp. 185–188 are repeated in place of pp. 209–212. In the Field copy Webster has marked this, and also made a change in the preface.

[6]Ibid.

5. Webster wrote to his son on October 10, 1835, "I mentioned to Sidney Babcock that I would be willing he should publish my History of the U.S. Durrie & Peck have taken offense at this, & claim that they have some right to the work, on account of their exertions to introduce it. They forget that I did something myself, & that they had a right a *cent* below the common premium. But they tell Mr. Babcock that when you took the plates, you told them they would have the printing of it on this side of the mountains, or that they would have the preference—or something of this sort. Is that the fact? If so, they ought to have it—& I am willing they should. I shall be glad to learn the truth from you. I have recd the balance due from D & P. . . ."[7]

564

——— New Haven: Published by S. Babcock. 1837.

324 pp., incl. frontis., illus. 14 cm.
NBLiHi, NN.

NOTES

1. Like Babcock's 1836 edition in reverting to the original contents; stereotyped by Redfield and Lindsay, New York. Catalogued as the ninth edition by The New York Public Library, probably on the basis of a cover imprint since destroyed by rebinding.

2. Reviewed in the *Knickerbocker*, December, 1838 (Vol. XII, pp. 543–544).

565

——— Cincinnati: Burgess and Crane. 1838.

318 pp., illus. 14 cm.
NN.

NOTES

1. Has the revised contents of 1835.

2. Burgess and Crane advertised Webster's History for sale in May, 1837, and again—as their own publication—in October, 1837. Since no copy with their imprint has been located earlier than 1838, it is possible that these references are to Title 561, published by their predecessor firm.

[7]Pierpont Morgan Library.

3. On May 15, 1838, Webster wrote his son, "Burgess & Crane owe premiums on about 1000 histories, which they write, will be sent with payment for that on the Speller,"[8] and on August 27, 1839, he wrote to "Friend" Morgan (probably Ephraim), "I learn by the public prints that you have met with heavy losses by fire—I hope you are indemnified by insurance, & that the plates of my History are not among your losses."[9]

566

——— New Haven: Published by Sidney Babcock. [1839?]

358 pp., incl. frontis., illus. 14 cm.
MWA, NN.

NOTES

1. In contents this is a cross between the two earlier forms, for it uses the original preface and all original chapters, but adds the "Continuation" as an appendix. There are no illustrations in the "Continuation." Stereotyped by Redfield and Lindsay, New York.

2. The front cover imprint adds the year 1839.

3. One of the New York Public Library copies contains Webster's MS corrections for a new printing.

4. Webster wrote to Thomas Robbins on June 13, 1839, "I wish my fellow citizens would compare my History of the U States with others. It contains some articles no where else to be found. I think this or other History of our country should be a *common reading book* in all schools; & even read by pupils before they can fully understand all parts of it. Continued repetition impresses the statements on the mind, & these will be recollected & applied in subsequent periods of life, without any effort. The doctrine that a child must read nothing which he does not fully understand is, in my view, erroneous. The memory of children is the first faculty to be employed, & this will treasure up stores of facts in advance of the understanding. . . ."[1]

567

——— New Haven: Published by Sidney Babcock. [1839?]

[8] Webster Papers, New York Public Library.
[9] Department of Special Collections, Columbia University Library.
[1] Thomas Robbins Papers, Connecticut Historical Society.

358 pp., incl. frontis., illus. 14 cm.
CT, MB, MH, MIDEAED, NN, Merriam.

NOTES

1. Identical with the preceding except that the corrections marked by Webster have been incorporated—e.g., p. 224, fourth line from the bottom, "The next day" changed to "The same day."

2. The front cover is dated 1839 in the Connecticut State Library and Merriam copies; the New York Public Library copy is catalogued as the twelfth edition and dated 1840, probably on the basis of covers since destroyed by rebinding.

568

——— Columbus: Published by I. N. Whiting. 1841.

318 pp., illus. 16 cm.
DLC, OC, OCLW, OCLWHI.

NOTES

1. The contents are the same as the 1835 Cincinnati edition, except for the addition, on p. [1], of a synopsis and recommendations.

2. On some copies the front cover imprint is dated 1845.

3. In writing to Webster on September 30, 1841, to settle accounts, Whiting stated that he had published an edition of 500.[2]

[2]Ellsworth Papers, Connecticut Historical Society.

PART FIVE: THE TEACHER

569

The teacher; a supplement to The elementary spelling book. By Noah Webster, LL.D. New Haven. Published by S. Babcock. 1836.

155, (1) pp., incl. frontis., illus. 18 cm. P. [1], blank. P. [2], frontispiece by J. W. Barber, the same as that in Webster's *Instructive and Entertaining Lessons*, 1835 (Title 528). P. [3], title-page. P. [4], copyright notice to Webster, District of Columbia, 1836. P. [5], preface, unsigned, dated New Haven, March, 1836, explaining that the book contains material too bulky to be compressed into the speller. Pp. [6]–155, text. P. [156], errata.

CT, CTHI, CTNHHI, MH, MWA, MIDEAED, MNU, NN, NNC, NNC-T, NHD, OCLWHI, VTMIDBC.

NOTES

1. The text includes lists of various types of words and names; weights, measures, and coinage; articles on the orders of architecture, banking, and the solar system; prefixes and affixes; accentuation; Latin and Greek derivations; "A Moral Catechism" (see Title 36); and "Wisdom and Benevolence of God." The cuts illustrate the orders of architecture and the solar system.

2. Reviewed: *Connecticut Courant*, June 13, 1836 (a clipping in The New York Public Library is marked by Webster, "Said to be by W. M. Holland"); *Cincinnati Daily Gazette*, October 10, 1836; and elsewhere.

570

——— New Haven: Published by S. Babcock. 1837.

156 pp., incl. frontis., illus. 18 cm.

CT, CTHT-W, CTY, MH, NNUT.

Similar to the first edition except that the errata noted therein have been corrected. P. 156 has new matter, "Stanzas from Addison's Hymn to Gratitude." On p. [4], below the copyright entry, is added "Stereotyped by Redfield and Lindsay, 13 Chambers Street—New York."

571

[Identical title-page.]

192 pp., incl. frontis., illus. 18 cm.

CtHT-W, MB, MiDeaEd, NN.

The same as the preceding, with the addition of pp. [157]–192, which consist of four sections, ". . . on Farming," "Of the Materials of Clothing, Food, and Utensils," "Of Government, Laws, Crimes, Trespasses, Contracts, and Courts of Justice," and "Human Ignorance." The first two and the fourth are taken from Webster's *Instructive and Entertaining Lessons for Youth*, 1835, with slight additions in the second. Webster refers to this added material in letters in October, 1837.

572

The practice of putting into the hands of children. . . . N. Webster. New Haven, Sept. 1837.

Broadside, 25 x 20 cm.

MiDeaEd, NN (each pasted in a copy of *The Teacher*).

A circular letter intended to be sent with copies of the book, asking school authorities to examine the work and let Webster know if they intend to use it. The text opens with a discussion of education, objecting to giving light and entertaining reading to children. Webster says that since they go to school to learn "what they *do not know*," lessons should be in advance of their knowledge.

573

The teacher. . . . New Haven: Published by S. Babcock. 1839.

156 pp., incl. frontis., illus. 19 cm.

NBuG.

Similar in content to Title 570.

PART SIX: MANUAL OF USEFUL STUDIES

Roorbach's Bibliotheca Americana, *Allibone's* Dictionary, *and Stone's* First Editions of American Authors *all list an edition of this work in* 1832, *but the compiler has not found any trace of an edition before* 1839, *in which year Webster referred to the work as "a recent publication."*[3] *The* 1832 *date is almost certainly an error, possibly for* 1842.

574

A manual of useful studies: for the instruction of young persons of both sexes, in families and schools. By Noah Webster, LL.D. New Haven: Printed and published by S. Babcock. 1839.

248 pp., incl. frontis., illus. 19 cm. P. [i], blank. P. [ii], frontispiece, a diagram of the solar system. P. [iii], title-page. P. [iv], copyright notice, 1839. Pp. [v]–vi, preface, initialled and dated New Haven, April, 1839, stating that Webster had spent much time in early life learning what proved useless later, cautioning young men against accepting the opinions of authors without investigation and against publishing their own prematurely, and setting forth "practical utility" as the purpose of the volume. Pp. [vii]–viii, table of contents and errata list. Pp. [9]–248, text, in twenty chapters.

CT, CTHT-W, CTY (with Webster's MS corrections), DLC, ICN, IU, MA, MB, MH, MWA, MIDEAED, NHI, N, NN (imperfect), NNC, OCLW, OO, PPM, VIU, Merriam, British Museum.

Sabin 102368.

NOTES

1. The chapters are: I, "The Solar System," reprinted in part from *The Teacher*, 1836. II, "Geology." III, "The Atmosphere." IV, "Animals."

[3]To Thomas Robbins, June 13, 1839; Thomas Robbins Papers, Connecticut Historical Society.

V, "Of Man. . . ." VI, "Moral System. . . ." VII, "The Laws respecting Females. . ." in various states, drawn from various sources, portions being written by William M. Holland and Charles Chauncey. VIII, "Property. . . ." IX, "Of Government, Laws, Crimes, Trespasses, and Courts of Justice," reprinted from *The Teacher*. X, "Rules of Logic." XI, "Rhetoric, Composition, Style." XII, "Rules of Orthography." XIII, "A Specimen of Definitions." XIV, "Illustrations of Grammar" (new material, not drawn from his grammars). XV, "Chronology." XVI, "Orders of Architecture," reprinted from *The Teacher*. XVII, "Banking Institutions," reprinted in part from *The Teacher*. XVIII, "Punctuation." XIX, "Prosody—Laws of Versification," reprinted from the *Philosophical and Practical Grammar*, 1807. XX, "Explanation of Prefixes, Affixes or Suffixes, and Terminations," reprinted in part from *The Teacher*. On the last page there is a short section headed "Reflections on Closing the Author's Literary Labors."

2. Reviewed: *New Haven Record*, May 18, 1839; *Middletown* (Conn.) *Constitution*, June 12, 1839; *New Haven Palladium*, June 15, 1839. On a clipping of the last Webster has written "Note Dr Miner."

3. Webster's correspondence with William C. Fowler from February, 1839, when the book went to press, until May, when it was published, is full of references to the work, and later letters to Fowler and others often mention the problem of getting it introduced in the schools. In a letter of May 3, 1839, Webster refers to the work as in the hands of the binder.[4]

575

——— New Haven: Published by the Author. 1842.

248 pp., incl. frontis., illus. 18 cm.
CtY, MB, NBuG, NN.

NOTES

1. The contents are the same as the first edition except that the errors there noted have been corrected.

2. On p. [iv], there is a stereotype notice of Redfield and Savage, New York. On November 9, 1841, Webster wrote Redfield, "I wish to countermand, in part, my direction respecting the Stereotyping of the Manual. Some of my friends think the Manual, *as it is*, will be better than with the

[4]To Samuel Parker; Webster Papers, New York Public Library.

additional articles from the *Lessons for Youth.* You may therefore stereotype the Manual as it is . . ., but lay aside the *Lessons for Youth,* till further orders. I may hereafter make the addition."[5]

576

——— Philadelphia: Published by Jesper Harding. . . . 1846.

248 pp., incl. frontis., illus. 18 cm.
MB, MBAt, MH, NN.

[5] In the possession of Prof. Harry R. Warfel, who kindly provided a transcript.

Section Three

DICTIONARIES

GENERAL NOTE ON THE DICTIONARIES

The compiler did not collect as extensive a mass of material on the dictionaries as on Webster's other works, though she planned to include them in the bibliography. It has not seemed wise to carry the editions of the *American Dictionary* and its modifications up to the present, or to include the many other dictionaries issued by the legal successors to Webster's work and by others. These editions, with the "War of the Dictionaries" of the 1850's, are a separate study in themselves.

The death of Webster in 1843 does not mark a clear-cut dividing line, since versions prepared by him were later reprinted, and since he left unpublished revisions which were later used. The editions of the dictionaries have therefore been carried to 1847, the point at which the G. and C. Merriam Company published a complete revision of the major dictionary, made by a different hand (Chauncey A. Goodrich, one of Webster's sons-in-law), and rejecting some of Webster's more extreme views. This was not, however, the first "Merriam-Webster" dictionary, for in buying the rights from the heirs the company acquired sheets of earlier printings and certain MS revisions, and their imprint first appears on a modification of an earlier edition (Title 588).

It was Webster's custom, and that of his successors, to issue broadsides, posters, and pamphlets containing recommendations and reviews of his dictionaries. These have not been listed here; of the vast amount of newspaper advertising, only a few items bearing on the initial publication of some of the titles are included. For a discussion of foreign language dictionaries based on Webster, see the note at the end of rubric B of Part Seven below.

When Webster's *Essays* were published in 1790, Daniel George, a printer in Portland, Maine, wrote him suggesting that he compile a dictionary along the lines of his new orthography. Webster apparently replied that he had thought of such a project, but that he doubted if the public was "prepared for the reception" of a dictionary of reformed orthography, and suggested that his youth and lack of influence rendered such a project impracticable.[6]

[6]Daniel George to Webster, September 27 and November 23, 1790, Webster Papers, New York Public Library; Ford's *Notes*, Vol. I, pp. 290–292. Webster's letter has not been found, and its contents have to be deduced from George's reply.

Webster did, however, begin compilation of a dictionary. On June 4, 1800, there appeared in the *Connecticut Journal* an article beginning "Mr. Webster of this city, we understand, is engaged in completing . . . ," very possibly written by Webster himself. The article is, as far as the compiler has been able to determine, the first public announcement of Webster's dictionary project. It outlines his plans for a dictionary of the American language, with a "small Dictionary for schools, one for the counting-house, and a large one for men of science." This drew forth a series of comments in various newspapers and magazines, most of them ridiculing the project, though some supported it. The most immediate were in the *Aurora*, June 7, and the *Gazette of the United States*, June 10, the latter signed "An Enemy to Innovation." Some of the attacks dragged in Webster's political beliefs and other non-lexicographical factors. The article itself was reprinted in the *Philadelphia Gazette*, June 7, the *Commercial Advertiser*, June 9, the *Mercantile Advertiser*, June 10, the *Impartial Register*, June 12 and 19, and the *Salem* (Mass.) *Gazette*, June 13.

PART ONE: COMPENDIOUS DICTIONARY

577

A compendious dictionary of the English language. [*twenty-eight lines, summarizing contents.*] By Noah Webster, Esq. From Sidney's Press. For Hudson & Goodwin, book-sellers, Hartford, and Increase Cooke & Co. book-sellers, New-Haven. 1806.

xxiii, (1), 408 pp. 17 cm. P. [i], title-page. P. [ii], copyright notice, January 15, [1806]. Pp. [iii]–xxiii, preface, unsigned, dated New Haven, January, 1806. P. [xxiv], abbreviations and pronunciation. Pp. [1]–355, text. Pp. 356–408, tables and lists.

CL, CLU, CSmH, Ct, CtHT, CtHT-W, CtHi, CtNhHi, CtY, DFSA, DLC, IC, ICHi, ICN, MA, MB, MBAt, MH, MNF (imperfect), MWA, MWiW-C, MiDeaEd, MiU, N, NBuG, NHi, NN, NNC (imperfect), NRU, NcD, NhD, NjR, OC, OO, PHi, PU, ViU, ViW (imperfect), VtMidbC, VtU, Merriam, British Museum.

Sabin 102347.

NOTES

1. Announced as in preparation in "Literary Notices" in the *Connecticut Courant*, June 6, 1804, reprinted in the *Commercial Advertiser*, June 8, the rural edition of the *Gazette of the United States*, June 12, and the *New Haven Visitor*, June 14. Advertised as "this day . . . published," *Connecticut Herald*, February 11 and 18, 1806; *Connecticut Courant*, February 19 and later; *Spectator*, March 1; and elsewhere.

2. Reviewed: (a) *Panoplist*, May, 1806 (Vol. I, pp. 550–554). Webster felt this review was too brief, and unsatisfactory. It is mentioned in the *Connecticut Journal*, June 26, and the *Connecticut Herald*, July 1.

(b) By "C," *Albany Centinel*, July 29, 1806. This Webster countered with articles in the *Connecticut Herald*, August 12, and the *Commercial Advertiser*, August 20. This exchange was remarked upon in the *Columbian Centinel*, September 13.

(c) *Eclectic Review* (London), January, 1807 (Vol. III, pp. 82–86), generally hostile. Webster wrote a reply to this which he sent to Jedidiah Morse, editor of the *Panoplist*, who ran it in the issues of July and August, 1808 (Vol. III, pp. 78–84, 123–128). The *Eclectic Review* countered with a reply in its issue of May, 1808 (Vol. IV, pp. 469–473).

(d) There was a brief notice of the work in the *Medical Repository*, May–July, 1807 (2nd Hexade, Vol. V, p. 72).

(e) *Monthly Anthology*, October, 1809 (Vol. VII, pp. 246–264), derogatory. This journal was the organ of the Anthology Society (Boston), the members of which were hostile to Webster and all his views and works, and had discussed the dictionary frequently before publishing the review. The Society's minutes from April 11, 1806, to December 12, 1809, contain periodic references to the work; it was assigned to four or five different members before James Savage finally produced a review, which he read on October 10, 1809. This was not the review which was printed, however. The manuscript of the Savage review was lent to Webster, who replied with a long letter which was read at the meeting of December 12, 1809.[7]

3. The price was $1.50; the edition was 7,000.

4. John Quincy Adams' letter of acknowledgment of a copy of this dictionary will be found in Ford's *Notes*, Vol. II, pp. 9–12.

[7] *Anthology Society. Journal of the Proceedings*..., edited by M. A. DeWolfe Howe (Boston, 1910), pp. 71, 81, 93, 121, 193, 199, 207, 208, 216.

PART TWO: COMMON SCHOOL DICTIONARY

578

A dictionary of the English language; compiled for the use of common schools in the United States. By Noah Webster, Esq. From Sidney's Press, N. Haven. Printed for John and David West, Boston[;] Brisban and Brannan, N. York[;] Lincoln and Gleason, and Oliver D. Cooke, Hartford[;] and I. Cooke and Co. New-Haven. 1807.

v, (1), 306 pp. 16 cm. P. [i], title-page. P. [ii], copyright notice, August 14, 1807. Pp. [iii]–v, preface, unsigned and undated. P. [vi], abbreviations and pronunciation. Pp. [1]–303, text. Pp. [304]–306, chronological tables.

CT (imperfect), CTHI, CTNHHI, CTY, DLC, ICN, ICU, IU, MA, MH, MWA, MIDEAED, MIU, NN, NNC, NJR, OO, PHI, PP, PPM, RPB, Merriam.

NOTES

1. Advertised in the *Connecticut Herald*, December 15, 1807, and in the *Connecticut Journal*, February 18, 1808, and later.

2. The edition was 4,000.

3. This work is sometimes referred to as an abridgment of the *Compendious Dictionary*; that it was not is shown in the following extract from a letter from Webster to Joel Barlow, October 19, 1807:

"I have in the press an abridgement of my Complete [i.e., American] Dictionary for common schools, omitting obsolete, and technical terms, and reducing it to a dollar book. With the profits of these I hope to be able to finish my Complete Dictionary.... It will require the incessant labor of from three to five years...."[8]

[8]Ford's *Notes*, Vol. II, p. 30.

579

—— Hartford: Printed by George Goodwin & Sons. 1817.

v, (1), 366 pp. 13 cm.

CT, CTHI, CTNHHI, CTY, ICU, IU, MH, MWA, NN, VTMIDBC, Merriam.

A paragraph has been added to the preface, more words are included, and the chronological table is omitted.

PART THREE: AMERICAN DICTIONARY, UNABRIDGED

A. *Prospectuses and Preliminaries, 1806–1826*

580

Circular. To the Friends of literature in the United States: When I first contemplated. . . . Noah Webster, jun. New-Haven, February 25, 1807.

4 pp. 32 cm. P. [1], caption title and statement of Webster's plan of compiling a large dictionary. Bottom of p. [1]–4, commendations of the *Compendious Dictionary* and other works from the presidents and faculty members of various colleges—Yale, Princeton, Dartmouth, Williams, and Middlebury—and other persons. The text concludes with a notice of the publication of Volume III of the *Elements of Useful Knowledge.*

CtNhHi, MSaE, NN.

NOTES

1. This circular was discussed and summarized in the *Connecticut Courant,* March 11, 1807 (reprinted in the *Connecticut Herald,* April 14); and was reprinted in the *Commercial Advertiser,* July 31 (*Spectator,* August 5), and in *Poulson's American Daily Advertiser,* August 6. A parody of the circular, in exaggerated phonetic spelling, appeared over the anagram "hoan strewbe" in the *United States Gazette,* April 2, 1807 (and in its rural edition for April 6). This drew forth a mild reply in the issue of April 4 (April 9), which Webster, on a clipping, attributed to Hezekiah Howe. Webster himself wrote the editor on April 18,[9] but no reply to or publication of this letter has been located.

2. The text of the circular was partially reprinted in *Education of Youth* (Title 754).

[9] Webster Papers, New York Public Library.

581

To the friends of literature in the United States. Having been several years engaged.... N. Webster. New-Haven, August, 1807.

Broadside, 39 x 24 cm.
CtNhHi, CtY (Manuscript Division), NN.

NOTES

1. A subscription blank, headed with an appeal for support in the project. Webster's record of subscriptions received is printed as Appendix XXVII of Ford's *Notes*.

2. Reprinted in Warfel's *Letters of Noah Webster*, pp. 279–281.

"To the Friends of Literature," a signed article by Webster in the Panoplist, *February,* 1810 (*Vol. II, pp.* 428–431), *discussed his lexicographical labors and asked support for a major dictionary, which would probably be published in three octavo volumes "at less than twelve or fifteen dollars." The article, part of which is headed "Prospectus of a new and complete Dictionary of the English Language," was reprinted in the* Monthly Anthology, *March,* 1810 (*Vol. VIII, pp.* 207–211). *A parody, "Proposals for a New Dictionary—humbly recommended to Noah Webster, jun. esq. by Tom the Tinker, esq. Laureat...," appeared in the Raleigh, North Carolina,* Star, *November* 15, 1810.

A further "prospectus" was published as an advertisement by Sherman Converse in the Connecticut Herald, *May* 2, 1826. *The text was probably written by Webster; there are also fourteen recommendations from prominent men. This was widely reprinted—e.g., in the New York* Evening Post, *May* 16, *with an editorial note recanting the paper's censure when Webster first announced his project twenty years earlier. This prospectus may well have appeared as a separate broadside or circular, though the compiler has found no such printing.*

582

The following is a specimen of the lexicography of Webster's dictionary; but not of the type.... [New Haven? 1826?]

4 pp. 26 cm.
DLC (Madison Papers, Vol. 80, p. 27).

NOTES

1. Consists of a caption title and sample words from the dictionary, taken from A through G, mostly from C.

2. Dated 1826 by the Library of Congress.

Other announcements of the dictionary, with pleas for support, appeared in the Quarterly Christian Spectator, *May*, 1826, (*Vol. VIII, pp.* 260–261) *and August*, 1827 (*Vol. VIII, pp.* 442–443).

The two-page "Advertisement" dated New Haven, November 28, 1828, *which forms part of the preliminaries of the first edition of the dictionary may be mistaken for a separate Webster item if encountered independently.*

B. *The First Edition*

583

An American dictionary of the English language: [*twelve lines, summarizing contents.*] By Noah Webster, LL.D. In two volumes. Vol. I [II]. [*one line of quotation.*] New York: Published by S. Converse. Printed by Hezekiah Howe—New Haven. 1828.

2 vols., not paged, frontis. in Volume I. 20 cm. Collation by signatures: Volume I, [A]^4, B–K^4 (including both I and J), [1]^4, 2–113^4, 114^2; Volume II, title-page not signed, 1–115^4, 116^2. Contents: Volume I: Frontispiece, the Morse portrait of Webster, engraved by Asher B. Durand and printed by James R. Burton. P. [A]$_1^r$, title-page, with copyright notice, April 14, 1828, on verso. Pp. [A]$_2^r$–[A]$_3^r$, preface, signed and dated 1828. P. [A]$_3^v$, blank. Pp. [A]$_4^r$–G$_2^v$, introduction. Pp. G$_3^r$–K$_3^r$, "Practical and Philosophical Grammar," consisting of an "Advertisement," four pages, and text, twenty-nine pages. Pp. K$_3^v$–K$_4^r$, key to pronunciation. P. K$_4^v$, alphabets. Pp. [1]$_1^r$–114$_2^r$, text, A–I. Volume II: Title-page, with copyright notice on verso. Pp. 1$_1^r$–116$_1^v$, text, J–Z. Pp. 116$_2^{r-v}$, additions and corrections.

CL, CLU, CSt, CSmH, CU, Ct, CtHT, CtHT-W, CtHi, CtNhHi, CtY, DLC, IC, ICHi, ICN, ICU, IU, M, MA, MB, MBAt, MCM, MH, MHi, MWA, Mi, MiDeaEd, MiU, N, NBLiHi, NBuG, NN, NNC, NNS, NRU, NUt, NcU, NhD, NjHi, NjP, O, OC, OClWHi, OO,

OOxM, PHC, PP, PPAmP, PU, RPB, ViU, ViW, VtMidbS, VtU, WaU, Merriam.

Sabin 102335.

NOTES

1. A two page "Advertisement," dated November 28, 1828, is usually found either tipped or bound into Volume I. It is apparently intended to be part of the work, though it is outside the regular signaturing of the volume; it is definitely a part of the preliminaries of the English editions.

2. Reviewed: *North American Review*, April, 1829 (Vol. XXVIII, pp. 433–480) [by James L. Kingsley], published also as a separate, repaged [1]–47. *Southern Review*, May, 1830 (Vol. V, pp. 337–381). *Middlesex Gazette*, date unknown, by "T. M.," whom Webster has identified as Thomas Miner on a clipping of a reprint from an unidentified newspaper, in the Webster Papers. In England, *Westminster Review*, January, 1831, and *Quarterly Review*, September, 1835; for details see these reviews as listed under Title 589. There were occasional favorable articles about this dictionary in the *New York Mirror* in 1831 (e.g., March 26, May 14).

3. Later Webster recorded: "I finished writing my dictionary in January 1825, at my lodgings in Cambridge, England. When I had come to the last word, I was seized with a trembling, which made it somewhat difficult to hold my pen steady for writing. The cause seems to have been the thought that I might not then live to finish the work, or the thought that I was so near the end of my labors. But I summoned strength to finish the last word, & then walking about the room, a few minutes, I recovered."[1]

4. The preface, in which Webster outlines his ideas about English and American idiom, was reprinted in *Encore*, July, 1943 (Vol. IV, pp. 90–95).

5. The "Practical and Philosophical Grammar" in the preliminary pages had previously been published as a separate work, with the adjectives of the title reversed.

6. The edition was 2,500 and the price $20.00. The edition moved slowly, but on September 19, 1836, an advertisement in the New Haven *Daily Herald* announced that the edition was exhausted, and that the demand would be filled with copies of the English edition.

7. On January 11, 1827, Converse contracted with James Gates Perci-

[1]Undated memorandum (on a sheet with another dated July, 1833), Webster Papers, New York Public Library; reproduced in Ford's *Notes*, Vol. II, facing p. 293. He also made the same statement in slightly different words in a letter which has been published (to Thomas Miner, November 21, 1836—see Appendix C).

val, geologist, poet, and editor, to proofread the dictionary, but on May 3 Percival wrote a friend that the printing had not commenced because the special paper and types had not come, though they were hourly expected. On July 4 a supplemental clause to the contract provided for Percival also to go over the MS before it was printed. His letters occasionally refer to the progress of the work, which he came to find most arduous. He gave up his connection with the editing in the autumn of 1828, before publication was finished, for he and Webster did not work well together —Percival wanted such a high degree of accuracy that he took limitless time, while Webster saw the need for getting the volumes out without undue concern over minor omissions and inaccuracies. Years later, in 1843, Percival assisted William G. Webster in compiling addenda to the unabridged dictionary, and in 1847 he assisted Chauncey Goodrich in the first major revision, though again he did not see the work through.[2]

8. Daniel Barnes, who was preparing a revision of William Bearcroft's *Red Book, Practical Orthography* (York, Pa., 1824; New York, 1828), was given access to the proof sheets of this dictionary, and records (p. 347) that at the end of May, 1828, the dictionary was one half printed.

9. A pamphlet which is in part about this dictionary is Roswell Judson, *Two Epistles of Free Stricture, On the American Dictionary of Mr. Webster, on the Hebrew Grammar and Hebrew Chrestomathy of Mr. Stuart, and on the Manual Hebrew Lexicon of Mr. Gibbs*... (second edition, "revised, corrected, and enlarged," New Haven, 1830; the compiler has not located the first edition).

10. Five years after the appearance of this work the Shaker community in East Canterbury, New Hampshire, published a pamphlet of twelve pages consisting of the section on punctuation from the "Practical and Philosophical Grammar": *Rules of Punctuation from Webster's Dictionary, Quarto Edition of* 1828. Canterbury, N.H., 1833. (Copy in the Williams College Library).

C. *Prospectuses and Preliminaries for a Second Edition, 1838–1841*

A proposal to issue an octavo edition of the quarto American Dictionary *was published in the* Middletown Sentinel and Witness, *July* 27, 1838, *reprinted*

[2]Julius H. Ward: *Life and Letters of James Gates Percival* (Boston, 1866), passim (see index). The contract between Percival and Converse is printed in full on pp. 265–267.

in the New Haven Daily Herald, *July* 27, *the* Boston Recorder, *August* 10, *the* People's Press and Addison County Democrat, *September* 4, *and the* Connecticut Observer, *September* 8.

An article praising the American Dictionary *and calling attention to the fact that a new edition was in press appeared in the* New Haven Record, *March* 28, 1840, *reprinted in the* National Intelligencer, *April* 9, *the* Hartford Patriot and Democrat, *April* 18, *and the* Hartford Daily Courant, *April* 20.

584

For subscription. In February next will be published.... [New Haven? 1840.]

Broadside, 25 x 20 cm.
NN (Webster Papers).

NOTES

1. A short announcement and subscription blank. All the copies located (which have been used by Webster as scratch paper) consist of only one leaf, so the item is here described as a broadside. However, all look as if the left side had been torn; the original format was probably two leaves, printed only on the recto of the first.

2. A blank space is left for the price to be entered.

3. Undated, but doubtless issued in 1840. Probably printed in New Haven.

585

In the press, and in February next will be published.... New Haven..., Oct., 1840....

Two leaves, printed only on the recto of the first. 25 x 20 cm.
NN (Webster Papers).

The wording is substantially the same as that of the preceding item. The prices are given as $14.00 in calf, gilt, and $13.00 in sheep.

An announcement and plea for support, addressed "To the Citizens of the United States," signed by Webster, appeared in the New Haven Evening Palladium, *January* 1, 1841, *reprinted in the New Haven* Daily Herald,

January 2, *the* Boston Courier, *January* 5, *the* Connecticut Courant, *January* 16, *and probably elsewhere.*

An unsigned article headed "Webster's Lexicon" in the New Haven Daily Herald, *January* 28, 1841, *reprinted in the* Boston Courier, *February* 1, *announced that Webster had finished the proof sheets.*

D. *The Second Edition*

586

An American dictionary of the English language; first edition in octavo, [*nine lines summarizing contents.*] By Noah Webster, LL.D. [*six lines of his memberships, honors, etc.; eight lines further summarizing contents.*] In two volumes. Vol. I [II]. New Haven: Published by the author. Sold by Crocker & Brewster, Boston; F. J. Huntington & Co., New York; Thomas, Cowperthwait & Co., Philadelphia; Cushing & Brother, Baltimore; and E. Morgan & Co., Cincinnati. Printed by B. L. Hamlen. 1841.

2 vols.: frontis., lxxvi, 938; 1004 pp. 25 cm. Volume I: Frontispiece (see below). P. [i], title-page. P. [ii], copyright notice, September, 1840. P. [iii], "Advertisement." P. [iv], blank. Pp. [v]–viii, preface, signed and dated New Haven, 1840. Pp. [ix]–lxxi, introduction. Pp. lxxi–lxxiii, "English Alphabet," an explanation of pronunciation. P. lxxiv, abbreviations. Pp. lxxv–lxxvi, alphabets. Pp. [1]–938, text, A–I. Volume II: P. [1], title-page. P. [2], copyright notice, September, 1840 (see Note 7 below). Pp. [3]–984, text, J–Z. Pp. [985]–1004, addenda.

CT, CTHT, CTNHHI, CTY, DLC, ICU, IU, MBAT, MH, MNF, MWA, NN, NHD, PHI, VI, Merriam, British Museum.

NOTES

1. The frontispiece is the Morse portrait of Webster; in some copies it is engraved by James R. Burton, in others the engraver is not indicated.

2. Advertised as "now being published," New Haven *Daily Herald*, March 24, 1841; and as on sale, *Boston Recorder*, September 10 and 17, *New York Observer*, September 18, New Haven *Daily Herald*, September 27, and elsewhere.

3. This edition was in the press well over a year. On the flyleaf of a copy now in the Connecticut State Library Webster wrote, "First signature of this edition impressed Oct. 22, 1839. Last sheet impressed January 30, 1841 15 months & 8 days."

4. A letter from Chauncey A. Goodrich to Webster, July 28/29, 1839,[3] shows that Webster had originally planned to publish four or even five thousand copies, but was persuaded to reduce the edition to three thousand, in view of the bad times. This was fortunate, for the edition sold slowly, and 1,420 copies were still on hand in sheets at the time of Webster's death.[4] Although the prospectus listed above gives $13.00 and $14.00 as the prices, McKeon's and Leavitt's works refer to it as $15.00.

5. "First edition in octavo" signifies first *unabridged* octavo edition, for there had already appeared several octavo printings of the Worcester abridgment (below, Part Five, rubric B).

6. Robert K. Leavitt, *Noah's Ark, New England Yankees, and the Endless Quest* ([Springfield, Mass.], 1947), p. 36, gives "2nd Edition, Corrected and Enlarged" as part of the title, but the compiler has not found any copy with this wording. He also says that the first copies were dated 1840; the compiler has found only a Volume II with this date (see following note).

7. The New York Public Library has a working copy of this edition, interleaved and added to in manuscript by Noah and William G. Webster. Volume I has the 1841 title-page described above, and lacks the frontispiece and pp. [iii]–viii. Volume II has a variant title-page, dated 1840, the verso of which bears a copyright entry dated June, 1840, instead of September. The summary of contents is briefer, and there are no honors following Webster's name; the firm names in the imprint are the same.

E. *Later Editions*

587

——— Amherst, Mass. Published by J. S. and C. Adams. . . . 1844.

2 vols.: frontis., lxxvi, 938; 1020 pp. 27 cm.
CtNhHi, MA, MH.

[3]Ellsworth Papers, Connecticut Historical Society.

[4]Newton F. McKeon and Katharine C. Cowles, *Amherst. . . Imprints, 1825-1876* (Amherst, 1946), p. 15.

NOTES

1. The same as Title 586 through p. 984 of Volume II. At this point there is a half-title, not included in either the pagination or the signaturing, "Supplement to an American Dictionary of the English Language by Noah Webster, LL.D." On the verso is a copyright notice, 1843, to William W. Ellsworth and Henry White, executors. Pp. [985]–1020, addenda, ending with a note initialled N.W.

2. Except for the addenda, this edition is made up from unsold sheets of the 1841 edition. See Newton F. McKeon and Katharine C. Cowles, *Amherst. . . Imprints*, 1825–1876 (Amherst, 1946), pp. 15–16, for details of the edition; they reproduce as their frontispiece Adams' advertising matter which lists the work at $12.50 in sheep and $11.50 unbound.

588

——— Springfield, Mass., Published by Geo. & Chas. Merriam. . . . 1845.

2 vols.: frontis., lxxvi, 944; 1020 pp. 26 cm.

MB, MiDeaEd, NN, NNC, PPFrankI, Merriam, British Museum.

NOTES

1. The contents are the same as the preceding except that there is an addendum in Volume I, pp. [939]–944.

2. This edition too may have been made up from the sheets of the 1841 edition, for the Merriams acquired the stock when they took over the contract for publication. The title-page still says "First edition in octavo," though pages have been added to both volumes since the 1841 printing.

3. Added vendors in the imprint are Carey & Hart, Philadelphia; Mark H. Newman, New York; Little & Brown and B. B. Mussey, Boston; "and booksellers generally."

PART FOUR: DICTIONARY OF THE ENGLISH LANGUAGE

(American Dictionary, unabridged, English edition)

The first English edition of the American Dictionary, *which was reworked by the English editor, E. H. Barker, and was not merely a reprinting, appeared in twelve parts, beginning in 1830, and was published as a complete work in 1832. Since the preliminary matter in the two forms varies, they will be described separately, as far as possible.*

589

Part I. Price 9s A dictionary.... Conditions of publication.... London: Printed for Black, Young and Young.... MDCCCXXX.

Pagination varies (see below). 28 cm.
CtY, Parts I–IV only, in original wrappers.

NOTES

1. The contents of the first four parts are: Part I: Pp. [i]–xl of the introduction and the first 120 pages of the text. List of subscribers on back cover.

Part II: Pp. xli-xlvii (end) of the introduction; p. [xlviii], blank; pp. [xlix]–lxxii of the Philosophical and Practical Grammar; 128 pages of text. List of subscribers on back cover.

Part III: List of subscribers, two unnumbered pages; pp. lxxiii–lxxx (end) of the Philosophical and Practical Grammar; 152 pages of text. Excerpts from reviews on the back cover.

Part IV: Pp. [1]–2, expanded list of subscribers, dated July 31, 1830; 160 pages of text. Additional excerpts from reviews on the back cover.

2. Reviewed: Part I in the *Dublin Literary Gazette*, April 17, 1830 (No. 16, p. 251), and noted in the *Examiner*, April 25 (No. 1160, p. 265). Part II, *Dublin Literary Gazette*, May 22, 1830 (No. 21, pp. 327–

328). Parts I and II, *Gentleman's Magazine*, May, 1830 (Vol. 147, pp. 439–440). Parts I through V and the New York edition of 1828, *Westminster Review*, January, 1831 (Vol. XIV, pp. 56–93). The manuscript of a reply by Webster to the editor of the last-named, April 11, 1831, apparently unpublished, was sold at the American Art Association-Anderson Galleries, November 10, 1936 (transcript in Webster Papers).

Other reviews quoted on the wrappers of Parts III and IV but not verified by the compiler include the *Cambridge Independent Press*, April 3, 1830; *Atlas*, June 20 and 27 and July 4, 1830; and *Edinburgh Literary Journal*, date unspecified. The reference to the *Mechanics' Magazine*, April 10 and 17 [and 24], 1830, is to two letters, one of them by the English editor, in response to an editorial footnote incorrectly referring to Webster's dictionary as a revision of Dr. Johnson's.

3. E. H. Barker announced his intention of publishing this work "with all possible expedition" in the *Gentleman's Magazine*, June, 1829 (Vol. 145, p. 542). Some of his correspondence with Webster on the subject is printed in Ford's *Notes*, Vol. II, pp. 305–309, 328–330.

4. Part I, published about February 10, 1830, promises Part II on April 10; Part II promises Part III on June 1; Part III promises Part IV on August 1; and Part IV promises Part V on October 1. If this schedule was maintained, the twelfth and final part appeared about December 1, 1831.

5. The price per part was 7 shillings to subscribers and 9 to non-subscribers, or a total of £ 4/4 and £ 5/8, respectively. Subscriptions were accepted until the publication of Part III, later extended to August 1, the publication date of Part IV.

589a

A dictionary of the English language: [*fourteen lines summarizing contents.*] By Noah Webster, LL.D. New York, 1828. In two volumes. [*one line of quotation.*] Reprinted by E. H. Barker, Esq., of Thetford, Norfolk, from a copy communicated by the author, and containing many manuscript corrections and additions. Vol. I [II]. London, Published by Black, Young, and Young . . ., MDCCCXXXII.

2 vols., preliminaries only paged. 27 cm. Volume I: P. [i], title-page. P. [ii], imprint of Richard Taylor. Pp. [iii]–v, "Advertisement," signed and dated New Haven, November 28, 1828. Pp. [vi]–viii, preface, signed and dated New Haven, 1828. Pp. [ix]–xlvii, introduction. P. [xlviii],

blank. Pp. [xlix]–lxxxi, Philosophical and Practical Grammar. Pp. [lxxxii]–c, synopsis of words differently pronounced by different authorities. P. [ci], alphabets. Pp. [cii]–civ, pronunciation. Text, A–I, not paged. On the last page is Taylor's imprint; this is followed by a leaf of publisher's advertisements. Volume II: Title-page, with Taylor's imprint on verso. Text, J–Z, not paged, with Taylor's imprint on last page. Leaf of publisher's advertisements.

DAFM, DLC, ICN, MHi, MiDeaEd, MiU, NBLiHi, NN, OO, Merriam, British Museum.

NOTES

1. Reviewed in the *Quarterly Review*, September, 1835 (Vol. LIV, pp. 304–309), together with the New York, 1828, edition.

2. The preliminaries of this edition combine those of the 1828 quarto and Worcester's abridgment thereof.

3. One of the New York Public Library copies has the Hall engraving of the Morse portrait of Webster as a frontispiece in Volume I, but this appears to be an insertion.

4. A news item about the English edition appeared in the *New York Evangelist*, April 14, 1832, credited to the "National Republican"; this was probably the Cincinnati paper of that name, but the compiler has been unable to trace the article.

5. When Henry G. Bohn acquired the unsold portion of the edition in 1835, he reduced the price to £2/12/6.

6. The English publishers of Webster's dictionary projected a supplement, of which only the first two parts were issued. No general title-page appears to have been printed; the wrapper title is *Boucher's Glossary of Archaic and Provincial Words, edited by the Rev. Joseph Hunter. . .forming a Supplement to the Dictionaries of the English Language, particularly those of Dr. Johnson and Dr. Webster,. . .by the Late Rev. Jonathan Boucher. . . .* London; Printed for Black, Young and Young. . . MDCCCXXXII. Richard Taylor, Printer. . . . These two parts, which contain an introduction and the text through "Blade," were uniform in size and appearance with the parts of Webster's dictionary as issued by the same publishers.

590

——— London: Published by Henry G. Bohn. . . . MDCCCXL.

2 vols., preliminaries only paged. 27 cm.
NN.

American Dictionary, English Edition

The contents are identical with the preceding, page for page, with the following exceptions: the Taylor imprint is omitted from the verso of the title-page of Volume I (though it is present on that of Volume II, and on the final text page of each volume); the added leaf of Black, Young and Young advertisements is not found in Volume II.

PART FIVE: AMERICAN DICTIONARY, ABRIDGED

Although it appeared many years earlier, the Common School Dictionary *of* 1807 *was referred to by Webster as an abridgment of this work; see the letter quoted under Title* 578.

A. *Webster's Abridgment*

591

[A dictionary of the English language. . . . New Haven, Hezekiah Howe, 1829.]

Ford's *Notes*, Vol. II, p. 537, locates a copy in The New York Public Library. None with such an imprint is to be found there, but there is a copy lacking a title-page, catalogued as 1829, which may be the edition meant. The fact that the copyright was taken out in May, 1829, suggests that the book was first published in that year, though the preface is not dated until December.

The contents of this copy agree with those of the following entry from pages [i] to 512 except that between vi and [7] there are four intrusive pages, numbered [i]–iv, consisting of advertising for and commendations of Webster's "Series of Books." The tables begin on p. 513 and break off at p. 532, the last page present in this copy. The last signature calls for one more leaf; perhaps this edition ran to p. 533, like Title 593, but did not include pp. 534–536 of that edition.

592

A dictionary of the English language; abridged from The American dictionary, for the use of primary schools and the counting house.

American Dictionary, Abridged

By Noah Webster, LL.D. New-York: White, Gallaher, & White . . ., Sold also by Webster and Skinner, Albany; Richardson, Lord, and Holbrook, Boston; Kimber and Sharpless, and Towar and Hogan, Philadelphia; Cushing and Sons, Baltimore; D. F. Robinson and Co. Hartford; O. Steele, Albany; Steele and Faxon, Buffalo; Hogan and Co. Pittsburg [sic]; J. [sic, for I.] N. Whiting, Columbus O. Stereotyped at E. White's Type and Stereotype Foundery. 1830.

(4) or (8), 532 pp. 14 cm. 1st unnumbered page, title-page. 2nd, copyright notice, May 22, 1829. (3rd–5th, commendations for the *American Dictionary*. 6th, blank.) 7th, "Key." 8th, blank. Pp. [i]–iv, preface, unsigned, dated New Haven, December, 1829. Pp. [v]–vi, directions and abbreviations. Pp. [7]–511, text, with additions at the bottom of 511. P. [512], blank. Pp. 513–532, tables.

DLC, MWA, MiDeaEd.

Not all copies have the two leaves containing commendations.

592a

—— New-York: White, Gallaher, & White. . ., Sold also by Webster and Skinner, Albany; Richardson, Lord, and Holbrook, Boston; Holbrook and Fessenden, Brattleborough; Kimber and Sharpless, Philadelphia; Cushing and Sons, Baltimore. Stereotyped at E. White's Type and Stereotype Foundery. 1830.

MWA.

593

[Title-page identical with 592a.]

(8) or (12), 536 pp. 14 cm.

Ct, MWA, NN.

The same as the preceding except that the tables run onto p. 533 and there are three added pages (534–536) containing advertising for Webster's "Series of Books." The Connecticut State Library copy has, between p. vi and p. [7], the four intrusive pages described under Title 591.

594

——— New-York: Published by White, Gallaher, & White..., Stereotyped at E. White's...Foundery. 1831.

(8), 532 pp. 14 cm.
CL, CtNhHi, DLC, MH, MiDeaEd, NN, Merriam.

595

——— New York: Published by N. and J. White.... Stereotyped at E. White's...Foundery. 1832.

(8), 524 [i.e., 536] pp. 14 cm.
MH.

The copy located is slightly different in content from other editions, and has a discrepancy in its pagination. It follows the description of Title 592 through p. 511. Pp. 512–524 are foreign words and phrases, and then the pagination repeats 513–524, which are the tables.

596

——— Ninth edition. New-York: Published by N. and J. White,... Stereotyped at E. White's...Foundery. 1832.

(4), 536 pp. 14 cm.
CtY (imperfect), MiDeaEd, NhD, RPB, Merriam.

The contents are similar to the preceding printings, though there are fewer preliminary pages. The Key is on the verso of the title-page with the copyright notice, and the recommendations occupy only two pages. Pp. 512–524 are foreign words and phrases, and pp. 525–536 are tables.

597

——— Tenth edition. New-York, Published by N. and J. White,... Stereotyped at E. White's...Foundery. 1832.

(4), 536 pp. 14 cm.
CtY, Nh, OO.

598

——— Eleventh edition. New-York: Published by N. & J. White, ...Stereotyped at E. White's...Foundery. 1833.

(4), 536 pp. 14 cm.
CtY, MB, MH, MiDeaEd, MiU, NN, NNC-T, Merriam.

599

——— Thirteenth edition. New-York: Published by N. & J. White,... Stereotyped at E. White's...Foundery 1833.

(4), 536 pp. 14 cm.
MWA, NNU-W, Merriam.

600

——— Seventeenth edition. New-York, Published by N. and J. White,... Stereotyped at E. White's...Foundery. 1835.

(4), 536 pp. 14 cm.
MiDeaEd.

601

——— Nineteenth edition. New-York: Published by N. & J. White,... Stereotyped at E. White's...Foundery 1836.

(4), 536 pp. 14 cm.
DLC.
In the copy located the title-page is a little shorter than the rest of the pages, and may be an insertion, since this is a copyright deposit copy.

Correspondence between N. and J. White and Webster in March and April, 1837,[5] *shows that during that period the Whites were negotiating with Francis J. Huntington of Hartford (who was setting up a New York office) for him to take over the rights to this abridgment and the* Dictionary for Pri-

[5]N. and J. White to Webster, March 30 and April 6, 1837, Ellsworth Papers, Connecticut Historical Society.

mary Schools; *when Webster approved, the transfer was effected. At the same time the Whites surrendered to William G. Webster their rights to the spelling book west of the Alleghenies.*

Note that after the Huntington firm took over this dictionary almost all printings continue to repeat "nineteenth edition." For possible printings in 1837, 1838, *and* 1841, *see the note on Martinson & Co., below, page* 257.

602

—— Nineteenth edition. New-York: Published by F. J. Huntington & Co.... Stereotyped at E. White's... Foundery 1839.

(4), 536 pp. 15 cm.
MiDeaEd, NjP.

603

—— Nineteenth edition. New-York: Published by F. J. Huntington & Co.... Stereotyped at E. White's... Foundery 1840.

(4), 536 pp. 13 cm.
DLC.

604

—— Nineteenth edition. New-York: Published by F. J. Huntington & Co.... Stereotyped at E. White's... Foundery 1842.

(4), 536 pp. 14 cm.
DLC.

605

—— Nineteenth edition. New-York: Huntington and Savage..., Stereotyped at E. White's... Foundery 1843.

(4), 536 pp. 14 cm.
IU, MWA, NHi, Merriam.

606

—— New-York: Huntington & Savage.... 1845.

(4), 536 pp. 15 cm.
MH.

B. *Worcester's Abridgment*

607

S. Converse proposes to publish by subscription an abridgment... by J. E. Worcester.... New York, April, 1829.

Broadside, 32 x 18 cm. (trimmed).

CtY (Yale Manuscripts).

The copy located is trimmed and bound into a small volume, with blank pages for signatures, of which there are fifty-five, headed by B. Silliman.

608

An American dictionary of the English language... abridged from the quarto edition... and Walker's Key to the pronunciation of Greek, Latin, and Scripture proper names. New York, Published by S. Converse, stereotyped at the Boston Type and Stereotype Foundry. 1829.

xxiii, (1), 1011 pp. 24 cm. P. [i], title-page. P. [ii], copyright notice, July 10, [1829] in the Connecticut District, and July 13, 1829, in the Massachusetts District, to Webster and Worcester. Pp. [iii]–v, preface, dated New Haven, June 1, 1829. P. [vi], blank. Pp. [vii]–xxiii, "Synopsis of words differently pronounced by different orthoëpists." P. [xxiv], explanation of the "pointed letters" (diacritical marks) and abbreviations. Pp. [1]–940, text. P. [941], separate title-page for Walker's *Key*, dated 1829. P. [942], blank. Pp. 943-1011, Walker's text, with its own preface, introduction, etc.

CtY, ICN, MB, MH, MiDeaEd, MiU, NjR, Merriam.

NOTES

1. Some copies (e.g., Harvard) have the text ending with Z on p. 940; others, no doubt later, have additions printed in the blank portion of that page.

2. In order to have on the market a lower priced dictionary than the unabridged *American*, Webster engaged Joseph E. Worcester to make this abridgment, which sold for $6.00.

609

—— Second edition. New York: Published by S. Converse, for John P. Ayres. 1830.

xxiii, (1), 1011 pp. 25 cm.
MiU.

NOTES

1. Not seen; data provided by library.
2. The Walker title-page retains the 1829 date in the 1830 editions.

610

—— Third edition. New York: Published by S. Converse. Stereotyped at the Boston Type and Stereotype Foundry. 1830.

xxiii, (1), 1011 pp. 25 cm.
CtY, DLC, MH, MiDeaEd, PP.

611

—— Fourth edition. New York: Published by S. Converse. Stereotyped at the Boston Type and Stereotype Foundry. 1830.

xxiii, (1), 1011 pp. 25 cm.
MH, N, NBuG.
The University of Michigan has a printing which agrees with this in edition statement, collation, and date of the Walker title-page, but the date in the imprint is 1832, not 1830.

612

—— Fifth edition. New York: Published by S. Converse. Stereotyped at the Boston Type and Stereotype Foundry. 1830.

xxiii, (1), 1011 pp. 24 cm.
MA, NN, ViU, ViW, British Museum.

613

—— Sixth edition. New York: Published by S. Converse. Stereotyped at the Boston Type and Stereotype Foundry. 1830.

xxiii, (1), 1011 pp. 24 cm.
MWA, MIDEAED (imperfect), OCLWHI.

614

—— Seventh edition. New York: Published by S. Converse. Stereotyped at the Boston Type and Stereotype Foundry. 1831.

xxiii, (1), 1011 pp. 25 cm.
MIU.

NOTES

1. Not seen; data provided by library.
2. The Walker title-page is still dated 1829.

No eighth edition has yet been found. It is possible that the University of Michigan copy of Title 611, which is dated 1832, fills this gap.

615

—— Ninth edition. New York: Published by S. Converse, for White, Gallaher and White.... 1832.

xxiii, (1), 1011 pp. 25 cm.
MWA.

NOTES

1. The Walker title-page is dated 1831 in the 1832 editions.
2. From this point, the stereotype notice of the Boston Foundry is found on the verso of the title-page.

616

—— Tenth edition. New York: Published by S. Converse, for White, Gallaher and White.... 1832.

xxiii, (1), 1011 pp. 25 cm.
MH.

617

—— Eleventh edition. New York: Published by N. and J. White ..., 1834.

xxiii, (1), 1011 pp. 25 cm.
NNU, NJR (imperfect).
The Walker title-page is dated 1834 in the 1834 editions.

618

—— Thirteenth edition. New York: Published by N. and J. White..., 1834.

xxiii, (1), 1011 pp. 24 cm.
DLC, MH, NBuHi, NN, Merriam.

619

[—— Fourteenth edition. New York: N. and J. White, 1835.]

A copy is recorded in the card catalogue of the G. and C. Merriam Company, but they were unable to locate the volume when the editor was verifying the dictionaries.

620

—— Fifteenth edition. New York: Published by N. and J. White.... 1835.

xxiii, (1), 1011 pp. 24 cm.
MWA, MiU.

From this point, except as noted, all editions are numbered fifteenth, and the Walker title-page date agrees with that of the main title-page.

621

—— Fifteenth edition. New York: Published by N. and J. White..., 1836. E. Sanderson, printer.

xxiii, (1), 1011 pp. 24 cm.
DLC, MH, MWA, MiDeaEd, NN, OO, RPB, Merriam.
In the New York Public Library copy the Walker title-page is dated 1835.

622

——— Fifteenth edition. New York: Published by N. and J. White, Printed by E. Sanderson, Elizabethtown, N.J. 1837.

xxiii, (1), 1011 pp. 24 cm.
C-S, CtY (imperfect), MiDeaEd (imperfect), OClW.
In the Sutro and Yale copies the Walker title-page is dated 1835, but in the Henry Ford Museum and Western Reserve copies it is dated 1837.

623

——— Fifteenth edition. New York: Published by N. and J. White. Printed by E. Sanderson, Elizabethtown, N. J. 1838.

xxiii, (1), 1011 pp. 24 cm.
CtHT-W, DLC, IU, MH, MiDeaEd, MiU, NHi, NN, ViU, Merriam.

624

——— Stereotype edition. New York: Published by N. & J. White. Printed by E. Sanderson, Elizabethtown, N.J. 1839.

xxiii, (1), 1011 pp. 24 cm.
MH, MiDeaEd, MiU, N, NNU, Merriam.

624a

——— Stereotype edition. New York: Published by White & Sheffield. Printed by E. Sanderson, Elizabethtown, N.J. 1839.

DLC, MB, MiDeaEd, PHi, Merriam.

625

[—— Stereotype edition. New York: Published by N. & J. White. Printed by E. Sanderson, Elizabethtown, N.J. 1841.]

[xxiii, (1), 1011 pp. approx. 24 cm.]
Entry made from catalogue card at Harvard, by analogy with other editions of the same firm; the Harvard copy, the only one located by the compiler, was discarded as waste paper in 1954.

C. *Worcester's Abridgment, Revised*

626

An American dictionary..., abridged from the quarto edition.... Revised edition; with an appendix.... New York: Published by White & Sheffield. Printed by E. Sanderson, Elizabethtown, N.J. 1841.

xxiii, (1), 1079, (1) pp. 24 cm.
CtH, CtHT-W, MH, MWA, MiDeaEd, NBuG, Merriam.

NOTES

1. The contents are similar to the earlier editions except as follows: P. [ii], added copyright notice, 1841, for the appendix, in Webster's name; no stereotype notice. P. [vi], added "Preface to the Revised Edition," dated New Haven, July 1, 1841. Pp. [941]–1008, "Appendix" (i.e., addenda). The Walker portion is now paged [1009]–1079. P. [1080] contains an advertisement for the unabridged dictionary, second edition.

2. Although the Walker portion of the volume has been repaged, its table of contents was not altered, and so is not correct.

627

—— New-York: Published by White & Sheffield. Printed by E. Sanderson, Elizabethtown, N.J. 1842.

xxiii, (1), 1079, (1) pp. 25 cm.
CtY, ICU, MWA, MiDeaEd, NN.

628

—— New-York: Published by White & Sheffield. Printed by E. Sanderson, Elizabethtown, N.J. 1843.

xxiii, (1), 1079, (1) pp. 25 cm.
MA.
Not seen; data provided by library.

629

—— New-York: Published by Harper & Brothers..., 1843.

xxiii, (1), 1079, (1) pp. 25 cm.
Ct, MH, MWA, MiDeaEd, NNU, Merriam.

630

—— New-York: Published by Harper & Brothers..., 1844.

xxiii, (1), 1079, (1) pp. 25 cm.
CU, CtNhHi, CtY, MB, MH, MiDeaEd, N, NN, OClWHi, OO, Merriam.

631

—— New-York: Published by Harper & Brothers..., 1845.

xxiii, (1), 1079, (1) pp. 25 cm.
IU, MB, MiDeaEd, NNC, Merriam.

632

—— New-York: Published by Harper & Brothers..., 1846.

xxiii, (1), 1079, (1) pp. 24 cm.
MB, MH, MWA, MiDeaEd, N, NN, Vi, Merriam.

Editions of this abridgment continued to appear after the terminal date of the present list.

PART SIX: PRIMARY SCHOOL DICTIONARY

633

A dictionary for primary schools.... New York: Published by N. and J. White.... New Haven: Durrie & Peck. Stereotyped by A. Chandler, New York. 1833.

341, (3) pp. 13 cm. P. [i], title-page. P. [ii], copyright notice, 1833. Pp. [iii]-vi, rules for spelling, directions, abbreviations, key. Pp. [7]-341, text. The verso of 341 is blank, and there is a flyleaf with recommendations for the work on both sides.

CSmH, CtNhHi, DLC, ICN, IU, MA, MH, MWA, MiDeaEd, MnU.

The Huntington Library copy belonged to Abraham Lincoln.

634

——— New York: Published by N. & J. White.... New Haven: Durrie & Peck. Stereotyped by A. Chandler, New York. 1834.

341, (3) pp. 13 cm.

CtNhHi, CtY, MH, MWA, MiDeaEd, NN.

P. [ii] has, in addition to the copyright notice, a short recommendation, and in some copies the imprint, "Jas. Van Norden, Printer, 49 William-street." In the New York Public Library copy the first signature was wrongly imposed, so that p. vi is on the verso of [iii] and p. iv on the verso of v.

635

——— New York: Published by N. & J. White.... New Haven: Durrie & Peck. Stereotyped by A. Chandler, New York. 1835.

341, (3) pp. 13 cm.
IU, MiDeaEd, NN, NhD.
Has the recommendation on p. [ii], which appears to be normal from this edition on.

636

——— New York: Published by N. & J. White. . . . Stereotyped by A. Chandler. . . . 1836.

341, (3) pp. 13 cm.
MWA, OO, Merriam.

637

——— New York: Published by N. & J. White. Printed by E. Sanderson, Elizabethtown, N.J. 1837.

341, (3) pp. 13 cm.
MH, MiDeaEd.

638

——— New-York: Published by F. J. Huntington and Co. . . . 1838.

341, (3) pp. 14 cm.
CtHt-W, CtNhHi, MWA, MiDeaEd, NN, Merriam.

NOTES

1. For the transfer of this dictionary from N. and J. White to F. J. Huntington, see the general notc on p. 247 above.
2. This printing does not have the recommendation on p. [ii].
3. On p. [ii] is the imprint of "Martinson & Co., Printers," of Hartford.

Although the imprint of Martinson and Company does not appear in all subsequent printings of this dictionary, the firm seems to have done a good deal of work for F. J. Huntington. In the Ellsworth Papers, Connecticut Historical Society, there is a sheet listing editions printed by Martinson, sometimes as many as seven printings in a year. Those headed "Small letter" total 19,500 *for* 1838, 20,000 *for* 1839, 3,500 *for* 1840, 23,000 *for* 1841, 10,000 *for*

1842, *and* 20,000 *for* 1843. *This heading probably designates this dictionary. There is another column headed "Large letter," in which the totals are* 2,000 *for* 1837, 4,000 *for* 1838, 3,000 *for* 1840, 2,000 *for* 1841, 2,500 *for* 1842, *and* 2,000 *for* 1843. *Since this document is an accounting with the Huntington firm, it seems probable that "Large letter" refers to the other dictionary he was publishing, Webster's abridgment (rubric A of this part).*

There are also listed on the same sheet under "Large letter" for 1843 5,000 *"Case"; and under "Small letter," "Some printed by Case Tiffany & [Co.] about April* 1841 *I believe* 5000." *This was also a Hartford firm; it is still in existence, but has no surviving records from this period.*

639

——— New-York: Published by F. J. Huntington and Co.... 1839.

341, (3) pp. 13 cm.

CtY, MH, MNF, MWA, MiDeaEd, N, NN, NNC-T, NNU-W, Merriam.

Some copies follow the previous arrangement of a blank verso on p. 341, with advertising on both sides of an unpaged leaf; others have the advertising on the verso of 341 and the recto of the next leaf, its verso being blank. From this point both variants occur.

640

——— New-York: Published by F. J. Huntington and Co.... 1841.

341, (3) pp. 13 cm.

CtNhHi, CtY, MiDeaEd, N, Merriam.

641

——— New-York: Published by F. J. Huntington and Co.... 1842.

341, (3) pp. 13 cm.

MWA, MiDeaEd, NN, Merriam.

642

——— New-York: Huntington and Savage.... 1843.

341, (3) pp. 13 cm.
CT, CTY, DLC, MWA, MIDEAED, Merriam.

643

——— New-York: Huntington and Savage.... 1844.

341, (3) pp. 13 cm.
Merriam.

644

——— New-York: Huntington and Savage.... [1845?]

341, (3) pp. 13 cm.
CTHT-W, CTHI, CTNHHI, CTY, DFSA, MH, MWA, MIDEAED, NN, NNC, NJR, Merriam.

NOTES

1. Some copies have the recommendation added on p. [ii], others do not.

2. There is no date in this printing other than the 1833 copyright entry, and this is the year under which some libraries catalogue it. In Ford's *Notes* (Vol. II, p. 540) the date 1835 is supplied, but without any evidence being given. The firm name of Huntington and Savage does not appear in New York city directories until 1842/43, and the earliest dated imprint of the firm in the present bibliography is 1843. Since the firm issued dated printings in 1843 and 1844, it is suggested that this one appeared about 1845.

PART SEVEN: RELATED DICTIONARIES AND POSTHUMOUS ABRIDGMENTS

A. *The Elementary Dictionary*

Although this work was issued after Webster's death, it is entered because it is connected with his speller and because it appeared so soon after his death that it was almost certainly based on his own lexicographical work rather than on that of his successors.

645

An elementary dictionary; containing a selection of the most useful words in the English language; being a sequel to Webster's Elementary spelling book. By William G. Webster, son of the late Noah Webster, LL.D. New York: Published by George F. Cooledge & Brother.... [1844?]

(6), 168 pp. 18 cm. (See below for preliminary matter). P. [1], title-page. P. [2], copyright notice to the Cooledges, 1844, and "Stereotyped by Redfield and Savage..., New York." Pp. [3]–4, preface, initialled W.G.W. and dated New York, July, 1844. Pp. [5]–6, "Key." Pp. [7]–168, text.

CtNhHi, NN.

NOTES

1. The signaturing calls for four leaves before the title-page. The recto of the first is the paste-down to the front cover. On its verso and the recto of the second is an essay, "National Language," about Webster's works on the English language. On the verso of the second leaf and the recto of the third are commendations for the speller and the dictionaries. On the verso of the third and recto of the fourth is advertising matter for the "Pictorial Edition" of the *Elementary Spelling Book*, with specimen illustrations. The verso of the fourth leaf is blank. In the New York Public

Library copy these preliminary leaves have been disarranged in rebinding.

2. In addition to being the copyright date, 1844 seems the most likely year of publication, since advertising matter refers to a work to be published January 1, 1845.

646

—— Second edition of ten thousand. New York: Published by George F. Cooledge & Brother.... [1844?]

(7), 168 pp. 18 cm.
CtHT-W, Merriam.

NOTES

1. The verso of the fourth preliminary leaf has Cooledge advertising matter for Pierpont's reader.

2. The cover title is "A Sequel to Webster's Elementary Spelling Book; or a Speller and Definer; containing a Selection of 12,000 of the Most Useful Words in the English Language. With their Definitions; intended to be used as a Spelling Book and a Dictionary." This becomes the wording of the title-page in later editions, of which the compiler has located many, including a fortieth, seventieth, eightieth, one hundredth, three hundredth (and third hundred), fourth hundredth, fifth hundredth, and sixth hundred thousand, published in New York, Philadelphia, and Louisville, all without imprint date. The third edition, "revised and greatly improved," with a Louisville (Morton and Griswold) and New York (Cooledge and Brother) imprint has the 1844 copyright date but a July, 1845, date in the preface. The same with only a New York imprint (Cooledge and Brothers—note the change to the plural) has both dated 1845. (Copies of the former are to be found in the Federal Security Agency and Indiana State Libraries, and of the latter in the New Haven Colony Historical Society.)

B. *Hawaiian Translation*

647

He hoakakaolelo no na huaolelo Beritania, i mea kokua i na kanaka Hawaii e ao ana ia olelo. Lahainaluna: Mea pai palapala o ke Kulanui. 1845.

x, 184 pp. 23 cm. P. [i], title-page. P. [ii], blank. Pp. [iii]–iv, preface, in English, signed J[ohn] S. Emerson, dated Seminary, Lahainaluna, August, 1845. Pp. iv–x, preliminaries, in Hawaiian. Pp. [1]–184, English-Hawaiian vocabulary.

CSmH, NN, NhD.

The preface states that "the present is mainly a translation of Webster's Abridgement still more abridged. . . ."

The above work is entered because it states specifically that it is translated from Webster. No attempt has been made to list dictionaries of European languages which are based in part on Webster's work, even though they may bear his name on the title-page, such as T. S. Williams' [German-] English Dictionary. . . principally extracted from. . . Webster and Johnson *(Hamburg, 1833) and Alexander Spiers'* General English and French Dictionary, newly composed from. . . Johnson, Webster. . . *(London, 1846), copies of both of which are in the British Museum.*

c. *Abridgments Published by Huntington and Savage*[6]

648

A dictionary of the English language: abridged from The American dictionary. Revised edition, [*eight lines summarizing contents.*] With a memoir of the author. New-York: Published by Huntington and Savage. . . . MDCCXLV.

(4), frontis., xvi, (1), [9]–556 pp. 21 cm. Two unpaged leaves with publisher's advertisements. Frontispiece, an engraving of the Ives bust of Webster. P. [i], title-page. P. [ii], copyright notice, 1845, to William W. Ellsworth and Henry White, executors; stereotype notice of Richard H. Hobbs, Hartford; and imprint of C. A. Alvord, New York. Pp. [iii]–iv, preface, unsigned, dated Amherst, October, 1845. Pp. [v]–x, memoir

[6]The Connecticut Historical Society has (Ellsworth Papers, Box 456) a copy of the printed contract between the executors of Noah Webster and Huntington and Savage, April 25, 1844, for publishing the "University" and "Pocket" editions hereunder described. The contract does not name the individual who was to make the abridgments, citing merely "a competent person or persons." At dates beyond the scope of the present list this firm issued further printings of these, as well as other versions of Webster dictionaries.

of Webster, unsigned (see below). Pp. [xi]–xvi, rules of pronunciation. P. [xvii], diacritical marks and abbreviations. P. [xviii], blank. Pp. [9]–483, text. P. [484], blank. Pp. [485]–534, lists of proper names. Pp. [535]–538, lists of variations from Walker's pronunciation. Pp. [539]–556, tables of coinages, weights, and measures.

CtY, MH.

NOTES

1. At head of title: "University edition."

2. According to Allibone, the abridgment was made by William G. Webster, but the editor may have been William C. Fowler, who had a strong connection with the work. The Yale copy belonged to him, and he stamped his name at the foot of the preface, suggesting his authorship of it, a suggestion strengthened by the Amherst dateline, Fowler being an Amherst College professor. In his *Elementary Grammar* (New York, 1859) Fowler says that he "superintended" the publication of this dictionary; and the unsigned memoir is attributed to him by Professor Warfel (*Noah Webster*, p. 443).

649

——— New-York: Published by Huntington and Savage.... MDCCCXLVI.

Frontis., 556 pp. 20 cm.

DLC, OC.

At head of title: "University edition."

650

A pocket dictionary of the English language: abridged from the American dictionary of Noah Webster, LL.D. [*two lines summarizing added matter.*] William G. Webster, editor. New-York: Huntington and Savage. 1846.

249 *or* 249, (3) pp. 14 cm. P. [i], title-page. P. [ii], copyright notice, 1846, to William W. Ellsworth and Henry White, executors; stereotype notice of Richard H. Hobbs, Hartford; imprint of C. A. Alvord, New York. Pp. [iii]–iv, "Advertisement," initialled W.G.W., dated Septem-

ber, 1846. Pp. [5]–6, rules for pronunciation. Pp. [7]–16, Latin and French proverbs, words, and phrases, United States mottoes. P. [17], pronunciation and abbreviations. P. [18], blank. Pp. [19]–249, text. In some copies the verso of p. 249 and an unpaged leaf contain publisher's advertisements.

CtHT-W, DLC (imperfect), MiDeaEd, NN. Merriam.

Section Four

PHILOLOGICAL, DIDACTIC, AND RELIGIOUS WORKS

PART ONE: DISSERTATIONS ON THE ENGLISH LANGUAGE

651

Dissertations on the English language: with notes, historical and critical. To which is added, by way of appendix, an essay on a reformed mode of spelling, with Dr. Franklin's arguments on that subject. By Noah Webster, Jun. Esquire. *Prima discentium elementa, in quibus et ipsis parum elaboratur.* TACITUS. Printed at Boston, for the author, by Isaiah Thomas and Company, MDCCLXXXIX.

410 pp. 21 cm. P. [i], title-page. P. [ii], blank. Pp. [iii]–vi, dedication to Benjamin Franklin, dated Hartford, May, 1789. Pp. [vii]–xiii, preface, unsigned and undated, discussing grammar and its teaching and the genesis of the present volume. Pp. [xiv]–xv, table of contents. P. [xvi], "Directions," explanation of diacritical marks. Pp. [17]–410, text, consisting of four numbered "dissertations," "Notes, Historical and Critical" (pp. [313]–390), and an appendix, "An Essay on the Necessity...of Reforming the Mode of Spelling..." (pp. [391]–410).

CLU-C, CSmH, CU, Ct, CtHT-W (fragment), CtHi, CtY, DFo, DLC, IC, ICN, IU, MA, MB, MBAt, MH, MHi, MSaE, MWA, MWiW-C, MdBE, MiDeaEd, MiU, N, NBuG, NHi, NN, NNC, NNS, NRU, NcD, NcU, NhD, NjP, NjR, OC, OU, PHi, PPAmP, RPB, RPJCB, ViU, VtMidbC, Merriam, British Museum.

Evans 22259, Sabin 102348.

NOTES

1. Webster planned as early as 1786 to publish his lectures on language, for on January 7 of that year he copyrighted in Maryland the title "Letters Critical and Practical on the English Language,"[7] and on May 24 he wrote to Benjamin Franklin enclosing a plan for a reformed alphabet

[7]Liber T.B.H., No. 1, folio 532, Maryland Record Office.

and asking permission to "inscribe my lectures to your Excellency, when I publish them, as it is probable I may do within a few months."[8] On July 29 Timothy Pickering urged on Webster speedy publication of his lectures, but suggested that they "be free from any comparison which the most prejudiced may deem invidious. Multitudes in the states southward of N. England are too proud and conceited to admit or think that they can receive instruction from that quarter."[9] In reply to this (August 10) Webster said that the work would probably be ready for the press during the next winter, but not until after he had visited Dr. Franklin, who wanted to discuss the subject of reformed spelling. He spoke of the good quality paper he wished to have made for the book, and added, "I propose to print 1500 copies, large Octavo, and it will make, probably 400 pages."[1]

Preparation of the book, however, was postponed until 1788. Late in that year Webster went from New York to Boston to supervise the publication, and the early months of 1789 are filled with letters referring to the progress of the work. On January 31 he wrote Mason F. Cogswell, "The book goes on, & about the month of May, you will see a large volume, well printed, full of criticisms, which some will call good sense & others, nonsense. People... will say, I have a wonderful knack at finding faults, where they before found beauties. I shall assert some strange things; some of them will be proved; and others, the world will say, are left unsupported. ...a host of adversaries, whose favorite authors I attack, will kick and flounce, till they fall themselves or throw me. Apropos: Some Great Men, with whose works I have taken liberties, stand with their mouths open, ready to devour the child as soon as it is born. But an author's brats are doomed to be the sport of a mad world; I have treated others as I thought they deserved; and probably mine will fare as well...."[2] The next day he wrote to James Greenleaf, a future brother-in-law, "I am correcting my book, which is now in the press, & will be finished in April or May.... If this work should sell well, it will help me—if not, it will be a further embarrassment. But I have done with making books...."[3]

Apparently, though, the contents were not completely fixed as late as March, for on the 15th of that month Webster wrote to Isaiah Thomas that his friends had dissuaded him from including essays on political

[8]American Philosophical Society; Ford's *Notes*, Vol. II, pp. 455–456.

[9]Pierpont Morgan Library; Ford's *Notes*, Vol. I, p. 117.

[1]Pickering Papers, Massachusetts Historical Society; the Society's *Proceedings*, Vol. 43, pp. 130–131; Ford's *Notes*, Vol. I, p. 163, n. 2.

[2]Jones Library, Amherst.

[3]Historical Society of Pennsylvania; Ford's *Notes*, Vol. II, pp. 407–409.

topics, and since the volume would run to 400 pages without them, "I have therefore called in the proposals that were sent out, & confine myself to the original limits of the volume. I would print another volume (about 500 copies) of Miscellaneous papers, but I dare not engage cash. So that unless you will contract for the Institute & pay in printing, I shall stop at one volume.[4] If you will take the Institute (First part)...& let the printing of the present volume be considered as part payment, I will either take the printing of another volume, or the books themselves in sheets @ 15/ for the remainder."[5] Thomas does not seem to have made such an arrangement, for in Webster's accounts for May, 1789, we find "By Printing 900 Dissertations and paper for the same... £148.17."

Copies were sent to both Washington and Franklin. The former acknowledged his on January 10, 1790: "The Book, entitled Dissertations on the English Language, which you was [sic] so polite as to send me on the 4th of December, has reached my hands: And your acceptance of my best thanks for this mark of attention will oblige...."[6] Franklin wrote on December 26, 1789: "I received some time since your 'Dissertations....' The Book was not accompanied by any Letter or Message, informing me to whom I am obliged for it; but I suppose it to be yourself. It is an excellent work, and will be very useful in turning the thoughts of our Country men to correct Writing. Please to accept my Thanks for it as well as for the great Honor you have done me, in its Dedication."[7] Webster printed Franklin's letter in the *American Mercury*, May 10 and 17, 1790, and it was reprinted in the *Massachusetts Spy* of July 23.

Despite Franklin's warm approval, the work—the price of which was ten shillings—did not sell well. On December 18, 1791, Webster admitted in a letter to Timothy Pickering that part of the edition might have to be sold as paper,[8] though in June, 1793, his hopes were raised by the news that the book was to be adopted as a text at Yale.[9]

2. A facsimile reprint of this work, with an introduction by Harry R. Warfel, was published in 1951 (Gainesville, Florida, Scholars' Facsimiles and Reprints), and portions of it have been reprinted as follows:

(a) Dedication. In part in Appendix XIII of Ford's *Notes.*

[4]However, he published—by subscription—his *Essays* in 1790.

[5]American Antiquarian Society.

[6]Presidential Papers, New York Public Library.

[7]Franklin Personal Papers, New York Public Library; Ford's *Notes*, Vol. II, p. 467.

[8]Pickering Papers, Massachusetts Historical Society; the Society's *Proceedings*, Vol. 43, pp. 134–135; Ford's *Notes*, Vol. I, pp. 308–309.

[9]Webster to James Greenleaf, June 22, 1793, Historical Society of Pennsylvania; Ford's *Notes*, Vol. II, pp. 423–425.

(b) Dissertation I. An excerpt in the *American Mercury*, June 8, 1789, and in the *Massachusetts Centinel*, July 18, 1789.

(c) Dissertation III. An excerpt in the *Gazette of the United States*, November 10, 13, 17, 20, and 27, 1790.

(d) Dissertation IV. Reprinted in part[1] in *An Explanatory Treatise on the Subjunctive Mode, being the Substance of Mr. Noah Webster's Fourth Dissertation on the English Language, With Numerous Additions, and Introductory Remarks*..., by H. J. H.... London, 1834.

(e) "Notes, Historical and Critical." Excerpt (consisting of the comments on Edward Gibbon) in the *Massachusetts Magazine*, July and August, 1789 (Vol. I, pp. 441–443, 475–476); in the *Gazette of the United States*, August 22 and September 23, 1789; in the *European Magazine and London Review*, December, 1794 (Vol. XXVI, pp. 407–409); and in the Kingston (Jamaica) *Diary*, March 7, 1796.

(f) Appendix. In the *Massachusetts Magazine*, October, November, and December, 1789 (Vol. I, pp. 605–608, 658–661, 743–746); in part in Webster's *Rudiments of English Grammar*, 1790 (which is in turn reprinted in his *Little Reader's Assistant* of the same year); and as *Old South Leaflet* No. 196 (Boston, [1908]).

3. Announced in the *Connecticut Courant*, March 30, 1789, and later and in the *Massachusetts Magazine*, April, 1789 (Vol. I, No. 4, back wrapper). Advertised as "just published" in the *Connecticut Courant*, June 1, 1789, and later, the *American Mercury*, June 8, 1789, and later, and elsewhere.

4. The work was praised by "An American" in the *Massachusetts Centinel*, July 4, 1789.

5. "M. D. Esquire," writing in the *Salem* (Mass.) *Gazette*, November 24, 1795, accused Webster of using, without acknowledgment, twenty pages from Bishop Percy's preface to Mallet's *Northern Antiquities*. The passage under attack is less than half the length asserted, and Webster in several places in his book acknowledges the use of Mallet, but it is true that for this passage his source is not directly indicated.

6. A London bookseller imported and offered this work in 1797. Its appearance in England brought forth hostile reviews in the *Monthly Review*, July, 1797 (Vol. XXIII, p. 356) and the *Critical Review*, October, 1797 (Vol. XXI, pp. 175–177).

[1] Pp. 222, "Verb," to 234 (except the last three words); 236, "For want of," to 277, "to notice them," with an occasional sentence omitted.

PART TWO: THE PROMPTER

In the list of Webster's writings at the end of Ford's Notes *the compiler includes (Vol. II, p. 534) an edition of the* Prompter *published by Thomas and Andrews in Boston in 1790, locating a copy in the possession of Albert C. Bates. This is almost certainly a ghost. The earliest located advertising for the work appears late in 1791, and the preface is dated in that year; no other copy or reference to such an edition has been found. Most of Mr. Bates' children's books were left to the Connecticut Historical Society, where no such edition can be found.*

652

The prompter; or A commentary on common sayings and subjects, which are full of common sense, the best sense in the world. "To see all others faults and feel our own." Hartford: Printed by Hudson and Goodwin, M,DCC,XCI. [Published according to act of Congress.]

94 pp., illus. 16 cm. P. [i], title-page. P. [ii], table of contents. Pp. [iii]–vi, preface, unsigned, dated Connecticut, 1791. Pp. [7]–94, text, consisting of 28 numbered homilies and a "Conclusion by the Prompter."

CtHT-W, CtHi, CtY, MB, MH, MWA (imperfect), NHi, NN, NhD, NjP (Hamilton Collection), RPJCB.

Evans 23969, Sabin 102378.

NOTES

1. Since three of the essays are in two parts, there are actually only twenty-five different titles. The essays are in the manner of Poor Richard; with plain expressions, short sentences, familiar illustrations, and quiet humor they satirize common follies and vices of the time, or give advice on the conduct of social intercourse and domestic economy. The two unsigned illustrations (pp. 87, 89) portray the first and last stages of a drunkard's progress.

Some of the essays are new, and some had appeared in the *Connecticut Courant*, as follows (in the original the sections bear Roman numerals):

1. A Bellows.	December 6, 1790
2. Green wood will last longer than dry.[2]	———
3. The Fidgets.	December 13
4. A Nose.	January 10, 1791
5. The Under-Lip.	January 17
6. The Grace of God in Dollars.	January 24
7. Every one to his notion.	January 31
8. He does not work it right.	February 14
9–10. It will do for the present.	February 21 and 28
11–12. How should I work it?	March 7 and 14
13. It is better to borrow than to buy.	March 21
14. Come, we'll take the t'other sip.	March 28
15–16. Any other time will do as well.	April 4 and 11
17. When a man's name is up, he may lay abed till noon.	May 9 (as "lie abed")
18. What is everybody's business is nobody's business.	May 16
19. When a man is going downhill, every one gives him a kick.	May 30
20. I told you so.	June 13
21. "Carpe diem." Horace. "Take time by the forelock." Plain English.	———
22. She carries the Bell.	———
23. He is sowing his wild oats.	———
24. He would have his own way.	———
25. If I was he.	———
26. It is just as the fit takes him.	———
27. A stitch in time saves nine.	———
28. He has come out at the little end of the horn.	———

2. Advertised as forthcoming in the *Gazette of the United States*, September 3, 1791, and the *Connecticut Gazette*, September 27, 1791, and as "just published" in the *Connecticut Courant*, October 31, 1791, and later, and elsewhere. (In his diary Webster recorded the publication date as November 1.) The price was 1/6, or 12/- a dozen.

[2]This replaces "A Pendulum without a Bob" of the newspaper series, probably omitted because it was political, ridiculing Jefferson's proposal to adopt the metric system in the United States.

3. This series of essays was extremely popular, and was widely reprinted in newspapers, pirated, and imitated. For newspaper reprintings, see Section Nine, Part Three, passim. The intention to print a pamphlet edition was mentioned in the *Connecticut Courant*, August 29, 1791, in an article headed "The Connecticut Prompter."

4. Webster very successfully altered his usual style, and even close friends and relatives did not at first recognize him as the author. Perhaps to help divert suspicion, in No. XXI he pokes fun at "learned wordmongers." His authorship was surmised by the editor of the *Oracle of the Day*, August 6, 1793, and was admitted in an advertisement in the *American Minerva* on January 16, 1796; it did not appear on a title-page until 1798, and that in England (Title 674).

653

[—— Albany: Charles R. and George Webster, 1792.]

Evans 25003; McMurtrie, Albany, 78.

Such an edition is suggested in Webster's letter of March 10, 1792, quoted below under Title 657, but the compiler has not located a copy.

654

—— Printed at Boston, by I. Thomas and E. T. Andrews.... MDCCXCII.

96 pp., illus. 16 cm.

CLU, CSmH, CSt, Ct, DLC (imperfect), ICN, MB, MH, MSaE (imperfect), MWA (imperfect), MiDeaEd, NHi, NN, NNC, PPL, RPJCB, Merriam, British Museum.

Evans 25004, Sabin 102379.

NOTES

1. The contents are the same as the first edition, with slight changes in spelling and phraseology.

2. Advertised in the *Columbian Centinel*, June 9, 1792, and later, and elsewhere.

655

The prompter: to which is added The whistle, a true story; by Dr. Franklin. I have seen, and I have not seen; by Governor Livingston.

Remarkable speeches of good old Roger Pindar, Esq. A vulgar error. The bee. The drone, in answer to the above. &c. &c. Being American productions, and calculated to instruct and amuse the reader. Burlington, Printed by Isaac Neale. M.DCC.XCII.

50 pp. 16 cm.
NN (imperfect), NJR, PHI.
Evans 25007, Sabin 102394.

NOTES

1. Contains only ten of the original twenty-five essays (Nos. 8, 11–12, 17, 19, 14, 20, 13, 15–16, 9–10, and 18); as indicated on the title-page, several similar items by other authors are added, notably Franklin's "The Whistle."

2. Advertised in the *General Advertiser*, May 10, 1792, and later.

3. Neale used one of Webster's essays, "He does not work it right," as a point of departure for an essay in his *New Jersey and Pennsylvania Almanac* for 1793.

656

[——— New London: Timothy Green and Son, 1792.]

Evans 25005.

The compiler has found no evidence for such a printing; advertisements in the *Connecticut Gazette*, August 16, 1792, and later, merely announce the work as for sale by the Greens.

657

[——— Philadelphia: Charles Cist, 1792.]

Evans 25006.

No copy located, but there is the following evidence suggesting its publication: Webster wrote to Timothy Pickering in Philadelphia on December 18, 1791, "A small impression here [Hartford] sells rapidly, it probably would in Philadelphia. . . . If an impression of 1000 or 1500 would sell in Philadelphia, a license for printing it might be obtained. . . ." On March 10, 1792, he wrote him again, "Enclosed . . . a Copy of the Prompter, which I will thank you to get printed in Philadelphia. Experiment proves it will sell. One impression here is gone, another at Albany is selling rapidly. I am willing to take the risk of an impression of 1500 or 2000 in Philadelphia...," and he continued with details about format, type, paper, etc., and the necessity of preserving his anonymity.

Some doubt, however, is thrown in a later letter (March 31, 1792), for although Webster says, "I highly approve of your employing Mr. Cist to print the Prompter," he adds, "I must suspend the printing at present for want of money...if the printer expects ready pay, which I suppose he does. I am also doubtful about so large a number as 1800...." Finally, November 11, 1792, "By last evenings mail I received 50 dollars from Mr. Cist on account of sales of my *books*; but he does not say *what* books. I have no way of accounting for this, but by supposing he has printed the *Prompter*; if so, I am indebted for it to your negotiation, and beg you to accept my thanks."[3]

658

The prompter; or A commentary.... Published according to act of Congress. Printed at Boston, by I. Thomas and E. T. Andrews.... MDCCXCIII.

96 pp., illus. 16 cm.

CT, CTHI, MA, MHI, MWA, MIDEAED, MIU-C, NN, NCD, NJP (Hamilton Collection), Merriam.

Evans 26451, Sabin 102380.

NOTES

1. The contents are the same as the first edition.

2. Andrews wrote Thomas from Boston, May 9, 1793, "Cannot make any terms with Webster for the Copyright as yet—he will be here soon he says," and on June 9, "Webster is now in town—he chooses not to sell the copyright of the Prompter at present." On July 28 Andrews wrote his partner that "The Prompter is not yet out."[4]

659

——— Printed at Newark, New-Jersey, by John Woods. 1793.

[3]All in Pickering Papers, Massachusetts Historical Society; the Society's *Proceedings*, Vol. 43, pp. 134–135, 136, 137; Ford's *Notes*, Vol. I, pp. 308–310, 311–312, 314–315.

[4]All in the American Antiquarian Society.

58 pp. 18 cm.
NHi (imperfect), NN, NjHi (imperfect).
Evans 45692, Sabin 102381, Hill and Collins 6.

NOTES

1. Includes the original items in slightly different order and adds Webster's "Rags! rags!" originally published in newspaper form (*Connecticut Courant*, June 4, 1792) and three or four small items from other sources.

2. In 1797 or later Woods bound up copies of this printing, without the title-page, with a work he published in that year, *A Collection of Essays on a Variety of Subjects*. He seems to have added to this *Collection* various small works he had on hand, and of the three copies in the New Jersey Historical Society no two agree in contents, only one (Ely N11a) containing the *Prompter*.

660

——— The fourth edition. New-York; Printed by George Bunce, & Co.... M.DCC.XCIII. [Published according to act of Congress.]

96 pp., illus. 17 cm.
MWA, NN, WaU.
Evans 26450, Sabin 102382.

NOTES

1. The contents are the same as the first edition, with the addition of a twenty-ninth number, "Stolen waters are sweet," which had previously appeared in a newspaper (*Connecticut Courant*, July 8, 1793).

2. Advertised in the *Minerva*, December 9, 1793, and later.

3. This edition was printed under Webster's personal supervision, since he was a partner in the firm. He noted in his diary on November 26, 1793, "Begin printing with the Prompter."

4. If all the editions hypothecated for 1792 existed, this would be more than a fourth edition; possibly Webster knew only those of Hartford, 1791, and Boston and Albany, 1792.

5. Copies were imported into England by the London bookseller Charles Dilly; the work was reviewed in the *Monthly Review*, September, 1797 (Ser. 2, Vol. 24, p. 105).

661

——— Printed at Boston, by I. Thomas and E. T. Andrews.... MDCCXCIV.

84 pp., illus. 13 cm.
CtHi, DLC, ICN, MWA, MiDeaEd, NN, NjR.
Evans 28049, Sabin 102384.
The contents are the same as Thomas and Andrews' earlier editions, the smaller number of pages being accounted for by the use of smaller type.

662

——— Boston: Printed and sold by John W. Folsom.... M,DCC.-XCIV.

96 pp. 14 cm.
CtHi, MiDeaEd, PU, RPJCB (imperfect).
Evans 28050, Sabin 102383.

663

[——— New York: George Bunce and Co., 1794.]

Evans 28051.
The compiler has found no evidence of such an edition.

664

[——— Philadelphia: Mathew Carey, 1794.]

Evans 28052.
The compiler doubts that such an edition was printed, for Carey seems to have inquired about purchasing copies of Bunce's edition of 1793; on February 19, 1794, Webster wrote him, "The Prompter we have at 10 dollars a hundred in sheets—perhaps something less by a larger number."[5]

[5]Lea and Febiger Papers, Historical Society of Pennsylvania.

665

[——— Leominster, Mass.: Charles Prentiss, 1795.]

Evans 29856.

The compiler doubts the existence of such an edition, believing Evans to have entered under the wrong year a reference to the 1796 or 1797 Leominster editions.

666

——— New-York: Printed and sold by Samuel Campbell.... M,DCC,XCV.

108 pp. 14 cm.

CtY, MWA, NN.

667

——— Leominster: Printed by Charles Prentiss. MDCCXCVI.

44 pp. 18 cm.

MLeo, MWA.

Evans 31597, Sabin 102385.

668

[——— New York: George Bunce and Co., 1796.]

Evans 31598.

It is true that Webster's paper, the *American Minerva*, advertised the work as "now published" in the January 11, 1796, and subsequent issues, but the loose terminology of that period does not make it certain that this represents a new printing. In the same paper for March 23 and later Webster advertised an auction on March 30, to include "4000 copies of the Prompter, in sheets."

669

——— Philadelphia: Printed for Mathew Carey.... 1796.

95 pp. 17 cm.

DLC, ICHi, MA, MH, MWA, NN, NNU, NjP, NjR, PU, British Museum.

Evans 31599, Sabin 102386.

670

—— Printed at Boston, by I. Thomas and E. T. Andrews.... Aug. 1797.

84 pp. 14 cm.
CtY, MWA, NN.
Evans 33185, Sabin 102387.
Evans calls for two pages after p. 84, but these are not in the New York Public Library copy, which he is describing, nor has the compiler found them elsewhere.

671

—— Second Leominster edition. Printed by Charles Prentiss. Sept. 1797.

91, (2) pp. 17 cm.
DLC, MWA, PU, Merriam.
Evans 33186, Sabin 102388.
The verso of p. 91 and the recto of the following leaf contain publisher's advertisements.

672

—— New Brunswick, Printed by Abraham Blauvelt. 1797.

84 pp. 12 cm.
NN (imperfect).
Evans 33187, Sabin 102389.
Contains all the essays of the original edition, though in different order, and adds "Rags! rags!"

673

—— Wilmington; Printed and sold by Peter Brynberg..., 1797.

96 pp. 13 cm.
NN (imperfect).

674

Sentimental and humorous essays;... By Noah Webster.... London: Printed for J. and A[.] Arch...; Knight and Triphook...; and H. D. Symonds.... M,DCC.XCVIII.

(8), 64 pp. 14 cm. P. [i], title-page. P. [ii], table of contents. Pp. [iii–iv], "Address to the Reader," signed "The Editor," in which he says that Americanisms have been retained "as it would have been uncandid to cover American Ground with English Leaves." Pp. [v–viii], Webster's preface. Pp. [1]–64, text.
CtY, N.

NOTES

1. Contains the added essay, "Stolen waters are sweet." The English editor has changed "If I was he" to "If I were he," and there are some alterations of colloquialisms, spelling, and grammar.

2. Reviewed in the *Gentleman's Magazine*, May, 1798 (Vol. LXVIII, p. 415); *Monthly Review*, September, 1798 (Ser. 2, Vol. 27, p. 112); and *Monthly Mirror*, November, 1798 (Vol. VI, pp. 291–292), the last named quoting in full one of the essays, "I told you so." The *Monthly Review* had previously noticed the New York, 1793, edition, and merely cited that review (though the reference to the issue of September, 1795, is an error for September, 1797). In July, 1798 (Vol. V, p. 512), the *Monthly Magazine* mentioned the work in a "Retrospect of the domestic Literature of the last six months," but called it *The Prompter*.

3. This is the first edition to bear Webster's name on the title-page; it did not appear on an American edition until 1833, though his name appeared as the copyright holder in 1803.

675

The prompter: or, A commentary.... Chambersburg: Printed by Robert Harper, for Mathew Carey, Philadelphia. M,DCC,XCVIII.

85 pp. 16 cm.
DLC (Toner Collection), NN.
Sabin 102390.

676

——— Printed in the year 1798.

[86] pp. (the last misnumbered 66). 13 cm.
PP.
Sabin 102391, Rosenbach 243.
Adds to the original essays "Stolen waters are sweet."

677

Sentimental and humorous essays.... London: Printed for W. West...; E. Harding...; sold also at the Juvenile Libraries of Crowder, Ripley, and West, Croydon. 1799.

72 pp. 14 cm.
NN, British Museum.

NOTES

1. The contents are the same as those of the 1798 English edition, although differently arranged. On pp. [2–3] are advertisements of schools. On p. 72 the imprint, "W. Dyde, Printer, Tewkesbury."

2. Advertised in the *Monthly Magazine*, September, 1800 (Vol. X, p. 173). The price was one shilling.

678

The prompter; or A commentary.... Printed for, and sold by the book-sellers. Dec. 1799.

72 pp. 14 cm.
CLU, CSt, Ct, CtHi, CtY, MB, MHi, MWA, MiDeaEd, MiU-C, N, NBuG, NN, NcD, NjP, OU, RPB, RPJCB.
Evans 36688, Sabin 102392.

679

—— The third Albany edition. Printed in Albany, by Charles R. & George Webster.... 1800. With privilege of copy-right.

95, (1) pp., illus. 14 cm.
MWA, N (imperfect), Merriam.
Evans 39050; McMurtrie, Albany, 271.

P. [vi] and the final unnumbered page contain publisher's advertisements.

680

——— Alexandria: Printed and sold by J. & J. D. Westcott.... 1800.

102 pp. 15 cm.
DLC, NN.
Evans 39051.

NOTES

1. The contents are those of the original edition, the greater bulk being accounted for by larger type.
2. The spelling "Alexander" for the place of printing, found on the Library of Congress printed card, is an error.

681

——— Printed in the year 1801.

86 pp. 14 cm.
IU, NNC.
Pages 78 and [79] have been reversed in printing.

682

——— Philadelphia: Printed by Joseph Charless,... 1802.

80 pp. 17 cm.
IC, MWA, MiU-C, NHi, NN.

683

——— A new edition, improved and enlarged. New Haven: Printed by Joel Walter. 1803.

137, (1) pp. 17 cm. P. [i], title-page. P. [ii], "Registered according to Law." Pp. [iii]–iv, preface (same as first edition). P. [v], blank. P.

[vi], "Advertisement to the Revised Edition," unsigned, dated New Haven, November, 1802. Pp. [7]–137, text (see below). P. [138], copyright entry, April 16, [1803], to Noah Webster, Jun.

CT, CTY, CTHT, ICN, ICU, MWA (imperfect), NBUG, NN, Merriam.

NOTES

1. Of the original contents No. VI, "The Grace of God in Dollars," and the Conclusion have been omitted; "Stolen Waters are Sweet," which had previously been added in some editions, now becomes No. XXVIII. The essays from p. [75] to the end are new, under the heading "Additional Numbers Written and First Published in 1803." These are: XXIX–XXX, "A Gillotin" (sic). XXXI, "Pride." XXXII, " 'Lord I thank thee, that I am not as other men.' " XXXIII, "Political Economy." XXXIV, "Prejudice." XXXV–XXXVI, "Popular Discontent." XXXVII, "Liberty and Equality." XXXVIII–XXXIX, "Inconstancy of the Populace." XL, "Popular Delusion." XLI, " 'Behold, how great a matter a little fire kindleth.' " XLII, "Parental Indulgence." XLIII, "The Counsels of Old Men Despised, or, Revolt and Division of Empire." XLIV, "Envy and Deception." XLV, "Envy and Malice." XLVI, "Envy, Hatred and Revenge Punished." XLVII, "Charity and Humanity." There are slight changes in some of the original sections.

2. Advertised "In Sheets, Boards, Half bound and Full Bound" in the New Haven *Visitor*, May 17, 1803, and later, and elsewhere. In the initial advertisement the price was in shillings and pence; the insertion of June 21 quoted fifty cents for full bound copies, thirty-seven and a half cents for half bound or boards.

3. The New York Public Library copy was Webster's and contains his MS corrections. It also contains a short MS (in the nature of a prefatory note to *The Prompter*) entitled "Tell me a Story."

684

[——— New Haven: W. W. Morse, 1803.]

Advertisements in the New Haven *Visitor* of January 1 and 25, 1803, announced that Morse had an edition in press. No trace of such an edition has been found by the compiler; these references may represent Title 683's having experienced a change of publishers between its inception and its appearance.

685

—— Wilmington: Printed & sold by Peter Brynberg.... 1804.

96 pp. 13 cm.
MiU (imperfect), NN.
The contents are those of the original edition.

686

—— By Noah Webster, author of The effects of slavery, &c. To which is added, The way to wealth. By B. Franklin, LL.D. Coventry: Printed by and for Pratt, Smith, & Lesson. Also sold by Longman, Hurst, Rees, & Orme; Craddock & Joy, and R. Scholey, London. 1808.

Frontis., (8), 88 pp. 18 cm. Frontispiece, "An Old Maid in the Fidgets," unsigned. P. [i], title-page. P. [ii], blank. Pp. [iii–iv], "Advertisement" to this edition, declaring that the original title has been restored "upon the ground that an author ought to be sufficient authority for the propriety of the title he chooses...." Pp. [v–vii], original preface. P. [viii], table of contents. Pp. [1]–70, text, like that of London, 1798. Pp. [71]–88, half-title for and text of "The Way to Wealth." On p. 88 is the imprint of Pratt, Smith, and Lesson, Coventry.
Ct, CtY, MWA, NN, PHi, PPL, VtMidbC.

687

—— Philadelphia: Published by D. Hogan,... L. Dobelbower, printer. 1810.

108 pp. 14 cm.
NN.
The contents are those of the original edition, with the addition of six "Letters of Advice" by Benjamin Franklin, pp. [79]–101. P. [102] is blank, and [103] to 108 are publisher's advertisements.

688

—— Philadelphia: Printed for B. & T. Kite,... Jane Aitken, pkinter [sic]. 1811.

108 pp. 14 cm.
MWA.
The front cover bears the imprint, "Philadelphia. Published by Johnson & Warner,... 1811."

689

——— The fifth edition. Lexington, K. Printed by Thomas T. Skillman, for Maccoun, Tilford & Co. 1812.

72 pp. 15 cm.
NN.
In the Webster Papers, New York Public Library, are several letters from Henry Clay between 1812 and 1816, showing that he acted as Webster's agent in trying to collect royalties due from Maccoun, Tilford and Co

690

About a quarter of the original text (Nos. 9, 11-12, 15, 19, 20, 27, and 28) appeared in:

The pirates. A tale for the amusement and instruction of youth. Embellished with cuts. To which is added: several select pieces in prose and verse. Philadelphia: Published by Johnson & Warner. William Greer, printer. 1813.

108 pp. 13 cm.
NHi, PHi, PP.
Sabin 102376, Rosenbach 479.
The *Prompter* excerpts appear on pp. 47–94, under the heading of "Select Pieces," without ascription of authorship. The volume also contains five verse selections—unquestionably not by Webster—and (pp. [5]–46) the title story. Dr. Rosenbach believed that Webster wrote this story. On April 22, 1916, he wrote the compiler that his uncle, Moses Polock, who had succeeded to the business and papers of Johnson and Warner, told him that he had their contract with Webster. Such a contract, however, might have covered only so much of the compilation as came from the *Prompter*. The compiler is inclined to feel that the style, bold subject matter, and incorrect grammar and spelling of "The Pirates"

militate against its being by Webster. He was deeply immersed in his dictionary project at this time. Further, he did not approve of fiction, and the *Prompter* is the farthest he is known to have gone in that direction.

691

The prompter, or A commentary.... Pittsburgh. Printed by Cramer, Spear and Eichbaum.... 1814.

108 pp. 13 cm.
PMA, OClWHi (imperfect).

692

——— New-York: Published by E. Duyckinck..., G. Long print. 1815.

108 pp. 13 cm.
CtHT-W, CtY, DLC, MWA, NN, NjHi, British Museum.

693

The English ship of war righting herself, after twenty years hard fighting! (In allusion to the present times) or, Thirty practical essays, founded on common sense; proving, in the most familiar way how every man, in any sphere of life, may right himself and his concerns even in such times as these! After the manner of Dr. Franklyn [sic], "When a man is going down hill, every one gives him a kick." But I will strive to lift him up. *Nil desperandum.* By Noah Webster, author of The effects of slavery &c. Including a plan, addressed to Francis Freeling, Esq. in August, 1816, for giving immediate employ to the poor and mechanics in general. To which is added, Dr. Franklyn's [sic] "Way to wealth." and "The plague of wealth," Bristol, printed for the editor, and sold wholesale and retail, by T. Long, Broadmead; and the other booksellers. [Entered at Stationers' Hall.] [1816?].

(6), 68 pp. 18 cm. P. [i], title-page. P. [ii], blank. P. [iii], "Address to the Reader," stating that twenty-eight of the essays were printed in America some years earlier, and "it was therefore thought advisable to alter the Title." Pp. [iv–v], original preface, with minor changes. P. [vi], table of contents. Pp. [1]–52, text (see below). Pp. [53]–68, Franklin's "Way to Wealth" and "Plague of Wealth."

CSmH, MB.

Sabin 102351.

The first twenty-eight numbers are the original *Prompter* essays, in different order, with "The Grace of God in Dollars" omitted and "Stolen Waters are Sweet" added. Nos. XXIX, "Bad Habits easily acquired not soon shaken off," and XXX, "Public Good is direct common sense," are not by Webster. No. XXX—which is the "Plan, addressed to Francis Freeling" called for on the title-page—is subscribed "A Bristol Patriot, The Editor. Bristol 1st, Sep. 1816."

694

The prompter; or Essays.... London: Printed by and for R. Edwards...; and sold by Sherwood Neely and Jones, and T. Hamilton...; W. Kent...; and all other booksellers. 1818.

120 pp. 15 cm. P. [i], title-page. P. [ii], blank. Pp. [iii]–iv, "Advertisement" to this edition. Pp. [v]–ix, preface, substantially the same as the first edition. P. [x], blank. Pp. [11]–102, text, following the London, 1798, edition. Pp. [103]–120, Franklin's "Way to Wealth."

CtY, MB, NN, British Museum.

695

—— Brunswick [Maine]: Printed by J. Griffin. 1821.

90 pp. 13 cm.

ICU, MWA, MiDeaEd, NN, NjR.

NOTES

1. The contents are those of the original edition, much rearranged and altered; "He would have his own way" has been omitted.

2. The cover imprint adds as vendors W. F. Lane, Hallowell; Wm. Hyde, Portland; H. Gray, Portsmouth; N. Burrill, Haverhill; and C. Ewer, Boston. It gives the price as eighteen and one-half cents.

The prompter, a series of essays on civil and social duties. Published originally in the Upper Canada Herald *(Kingston, Ontario, 1821) is a different work, though similar in style and subject matter to Webster's.*

696

——— Windsor, Vt. Published by Simeon Ide. 1827.

96 pp., illus. 12 cm.

CT (imperfect), MB, MBAT, MH, MWA (imperfect), NN, British Museum.

The contents are those of the original edition with frequent minor changes. Pp. [91]–96 consist of an "Appendix Selected by Philo Prompter," including short homilies from other sources. The cuts illustrate a drunkard's progress, but differ from those used earlier.

697

——— Cleaveland: Published by R. Pew & Co. David B. M'Lain, printer. 1830.

88, (2) pp. 11 cm.

OCLWHI.

The contents are the same as the original edition. A leaf after the text contains publisher's advertisements.

698

——— By Noah Webster,... Claremont, N.H. Published by John Wilcox. 1833.

77 pp. 10 cm.

MB, MH, MHI, MWA, MIDEAED, NN, NHD, NHHI, PU, British Museum.

NOTES

1. The contents are basically those of the original edition, with deletions in the preface; "The Fidgets," "The Grace of God in Dollars," and "It is just as the fit takes him" are omitted, and "Stolen waters are sweet" and "Tell me a story" are added; the latter is entirely new. On p. [ii] is a new copyright entry, to Webster, dated 1833; on the same page is the stereotype notice of Cofnin and Roby, Concord, N.H.

2. This is the first edition in the United States to bear Webster's name on the title-page.

3. A draft of "Tell me a story" in Webster's hand is laid in the New York Public Library copy of the New Haven, 1803, edition.

699

——— By Noah Webster,... Newport, N.H. Published by John Wilcox. 1833.

77 pp. 11 cm.

Ct, DLC, MWA, NN.

Identical with the preceding except for the place of publication in the imprint.

700

——— Rochester: Marshall & Dean, printers. 1834.

143 pp. 10 cm.

CtHi, CtY, MiU, N, NN, NRU, OClWHi.

The contents are the same as the original edition, with the addition of "The Way to Wealth" and other selections from Benjamin Franklin, pp.[107]–143.

701

[——— Cincinnati, 1836(?).]

A possible Cincinnati edition about 1836 is indicated in several letters from William G. Webster to his father from there. On July 22, 1835, he wrote, "The Prompter we shall Stereotype immediately...." September 16, "...an edition of the Prompter is in press—(stereotyped.)" November 24, "The Prompter has been delayed on account of the person who is to design the cuts. He is not yet ready. . . ." March 5, 1836, "The Engravers are going on with the cuts of the prompter."[6]

702

——— By Noah Webster, . . . New Haven: Published by S. Babcock. 1839.

94 pp. 10 cm.
CT, CTH, MH, MWA, NN.

NOTES

1. The contents are those of the Wilcox editions of 1833.
2. The Harvard copy has a cover imprint of 1843.

703

——— By Noah Webster, . . . Dayton Printed & published by B. F. Ells. 1849.

80 pp., incl. frontis., illus. 16 cm. P. [1], blank. P. [2], frontispiece, a rural scene, signed "Whitridge Del" and "Grosvenor." P. [3], title-page. P. [4], "Stereotyped, Printed, Published, and Sold by B. F. Ells, Fair Mount, Western Suburb of Dayton, O." P. [5], abbreviated version of the original preface. P. [6], table of contents. Pp. [7]–80, text.

MA, MB, NN, NNC, OCLWHI.

Six of the original selections are omitted: "The Fidgets," "The Grace of God in Dollars," "He would have his own way," "If I was he," "It is just as the fit takes him," and "A stitch in time saves nine." There are illustrations scattered throughout the volume, usually of rural or agricultural scenes. Some are obviously meant to illustrate the fables in Webster's speller.

[6] Webster Papers, New York Public Library.

PART THREE: LETTER TO THE GOVERNORS

704

A letter to the governors, instructors and trustees of the universities, and other seminaries of learning, in the United States, on the errors of English grammars. By Noah Webster, jun. New-York: Printed by George F. Hopkins, for the author. 1798.

36 pp. 22 cm. P. [1], title-page. P. [2], blank. Pp. [3]–36, text, dated New York, January, 1798, on errors in English grammars, with particular reference to the subjunctive mood.

CSmH, CtHT-W, CtHi, CtNhHi, CtY, DLC, MB, MBAt, MH, MWA, MWiW, N, NHi, NN, NNC, NNUT, PHi, PPM, RPJCB, British Museum.

Evans 34981, Sabin 102362.

NOTES

1. Advertised in the *Commercial Advertiser*, February 12, 1798, and the *Spectator*, March 31.

2. Reprinted in Warfel, *Letters of Noah Webster*, pp. 173–177.

PART FOUR: LETTER TO DR. RAMSAY

705

A letter to Dr. David Ramsay, of Charleston, (S.C.) respecting the errors in Johnson's Dictionary, and other lexicons. By Noah Webster, Esq. New-Haven: Printed by Oliver Steele & Co. 1807.

28 pp. 20 cm. P. [1], title-page. P. [2], blank. Pp. [3]–28, text, dated New Haven, October, 1807.

CSt, Ct, CtHT-W, CtHi, CtY, DAFM, DLC, MB, MBAt, MH, MHi, MWA, MiD-B, N, NHi, NN, NNNAM, NhD, OClW, PU, British Museum.

Sabin 102360.

NOTES

1. Reprinted in Warfel, *Letters of Noah Webster*, pp. 282–292.

2. Reviewed in the *Monthly Anthology*, December, 1807 (Vol. IV, pp. 670–675). Ridiculed in an article signed "The Wounds of a Friend," in the *Norfolk Repository*, December 22, 1807.

PART FIVE: PECULIAR DOCTRINES OF THE GOSPEL

706

The peculiar doctrines of the Gospel, explained and defended. [*seven lines of editorial introduction, ending* "Editors."] [New York, J. Seymour, 1809.]

23, (1) pp. 23 cm. P. [1], caption title and beginning of text. Pp. 2–23, text, signed at end. P. [24], imprint, "J. Seymour, Printer, New-York."

CSt, Ct, CtHT-W, CtY, DLC, MH, MWA, MiDeaEd, N, NHi, NN, NNG, NNS, NNUT, NcD, NjR, PHi, PPAmP, PPPrHi, RPB, VtU, Merriam, British Museum.

NOTES

1. In 1808 Webster and Judge Thomas Dawes of Boston, one of his wife's brothers-in-law, discussed religion in their correspondence. Webster, on December 20, 1808, wrote a detailed letter summarizing his religious experiences and beliefs; Dawes acknowledged it on February 6, 1809, expressing rather liberal views, and on February 23 Webster wrote a long answer, which became the present text.[7]

Moses Stuart, pastor of the First Congregational Church, New Haven, saw a copy of the February letter and told Jedidiah Morse about it, urging him to secure Webster's permission to print it in the *Panoplist and Missionary Magazine United*, which Morse edited. A month later Stuart wrote that he had secured Webster's consent to the publication of the February letter, but not the earlier one of December, which was more personal.[8] Webster revised the letter for publication, and Dawes went

[7]Webster Papers, New York Public Library; Ford's *Notes*, Vol. II, pp. 40–48, 58–59.

[8]Stuart to Morse, May 11 and June 14, 1809. Transcripts provided by Prof. Harry R. Warfel.

over it also.[9] It was published in the *Panoplist* for July, 1809 (n.s., Vol. II, pp. 58-74). The title "Peculiar Doctrines..." was given to the piece by Morse.

The compiler believes this printing to have been the first separate edition. On September 15, 1809, Samuel Whiting wrote Webster, "A few individuals are desirous of printing it in a small *Tract form* for gratuitous distribution," and asked if Webster had "any additions or variations which would render the letter more useful as a tract."[1]

2. The verso of the front wrapper and both sides of the back contain publisher's advertisements. The wrapper title is: A letter from Noah Webster, Esq. of New-Haven, Connecticut, to a friend, in explanation and defence of the distinguishing doctrines of the Gospel. Published by subscription, at New-York, and sold at the Theological and Classical Bookstore of Williams and Whiting.... J. Seymour, printer. 1809.

3. The pamphlet was replied to in *Observations on a Letter from Noah Webster.... Published in the Panoplist, and republished in New-York. By an Old-Fashioned Churchman* (New Haven, 1809). The author was John Bowden, not Governor James Bowdoin, as stated in Ford's *Notes*, Vol. II, pp. 48, 78. In the Webster Papers is the MS of an unpublished reply, "A word to an old fashioned churchman," signed by Webster as "A Calvinist." The endorsement shows that Webster identified Bowden as the "Old-Fashioned Churchman."

4. The pamphlet and its answer became part of the three-cornered wrangle then going on between the Calvinists, the Unitarians, and the Episcopalians, especially in the columns of the *Panoplist* and the *Monthly Anthology* of Boston. Later, some of the Massachusetts Unitarians allowed these religious differences to color their evaluation of Webster's philological work.

5. The letter of December 20, 1808, is reprinted in Ford's *Notes*, Vol. II, pp. 42–48, and in Warfel, *Letters of Noah Webster*, pp. 309–315 (though it is not in the *Panoplist*, as indicated by Warfel).

6. One paragraph and portions of two others of this text were reprinted, with an editorial note, in *Renunciation of Unitarianism: or, the Conversion of Dr. J. E. Stock, of Bristol, England. With an Appendix, containing Extracts of a Letter from Noah Webster, Esq....* (Worcester, 1818).

[9]Dawes to Webster, July 13, 1809, Webster Papers, New York Public Library; Ford's *Notes*, Vol. II, pp. 63–65.

[1]Webster Papers, New York Public Library; Ford's *Notes*, Vol. II, pp. 73–74. In the latter Whiting's letter is said to apply to Webster's December letter, but it seems likely that it applies to the February letter, which was the one that Whiting actually printed.

707

[Same caption title.]

23 pp. 18 cm.
MA, MWA.
The same in content and collation as the preceding except for slight differences in the caption title and introductory paragraph, the last word of which is "Panoplist." There is no imprint on the verso of p. 23. Neither copy has covers.

708

—— By Noah Webster, Esq. in a letter to his friend in Boston. Poughkeepsie: Printed by Joseph Nelson, for Chester Parsons & Co. . . . , 1809.

15 pp. 21 cm.
CSmH, Ct, CtHT-W, DLC, NN, PHi.
The same text, but this edition has a title-page, and the caption title (p. [3]) is "The Gospel Vindicated."

709

—— [Trenton, George Sherman, 1810.]

23 pp. 23 cm.
NN.

NOTES

1. There are slight changes in the text, mainly in the paragraphing.
2. The cover title is the same as that of Title 706 through "Gospel," and adds the imprint, "New-York—printed, Trenton, Re-printed by Geo: Sherman. 1810."

710

—— In a letter from Noah Webster, Esq. to a friend in Boston. Third edition. Portland: Published and sold by A. Lyman & Co. . . . J. M'Kown, printer. 1811.

50 pp. 14 cm.

CtHT-W, DLC, MA, MB, MBAt, MWA, N (imperfect), NBLiHi, NN, NcD, British Museum.

Noyes 578.

To the caption title on p. [3] is added "New-Haven, Feb. 23d, 1809," and the editorial note is omitted. Signed at the end with Webster's name.

711

—— In a letter from the celebrated Noah Webster, Esquire, to a friend in Boston.

22 pp. 19 cm.

NN.

NOTES

1. Caption title. The original text, with a change in paragraphing. The editorial note is omitted.

2. There is nothing to indicate the place or year of printing; possibly the use of the word "celebrated" suggests a later date than the other editions.

PART SIX: LETTER TO JOHN PICKERING

712

A letter to the Honorable John Pickering, on the subject of his Vocabulary; or, Collection of words and phrases, supposed to be peculiar to the United States of America. By Noah Webster. Boston: Published by West and Richardson, . . . T. W. White, printer. 1817.

60 [i.e., 52] pp. (41–48 omitted). 24 cm. P. [1], title-page. P. [2], copyright entry by West and Richardson, 1817. Pp. [3]–60, text, dated Amherst, December, 1816. On p. 60 there are a note on authorities and a list of errata.

CtHT-W, CtY, DLC, ICU (imperfect), MA, MB, MBAt, MH, MHi, MWA, MiD-B, N, NN, NNS, PHi, RPJCB.

Sabin 102363.

NOTES

1. A criticism of Pickering's *Vocabulary*, published in Cambridge in 1815 and in Boston in 1816. Pickering was the son of Webster's college classmate and friend, Timothy Pickering.

2. Reprinted in Warfel, *Letters of Noah Webster*, pp. 341–394.

3. Reviewed in the *North American Review*, May, 1817 (Vol. V, pp. 82–98). Unsigned, but by Sidney Willard, a Harvard professor.

4. Allibone's *Dictionary* and Stone's *First Editions of American Authors* list an edition of Amherst, 1816, apparently an error caused by taking the year of the letter as the year of publication. The compiler has found no trace of an 1816 edition.

PART SEVEN: VALUE OF THE BIBLE

713

Value of the Bible, and excellence of the Christian religion: for the use of families and schools. By Noah Webster, LL.D. New Haven: Published by Durrie & Peck. 1834.

180 pp. 14 cm. P. [1], title-page. P. [2], copyright notice, 1834, to Webster, and imprint of Hezekiah Howe & Co. P. [3], "Advertisement" (preface), dated New Haven, May, 1834. P. [4], blank. Pp. [5]–180, text.

MiDeaEd, NN, NjR, British Museum.

NOTES

1. The preface states that "the general object of this little book, is, to show the excellence of the Christian religion, and...to prove the inestimable value of the book in which this religion is revealed and inculcated."

2. Listed by the publishers, under date of August 1, 1834, on p. [1] of their 1831 edition of the *Elementary Spelling Book* (Title 277), apparently a leaf substituted or added in copies still unsold in 1834. Advertised, with an extract, in the *Connecticut Journal*, August 12, 1834, and later.

PART EIGHT: BRIEF VIEW

714

A brief view 1. Of errors and obscurities in the Common Version of the Scriptures; addressed to Bible societies, clergymen and other friends of religion. 2. Of errors and defects in class-books used in seminaries of learning; including dictionaries and grammars of the English, French, Greek and Latin languages; addressed to instructors of youth, and students, with a few hints to statesmen, members of Congress, and heads of departments. To which is added, 3. A few plagiarisms, showing the way in which books may be made, by those who use borrowed capital. By Noah Webster, LL.D. [New Haven, 1834?]

24 pp. 23 cm. P. [1], caption title and beginning of text. Pp. 2–24, text (see below).

CT, CTHT-W, CTY, DLC, MB, MHI, MWA, MID-B, N, NHI, NN, NNC, NNC-T, NNUT, PPPRHI, Merriam.

Sabin 102342.

NOTES

1. The first section, pp. [1]–6, deals with inaccuracies and misreadings in Biblical translations. The second section, pp. 6–20, headed "To Those Who Write, and Those Who Teach, the English Language," is divided into orthography, pronunciation, definition, grammar, errors, and mistakes in grammars, and discusses various writers on these subjects. The third section, pp. 20–24, headed "Plagiarisms," accuses Lindley Murray and Joseph Worcester of plagiarizing from Webster's speller, *Elements of Useful Knowledge*, *Letters to a Young Gentleman*, and *History of the United States*.

2. Reprinted in Webster's *Collection of Papers*, 1843.

3. The year of publication seems almost surely to be 1834, for the following reasons: there is a reference to that year in the text; the Boston

Public Library copy is so dated in what appears to be a contemporary hand; and an anonymous writer in the *Connecticut Journal* of December 16, 1834, cites the work as "just published." Allibone, however, implies a date of 1839, which is the date given in Ford's *Notes* (Vol. II, p. 525).

4. One of the New York Public Library copies contains MS corrections by Webster which were incorporated in the reprint.

PART NINE: MISTAKES AND CORRECTIONS

715

Mistakes and corrections. 1. Improprieties and errors in the Common Version of the Scriptures; with specimens of amended language in Webster's edition of the Bible. 2. Explanations of prepositions, in English, and other languages. These constitute a very difficult part of philology. 3. Errors in English grammars. 4. Mistakes in the Hebrew lexicon of Gesenius, and in some derivations of Dr. Horwitz. 5. Errors in Butter's Scholar's companion and in Town's Analysis. 6. Errors in Richardson's Dictionary. By Noah Webster, LL.D. New Haven: Printed by B. L. Hamlen. 1837.

28 pp. 23 cm. P. [1], title-page. P. [2], blank. Pp. [3]–26, text. Pp. 26–28, recommendations for Webster's works.

CtHT-W, CtHi, CtY, DLC, MB, MBAt, MH, MHi, MWA, N, NN, NNUT, NUt, NjR, OClW, PU, Merriam, British Museum.

Sabin 102370.

NOTES

1. Some of the copies are in yellow wrappers with the cover title "Mistakes and Corrections."

2. In the January, 1837, issue of the *Knickerbocker* (Vol. IX, p. 98) the editor acknowledges receipt of this pamphlet and expresses regret that he cannot reprint it.

3. The draft of the section on Richardson's *Dictionary* is in the Webster Papers. This section is reprinted in Warfel, *Letters of Noah Webster*, pp. 460–478.

PART TEN: OBSERVATIONS ON LANGUAGE AND COMMERCE

716

Observations on language, and on the errors of class-books; addressed to the members of the New York Lyceum. Also, Observations on commerce, addressed to the members of the Mercantile Library Association, in New York. By N. Webster. New Haven. Printed by S. Babcock. 1839.

39 pp. 18 cm. P. [1], title-page. P. [2], dedication to the New York Lyceum and the Mercantile Library Association, in lieu of lectures Webster was unable to present in person. Pp. [3]–32, "Observations on Language." Pp. [33]–39, "Observations on Commerce, and the Political Condition of the United States."

CSmH, Ct, CtH, CtHT-W, CtHi, CtY, DLC, MAJ, MB, MH, MHi, MWA, MiD-B, N, NBLiHi, NHi, NN, NNC, NNC-T, NjR, VtMidbC, Merriam, British Museum.

Sabin 102371.

NOTES

1. Reviewed: By "A.N.," *New Haven Record*, November 23, 1839, reprinted in the *Daily National Intelligencer*, December 10, and the *Peoria* (Ill.) *Register and North Western Gazetteer*, November 27, 1840; New Haven *Daily Herald*, November 23, 1839; *American Quarterly Register*, February, 1840 (Vol. XII, p. 301).

2. Cover title, "Observations on Language and Commerce."

3. Extracts from the first section were printed in the first review cited. Extracts from the second section were printed in the tri-weekly edition of the *Hartford Times*, February 10, 1840, and the weekly edition, February 15. The editor added comments of his own, in reply to which Webster wrote a letter, February 15, which was apparently never published.[2]

[2]Original in the possession of Mrs. J. Saunders Taylor.

Section Five

POLITICAL WORKS

PART ONE: SKETCHES OF AMERICAN POLICY

717

Sketches of American policy. Under the following heads: I. Theory of government. II. Governments on the eastern continent. III. American states; or the principles of the American constitutions contrasted with those of European states. IV. Plan of policy for improving the advantages and perpetuating the union of the American states. By Noah Webster, Jun'r. Esq. Hartford: Printed by Hudson and Goodwin. M.DCC.LXXXV.

48 pp. 23 cm. P. [1], title-page. P. [2], "Advertisement" (preface), unsigned and undated. Pp. [3]–48, text.

CtHT-W, CtHi, CtY, DLC, MBAt, MH, MWA (imperfect), N, NN, NNP (George Washington's copy), British Museum.

Evans 19366, Sabin 102399. Evans errs in listing the *Maryland Gazette* version as the first printing.

NOTES

1. In the preface Webster states that "before the appearance of Dr. Price's Pamphlet,[3] I had formed a design of publishing some Remarks on the American Constitutions and on the Federal Government.... If the following observations, thrown together in haste and without much regard to method, can have any merit, it is this, that they are dictated by an honest intention and full conviction of their truth."

2. Reprinted in *State Gazette of South Carolina*, December 22, 1785, to February 6, 1786, and the *Maryland Gazette*, December 27, 1785, to January 17, 1786; the latter contains added notes and minor changes

[3]Richard Price, *Observations on the Importance of the American Revolution* (London, 1784; Boston, 1784; etc.). Webster sent a copy of his work to Price in England, who acknowledged it on August 2, 1785.

which were probably by Webster himself. Section IV was reprinted in the *Pennsylvania Journal*, January 21 and 25 and February 1, 1786; in part in the *New York Daily Advertiser*, April 11, 12, and 15, 1786; and in *Old South Leaflets* No. 197 (Boston, [1908]), pp. 1–18. A facsimile reprint of the entire volume, with three pages of introductory matter by Harry R. Warfel, was published in the Scholars' Facsimiles and Reprints Series (New York, 1937).

3. Advertised in the *Massachusetts Spy*, March 3, 1785; *Connecticut Courant*, March 8; and *New Haven Gazette*, March 31 and later.

4. The last five pages are set in smaller type than the rest.

5. The New York Public Library copy was Webster's own; on the flyleaf he has written, "The following sketches were written in the month of February 1785, before any proposal had ever been made to new model the government of the States. In May I carried one Copy of them to Virginia & presented it to Genl. Washington. Mr Maddison [sic] saw & read it at the General's soon after, & in November the same year, he, in conversation with me, expressed a warm approbation of the sentiments it contains. . . ."

Stephen Hopkins, once colonial governor of Rhode Island, thought the ideas of the pamphlet "too democratic" for him in 1785,[4] and in the course of time Webster came to agree with him. On July 24, 1797, he wrote to Jedidiah Morse, "It is a little too democratic for my present notions. I was once a visionary and should now leave out a few [views?] contained in it. It contains also a few remarks on the Southern States which I should suppress. On the whole however, I agree with myself in 1785."[5] By 1800 he was less inclined to agree with himself. In that year he endorsed the letter containing Governor Hopkins' opinion, "The sentiments of that Pamphlet are too democratic for the author. . . . We grow wiser with age." His marginal notes in his copy of the work, written apparently at different times—some as late as Van Buren's administration—are even more outspoken, such as: "Great mistake;" "Many of these notions, taken from Rousseau's *Social Contract*, are found to be chimerical;" "Most of this is the reverse of the truth;" "Shortsighted as I was; I did not foresee the force of party;" or "The Three first Sketches contain many . . . notions . . . which can never be reduced to practice."

6. At first Webster declined to allow extracts to be printed in the newspapers, but in December he agreed; he had no copy with him in Virginia, and had to write to George Washington and borrow the copy

[4]Asher Robbins to Webster, April 14, 1785, bound in the New York Public Library copy of the work.

[5]Yale University Library.

he had given him in May.[6] In sending it, Washington said, "I . . . conceive that the publication of extracts therefrom will be pleasing, and may be beneficial."[7]

7. In the succeeding years much ink was spilled on the subject of Webster's priority and significance in proposing the form of government which was evolved in the Constitution. The modern evaluation is summarized in Warfel's biography, pp. 117–118.

[6]December 16, 1785, Historical Society of Pennsylvania.

[7]December 18, 1785, Presidential Papers, New York Public Library; Ford's *Notes*, Vol. I, pp. 109–110.

PART TWO: EXAMINATION OF THE CONSTITUTION

718

An examination into the leading principles of the Federal Constitution proposed by the late Convention held at Philadelphia. With answers to the principal objections that have been raised against the system. By a citizen of America. *Ut patria sua felicitate caeteris praestaret, efficit.* XENOPH. LACEDAEM. RESP. Philadelphia: Printed and sold by Prichard & Hall.... M.DCC.LXXXVII.

55 pp. 20 cm. P. [1], title-page. P. [2], blank. P. [3], dedication to Benjamin Franklin, Philadelphia, October 10, 1787. P. [4], blank. Pp. 5–55, text, comparing the proposed American Constitution with the Roman and British constitutions, and favoring its adoption.

CSmH, CtHT-W, CtY, DLC, ICU, MBAt (George Washington's copy), MH, MWA, MiU, N, NBLiHi, NHi, NN, PHi, PPAmP, PPL, RPJCB.

Evans 20865, Sabin 102352.

NOTES

1. An extract was published in the *New Hampshire Gazette*, November 29, 1787. Reprinted in full on pp. [25]–65 of Paul Leicester Ford's *Pamphlets on the Constitution... 1787–1788* (Brooklyn, 1888), with Webster's corrections and additions given as footnotes. A few separates were made of this printing, repaged [1]–41.

2. Advertised as "this day...published," *Pennsylvania Packet*, October 18, 1787, and later; advertised in the same paper November 28 and December 1 and 5 as almost out of print.

3. The New York Public Library copy was Webster's own, on the flyleaf of which he wrote, "This is a hasty production written at the request of Mr. Fitsimmons [sic], a member of the Convention." In his diary for 1787 he records Thomas Fitzsimmons' request on September 15, the writing of the pamphlet on October 9, and its publication on October 17.

PART THREE: ATTENTION, OR NEW THOUGHTS

719

Attention! or, New thoughts on a serious subject; being an enquiry into the excise laws of Connecticut; addressed to the freemen of the state. By a private citizen. Hartford: Printed and sold by Hudson and Goodwin. M.DCC.LXXXIX.

18 pp. 21 cm. P. [1], title-page. P. [2], blank. Pp. [3]–18, text, questioning the rights of individual states to levy excise duties.

CtHT-W, CtY, DLC, M, MH, MHi, MiD-B, MiU-C, NN.

Evans 22258, Sabin 102339.

NOTES

1. Reprinted in the *Norwich* (Conn.) *Packet*, January 8, 15, and 22, 1790. Extracts in the *Massachusetts Centinel*, January 20 and 23, 1790.

2. Advertised in the *American Mercury*, December 28, 1789, as "just published." The price was nine pence.

3. Webster recorded in his diary for 1789 that on December 9 a discussion group at Mr. Trumbull's decided that state excise taxes were inconsistent with the new Federal system, and that he wrote on the subject on December 17 and 18.

4. At the time of publication of this pamphlet there was a series of articles signed "Observer" running in the *American Mercury*. In No. XII (January 4, 1790), "Observer" mentions having seen the pamphlet, and in No. XIV (January 11) he quotes from it extensively. This article with its extracts from Webster's work was reprinted in the *Connecticut Courant*, January 14, and in half a dozen other papers between January and April.

PART FOUR: EFFECTS OF SLAVERY

720

Effects of slavery, on morals and industry. By Noah Webster, Jun. Esq. Counsellor at law and member of the Connecticut Society for the Promotion of Freedom. *The gods are just, and of our pleasant vices Make instruments to scourge us.* SHAKESPEAR. Hartford (Connecticut) Printed by Hudson and Goodwin. M,DCC,XCIII.

56 pp. 20 cm. P. [1], title-page. P. [2], blank. P. [3], dedication to the Connecticut Society for the Promotion of Freedom and the Relief of Persons unlawfully holden in Bondage. P. [4], preface, dated Hartford, May 9, 1793. Pp. [5]–49, text, showing "the pernicious consequences of slavery." Pp. 50–56, appendices I–IV.

CT, CTHT-W, CTHI, CTY, DLC (imperfect), ICN, ICU, MA, MB, MBAT, MH, MHI, MWA, MID-B, MIDEAED, MIU-C, NHI, NN, NJR, OU, PHI, PPAMP, PPL, PU, RPJCB, VIU, Merriam, British Museum.

Evans 26448, Sabin 102349.

NOTES

1. Advertised in the *Connecticut Courant*, May 20, 1793, and elsewhere.

2. Reviewed in the *Critical Review* (London), August, 1797 (Ser. 2, Vol. XX, pp. 448–450).

3. In his diary Webster records his election to "the Abolition Society" (May 12, 1791), his appointment to deliver the annual oration (May 10, 1792), and his performance of the task (May 9, 1793).

4. As the abolition movement grew more violent and Webster grew more conservative with age, he disapproved of the course of events.

5. Extracts appeared in the *American Minerva*, December 14, 1793.

6. One of the New York Public Library copies has MS corrections and annotations by Webster, one dated 1832. The changes are mostly in spelling and word form, such as "held" for "holden" in the dedication.

PART FIVE: REVOLUTION IN FRANCE CONSIDERED

721

The Revolution in France, considered in respect to its progress and effects. By an American. [*thirteen lines of quotations in Latin and English.*] New-York: [Printed and published according to act of Congress.] By George Bunce, and Co. . . . M,DCC,XCIV.

72 pp. 20 cm. P. [1], title-page. P. [2], table of contents. Pp. [3]–4, preface, unsigned and undated, stating that his enthusiasm for the French Revolution had waned as it became more bloody and atheistic. Pp. [5]–72, text, under the headings: Introduction, Jacobin Society, Commissioners, National Treasury, Probable Event [i.e., outcome] of the War, Debts, Agriculture, Manufactures, Commerce, Arts and Science, Religion, Morality, Government, Remarks, Application, Appendix, and Conclusion.

CSmH, CSt, CtHT-W, CtHi, CtY, DLC, ICN, ICU, MB, MBAt, MH, MHi, MWA, MiU-C, NN, NNC, NcD, NjP, NjR, RPJCB, VtMidbC, Merriam.

Evans 28053, Sabin 102395.

NOTES

1. Reprinted in Webster's *Collection of Papers*, 1843, incorporating most of the corrections marked in his copy of the original edition. Extracts were printed in the *New York Magazine*, April, 1794 (Vol. V, pp. 235–240), and Webster himself quoted from the pamphlet in the *American Minerva*, June 5, July 5, October 11, and October 16, 1794.

2. Advertised in the *American Minerva*, April 19, 1794, and later as "just published." The price was twenty-five cents.

3. The New York Public Library owns Webster's copy, with annotations, one of which (p. 32) draws attention to the word "demoralize," which Webster said was the only word he ever coined.

4. Two paragraphs from the pamphlet were quoted, with approbation, at the conclusion of a Thanksgiving sermon by the Reverend David Osgood of Boston, published as *The Wonderful Works of God are to be Remembered* (Boston, 1794, etc.; Sabin 57776) and in part in various newspapers, e.g., *Columbian Centinel*, December 27, 1794. Osgood's use of the pamphlet served to advertise it in Boston, which is ironic, since he did not like Webster's reformed orthography, and refused to read the work until requested to do so as a favor to a friend. Mrs. Webster's brother-in-law Thomas Dawes related this in a letter to Webster, February 9, 1795. In October, he said, Chief Justice Dana had referred to the pamphlet and Dawes was embarrassed because he had never heard of it. He added, "Since Osgood has raked it up it has been borrowed all around the Town & is as much admired as you would have it."[8]

[8]Webster Papers, New York Public Library; Ford's *Notes*, Vol. I, pp. 396–398.

PART SIX: TEN LETTERS TO PRIESTLEY

722

Ten letters to Dr. Joseph Priestly [sic], in answer to his Letters to the inhabitants of Northumberland. From Noah Webster, Jun. New Haven: Printed by Read & Morse. 1800.

29 pp. 19 cm. P. [1], title-page. P. [2], blank. Pp. [3]–29, text, consisting of ten "letters" and a "Postcript," dealing with the French Revolution and Napoleon's seizure of power.

CT, CTHT-W, CTHI, CTY, DAFM, DLC, ICN, MB, MBAT, MH, MHI, MWA, NHI, NN, PHI, PPAMP, PPL, PU, British Museum.

NOTES

1. Reprinted in the *Commercial Advertiser*, June 25, 28, and 30 and July 1, 2, 3, 5, 11, 12, and 14, 1800, and in the *Spectator*, June 28 and July 2, 5, 9, 12, and 16. Warfel, *Letters of Noah Webster*, pp. 204–215.

2. Announced in the New Haven *Messenger*, January 30, 1800, and advertised therein as "just published" February 6 and later.

3. The work to which this is an answer is Priestley's *Letters to the Inhabitants of Northumberland and its Neighbourhood* (Northumberland, 1799).

4. Allibone (s.v. Priestley) lists a second edition, 1801, of which the compiler has been unable to find any trace.

5. Ridiculed by the editor of the *Aurora* in his editorial notes of June 28, 1800, and by "Timothy Plain" in a series of three articles in the *American Citizen*, July 11 and 19 and August 6, 1800.

PART SEVEN: A ROD FOR THE FOOL'S BACK

723

A rod for the fool's back. [*four lines of quotations from the Bible.*] [New Haven? 1800.]

11 pp. 21 cm. P. [1], title-page. P. [2], blank. Pp. [3]–11, text, a scathing analysis of Abraham Bishop's *Connecticut Republicanism, an Oration* (New Haven, [1800] etc.).

CtH, CtY, DLC.

Evans 39054, Sabin 102396.

NOTES

1. Part of p. 10 and p. 11 are in smaller type than the rest. From this, the lack of an imprint, and other indications, the compiler believes this issue to have been the first, published probably about September 18, 1800. Probably printed in New Haven.

2. Reprinted with favorable comment in the *Connecticut Courant*, September 22, 1800, the *Middlesex Gazette*, September 26, 1800, and the *Commercial Advertiser*, June 9, 1801.

3. Witheringly reviewed in the *American Citizen*, July 28 and 29, 1801, reprinted in the *Republican Watch Tower*, July 29.

4. This work is sometimes confused with "*A Rod for the Fool's Back;" or an Examination of a Pamphlet entitled Republican Economy. By a Plain Man* (Newbern, North Carolina, 1803).

724

—— [New Haven?] 1800.

12 pp. 19 cm.

CtY.

Evans 39053.

The text, being set in the same size type throughout, runs on to p. 12. The compiler believes this to be the second issue. Probably printed in New Haven.

725

——— New Haven: Printed by Read and Morse.... 1800.

10 pp. 21 cm.
CtHi, CtY, NN (photostat).
Evans 39052.

726

An oration, "On the extent and power of political delusion", has lately been re-printed and issued from the press of Citizen Haswell: the public are in turn presented with A rod for the fool's back; or Abraham Bishop unmask'd. By a citizen of Connecticut. [*nine line, of quotation.*] Reprinted at Bennington, by Wm. Stockwell, and Company.... [1800?]

15 pp. 17 cm.
ICN, MB, MWA, NN (photostat), RPJCB, VtHi, VtU.
Evans 39049, Sabin 5598 and 102396.
The text is dated at the end New Haven, September 16, 1800.

PART EIGHT: LETTER TO GENERAL HAMILTON

There are at least six printings of this pamphlet, all probably issued in 1800, though only one has an imprint. There are minor textual variations, but only differences in the title and pagination are listed here, since these are sufficient to distinguish the printings. Notes which cannot be assigned to specific printings are lumped at the end. Evans 39045–39047, Sabin 29960 and 102361.

727

A letter to General Hamilton, occasioned by his letter to President Adams. By a Federalist. [New York? 1800.]

The caption title is in six lines, with "Letter" in roman type, "Occcasioned" in roman type, and "By a Federalist" in black letter. The page numbers are not set off by any ornament.

8 pp. 21 cm.

MWA, NHi, NN, NNC, NhD.

Felt by the compiler to be the first issue, probably published in New York about November 1, 1800. The Columbia University copy has an ownership inscription dated 1800.

728

———

The caption title is in six lines, with "Letter" in roman type, "Occasioned" in roman type, and "By a Federalist" in italic type. The page numbers are enclosed in square brackets.

8 pp. 21 cm.

PPAmP.

729

The caption title is in six lines, with "Letter" in roman type, "Occasioned" in italic type, and "By a Federalist" in italic type. The page numbers are enclosed in parentheses.

8 pp. 23 cm.

DLC (Duane Pamphlets), MBAT, MIU-C, NN, PPL.

Although the New York Public Library copy contains a note by Wilberforce Eames suggesting that it was printed in New York, the Library of Congress, at the compiler's request, made in 1934 a detailed study of the variant printings and concluded that this one was done by William Duane in Philadelphia, from the same type used in the printing of this text in his paper, the *Aurora*.

730

The caption title is in seven lines, with "Letter" in italic type, "Occasioned" in italic type, and "By a Federalist" in roman type. The page numbers are enclosed in parentheses. The caption title is distinguished from the following entry only by the fact that in this "Occasioned" is spelled with a long s and "By a Federalist" is set off by rules rather than by ornamental bars—but the pagination readily distinguishes the two printings.

8 pp. 21 cm.

CSMH, DLC (Force Collection; Waterman Pamphlets), ICN, MB, MBAT, MHI, MSAE, MIU-C, NN, NNC, RPJCB.

731

See the preceding entry for the distinguishing features; "Occasioned" is spelled with a modern-form s.

[8] pp. (numbered [3]–10). 23 cm.

CTHT, CTNHHI, CTY, DLC (Wolcott Pamphlets), M, MHI, MWA, NN, PPL, VIU.

Pagination beginning with [3] suggests that a title-page or other preliminary page was intended or printed, though the item is a complete signature as it stands.

732

——— New-York: Printed by E. Belden, & Co. 1800.

15 pp. 19 cm.

MHi, MiD-B, N.

A title-page and different pagination make this printing easily distinguishable from the others. The compiler feels that this is the latest because Webster tried to remain anonymous and was not likely at first to have used the imprint of Ebenezer Belden, who was the printer of Webster's newspapers at the time.

GENERAL NOTES

1. Signed "Aristides," this is a scathing attack on Hamilton for his secret maneuvers within the Adams administration and his support of a standing army.

2. Reprinted: *Aurora*, November 5, 1800; *American Mercury*, November 6, 1800; *Federal Gazette* (Baltimore), November 11, 1800; *Boston Gazette*, November 13, 1800; Charleston *City Gazette*, November 24, 1800; *South-Carolina State Gazette*, December 1, 1800; Boston *Democrat*, February 13, 1805; *National Aegis*, September 27, 1809; and in part in other contemporary papers. Warfel, *Letters of Noah Webster*, pp. 222–226.

3. Advertised: *Boston Gazette*, November 6, 1800, and later, as "just published"; *Aurora*, November 11, 1800, as "this day published," price six cents; *New York Gazette*, November 12, 1800, and later, as "this day published"; *Commercial Advertiser*, November 26, 1800, and later, as "this day published"; and elsewhere. Probably at least one of the issues was printed in New England; this is borne out by an advertisement in the *Salem Gazette*, December 12, 1800: "Joshua Cushing has this day reprinted, from a Newyork edition, and has for Sale at his Printing Office in County Street, Salem, A Letter to General Hamilton.... Price 25 cents...."

4. Reviewed: Temperately in the *Monthly Magazine and American Review*, November, 1800 (Vol. III, pp. 379–380); virulently in the *New York Gazette*, November 24, 1800. The latter said, "A more puerile, catch penny production never blotted paper.... The creature...appears from his work about as well qualified for the task, as a Billingsgate oyster is to contemplate the principles of Newtonian philosophy."

5. Webster's authorship was suggested as early as the *Aurora* reprint of November 5, 1800.

PART NINE: MISCELLANEOUS PAPERS

733

Miscellaneous papers, on political and commercial subjects. I. An address to the President of the United States, on the subject of his administration. II. An essay, on the rights of neutral nations, in vindication of the principles asserted by the northern powers of Europe. III. A letter, on the value and importance of the American commerce to Great-Britain. IV. A sketch of the history of banks and insurance companies, in the United States. By Noah Webster, Jun. New-York: Printed by E. Belden & Co. 1802. [Copy-right secured.]

viii, 227, 48 pp. 21 cm. P. [i], title-page. P. [ii], "Corrections" and "Note" to Section IV. Pp. iii–viii, preface, unsigned, dated New Haven, March, 1802. Pp. [1]–76, Section I. Pp. [77]–215, Section II. P. [216], blank. Pp. [217]–227, Section III. P. [228], blank. P. [1], "Advertisement" for Section IV. P. [2], blank. Pp. [3]–48, Section IV.

CT, CTNHHI, CTY, DLC, ICU, MB, MBAT, MH, MNF, MWA, MIDEAED, MOSHI, N, NHI, NN, NHD, NJP, NJR, PPAMP, PPM (imperfect), PU, British Museum.

Sabin 102369.

NOTES

1. Reprinted: Section I: Warfel, *Letters of Noah Webster*, pp. 240–245.

Section II: In Webster's *Collection of Papers*, 1843.

Section IV: The first four pages, in Webster's *Collection of Papers*, 1843. This section was heavily drawn upon, with credit to Webster, in Joshua Montefiore's *Commercial Dictionary* (3 vols., Philadelphia, 1804). In Ford's *Notes* (Vol. I, p. 526n) is printed a letter from Samuel Bradford of Philadephia to Webster, with an endorsement by Webster, regarding unauthorized use of Webster's material in a work published by [James ?]

Humphrey[s], and then used by Bradford—with Humphreys' permission —in an encyclopedia. It has not been possible to identify these works, though James Humphreys was the publisher of Montefiore's work, which may thus be the title concerned in this incident; since Bradford admits in the letter that he had read only a few paragraphs of whatever item it was that was in dispute, he may have seen the material on banks in Montefiore but failed to notice at the end the attribution of the information to Webster.

2. Advertised in the *Commercial Advertiser*, March 31, 1802, as "just published." This advertisement contains a copyright notice, March 29, [1802], which is not in the book. The work was still advertised as "just published" in the same paper as late as January 15, 1804. The price was $1.25.

3. Reviewed in the *American Review and Critical Journal*, April–June, 1802 (Vol. II, pp. 193–204).

4. Hamilton B. Tompkins, in his *Bibliotheca Jeffersoniana* (New York and London, 1887), lists (p. 165) an "Address to the President of the United States on the subject of his Address," 1802, crediting it to Noah Webster. The compiler has found no such imprint, but it may represent a separate printing of Section I.

5. The fact that the fourth section is called for on the title-page and is included in the corrigenda on p. [ii] shows that it was intended to be part of the volume, but its separate pagination and signaturing suggest the possibility of separate publication, although none has been located by by the compiler.

6. The first three sections had previously been published in Webster's *Commercial Advertiser*, as follows: Section I, September 26 to November 6, 1801; Section II, November 24 and 27, 1801; and Section III, November 10 and 11, 1801. Some changes and additions were made in the present printing.

7. One of the New York Public Library copies was Webster's and has marginal corrections and revisions, partly cut away by the binder.

PART TEN: ADDRESS TO THE CITIZENS OF CONNECTICUT

734

An address to the citizens of Connecticut. [New Haven.] J. Walter, Printer. [1803.]

24 pp. 20 cm. P. [1], title-page. P. [2], blank. Pp. [3]–24, text, signed "Chatham," attacking the local Republican party and Thomas Jefferson.

CSmH, Ct, CtH, CtHT-W, CtHi, CtNhHi, CtY, DLC, MHi, MWA, MiU-C, MoSHi, N, NHi, NN, NNUT, OC, PHi, PPAmP.

Sabin 15640 and 102333.

NOTES

1. Reprinted in the *Middlesex Gazette*, March 21 and 28, 1803.

2. Called forth by an invitation to a Republican meeting to be held on March 9, 1803, published in the *American Mercury*, January 27, and elsewhere, and a "Circular" published in the *Connecticut Courant*, February 16, and elsewhere. Webster attacked these two documents over his own name in the *Connecticut Journal*, February 24, reprinted in the New Haven *Visitor*, March 22.

3. Webster's authorship was attributed at the time by his opponents; e.g., "N. Webster. On the 9th of March this man. . . published *two pence* worth of federalism in a small pamphlet, signed Cheatham [sic]. . ." (*American Mercury*, March 17). The pamphlet was also attributed to him in an article in the same paper on March 24.

4. This address was extensively quoted from (after March 12) in a series of articles on the subject in the *Commercial Advertiser*, February 16 to March 16 (*Spectator*, February 19 to March 19). This whole series may have been written by Webster.

PART ELEVEN: LETTER TO DANIEL WEBSTER

735

A letter to the Hon. Daniel Webster, on the political affairs of the United States. By Marcellus. Philadelphia: Printed by J. Crissy.... 1837.

34 pp. 21 cm. P. [1], title-page. P. [2], blank. Pp. [3]–34, text, signed "Marcellus," discussing various political concepts which had been mentioned in Daniel Webster's speeches.

CtHT-W, CtY, ICN, MH, MHi, NN, NhD, PHi, PPL.

Sabin 44480.

NOTES

1. Reprinted: *Hartford Times*, June 13, 1838. Quoted from extensively in an article, "Whig Activity and Objects," *New Era*, June 14, 1838; the paper promised a full reprint, which the compiler has been unable to locate. In Webster's *Collection of Papers*, 1843. Warfel, *Letters of Noah Webster*, pp. 478–504.

2. The cover title is "A Letter to the Hon. Daniel Webster."

3. The 1843 republication served as the basis of an anonymous review article, "The Dangers of our Country," *New Englander*, October, 1843 (Vol. I, pp. 492–502).

4. A private letter on political matters, written to Daniel Webster by Noah Webster in 1834, was first printed in 1903; see Appendix C, September 6, 1834.

PART TWELVE: APPEAL TO AMERICANS—VOICE OF WISDOM

736

Appeal to Americans. Fellow Citizens! The following essay.... [New York? 1838?]

8 pp. 21 cm. P. [1], caption title and introductory note. Pp. [2]–8, "A Voice of Wisdom" by "Sidney," reprinted from the *Commercial Advertiser*, November 20, 1837. As a filler at the foot of p. 8 is a paragraph entitled "Hard Money."

DLC, NHi, NN.

Sabin 102338.

NOTES

1. For the subject matter, the identification of Webster as "Sidney," and the newspaper debates which raged over this article, see Section Nine, Part Three, No. 289, and Part Four, rubric L. Probably printed in New York.

2. Published, not by Webster or his friends, but by someone opposed to his views, in order to draw attention to "these monarchical doctrines"; the note on p. [1] is sharply critical of the text. In this version italics and capitalization vary from the newspaper printing, and "Appeal to Americans" is a title given by the anonymous publishers.

3. The introductory note contains a quotation from the *Commercial Advertiser* of December 2, 1837, so the pamphlet cannot have been issued earlier than that date.

Section Six

PUBLISHED SPEECHES

PART ONE: ORATIONS AND LECTURES
1776–1786

"Juventutem bene actam . . . ," a student Latin oration of May 4, 1776, was published in 1926 and 1954; see Title 770.

Webster's senior class "Cliosophic Oration" at Yale was published in the New York Magazine *a decade after its delivery; see Section Nine, Part Three, No. 74.*

Webster's series of lectures on the English language and education, delivered in various cities in 1785, '86, and '87 (see Appendix B), was not published except insofar as the ideas were incorporated in his Dissertations, *1790. There was, however, the following printed prospectus:*

737

A syllabus of Mr. Webster's Lectures on the English language and on education. . . . New-Haven, June 15, 1786.

Broadside, 33 x 20 cm.
CtNhHi, CtY, NN (photostat).
Sabin 102400.
Reprinted in the *American Historical Magazine*, January, 1836 (Vol. I, pp. 22–23).

PART TWO: FOURTH OF JULY ORATIONS

738

An oration pronounced before the citizens of New-Haven on the anniversary of the independence of the United States, July 4th 1798; and published at their request. By Noah Webster, Jun. New-Haven: Printed by T. and S. Green. [1798.]

16 pp. 21 cm. P. [1], title-page. P. [2], blank. Pp. [3]–16, text.

CSmH, Ct, CtHT-W, CtHi, CtY, DLC, MB, MBAt, MH, MHi, MWA, N, NHi, NN, PHi, RPJCB, Merriam, British Museum.

Evans 34984, Sabin 102373.

NOTES

1. Reviewed in the *Time Piece*, July 30, 1798 (hostilely).
2. The text was printed in the *Commercial Advertiser*, July 24, 1798, probably a later printing than the pamphlet.
3. After having read the oration, Benjamin Rush of Philadelphia wrote Webster, July 20, 1798, "But Alas! my friend, I fear all our attempts to produce political happiness by the solitary influence of human reason, will be as fruitless [as] the search for the philosopher's stone."[9]
4. Abraham Bishop, Webster's political opponent, characterized this oration as "milk and water" in the appendix to his *Oration Delivered in Wallingford, on the 11th of March 1801, before the Republicans of the State of Connecticut* (New Haven, 1801).

739

An oration pronounced before the citizens of New Haven, on the anniversary of the Declaration of Independence; July, 1802. And published at their request. By Noah Webster, Jun. [*two lines of quotation.*] New Haven: Printed by William W. Morse. 1802.

[9] Webster Papers, New York Public Library; Ford's *Notes*, Vol. I, p. 466.

30 pp. 21 cm. P. [1], half-title, "Mr. Webster's Oration." P. [2], blank. P. [3], title-page. P. [4], blank. Pp. [5]–30, text, including "Erratum," p. 30.

CSmH, Ct, CtNhHi, CtY, DLC, MB, MBAt, MH, MWA, MiU-C, N, NBLiHi, NHi, NN, NjP, NjR, PPM, PU.

Sabin 102372.

NOTES

1. Advertised as ready "Thursday next," New Haven *Messenger*, July 12, 1802; as "just published" in the same, July 19.

2. "Another issue" mentioned in Sabin, drawn from the compiler's annotations to Ford's *Notes* (Vol. II, p. 533), is apparently a ghost.

3. This oration was cited in "Republican Festival," an attack on Connecticut Federalists, in the *American Mercury*, February 10, 1803.

740

An oration, pronounced before the Knox and Warren branches of the Washington Benevolent Society, at Amherst, on the celebration of the anniversary of the Declaration of Independence, July 4, 1814. By Noah Webster, Esq. Northampton, printed by William Butler: 1814.

32 pp. 23 cm. P. [1], title-page. P. [2], vote of thanks to Webster by the committee of "arrangement and advertisement." Pp. [3]–27, text. Pp. 27–32, supplementary material, including Jefferson's letter to Mazzei of January 1, 1797.

CSmH, Ct, CtHT-W, CtY, DLC, MA, MBAt, MH (imperfect), MWA, N, NBLiHi, NHi, NN, NjR, Merriam.

Sabin 102374, Gilmore 234.

NOTES

1. The Boston Athenaeum copy was presented by Webster to Thomas Dawes, and that in the Watkinson Library to General Nathaniel Terry.

2. The occasion was described in the *Hampshire Gazette*, July 20, 1814, but the editor forbore comment on the oration, "as it will probably soon appear in print. . . ."

PART THREE: AGRICULTURAL SOCIETY ADDRESS

741

An address, delivered before the Hampshire, Franklin and Hampden Agricultural Society, at their annual meeting in Northampton, Oct. 14, 1818. By Noah Webster, Esq. Vice President of the Society. Published at the request of the Society. Northampton: Printed by Thomas W. Shepard & Co. 1818.

28 pp. 21 cm. P. [1], title-page. P. [2], blank. Pp. [3]–28, text, which treats of horse raising, wool, potatoes, and currency, and denounces war, gaming, theaters, circuses, and brutal sports.

CSmH, CtHT-W, CtY, DLC, ICN, IU, MA, MBAt, MH, MWA, MWiW, NHi, NN, Merriam.

Sabin 102332, Gilmore 266.

NOTES

1. Reprinted: *Hampshire Gazette*, February 16 and 23 and March 2, 1819; *Connecticut Courant*, March 2, 9, 16, and 23, 1819; Webster's *Collection of Papers*, 1843.

2. Reviewed in the *Panoplist*, December, 1818 (Vol. XIV, pp. 542–546).

3. In acknowledging receipt of a copy, Josiah Meigs wrote from Washington, December 3, 1818, remarking that "Attention to Manure is the *sine qua non*; it is like *Grace* in Religion—without it all is vain."[1]

[1] Webster Papers, New York Public Library; Ford's *Notes*, Vol. II, pp. 154–156.

PART FOUR: AMHERST CORNERSTONE ADDRESS

742

A plea for a miserable world. I. An address, delivered at the laying of the corner stone of the building erecting for the Charity Institution in Amherst, Massachusetts, August 9, 1820, by Noah Webster, Esq. II. A sermon delivered on the same occasion, by Rev. Daniel A. Clark, pastor of the First Church and Society in Amherst. III. A brief account of the origin of the institution. Boston: Printed by Ezra Lincoln.... 1820.

48 pp. 23 cm. P. [1], general title-page. P. [2], blank. Pp. [3]–4, account of the occasion. P. [5], Webster title-page. P. [6], blank. Pp. [7]–11, Webster text. P. [12], blank. P. [13], Clark title-page. P. [14], blank. Pp. [15]–39, Clark text. P. [40], blank. Pp. [41]–48, text of the historical account.

CSmH, CSt, Ct, CtHT-W, CtHi, CtY, DLC, ICN, ICU, IU, M, MA, MB, MBAt, MH, MHi, MNF, MWA, MiD-B, MiU-C, N, NBLiHi, NHi, NN, NNC-T, NNUT, Nh, NhD, NjP, NjR, OClWHi, PHi (Section I only), PPPrHi, RPB (Section I only), Merriam.

Sabin 1314.

NOTES

1. "A Plea for a Miserable World" refers to the sermon and not to Webster's address. The Webster title-page adds after his name "Vice President of the Board of Trustees of Amherst Academy."

2. An account of the occasion, containing extracts from Webster's address, was published in the *Boston Recorder*, March 24, 1821.

3. Webster may well have had a hand in the preparation of the historical account.

For newspaper printings of speeches made by Webster in the Connecticut and Massachusetts legislatures, see Appendix G.

Section Seven

MISCELLANEOUS WORKS

PART ONE: TWO CARRIER'S ADDRESSES

743

The carrier of the American Mercury, presents.... Hartford, January 1st, 1790.

Broadside, 27 x 22 cm.
NHi, NN (photostat).
Evans 22306.

NOTES

1. Extracts were printed in the *Gazette of the United States*, January 9, 1790; the *Massachusetts Centinel*, January 20; *Providence Gazette*, February 6; *Maryland Journal*, January 19; and Warfel, *Poems by Noah Webster*, p. 12.

2. The poem is unsigned, and begins, "The rising glory of my nation...." The poem is not found to have been acknowledged by Webster, but it is attributed to him by Professor Warfel, and there is the following contemporary attribution: Dr. Daniel Greenleaf, a brother of Mrs. Webster, wrote Webster from Boston on January 24, 1790, "Your New Years Wish, hath been highly complimented here—it was reprinted in the Centinel with '*What tones*, when *Genius* strikes the lyre!' as a Caption...."[2]

744

[Connecticut Courant. The news-boy's address to his customers. Hartford: Hudson and Goodwin, 1790.]

Evans 22429.

Evans locates no copy, but describes this as a broadside. The poem, which is unsigned, begins, "Behold another year is past...." It is reprinted in the issue of January 7; the *Gazette of the United States*, January

[2]Webster Papers, New York Public Library; Ford's *Notes*, Vol. I, p. 278.

13; the *Massachusetts Centinel*, January 23; the *Middlesex Gazette*, January 23; the *Salem Gazette*, February 2; and in Warfel, *Poems by Noah Webster*, pp. 9–11. Authorship is acknowledged (by signature and initials) in the New York Public Library file of the *Courant* and in the Yale file of the *Gazette of the United States*.

PART TWO: COLLECTION OF ESSAYS

745

A collection of essays and fugitiv writings. On moral, historical, political and literary subjects. By Noah Webster, Jun. Attorney at law. [*three lines of quotations.*] Printed at Boston, for the Author, by I. Thomas and E. T. Andrews.... MDCCXC.

xvi, 414 pp. 21 cm. P. [i], title-page. P. [ii], blank. Pp. [iii]–vi, list of subscribers. P. [vii], dedication, to the President, Vice-President, Senators, and Representatives, dated Hartford, June, 1790. P. [viii], errata list. Pp. [ix]–xi, preface, unsigned, dated Hartford, June, 1790, explaining the origin of the pieces, and also the inconsistent orthography. Pp. [xii]–xvi, table of contents, in which the entries do not always jibe with the headings in the body of the work. Pp. [1]–414, text, in thirty numbered pieces.

C, CSmH, Ct, CtH, CtHT–W, CtHi, CtY, DLC, IC, ICN, IU, MA, MB, MBAt (George Washington's copy), MH, MHi, MWA, MWiW, MdBE, MiDeaEd, MiU-C, MnU, N, NBuG, NHi, NN, NNC, NNG, NNUT, NjP, NjR, OC, OU, PPL, PU, RPB (imperfect), RPJCB, VtMidbC, Merriam, British Museum.

Evans 23053, Sabin 102344.

NOTES

1. The titles and sources of the selections are:

I. "On the Education of Youth in America," dated New York, 1788. Reprinted, with minor changes, from the *American Magazine*, where it ran in six installments from December, 1787, to May, 1788. For other reprintings see the magazine entry, Section Nine, Part One.

II. "Principles of Government and Commerce," dated New York, 1788. Reprinted from the *American Magazine*, December, 1787.

III. "Bills of Rights," dated New York, 1788. Reprinted, with minor changes, from thc same.

IV. "On Government," dated New York, 1788. Reprinted, with minor changes, from the same, January, 1788.

V. "On Government," dated New York, 1788. Reprinted, with minor changes, from the same, February, 1788.

VI. "On Government," dated New York, 1788. Reprinted, with minor changes, from the same, March, 1788.

VII. "Remarks on the Manners, Government, and Debt of the United States," dated Philadelphia, 1787. First published in the *Pennsylvania Packet*, February 15, 17, 19, and 21, 1787, and then in the *Pennsylvania Herald*, February 21, 24, and 28, 1787; used by Webster in revised form in his *American Selection*, 1787; reprinted as revised in the *American Museum*, March and April, 1789 (Vol. V, pp. 269–272, 349–353). The text here follows the original newspaper issue, with minor changes.

VIII. "On Paper Money." Reprinted from the *Maryland Journal*, August 9, 1785.

IX. "On Redress of Grievances," dated Newburyport, 1786. Reprinted from the *Essex Journal*, September 13, 1786.

X. "The Devil is in you," dated Providence, 1786. Reprinted from the *United States Chronicle*, September 28, 1786.

XI. "Desultory Thoughts," dated New London, October, 1786. Reprinted from the *Connecticut Gazette*, October 20, 1786.

XII. "Advice to Connecticut Folks," dated New Haven, December, 1786. Reprinted, with one slight change, from the *New Haven Gazette*, December 14, 1786.

XIII. "To the Dissenting Members of the late Convention of Pennsylvania," dated New York, December, 1787. Reprinted from the *Pennsylvania Gazette*, January 23 and 30, 1788.

XIV. "On Test Laws, Oaths of Allegiance and Abjuration, and Partial Exclusion from Office," dated Philadelphia, March, 1787 [sic]. Reprinted from the *Pennsylvania Evening Herald*, March, 1786.

XV. "Sketches of the Rise, Progress and Consequences of the late Revolution...now republished, with material corrections, and a Letter from [George Washington]...." Reprinted, with the omission of a few paragraphs, from Webster's contribution to Morse's *American Geography* (see Note 9).

XVI. "Remarks on the Method of Burying the Dead among the Nativs of this Country...," dated New York, January 20, 1788. Reprinted, with changes and a prefatory note indicating that his opinions had changed, from the *American Magazine*, February, 1788.

XVII. "On the Regularity of the City of Philadelphia," dated New York, February, 1788. Reprinted from the same.

XVIII. "A Dissertation concerning the Influence of Language on Opinions...," dated New York, May, 1788. Reprinted, with changes, from the same, May, 1788. The New York Public Library copy of the volume contains here a MS note: "This Dissertation contains many errors. N.W. 1835."

XIX. "On Vocal Music," dated Philadelphia, 1787. First printed in the *Pennsylvania Packet*, April 24, 1787, then with changes in the *American Magazine*, June, 1788; the latter version is reprinted here.

XX. "On Morality," dated New York, June, 1788. Reprinted from the *American Magazine*, July, 1788.

XXI. "A Letter from a Lady..." and reply, dated New York, June, 1788. Reprinted from the same.

XXII. "A Letter to the Author...," dated New York, July, 1788. Reprinted, with minor changes, from the same.

XXIII. "An Enquiry into the Origin of the Words Domesday, Parish, Parliament...," dated Boston, March, 1789. Probably one of his lectures, and very possibly printed in a newspaper, but the compiler has not found an earlier printing.

XXIV. "The Injustice, Absurdity, and Bad Policy of Laws against Usury," dated Hartford, September, 1789. Possibly printed earlier in a newspaper, but not located. Reprinted in the New York *Minerva*, February 2, 1795 (*Herald* extra, February 4).

XXV. "On Allegiance," dated Hartford, October, 1789. No earlier printing found.

XXVI. "Explanation of the Reezons, why Marriage iz Prohibited between Natural Relations," dated Hartford, July, 1789. No earlier printing found.

XXVII. "Miscellaneous Remarks on Divizions of Property, Guvernment...," dated Hartford, February, 1790. No earlier printing found.

XXVIII. "On a Discrimination between the Original Holders and the Purchasers of the Certificates of the United States," dated Hartford, March, 1790, with a note beginning, "The following iz part of an 'Essay on the Dets of the United States,' written in 1787, but never before published." The same ideas, sometimes in the same words, had been set forth by Webster in the *Pennsylvania Gazette*, March 21, 1787.

XXIX. "An Address to Yung Gentlemen," dated Hartford, January, 1790. Quoted in the *Gazette of the United States*, July 31, 1790, and printed in the sixth edition of Webster's *American Selection* (Newport, 1789). The date of the latter would suggest that it was the first printing of the piece, but since the essay appears in only certain copies of the sixth edition, on added pages, the situation is not clear. See the following paragraph.

XXX. "An Address to Yung Ladies," dated New York, 1788. Reprinted, with slight changes, from the *American Magazine*, March, 1788. This essay too appears in some copies of the sixth edition of the *American Selection;* that the version there agrees with the magazine publication rather than with this book suggests that the use in the reader preceded this appearance.

2. A "Proposal, for Printing by Subscription" this work was printed on the back cover of the *Massachusetts Magazine* for October, 1789. Advertised as in press in the *American Mercury*, June 21, 1790. Advertised as "this day published" in the *Gazette of the United States*, July 28, 1790, and later, and elsewhere; and as "just published" in the New York *Daily Advertiser*, August 4, 1790, and later, and elsewhere.

3. Reviewed in the *Gazette of the United States*, July 28, 1790, and the *Universal Asylum and Columbian Magazine*, October and November, 1790 (Vol. V, pp. 253–259, 326–333). Webster wrote a letter to the editor of the latter publication, which was printed in September and October, 1791 (Vol. VII, pp. 191–192, 259–264), with the editor's rebuttal (pp. 265–266).

4. Both the New York Public Library and the Rutgers University Library copies contain MS annotations in Webster's hand.

5. Nathaniel W. Appleton, a brother-in-law of Mrs. Webster, acted as Webster's agent in Boston for securing subscriptions and seeing the volume through the press. The Webster Papers contain several letters from him on these subjects. He did not approve of Webster's changing the orthography in quotations (letter of May 16, 1790).

6. The cost appears in Webster's account books thus: "June 23, 1790. By printing 500 copies of Essays. 27 sheets at £5.0.0. 135.0.0." The retail price was $1.67. The sale was not good; on December 18, 1791, Webster wrote Timothy Pickering, "Some of my Essays found a sale, perhaps a third; the remainder will probably be a dead loss...."[3]

7. In acknowledging receipt of a copy of this book, Ezra Stiles wrote, August 27, 1790, regarding the orthography, "You will make a thoro' Experiment upon the public.... I suspect you have put in the pruning Knife too freely for general Acceptance."[4]

8. In the fifth essay Webster took issue with some of Thomas Jefferson's points in *Notes on Virginia*. In sending Jefferson both copyright and personal copies of the work, Webster expressed the hope that this

[3]Pickering Papers, Massachusetts Historical Society; Ford's *Notes*, Vol. I, pp. 308–309.

[4]New York Public Library, bound in copy 2 (Webster's own) of Webster's edition of Winthrop's *Journal* (Hartford, 1790).

would give no offense.[5] Jefferson replied at length, elaborating upon his views, but saying, "In mentioning me in your essays, and canvassing my opinions, you have done what every man has a right to do, and it is for the good of society that this right should be freely exercised."[6]

9. The Reverend Jedidiah Morse was the first person to publish geography texts in the United States. He had a manuscript text which he used in teaching school, and which he published in New Haven in 1784 as *Geography Made Easy*. In 1789 he published a more substantial work, *The American Geography*, which was printed in Elizabethtown, New Jersey. He requested Webster to write for him the summary of United States history which was included, consisting of pp. 94–126 of the first edition. The Webster contribution appears in the succeeding editions of Morse's geography, 1793, 1796, 1802, and 1805, and London, 1792 and 1794 (some editions being entitled *American Universal Geography*).

The contribution is listed on the title-page of the work as "History; Concise Account of the War, and of the Important Events which have Succeeded." This section is followed by four biographical sketches which are probably not by Webster. There is no indication in the volume that this portion was not written by Morse. Webster's authorship, however, is clearly shown in his diary and correspondence, in the fact that some paragraphs are taken bodily from the historical sketch in his *American Selection*, 1788, and in his use of the essay in the present work.

It was while he was preparing this essay that Webster wrote to George Washington for information about the battle of Yorktown. The exchange of letters was published in the *Essays* and elsewhere (Title 765). Webster himself admitted, in a letter to his brother-in-law James Greenleaf, that there were errors in the section. He pleaded as an excuse that "I was sick when I wrote it, & hardly able to hold a pen, much less to examine authorities. . . ."[7]

The description of New York city on pp. 253–258 of Morse's *American Geography* was, as acknowledged in a footnote, taken principally from a description which Webster had written for his *American Magazine*, March, 1788 (Vol. I, pp. 220–228). It too was used in later editions of Morse, though somewhat altered, and also appeared in the 1790, 1791, and 1794 editions of *Geography Made Easy*; for other reprints of this

[5]October 14, 1790, Jefferson Papers, Manuscripts Division, Library of Congress.

[6]December 4, 1790, Presidential Papers, New York Public Library. This letter was printed in the *New Haven Palladium*, June 14, 1843, just after Webster's death; he may well have sent it to the editor himself.

[7]October 12, 1789, Historical Society of Pennsylvania; Ford's *Notes*, Vol. II, pp. 412–413.

description, see Section Nine, Part One, *American Magazine*, March, 1788.

In return for these contributions, Morse gave Webster for use in the *American Magazine* the plate of a map of Virginia. The relations between the Morse and Webster families were long and cordial; the best-known portrait of Webster was painted by S. F. B. Morse, son of Jedidiah.

PART THREE: TWO UNFINISHED PROJECTS

746

Circular. To the clergymen or other well informed gentlemen in the several towns in Connecticut.... N. Webster, junr.... New-Haven, May 7, 1798.

Two leaves, printed only on recto of first. 30 x 20 cm.
CtNhHi, NN.
Evans 34985, Sabin 102343.

NOTES

1. A request for statistical information on which to base an accurate account of the "civil and domestic economy" of Connecticut.

2. Reprinted in the *Medical Repository*, May–July, 1799 (Vol. II, pp. 112–113).

3. One New York Public Library copy is endorsed by Webster, "Circular for Statistics May 7, 1798 N W This project was never carried into effect—but it may have had an influence in exciting other Gentlemen to form the Connecticut Academy...." Another copy in the same library has written on it the desired information for Saybrook.

747

New-Haven, [*space for date*] 1801. Sir, With a view to collect authentic facts.... Noah Webster, jun.

Two leaves, printed only on recto of first. 23 x 18 cm.
NN.

NOTES

1. A request for information on the history of the newspapers of a given place, blanks being left for the date and name of the place.

2. The compiler's files contain a photostat of a copy addressed to the town of Walpole, N.H., dated June 17; the location of the original is not recorded.

3. Ford's *Notes* (Vol. I, pp. 509–510n) lists fourteen replies that Webster received. The project did not result in any publication. See Allen Walker Read, "Noah Webster's Project in 1801 for a History of American Newspapers," *Journalism Quarterly*, September, 1934 (Vol. XI, pp. 258–275).

PART FOUR: EPIDEMIC AND PESTILENTIAL DISEASES

748

A brief history of epidemic and pestilential diseases; with the principal phenomena of the physical world, which precede and accompany them, and observations deduced from the facts stated. In two volumes. By Noah Webster, [*six lines of memberships and other identification*]. Vol. I [II]. Hartford: Printed by Hudson & Goodwin. 1799. [Published according to act of Congress.]

2 vols., xii, [9]–348; (4), 352 pp. 21 cm. Volume I: P. [i], title-page. P. [ii], "Advertisement," concerning authorities cited. P. [iii], table of contents. P. [iv], errata notice. Pp. [v]–xii, introduction. Pp. [9] (sic)–348, text, Sections I through VIII. Volume II: P. [i], title-page. P. [ii], blank. P. [iii], table of contents. P. [iv], errata notice. Pp. [1]–352, text, Sections IX through XVIII, and Addenda. Dated at end, New Haven, November, 1799.

CSmH, CU, Ct, CtHT-W, CtHi, CtNhHi, CtY, DAFM, DLC, IC, ICJ, ICN, ICU, IU, MA, MB, MHi, MWA, MWiW, MiU, N, NBLiHi, NHi, NN, NNC, NNNAM, NRU, NcD, NcU, NhD, NjR, OC, OClW, OClWHi, OO, PMA, PPL, PU, ViU, VtMidbC, Merriam, An-C-M, British Museum.

Evans 36687, Sabin 102341.

NOTES

1. In an unsigned editorial on South Carolina quarantine laws in the *Commercial Advertiser*, January 20, 1798 (*Spectator*, January 31), Webster spoke of data he had gathered on yellow fever and said, "These will be laid before the public in the course of the ensuing spring." He recorded in his diary that on April 10, 1798, he began to write this work "from materials which I have been three months collecting." The Webster Papers contain several affidavits from relatives concerning the circumstances of various deaths from fevers, eyewitness accounts of epidemics in various places, meteorological observations, and mortality statistics

gathered by Webster—some of them later than the publication of this book—to document his theories.

A "Proposal. For Publishing by Subscription, An Enquiry into the Origin of Epidemic Diseases...," signed by Webster, appeared in the *Commercial Advertiser*, March 17, 1798, and later (*Spectator*, March 21 and later), and the *Merchant's Daily Advertiser*, March 24 and later. It is reprinted in Warfel, *Letters of Noah Webster*, pp. 179–180.

In the *Connecticut Journal* of August 29 and September 12, 1798, appeared "To the Public. A Request," signed by Webster, asking for statistics. In the issue of September 19 there appeared another signed notice thanking those persons who had sent information, though saying that the data were not precise and detailed enough.

The book did not actually come out until very late in 1799. The edition was 950 copies. In Webster's accounts he entered under December 4, 1799, that he owed Hudson and Goodwin £159/6 [sic, for £160/4] for 44 ½ sheets at 72/-. The binding was additional, though not all the edition was bound at once. The retail price was $4.00.

2. Advertised: Announced (as "History of Pestilential Diseases") as probably ready in January, 1799, in the *Commercial Advertiser*, November 27, 1798 (*Spectator*, November 28), and the *Salem Gazette*, January 1, 1799. Announced as in press and ready in about three weeks in the *Connecticut Courant*, November 11, 1799, the *New York Gazette*, November 15, the *Commercial Advertiser*, November 16 (*Spectator*, same date), and elsewhere during November. Advertised as "now published" in the *Connecticut Journal*, December 26, 1799, and later, the *Commercial Advertiser*, December 28 and later, and elsewhere.

3. Reviewed: *Monthly Magazine and American Review*, January, February, March, and April, 1800 (Vol. II, pp. 30-36, 108–115, 208–213, 289–296); in a series of articles by James Tytler in the *Salem Gazette*, February 18 and 28, March 11 and 21, and April 15 and 22, 1800; in the *Medical Repository*, [January] and [April], 1800 (Vol. III, pp. 278–288, 390–399); and elsewhere. Webster's reply to the first-mentioned review was printed in his *Commercial Advertiser*, October 16, 1800, and later, and reprinted in the *Monthly Magazine* in November, 1800 (Vol. III, pp. 332–339, with the editor's reply on pp. 339–340). William Cobbett poked fun at Dr. Rush and "that pestilential writer" Webster in his *Rush Light*, March, 1800 (reprinted in his works [London, 1801], Vol. XI, pp. 252–253).

In 1801 the *Medical Repository* printed (Vol. V, pp. 32–36) a letter from Joseph Priestley to Benjamin Rush, dated May 4, 1801, consisting of a critique of the book; this was reprinted in various newspapers, as were many other reviews, replies to reviews, letters to the editor, etc. Many references to Webster's book occur in the various pamphlets and books which were appearing at this time on the much debated subjects of contagion and fevers. An example is found in Dr. William Currie's *Sketch of the Rise and Progress of the Yellow Fever...in...Philadelphia, in ...1799* (Philadelphia, 1800). Currie was particularly critical of Webster's views since late in 1797 Webster had published a series of "letters" attacking Currie's theories (see Section Nine, Part One, rubric C, No. 8).

4. Sir William Osler called this work "the most important medical work written in this country by a layman."[8] For special discussions of this work and Webster's position in the field, see Aldred S. Warthin, "Webster as Epidemiologist," *Journal* of the American Medical Association, March 17, 1923 (Vol. 80, pp. 755–764), and Charles-Edward A. Winslow, "The Epidemiology of Noah Webster," *Transactions* of the Connecticut Academy of Arts and Sciences, January, 1934 (Vol. 32, pp. 21–109). The latter was also issued as a separate, with two illustrations.

5. A physician who was much impressed by Webster's book, Ennalls Martin of Maryland, later dedicated to him a work of his own on the same topic, *Essay on the Epidemics of the Winters of 1813 and 1814, in Talbot and Queen-Anne's Counties...Maryland* (Baltimore, 1815).

6. Large portions of the work were taken over, without credit to Webster, by Edward Bascome in his *History of Epidemic Pestilences* (London, 1851).

7. In October, 1845, Dr. Joseph Barratt, a physician and botanist of Middletown, Connecticut, read before the Middlesex County Medical Society a paper entitled "Diseases of the United States for the last Forty-Six Years," which he stated was a continuation of Webster's book.[9]

8. One of the New York Public Library copies is Webster's own, with MS corrections and revisions for a reprinting. In 1832 a new edition was proposed (see Title 750). The following year a contributor to a New York newspaper ("Prudens" in the *Commercial Advertiser*, June 17, 1833) asserted that the work was being translated in Germany, but the compiler has not found any German translation. In September, 1849, after Webster's death, his son William urged Harper & Brothers to bring out a new edition, incorporating Webster's changes, but nothing came of the proposal (correspondence in the Webster Papers).

[8]"Some Aspects of Medical Bibliography," *Bulletin* of the Association of Medical Librarians, July–October, 1902 (Vol. I, pp. 19–32, the quotation being from p. 27).

[9]Frank K. Halleck, "Joseph Barratt, M.D...," *Bulletin* of the Society of Medical History of Chicago, January, 1923 (Vol. III, pp. 151–167).

9. The Library of Congress has a second copy in which the title-page has been reset in different type, though the wording is identical. The most easily observable difference is that in the variant the line endings in the paragraph below Webster's name are Works, the, in, Sci-, Mass- instead of other, Sciences, Man-, Academy, Histori-.

749

——— London: Printed for G. G. and J. Robinson, Paternoster-Row, by G. Woodfall, Paternoster-Row. 1800.

2 vols., xvi, 559; iv, 526 pp. 21 cm.

CSt, DAFM, DLC, MH, MHi, MdBE, MiDeaEd, NN, NNNAM, NjP, NjR.

NOTES

1. The phrase "In two volumes" is dropped from the title, and the lines are not divided at the same points. Except for Anglicized spelling, the text follows the American edition.

2. Reviewed: *Monthly Magazine or British Register*, July, 1800 (Vol. IX, p. 649); *British Critic*, August, 1800 (Vol. XVI, pp. 160–168); *Critical Review*, March, 1801 (Ser. 2, Vol. XXXI, pp. 260–268); *Monthly Review*, April, 1802 (ser. 2, Vol. XXXVII, pp. 404–407). The last was quoted in the *Commercial Advertiser*, August 30 (*Spectator*, September 1) and the Hudson (N.Y.) *Bee*, September 14. On May 13, 1801, the *National Intelligencer* reprinted a review from "The London Review," which periodical has not been identified by the compiler.

3. Rufus King, who was then in London, handled the details of British publication. On February 18, 1800, Webster wrote Benjamin Rush, "I have rec'd a letter from Mr. King Dated Decr 13th in which he informs me that he has sold [the] MS. Hist. of Pestilence to Mr. Robinson & Co. for 100 Guineas, for the first impression of 1000 copies; & 100 more in case a second impression should be printed."[1] The price of the English edition was eighteen shillings.

750

Proposal for publishing by subscription.... L. H. Young. New Haven, June, 1832.

Broadside, 32 x 20 cm.

[1] Webster Papers, New York Public Library; Ford's *Notes*, Vol. I, pp. 475–476.

NOTES

1. The compiler's notes record this broadside, but do not locate a copy. The one described is recorded as endorsed by Webster, "Young's proposal for publishing Hist. of Epidemics."

2. Reprinted in the *Connecticut Herald*, July 3 and 10, 1832.

3. Despite Young's signature on the broadside, the compiler feels that the text—which includes commendations and reviews of the first edition—was compiled by Webster. The edition did not mature.

PART FIVE: WEBSTER GENEALOGY

751

Genealogy. The following account has been compiled by N. Webster.... [New Haven, 1836.]

8 pp. 23 cm. P. [1], caption title and beginning of text; dated at end New Haven, January, 1836.

CtHi, CtNhHi, DLC, ICN, MB, MWA, N, NBLiHi, NN, PHi, VtHi.

Sabin 102354.

This pamphlet was printed but not published, copies being given to each of Webster's children and grandchildren "for the purpose of preserving the history of the family...and to correct an error in Dr. Trumbull's History of Connecticut...."[2]

752

Webster genealogy. Compiled and printed for presentation only by Noah Webster. New Haven: 1836. With notes and corrections by his great-grandson, Paul Leicester Ford. Brooklyn, N.Y. Privately printed. 1876.

[Frontis.], (3), 9, (3) leaves, printed on rectos only, illus. 30 cm. Leaf [i], half-title. Leaf [ii], title-page. Leaf [iii], editor's note, signed "P.L. F. Brooklyn, N.Y. November, 1876." Leaves 1–9, text, incorporating MS corrections made by Webster in a copy of the original edition. Leaves [10–11], a "pre-print" of Horace Scudder, "Great-Grandfather's Books and Pictures," which appeared in *St. Nicholas Magazine*, January, 1877 (Vol. IV, pp. 193–197). Leaf [12], genealogical data on the immediate family of Gordon L. Ford.

[2]Webster to William G. Webster, January 23, 1836, Pierpont Morgan Library; Ford's *Notes*, Vol. II, p. 351.

CSmH, Ct, CtNhHi, DLC, MB, MNF, MWA, N, NBLiHi, NN, NjR, PHi, PPPrHi, British Museum.

NOTES

1. 250 copies, gray paper wrappers. Some contain the conjugate frontispiece and title-page of a Merriam-Webster dictionary of the period. The frontispiece thereof, the Morse portrait of Webster engraved by H. B. Hall and Sons, serves as a frontispiece in these copies (facing the title-page); and the dictionary title-page appears as a tailpiece, facing the blank verso of leaf [12].

2. One copy in The New York Public Library has, after leaf [12], two added charts of the Ford and Burnham descent of Gordon L. Ford.

PART SIX: COLLECTION OF PAPERS

753

A collection of papers on political, literary and moral subjects. By Noah Webster, LL.D. New York: Webster & Clark.... Boston—Tappan & Dennett. Philadelphia—Smith & Peck. 1843.

(4), 4, 373 pp. 23 cm. P. [i], title-page. P. [ii], copyright notice, 1843, and "New Haven: Printed by B. L. Hamlen." P. [iii], "Advertisement" (preface), unsigned and undated. P. [iv], table of contents. At this point there is an intrusive signature, pp. [1]–4, with advertising matter for Webster's other works. Pp. [1]–373, text.

CLU, CSmH, CU, Ct, CtHT, CtNhHi, CtY, DLC, IC, ICN, ICU, IU, M, MA, MB, MBAt, MH, MHi, MSaE, MWA, MWiW, MdBE, MiDeaEd, MiU, N, NBLiHi, NBuG, NHi, NN, NNC, NNS, NNUT, NRU, NcD, NcU, Nh, NjHi, NjN, NjP, O, OC, OClWHi, OO, OU, PHi, PHC, PU, RPB, VtMidbC, Merriam, British Museum.

Sabin 102345.

NOTES

1. The sections and their sources are:

I. "Revolution in France," reprint of Title 721, with minor changes which incorporate Webster's MS corrections.

II. "The Rights of Neutrals," reprint of Section II of Webster's *Miscellaneous Papers*, 1802, with a "Postscript," but omitting the "Appendix" of the original printing. This incorporates most of the corrections and changes made in Webster's marked copy (New York Public Library).

III. "On the Supposed Change in the Temperature of Winter," reprinted from the *Memoirs* of the Connecticut Academy of Arts and Sciences, Vol. I (1810), pp. 1–68, with minor changes.

IV. "Origin of the first Bank in the United States," reprint of the introductory portion of Section IV of Webster's *Miscellaneous Papers*, 1802, incorporating some MS corrections.

V. "Letter from General Washington," previously printed as a footnote in No. XV of Webster's *Essays*, 1790. It incorporates a correction made in MS in Webster's copy.

VI. "Correspondence with the Hon. Jas. Madison, on the Origin of the Constitution," apparently not previously published.

VII. "Origin of the Copy-Right Laws in the United States," reprinted from the *Commercial Advertiser*, June 21, 1831.

VIII. "Vindication of the Treaty of Amity, Commerce and Navigation with Great Britain," reprinted from the *Minerva*, July 18–August 5, 1795, with minor changes.

IX. "Origin of Amherst College in Massachusetts," apparently not previously published (see Note 6).

X. "An Address before the Agricultural Society in Northampton, October 14, 1818," reprint of Title 741.

XI. "A Letter to the Honorable Daniel Webster," reprint of Title 735, with minor changes.

XII. "Answer to His Exc. John Brooks, Governor of the Commonwealth of Massachusetts," reprinted from the *Columbian Centinel*, June 5, 1819.

XIII. "A Letter to the Rev. Samuel Lee, Professor of Arabic in the University of Cambridge," reprinted from "Philology" in the *New England Magazine*, November 1, 1831 (Vol. I, pp. [369]–380).

XIV. "Reply to a Letter of David McClure, Esq., on the Subject of the Proper Course of Study in the Girard College, Philadelphia," reprinted from the *National Intelligencer*, November 2, 1836.

XV. "Letter to a Young Gentleman Commencing his Education," reprint of Letter I of *Letters to a Young Gentleman*, 1823, with minor changes.

XVI. "Form of Association for Young Men," apparently not previously published.

XVII. "Modes of Teaching the English Language," apparently not previously published.

XVIII. "Origin of the Hartford Convention in 1814." A fuller account than that given in the 1835 and later editions of Webster's *History of the United States*.

XIX. "A Brief History of Political Parties in the United States," apparently not previously published. It is drawn in large part from Webster's unpublished speech before the Connecticut Historical Society, 1840 (MS in the Webster Papers), and basically goes back to articles he published in the *Connecticut Courant* in 1783 (see Section Nine, Part Three).

XX. "State of English Philology," not previously published in this form, but drawn in part from various of Webster's philological writings.

2. Section VI was reprinted in *Old South Leaflet* No. 197 (Boston, [1908]), pp. 18–23, and Section IX in the *Amherst Graduates' Quarterly*, May–November, 1946 (Vol. 35, pp. 237–248, 391–402; Vol. 36, pp. 12–21).

3. Announced in the New Haven *Daily Herald*, April 15, 1843, and the *Hampshire Gazette*, April 25, and advertised as "just published" in the *Hartford Daily Courant*, May 13, 1843, and later, and elsewhere. The price was $1.37½.

4. Reviewed: New Haven *Daily Herald*, May 11, 1843; *New York Evangelist*, May 25, reprinting Section XV; *New York Daily Tribune*, May 30; *Boston Recorder*, June 29.

5. Webster wrote to his son-in-law William Chauncey Fowler, April 11, 1843, "I am now bringing all my literary labors to a close. I have in the press a collection of papers, which will be published in about a month. This closes my literary pursuits. . . ."[3]

6. The history of Amherst (Section IX) had apparently existed in MS for some time, for on June 16, 1840, Webster had written to Fowler, "Dr Coggswell of Boston has my MS History of Amherst College for insertion in the Quarterly Register; but he has delayed printing it, by request of Dr. Humphrey, for the purpose of having an addition to it. But I do not approve of this—I wish the History, if published at all, to be soon published by itself—& the MS returned to me. It is a part of my family-papers, which I am unwilling to have lying in Boston."[4]

[3]In the possession of Mrs. Howard B. Field; transcript provided by Prof. Harry R. Warfel.

[4]Ibid.

PART SEVEN: ADVERTISEMENTS, RECOMMENDATIONS, AND DEFENSES OF WEBSTER'S PUBLICATIONS

Included in this section are broadsides and pamphlets which refer to more than one of Webster's works, those which bear on single titles being entered under the title. A further limitation is that only those are listed which contain some text written by Webster, thus omitting a few examples of commendations of his works published without commentary.

A. *Education of Youth*

754

Education of youth in the United States. The principles of the sciences. . . . [New Haven? 1807.]

Broadside, 47 x 27 cm.
NN.

NOTES

1. Advertising matter for six of Webster's works, consisting of a brief introduction, a short descriptive note for each work, and recommendations. These are followed by a long list of "Proprietors and Publishers of the Foregoing Works." The text ends with an appeal by Webster for the purchase of his textbooks, in order to enable him to continue work on his large dictionary.

2. The latest internal date is December 15, 1807, and two copies in The New York Public Library are endorsed by Webster, "Recommendations, 1807." They also bear his MS correction of "American" to "Connecticut" Academy. Probably printed in New Haven.

B. *Series of Books*

755

Series of books for systematic instruction in the English language, by N. Webster, LL.D. [New Haven, 1830?]

16 pp. 23 cm. P. [1], caption title and beginning of text, which continues to p. 7, consisting of many recommendations of various of Webster's writings. Pp. 7–16, essay by Webster, "Discrepancies of English Orthography. . . ." On p. 16, imprint "H. Howe, Printer, New Haven."

CTY, DLC, MB, MBAT, MH, MWA, N, NN, NHD, Merriam, British Museum.

Sabin 102398.

NOTES

1. The pamphlet cannot be earlier than March, 1830, for that is the date of one of the recommendations (p. 4); but it appears to have been printed soon after that, for Webster wrote on April 12, 1830, to his son-in-law William C. Fowler, sending him an imprint which must surely be this, for he says it contains "testimonials respecting my books, with some authorities & explanatory remarks on orthography. . . ."[5]

2. There are two preliminary forms of this pamphlet, with the same title, which do not contain any text by Webster:

(a) Two leaves, printed only on the recto of the first, 32 x 20 cm. This consists of one recommendation, signed by President Day of Yale and others. There are three copies in the Webster Papers, New York Public Library, each of which had been sent to a prominent person and returned with a further recommendation added in MS. These recommendations were incorporated in the later forms. The earliest of these was sent by Webster on January 9, 1830, so the piece was printed before that date.

(b) An eight-page pamphlet in the New York State and New-York Historical Society libraries. The text is as described through p. 7; the balance of 7 and p. 8 contain a review of the *American Dictionary* reprinted from the *Edinburgh New-Philosophical Journal.*

3. Apparently this pamphlet prompted Lyman Cobb to publish his *Critical Review of the Orthography of Dr. Webster's Series of Books* (New York, 1831); see Section Nine, Part Four, rubric J.

[5]In the possession of Mrs. Howard B. Field; transcript courtesy of Prof. Harry R. Warfel.

756

[Same caption title, different setting of type.]

16 pp. 21 cm.
CtY, MWA.

NOTES

1. Similar to the preceding. There are additional recommendations, additions to the essay, and an added passage by Webster describing his work. The "Discrepancies" section in this printing begins on p. 9 instead of p. 7, and runs all the way to the bottom of p. 16. There is no imprint.

2. Probably printed early in April, 1831, for on April 20 Webster wrote Fowler, "I send you a pamphlet reprinted with additions."[6]

757

Advertisement. A new edition of the Bible.... [1832(?)]

16 pp. 23 cm.
Ct.

NOTES

1. Another version of the *Series of Books*. P. [1] consists of an advertisement for Webster's forthcoming edition of the Bible. On p. 2 is the caption title "Series of Books...," and the beginning of a series of testimonials, which runs to p. 13. Pp. 13–16, "Discrepancies...," a shortened version of Webster's essay in the earlier printings.

2. Not earlier than 1832, since some of the recommendations bear that date. 1832 and 1833 were the years in which Webster was preparing and advertising his Bible.

c. *Attacks on Lyman Cobb*[7]

758

To the public. Lyman Cobb has lately published.... New Haven, November 15, 1831. N. Webster.

[6]Ibid.
[7]See Section Nine, Part Four, rubric J for Webster's long feud with Cobb.

Broadside, 25 x 20 cm.
NN.
In this Webster parries the charges of discrepancy and inconsistency made in Cobb's *Critical Review*.

759

To the friends of American literature. Lyman Cobb has been... attempting to disparage Dr. Webster's school books.... [New York? 1831?]

8 pp. 21 cm. P. [1], caption title and beginning of text, which runs to p. 8, discussing Cobb's attacks on Webster's works, signed "A Friend to American Literature." Following this is a review of Cobb's *Critical Review*, reprinted from the New York *Daily Advertiser*, November 22, 1831.
CtHi, CtY, NN.

NOTES

1. Probably published late in 1831, perhaps in New York.
2. The identity of the author is not known, but the compiler believes that this pamphlet was written by Webster, though apparently Robert C. Sands, editor of the *Commercial Advertiser*, had a hand in it (see N. and J. White to Webster, January 30, 1835, quoted under the following entry).
3. An extract was printed in the *Indiana Democrat*, May 3, 1837.

760

[To the friends of American literature(?). New York, 1835.]

Some sort of pamphlet or broadside counter-attacking Cobb, perhaps a revision of the preceding, was published in New York about the middle of February, 1835, as evidenced by the following extracts from letters from N. and J. White of that city to Webster.[8]

January 22, 1835. "Yours of the 19– came duly to hand & contents noted. In compliance with your request we return the papers which you sent us. We fully coincide with you that a short defense of your books against Cobbs attacks accompanied by a brief criticism of his books... would do good. Let it be *short*. The public will not read long criticisms—

[8] All in the Ellsworth Papers, Connecticut Historical Society.

& then have it circulated privately amongst teachers & others in those sections where Cobb is so busily at work. We would not think it best to put it in the public prints, at least, for a time. Will not some teacher in N Haven under your direction prepare such an article—we will see that they [sic] are circulated...."

January 30, 1835. "We have barely had time to glance at your Criticisms of Cobbs Books but would suggest [i.e., ask] whether the article prepared by yourself & Mr Sands 2 or 3 y^{rs} since headed 'To the Friends of Am. Literature' with slight alterations would not be quite to the point, if so it could be reprinted & circulated as before.... If you will revise it & send it to us, we will be at one half the expense & all the trouble of Printing and Circulating them [sic]...."

February 9, 1835. "We are printing the Criticisms."

February 19, 1835. "We have printed the remarks on Cobbs Books and have charged one half of the expense to your acct $13.20.... We shall send 100 to you by first boat...."

761

[To the friends of American literature(?). Cincinnati, 1835.]

One of Webster's pamphlets against Cobb, probably the one just discussed, was republished in Cincinnati in mid-1835. The evidence is contained in two letters from William G. Webster to his father. On July 22, 1835, he wrote that Cobb's agents were very active in the area, so "we thought it expedient to print *five thousand* of the little pamphlets & shall circulate them diffusely," and on July 27 he wrote, "We have published 5000 copies of the pamphlet & are scattering them abroad...."[9]

D. *To the Friends of Literature*

762

To the friends of literature. Great attention is now given.... New Haven, October, 1836.

Broadside, 51 x 30 cm.
NN.

[9] Webster Papers, New York Public Library.

NOTES

1. An essay discussing orthography and pronunciation and the books which record and teach them, with particular reference to Webster's series of books. This is followed by a testimonial subscribed by thirty-one Senators and seventy-three Representatives, and several other recommendations and reviews of various of Webster's works.

2. The compiler believes that the introductory matter and connective notes were written by Webster.

763

[Same caption title.]

12 pp. 18 cm. P. [1], caption title and beginning of text, which is the same as the preceding title as far as the end of the Congressional testimonial; in this version the names are not given individually. From this point the text and recommendations are partly the same, partly new, the latest date being January, 1839. At the end is an advertisement of S[idney] Babcock, which suggests New Haven as the place of publication.

NN.

Reprinted, with two additional paragraphs, in the Watertown (N.Y.) *Jeffersonian*, July 15, 1839.

E. *Commendations*

764

Commendations of Dr. N. Webster's books.... [New Haven? 1841?]

30 pp. 23 cm. P. [1], caption title and beginning of a group of about fifty testimonials, which run through p. 10. These are followed by three essays by Webster: pp. 11–15, "State of English Philology"; pp. 15–25, "Grammatical Errors in the Common Version of the Scriptures...;" and pp. 25–30, "Gesenius."

CtHT-W, CtY, MHi, MiDeaEd, NBLiHi, British Museum.

NOTES

1. The "State of English Philology"—really a discussion of the English translations of the Bible—is not the same as the essay of that title in

Webster's *Collection of Papers*, 1843, though it covers in part the same ground. The other two essays are similar in title and content to, but not the same as, two parts of his *Mistakes and Corrections*, 1837.

2. Probably published early in 1841. On February 27 of that year Webster wrote to his son, "I have sent my pamphlet of *Commendations* to several of the Senators & Representatives. . . ."[1]

[1]Pierpont Morgan Library.

PART EIGHT: POSTHUMOUS PUBLICATIONS

Since the works in this part are in general modern works widely available, analysis of contents and locations of copies are not given. Copies of each are in The New York Public Library. For Webster letters printed in books not primarily concerned with him, see Appendix C.

765

1781. York Town. Letter from Noah Webster to George Washington and from George Washington to Noah Webster, from the original in the possession of Gordon L Ford. Brooklyn, N.Y., privately printed, 1881. [Elzevir Club series, No. 4.]

5 leaves, printed on the rectos only. 28 cm.

The text consists of Webster's letter of inquiry about the Battle of Yorktown, dated July 14, 1788, and Washington's reply of July 31. This is the first printing of the former; the latter had been published by Webster as a footnote to No. XV of his *Essays*, 1790, and as No. V of his *Collection of Papers*, 1843, and has since been published elsewhere. Both are printed in Ford's *Notes*, Vol. I, pp. 180–183.

766

Notes on the life of Noah Webster, compiled by Emily Ellsworth Fowler Ford, edited by Emily Ellsworth Ford Skeel. Volume I [II]. New York, privately printed, 1912.

2 vols., frontis., [xi], 567 pp., illus.; frontis., [vii], 555 pp., illus. 20 cm.

This work contains the first printing of certain Webster materials (other than letters), as follows:

Vol. I, p. 23. Extract from a student Latin oration of 1776; later separately published (Title 770).

Vol. II, p. 79. Extract from "A word to an old-fashioned Churchman," ca. 1810.

Vol. II, pp. 125–128. Circular letter, January 5, 1814 [sic], signed by Joseph Lyman but probably written by Webster; see Appendix A, No. 13.

Vol. II, p. 198. "Prayer before sailing to Europe," 1824.

Vol. II, pp. 482–483. Open letter "To the Abolitionists, so called," undated.

Passim. Diary, 1784–1794, 1798–1820; memoranda and scraps.

767

Poems by Noah Webster, edited by Ruth Farquhar Warfel and Harry Redcay Warfel. College Park, Maryland, Harruth Lefraw, 1936.

16 pp. 22 cm.

Nine poems, reprinted from the *American Magazine*, the *Connecticut Courant*, the *Gazette of the United States*, and the *American Spelling Book*, 1804.

Some previously unpublished Webster marginalia in a copy of his own Essays, *1790, are printed in Clarence E. Partch, "Noah Webster, the Schoolmaster of our Republic,"* Journal *of Rutgers University Library, June, 1939 (Vol. II, pp.* [*39*]*–45).*

768

Noah Webster: Letters on yellow fever addressed to Dr. William Currie, with an introductory essay by Benjamin Spector. Baltimore, The Johns Hopkins Press, 1947.

vi, 110 pp., illus. 25 cm.

At head of title: Supplements to the Bulletin of the History of Medicine... No. 9.

For the original publication of the letters, see Section Nine, Part One, rubric C, No. 8.

769

Letters of Noah Webster, edited with an introduction by Harry R. Warfel. New York, Library Publishers, [copyright 1953].

xlvi, 562 pp. 23 cm.

Personal letters, letters to newspapers, controversial pamphlets, and other material, some not previously published.

770

Noah Webster on youth and old age, a sophomore Latin exercise given at Yale College, May 4, 1776. [New York, The New York Public Library, 1954.]

[4] pp. 29 cm.

100 copies privately printed "as a keepsake." Latin text only. An extract from the Latin text was published in Ford's *Notes* (Vol. I, p. 23), and the complete text, with an English translation, was published in the *Yale Alumni Weekly*, November 19, 1926 (Vol. 36, p. 225) in an article, "Noah Webster as a Student Orator," by Theodore A. Zunder.

Section Eight

WORKS EDITED BY WEBSTER

PART ONE: THE NEW ENGLAND PRIMER

771

[New England primer, "amended and improved; by the author of the Grammatical Institute." Philadelphia: Young and M'Culloch, 1787.]

Evans 20546, Heartman (1934 ed.) 102.

No copy of this has been found, nor has the compiler been able to find the source of Evans' wording for the title, but the publication of such an edition is suggested by advertisements in contemporary newspapers, e.g., the *Pennsylvania Gazette* and the *PennsylvaniaHerald*, October 31, 1787, and later, in both of which Young and M'Culloch advertise a New England primer improved according to Webster's speller.

Heartman's entry is taken from Evans. As No. 103 he lists another edition, Philadelphia, Joseph Crukshank, 1787, without reference to Webster or "the author of the Grammatical Institute." The Crukshank edition is attributed to Webster in Richard B. Sealock, "Publishing in Pennsylvania, 1785–1790..." (unpublished M.S. thesis, Faculty of Library Service, Columbia University, February, 1935), but this seems to be a mistaken telescoping of Evans' and Heartman's entries.

772

[—— Hartford: Elisha Babcock, 1788(?).]

Evans 21989.

Evans enters this under 1789, presumably on the basis of newspaper advertising of January, 1789, but the compiler places the edition in the preceding year because she has located a newspaper advertisement in the *American Mercury*, December 8, 1788, in which the New England primer, "Amended and improved by the author of the Grammatical Institute," is announced as "just published." This advertisement contains the wording given by Evans in his hypothetical title.

773

The New-England primer, amended and improved. By the author of The grammatical institute. Embellished with cuts. New-York: Printed by J. Patterson. . . . 1789. Under protection of the statute.

72 unnumbered pp., illus. 10 cm. P. [1], title-page. P. [2], preface, unsigned and undated. P. [3], "Index or Key." Pp. [4–5], alphabets. P. [6], double letters. Pp. [7–24], Tables [I]–VIII, of words of one or more syllables. Pp. [25–29], simple sentences of moral tone, with a cut at the head of each page. Pp. [30–36], Stories [I]–IV, each with a cut. Pp. [37–61], Shorter Catechism. Pp. [62–72], hymns, verses, prayers, and Creed.

CtHi, MWA (imperfect).

Heartman (1934 ed.) 112.

The tables, the moral sentences, and three of the four stories seem to be Webster's. The first story, that of the martyrdom of John Rogers, is from the old New England primer; the other three are "Of the boy, who was bit by a mouse in Albany county," "The boy who played truant in New-York," and "Of the two industrious girls in Poughkeepsie." The rhymed alphabet is not the traditional one; this version may be Webster's composition too, though the old text had already suffered changes at the hands of various editors. For some of these changes, see James H. Trumbull, "The New England Primer and its Predecessors," *Sunday School Times*, May 6, 1882 (Vol. XXIV, pp. 275–277).

774

The New-England primer, amended and improved by the author of The grammatical institute. Let children learn to lisp their Maker's praise. Under protection of the statute. Hartford, Printed by Elisha Babcock, M,DCC,XCIII.

80 pp., illus. 11 cm.

NRU.

Evans 25886.

NOTES

1. Not seen by the compiler; data provided by the library.

2. Advertised in the *American Mercury*, December 23, 1793, and later, as "just published."

775

[—— Hartford: Elisha Babcock for John Babcock, 1797.]

Evans 32527.

The compiler has found no evidence of such an edition. The work was being advertised for sale at the office of the paper in the *American Mercury*, September 27 and October 4, 1798, but it cannot be determined which version or edition this represents.

776

The New-England primer. Improved and adapted to the use of schools. By Noah Webster, Jun. Esq. Designed as an introduction to The American spelling book. Embellished with cuts. Hudson: Printed by Ashbel Stoddard, M,DCCCI.

96 unnumbered pp., illus. 10 cm.

MB.

Heartman (1934 ed.) 185.

The contents of this edition are closer to the original New England primers than were those of the New York, 1789, edition. The alphabet is the traditional one, beginning "In Adam's fall We sinned all;" and the stories and verses include more of the early ones and less new material.

In an edition published by Isaiah Thomas in Worcester in 1802, the words of the familiar prayer are changed from "I pray the Lord my soul to keep" to "I pray thee, Lord, my soul to keep." James H. Trumbull in "The New England Primer and its Predecessors," Sunday School Times, *May 6, 1882 (Vol. XXIV, pp. 275–277), suggests that this change was made by Webster. It does not, however, appear in any of the editions with which Webster had known connection.*

777

[—— Hudson, N.Y.: Ashbel Stoddard, 1804.]

Heartman (1934 ed.) 205.

Heartman cites as authority a primer advertisement in another book published by Stoddard. The compiler has found no other evidence of this edition, and Mr. Heartman was unable to tell her where he had seen the other work—which the Library of Congress could not locate—and she suspects the edition to be a ghost. Perhaps Heartman's entry is a garbled reference to the following edition.

778

——— Hudson. Printed by Ashbel Stoddard. . . . 1805.

96 unnumbered pp., illus. 11 cm.
MWA (imperfect).
The contents are similar to Stoddard's edition of 1801.

779

——— Hudson. Printed by Ashbel Stoddard, for William E. Norman. 1805.

92 unnumbered pp., illus. 11 cm.
NN, Columbia County Historical Society, Valatie, N.Y.
There are slight differences in the contents from the preceding.

780

——— Hudson: Printed by Ashbel Stoddard. . . . 1818.

92 unnumbered pp., illus. 11 cm.
MWA, PPPM.
The contents are only slightly different from the preceding entry.

PART TWO: WINTHROP'S JOURNAL

781

A journal of the transactions and occurrences in the settlement of Massachusetts and the other New-England colonies, from the year 1630 to 1644: written by John Winthrop, Esq. First governor of Massachusetts: and now first published from a correct copy of the original manuscript. [*three lines of quotation.*] Hartford: Printed by Elisha Babcock. M,DCC,XC.

(8), 364, (4) pp. 20 cm. P. [i], title-page. Pp. [ii–iv], blank. Pp. [v–vi], preface, unsigned, dated Hartford, July, 1790. P. [vii], dedication to Winthrop's descendants. P. [viii], blank. Pp. [1]–364, text. Pp. [365–368], table of contents.

CSmH, CU, Ct, CtHi, CtY, DLC, ICN, ICU, MB, MH, MHi, MSaE, MWA, MWiW-C, MiU-C, N, NHi, NN, NNC, NjP, PHi, PPAmP, PPL, RPJCB, ViU, British Museum.

Evans 23086, Sabin 104847.

NOTES

1. Advertised as in press, *American Mercury*, May 24, 1790, and later, and as "just published" in the same, July 19 and later. Webster's diary gives July 29 as the publication date.

2. Webster had this book in mind as early as May 1, 1788, the date of an unsigned letter "To the Publick," published in the *Impartial Gazetteer*, June 14, 1788, in which he proposed to publish the work by subscription. A second letter, dated Boston, May 1, 1789, appeared in the *Massachusetts Magazine*, April, 1789 (inside front cover) and in the *Massachusetts Spy*, May 14, 1789, and later, repeating the proposal and naming Isaiah Thomas as the printer. Neither of these plans matured, however.

3. One of the New York Public Library copies was Webster's own, with MS annotations and inserted related correspondence.

4. Webster just broke even on the cost of publishing this work; in an article in the *Boston Recorder*, August 18, 1837, he wrote of it, "The sale of the edition enabled me to pay for the printing, but afforded me no profit."

5. A small portion of the text was reprinted as "Curious Extracts" in the *Massachusetts Magazine*, June, 1791 (Vol. III, pp. 356–357), and part of the preface is reprinted in Appendix XXII of Ford's *Notes*.

PART THREE: COLLECTION OF PAPERS ON BILIOUS FEVERS

782

(Circular.) To the physicians of Philadelphia, New-York, Baltimore, Norfolk and Newhaven.... Noah Webster, Jun. New-York, Oct. 31, 1795.

Two leaves, printed only on the recto of the first. 33 x 20 cm.
PPL (Rush MSS).

NOTES

1. Reprinted: In the book, pp. [vi]–x; *American Minerva*, October 31, 1795; New York *Daily Advertiser* and New York *Diary*, November 2; *Aurora* and *Gazette of the United States* and New York *Herald*, November 4; *Argus* and *American Mercury*, November 9; Norfolk, Va., *Herald*, November 12; *Albany Gazette*, November 13; *Federal Orrery*, November 16; *New Jersey State Gazette* and *South Carolina State Gazette*, November 17; *Wood's Newark Gazette*, November 18; *Connecticut Journal*, November 19; Warfel, *Letters of Noah Webster*, pp. 130–133.

2. Probably printed in New York.

3. An announcement of Webster's plan of compiling this work and a request for assistance from physicians. Its publication in the newspapers brought an ironic reply signed "A Fellow of the College of Physicians," published in the *Aurora*, November 6, and reprinted in the New York *Argus*, November 10, and the *Federal Orrery*, November 20. A clipping from the *Aurora* in The New York Public Library is endorsed by Webster, "Insulting answer to N Webster's humane proposals to collect facts on yellow fever." Other sarcastic replies appeared in the New York *Daily Advertiser*, November 12 (reprinted in the *Federal Orrery*, November 26); the New York *Argus*, November 14; and the *Salem Gazette*, November 24 (reprinted in the *Argus* and the *New York Journal*, December 5).

4. There is an undated personal letter from Webster to Benjamin Rush on the recto of the second leaf of the copy located; perhaps there was a personal approach on each copy.

783

A collection of papers on the subject of bilious fevers, prevalent in the United States for a few years past. Compiled by Noah Webster, Jun. [*five lines listing memberships.*] New-York: Printed by Hopkins, Webb and Co.... 1796. [Published according to act of Congress.]

x, ix, 52, (1), [53]–246 pp. 21 cm. (See Note 1 for analysis of contents.)

CSmH, CtHT-W, CtHi, CtY, DAFM, DLC, MB, MHi, MWA, MiU, N, NBLiHi, NHi, NN, NNNAM, NNS, NRU, NjR, PHi, PP, PPCP, PPL, British Museum.

Evans 31593, Sabin 102346.

NOTES

1. Contents: P. [i], title-page. P. [ii], blank. P. [iii], table of contents. Pp. [iv]–v, "Advertisement," signed and dated New York, July 1, 1796. Pp. [vi]–x, "Circular," a reprint of the preceding entry.

Here follows the title-page of *An Account of the Epidemic Yellow Fever, as it Appeared in the City of New-York in the Year 1795...*, by Valentine Seaman, M.D., with a Hopkins, Webb and Co. imprint, 1796. The ensuing section is made up of sheets of the original printing of Seaman's work, according to Sabin. In any case, this section begins a new Roman numeration; it also begins a series of signature marks which continues through the whole volume. This title-page being [i], [ii] is blank. P. [iii], dedication to Benjamin Rush. P. [iv], blank. P. [v], second dedication, to the "Surviving Members of the Committee of Health of New-York for 1795." P. [vi], blank. Pp. [vii]–ix, preface. P. [x], blank. Pp. [1]–52, text. This portion is described in the table of contents of the volume as "I. Account of the Yellow Fever in New-York in 1795—by Dr. Valentine Seaman."

Then there is a half-title, which is not in the pagination of the volume, though it is in the signaturing: "Letters to William Buel, Physician, on the Fever Which Prevailed in New-York in 1795. By E. H. Smith. To Which is Prefixed an Account of the Febrile Diseases of Sheffield (Massachusetts) in the Years 1793, 1794 and 1795. By W. Buel." The verso is blank. Pp. [53]–144, text. This section is listed in the table of contents as "II. Account of the same, by Dr. Elihu H. Smith: to which is prefixed,

III. An account of the Fevers that prevailed in Sheffield, State of Massachusetts, in 1794 and 1795—by Dr. Buel."

P. [145], half-title, "Letter from Doctors Taylor and Hansford to the Publisher." P. [146], blank. Pp. [147]–153, text. This is listed in the table of contents as "IV. An account of the Fever at Norfolk, Virginia, in 1795—by Doctors Taylor and Hansford."

P. [154], caption title, "Extract of Dr. Ramsay's (of Norfolk, Virginia) Letter to Mr. Mitchill;—Concerning the Pestilential Sickness in Norfolk, in the Summer and Autumn of 1795," and beginning of text, which runs through p. 156. This section is listed in the table of contents as "V. Letter from Dr. Ramsay on the same subject."

P. [157], caption title, "Summary View of Dr. Mitchill's Opinion Concerning the Causes of Epidemic Distempers," and beginning of text, which runs through p. 170. This section is listed in the table of contents, *after the following section*, as "VII. Dr. Mitchill, on Contagion."

P. [171], half-title, "Two Letters Relative to the Yellow Fever, as it appeared in New-Haven, in the State of Connecticut, in the Year 1794. I. Letter from Dr. Monson, jun. to the Publisher, on the Origin, Symptoms, Progress, and Disappearance of the Yellow Fever, in New-Haven —&c. &c. II. Letter from Dr. Monson, sen. on the Treatment pursued, and most successful, in the Cure of the Yellow Fever in New Haven—&c. &c." P. [172], blank. Pp. [173]–193, text. P. [194], blank. In the table of contents this section is listed as "VI. An account of the Fever at New-Haven in 1794—by Dr. Eneas Monson, and his Son."

P. [195], caption title, "Letter of Dr. Reynolds, to the Publisher," and beginning of text, which runs through p. 199. P. [200], blank. This section is listed in the table of contents as "VIII. Letter from Dr. Reynolds, on the Fever in Montgomery County."

P. [201], caption title, "Remarks on Certain Causes of Disease in Large Cities, and the Means of Preventing Them. Written in December, 1795," and beginning of text, which runs to the middle of p. 220. This section is listed in the table of contents as "IX. Remarks on Cleanliness and Ventilation, by the Compiler."

P. 220, caption title, "The following Remarks are judged worthy of a place in this Collection. From the French and American Gazette. Medical Observations," and beginning of text, which runs to the middle of p. 224. P. 224, caption title, "The following Observations from the *Manchester Mercury*, contain useful hints, and cannot be inapplicable to many situations in the United States," and beginning of text, which runs through p. 231. P. 232, caption title, "Prevention and Suppression of Fever. Extracts of a letter from Dr. Haygarth, of Chester, to Dr. Percival, dated January 6th, 1796," and beginning of text, which runs to the middle of p. 233. These sections are not listed in the table of contents.

P. 233, caption title, "Concluding Observations," and beginning of text, which runs through p. 239. This section is listed in the table of contents as "X. Concluding Remarks, by the same." P. 240, caption title, "Additional Remarks," and beginning of text, which runs through p. 245. P. 246, table, "Number of Persons who died of the Fever in New-York,—in 1795."

2. Advertised as in press in the New York *Diary*, May 10, 1796, and later, and the *Minerva*, May 11, and as "lately published" in *Porcupine's Gazette*, September 16, 1797. The price was $1.00, in boards.

3. Reviewed by "C" in the New York *Diary*, June 12, 1796, reprinted in the *Federal Orrery*, July 28.

4. A "Circular Address" signed by Samuel Latham Mitchill, Edward Miller, and E. H. Smith, dated November 15, 1796, and printed in the *Farmer's Weekly Museum*, May 29, 1797, referred to this work as a "benevolent attempt," saying that its "partial success...is rather encouraging than disheartening since its failure is attributable to causes not necessarily connected with the design, and since there is good ground to believe, that a little perseverance would have given it stability and reputation. ...too much reliance was probably placed on public solicitation, with so limited a time for the collection of materials." (Quoted in Samuel Miller, "Biographical Sketch of Dr. Edward Miller," in the *Medical Works of Edward Miller*... [New York, 1814].)

5. The New York Public Library copy was Webster's own, and has manuscript notes, partly cut away by the library binder.

6. A writer in the New York *Diary*, September 18, 1797 (reprinted in the *Minerva*, September 20, and the *Herald*, September 23), asserted that the work was being translated into German by [Gottfried Christian] Reich; the compiler has not been able to find any such translation.

PART FOUR: THE HOLY BIBLE AND NEW TESTAMENT

784

The Holy Bible, containing the Old and New Testaments, in the Common Version. With amendments of the language, by Noah Webster, LL.D. New-Haven: Published by Durrie & Peck. Sold by Hezekiah Howe & Co., and A. H. Maltby, New Haven; and by N. & J. White, New York. 1833.

xvi, 907 pp. 22 cm. (Issued in one volume, but copies are found re-bound in two or even three volumes.) P. [1], title-page. P. [ii], list of the books of the Bible; copyright notice, 1833; and "Printed by Hezekiah Howe & Co." Pp. [iii]–v, preface, initialled and dated New Haven, September, 1833. P. [vi], blank. Pp. [vii]–xvi, introduction, explaining the nature of the alterations in the language. Pp. [1]–690, Old Testament. P. [691], title-page for New Testament. P. [692], blank. Pp. [693]–907, New Testament. Some copies have an errata slip (see Note 6).

CT, CTNHHI, CTY, DLC, ICU, MA, MB, MWA, MIDEAED, MIU, NBUG, NN, NNUT, NJR, OCLWHI, PPL, PPPRHI, RPB, Merriam, British Museum.

O'Callaghan, p. 222.

NOTES

1. Announced in the *Connecticut Journal*, May 7, 1833, in the *Palladium and Republican*, September 21, and in the *New York Evangelist*, November 24, quoting from the *Literary Tablet* (original reference not found). Advertised in the *Religious Intelligencer*, September 21, 1833, *Connecticut Journal*, September 24 and October 8, and elsewhere. The edition continued to be advertised sporadically by booksellers for the next three or four years, and Webster from time to time issued broadside throw-aways reprinting various testimonials for the work.

2. Reviewed: *Connecticut Journal*, September 24, 1833; *New York Spectator*, September 30; *Palladium and Republican*, October 19; *Quarterly*

Christian Spectator, December, 1833 (Ser. 3, Vol. V, pp. 655–656) [by Leonard Bacon]; *Religious Intelligencer*, December 14; all favorable. There was a series of review articles and letters to the editor for several years, many of them quite hostile, some taking a half-way position. Selected items include: *New York Evangelist*, March 15, 1834, a letter signed "C," from Illinois; *Commercial Advertiser*, July 7, 1835; *New York Mirror*, September 5, 1835; *Massachusetts Eagle*, September 24, 1835 (widely reprinted); *Lexington* (Ky.) *Intelligencer*, December 25, 1835; *New York Transcript*, January 26, 1836; *Boston Courier*, December 1, 1836, with follow-ups on December 8, 19, and 31; same, August 29 and 31, 1837; *Connecticut Observer*, January 19, 1839, by Zebulon Crocker; *New York Mirror*, February 22, 1840; New Haven *Daily Herald*, May 21, 1840, with follow-ups on May 22 and 23; same, December 1, 1840; *Chronicle of the Church*, July 10 and 17, 1840, by Calvin Chapin. In the issue of January 14, 1837, the editor of the New Haven *Palladium* told a contributor that he was declining to print a letter critical of the edition because it was not based on an examination of the book.

3. Webster had long been interested in the subject of mistranslations in the Bible. In 1784 in his *Grammar* he pointed out what he considered a mistranslation in Matthew XXIII, 24; in 1788 in his *American Magazine* (October, p. 775 n), he mentioned that a gentleman in New York—perhaps referring to himself—was translating the prophets "into the language of our country"; and in his *Essays*, 1790, he remarked (p. 228) on misunderstood phraseology of the Bible. By 1822 he had begun his reworking of the text, for in that year Moses Stuart, an Andover professor, wrote him the reactions of "our little club" to Webster's version, of which he seems to have sent them some manuscript for discussion. The project was definite by 1831, in which year Webster sent out a manuscript circular letter to various clergymen, asking their opinion on the desirability of publishing such a version. The only reply the compiler has found attempted to dissuade him.[2]

4. The actual printing of the work took considerable time. On December 27, 1832, Webster wrote his son-in-law William C. Fowler, "I am now occupied constantly with the Bible. More than a hundred pages of my edition are printed.... The corrections & the reading of proof-sheets keep me busy. It will require 8 or 9 months to bring it before the public.... It will be an octavo elegantly printed, & is intended for a

[2]Undated draft of circular letter, [1831]; James Milnor to Webster, January 30, 1832, Webster Papers, New York Public Library. (The letter which Milnor received was dated October 24, 1831.)

family Bible."[3] On May 16, 1833, he wrote the same addressee that, although a cold had forced him to give up reading for a while, he had finished the copy for the whole work, and the printing "is advanced to Jeremiah, but will not be published so early as I stated in the paper—I think it will not be finished till the last of August."[4] On July 30 he wrote to Harriet Webster Fowler, "...the printing is finished to *Acts*, & I trust will be completed in September...,"[5] in which month it did come out.

5. The published price was three dollars, but later it was reduced. On January 18, 1836, Webster wrote to N. and J. White in New York, "As I intend to close all my concern with book-selling as soon as practicable you may sell my bibles if you can at 2 dollars each. If I could dispose of the whole I would take less."[6] In July, 1841, when he was preparing a new edition, he authorized the sale of the old one at $1.50,[7] at which figure it had been advertised by some booksellers as far back as 1836.

6. The errata slip unintentionally introduced a new confusion, for it refers to a question of wording as given in a French translation in "Job xvii. 13," which is an error for Jeremiah.

7. Webster's serious-mindedness and determination to improve his fellow man whether he wished it or not are reflected in his reaction to the reception his Bible received. On February 24, 1834, he wrote to the editor of the New York *Observer*, "I suppose by your not publishing the address before, as you encouraged Mr White to believe you would, that you are not friendly to my design. But I consider this emendation of the common version as the most important enterprise of my life, & as important as any benevolent design now on foot; & I feel much hurt that my friends should discountenance the design."[8] He wrote to Fowler on November 16, 1835, "I wish a few clergymen would summon courage enough to commend my Bible to the public. It wounds my feelings to observe how indifferent the public are, & especially clergymen, to the correction of faults in the common version...."[9]

To Daniel Webster he wrote on March 30, 1837, "Having nearly lost all hope of benefiting my country in correcting the disorders of our

[3]In the possession of Mrs. Howard B. Field; transcript provided by Prof. Harry R. Warfel. [4]Ibid. [5]Ibid.

[6]Lehigh University Library, autograph letter no. 258; transcript provided by Prof. Harry R. Warfel.

[7]Webster to Fowler, July 7, 1841, in the possession of Mrs. Howard B. Field; transcript provided by Prof. Harry R. Warfel.

[8]Webster Papers, New York Public Library.

[9]In the possession of Mrs. Howard B. Field; transcript provided by Prof. Harry R. Warfel.

language, but unwilling to believe that the labors of my life must all be fruitless, I still indulge a hope that my efforts to render the language of our English Bible less exceptionable, & in many passages, more intelligible, may not be wholly unsuccessful."[1] And the voice was still crying in the wilderness in 1839, when he wrote another son-in-law, William W. Ellsworth, "I think it high time that the public attention should be called to the mistakes and inaccuracies in the language of the Common Version of the Bible. I do not think the Christian world can be justified in neglecting the subject. . . ."[2]

Unfortunately for Webster, the Christian world's reaction seems on the whole to have been that of "F.B.P.," who wrote on the flyleaf of his copy of Webster's edition, "Give[n] me by Aunt N., Oct. 17, 1859. Sent to her for missionaries' use evidently wrongly. They don't want the word of Webster, but the Word of God."[3]

8. For discussions of this work and its content and reception, see, in addition to Chapter XVIII of Warfel's biography, G[ordon] L[ester] F[ord], "A Forgotten Book. . .," *New York Tribune*, January 11, 1880; Allen Walker Read, "Noah Webster as a Euphemist," *Dialect Notes*, July, 1934 (Vol. VI, pp. 385–391); and Harry R. Warfel, "The Centenary of Noah Webster's Bible," *New England Quarterly*, September, 1934 (Vol. VII, pp. 578–582). In the case of the last-named, the writer informed the compiler that the editors added sentences with which he does not agree.

785

The New Testament in the Common Version. With amendments of the language by Noah Webster, LL.D. New Haven, Published by S. Babcock. Stereotyped by J. S. Redfield, New York. 1839.

267, (1) pp. 18 cm. P. [1], title-page. P. [2], list of books and copyright notice, 1833. Pp. 3–267, text. P. [268], three testimonials for Webster's edition of the Bible. Some copies have two front flyleaves containing "Specimens of emendations of language in this edition of the New Testament."

CtHT, CtHT-W, CtNhHi, CtY, ICN, MB, NN, NNUT, Merriam.
O'Callaghan, p. 264.

[1]Daniel Webster Papers, Library of Congress.
[2]November 26, 1839, Pierpont Morgan Library.
[3]*Catalogue of the American Library of the Late Mr. George Brinley*. . . (5 vols., Hartford, 1878–1897), No. 7297 (Pt. IV, p. 156).

NOTES

1. Announced in the *Connecticut Observer*, December 8, 1838, and advertised in the *New Haven Record*, May 11, 1839, and later, and elsewhere.

2. Some of the copies have an 1840 date on the front cover.

3. An article announcing the adoption of this work in the city schools of New Haven appeared in the New Haven *Daily Herald*, May 19, 1840.

786

The Holy Bible.... New Haven: Published by N. Webster. M.DCCC.XLI.

852, 260 pp. 12 cm. P. [1], title-page. P. [2], list of the books, copyright notice, 1833, and "Stereotyped at the Boston Type and Stereotype Foundry." Pp. [3]–6, preface, like the 1833 edition. Pp. [7]–21, introduction, with minor changes from the earlier edition. P. [22], blank. Pp. [23]–852, Old Testament. P. [1], title-page of New Testament. P. [2], list of the books, copyright notice, and stereotype notice. Pp. [3]–255, New Testament. P. [256], blank. Pp. 257–260, table of names. With this pagination it was possible to issue the New Testament separately (see the following entry).

CT, CTHT, CTHT-W, CTY, DLC, ICN, MB, MWA, N, NN, NNC, OC, Merriam.

O'Callaghan, p. 269.

NOTES

1. Advertised in the *Boston Recorder*, October 15, 1841, and later, and May 13, 1842, and later; New Haven *Daily Herald*, December 10, 1841; and elsewhere.

2. Reviewed in the *Christian Watchman*, October 29, 1841.

3. One of the New York Public Library copies is inscribed by Webster to his daughter Louisa, and one of the Yale copies to his grandson Oliver Ellsworth.

787

The New Testament.... New Haven: Published by Noah Webster. M.DCCC.XLI.

260 pp. 12 cm.

MWA.

A separate publication of part of the preceding. That it was issued in this form and is not a fragment is shown by contemporary advertisements, e.g., New Haven *Daily Herald*, December 10, 1841: "... the New Testament may be purchased separate from the Old if desired...." A bookseller's catalogue of 1914 (Garret Book Shoppe) listed a 32mo Webster New Testament, New Haven, 1842; if this date is correctly recorded, it may have come from a cover title which was dated a year later than the title-page—otherwise the compiler has found no trace of an 1842 edition.

Section Nine

PERIODICALS

GENERAL NOTE ON PERIODICALS

The compiler and her research assistants expended much time and energy in searching newspaper files from the 1770's to the 1840's, and turned up an enormous amount of material by and about Webster, including advertisements and reviews of his works. Reviews and selected advertisements have been cited in the preceding sections, with the work to which they apply. In the present section it has not been possible to be as inclusive as the compiler planned. Reduction of bulk has been effected in two directions : by avoiding detailed descriptions of articles which evoked Webster's own contributions, or which are replies to him; and by omitting most of the doubtful ascriptions to Webster. The compiler's full notes on both these types are on file in The New York Public Library.

Reprintings of newspaper items are recorded only under the date of the original, and are not given separate chronological entries or cross-references. Series are entered only under the initial date. Reprints from Webster's writings which were first published in book or pamphlet form have already been listed under the original form in the preceding sections. Material by Webster which he himself reprinted in his own periodicals is listed in the present section, because this demonstrates his literary methods.

Periodicals are cited by the form of the title appearing on the issue concerned; a list identifying those whose titles are not self-explanatory will be found on p. xxvii. When the compiler began her work, over forty years ago, she felt it desirable to record the location of files of the periodicals she cited. Now, however, the availability of Clarence S. Brigham's *History and Bibliography of American Newspapers*, 1690–1820 (2 vols., Worcester, Mass., 1947) and other reference works makes such a record unnecessary, and locations are mentioned only for marked copies. It has also seemed acceptable to omit the background of the controversies reflected in newspaper contributions; Webster's major newspaper writings are set in their context in Warfel's biography.

In the case of unsigned articles, attribution to Webster is based on his acknowledgment of authorship in his own files of the papers, his later use of the material in his books, references in his diary or correspondence, or closeness of the subject matter to his known interests, though the last-named is used only as added weight, and is not taken as evidence by itself.

The arrangement is by year, then month, then day. Items which are dated by quarter or month only are entered at the beginning of that quarter or month. The following distinctions should be carefully noted: "signed" (unless followed by a pseudonym or the name of a different person) or "initialled" means that Webster's name or initials appear *in print* on the item described; "autographed" or "paraphed" means that there is no printed indication of the writer's name, but that Webster has written his name or initials on the item in one or more copies of the periodical. Most of these marked files are to be found in The New York Public Library or at Yale. In such files and on an occasional single copy or clipping Webster sometimes placed marks or notes to draw attention to points in which he was interested. In a few cases the marks seem to suggest his authorship, though there is not a standard mark for this purpose. The compiler has used her best judgment in including a few instances in which she thinks Webster the possible writer of the article.

In order to present as lucidly as possible the involved newspaper and pamphlet disputes in which Webster engaged, any exchange involving more than six items has been considered a "controversy," and is treated separately in Part Four of this section.

PART ONE: PERIODICALS EDITED BY WEBSTER

A. *American Magazine*

788

The American magazine. Containing a miscellaneous collection of original and other valuable essays, in prose and verse, and calculated both for instruction and amusement. [one line of quotation.] For December 1787 [–November, 1788]. Contents. . . . New York, Printed by Samuel Loudon, and sold by the printer, by Messieurs Berry and Rogers, Mr. R. Hodge, Mr. S. Campbell, Mr. T. Allen, and Mr. T. Greenleaf. [1787–1788.]

Twelve issues, constituting one volume of 882 pp., illus. 19 cm.

Complete and partial files can be located through the *Union List of Serials*. The New York Public Library copy contains MS annotations by Webster, as does a copy formerly in the possession of Goodspeed's Book Shop, Boston. The present location of the latter volume is unknown, and it is referred to here as the Goodspeed copy. The complete volume is reproduced as No. 3 of the "American Periodical Series: Eighteenth Century" of University Microfilms, Ann Arbor, Michigan.

Evans 20191, Sabin 1135. See Sec. III of Chap. 10 of Lyon N. Richardson, *History of Early American Magazines* (New York, 1931).

Late in November, 1787, Webster moved from Connecticut to New York and founded this magazine, the first monthly to appear there. His diary and letters of the time record its progress. He noted on December 3, 1787, "Making a contract with M^{r} [Samuel] Loudon, where I take tea;" on the 4th, "Make the bargain for printing the American Magazine & get the paper on Shore;" and on the 5th, "The work is begun." The first number, dated December, 1787, apparently appeared late in the month;

at that time it was the practice for magazines to bear the date of the month preceding their publication and the introduction to Webster's first number is dated January 1, 1788.

The price was $2.50 a year, twenty-five cents a number, though Connecticut neighbors of Webster's father were allowed to pay him in kind. Indications of the news-stand sale of the magazine are found in a letter from Webster to William Young in Philadelphia, June 23, 1788, referring to his disposing of a dozen copies, and one from William Spotswood (publisher of the *Columbian Magazine*, Philadelphia) to Jeremy Belknap, October 9, 1788, speaking of a monthly sale in Charleston, South Carolina, of only five or six copies.[4] (For newspaper advertisements of the magazine, see Richardson as cited above.)

The magazine lasted a year, a good record at that time for a periodical published by an individual rather than a group. In February, 1788, Webster was thinking of forming a corporation, with ten "proprietors" distributed throughout the country. He wrote various people about this plan, but nothing came of it.[5]

In the following analysis of Webster's contributions to the magazine, purely editorial notes (such as "Ethicus is under consideration") which appear on the verso of the title-pages are omitted, as are footnotes and editorial comments added to the contributions of others, and single paragraphs or short items appearing under such headings as "Miscellany," "Anecdote," or "Intelligence." The book reviews—which were not a usual feature of American magazines of the time—were presumably by Webster, and have been listed unless there is evidence to the contrary. Webster's annotations in the two files mentioned have been heavily relied upon, though he does not seem to have marked all his own work, particularly book reviews.

December, 1787, issue (pp. [1]–64)

1. "Introduction," unsigned, dated New York, January 1, 1788, setting forth the plan of the magazine; pp. 3–4. Reprinted as Appendix XI of Ford's *Notes*.

2. "Advice to Masons...," signed "Fact," on the art of building good chimneys; p. 8. Paraphed in the Goodspeed copy.

[4]Yale University Library and Massachusetts Historical Society *Collections*, Ser.6, Vol. IV, p. 421, respectively.

[5]Webster to Jeremy Belknap, February 9, 1788, ibid., pp. 385–386; Webster to Benjamin Rush, February 10, Rush MSS, Library Company of Philadelphia; Rush to Webster, February 13, and Webster to Rush, February 24, Webster Papers, New York Public Library. The last two are printed in Ford's *Notes*, Vol. I, pp. 177–178.

3. "Principles of Government and Commerce," signed "American"; pp. 9–12. Paraphed and corrected in the Goodspeed copy. Reprinted in Webster's *Collection of Essays*, 1790, *Rudiments of English Grammar*, 1790, and *Little Reader's Assistant*, 1790.

4. Series of four articles on the Constitution, the last three headed "Government," signed "Giles Hickory"; pp. 13–15, 75–80, 137–145, 204–210. Reprinted with changes as Nos. III–VI of Webster's *Collection of Essays*, 1790. These are probably reworkings of some of his lectures.

5. Series of three signed letters headed "Antiquity," addressed to Ezra Stiles, President of Yale, on the subject of the aboriginal mounds found west of the Alleghenies; pp. 15–19, 87–93, 146–156. Reprinted in the *Massachusetts Spy*, May 29, 1788, and later, the *American Museum*, July, 1789, and later, and in *Letters and Papers of Ezra Stiles* (New Haven, 1933), pp. 80–105. Webster reprinted the third letter as No. XVI of his *Collection of Essays*, 1790. Replies from Stiles appeared in the March, 1788, issue, pp. 246–[247], and the April issue, pp. 291–294. A dissenting view was expressed in "Observations on the Travels. . .of Ferdinand De Soto" in the *Columbian Magazine*, September, 1788 (Vol. II, pp. 477–489); that this anonymous article was by Jeremy Belknap is shown in his correspondence with Ebenezer Hazard (Massachusetts Historical Society *Collections*, Ser. 5, Vol. III). Webster replied with a signed letter, printed in the *Columbian Magazine*, November, 1788 (Vol. II, pp. 645–646), admitting the cogency of the criticisms. See G. Hubert Smith, "Noah Webster, the Archaeologist," *American Anthropologist*, October–December, 1931 (Vol. 33, pp. 620–624).

6. Two-part unsigned abridgment of John Smith's *History of Virginia*; pp. 19–22, 156–158. Paraphed by Webster in the Goodspeed copy. Later Ezra Stiles sent Webster an abridgment of Smith made by his son; the relation between the two abridgments is not clear.[6]

7. Series of six unsigned articles headed "Education," discussing the principles and practice of education, including that of women; pp. 22–26, 80–82, 158–161, 210–216, 311–313, 367–374. Paraphed by Webster in the Goodspeed copy, and reprinted with changes as No. I of his *Collection of Essays*, 1790. Also reprinted—from the book version—in the *American Museum*, July to December, 1792 (Vol. XII, pp. 41–44, 98–102, 173–175, 237–241, 278–283, 309–313); in the *Hampshire Gazette*, July 10–August 21, 1793; and in part in the *American Journal of Education*, April, 1876 (Vol. XXVI, pp. 196–200).

[6]Stiles to Webster, February 27, 1788, Webster Papers, New York Public Library.

8. Letter to the editor signed "Jemima Loveleap," wishing the new magazine luck and expressing the hope that the new year will see the ratification of the proposed Constitution; pp. 26–27. Not acknowledged by Webster, but believed by the compiler to be his; see the comment on No. 12 below.

9. Unsigned article beginning, "Some laws enacted...," discussing early colonial laws; pp. 51–52. Paraphed by Webster in the Goodspeed copy.

10. Unsigned "Verses on the New Year..."; p. [56]. Autographed by Webster in both the New York Public Library and Goodspeed copies, and reprinted in his *Instructive and Entertaining Lessons*, 1835, and in Warfel, *Poems by Noah Webster*, p. 5.

January, 1788, issue (pp. [65]–128)

With this issue the list of vendors is expanded to add S. and R. Campbell, F. Childs, and J. Reid, New York; J. Hastings, Boston; Hudson and Goodwin, Hartford; J. [i.e., I.] Beers, New Haven; A. Stoddard, Hudson, N.Y.; W. Falconer and Co., Albany; Young and M'Culloch, Philadelphia; and Mrs. A. Timothy, Charleston.

11. Unsigned "Theological Remarks," comparing various religions through their superstitions; pp. 69–71. Paraphed by Webster in the Goodspeed copy. On the verso of the title-page a continuation of these remarks was promised, but it never appeared.

12. Series of four numbered letters signed "Belzebub" [sic], commenting on the first two parts of the "Education" series (No. 7 above); pp. 82–86, 161–163, 389–390. Not acknowledged by Webster, but the compiler thinks it probable that he wrote them. He was given to commenting on his own work; in a letter of April 30, 1788, Ebenezer Hazard said to Jeremy Belknap, "N.W. goes on publishing letters to himself."[7]

13. Unsigned "General Description of Philadelphia"; pp. 97–99. Paraphed by Webster in the Goodspeed copy, and reprinted as part of No. XVII of his *Collection of Essays*, 1790.

14. Two letters headed "The Art of pushing into Business, and making way in the world," signed "Peter Pickpenny," satirizing pretentiousness and preference for foreign books; pp. 103–105, 166–170. Paraphed by Webster in the Goodspeed copy.

February, 1788, issue (pp. [129]–192)

15. Long, unsigned editorial note thanking subscribers for support, announcing plans, and complaining of "trespasses" on his literary prop-

[7]Massachusetts Historical Society *Collections*, Ser. 5, Vol. III, p. 33.

erty; p. [130]. Reprinted in the New York *Daily Advertiser*, March 5, 1788.

16. Prose "Rhapsody. Par Mons——— ———," on "the laws of nature," translation with French and English in parallel columns; pp. 131–133. The compiler thinks it likely Webster did the translation.

17. Unsigned essay in "Miscellanies" beginning, "Well, how do you like Boston?" comparing various American cities; pp. 164–166. Paraphed and corrected by Webster in the Goodspeed copy, and reprinted as part of No. XVII of his *Collection of Essays*, 1790; also reprinted in the *American Museum*, May, 1789 (Vol. V, pp. 491–493).

18. Three unsigned "Extracts from Ancient Records, with Remarks," quoting from early New England laws; pp. 170–172, 324–325, 420. The first two paraphed by Webster in the Goodspeed copy.

19. Unsigned "Lines written by a Youth on the Death of Mr. S——, of Sharon"; pp. 180–181. Not acknowledged by Webster, but the compiler is inclined to identify these with "ye few sympathetic lines" which Webster sent the Reverend Cotton Mather Smith of Sharon on the death of a son in 1782 (Ford's *Notes*, Vol. I, p. 48). It looks as if, in order to fill his columns, Webster was digging up his youthful poetry—see No. 23 below.

March, 1788, issue (pp. [193]–272)

With this issue the imprint changes to S. and J. Loudon, the latter being Samuel's son John.

20. Unsigned "General Description of the City of New York"; pp. 220–229. Paraphed by Webster in the Goodspeed copy. Reprinted with some changes and additions as "Description of the City of New-York" in Jedidiah Morse, *American Geography*, 1789 and later (see Note 9 to Title 745). Although it is not part of the original edition, this sketch is included in certain reprints of the first New York city directory, 1786 (e.g., New York, Trow City Directory Co., [1886]; New York, H. J. Sachs and Co., 1905).

21. "An Address to the Ladies," signed "Alphonzo," replying to a letter from "Eliza," discussing the relations between the sexes, education, etc.; pp. 241–246. Paraphed by Webster in the Goodspeed copy and reprinted in some editions of his *American Selection*, 1787, and as No. XXX of his *Collection of Essays*, 1790.

22. Unsigned review of *An Academy for Grown Horsemen*, by Geoffrey Gambado (pseudonym of Henry B. Williams), [London, 1787]; pp. [248]–251 (248 misnumbered 448).

The compiler does not believe that Webster wrote the review of The Federalist, *pp. 260–261, 337–341, 423–424, and 503–507, though it agrees with his views.*

23. Unsigned poem, "To the Author of the Conquest of Canaan. Written by a Youth of Nineteen"; pp. 265–266. Autographed or paraphed by Webster in both marked files, and acknowledged when reprinted in his *Instructive and Entertaining Lessons,* 1835. This praise of Timothy Dwight was written shortly after September 10, 1777.

April, 1788, issue (pp. [273]–352)

24. Letter signed "Alphonzo," a follow-up to No. 21 above; pp. 333–334. Not acknowledged by Webster, but very likely his, since the earlier one was.

25. Unsigned book reviews of [John Jay], *Address to the People of the State of New-York, on the Subject of the Constitution; An Address to the People of the State of New-York, Shewing the Necessity of Making Amendments... By a Plebeian*; and Nicholas Pike, *New and Complete System of Arithmetic*; pp. 341–343.

26. Unsigned poem, "Ode to Spring"; p. 346. Marked by Webster in the New York Public Library file with a mark sometimes used to designate his own writings, but not otherwise identified as his.

May, 1788, issue (pp. [353]–432)

27. "A Dissertation concerning the Influence of Language on opinions and of opinions on Language," unsigned; pp. 399–403. Paraphed, annotated, and corrected by Webster in the Goodspeed copy, including a remark dated 1832 that "Much of this is in error." Reprinted as No. XVIII of his *Collection of Essays,* 1790.

28. Unsigned and untitled "...Remarks...read before the Philological Society...," discussing motives of writers, style, etc.; pp. 404–405. Not acknowledged, but presumably by Webster, who was the leading spirit of this Society. He recorded in his diary for April 28, 1788, "At evening attend the philological Society and read a Dissertation. Ordered to be published," which might apply either to this or to the preceding entry.

29. Unsigned reviews of some pamphlets on the Constitution; pp. 422–423.

30. Unsigned poem beginning, "Let sage discretion the gay world despise..."; pp. 427–428. Marked by Webster in the New York Public

Library file with a mark sometimes used to designate his own writings, but not otherwise identified as his.

June, 1788, issue (pp. [433]–512)

With this issue S. Hall replaces J. Hastings as the Boston vendor.

31. "To the Public," signed "Orpheus," advocating music as part of the school curriculum; pp. 448–450. Autographed by Webster in the New York Public Library copy, and reprinted as No. XIX of his *Collection of Essays*, 1790. This had originally appeared, in somewhat different form, in the *Pennsylvania Packet*, April 24, 1787.

July, 1788, issue (pp. [513]–602)

32. Unsigned essay, "Morality"; pp. 526–530. Not acknowledged by Webster in the marked files, but used as No. XX of his *Collection of Essays*, 1790.

33. "Rules for Genteel Behavior," signed "Peter Punctilio," a satire on lack of manners; pp. 530–531. Paraphed by Webster in the Goodspeed copy.

34. "A Letter from a Lady, with Remarks," the letter signed "Constantia" and the remarks "E.," discussing courtship; pp. 531–534. Paraphed by Webster in the Goodspeed copy, and reprinted as No. XXI of his *Collection of Essays*, 1790.

35. Unsigned letter, "Remarks on Gibbon's Style," sharply critical of Gibbon and disagreeing with the "Account of Edward Gibbon, Esq." which had been published in the preceding issue (pp. 466–469); pp. 536–537. Paraphed by Webster in the Goodspeed copy. Webster's criticisms of Gibbon which appeared in the *Massachusetts Magazine*, July and August, 1789, and in the *Gazette of the United States*, August 22 and September 23, are taken from his *Dissertations* and not from these "Remarks."

36. Signed letter to Ezra Stiles, dated July 4, 1788, discussing American Indian customs, a follow-up to the "Antiquity" series (No. 5 above); pp. 537–541.

37. Letter "To the Authors of the London Review," signed "An American," dated July 4, 1788, defending Timothy Dwight's *Conquest of Canaan* against hostile English reviews; pp. 562–566. The letter incorporates extracts from a letter from Dwight, June 6, 1788 (erroneously given as July in the article). Paraphed by Webster in the Goodspeed copy. See Theodore A. Zunder, "Noah Webster and *The Conquest of Canaan*," *American Literature*, May, 1929 (Vol. I, pp. 200–202), in which Dwight's letter is quoted in full.

38. Untitled letter signed "A Young Bachelor," dated July, 1788, commenting on education for women, as an introduction to a letter written by a twelve-year old girl of Bethlehem, Pennsylvania; pp. 567–568. Paraphed by Webster in the Goodspeed copy.

39. Letter "To a Subscriber," signed "E.," discussing education, in reply to a letter signed "Subscriber"; pp. 583–585. Paraphed by Webster in the Goodspeed copy, and both items reprinted as No. XXII of his *Collection of Essays,* 1790. He may have written the inquiry as well as the reply.

40. Unsigned book reviews of Jonathan Edwards, *Observations on the language of the Muhhekaneew or Mohegan Indians* and [Timothy Dwight], *Triumph of Infidelity*; pp. 587–590. The former is not acknowledged by Webster, but the latter has in the table of contents of the New York Public Library file a mark which usually designates Webster's own writings.

The second review was reprinted in the New York *Daily Advertiser,* August 9, 1788, and in the *Massachusetts Centinel,* August 23. Its appearance in the New York paper touched off a dispute in its columns, to which Webster contributed another article (Part Three below, No. 63).

In the section "American Intelligence," on pp. 600–601, there is a paragraph about the procession in New York held to celebrate the adoption of the Constitution, promising a detailed account, which, however, never appeared. Webster marched in this procession and wrote a description of it which was first printed on August 2, 1788, in the New York Daily Advertiser *(see Appendix A, No. 1).*

August, 1788, issue (pp. [603]–682)

This issue, which contains a map of the southeastern United States, was advertised at "two-thirds of a dollar" in the New York *Daily Advertiser,* September 3, and the *New York Packet,* September 5, and later. The map had been engraved for Morse's *American Geography*; Morse allowed Webster to use it in return for a contribution to that work (see notes to Title 745). Nothing in this issue beyond editorial notes can definitely be ascribed to Webster, though the unsigned essay "Practicability of well amusing the latter years of life" (pp. 626–627) seems like his style and subject matter.

September, 1788, issue (pp. [683]–754)

41. Unsigned book reviews of Peter Markoe, *The Times, A Poem; An Account of the Conversion of. . . John Thayer;* George R. Minot, *History*

of the Insurrections in Massachusetts; David Humphreys, *Essay on... Major General Israel Putnam; Thoughts on the Political Situation of the United States;* and some medical works and volumes of sermons and orations; pp. 729–747, 799–807.

42. Unsigned poem, "The Negroes [sic] Complaint"; p. 751. Marked by Webster in the New York Public Library file with a mark sometimes used to designate his own writings, but not otherwise identified as his. This is not Cowper's poem of the same title, written the same year.

October, 1788, issue (pp. 755]–818)

On p. [756], the verso of the title-page, is an editorial notice which reads:

"As the *twelfth* number of the Magazine will complete this volume and fulfil the proprietor's engagements with the public; and as business will require him to leave this city, immediately upon the delivery of that number, subscribers and persons entrusted with Magazines on commission, are requested to settle their accounts, within the month of November.

"Whether the most flourishing city in America, and the seat of the Federal Legislature will continue and support this *periodical publication*, remains yet to be determined. A beginning has been made by an individual under every possible disadvantage, and the experiment will warrant a continuation of the work, by persons whose business, citizenship and connections shall command more general patronage. It is not consistent with the proprietor's interest and views in life to devote his whole time to a work of this kind; but he will ever be happy to contribute his share towards the support of a publication, which has public utility for its object."

Except for editorial notes and the continuation of two book reviews (pp. 799–807), nothing in this issue is ascribed to Webster.

November, 1788, issue (pp. [819]–882)

43. "Remarks on the late Meteor," signed "E.," incorporating a letter "from a gentleman at New-town"; pp. 867–871. Paraphed by Webster in the Goodspeed copy.

As indicated by the note in the October issue, there was doubt about the survival of the publication, but Webster was sanguine, and the notes on the verso of the title-page of the November issue refer to matter "reserved for the second volume." On October 2, 1788, Mrs. Ann Timothy of Charleston, one of the distributors named in the imprint, advertised the second volume in the State Gazette of South Carolina, *mentioning several maps to be published therein.*

*Webster, however, was thinking in terms of a group of proprietors, as had earlier been proposed, and the first half of November was filled with negotiations. He recorded in his diary for November 6, "Wait on M*r *[Ebenezer] Hazard, dine with M*r *[Francis] Childs;" for November 7–8, "busy endeavoring to form a Society for publishing The American Magazine & Universal Register. succeed;" and for December 5–6, "Sign articles of agreement for the publishing of a Magazine & Register, with M*r *F Child[s] & M*r *E. Hazard." The upshot of the arrangements early in November was a long advertisement, dated November 10, 1788, published in the New York* Daily Advertiser, *November 13, announcing that "On the first day of February next, will be published in this city, The American Magazine, and Universal Register: for January, 1789. Being No. I of Volume II. By a Society of Gentlemen. . . ." The advertisement explained the desirability of group effort and the intended inclusion of a "register," which was to be a supplement of historical and state papers, separately paged and on better paper, which could be bound independently. It was promised that each issue would consist of 56 pages of magazine and 48 of "register." The price was to be half a guinea for the magazine alone, or three dollars for both parts, payable at the end of each six months. Childs was named as the printer, and his address was given for the editorial office. This advertisement was reprinted, with changes, in the* New-Jersey Journal, *November 26 and later, the* State Gazette of South Carolina, *December 4, the* Massachusetts Centinel, *December 6 and later, the* Newport *(R.I.)* Herald, *December 11, the* Albany Gazette, *December 26 and later, the* American Mercury, *January 5, 1789, and later, and the* Connecticut Gazette, *January 9 and later.*

An actual start was made on the publication, for a letter from Ebenezer Hazard to Jeremy Belknap, November 22, 1788, relates that Webster had printed six sheets of the January "register," containing Winthrop's Journal, but that he would have to sacrifice the cost of these sheets since he had decided to publish the "register" on better paper.[8] *Webster wanted Hazard as a proprietor of the expanded journal because he had formed a large collection of historical papers.*[9] *Although he cooperated with Webster, Hazard did not particularly*

[8]This letter and the others referred to in this paragraph are in the Massachusetts Historical Society. The Belknap–Hazard correspondence is printed in that Society's *Collections*, Ser. 5, Vols. II and III, and Ser. 6, Vol. IV. Webster later published Winthrop's Journal as a book (Title 781).

[9]For Hazard's proposal to collect and publish "American State Papers" as early as 1774, see Isabel M. Calder, ed., *Letters and Papers of Ezra Stiles* (New Haven, 1933), pp. 40–41, and Fred Shelley, "Ebenezer Hazard: America's first historical editor," *William and Mary Quarterly*, January, 1955 (Ser. 3, Vol. XII, pp. [44]–73).

like him, and his extensive correspondence with Belknap is full of sneering remarks on the part of both writers. Hazard felt that Webster's name in conjunction with the new venture was a drawback rather than an asset. Belknap felt that Isaiah Thomas' Massachusetts Magazine was too strong a rival, and that it would drive the Columbian Magazine (Philadelphia) out of the Boston market.

In regard to the Massachusetts Magazine, however, Webster had other ideas, for his diary entry for January 4, 1789, records, "Do some business with Mr Thomas & form a plan for uniting the American & Massachusetts Magazine[s]." Apparently he communicated this to Hazard, for the latter wrote to him on January 11, "I like the idea of an Union, but have not had time to consider the Terms proposed yet. Qu. can not we extend it, & take in the Columbian too, so as to monopolize a Magazine in the States[?]"[1] Two days later Hazard wrote Webster again, advising against the consolidation; in the letter differences of opinion became quite apparent, especially regarding the value of the "register," and Hazard says, "The paper is come, but our first number cannot appear at the time proposed, nor will it at all, unless there should be such a list of Subscribers as will afford a rational prospect of Success. When we do publish, it will be upon our first Plan, & as you declare yourself 'unwilling to continue the Magazine and Register upon that Plan,' I suppose the other Proprietors will have no Objections against releasing you from your obligations upon Payment of your proportion of the Expence already accrued."[2]

Webster seems to have been sulking in his tent. On February 1 he wrote to James Greenleaf, a future brother-in-law, "Since my last I have exchanged my residence: You will hear of me in future in Boston.... There is a company formed for carrying on the Magazine in N York; but I am doubtful of its success— & not very anxious about it...."[3] Perhaps he had not seen the long advertisement in the New York Daily Advertiser of January 27 and later, indefinitely postponing the appearance of the magazine. The postponement, however, turned out to be permanent, though in February Abiel Holmes was writing Webster enthusiastically about gathering subscriptions in the vicinity of Medway, Massachusetts.[4]

[1]Pierpont Morgan Library.
[2]Webster Papers, New York Public Library.
[3]Historical Society of Pennsylvania; Ford's *Notes*, Vol. II, pp. 407–409.
[4]Webster Papers, New York Public Library; Ford's *Notes*, Vol. I, pp. 194–195.

B. *The Minerva and Herald*

789

The American Minerva, patroness of peace, commerce, and the liberal arts. Published (daily) by George Bunce & Co. No. 37, Wall-street, nearly opposite the Tontine Coffee-house, at six dollars per annum.

Vol. I, No. 1, to Vol. IV, No. 1162, December 9, 1793–September 30, 1797. Approx. 42 x 25 cm.

In 1793 Alexander Hamilton, Rufus King, James Watson, and other leaders of the Federalist party induced Webster to move from Hartford to New York in order to establish and edit a daily newspaper devoted to the party's interest. To initiate the project these men raised about $1,500, which was repaid (without interest) over a period of five years. The paper was christened *The American Minerva*, and the first number appeared December 9, 1793. In June, 1794, a semi-weekly edition for the country was added (see below).

For the first two years Webster did all the editorial work himself, not having even a clerk; later he was able to engage an assistant editor and a clerk, but he continued to be the moving spirit of the papers for at least the first five years. Initially the publishers were George Bunce and Co. This firm was succeeded by Hopkins, Webb and Co. in May, 1796, and they in turn by E. Belden and Co. in July, 1799. Webster was the "and Co." in each of these firms, and he had a close tie with the last-named, since Ebenezer Belden was his nephew. In 1803 the papers, by then bearing different names, were sold to Reverend Zachariah Lewis, though Webster continued to contribute occasionally to their columns.

"Proposals" for the *Minerva*, dated December 2, were printed in the first issue, and it is likely that these had first been circulated in broadside form, but no copy has been located. In his diary for December 2–3, Webster noted, "Issue proposals for the Minerva."

Even more than in the case of the *American Magazine*, large parts of each issue must have been written by Webster, and the compiler has listed hundreds of unsigned editorial notes. In the following listing, however, only articles signed by Webster, acknowledged by him in marked copies or elsewhere, or attributed to him on good evidence of other sorts are entered. The New York Public Library file was Webster's, annotated by him. Also listed, whether signed or not, are a few items which throw light on the history or policies of the papers.

1793

1. December 9. Signed "Proposals, for publishing...The American Minerva...," announcing the plans and policies of the paper, which was to be "chaste and impartial," to avoid personalities whenever possible, and to support the Administration. Also in this and following issues appeared a note, "This paper will be enlarged and improved in proportion to the encouragement it receives."

2. December 9. Unsigned "Editor's address to the public," on the value of newspapers in learning, politics, agriculture, and science. This was repeated in succeeding issues and reprinted—without acknowledgment—in the *Philadelphia Gazette*, January 1, 1794. Webster complained of this larceny in an unsigned editorial in his *Minerva*, February 6, 1794. Paraphed by Webster in the New York Public Library file; against the passage stating that a general diffusion of knowledge seems to be the foundation of all free government, Webster has written, "Events have very much weakened my hopes. 1837. N.W."

3. December 9. First of an unsigned series, "Sketches of the History & Progress of Commerce," which continues in the issues of December 10, 12, 13, 14, 17, 23, 24, 25, 30, and 31 and January 15, 1794. All except the last paraphed by Webster in the New York Public Library file. The last installment cited promised further articles, which did not, however, appear.

4. December 9. Article beginning, "The Presidents address to Congress...," signed "A Stable Republican," discussing American independence and the tax on newspapers. Paraphed in the New York Public Library file.

5. December 10. "On the Dignity of our National Character," signed "Brutus," discussing the attacks of North African pirates on American shipping. Paraphed and corrected in the New York Public Library file.

6. December 11. Letter signed "A Freeman," attacking party spirit. Paraphed in the New York Public Library file. Reprinted in the *Federal Gazette* (Philadelphia), December 14, and *Gazette of the United States*, December 16.

7. December 17. Unsigned editorial beginning, "The question of putting our country...," on the need of an adequate navy. Paraphed in the New York Public Library file. Reprinted in *Edwards's Baltimore Daily Advertiser*, December 26; the *Baltimore Daily Intelligencer*, Decem-

ber 26; the *Newport* (R.I.) *Mercury*, January 7, 1794; and the *South Carolina State Gazette*, January 21.

8. December 18. Unsigned editorial beginning, "Incredible pains. . . ," defending the Secretary of the Treasury's funding system. Paraphed in the New York Public Library file. Reprinted in the *Gazette of the United States*, December 20; and the *Columbian Centinel*, December 28.

9. December 20. Unsigned editorial beginning "A correspondent remarks. . . ," criticizing the resolutions of the Kentucky Democratic Society on the subject of Western lands (published in the paper the preceding day). Paraphed in the New York Public Library file.

With the issue of December 23 "The" was dropped from the title.

10. December 26. "A Candid address to the Minister of the French Republic," signed "Scipio," objecting to Genet's interference in domestic affairs. Paraphed, corrected, and annotated in the New York Public Library file.

11. December 30. "Remarks," signed "Ed.," on an extract from Arthur Young's account of the White Boys in Ireland, contrasting the lot of the common people in Ireland and the United States. Paraphed in the New York Public Library file.

12. December 30. Unsigned editorial beginning, "It is with pleasure. . . ," concerning restrictions placed on American commerce by foreign countries. Paraphed in the New York Public Library file. Reprinted in the *Columbian Centinel*, January 15, 1794, and the *Georgia Journal*, January 18.

13. December 30. "The petition of the ancient participle stricken," signed "Stricken," humorous discussion favoring the form "struck." Paraphed in the New York Public Library file.

1794

14. January 8. Unsigned editorial "On Public Schools," praising particularly those in Connecticut. Paraphed in the New York Public Library file.

The issues of January 27 and 28 each consisted of one sheet only because of the journeymen printers' demand for higher wages, as explained in an unsigned note in the former issue.

15. January 29. Unsigned editorial, "Tobacco," comparing James I's fears on that subject with Genet's about possible aristocratic tendencies in America. Paraphed in the New York Public Library file.

16. January 31. Letter "To W[illiam] W[ilcox]," signed "A real Friend to Republicanism," objecting to Wilcox' proposal to abolish such terms as "excellency," "esquire," and "honor." Paraphed in the New York Public Library file. The argument continued in the issues of February 15, 21, and 27.

At this point the numeration of the paper slipped a cog; the January 31 issue was numbered 48 instead of 47, and the skipped number was never picked up.

17. February 10. Unsigned essay, "A Fop," satirizing the species. Paraphed in the New York Public Library file.

18. February 11. Letter, "Alarm! Alarm!", signed "Democrat," objecting to such monarchical street names as King, Queen, Princess, and Duke. Paraphed in the New York Public Library file. Webster intended this as satire, but it backfired; he annotated the article, "This burlesk had an effect contrary to what was intended. The Corporation of New York met soon after and changed the names of those streets." Opposition to the Corporation's act was expressed in the *Minerva* of April 19 and 30 and October 30.

19. February 12. "Remarks occasioned by the Review of 'An enquiry into the principles and tendency of certain public measures'...," signed "Portius," replying to certain arguments against the Bank of the United States and the funding system. Paraphed in the New York Public Library file. The review originally appeared in the *Philadelphia Gazette* of February 4, and was reprinted in the *Minerva* of February 7.

20. February 26. "The editor...to Justitius," signed with initials, discussing that contributor's suggestions for improvements in the paper, which had been printed in the issue of February 24.

21. February 27. "To the man who stiles himself W. W....," signed "A real Friend to Republicanism," the final gambit in an exchange which began January 31 (q.v.).

With March 19 the paper changed its size to 48 x 31 centimeters, and used a new masthead containing a cut. This and a few succeeding issues had an unsigned editorial note explaining the symbolism of the cut and the paper's motto. (The issues from March 19 through April 10 and many later numbers are missing in the marked file in The New York Public Library.)

22. March 19 and later. Signed editorial announcement, headed "To the Public," concerning the enlargement of the paper, terms, etc. The title became *American Minerva, and the New-York (Evening) Advertiser.*

In the same issues is an unsigned note asking for a person qualified to translate from the French, a task to which Webster himself gave a good deal of time. (An article in the issue of August 21 specifically mentions that a document quoted therein was translated by the editor.)

23. April 1. First of an unsigned series entitled "The Times," editorials on contemporary events and problems. Thirteen appeared in the issues of April 1, 7, 10, 11, 14, 16, 18, 19, 23, and 30 and May 2, 6, and 10; the series was resumed on October 11, 1796, q.v. Various of the first thirteen numbers were extensively reprinted in other newspapers, especially in April, May, and June, and even as late as January, 1802. Not acknowledged by Webster, but doubtless his.

24. April 12. Unsigned "Advertisement Extraordinary. The ship *Minerva*...," an allegory appealing for patriotic articles for the paper.

In the issue of May 7 Webster published, without its signature, a letter praising his Revolution in France Considered. *It was written by Oliver Wolcott, May 3, 1794. The original is in the Webster Papers, New York Public Library.*

25. May 21 and later. Signed announcement, "To the Public," consisting of most of the text of the broadside described below. Reprinted in the new *Herald* on June 4 and 7.

26. June 4. Announcement of the publication of the first number of the *Herald*, signed "The Publishers," printed also in the *Herald*, June 4 and 7.

790

To the Public. It is a subject.... Noah Webster Jun. Compiler. George Bunce, & Co. Publishers. New-York, May 7th, 1794....

Broadside, 40 x 33 cm.

NN.

An announcement and subscription blank for the publication, under the name of *The Herald*, of a weekly edition of the *Minerva*, to contain selected articles and much less advertising, for circulation in the country. The copy located bears the signatures of several subscribers. See Arnold Berthold, "Launching the Herald," *Bulletin* of The New York Public Library, July, 1935 (Vol. 39, pp. 519–520).

791

The Herald; a gazette for the country. Published Wednesdays and Saturdays, by George Bunce & Co. No. 12, Wall-street, near the City-hall, at Three Dollars per annum.

Vol. I, No. 1, to Vol. IV, No. 343, June 4, 1794–September 30, 1797. Approx. 50 x 31 cm.

Since *Herald* articles are almost always reprints from the *Minerva*, they are not listed separately unless they are original. The initial date in the entries below represents the *Minerva*, and dates in parentheses the *Herald* appearance of the same item. (See the last two *Minerva* entries, above, for introductory material printed in the first two issues of the *Herald*.)

1. June 5 (7). Unsigned editorial, "On the French Revolution." Not acknowledged by Webster but probably written by him, since it points out the accuracy of the predictions in his pamphlet *The Revolution in France Considered*. Cf. No. 5 below.

2. June 10 (16). Signed essay, "To the Public," demonstrating that slave labor is less productive than free. Intended to supplement Webster's *Effects of Slavery*. This and the following entry are reprinted in Warfel, *Letters of Noah Webster*, pp. 118–123.

3. June 11 (16). Signed article, "To the Public," an amendment to the essay on slavery in the preceding issue.

4. June 13 (16). Translation of official papers concerning the partition of Poland, from the *Leyden Gazette*. The translation is credited to "The Compiler" of the paper.

An unsigned article in the Herald, *June 19, proposed to exchange that paper rather than the* Minerva *with rural editors, and asked country subscribers to indicate which paper they wished to receive.*

5. July 5 (7). Unsigned article quoting from Webster's *Revolution in France Considered*, probably written by him. Cf. No. 1 above.

An unsigned note in the Herald *of July 24 asks that correspondence and papers be addressed to the printer rather than to the editor.*

6. August 4 (7). Unsigned editorial beginning, "The present period of revolutions...," severely critical of Thomas Paine's *Age of Reason*. Not acknowledged, but attributed to Webster in an anonymous attack on

him in the *American Citizen*, October 20, 1801 (reprinted in the *Republican Watch Tower*, October 21). The editorial was reprinted in the *Norwich* (Conn.) *Packet*, August 21, 1794.

7. August 15 (18). Unsigned article beginning, "We hear the Insurgents at Pittsburg [sic]...," on anti-tax riots there. Paraphed in the New York Public Library file of the *Minerva*.

An unsigned note in the Herald *of August 18 discusses the impossibility of delivering the paper to ships.*

8. August 26 (28). Although it is not acknowledged by Webster, he probably wrote the review of Benjamin Rush, *An Account of the Bilious remitting Yellow Fever...in...Philadelphia, in...1793* (Philadelphia, 1794), because of his interest in the subject.

An unsigned note in the Herald, *September 1, records the completion of its first quarter, and asks for remittances on subscriptions, and another note in the issue of September 4 apologizes for non-delivery of some copies.*

9. September 25. "Proposals for Publishing by Subscription, a Register of the Times...," signed by Webster and Bunce, proposing publication of official papers relating to the French Revolution and subsequent history, and perhaps a compilation of American state papers. Webster had earlier projected a similar "register" to accompany the *American Magazine*; neither materialized.

10. September 25 and later (29). Unsigned announcement of the formation of the Massachusetts Historical Society, soliciting contributions of historical papers and objects. Webster is named as a Corresponding Member in New York, to whom material may be given for forwarding to Boston.

11. October 1 (2). Unsigned editorial beginning, "In a sincere wish...," hoping that France will not engage in wars of aggression or try to liberate other peoples by force. Paraphed in the Boston Athenaeum file of the *Minerva*.

12. October 20, 21, 28, 30, and 31 and November 3, 4, 8, 15, 21, and 24 (October 23 and 30 and November 3, 6, 10, 17, 24, and 27). Unsigned series entitled "Revolution in France," analyzing the reasons why it has taken such a sanguinary turn. Not acknowledged by Webster, but attributed to him by the compiler; it is not the same in content as his pamphlet on the subject. Eight of the installments were reprinted in the *Gazette of the United States*, October 22–November 28, one in the

Columbian Centinel, November 15, and one in the *American Apollo*, November 20.

A note in the Herald *of October 20, signed "The Publishers," reprints part of the prospectus for the paper, concerning price, payment, and delivery, and congratulates itself on lack of complaints from subscribers.*

During late October and early November two separate wrangles filled the columns of Webster's papers and those of the New York Journal, *edited by Thomas Greenleaf, an arch-rival. One, between Greenleaf and "Argus" and "Civis," concerning the reliability of Greenleaf's edition of Rabaut's* History of the Revolution in France; *the other, between "A." on one side and "Curtius," "A.K.," "Fair Play," and "Regulator" on the other, concerned Jay's mission to England.* *See Part Four below, rubrics C and D.*

13. November 14 (17). Unsigned note, "It is the determination of the Director of this Payer [sic] to render it the most complete Register of all political and other important transactions, now published in America."

14. November 26. Unsigned note announcing that new types had been acquired and that the circulation was increasing.

15. November 29 (December 1). Editorial "To the Public," signed "The Editor," defending himself against the *New York Journal's* charges (in their issue of November 29) of delaying and garbling news favorable to the French.

16. December 4 (8). Unsigned note announcing the *Minerva's* intention of publishing the debates of Congress.

17. December 11 (13). Unsigned editorial beginning, "The speech of Mr. Baldwin...," concerning wider diffusion of the proceedings of Congress. Autographed in the Boston Athenaeum file of the *Minerva.* Reprinted in the *New Jersey State Gazette*, December 23, the *Western Star*, December 30, and in part in the *Columbian Centinel*, December 31.

18. December 29 (31). Unsigned announcement beginning, "The Editor is preparing...," announcing forthcoming publication of translations of two important reports made to the French National Convention.

An unsigned "Notice" in the Herald *of December 31 comments on the increasing demand for the paper.*

1795

19. January 3 (7). Unsigned editorial note headed "Ominous," ascribing the recent burning of the German Lutheran Church in Philadelphia to

a meeting therein of the German Republican Society and the "Fiery address" which it adopted. Not acknowledged by Webster, but attributed to him by those who replied to it. Reprinted in the *Aurora*, January 8, and the *Columbian Centinel*, January 14. Replied to by "A German" in the *Aurora*, January 8, and "A Lutheran" in the same paper, January 9 (reprinted in the *Independent Chronicle*, January 19); also mentioned hostilely in James T. Callender's *American Annual Register*... 1796, pp. 89–90. In this instance Webster's zeal in never missing an opportunity to attack Republican clubs carried him too far, and his editorial was castigated as being both tactless and untrue (the meeting was not held in the church). Webster retracted the statement in his issue of January 9 (January 10), reprinted in the *Columbian Centinel*, January 21, and—with adverse comment—the *Independent Chronicle* and *Boston Gazette*, January 22.

20. January 8. Note, signed "The Publishers," explaining the reasons for an increase in price of the *Minerva*, to seven dollars a year.

Webster's role as editor of the Minerva *is referred to in "A Typographical Eclogue," in the* Federal Orrery, *January 8. This is an anonymous poetic treatment of the leading editors of the day, in which Thomas Greenleaf, editor of the* New York Journal, *is made to say to the editor of the* Gazette of the United States,

> *"John Fenno, brother Bache's a dunce,*
> *Compared with him, who prints with Bunce;*
> *That Webster mocks the power of speech,*
> *Or the vast stretch, that thought can reach:*
> *He watches every step, I take—*
> *Exposes every* slip, *I make—*
> *Rails at our clubs, our plots descries,*
> *And, after all, our power defies!"*

21. February 2 (4, extra). Reprint of Webster's essay on usury laws, No. XXIV of his *Collection of Essays*, 1790.

22. February 14 (18). Unsigned editorial beginning, "The public will take notice...," regarding an implied attack on Webster in the *New York Journal*, for trying to stir up anti-French feeling by printing atrocity stories. The *Journal's* reply, February 18, makes the charge specific; to this Webster replied in "At length the publisher...," February 18 (21).

With the May 6 issue the title of the daily paper changed to American Minerva and Evening Advertiser.

23. May 13, 14, and 15 (16). Unsigned editorial, in three installments, the first beginning "Nothing is more common...," the second, "If men are forever influenced...," and the third, "The remarks already published...," citing ancient history and current events in France to show that self-interest is a natural, effective, and beneficial motivation in governmental action. Paraphed in the Yale file of the *Herald*. Reprinted in part in the *Gazette of the United States*, May 15 and 19, the *American Mercury*, May 25, and the *Farmer's Museum*, June 9. Replied to by B. F. Bache in the *Aurora*, May 19, reprinted in the *Gazette of the United States* of the same date.

An unsigned note in the Herald, *May 30, records the completion of a year of publication and announces the forthcoming publication of an index. The compiler has not found that any such index was printed.*

24. July 4 (8). Unsigned essay, "Candid remarks on the treaty...," discussing in detail and approving Jay's treaty. Not acknowledged by Webster, but probably his, since he replied to "Decius," who attacked this article. See Part Four below, rubric D.

25. July 18, 20, 21, 22, 23, 24, 27, 29, and 30 and August 1, 4, and 5 (July 22, 25, and 29 and August 1, 5, and 8). Series of twelve numbered articles, "Vindication of the Treaty...," signed "Curtius." See Part Four below, rubric D, for this series and the replies to it.

26. August 6 (8). Unsigned editorial note stating that the editor of the *Minerva* "waves" the honor of being the "colussos" of the aristocratic faction, of which the *Aurora* had accused him on August 4.

27. September 3 (5). Unsigned editorial about Pennsylvania. See Part Four below, rubric E, for this and the resultant controversy.

28. October 21 (November 4). Signed "(Circular.) To the Physicians of Philadelphia...," issued also as a separate publication; see Title 782.

29. October 29 (31). Unsigned editorial, Webster's(?) first contribution to the "Calm Observer" controversy; see below, Part Four, rubric F.

1796

30. January 20. Unsigned note that a new carrier has been employed to deliver the *Minerva* in the western parts of the city.

31. February 15 (17). Unsigned editorial about Virginia. This became part of the "Harrington" controversy; see below, Part Four, rubric G.

32. April 29 (30). Unsigned note asking that accounts be settled, since at the end of the month the partnership is to be dissolved and a new firm is to take charge of the newspapers.

With the issue of May 2 the name of the daily paper became The Minerva & Mercantile Evening Advertiser.

33. May 2 (4). Signed announcement, dated May 1, "To the Public," using a change in partnership (from that in George Bunce & Co. to one in Hopkins, Webb & Co.) as a point of departure for an explanation of Webster's policies, views, and ideas about newspapers, claiming that despite party spirit he has attempted to be impartial and independent in judgment. Reprinted in Warfel, *Letters of Noah Webster*, pp. 134–136.

34. June 13 (15). Unsigned editorial beginning, "Scarcely a week passes...," parrying charges by the *Aurora* that the *Minerva* is the mouthpiece of Alexander Hamilton, and setting forth Webster's political beliefs. Reprinted, with the heading "Confession of Faith of the Editor of the (New-York) Minerva...," and with comment, in the *Aurora*, June 16. The editorial is not specifically acknowledged by Webster, but is certainly his.

35. June 14 (15). Unsigned editorial beginning, "It is a remark worthy of notice...," asserting that opposition parties receive their strength from the poor and ignorant. Reprinted in the *Gazette of the United States*, June 20. See No. 37 below.

36. June 25 (29). Signed "Notice" requesting that business correspondence be addressed to Hopkins, Webb & Co., and that only editorial matters be addressed to Webster.

During the summer of 1796 there were various articles in the Minerva *about yellow fever in different localities; although not acknowledged by him, these were probably written by Webster, especially those of July 11 (13) and July 13 (16), which quote from his book on the subject. The* Aurora *of July 18 charged him with arrogance in this field.*

37. July 19 (20). Unsigned editorial beginning, "There are but few numbers of the Aurora...," defending his editorial of June 14 against attacks in the *Aurora*, June 29, which charged him with aristocratic leanings. Reprinted in the *Argus*, July 22, the *Aurora*, July 26, the *Washington Gazette*, August 3, and in Warfel, *Letters of Noah Webster*, pp. 138–141.

38. September 10, 14, 21, 27, and 28, October 4 and 5, and November 1, 7, and 9 (September 14, 17, 24, and 28, October 1, 5, and 8, and

November 2, 9, and 12). Unsigned series of ten numbered articles titled "Political Fanaticism," concerning the abuse of power through religious or political fanaticism. Probably written by Webster, though not acknowledged by him. Portions were reprinted in the *Columbian Herald*, October 6, the *Farmer's Museum*, September 27 and October 11, the *Salem Gazette*, November 1, and the *Maryland Herald*, November 22.

39. October 11, 21, and 31, November 8, December 1, 20, and 28, January 9, 18, and 25, and March 15, 1797 (October 12 and 22, November 2 and 9, December 3, 21, and 31, January 11, 21, and 28, and March 18). Nos. XIII to XXIII of the editorial series "The Times," probably written by Webster. The first twelve had appeared April 1–May 10, 1794, q.v.

40. October 19 (20). Unsigned article, "We told you so," quoting predictions from Webster's *Revolution in France Considered* which had been fulfilled. Not acknowledged, but almost certainly by Webster. He also pointed out the validity of his predictions in an editorial note beginning "The Directory have officially. . . ," in the issue of October 24 (26).

41. October 31 (November 2). Unsigned editorial note appended to a letter from "Your friend and subscriber," printed in the same issue, asking Webster to explain apparent inconsistencies in the attitude of his papers toward the French Revolution. In the reply, he explains that he approved of the French people's efforts to gain their own liberty, but changed his opinion when they carried aggression beyond the country's borders. In Nos. II, III, IV, and VI of a series of anonymous essays headed "The Patriot," in the New York *Diary*, November 5, 11, 14, and 28, and reprinted in part in other papers, Webster and others are attacked for their opposition to France, and he is accused of being a British tool. No. VI quotes this editorial, but the series replies to Webster's over-all policy and not to any single editorial or article.

42. December 14, 17, 27, and 28, January 4 and 20, February 8, 16, 21, and 27, and March 1, 1797 (December 17, 21, 28, and 31, January 7 and 21, February 11, 18, and 22, and March 1 and 4). Unsigned series of eleven numbered articles, "To the People of the United States," analyzing French foreign policy and interference in American domestic affairs. Not acknowledged—except in that the last article is signed "W."—but almost certainly by Webster. Partially reprinted in the *Columbian Centinel*, December 28 and January 11, *Wood's Newark Gazette*, December 28, January 4, and February 1, and the *Oracle of the Day*, January 4, 11, 18, and 25, February 1, and March 29. The final installment is reprinted in part in Warfel, *Letters of Noah Webster*, pp. 145–147.

1797

43. January 2. "The great rise of paper and wages compels us to set the Daily Paper at eight dollars a year," unsigned.

44. January 12, 16, 17, 18, and 27 (14, 18, 21, and 28). Series of five untitled, unsigned editorials beginning, "It gives us great pleasure...," "All social establishments...," "The situation of the poor...," "I will at present confine...," and "Another essential article...," remarking on the increased circulation of the papers, and reviewing some of the practical ideas which they have sponsored, such as improved construction of chimneys and a system of insurance to cover workmen injured in the course of duty or otherwise rendered unable to earn, and widows and children of men killed at work. Further self-congratulation on increased circulation, beginning "The rapid increase...," appeared on January 30 (February 1).

45. February 7 (8). Unsigned note beginning, "The publishers of this paper are sorry...," regarding the charge that some rural postmasters who are also printers delay the delivery of urban newspapers in order to give their own papers precedence.

46. March 13, 14, 16, 18, 27, 28, and 29 and April 1, 7, 11, 14, 15, and 20 (March 15, 18, 22, and 29 and April 1, 5, 12, 15, 19 and 22). Series of thirteen numbered "Political Sketches," the last signed "N.W.," analyzing American commerce, industry, finance, etc. Three of the series were reprinted in the *State Gazette of South Carolina*, April 11 and May 1 and 5, and one in the Baltimore *Federal Gazette*, April 26.

47. March 21 (22). Statement of political views, signed "W.", beginning "In a late paper...." This referred to "Peter Porcupine" (William Cobbett), who replied in *Porcupine's Gazette*, March 25, and reprinted both items in *Porcupine's Political Censor*, March, 1797 (pp. 75–80). Webster's article was also reprinted in *Carey & Markland's Daily Advertiser*, March 25, the *Newport* (R.I.) *Mercury*, April 11, and the *State Gazette of South Carolina*, April 13.

In the Herald *of April 5 is a notice, signed "The Publishers," warning subscribers whose payments are in arrears, and explaining the necessity of an additional charge for wrapping moist papers to comply with the new postal regulation about drying newspapers before mailing.*

48. May 4 (6). Unsigned review of Dr. Alexander Hosack's *Inaugural Essay on the Yellow Fever* (New York, 1797). Probably by Webster, since he is mentioned in the work, and was a friend of the author. Re-

printed in the *Merchant's Daily Advertiser*, May 8, and the *Farmer's Museum*, May 23.

49. May 6. "Notice," signed by Webster and George F. Hopkins, dated May 6, announcing the dissolution of Hopkins, Webb & Co. The notice asserts that Joseph D. Webb had violated his agreement with his partners.

50. May 8. "Notice," signed by the same two persons, dated May 8, announcing that an account of the difficulties would be published the following day, Webb having written the paper a letter (printed in the same issue) requesting their statement, since he claimed to be the injured party.

51. May 9. "To the Public," signed by Webster, dated May 9, setting forth his and Hopkins' side of the argument.

52. May 13. "Notice," signed by Webster and Hopkins, dated May 13, announcing that the firm is once again functioning smoothly, and is to be known as Hopkins and Co.

53. May 17. Unsigned editorial note refusing to heed Webb's complaints.

54. May 27. Unsigned notice beginning, "The public are informed...," stating that by an injunction Joseph D. Webb is prohibited from receiving any moneys due Hopkins, Webb and Co. until the case has been settled in court.

55. June 10 (14). Unsigned editorial note (beginning, "We have good authority...") regarding Jefferson's famous letter to Philip Mazzei, urging support of all administration measures in regard to France. Paraphed by Webster in the Henry Ford Museum file of the *Herald*.

56. June 13 (14). Unsigned editorial beginning, "Not only sentiments of humanity...," calling for peace in Europe and hoping that France will recover from her sanguinary follies. Paraphed by Webster in the Henry Ford Museum file of the *Herald*. Reprinted in the *Merchant's Daily Advertiser*, June 19, the *Southern Centinel*, July 6, and the *South Carolina State Gazette*, July 10.

57. June 20 (21). Unsigned announcement that, in order to assist the mercantile and agricultural interests of the country, the papers would from time to time publish new federal laws. This practice began in the *Minerva's* issues of June 21 and 23.

58. June 26 (28). Unsigned editorial beginning, "Peace is at length...," on the cessation of hostilities in Europe. Paraphed by Webster in the Henry Ford Museum file of the *Herald*. Reprinted in the *Aurora* and the *South Carolina State Gazette*, July 20.

59. June 27 (28). Unsigned editorial beginning, "Some of our best informed politicians...," on the situation in Europe and the beneficial

effects of a general peace. Paraphed by Webster in the Henry Ford Museum file of the *Herald*. Reprinted in the *Federal Gazette* (Baltimore) and the *Merchant's Daily Advertiser*, June 30, *Bartgis's Federal Gazette* (Fredericktown, Md.), July 5, the *Albany Centinel*, July 11, and the *South Carolina State Gazette*, July 20.

60. July 7 (8). Unsigned editorial beginning, "The alarming state. . .," predicting continued war in Europe and possible involvement of the United States. Paraphed by Webster in the Henry Ford Museum file of the *Herald*.

61. July 12 (15). Unsigned editorial beginning, "The restless, turbulent ambition. . .," decrying the influence on government of unscrupulous men of ambition and of men without property. Paraphed by Webster in the Henry Ford Museum file of the *Herald*.

62. July 13 (15). Unsigned editorial note (beginning, "Captain Bray. . .") on news of the English naval mutiny at Portsmouth and other events, brought by a ship from Lisbon. Paraphed by Webster in the Henry Ford Museum file of the *Herald*.

63. July 13 (19). Notice beginning, "Our customers are informed. . .," signed by Webster and Hopkins, dated July 13, announcing that because of the break with Webb their accounts will be audited, and any errors in regard to customers adjusted.

64. July 15 (19). Unsigned editorial beginning, "A gentleman recently. . .," on the agricultural advantages of the Genesee region in New York. Paraphed by Webster in the Henry Ford Museum file of the *Herald*. Reprinted in the *Merchant's Daily Advertiser*, July 19.

65. July 28 (29). Unsigned editorial comment (beginning, "The remarks published. . .") on an extract from a French newspaper which had been published in the *Minerva* on July 26, about conditions in France. Paraphed by Webster in the Henry Ford Museum file of the *Herald*.

66. August 2 (5). Unsigned editorial beginning, "The reputation of our papers. . .," announcing a policy of avoiding personal remarks and letting facts speak for themselves, and declaring that the large circulation of the papers is proof of their excellence. Derided by "Ferula" in the *Argus*, August 4, who called Webster "Domine Syntax." Webster made no reply to this, for which he was twitted by "Vox Populi Americani" in the *Argus* for August 14.

67. August 14 (16). Signed editorial replying to "Vox Populi Americani." Reprinted, with the letter to which it replies, in the *Aurora*, August 17.

68. August 14 (16). Unsigned editorial beginning, "Should it be true. . .," about the demand of the French Directory for a special em-

bassy, reflecting on the tendency of men of all types to become despotic with power. Paraphed by Webster in the Henry Ford Museum file of the *Herald*. Reprinted in the *South Carolina State Gazette*, September 2.

69. August 15 (16). Unsigned note beginning, "It is amusing to see...," denying authorship of an article on the boundaries of France which had appeared in the *Minerva* of July 26, saying it was material taken from foreign papers. Webster further denied authorship in the *Minerva* of August 19.

70. August 17 (19). Unsigned editorial beginning, "The French will...," comparing religious and political bigotry and censuring the *Aurora* and *Porcupine's Gazette* for partiality to the French and the English, respectively. Paraphed by Webster in the Henry Ford Museum file of the *Herald*. Reprinted in part and replied to in the *Aurora*, August 26.

71. August 17 (19). Unsigned editorial beginning, "The following remarks...," on the release of the American ship *Juliana* by a court in Le Havre, with political reflections. Paraphed by Webster in the Henry Ford Museum file of the *Herald*.

72. August 18 (19). Unsigned editorial beginning, "In our former observations...," on the fall of ancient empires from military ambition and unwieldy size, predicting a like fate for France. Paraphed by Webster in the Henry Ford Museum file of the *Herald*.

73. September 21 (23). An unsigned editorial beginning, "We may rail at the French..." was paraphed by Webster in the Henry Ford Museum file of the *Herald*, though in print it is credited to a London paper.

Because of the differences between Webster, Hopkins, and Webb, the Minerva *and* Herald *ceased publication with their issues of September 30. New papers were instituted immediately, however, and advertising matter which still had time to run continued in them.*

C. *The Commercial Advertiser and Spectator*

792

Commercial Advertiser. [colophon:] Published, (Daily) at No. 40 Pine-street, by Geo. F. Hopkins....

Vol. I, No. 1 [to Vol. VII, No. 1882], October 2, 1797 [–November 2, 1803]. Approx. 51 x 35 cm.

793

The Spectator. [colophon:] Published by G. F. Hopkins, at No. 40 Pine-street.

Vol. I, No. 1 [to Vol. VII, No. 652], October 4, 1797 [–November 2, 1803]. Approx. 51 x 35 cm.

The former arrangement of a daily (except Sunday) and a semi-weekly rural edition was continued, the *Spectator* being the semi-weekly. The daily cost $8.00 a year and the semi-weekly $3.50. George F. Hopkins appeared as sole proprietor of both papers, but Webster was a silent partner, a fact not unknown to rival editors. The *Argus* of October [3] contains a mock obituary of the *Minerva*, detecting Webster's hand in the new papers.

As with the precedent papers, the initial dates in the following entries are those of the daily, and dates in parentheses are those of republication of the same item in the semi-weekly.

1. October 2 and later (4 and later). Notice, "To the Public," signed by Hopkins, dated October 2, announcing the discontinuance of the two earlier papers and the establishment of the new, quoting terms, and declaring that the papers will be friendly to the government, moral, and truthful, and that foreign news will be based upon authentic and reliable sources.

2. October 2, 9, 16, and 24 (4, 11, 18, and 25). Series of four numbered, unsigned essays entitled "The Tickler," humorously discussing the vulnerable spots in human nature. The first was paraphed by Webster in the Henry Ford Museum file of the *Spectator*. Reprinted in part in the Baltimore *Federal Gazette*, October 9, 24, and 31, the Alexandria, Va., *Times*, October 12, the *Merchant's Daily Advertiser*, October 19, the *New Jersey State Gazette*, October 24, the *Farmer's Museum*, October 30, the *NewHampshire Gazette*, November 1, the *South Carolina State Gazette*, November 1, the *Columbian Mirror*, November 2 and 4, the *Whitestown* (N.Y.) *Gazette*, November 7, and the *Farmer's Oracle*, November 28. Satirical replies appeared in the New London *Bee*, October 25 (reprinted in the *Aurora*, October 30), and in the *Chelsea Courier*, November 1 (reprinted in the *American Mercury*, November 13). Both writers guessed that Webster was the author. Presumably with this series he was trying to repeat the success of the *Prompter*, but failed. With the first of the series there is a notice of copyright entry of "The Tickler: Being a Series

of Periodical Papers, Descriptive of Life and Manners" as a book, copyrighted to Hopkins, October 2. The compiler has found no separate edition.

An unsigned note in the first issue of the Spectator *announces that the paper will be conducted on the same principles that the* Herald *had been, gives terms and postage rates, and asks for agents.*

3. October 5. Unsigned editorial note (beginning, "To the Merchants of New-York...") denying the accusations of James Oram that the paper's "Prices Current" feature plagiarizes Oram's *New York Prices-Current.*

4. October 6. Note signed by Webster correcting a misprint in the preceding day's issue and disclaiming responsibility for the business end of the paper, outlining his province as the "political, moral, literary and philosophical department." This phrase was quoted satirically against Webster in the *New York Gazette*, October 19.

5. October 6 (7). Unsigned editorial beginning, "The numberless evils...," philosophizing on the troubles of mankind, especially as they arise from uncontrolled passions. Paraphed by Webster in the Henry Ford Museum file of the *Spectator*.

6. October 16 and 17 (18). Two unsigned editorial notes (beginning "Among all the writers..." and "Since writing the observations...") on plagues, upholding the domestic origin of yellow fever; these are more or less introductory to the series of letters to Dr. Currie which began on October 26. Paraphed by Webster in the Henry Ford Museum file of the *Spectator*. The first reprinted in the *New Jersey State Gazette*, October 24, and the Lansingburgh, N.Y., *Northern Budget*, November 28, and both in the *Aurora*, October 19 and 20, with critical comment on October 21. Although not acknowledged by Webster, another note on yellow fever (beginning, "It has often been noticed...") on October 24 (25) was probably also by him.

7. October 17 (18). Unsigned editorial beginning, "Most governments regulate...," discussing recent acts of the French Directory. Paraphed by Webster in the Henry Ford Museum file of the *Spectator*. Reprinted in the *Aurora*, October 20.

8. October 26, 28, and 30, November 1, 2, 7, 11, 13, 15, 17, 21, 22, 24, 27, and 29, and December 1, 5, 6, 8, 9, 13, 14, 15, 18, and 20 (October 28, November 1, 4, 8, 15, 18, 22, 25, and 29, and December 2, 6, 9, 13, 16, 20, and 23). Signed and numbered series of twenty-five open letters "To Dr. William Currie" on yellow fever. Reprinted in part in the *Merchant's Daily Advertiser*, November 10 and 11, the *Salem Gazette*,

December 15, the Baltimore *Telegraphe*, November 3, 14, 15, 16, and 18, and the Baltimore *Federal Gazette*, November 24. Contemporary references in letters and periodicals—including Webster's own, December 14 (16)—show that Webster seriously considered a pamphlet reprint of the series, but no such edition has been located. Benjamin Rush wrote Webster of an Academy of Medicine formed in Philadelphia by the physicians who believed in the domestic origin of the fever, and said that the Currie letters would be included in their first annual volume of transactions,[5] but the organization apparently did not survive long enough to print such a volume. Mathew Carey also seems to have asked permission to reprint the letters.[6] The series was reprinted in recent years as a monograph (Title 768), and in part in Warfel, *Letters of Noah Webster*, pp. 161–170.

9. November 3 (4). Unsigned editorial beginning, "The Maritime Courier of Havre...," analyzing a memorial of the merchants of Le Havre, the text of which is given in the *Commercial Advertiser*. Paraphed by Webster in the Henry Ford Museum file of the *Spectator*. Reprinted in the Baltimore *Telegraphe*, November 8, the *Columbian Mirror*, November 9, the *South Carolina State Gazette*, November 25, and the *Southern Centinel*, December 7.

10. November 9. Signed letter "To Dr. Benjamin Wynkoop of Philadelphia," on the yellow fever there. Dr. Wynkoop's reply, first printed in the *Merchant's Daily Advertiser*, November 20, was reprinted in the *Commercial Advertiser* on November 23.

11. November 9 (11). Unsigned editorial beginning, "As many of our readers...," on recent political parties and activities in France. Paraphed by Webster in the Henry Ford Museum file of the *Spectator*. Replied to in *Porcupine's Gazette*, November 15.

12. November 11 (15). Unsigned editorial beginning, "The intelligence from France...," attacking the recent proscriptions by the French Directory. Paraphed by Webster in the Henry Ford Museum file of the *Spectator*. Reprinted in part in *Porcupine's Gazette*, November 16 (with critical comment), and in *Porcupine's Works*, Vol. VII, pp. 295–298.

13. November 16 (18). Unsigned editorial beginning, "The news from Boston...," on recent events in France and the apparent French intention of revolutionizing the world. Paraphed by Webster in the Henry Ford Museum file of the *Spectator*.

14. November 16 (18). Unsigned editorial beginning, "It is hardly

[5] December 29, 1797, Webster Papers, New York Public Library.

[6] Webster to Carey, January 22, 1798, Lea and Febiger Papers, Historical Society of Pennsylvania.

conceivable...," attacking the lack of respect shown the President by the American "Jacobins." Paraphed by Webster in the Henry Ford Museum file of the *Spectator*.

15. November 17 (18). Unsigned editorial beginning, "We notice with regret...," on the likelihood of continued French depredations on American commerce. Paraphed by Webster in the Henry Ford Museum file of the *Spectator*.

16. November 18 (22). Unsigned editorial beginning, "The revolt of the provinces...," on the revolt of the German provinces. Paraphed by Webster in the Henry Ford Museum file of the *Spectator*.

17. November 22 (25). Unsigned editorial beginning, "In the sitting of the council...," on the rise of the Sans-culottes to power in France. Paraphed by Webster in the Henry Ford Museum file of the *Spectator*. Reprinted in the *North Carolina Journal*, December 18.

18. November 27 (29). Unsigned editorial beginning, "Should the war in Europe continue...," on the probable alignment of forces should the war continue in Europe. Paraphed by Webster in the Henry Ford Museum file of the *Spectator*. Reprinted in *Boston Prices Current*, December 4, the *New Jersey State Gazette*, December 5, the *Connecticut Gazette*, December 6, the *South Carolina State Gazette*, December 20, and the *New Jersey Journal*, December 26.

19. November 30 (December 2). Unsigned short editorial paragraph (beginning, "The purchasers...") about the purchasers of confiscated properties in France. Paraphed by Webster in the Henry Ford Museum file of the *Spectator*.

20. December 6 (9). Unsigned editorial beginning "Our readers will observe...," justifying the amount of attention given to the French Revolution because of the principles and momentous changes involved. Paraphed by Webster in the Henry Ford Museum file of the *Spectator*. Ridiculed in the *Aurora*, December 11.

21. December 12 (13). Unsigned editorial beginning, "Zimmerman [sic] on National Pride...," commending Johann Georg von Zimmermann's *Essay on National Pride* (London, 1797) as being frank about the vices and prejudices of various nations. William Cobbett considered this to be by Webster, for he headed a reply "Zimmerman [sic], Noah Webster, and Peter Porcupine," in *Porcupine's Gazette*, December 15 (reprinted in *Porcupine's Works*, Vol. VII, pp. 425–428).

22. December 13 (16). Unsigned editorial beginning, "The extension of the revolution...," predicting great power and extent for France if she can realize her plans. Paraphed by Webster in the Henry Ford Museum file of the *Spectator*.

23. December 14 (16). Unsigned editorial beginning, "The Romans, after a long war...," on the revengeful and dictatorial policies of the French. Paraphed by Webster in the Henry Ford Museum file of the *Spectator*.

24. December 14 (16). Unsigned editorial beginning, "The destruction of wood...," deploring waste of wood and suggesting tree plantings. Paraphed by Webster in the Henry Ford Museum file of the *Spectator*. Reprinted in the *Aurora*, December 18, and the *New Jersey State Gazette*, December 19.

1798

25. January 4, 5, 8, and 9 (6 and 10). Series of four letters signed "Observer," opposing a bill before the state legislature to limit the rate of interest on loans. Paraphed by Webster in the Henry Ford Museum file of the *Spectator*. The third reprinted in *Porcupine's Gazette*, January 31. An article from the *Albany Gazette* presenting the other side of the argument was printed in the issue of February 6 (February 17), and news items about the progress and defeat of the bill appeared at later dates.

26. January 8 and 9. Signed note "To the Sextons of the several Churches and congregations of New-York," asking them for the death records of their parishes, 1785–1797, and offering to pay for statistics delivered.

27. January 10 (13). Signed letter "To Mr. Benjamin Wyncoop [sic]...," acknowledging that gentleman's reply to No. 10 above.

28. January 22 (24). Unsigned editorial beginning, "There never was a sample...," censuring James Monroe for the nature of his dealings with the French foreign ministry. Paraphed by Webster in the Henry Ford Museum file of the *Spectator*. Reprinted in the *Farmer's Weekly Museum*, February 6.

29. January 30 (31). Unsigned editorial beginning, "Governor Pinckney...," about South Carolina quarantine measures, leading into a general discussion of yellow fever. Paraphed by Webster in the Henry Ford Museum file of the *Spectator*.

30. February 2 (3). Signed letter "To Mr. Joseph Scott, of Philadelphia...," regarding charges of plagiarism exchanged between Scott and Jedidiah Morse, saying that Morse had Webster's permission to use his descriptive material on New York (see above, Note 9 to Title 745, and rubric A of this part, No. 20). Reprinted in Warfel, *Letters of Noah Webster*, p. 178.

31. February 10 (14). Unsigned editorial beginning, "There must in all governments...," on Congress' power to tax and the chief exec-

utive's to make diplomatic appointments. Paraphed by Webster in the Henry Ford Museum file of the *Spectator*.

32. March 1 (3). Unsigned editorial beginning, "It is suggested . . . ," regarding asserted French tampering with mails from the United States. Paraphed by Webster in the Henry Ford Museum file of the *Spectator*. Attacked in the *Argus*, March 3, and reprinted in the *Columbian Centinel*, March 10, and the *Massachusetts Spy*, March 14.

33. March 7 (10). Unsigned editorial beginning, "No people of the earth . . . ," contrasting the expenditures for a federal capital city with the neglect of the roads leading to it. Paraphed by Webster in the Henry Ford Museum file of the *Spectator*. Reprinted, with approval, in the *Aurora*, March 14, and in the Charleston *City Gazette*, April 6.

34. March 10 (14). Unsigned editorial note (beginning, "It is with regret . . .") apologizing for the necessity of abridging foreign news, and giving comparative costs and sizes of American, English, and French newspapers.

35. March 16 (17). Unsigned editorial beginning, "We have had occasion . . . ," on France and her plans of European conquest. Paraphed by Webster in the Henry Ford Museum file of the *Spectator*. Reprinted in the *Connecticut Courant*, March 26.

36. March 28. Unsigned "Notice" reminding subscribers, especially those in Canada, that their papers will be discontinued unless payment is made in advance.

37. March 28 (31). Unsigned editorial beginning, "Much clamor is raised . . . ," deploring demands that the President publish in full dispatches from American commissioners in Paris, in reply to an editorial in the *Aurora* of March 27. Paraphed by Webster in the Henry Ford Museum file of the *Spectator*. Reprinted in the *Albany Gazette*, April 6.

On April 1, 1798, Webster moved from New York to New Haven, and so less of the content of the papers thereafter is attributable to his pen.

38. June 8, 11, 13, and 16 (9, 13, 16, and 20). Series of four unsigned articles, "To the Young Men. . . ." The first three discuss the situation in Europe and the fourth appeals to young Americans to join the militia and to be neither pro-French nor pro-British. The fourth paraphed by Webster in the Henry Ford Museum file of the *Spectator*.

39. June 15 (16). Letter to the editor, signed "Amicus," probably by Webster. This was part of the controversy about Josiah Coit; see Part Four below, rubric H.

40. June 16 (20). Unsigned editorial beginning, "There are a few . . . ,"

observing that no nation has procured durable peace with loans, bribes, or tribute. Paraphed by Webster in the Henry Ford Museum file of the *Spectator*. This contains Webster's frequently-made point that the Jay Treaty was not a cause of French hostility to the United States; this view was attacked in the *Argus*, June 19, and the *Time Piece*, June 20.

41. June 19 (20). Unsigned editorial beginning, "It is common to hear...," minimizing the threat of an invasion of the United States and predicting that French plans for world domination would fail. Paraphed by Webster in the Henry Ford Museum file of the *Spectator*.

42. June 25 (27). Unsigned editorial beginning, "We have said...," urging the creation of an adequate army and navy in view of possible French domination of the seas. Marked by Webster ("N.W. on Navy") in the Henry Ford Museum file of the *Spectator*. Reprinted with a reply in the *Aurora*, June 28 (both reprinted in the *Independent Chronicle*, July 12); also replied to in the *Aurora* of June 29.

43. July 4 (7). Unsigned editorial, headed "Birth day of American Liberty," calling for resistance to French demands for tribute. Paraphed by Webster in the Henry Ford Museum file of the *Spectator*.

44. July 11 (14). Unsigned editorial, very possibly by Webster, which precipitated a small newspaper controversy about British atrocities in the Revolution. See Part Four below, rubric I.

45. July 18. Signed letter to the acting editor, George Hopkins, dated New Haven, July 16, discussing some cancellations of subscriptions which resulted from an article in the paper for July 5 reflecting on England. See Part Three below, No. 114.

46. July 21 (25). Unsigned editorial beginning, "Nothing is so degrading...," calling for a strong navy. Paraphed by Webster in the Henry Ford Museum file of the *Spectator*. Replied to in *Russell's Gazette*, July [30], and *Porcupine's Gazette*, August 3.

47. July 24 (25). Webster's Fourth of July oration at New Haven; it was later printed in separate form (Title 738).

48. July 26 (28). Unsigned editorial beginning, "It is a popular doctrine...," calling for a strong navy and cautioning against imperialism and entangling alliances. Paraphed by Webster in the Henry Ford Museum file of the *Spectator*. Replied to in the *Aurora*, July 31 (reprinted in the *Time Piece*, August 3).

49. July 27 (28). Unsigned editorial beginning, "On the great fundamental maxim...," pointing out that the United States' lack of colonies and isolation by sea reduce the cost of defense, making a militia and small navy adequate. Paraphed by Webster in the Henry Ford Museum file of the *Spectator*.

50. July 30 (August 1). Unsigned "Communication from Providence, R.I.," contrasting the forty-five "Gentlemen of the first respectability" there who subscribe to the *Spectator* with the one "notorious swindler" who subscribed to *Porcupine's Gazette,* "but was obliged to elope even before" receiving his first number.

An unsigned "Notice—Notice" in the Spectator *of August 4 calls on subscribers to remit promptly or be dropped.*

An unsigned note in the Spectator *of September 22 explains the necessity of reducing the paper to a single sheet because of an epidemic.*

51. August 16 (18). Unsigned editorial beginning, "In the first alarm...," on epidemics, speculating that there must be some cause beyond filth, heat, and uncleanliness. Paraphed by Webster in the Henry Ford Museum file of the *Spectator.*

52. September 26 and 27 and October 1, 5, 6, and 8 (September 29 and October 3, 6, and 10). Series of six articles on the plague, the first signed by Webster. Reprinted in part in *Russell's Gazette,* October 8, the *Hampshire Gazette,* October 10, the *Independent Chronicle,* October 11, the *Columbian Centinel,* October 13, the *American Farmer,* November 1, the *Newark Gazette,* December 4, and the *Oracle of the Day,* July 13, 1799.

53. October 30 (November 3 and later). Unsigned "Notice" requesting customers to settle accounts promptly because of the difficulties of conducting the papers during the epidemic.

54. November 16 (17). Letter "To Joel Barlow," signed "W.," criticizing Barlow's pro-French letter to Abraham Baldwin, first printed in the *Connecticut Courant,* November 5, and widely reprinted, including the *Commercial Advertiser,* November 10 and 12. Webster's letter was reprinted in the *Hampshire Gazette,* November 28, the *American Mercury,* November 29, the *Albany Centinel,* December 4, the *Columbian Centinel,* January 2, 1799, and in Warfel, *Letters of Noah Webster,* pp. 187–194; Barlow's letter was reprinted in 1806 in a pamphlet published in New Haven entitled *Two Letters to the Citizens of the United States,* with an introductory note in which Barlow states that although the letter is basically his, it has been garbled, added to and deleted from, and otherwise mutilated and changed from his language and content.

55. December 6 (8). Unsigned editorial note (beginning, "The great mortality...") in which the *Commercial Advertiser* preens itself that because of the preventive measures followed in its office there were no deaths there during the epidemic.

56. December 29 (January 2 and later). Unsigned editorial note asking the person who borrowed a file of the *Spectator* to return it.

1799

57. January 1 (2). Unsigned "Reflections, for January 1. . . ," on the events of the preceding year. Paraphed by Webster in the New York Public Library file of the *Spectator*. Reprinted in the *Philadelphia Gazette*, January 3.

58. January 28. Unsigned editorial note beginning, "The publisher. . . ," denying the rumor that the *Commercial Advertiser* is about to suspend publication, claiming an output of "between 7 and 8000" papers a week—i.e., over a thousand copies of each issue.

59. February 2 (6). Unsigned editorial beginning, "In the September session of the Assembly. . . ," regarding yellow fever. Paraphed by Webster in the New York Public Library file of the *Spectator*.

60. March 9 (13). Unsigned "Communication" regarding inconsistencies in state and federal laws against usury. Paraphed by Webster in the New York Public Library file of the *Spectator*.

61. March 23 (27). Signed letter "To the Citizens of New-York and Philadelphia," about yellow fever. Reprinted in *Russell's Gazette*, April 1, the *Salem Gazette*, April 2, the *South Carolina State Gazette*, April 16, the Charleston *City Gazette*, May 6, and the *Georgetown* (S.C.) *Gazette*, May 22. Fun was poked at Webster for riding yellow fever as a hobby horse in the *Argus*, March 26 and 30 and September 20.

62. May 29 and 30 and June 1, 3, 4, and 6 (June 1, 5, and 8). Series of six unsigned articles, "To the People of America," on the world situation and American commerce. Paraphed by Webster in the New York Public Library file of the *Spectator*. Reprinted in full in the *Newport* (R.I.) *Mercury*, June 18–July 16, in part in the *South Carolina State Gazette*, June 20, and in the *Salem Gazette*, July 12.

63. July 1 and later (3 and later). "Notice. The Partnership of Noah Webster, jun. and George F. Hopkins, is this day dissolved, by mutual consent," signed by both; and signed announcement of a new partnership, consisting of Webster and Ebenezer Belden, as E. Belden & Co., which is empowered to collect debts due the former partnership, and which will continue the publication of the papers. Belden was Webster's nephew.

An unsigned note in the issue of July 1 (3) announces the gift of files of the Spectator *to "the Library of New-York—of Columbia College—of Princeton College—of Yale College—of Providence College—of Harvard College—of Dartmouth College—of the Massachusetts Historical Society, and of Philadelphia," and suggests that other publishers follow the example, to assist research workers.*

Another note in the same issues announces that several gentlemen, who must remain anonymous, will write for these papers critical discussions oj religion, government, and ethics, and solicits such contributions.

64. July 19. Unsigned announcement that the *Commercial Advertiser* will publish accounts of Custom House entries and clearances. The editor of the *New York Mercantile Advertiser* claimed (July 16) that both the *Commercial Advertiser* and the *New York Gazette* were poaching on his domain.

65. July 24 (27). Unsigned editorial beginning, "It is curious to observe...," on Jacobinism in the United States, and asserting that the readers of the *Spectator* were of higher caliber than those of rival papers. Paraphed by Webster in the New York Public Library file of the *Spectator*. This of course brought replies, in the *Argus*, July 26, 27, and 30, the first claiming that Webster was whistling in the dark because of falling circulation.

66. July 30 (31). Unsigned editorial beginning, "The Modern French philosophers...,"pointing out the inconsistency between French scientific thought and French political thought. Paraphed by Webster in the New York Public Library file of the *Spectator*. Reprinted in the *Philadelphia Gazette*, August 3, and in part in the *Newport* (R.I.) *Mercury*, August 13.

67. September 24 (28). Editorial signed "W.," beginning, "Nothing can equal the vanity...," on the yellow fever. Paraphed by Webster in the New York Public Library file of the *Spectator*.

68. September 25 (28). Unsigned review of an anonymous pamphlet, *A Hint for Free-Masons* (Newfield, Conn., 1799). Paraphed by Webster in the New York Public Library file of the *Spectator*. His copy of the pamphlet is now in the Watkinson Library, Trinity College, Hartford.

69. October 1 (5). Editorial signed "W.," beginning, "Will not our cities...," about recurrent diseases. Paraphed by Webster in the New York Public Library file of the *Spectator*. Reprinted in the *Salem Gazette*, October 22.

70. October 21, 23, 25, 28, and 30, November 1, 4, 6, 8, 11, 19, 21, 23, 27, and 30, and December 3, 5, 9, and 13 (October 23, 26, and 30, November 2, 6, 9, 13, 20, 23, 27, and 30, and December 4, 7, 11, and 14). Series of nineteen unsigned, numbered articles headed "Barruel Amended," assaulting Jacobinism. Not acknowledged by Webster but considered to be by him by all those who replied in other papers. Parts of the series were widely reprinted.

1800

71. January 20 (22). Unsigned editorial beginning, "No hostile attempts...," stating that the papers' editorials on Washington's death were not meant to revive party spirit, but merely to point out—especially to Europeans—that the republic is not dependent on the life of any one man.

72. February 3, 6, and 11 (8 and 12). Series of three signed letters from Webster, dated at New Haven, January 24, 27, and 30, giving data to supplement his books on epidemic and pestilential diseases, and discussing statistics and scientific observation. The second letter was reprinted in the *Columbian Centinel*, February 15, the *Salem Gazette*, February 18, and the *Hampshire Gazette*, February 26. Replied to in the *Argus*, February 11, and especially in a series of letters from James Hardie in the *New York Gazette*, February 11 to March 24. An unsigned letter about atmospheric phenomena in England in the *Columbian Phenix*, February, 1800 (p. 107), reprinted in the *New York Weekly Museum*, March 29, mentions Webster and probably was evoked by these letters.

73. February 17, 18, 20, 21, 24, 25, and 26 (February 19, 22, and 26 and March 1). Series of seven numbered, unsigned editorials in support of bicameral legislatures. I, II, III, and VII paraphed by Webster in the Henry Ford Museum file of the *Spectator*. Replied to in the *Aurora*, February 20 and 28.

Two announcements in the Spectator *of March 8 give (1) reasons for having to set a different price for subscriptions not paid in advance, and (2) a list of agents for the paper in various towns.*

74. March 21 (22). Signed note suggesting that on January 1, 1801, every clergyman preach a "Century Sermon" on the history of his town. Reprinted in the New Brunswick *Guardian*, March 25, the *Salem Gazette*, April 8, the Alexandria, Va., *Times*, April 10, the *Columbian Mirror*, May 1, and the *Newark Gazette*, May 27.

75. March 22 (26). Unsigned editorial beginning, "In consequence of...," on the abuse of the press, declining to print anything which smacks of personal calumny. Paraphed by Webster in the Henry Ford Museum file of the *Spectator*.

76. March 27 and 28 and April 1, 2, and 3 (March 29 and April 2 and 5). Series of five unsigned editorials, "Remarks on the New Constitution of France." Paraphed by Webster in the Henry Ford Museum file of the *Spectator*.

77. April 22 (26). Unsigned editorial beginning, "In the letter from Thomas Cooper. . . ," on Jacobin principles in the United States. Marked by Webster in the Yale and Henry Ford Museum files of the *Spectator*. A letter to the printers in the issue of April 30 (May 3) complains of changes which they made in the copy.

78. April 25 (30). Unsigned editorial beginning, "The public prints. . . ," using news reports of a rain of sulphur as an opportunity to discuss the connection of atmospheric disturbances and disease, and the need for reliable statistics. Paraphed by Webster in the Henry Ford Museum file of the *Spectator*.

79. May 19 (21). Unsigned editorial beginning, "It seems to be. . . ," citing recent instances of atmospheric disturbances and plague as supporting Webster's views in his book on fevers; very likely written by him. Another article citing recent events to support his views appeared in the issue of June 25 (28).

80. June 25, 28, and 30 and July 1, 2, 3, 5, 11, 12, and 14 (June 28 and July 2, 5, 9, 12, and 16). "Ten Letters to Dr. Joseph Priestly [sic]," of which only the last is signed, reprinted from the pamphlet edition (Title 722) with the note, "The following letters were originally published in a pamphlet; but the few copies printed not satisfying the demand we give them a place in our papers."

81. August 28 (30). Unsigned editorial beginning, "A very candid writer. . . ," on an anonymous pamphlet (by William Linn), *Serious considerations on the election of a President* (New York, 1800). Paraphed by Webster in the Yale file of the *Spectator*. Reprinted in the *Connecticut Gazette*, September 3, and the *Middlesex Gazette*, September 5.

82. October 15 (18). Unsigned editorial beginning, "The public attention. . . ,"discussing current diseases, quoting from Webster's book on them, and asking navigators from the Behring Straits area for data on volcanic eruptions. Paraphed by Webster in the Yale file of the *Spectator*.

83. October 16, 17, 22, and 25 (18, 25, and 29). Series of four articles, "The Author of the History of Epidemic and Pestilential Diseases, To the Editor of the Monthly Magazine and American Review" (Charles Brockden Brown), replying to a review therein. In addition to the heading as evidence of authorship, part of this series was paraphed by Webster in the Yale file of the *Spectator*. Reprinted in the *Monthly Magazine*, November, 1800 (Vol. III, pp. 332–339). See No. 85 below.

1801

84. January 1, 2, 5, 6, 7, and 8 (3, 7, and 10). Series of six unsigned articles, "Observations for the Commencement of the Nineteenth Cen-

tury," on history, politics, etc. Paraphed by Webster in the Yale file of the *Spectator*. Reprinted in the *Boston Gazette*, January 15 and 22.

85. January 9 (10). "To the Reviewer of the History of Pestilence," signed "W." and "N.W.," continuing the discussion described above as No. 83.

86. January 31 (February 4). Unsigned editorial beginning, "Our wiseacres have just discovered. . . ," on the desirability of dissolving state governments and becoming a single federal unit. Reprinted in the *American Citizen*, February 7, the *American Mercury*, February 12, and the New London *Bee*, February 18; these reprints are all accompanied by editorial notes replying to the original. Although not acknowledged by Webster, this contribution was attributed to him by the editors who replied to it.

87. February 5 (7). Unsigned editorial beginning, "Nothing demonstrates the narrow views. . . ," on undue despondency about unfortunate public events, such as Washington's death. Paraphed by Webster in the Yale file of the *Spectator*. Reprinted in the *Salem Impartial Register*, February 29.

88. February 9 (11). Unsigned editorial beginning, "When the Constitution. . . ," advocating a national bank instead of a multiplicity of banks, and ascribing contemporary political evils to defects in the Constitution. Paraphed by Webster in the Yale file of the *Spectator*. Reprinted in *Russell's Gazette*, February 23, the *Salem Impartial Register*, February 23, and the New London *Bee*, February 25.

89. May 2. "The Office of the Commercial Advertiser will be removed this afternoon to No. 131 Pearl-street." The same information was given in the *Spectator* of May 2 and later, which further mentions that the former address was 40 Pine Street, and that Pearl Street was formerly Hanover Square.

90. September 26 and 29, October 1, 3, 6, 8, 10, 13, 15, 19, 21, 23, 26, 28, and 30, and November 2, 4, and 6 (September 30, October 3, 7, 10, 14, 17, 21, 24, 28, and 31, and November 4 and 7). Series of eighteen numbered, unsigned essays, analyzing the first six months of Jefferson's administration. Authorship demonstrated by Webster's use in his *Miscellaneous Papers*, 1802. Hamilton B. Tompkins' *Bibliotheca Jeffersoniana* (New York, 1887) implies (p. 153) a pamphlet edition, but the compiler has located none. Reprinted in the *Salem Gazette*, October 7 to December 1, the *Boston Gazette*, October 15 to December 17, and the *Connecticut Courant*, October 26 to January 18; and in part in the *Oracle of the Day*, November 21 to January 2, and the New Haven *Messenger*, January 5 to February 9, 1802. The first six installments were replied to in the *Amer-*

ican Citizen, October 3, 5, 8, 9, and 10, 1801, reprinted in the *Republican Watch-Tower*, October 7, 10, and 14; Webster's views were upheld in the *Columbian Centinel*, November 11, 1801. Professor Warfel calls this "the angriest, most incisive, most explosive analysis of the new administration yet made."

91. October 5 (7). Unsigned "Remarks on the Population of the United States," discussing population figures, migration, etc. Paraphed by Webster in the Yale file of the *Spectator*. Reprinted in the *Middlesex Gazette*, October 12.

92. November 10 and 11 (11 and 14). Unsigned "Letter, from an American gentleman to a character of distinction in London [Rufus King] on the Commercial interests of the United States and Great-Britain written in 1797." Authorship acknowledged by Webster's use in his *Miscellaneous Papers*, 1802. Reprinted in the *Salem Gazette*, December 15 and 18.

93. November 13 and later (14 and later). Unsigned "Card," announcing the addition of an associate editor, who is not named, and restating the papers' policies. The anonymous assistant was Samuel Bayard. Comments by other papers suggested that Webster needed help to meet the competition of the new *New York Evening Post* and that the latter had begun on a mild note in order to wean subscribers from the *Commercial Advertiser*. The new paper, which began publication on November 16, 1801, was edited by William Coleman, a partisan of Alexander Hamilton. Webster felt that the creation of a new Federalist paper was a slap at him because he had taken Adams' part against Hamilton. He expressed this belief to Oliver Wolcott, detailing his reasons for not having used more political material in recent months, his attempts to "collect the scattered remains of the party," and his lack of subsistence from any other source than the papers. He suggested that Coleman might either become the editor of the papers or else buy them from him, saying that if the new venture injured his investment in the papers, he would attack its backers and "exhaust the remaining powers of body and mind, to defeat the views of the party."[7] Wolcott returned a soft answer, saying that there was no personal hostility involved, and hoping that Webster and Coleman would come to a satisfactory agreement.[8] By the time Webster replied, however, he had been to New York, and was sure that the purpose of the new paper was to injure him; he said that if it constituted injury to his property he would seek redress, and claimed, "No man in America has labored so

[7] Wolcott Papers, Connecticut Historical Society; Ford's *Notes*, Vol. I, pp. 481–482.

[8] Wolcott Papers, Connecticut Historical Society.

incessantly to oppose anarchy as I have done from the peace of 1783 to this hour. I can show more columns written for this purpose than any twenty men in the United States."[9]

94. November 24 and 27 (25 and 28). Two unsigned essays, "The Rights of Neutral Nations." Authorship acknowledged by use in Webster's *Miscellaneous Papers*, 1802, and his *Collection of Papers*, 1843. The first installment was reprinted in the *Boston Gazette*, December 10.

1802

95. May 28 (29). Unsigned editorial, "Liberty and Equality," on their true nature. Paraphed by Webster in the Yale file. Reprinted in the *South-Carolina State-Gazette*, June 16. (This is not the same as No. XXXVII of the *Prompter*, which has the same title.)

An unsigned editorial note in the Spectator *of December 18 and later apologizes for the poor quality of the paper stock used, and promises a better grade in January.*

1803

96. September 12, 13, 14, 16, 19, 20, 21, 22, 23, and 24 (14, 17, 21, 24, and 28). Series of ten signed articles, "To the Citizens of the United States," on the yellow fever, discussing additional evidence and changing opinions since the publication of Webster's work on the subject in 1799. Reprinted in part in the *Hampshire Gazette*, September 28, October 12, 19, and 26, and in the *Medical Repository*, November–January 1803/4 (2nd Hexade, Vol. I, pp. 316–324). The latter apparently intended to publish more, as its extract ends with "To be continued." Coleman replied with a counter-series in the *New York Evening Post*, September 17, 22, and 26 and October 6 and 7.

97. September 27 (28). Signed letter "To the Editor of the Evening Post," discussing certain errors in Coleman's first reply.

98. October 13 (15). Signed letter "To the Editor of the Evening Post," a counter-reply to Coleman. Each accused the other of misrepresentation.

99. October 14 (15). Two affidavits signed by Webster, New Haven, October 1 and 3, 1803, with a third signed by another person, regarding the handling of the effects of a victim of yellow fever there.

[9] Ibid. Ford's *Notes*, Vol. I, pp. 522–523.

100. November 2 (5). "The Partnership of E. Belden, & Co. was dissolved by mutual consent, on the 31st of October," signed by Webster and Belden.

Upon this dissolution Webster sold the papers to the Reverend Zachariah Lewis, and with the issue of November 4 (5), Lewis appears as proprietor and Joseph Mills as printer. In January, 1804, the titles were altered to New-York Commercial Advertiser *and* New-York Spectator. *Webster's contributions to these papers after they left his control are listed in Part Three of this section.*

PART TWO: WEBSTER'S CONTRIBUTIONS TO PROCEEDINGS OF LEARNED SOCIETIES

794

"On the Theory of Vegetation." Article XXVI, *Memoirs* of the American Academy of Arts and Sciences, Vol. II (1793), Pt. I, pp. 178–185.

Signed and dated Hartford, June 12, 1790.

795

"Bill of Mortality, with Remarks on the history of the town of Hartford. . . ." *Collections* of the Massachusetts Historical Society, [Ser. 1,] Vol. III (1794), pp. 4–6.

Signed and dated Hartford, May, 1793. This paper appears to be the "Topographical Description of Hartford" that Webster is recorded as having communicated to a meeting of the Society in Boston on July 30, 1793 (p. 51 of Vol. I of the Society's *Proceedings* [1879]). It cannot have been delivered in person, however, for Webster was in Hartford on that date.

On pp. 92–[93] of the same volume appear "Remarks on Mr. Webster's Calculations," by John Mellen, Jr., and on p. 94, "Mr. Webster's Reply to Mr. Mellen's Remarks," dated January 22, 1794.

796

"Mr. Noah Webster on Raising Potatoes; in a Letter to Secretary [Samuel Latham] Mitchill." *Transactions* of the Society for the Promotion of Agriculture, Arts, and Manufactures (Albany), Vol. I, Pt. III (1798), pp. 90–91.

Dated New York, April 28, 1797. Dr. Mitchill returned the compliment with "A Letter...on the Operation of Manure. To Noah Webster Jun, Esq...," in the *Universal Magazine*, January, 1798 (Vol. II, pp. 204–205).

797

"On the Effects of Evergreens on Climate...." *Transactions* of the Society for the Promotion of Agriculture, Arts, and Manufactures (Albany), Vol. I, Pt. IV (1799), pp. [51]–52.

Signed and dated New York, March 16, 1795.

798

"Experiments respecting Dew.... By Noah Webster, Esq. F.A.A." Article XIV, *Memoirs* of the American Academy of Arts and Sciences, Vol. III (1809), pp. 95–103.

799

"A Dissertation on the supposed Change in the Temperature of Winter: Read before the...Academy...[June 10,] 1799. By N. Webster, Jun. Esq." Article I, *Memoirs* of the Connecticut Academy of Arts and Sciences, Vol. I (1810), pp. [1]–68.

Reviewed in *The General Repository*, October, 1813 (Vol. IV, pp. 313–356).

800

"Number of Deaths, In the Episcopal Church in New-York, in each month for ten years...1786, to...1795.... Communicated by N. Webster, Esq." Article V, *Memoirs* of the Connecticut Academy of Arts and Sciences, Vol. I (1810), pp. [97]–98.

801

"On the Decomposition of White Lead Paint." Article XIII, *Memoirs* of the Connecticut Academy of Arts and Sciences, Vol. I (1810), pp. [135]–136.

In the form of a letter to the secretary, signed and dated New Haven, October 30, 1804.

802

"Origin of Mythology. By Noah Webster, Jun. Esq." Article XVII, *Memoirs* of the Connecticut Academy of Arts and Sciences, Vol. I (1810), pp. [175]–216.

The volume containing Nos. 799–802 was reviewed in the *Panoplist*, October, 1810 (Vol. VI, pp. 217–220), with specific mention of three of Webster's contributions. The four papers were commented on in the *Medical Repository*, February–April, 1810 (3rd Hexade, Vol. I, pp. 369–375).

PART THREE: WEBSTER'S CONTRIBUTIONS TO OTHER PERIODICALS

803

For convenience of reference, Webster's known or attributed contributions to periodicals not edited by him are lumped under this number.

Also included are a few items about Webster but not by him. Articles and advertising matter about his works are entered under the work above, and those about his lectures in Appendix B.

1771

1. Letter beginning, "Mr. Printers, After I have stated my case...," from "a lad, of about fourteen years of age," complaining that the musical activities of a group of young people in his church are not appreciated. *Connecticut Courant*, August 21. The compiler thinks it likely that this was written by Webster; the subject matter and style resemble his later writings. At this date he would not quite have reached his thirteenth birthday, but perhaps he stretched the truth a bit.

1778

The Connecticut Journal, *July 29, records the senior class examination at Yale, held on July 23, and on September 16 the commencement, held on September 9; Webster is listed in both articles. For his "Cliosophical Oration" on the former occasion, see below, No. 74.*

1779

2. Advertisement, signed N. Webster, dated February 20, for a pair of shoes lost on the road between New Haven and Wallingford. *Connecticut Journal*, March 10. It seems likely that this was the son rather than the father.

1780

3. Unsigned note to the printers requesting them to insert "a short extract," which consisted of a quotation from Ascham's *Schoolmaster* about poorly trained and paid schoolmasters. *Connecticut Journal*, August 10. This passage was quoted by Webster in his article "Education" in the *American Magazine*, March, 1788 (p. 213), and in his *Collection of Essays*, 1790, so it is quite possible he was the person who submitted it here.

4. Unsigned parody on Benedict Arnold's letter "To the Inhabitants of America." *Connecticut Courant*, October 31. Attributed to Webster in E. Wilder Spaulding, "The *Connecticut Courant*, a Representative Newspaper in the Eighteenth Century," *New England Quarterly*, July, 1930 (Vol. III, p. 458). The compiler does not agree with this ascription, though Webster was interested in the subject, for in his own file of the paper (New York Public Library) he wrote "Arnold" above the article.

1781

5. Advertisement, signed and dated Sharon (Connecticut), June 1, announcing Webster's proposed school there. *Connecticut Courant*, June 5 and later. Reprinted in Warfel's biography, pp. 40–41.

Webster's name appears in the list of M.A. degrees granted by Yale on September 12, in the Connecticut Courant, *September 25. His "Dissertation in English upon the Universal diffusion of Literature, as introductory to the universal diffusion of Christianity" is mentioned. See No. 75 below.*

6. Signed essay, on a subject not recorded. "The Clio, a Literary Miscellany," October. This was a manuscript magazine edited by Juliana Smith of Sharon. See Helen E. Smith, *Colonial Days and Ways* (New York, 1900), pp. 283–285, and p. 42 of Warfel's biography, where a frank comment on Webster by the young lady is quoted.

1782

7. Series of three numbered, unsigned essays, "Observations on the Revolution of America." *New York Packet*, January 17 and 31 and February 7. The Yale file contains Webster's note, "Written in Sharon, 1782. These expressions & many of the remarks must find an apology in the spirit of the times. They are the effervescence of youth and patriotism." Reprinted as part of a revised series (No. 13 below). No. I was reprinted in the *Salem Gazette*, January 31.

8. Signed advertisement, dated Sharon, April 16, announcing the opening of another school and calling particular attention to the education of women and to faults in the teaching of English grammar. *New York Packet*, April 16 and later. Reprinted in the *Historical Magazine*, August, 1858 (Vol. II, pp. 243–244), in *Etude*, January, 1939 (Vol. 56, pp. 15–16), in Ford's *Notes*, Vol. I, p. 42, and in Warfel's biography, pp. 49–50.

9. Letter headed "Of Orthography without Sense and Sense without Orthography," signed "A Detester of all Envious Productions." *Pennsylvania Packet*, November 9. This supports the view of "Lexiphanes," who had written an article "in one of last Tuesdays papers," which the compiler has not been able to locate. Both criticize Dr. Johnson; the compiler feels that one or the other was written by Webster—perhaps even both, to stir up interest. He was in Philadelphia in November.

1783

10. Series of eight articles dealing with the commutation question,[1] all except the first signed "Honorius." The first two are entitled "An Address to the discontented people of America" and the third "An address to the Officers of the Connecticut Line." *Connecticut Courant*, August 26, September 2, 9, 16, and 30, October 14 and 21, and January 27, 1784. Webster's authorship is evidenced in the New York Public Library file, in which are found his signatures, notes, and markings for a reprinting, probably made about 1789. There is a note dated 1832 saying that the republication was never effected. In these notes the series is retitled "An Address to the People of Connecticut." Reprinted in part in the *Connecticut Gazette*, September 5 and 12, and the *Salem Gazette*, September 18. Anonymous replies appeared in the *Freeman's Chronicle*, September 22 and November 3, the *Connecticut Gazette*, September 26 and October 31, and the *Connecticut Courant*, October 7. In view of Webster's life-long habit of writing for the press, the opening lines of the first installment are ironic: "I am not fond of scribling [sic] in public papers. It is a business by which little good is to be done and less reputation to be acquired. . . ."

11. Letter signed "Correspondent," to a committee in Killingworth, refuting its report on the commutation situation. *Connecticut Courant*, September 16. Autographed by Webster in the New York Public Library file. Replied to by "Respondent" in the issue of October 7 and by "Exit" in that of October 14. See No. 16 below for Webster's counter-reply.

[1] In March, 1783, Congress voted to commute the half-pay promised Revolutionary army officers to five years' pay in a lump sum. The measure evoked considerable discussion and difference of opinion.

12. Letter to the editor signed "Decency," also on the commutation question and the actions of Connecticut town meetings in regard to it. *Connecticut Courant*, September 16. Autographed by Webster in the New York Public Library file.

13. Series of six unsigned essays, "Observations on the Revolution of America." *Freeman's Chronicle*, September 22 and 29, October 6, 20, and 27, and November 3 and 10. These consist of three articles of the same title published earlier (No. 7 above) and three additional numbers, one of them in two installments. Autographed and annotated by Webster in the New York Public Library file.

14. Essay on the teaching of English grammar, initialled, supplementing an advertisement for Part One of the *Grammatical Institute. Connecticut Courant*, October 14. Reprinted in the *Freeman's Chronicle*, October 20.

15. Unsigned article beginning, "A Correspondent...," on the commutation question. *Connecticut Courant*, October 28. Autographed by Webster in the New York Public Library file.

16. Unsigned letter "To Mr. Respondent, Probus, Agricola, &c," on the commutation question. *Connecticut Courant*, November 25. Autographed by Webster in the New York Public Library file.

17. Unsigned satiric verses on the Middletown Convention, bearing on the commutation controversy. *Connecticut Courant*, December 30. Paraphed by Webster in the New York Public Library file, and also acknowledged on a flyleaf, where he refers to this as "N Webster's doggerel verse on the Middletown Convention." Quoted in part in Louie May Miner, *Our Rude Forefathers: American Political Verse, 1738–1788* (Cedar Rapids, Iowa, 1937), pp. 92-93. It was replied to, also in verse, in the issue of January 13, 1784.

18. Signed advertisement proposing to open an evening school to teach pronunciation. *Connecticut Courant*, December 30 and later. Reprinted in Ford's *Notes*, Vol. I, pp. 64–65.

1784

19. Article beginning, "The printers are informed...," signed "The Printers of the Connecticut Courant," concerning an attempt to alienate customers; also discussing commutation. *Connecticut Courant*, January 6. Paraphed by Webster in the New York Public Library file.

20. Article signed "A.Z.," attacking the Middletown Convention. *Connecticut Courant*, January 13. Paraphed, annotated, and corrected by Webster in the New York Public Library file, and given the title "An address to the Inhabitants of Connecticut." Replied to by "A Convention-Man" in the issue of February 3. See No. 22 below.

21. Signed notice of the time and place of the meeting of Webster's "Rhetorical School" (No. 18 above). *Connecticut Courant*, January 13.

22. Letter to the editor signed "A.Z.," in reply to "A Convention-Man" (No. 20 above). *Connecticut Courant*, February 10. Paraphed by Webster in the New York Public Library file.

23. Series of six unsigned articles, "Policy of Connecticut," setting forth Connecticut's true political and commercial interests. *Connecticut Courant*, February 24, March 2, 9, and 16, and May 18 and 25. Autographed, corrected, and annotated for a proposed reprinting in the New York Public Library file. Reprinted in full in the *Connecticut Gazette*, March 26 to June 4, and in part in the *Independent Gazette*, March 11.

24. Unsigned satirical article beginning, "Last Thursday was handed about...," on the Middletown Convention. *Connecticut Courant*, March 16. Autographed by Webster in the New York Public Library file.

25. Unsigned address "To the Members of the Convention...," replying to an address which had been circulated by the Convention as a handbill. *Connecticut Courant*, April 6. Autographed, annotated, and corrected for a projected reprint in the New York Public Library file.

26. Unsigned article beginning, "A Correspondent observes...," opposing faction and defending the Society of the Cincinnati in the commutation controversy. *Connecticut Courant*, May 4. Autographed by Webster in the New York Public Library file.

27. Unsigned article, "Majority for the Impost," approving a nation-wide impost. *Connecticut Courant*, May 25. Webster's markings on the following entry seem to indicate authorship of this item as well.

28. Unsigned note beginning, "Last Friday his Excellency...," on the retirement of Governor Trumbull. *Connecticut Courant*, May 25. Paraphed and autographed by Webster in the New York Public Library file.

29. Signed letter to the editor in reply to an attack on Webster's speller by "Dilworth's Ghost." *Freeman's Chronicle*, July 8. See Part Four below, rubric A.

30. Article addressed "To an Agrieved [sic] Freeman," signed "A Contented Freeman," criticizing a recent change in the method of appointment of Superior Court judges. *Connecticut Courant*, August 31. Autographed by Webster in the New York Public Library file.

1785

31. Series of seven unsigned articles, "The claims of Connecticut to Lands west of the Delaware, deduced from authentic records and fairly stated." *American Mercury*, January 3, 10, 17, 24, and 31, and February 7

and 21. The first installment in the *Connecticut Courant* reprint is endorsed in the New York Public Library file by Webster, "Written at the request of William Judd & others interested in Wyoming." His authorship is further shown in his diary, November 30, 1784: "...preparing to write a brief account of the settlement of that country, and the treatment of the Settlers by Pennsylvania." Reprinted in the *Connecticut Courant*, January 4–February 15, and the *Independent Chronicle*, January 13–March 17. An announcement of the series, probably by Webster, appeared in the *Connecticut Courant* of December 14, 1784, and the *American Mercury* of December 20.

32. Signed letter "To the Public," analyzing various spelling books. *American Mercury*, February 21. Reprinted in the *New Haven Gazette*, March 3, the *Salem Gazette*, March 15, and Warfel, *Letters of Noah Webster*, pp. 32–36. The *Salem Gazette* reprint drew forth a series of articles by "Philomathes" in the issues of July 5, 12, and 19, discussing various spellers in terms hostile to Webster.

33. Unsigned letter to the editor, condemning some resolutions passed by the freemen of Waterbury on the subject of a recent act of the Assembly relating to appointment of judges. *Connecticut Courant*, April 26. Autographed by Webster in the New York Public Library file.

34. Signed letter "To the Inhabitants of Baltimore," discussing the educational system there, and announcing Webster's plan of opening a school. *Maryland Journal*, May 27. Reprinted in Warfel's biography, p. 124.

35. Unsigned "Elegy on the Death of the Reverend Mr. [Allen] Mather...." *Connecticut Courant*, July 11. Paraphed by Webster in the Yale file.

36. Signed advertisement of the opening of a school of vocal music. *Maryland Journal*, July 19.

37. Letter to the editor, signed "Z.," on paper money. *Maryland Journal*, August 9. Authorship demonstrated by Webster's use in his *Collection of Essays*, 1790.

38. Unsigned letter dated Richmond, November 26, praising Webster's lectures. *Newport Mercury*, December 19. The compiler conjectures that Webster wrote this himself; see Appendix B.

1786

39. Unsigned "Extract of a Letter from a Gentleman in Virginia, to his Friend in this Town" (Baltimore), praising Webster's *Grammatical Institute* and his lectures. *Maryland Journal*, January 3. The compiler suspects that Webster wrote the letter. A similar extract "from a Gentle-

man in Annapolis" appeared in the *Maryland Gazette*, January 10; for further details see Appendix B.

40. Unsigned letter "To the Public," pointing out the uselessness and bigotry of test laws, oaths of allegiance, etc. *Philadelphia Evening Herald*, March 11. Authorship indicated by use in Webster's *Collection of Essays*, 1790. Reprinted in the *American Museum*, February, 1789 (Vol. V, pp. 157–158).

41. Signed letter to the editor, refuting criticisms on one of Webster's lectures, published in the paper on April 11. New York *Daily Advertiser*, April 13. Reprinted in Warfel, *Letters of Noah Webster*, pp. 47–49.

42. Letter "To the Printer of the Daily Advertiser," signed "Poplicola," discussing certain recent New York laws. New York *Daily Advertiser*, April 18. Paraphed by Webster in the Yale file.

43. Unsigned "Political Paragraphs," discussing the proceedings of the spring session of the state legislature. *Connecticut Courant*, June 12. Autographed by Webster in the Yale file. Reprinted in the *New Haven Gazette*, June 22, and the *Connecticut Gazette*, June 23.

44. Unsigned article commending Webster's efforts in language, though not mentioning him by name. *New Haven Gazette*, June 22. Not acknowledged by Webster, but perhaps his, since it employs part of the wording of the preface to the first edition of his reader. Reprinted in the *Independent Gazetteer*, July 1, and the *Massachusetts Gazette*, July 3.

45. "Redress of Grievances," signed "An Industrious Man," discussing the Massachusetts legislature and courts, lawyers, and the spending, for liquor, of money which should be devoted to paying taxes. *Essex Journal*, September 13. Authorship demonstrated by use in Webster's *Collection of Essays*, 1790. Reprinted in the *Massachusetts Centinel*, September 20, the *United States Chronicle*, September 21, the *New Brunswick Gazette*, October 5, the *American Museum*, February, 1787 (Vol. I, pp. 111–112), and in "A Summary View of the Politics of the United States, from 1783..." in [William Cobbett], *Porcupine's Works*, Vol. I, pp. 56–58.

46. Article beginning, "That the political body...," signed "Tom Thoughtful," discussing the weakness of the federal government, luxury and extravagance, paper money, extra-legal conventions, etc. *United States Chronicle*, September 28. Autographed by Webster in the Yale file of the *Connecticut Courant*, with the note, "Written at Providence while I was reading Lectures...." Reprinted in his *Collection of Essays*, 1790, with the title "The Devil is in you." Reprinted in the *Exchange Advertiser*, October 5, the *Independent Gazette*, October 20, the *Connecticut Gazette*, October 20, the *Connecticut Courant*, November 6, the *In-*

dependent Chronicle, November 9, the *Worcester Magazine*, second week of November (Vol. II, pp. 382–384), the *American Museum*, February, 1787 (Vol. I, pp. 116–119), the *Pennsylvania Gazette*, May 16, 1787 (where it is attributed to Webster), the *Hampshire Chronicle*, February 6, 1788, and in the "Summary View of the Politics of the United States, from 1783..." cited in the preceding entry (pp. 58–64).

47. Poem signed "William Wimble," bearing on a question of sale of public land by the state legislature. *Connecticut Courant*, October 9. Attributed to Webster by Louie May Miner in *Our Rude Forefathers* (Cedar Rapids, Iowa, 1937), p. 162, on the basis of a mark by Webster in the Yale file of the paper. The situation of which the poem was a part is described by Miner.

48. Unsigned article beginning, "A Correspondent observes...," on current problems in Connecticut. *Connecticut Gazette*, October 20. Authorship demonstrated by use in Webster's *Collection of Essays*, 1790 (as "Desultory Thoughts"). Reprinted in the *Massachusetts Centinel*, November 4, and the *Salem Mercury*, December 23.

49. Unsigned article beginning, "At the close of the late war...," on the public debt and party spirit. *Connecticut Courant*, November 20. Autographed by Webster in the Yale file, and annotated, "Written during the Insurrection in Massachusetts." Reprinted in the *Middlesex Gazette*, November 27, the *New Haven Gazette*, November 30, and the *Norwich Packet*, November 30.

50. Unsigned article, "A Bit of Advice to Connecticut Folks," on lawyers, extravagance, etc. *New Haven Gazette*, December 14. Authorship demonstrated by use in Webster's *Collection of Essays*, 1790. Reprinted in the *Massachusetts Centinel*, December 27, the *Independent Gazette*, January 11, 1787, the *Pennsylvania Packet*, January 15, the *Connecticut Gazette*, February 23, the *New Jersey Journal*, March 21, the *American Museum*, March, 1789 (Vol. V, pp. 261–263), the *Middlesex Gazette*, November 14, 1789, the *Gazette of the United States*, September 27, 1794, the *Farmer's Museum*, October 10, 1794, the Baltimore *Federal Gazette*, November 18, 1797, the *Connecticut Herald*, March 21, 1826, the *Hartford Courant*, September 20, 1871, and the *New York Times*, October 13, 1918. Some of the reprints alter "Connecticut" in the title to an appropriate designation for their place of publication.

1787

51. Note in the third person declining to reply to "Juvenis," who had attacked Webster's lecture announcements. *Independent Gazetteer*, February 8.

52. Series of four unsigned articles, "Remarks on Manners, Government, Law and the Domestic Debt of America, Addressed to the Citizens of the United States." *Pennsylvania Packet*, February 15, 17, 19, and 21. Authorship demonstrated by use in Webster's *American Selection*, 1787, and his *Collection of Essays*, 1790. Reprinted in the *Pennsylvania Herald*, February 21, 24, and 28, and the *American Museum*, March and April, 1789 (Vol. V, pp. 269–272, 349–353). These articles are drawn from Webster's lectures.

53. Signed letter to the editor, dated March 1, listing the copyright regulations of eleven states. *Pennsylvania Packet*, March 7. Reprinted in Warfel, *Letters of Noah Webster*, pp. 57–59. A virtually identical letter, signed but undated, and not quite so detailed, appeared in the *Pennsylvania Evening Herald*, March 10.

54. Unsigned "Thoughts on the Domestic Debts of the United States and the present state of affairs in Massachusetts, Addressed to the Governor of that Commonwealth. By a Citizen of Philadelphia." *Pennsylvania Gazette*, March 21. Part Four below, rubric B.

55. Unsigned announcement in the third person that Webster "has accepted of the place of Master of [the English] language in the [Protestant Episcopal] Academy" in Philadelphia. *Independent Gazette*, April 14. This drew a satiric note from "Seth" in the *Freeman's Journal*, precipitating another word-war, for which see Part Four below, rubric B.

56. Article "To the Public," signed "Orpheus," on the beneficial effect of music on morals. *Pennsylvania Packet*, April 24. Authorship demonstrated by use, with changes, in the *American Magazine*, June, 1788 (pp. 448–450), and in Webster's *Collection of Essays*, 1790.

In the Independent Gazetteer *for June 11 appeared a letter over Webster's signature, but it is satirical and was not written by him. See Part Four below, rubric B.*

57. "Anecdotes of Pocahunta." *Columbian Magazine*, July (Vol. I, pp. 548–551). Attributed to Webster by Lyon N. Richardson in his *History of Early American Magazines, 1741–1789* (New York, 1931), p. 285, n. 52. The compiler doubts this, especially since the story is taken bodily from the first English edition of Chastellux' *Travels in North America* (London, 1787).

58. "Address to all Federalists," signed "Curtius," dated New York, September 27, 1787. *American Museum*, October (Vol. II, pp. 381–384). Attributed to Webster by Richardson as cited in the preceding entry, p. 318, n. 232. Although the views expressed agree with Webster's, certain

personal references do not apply, and he was not in New York at the time; the compiler does not accept the attribution.

1788

59. Series of three articles, "To the Minority of the Convention of Pennsylvania," signed "A Freeman," discussing the proposed Constitution. *Pennsylvania Gazette*, January 23 and 30 and February 6. Authorship is indicated in Webster's diary (December 28, 1787) and by use of the series in his *Collection of Essays*, 1790. Reprinted in the *Pennsylvania Packet*, January 25 and 31 and February 7.

60. Unsigned article, "To the Publick," discussing America's historical records and proposing to publish an edition of Governor Winthrop's journal. *Impartial Gazetteer*, June 14. The project did not mature in the form proposed, though Webster later published the journal; see Title 781.

61. Signed legal notice of the granting to William Young of Philadelphia of certain vending rights in the *Grammatical Institute*. *New York Packet*, June 27 and later. This action was challenged, and a signed statement reaffirming the grant was published in the issue of July 18.

62. Article headed "Federal Procession," signed by Richard Platt, but written at least in part by Webster. New York *Daily Advertiser*, August 2. See Appendix A, No. 1.

63. Letter to the editor, signed "The Reviewer," replying to an article in the issue of August 27 attacking the review of Timothy Dwight's *Triumph of Infidelity* which had appeared in Webster's *American Magazine* for July (Part One above, rubric A, No. 40). New York *Daily Advertiser*, September 5. Although not acknowledged by Webster, this letter is characteristic of him, and the compiler believes that he wrote the original review.

64. Signed letter replying to an attack on one of his articles in the *American Magazine*. *Columbian Magazine*, November. See Part One above, rubric A, No. 5.

1789

65. Letter signed "W.," disapproving a New York proposal for a convention to consider amendments to the Constitution. *Connecticut Courant*, March 23. Marked by Webster in the Yale file.

66. Unsigned proposals for publishing an edition of Governor Winthrop's journal, similar to those published June 14, 1788. *Massachusetts Spy*, May 14 and later.

Notice of Webster's marriage to Rebecca Greenleaf appeared in the Middlesex Gazette, *October 31, 1789.*

1790

67. "The Tablet," Nos. LXXVIII, LXXIX, and LXXX, three unsigned essays on the defects of the American educational system. *Gazette of the United States*, January 9, 13, and 16. In the Yale file Webster has initialled the third and annotated the first, "Written the winter of 1779–1780. When I lived at Westdivision" (i.e., West Hartford).

68. "The Tablet. No. LXXXII," unsigned essay on the neglect of the education of women. *Gazette of the United States*, January 23. An editorial note suggests that the article was written by a woman. In the Yale file Webster has written, "This conjecture of the Editor is erroneous. I wrote the Essay when a Sophomore or Junior in College. It is quite Juvenile."

69. "The Tablet, No. LXXXV," unsigned essay on religious terminology and concepts of good and evil. *Gazette of the United States*, February 3. Endorsed by Webster in the Yale file, "Written at New York in 1788."

70. Letter setting forth a "Plan for discharging the domestic debt of America . . . ," signed "A Private Citizen." *Connecticut Courant*, February 25. A signature or note appears to have been cut from the Yale file at this point, so Webster may have acknowledged the article; it is similar in its ideas to his letter on the subject published March 21, 1787 (No. 54 above).

71. Initialled "Remarks on the Influenza." *American Mercury*, April 26. Reprinted in the *New York Packet*, May 18.

72. A series of "Remarks on the English Language," consisting of an introduction and fourteen numbered articles. *American Mercury*, May 10, 17, 24, and 31, June 7, 14, 21, and 28, July 5, 12, 19, and 26, August 9, 23, and 30, and September 6. The introduction—which quotes a letter from Benjamin Franklin, December 26, 1789, on Webster's *Dissertations on the English Language*, 1789—is signed in full and six of the installments are initialled. Reprinted in full or in part in the *Massachusetts Magazine*, June, 1790, to October, 1791 (divided differently); the *Massachusetts Spy*, July 23–November 18; the *Pennsylvania Packet*, August 2; the *Gazette of the United States*, August 21–December 1; the *Salem Gazette*, September 21; and the *Maryland Gazette*, October 22. The series was attacked by "Jocosus" in the *American Mercury*, June 7 and 14, and by "Z." in the same paper for June 28; it was defended by "Aristides" in the *Gazette of the United States*, September 22, 1790, and February 16, 1791.

73. "The Tablet. No. CXIII," unsigned essay on defects in education, with particular reference to law students. *Gazette of the United States*, May 12. Not acknowledged by Webster but felt by the compiler to be by him, since the ideas are his and the writer identifies himself as having been admitted to the bar in April, 1781, as interested in "philology, Belles

Lettres, and ancient history," and as having traveled two years in America —all of which fits Webster. Reprinted in the *Boston Gazette*, July 16, 1801.

74. "A Short View of the Origin and Progress of the Science of Natural Philosophy.... Delivered at the public Examination...Yale College, 23d, July, 1778, by Noah Webster, jun." *New York Magazine or Literary Repository*, June and July (Vol. I, pp. 338–340, 383–384).

75. "The Tablet," Nos. CXIX–CXXIII, five unsigned essays on "Whether the universal diffusion of literature will precede and prepare the way for the universal prevalence of religion?" *Gazette of the United States*, June 2, 5, 9, 12, and 16. Not acknowledged by Webster, but this seems almost certainly to be his M.A. thesis, "Dissertation...upon the Universal diffusion of Literature, as introductory to the universal diffusion of Christianity." This was a period in which he was contributing his college writings to the papers.

76. "On the means of Preserving the Union of the American States," initialled. *Gazette of the United States*, June 23. Reprinted in the *Vermont Gazette*, July 12.

77. "The Tablet. No. CXXXVI," unsigned essay on exercise and the ill effects of too much study, consisting of excerpts from No. XXIX of Webster's *Essays*, 1790 ("An Address to Yung Gentlemen"). *Gazette of the United States*, July 31. This printing does not employ the simplified spelling of the *Essays*. An anonymous reply, objecting to fencing as an exercise, appeared in the same paper, August 7, and was reprinted in the *Vermont Gazette*, August 23.

78. Unsigned article in the third person announcing that Webster had given Yale, from the proceeds of the *Grammatical Institute*, about twenty-five dollars annually as a prize for "the best treatise on ethics, moral philosophy, or belles letters." *American Mercury*, August 16. The article concludes, "One clause in the conditions of this premium is worthy of imitation: No person being allowed of as a competitor...who shall have been guilty of seduction, or shall be known to have ever given or accepted a challenge to fight a duel." Webster may have written the article himself.

Notice of Webster's admission as attorney and counsellor before the United States Circuit Court for Connecticut appeared in the Farmer's Journal, *November 16.*

79. Series of twenty unsigned essays, "The Prompter," later acknowledged by Webster. *Connecticut Courant*, December 6 and 13, January 3,

10, 17, 24, and 31, 1791, February 14, 21, and 28, March 7, 14, 21, and 28, April 4 and 11, May 9, 16, and 30, and June 13. Nineteen of these were reprinted in book form, 1791 (Title 652); the one not used was No. III, which ridiculed Jefferson's report on the metric system. One or more of the essays were reprinted scores if not hundreds of times in contemporary and later newspapers, and they were widely commented upon in the press and imitated. Additions to the series appeared in newspapers (Nos. 92 and 101 below). (Some of the added essays first published in book form in 1803 were reprinted in various newspapers during May, June, July, and August of that year.)

1791

80. Series of three unsigned articles, "On the Utility of Banks." *Connecticut Courant*, March 14, 21, and 28. Autographed by Webster in the Yale file.

81. Unsigned "Extract of a letter from a gentleman...dated March 27, 1791," ridiculing the idea of a federal city on the "Patowmac" and of a single tax on land. *Connecticut Courant*, April 11. Autographed by Webster in the Yale file.

82. Unsigned note beginning, "A Correspondent observes...," on the origin of juries and the etymology of "peer." *Connecticut Courant*, April 18. In the Yale file this bears a mark often used by Webster to indicate his own writings.

83. Series of five numbered, unsigned articles, "The Patriot," on agriculture, manufactures, labor supply, foreign trade, etc. *American Mercury*, April 18 and 25, May 2, 9, and 16. Not acknowledged by Webster, but recorded in his diary, March 9: "Writing, the Patriot, No. I." Reprinted in part in the *Gazette of the United States*, April 30–May 25, the *American Museum*, May (Vol. IX, pp. 250–251), the *Freeman's Journal*, May 11, the *Massachusetts Spy*, May 26, and the *Political Repository*, June 9, and in full in Warfel, *Letters of Noah Webster*, pp. 90–102. Cf. No. 89 below.

Webster advertised his services as a lawyer and notary public in Hartford in the New York Daily Advertiser, *August 12 and later.*

84. Note in the third person by "The Connecticut Prompter," promising separate publication of the Prompter essays. *Connecticut Courant*, August 29. Reprinted in the *Columbian Centinel*, September 7.

85. Signed letter to the editor, replying to a review of Webster's *Collection of Essays*, 1790, which had appeared in the issues of October

and November, 1790. *Universal Asylum and Columbian Magazine*, September and October (Vol. VII, pp. 191–192, 259–264).

86. Unsigned essays on the "Penal Laws," opposing capital punishment. *Connecticut Courant*, September 5 and 26. Autographed by Webster in the Yale file.

87. Letter to the editor, signed "P.Q.," a humorous criticism of dirty and crowded churches. New York *Daily Advertiser*, September 23. Autographed by Webster in the Yale file of the *Connecticut Courant*. Reprinted in that paper, October 3, the *Connecticut Journal*, October 5, and the *Massachusetts Spy*, October 20.

Webster advertised his services as a lawyer and notary public in the Connecticut Gazette, *October 6 and later, and the* Connecticut Courant, *October 17 and later.*

88. Unsigned article, "To the Citizens of Hartford," advocating a fund for relief of those suffering from sudden misfortunes. *Connecticut Courant*, December 12. Autographed by Webster in the Yale file. Reprinted in the *Connecticut Journal*, December 14.

1792

89. Series of seven numbered, unsigned articles, "The Patriot," on trade, banks, navigation, a Cape Cod canal, roads, etc. *Connecticut Courant*, January 2, 9, 16, 23, and 30, and February 6, 20, and 27. Autographed by Webster in the Yale file, and recorded in his diary, February 7: "Finish the Patriot, No. 7."

90. Signed recommendation for Gordon Johnson's *Introduction to Arithmetic* (Springfield, 1792), dated November 25, 1791. *Hampshire Chronicle*, February 15. Reprinted in the *Connecticut Courant*, March 19, and again January 7, 1793, and later, with the addition of another person's recommendation.

91. Letter to the editor, signed "Peter Puzzle," opposing the use of the eagle on United States coins. *Connecticut Courant*, April 30. Paraphed by Webster in the Yale file.

92. "Rags! Rags!" unsigned, another "Prompter" essay (see above, No. 79). *Connecticut Courant*, June 4. Widely reprinted, and used in the book form of the essays.

93. Two letters to the editor, signed "Viator," discussing the canker worms which attack apple trees and suggesting measures against them. *Connecticut Courant*, July 9 and August 6. Autographed by Webster in the Yale file.

94. "A Word to Parents and Masters," unsigned. *Connecticut Courant*, September 10. Attributed to Webster by Vera M. Butler in her *Education as Revealed by New England Newspapers prior to 1850* ([Philadelphia], 1935); the compiler doubts this ascription.

95. Letter to the editor beginning,"I was lately in company...," signed "A.B.," deriding the fear of the rise of an aristocracy in the United States. *Connecticut Courant*, September 17. Paraphed by Webster in the Yale file, which suggests that perhaps other contributions of the same period signed "A.B." were Webster's.

96. Signed letter "To the Public," dated Hartford, September 15, denouncing and denying the claim made in Samuel Campbell's fourteenth edition of Webster's spelling book (Title 28) that it contained the latest revisions. *Connecticut Courant*, September 17 and later. Reprinted in the *Connecticut Journal*, September 19, the New York *Daily Advertiser*, September 22, and the *Providence Gazette*, October 20. The publisher of this edition, Samuel Campbell of New York, replied in the *American Mercury*, November 5.

97. Unsigned letter "To the Inhabitants of Hartford," advocating a charity fund in the absence of compensation for workmen injured while at work. *American Mercury* and *Connecticut Courant*, October 1. Autographed by Webster in the Yale file. Reprinted in Warfel, *Letters of Noah Webster*, pp. 105–108.

98. Signed letter to the editor, in reply to Samuel Campbell's reply to No. 96. *Connecticut Courant*, November 12. In turn, Campbell replied to this in the *American Mercury*, December 31.

99. Notice signed by Webster as representative of the Charitable Society. See Appendix A, No. 2. *Connecticut Courant*, November 19.

100. Signed letter to the editor, another round in the battle with Samuel Campbell. *American Mercury*, December 31.

1793

101. "Stolen waters are sweet," unsigned, another "Prompter" essay (see above, No. 79). *Connecticut Courant*, July 8. Widely reprinted, and used in the book form of these essays.

102. Unsigned article beginning, "The melancholy state of Cape Francois...," on the French West Indian trade and its importance to the United States. *Connecticut Courant*, July 29. Autographed by Webster in the Yale file.

103. Two articles on the French Revolution and probable future events in France, signed "Candor." *Connecticut Courant*, July 29 and August 5. Autographed by Webster in the Yale file, with a note indicating

a later change in views. Reprinted in the *New Jersey State Gazette*, August 14 and 21, and the first article only in the *Washington Spy*, August 30, the *New Hampshire Gazette*, September 10, the *Hampshire Gazette*, September 12, the *Farmer's Journal*, October 11, the *Massachusetts Spy*, December 12, and the *Minerva*, January 4, 1794.

104. "True Republicanism," signed "A Million of true Republicans," setting forth the Federalist views on government and foreign affairs. *Connecticut Courant*, August 12. Autographed by Webster in the Yale file. Reprinted in *Dunlap's American Daily Advertiser*, August 17, the *Baltimore Daily Repertory*, August 22, the *Massachussetts Spy*, August 22, the *Connecticut Gazette*, August 22, the *Hampshire Gazette*, August 28, the *Farmer's Museum*, September 6, and the *New Jersey Gazette*, September 18.

105. Address from the citizens of Hartford to the President, at least partly written by Webster. *Connecticut Courant*, August 19. See Appendix A, No. 3.

106. "All persons indebted to the subscriber, are requested to make payment within twelve days; otherwise their notes and accounts will be put in suit. For sale, an elegant chaise, with harness compleat. Noah Webster, Jun. Hartford, September 2, 1793." *Connecticut Courant*, September 2.

1794

107. Letter to the editor, signed "Editor" (i.e., of the *Minerva*), regarding his having refused space to an article because of its scurrilous language. *New York Journal*, August 13.

1795

108. Letter to the editor in the third person from the editor of the *Minerva*, replying to insinuations about him made in the *Argus* of the preceding day, to the effect that he had used scornful language about the people. *Argus*, August 5.

109. Signed letter to the editor, dated November 10, complaining of his having withheld Webster's circular letter to physicians until he had an abusive reply to print with it. *Argus*, November 11. Reprinted in Warfel, *Letters of Noah Webster*, p. 133.

1796

110. Signed letters to Alexander J. Dallas, December 24 and [26], 1796. Nos. IV and VI of a series of letters on asserted irregularities in the Bank of Pennsylvania. *Argus* and *Diary*, December 31. In the *Diary*

the series is preceded by an editorial note stating that "republication of the correspondence between Mr. Dallas and Mr. Webster will be but an act of justice to the former...." Reprinted in the *Aurora*, January 3, 1797.

1797

111. Signed letter to the editor, protesting that the order in which the Dallas-Webster letters were printed (see preceding entry) gives a false impression. *Argus*, January 2.

112. Two articles signed "An American," condemning the prevalence of personal abuse and slander in American political discussion, particularly censuring William Cobbett ("Peter Porcupine"). *Massachusetts Mercury*, August 18 and 22. Apart from style and subject, the attribution is based on a letter from Webster to Jedidiah Morse, July 24, 1797, in which he says, "I have thrown together some thoughts on slander, aimed at our... printers. It will not do for *me* to publish them, because I have a paper and have sometimes been guilty of personalities, tho' not often," and suggests that they might be used in one of the Boston papers.[2]

113. Signed letter from Webster to Timothy Pickering, Secretary of State, dated New York, July 11, 1797, in the course of a series of documents annexed to a report of the Committee of Impeachment of Senator William Blount. *Philadelphia Gazette*, December 17. Reprinted in the *Merchant's Daily Advertiser*, December 21, and on pp. cxlvi–cxlvii of the *Report of the Committee of the House of Representatives...Appointed to Prepare...Articles of Impeachment against William Blount* ([Philadelphia, 1797]). The *Commercial Advertiser*, Webster's paper, published the committee report and some of the documents, but did not include this one.

1798

114. Signed letter dated New Haven, July 9, 1798, to a subscriber to the *Commercial Advertiser* who had cancelled his subscription. *Porcupine's Gazette*, July 28 (*Country Porcupine*, July 28–30). Reprinted in *Porcupine's Works*, Vol. IX (1801), p. 48, and in Warfel, *Letters of Noah Webster*, pp. 181–182. Without Webster's permission the addressee—a Mr. Waddington—sent his letter and Webster's reply to Cobbett for publication, about which Webster remarked in a letter to Timothy Pickering, "This is uncivil and perfidious. The public are welcome to the letter, but he is no gentleman that takes such liberties with private correspondence."[3]

[2]Yale University Library.

[3]July 17, 1798, Pickering Papers, Massachusetts Historical Society; Ford's *Notes*, Vol. I, pp. 464–465.

115. Signed letter to the editor, dated New Haven, August 6, refuting and dismissing charges against him published by Russell and Cobbett. *Russell's Gazette*, August 16. Reprinted in *Porcupine's Gazette*, September 1.

116. Signed letter "To the Public," requesting statistics on epidemics for his work on epidemic and pestilential diseases. *Connecticut Journal*, August 29 and later. The issue of September 19 contains a note of thanks to those who responded. See Title 748.

117. Signed letter "To Mr. Josiah Meigs," dated New Haven, October 30, asserting that Meigs had given a false account of an incident involving him and Webster which took place in New Haven on July 4, and denying any connection with an article on the subject in the *New York Daily Gazette* of July 19. *Connecticut Journal*, November 1. Reprinted in the Litchfield *Monitor*, November 7. Meigs' account had appeared in the *Connecticut Courant*, October 15, and the *Connecticut Journal*, October 24.

1799

118. Signed letter to the editor, objecting to the paper's consistent opposition to the government. New London *Bee*, June 12.

119. Letter signed "Philo-Barruel," urging newspapers to reprint the *Connecticut Courant's* abridgment of *Memoirs Illustrating the History of Jacobinism*, by Augustin de Barruel. *Connecticut Courant*, July 22. The compiler believes that Webster wrote this, though there is no documentary evidence. She also thinks it likely that he wrote the introductory remarks to the abridgment, in the issue of June 17.

120. Unsigned letter to the editor, beginning, "Some time since you published...," attacking Joel Barlow's enthusiasm for France. *Connecticut Courant*, August 19. Not acknowledged, but the compiler believes Webster wrote this. Reprinted in the *Commercial Advertiser*, August 21 (*Spectator*, August 24), the *Federal Gazette*, August 27, and the *South-Carolina State Gazette*, September 9.

121. Anonymous article announcing the incorporation of the Connecticut Academy of Arts and Sciences. *Connecticut Courant*, November 4. Probably written by Webster, who was Corresponding Secretary of the organization. Reprinted in the *Commercial Advertiser*, November 6 (*Spectator*, November 9); the *Argus*, New York *Daily Advertiser*, and *New York Gazette*, November 7; the *Middlesex Gazette*, November 8; and the New London *Bee*, November 13.

1800

122. Signed recommendation, dated December 12, 1799, as part of advertising for Nathan Daboll's *Schoolmaster's Assistant*. *Connecticut*

Courant, January 4 (supplement) and later. This was also used in the *Connecticut Gazette*, January 8 and later; the *Connecticut Journal*, March 11, 1802, and later; the Hudson, N.Y., *Bee*, August 24, 1802, and later; the New York *Morning Chronicle*, November 1, 1802, and later; and the *Middlesex Gazette*, January 10, 1803, and later.

123. Signed letter to the editor, discussing whether yellow fever is transmitted by ships from abroad and asking people to give him data. *Connecticut Journal*, January 30. Reprinted in the *Commercial Advertiser*, February 4 (*Spectator*, February 5).

124. Unsigned article in the third person, beginning, "Mr. Webster of this city, we understand, is...," outlining his plan for an American dictionary. *Connecticut Journal*, June 4. If not written by Webster, this was certainly written from material supplied by him. Reprinted in the *Philadelphia Gazette*, June 7, the *Commercial Advertiser*, June 9 (*Spectator*, June 11), the *Mercantile Advertiser*, June 10, the *Impartial Register*, June 12 and 19, and the *Salem Gazette*, June 13. An article in the *Farmer's Museum*, June 23, discussing the *Grammatical Institute* as part of a system of education and announcing the dictionary, is probably by Webster also.

125. "Important Political Investigation," signed "Marcus Aurelius," attacking Alexander Hamilton (as "Titus Manlius") for having gone over President Adams' head in advocating a standing army. *Boston Gazette*, October 13. Paraphed, annotated, and corrected by Webster on a clipping in The New York Public Library. Reprinted in the *Commercial Advertiser*, October 28. Replied to by "Civis" in the *Columbian Centinel*, October 18 and 25, and by "A Citizen" in the *Boston Gazette*, October 20; these two were in turn replied to by "Curto" in the latter paper, October 23 and 27. Webster's views on the subject were ridiculed in essays III and IV of "The Latitudinarian," *Columbian Centinel*, November 19 and 26, the latter reprinted in the *Aurora*, December 31.

1801

126. "On the Connection of Earthquakes with Epidemic Diseases, and on the Succession of Epidemics..., a letter from Noah Webster, jun. Esq. to Dr. Miller, dated New-Haven, Feb. 21, 1801." *Medical Repository*, February–April ([1st Hexade], Vol. IV, pp. 340–344).

127. "A Collection of Phenomena, relative to the Connection between Earthquakes, Tempests, and Epidemic Distempers; and a Vindication of the Doctrine of Equivocal Generation. By Noah Webster, jun. Esq. in a letter to Dr. Mitchill, dated New-Haven, March 2, 1801." *Medical Repository*, May–July ([1st Hexade], Vol. V, pp. 25–31). Reprinted in part

in the *Salem Gazette*, October 27, 1801, as "Equivocal Generation vindicated," and in Warfel, *Letters of Noah Webster*, pp. 229–230.

128. Remonstrance of New Haven merchants, probably written by Webster. *Connecticut Courant*, July 27. See Appendix A, No. 4.

129. Signed letter to the editor, dated New Haven, December 20, 1801, commenting on some remarks on the substance of the sun in an earlier number, referring to his opinions as given in the appendix to his *History of Epidemic and Pestilential Diseases*, 1799. *Medical Repository*, November–January, 1801/1802 ([1st Hexade], Vol. V, p. 371).

130. Signed letter to the editor, dated New Haven, November 10, 1801, replying to attacks on his plans for a dictionary, made in a series of articles by "Aristarchus" (John S. J. Gardiner). *Mercury and New-England Palladium*, November 20. Reprinted in Warfel, *Letters of Noah Webster*, pp. 245–247.

131. "Literary Intelligence. Noah Webster, jun. is at present engaged in compiling a System of Principles for the Education of Youth, on a plan new and more extensive than has yet appeared." *Mirror of the Times*, December 5. Perhaps contributed by Webster.

1802

132. Unsigned article, "Rights of Neutrals," summarizing and quoting from the essay on that subject in Webster's *Miscellaneous Papers*, 1802. New York *Daily Advertiser*, May 19. Although this is in the third person, the compiler believes that Webster wrote it himself. Reprinted in the *Commercial Advertiser*, May 19 (*Spectator*, May 22).

133. Signed letter to the editor protesting against some misrepresentations of his views in a review of his *Miscellaneous Papers* which had appeared in the preceding issue (pp. 193–204). *American Review and Literary Journal*, July–September (Vol. II, pp. 379–380).

1803

134. Signed letter to the editor, criticizing a circular letter announcing "A Republican festival," published in this paper and elsewhere. *Connecticut Journal*, March 3. Reprinted in the *Middlesex Gazette*, March 7, the *Commercial Advertiser*, March 8 (*Spectator*, March 9), and the New Haven *Visitor*, March 22. The circular precipitated much comment in the press, involving the character of Abraham Bishop, and attacks or defenses of Bishop and his father continued for some time.

135. "Remarks on the Connection between Catarrh and Malignant Fevers. . . , a letter from Noah Webster, Esq. to Dr. Miller, dated New-

Haven, Sept. 28, 1803." *Medical Repository*, August–October ([2nd Hexade], Vol. I, pp. 131–143).

136. "Additional Observations on the Nature of Fever, and on the Importance of Remedies applied to the Skin. In a Letter from Noah Webster, Esq. to Dr. Miller, dated New-Haven, Oct. 3, 1803." *Medical Repository*, November–January, 1803/1804 ([2nd Hexade], Vol. I, pp. 255–258).

137. "To the Citizens of the United States, the following remarks are addressed by their well-wisher, N. Webster." Ibid., pp. [316]–324. Running head, "On the Origin of Bilious Plague." At the end there is a "To be Continued" note, but nothing more appears to have been published.

1804

138. "For Sale, the Dwelling House of the subscriber, with its appurtenances. For terms enquire of N. Webster. New Haven, March 6." *Connecticut Post and New Haven Visitor*, March 8 and later.

139. "Critical Remarks on some Parts of [Erasmus] Darwin's Theory of Fever: In a letter from Noah Webster, Esq. dated New-Haven, Jan. 30, 1804." *Medical Repository*, May–July (2nd Hexade, Vol. II, pp. 25–35).

140. Unsigned "Literary Notices," announcing a new edition of Webster's speller and Volume II of his *Elements of Useful Knowledge*, and discussing his dictionary plans. *Connecticut Courant*, June 6. Very likely written by Webster. Reprinted in the *Commercial Advertiser*, June 8 (*Spectator*, June 9), the rural edition of the *Gazette of the United States*, June 12, and the *Connecticut Post and New Haven Visitor*, June 14.

141. Letter to the editor, signed "A Lover of Good Cider," on how to make good apple cider. *Connecticut Journal*, October 4. The compiler believes that Webster wrote this.

142. Signed letter congratulating the paper on its new "Farmer's Repository" section, and commenting on insects injurious to crops. *Connecticut Courant*, October 24. Reprinted in the *Pennsylvania Gazette*, November 14, the *Mirror of the Times*, March 20, 1805, and the *Petersburg Intelligencer*, April 2, 1805. See the next entry.

143. Signed "Letter II," about fruit trees and potatoes. *Connecticut Courant*, October 31. Reprinted in the *New England Palladium*, November 6, the *Pennsylvania Gazette*, November 14, the *Mirror of the Times*, December 1 (without naming the writer), and again on March 23, 1805 (with Webster's name), the *Universal Gazette*, April 18, 1805, the New Brunswick *Guardian*, April 18, 1805, the *New Haven Palladium*, Febru-

ary 4, 1837, and the *Worcester Palladium*, August 28, 1838. It was also reprinted in the *Massachusetts Agricultural Repository*, 1804 (pp. 43–47 of one of the volumes of papers issued that year).

144. Series of two signed articles, "Thoughts on Education, Addressed to Heads of Families in Connecticut...," discussing literacy, physical conditions in the school room, standards for teachers, curriculum and texts (with recommended titles, including some of his own), the importance of family life and home influence, etc. *Connecticut Herald*, December 24 and 31. In a postscript Webster says that he has not time enough to write a work on how to teach, but that he may prepare a dictionary of synonyms. The second article was repeated in the issue of January 1, 1805.

1805

145. Letter to the editor, signed "Inspector," on agriculture, particularly fertilizers. *Connecticut Herald*, February 12. Paraphed by Webster on a clipping in The New York Public Library.

146. Signed letter to the editor, on the relative severity of winters. *Connecticut Herald*, February 26. Reprinted in the Hudson, N.Y., *Bee*, March 12, the rural edition of the *Gazette of the United States*, May 20, the *Hampshire Gazette*, May 22, the *Mirror of the Times*, May 25, and the Charleston, S.C., *Times*, July 2.

147. "To the Citizens of New-Haven," signed "A Citizen," warning against undue alarm over yellow fever in the city. *Connecticut Herald*, August 13. Paraphed by Webster on a clipping in The New York Public Library. Reprinted in part in the *New England Palladium*, August 20 (attributing it to Webster), and the *Columbian Centinel*, August 24.

148. Signed letter, dated September 10, to Dr. David Hosack, on the yellow fever, with Hosack's reply, September 13, and Webster's reply to this, September 17. *Commercial Advertiser*, September 21 (*Spectator*, September 25). Reprinted in the Charleston, S.C., *Times*, October 15 and 17, and (Webster's initial letter only) in the *New York Times*, September 15, 1878. Hosack's letter of September 13 is reprinted in his *Essays on Various Subjects of Medical Science* (3 vols., New York, 1824–1830), Vol. III, pp. 427–437.

A series of fourteen numbered articles "On Early Education," signed "A.C.," appeared in the Connecticut Herald, *December 24, 1805, to March 25, 1806. These cover more or less the same ground as Webster's two articles of December 24 and 31, 1804, though in much greater detail. While the compiler does not attribute these to Webster, she does believe that he had a hand in the preparation of the series, perhaps in providing some of the material.*

1806

149. Unsigned review of Volume I of Abiel Holmes' *American Annals*. *Panoplist*, January (Vol. I, pp. 361–364). Webster's authorship is shown by a letter from Holmes, February 8, 1806,[4] and in later references by Webster. Two years later Jedidiah Morse, editor of the *Panoplist*, asked Webster to review Volume II,[5] but apparently no such review ever appeared.

150. Essay "American Literature," signed "Americus," maintaining that American inferiority to England lies not in abilities, but in background. *Connecticut Herald*, January 21. Autographed by Webster in the New York Public Library file.

151. Memorial by New Haven Chamber of Commerce, possibly written by Webster. *Connecticut Herald*, February 11. See Appendix A, No. 7.

152. Two letters to the editor, the second dated July 30. *New York Evening Post*, July 29 and August 5. There are no signatures, but Webster's name is given in the headings. These reply to a series of articles by William Coleman which had appeared in the paper on July 15, 16, 18, 19, 22, and 23, severely critical of Webster's first dictionary. Reprinted in the *New York Herald*, July 30 and August 6.

153. Signed letter to the editor, accompanied by a signed letter "To the Public," dated August 5, replying to criticisms of his dictionary by "C," which had appeared in the *Albany Centinel*, July 22. *Connecticut Herald*, August 12. Reprinted in the *Commercial Advertiser*, August 19 (*Spectator*, August 20), and in part (with editorial comment) in the *Albany Centinel*, September 9. Further comment appeared in the *Columbian Centinel*, September 13, reprinted in the *Connecticut Herald*, September 23, and the *Commercial Advertiser*, October 4 (*Spectator*, October 8).

1807

154. Article about the newly formed Charitable Society, signed "Franklin." *Connecticut Herald*, February 17. Paraphed by Webster on a clipping in The New York Public Library. He had also written the invitation to the organizational meeting, published a month earlier. See Appendix A, No. 9.

155. "On the affinity between the languages of Europe and Asia," signed "W." *Panoplist*, March (Vol. II, pp. 469–471). That this was Webster is shown by a letter from Webster to Jedidiah Morse, January

[4]Webster Papers, New York Public Library.
[5]Morse to Webster, May 31, 1808, ibid.

24, 1807, enclosing "a communication,"[6] and by an announcement in the February issue (p. 440).

156. Letter signed "Candidus," parrying Lindley Murray's attack on Webster's speller. *Commercial Advertiser*, March 23 (*Spectator*, March 25). Attributed to Webster by the compiler. This stirred up a flurry of comment, and some of the writers assumed Webster to be "Candidus."

157. Unsigned essay evaluating Webster's grammar, following an advertisement for the work. *Connecticut Herald*, June 9 and later. This may well have been written by Webster.

158. Signed article, dated New Haven, June 10, 1807, in reply to unfavorable reviews of his *Compendious Dictionary*, particularly that in the London *Eclectic Review*, January, 1807 (Vol. III, pp. 82–86). *Panoplist*, July and August (Vol. III, pp. 78–84, 123–128).

159. Series of five unsigned articles, headed "Literary," analyzing Dr. Johnson's and other dictionaries. *Connecticut Herald*, September 1, 22, and 29 and October 6 and 13. Webster's authorship is shown by the incorporation of this text, with changes, into his *Letter to Dr. Ramsay*, 1807.

160. Unsigned article, "The following proposition...," urging adoption of a proposal before the legislature for the better construction of bridges. *Connecticut Journal*, December 3. Autographed by Webster on a clipping in The New York Public Library.

1808

161. Signed letter to "Messrs. Steele & Co." (publishers of the *Connecticut Herald*), asking them to print a letter from James Hillhouse on the embargo. *Commercial Advertiser*, April 4 (*Spectator*, April 6). Although this item is headed "From the Connecticut Herald," it actually appeared here first, not being published in the paper to which it was addressed until April 5. Reprinted in the *Connecticut Courant*, April 6, the *Connecticut Journal*, April 7, the *Middlesex Gazette*, April 7, *Poulson's Daily Advertiser*, April 7, the Boston *Repertory*, April 8, and the *Albany Gazette*, April 11.

162. Article signed "Sidney," on the low state of the country after seven years of Democratic administration. *Connecticut Journal*, April 7. Attributed to Webster by the compiler; the opinions are certainly his, and in other instances he used "Sidney" as a pseudonym.

163. "To all American Patriots," signed "Public Spirit," complaining of the divided nature of the country and the weak defense of its shipping,

[6] Webster Papers, New York Public Library.

calling for increased nationalism and suggesting the formation of a patriotic association. *Connecticut Herald*, May 17. Webster's authorship is shown by the presence of the MS in the Webster Papers and by his correspondence (see Ford's *Notes*, Vol. II, pp. 36–38).

164. Memorial by the citizens of New Haven, written at least in part by Webster. *Connecticut Journal*, September 1. See Appendix A, No. 10.

1809

165. Resolutions by the residents of New Haven against the embargo. *Connecticut Herald*, January 31. Signed by Elisha Munson as town clerk, but written by Webster. See Appendix A, No. 11.

166. "The Peculiar Doctrines of the Gospel, Explained and Defended," signed. *Panoplist*, July (Vol. V [n.s., Vol. II], pp. 58–74). There is an editorial note identifying the text as a letter by Webster, but not naming the addressee. This appeared as a separate publication (Title 706), which see for further details.

167. Signed letter to Judge Dawes of Boston, dated New Haven, July 25, discussing language in general and the progress of Webster's lexicographical work. *Columbian Centinel*, August 2. Reprinted in Ford's *Notes*, Vol. II, pp. 65–71, and in Warfel, *Letters of Noah Webster*, pp. 318–324. Judge Dawes (a brother-in-law of Mrs. Webster) had first taken the letter to the Boston *Repertory*, but the editors of that paper refused to print it unless they could restore the "-our" and "-ick" spellings (Ford's *Notes*, Vol. I, p. 71).

168. Two signed letters to Judge Dawes, both dated New Haven, August 5, on Webster's and others' dictionaries and grammars. *Monthly Anthology*, September (Vol. VII, pp. 205–211). Reprinted in the Raleigh, N.C., *Star*, July 19, 1810 (with slight omissions) and in Warfel, *Letters of Noah Webster*, pp. 324–332. These letters served as a point of departure for a severe attack on Webster's works by "Steady Habits" (Benjamin D. Perkins, a New York bookseller), consisting of a letter in the December issue of the *Monthly Anthology* and a series of three articles in the issues of February, March, and April, 1810.

169. Signed letter to the editor, New Haven, October 24, objecting to the editorial remarks which had been attached to the preceding entry. *Monthly Anthology*, November (Vol. VII, p. 353).

1810

170. Signed "To the Friends of American Literature.... Prospectus of a new and complete dictionary of the English Language," discussing Webster's lexicographical work, his views, and the comments on his

work, and asking for financial support; followed by a recommendation signed by President Dwight of Yale and four professors. *Panoplist*, February (Vol. V [n.s., Vol. II], pp. 428–430). Reprinted in the *Monthly Anthology*, March (Vol. VIII, pp. [207]–212). This prospectus has not been located as a separate imprint, though there may well have been one.

171. Letter to the editor, signed "W.," on the derivation of "Yankee." *Connecticut Herald*, March 13. Not acknowledged, but almost certainly Webster's. Contemporary commentators on the article referred to it as his. Reprinted in the *Monthly Anthology*, April (Vol. VIII, pp. 244–245) and the *Boston Mirror*, May 19.

172. Signed advertisement offering for sale Webster's house on Water Street, New Haven, and a single share each in the Union School and New Township Academy. *Connecticut Herald*, June 12 and later.

173. Unsigned article, "Insurance." *Connecticut Herald*, October 30. Autographed by Webster on a clipping in The New York Public Library.

174. Recommendation for two gentlemen who proposed to open a school for boys in the New Township Academy, of which Webster was one of three signers. *Connecticut Herald*, November 13 and later, and April 9, 1811, and later.

1811

175. Resolutions of the citizens of New Haven, written by Webster. *Connecticut Herald*, May 7 and 28. See Appendix A, No. 12.

1812

176. Letter to the editor, initialled, about an earthquake which Webster had felt on Long Island on January 23. *Connecticut Herald*, January 28.

177. Announcement of the new quarter at the New Township Academy, signed by Webster as one of the three trustees. *Connecticut Herald*, May 5.

1813

178. Letter to the editor headed "The Question Stated," signed "Peace & Justice," blaming the War of 1812 on United States policy. *Hampshire Gazette*, March 24. Paraphed by Webster on a copy in The New York Public Library.

179. Signed "Strictures on an Article in the Christian Observer...," refuting statements about Hebrew names. *Panoblist*, September (Vol. IX, pp. 213–222).

1814

180. "To the Disciples of Washington," signed "A Disciple of Washington," urging financial aid to war-ravished Europe. *Hampshire Gazette,* July 13. Autographed by Webster on a clipping in The New York Public Library.

1816

181. Letter headed "Spurred Rye," signed "Probus," on the asserted dangerous nature of ergot, in response to articles on the subject in the *Boston Patriot* of March 9 and 16. *Hampshire Gazette,* April 3. Paraphed by Webster on a clipping in The New York Public Library. Further discussion appeared in the *Hampshire Gazette,* March 27, April 17, and May 1.

1817

182. Signed article, "Domestic Economy," on farming, conservation of forests and fuel, construction of houses, crop failures, etc. *Hampshire Gazette,* March 26. Reprinted in the *Connecticut Courant,* April 22, and the *Middlesex Gazette,* May 1. On a clipping in The New York Public Library Webster wrote, "The cold summer of 1816 discouraged farmers from planting maize. To counteract this effect N. Webster wrote on Economy."

183. Series of three signed letters on Webster's agricultural experiences, written at the request of the editors. *Hampshire Gazette,* November 19 and 26 and December 3.

1818

184. Signed letter beginning, "I observe in the Recorder...," discussing the advertisement of a new translation of the New Testament, by John Bellamy, and reporting on the progress of his own labors. *Hampshire Gazette,* May 13. Reprinted in part in the *Virginia Patriot,* June 9.

185. Letter about Amherst College, Webster being one of three signers. *Hampshire Gazette,* November 10. See Appendix A, No. 15.

1819

186. Letter beginning, "I was much pleased...," signed "B.," discussing two recent works, Samuel Worcester's *Christian Psalmody* and Timothy Dwight's *Theology Explained and Defended. Hampshire Gazette,* March 9. Autographed by Webster on a copy in The New York Public Library.

187. Massachusetts legislature's "Answer to the Address of the Governor," written by Webster. *Columbian Centinel*, June 5. See Appendix A, No. 16.

1821

188. "The Public are informed...," announcement signed by Webster as President of the Board of Trustees of Amherst Academy, listing the officers and rules for admission of the new college. *Hampshire Gazette*, June 20. Reprinted in the *Connecticut Courant*, July 3.

189. Letter headed "Amherst Academy," signed by Webster as President of the Board of Trustees, dated July 12, giving information on admission to the academy and the college. *Boston Recorder*, July 21. Reprinted in Frederick Tuckerman, *Amherst Academy* (Amherst, 1929), pp. 239–240. Webster may also have written the unsigned, unofficial description of the new college in the same paper, September 1.

190. "Amherst Collegiate Institution," unsigned article reporting the progress of the new school. *Boston Recorder*, October 6. Autographed by Webster on a clipping in the Webster Papers.

191. "Female Education," signed "Academicus," praising Emma Willard and certain steps toward education for women. *Connecticut Courant*, October 9. Not acknowledged by Webster, but attributed to him in Vera M. Butler, *Education as Revealed by New England Newspapers prior to 1850* ([Philadelphia], 1935); the compiler is inclined to accept this ascription.

192. Letter to the editor, signed "Senex," defending the new college and the suggested removal of Williams College to Amherst. *Hampshire Gazette*, December 19. A reply to "Academus," who, in the same paper, November 21, asserted that Amherst College was founded for the purpose of destroying Williams College. "Senex" may very well have been Webster. He was replied to by "Fair Play" in the issue of January 2, 1822.

1822

193. "Amherst Academy and College," signed "Observator," about the progress of the institutions. *Boston Recorder*, February 16. Autographed by Webster on a clipping in the Webster Papers. He may also have had some connection with the account, by "A Spectator," of the first commencement, published in the *Hampshire Gazette*, September 4.

1823

194. Signed recommendation, dated New Haven, June 28, for "D. Ritter's Patent Metallic Paste and Strap, for Razors...." *Middlesex Gazette*, July 24 and later.

The Yale commencement on September 10, at which Webster received the degree of LL.D., is recorded in the Religious Intelligencer, *September 13, and the* Connecticut Journal, *the* Connecticut Courant, *and the* Connecticut Herald, *September 16.*

195. Minutes of a meeting, resolutions, and an address on the subject of Greek independence, probably written by Webster. *Connecticut Journal*, December 23 and 30, and elsewhere. See Appendix A, No. 20.

1824

196. "On the origin and history of parties," signed "Aristides." *Connecticut Journal*, February 17. Autographed by Webster on a clipping in The New York Public Library.

1826

197. Letter signed "P.,"about the efforts of certain New York schoolmasters to discontinue the use of Webster's speller, the proposed revision of the speller to conform to the dictionaries, and the progress of the unabridged dictionary. *Connecticut Journal*, March 7. The compiler feels that this was probably written by Webster.

198. Signed letter "To the Public," dated New Haven, March, discussing Webster's series of elementary books, describing the success of the speller and its financial support of his work on his dictionary, and telling of his trip to England and other matters relating to the dictionary. *Connecticut Herald* and *Connecticut Journal*, March 14. An abstract appeared in the *Detroit Gazette*, April 18.

199. Signed letter to the editor discussing orthography and philology, and disclaiming pursuit of philological discussion through the newspapers. *Connecticut Journal*, April 4.

200. "To Gentlemen of Property in the United States," signed "Stark," pleading for support of Professor Silliman's *Journal of Science*. *Connecticut Journal*, December 5. Paraphed by Webster on a clipping in The New York Public Library.

1827

201. Signed letter to the editor, replying to part of a series of articles by "Examinator" (Lyman Cobb) attacking Webster's works. *Albany Argus*, December 14. See Part Four below, rubric J.

1828

202. Unsigned article beginning, "The printing of the American dictionary . . . ," announcing the completion of the unabridged dictionary. *New Haven Chronicle*, November 29. The compiler thinks it probable that Webster wrote this article, which also promises abridgments of the dictionary and a revision of the speller.

1829

203. Unsigned article, "Webster's Dictionary." *New York Evening Post*, May 28. Very likely written by Webster. Reprinted in the *Commercial Advertiser*, May 29 (*Spectator*, June 2) and the *Connecticut Courant*, June 2. See Part Four below, rubric J.

204. Signed letter to the editor, replying to the criticisms of Webster's dictionary made in a series of articles which had appeared in the New York *Morning Herald. Commercial Advertiser*, August 26 (*Spectator*, August 28). See Part Four below, rubric J.

205. Signed letter to the editor, dated August 31, discussing the English edition of Webster's dictionary and his labors with orthography, and announcing an abridgment of the dictionary by J. E. Worcester. *New Haven Advertiser*, September 4. Reprinted in the *Connecticut Journal*, September 8, and the *Connecticut Courant*, September 15.

During 1829 many unsigned articles on dictionaries and orthography appeared in the newspapers; some of them may have been by Webster.

206. "Good Breeding," unsigned, on quarrels, incivility to inferiors, education of the young in "good morals and good manners," etc. *Connecticut Journal* and *New Haven Advertiser*, December 22. Paraphed by Webster on a clipping in The New York Public Library.

1830

207. Testimonial headed "Lancasterian School," signed by Webster as one of three, in support of Miss Hotchkiss as a teacher. *New Haven Advertiser*, February 2.

208. "Winters becoming Milder," signed "W." *New Haven Advertiser*, March 16. Not acknowledged by Webster, but probably his, because of his known interest in the subject.

209. Letter to the editor, signed "W.,"protesting against the use of "republican" as a party term, severely criticizing Jefferson. *New Haven Palladium*, April 6. Not acknowledged by Webster, but very likely his because of style and content.

Reference to Webster's having received an LL.D. degree at Middlebury College is made in the Connecticut Journal *and* Connecticut Herald *of September 7.*

210. Signed letter "To the Public," dated October 4, 1830, discussing Webster's dictionaries and announcing the authorized edition of his school abridgment of the unabridged dictionary (Title 592). *Connecticut Journal* and *New Haven Advertiser*, October 5. Reprinted in the *New Haven Palladium*, October 18, the *Connecticut Observer*, October 25, the *Religious Intelligencer*, October 30, the *Connecticut Courant*, November 23, the *Connecticut Mirror*, November 27, the *Hampshire Gazette*, December 1, and the *Indiana Democrat*, December 4.

1831

211. Address about fire victims in Fayetteville, N.C., possibly written by Webster. *Connecticut Journal*, etc., June 14. See Appendix A, No. 22.

212. Unsigned article "The Copy Right Law," summarizing Webster's efforts in this direction. *New York Whig*, and *Commercial Advertiser*, June 21 (*Spectator*, June 24). Said by the editor of the *Commercial Advertiser* to be "from the pen of an old and highly valuable friend and correspondent." Partial clippings in The New York Public Library are marked and corrected by Webster, and he used the item in his *Collection of Papers*, 1843. Reprinted in the *Boston Courier*, June 25, and *Niles' Weekly Register*, July 2.

213. Signed letter admitting an erroneous definition in his dictionary. *Connecticut Journal* and *New Haven Advertiser*, August 16. The error had been pointed out by W.E.D. in the latter paper, August 12.

214. "To the Citizens of the United States," signed "Verity," lamenting that voters no longer consider the moral character of candidates for office. *New Haven Advertiser*, August 26. Paraphed by Webster on a clipping in The New York Public Library. Reprinted in the *Connecticut Journal*, August 30.

215. Signed letter, dated New Haven, September 10, on "staves" as an irregular plural. *New York Mirror*, September 17.

216. "To Farmers," signed "W.,"describing a new agricultural implement invented by a Maine farmer. *Connecticut Courant*, September 27. Paraphed by Webster on a clipping in The New York Public Library. The farmer was Dr. Southgate, father of one of Webster's sons-in-law.

217. Signed article, "Philology," discussing Webster's efforts in England to get scholars to confer on debated pronunciations. *New England Magazine*, November (Vol. I, pp. [369]–380). Reviewed in the

Connecticut Journal, November 8. Webster's letter of December 20, 1824, to Dr. Samuel Lee of Cambridge is incorporated in the article.

218. "To the Citizens of the U. States," signed "A Lover of his Country," proposing William Wirt for the presidency. *New Haven Advertiser*, November 25. Paraphed by Webster on a clipping of the reprint in The New York Public Library. Reprinted in the *Connecticut Journal*, November 29.

219. Signed letter to the editor defending his orthography against criticisms that had appeared in the paper on November 28; accompanied by elaborate editorial notes in rebuttal. *New England Weekly Review*, December 5.

1832

220. Letter to the editor, initialled, quoting from Webster's *History of Epidemic and Pestilential Diseases* and discussing cholera. Seen only as a clipping. The compiler believes the article appeared in the Cincinnati *National Republican* in January, 1832.

221. Signed letter to the editor, dated February 9, replying to some criticisms of his dictionary made by "A Farmer" in the issues of December 24 and 31, 1831. *Genesee Farmer*, March 3.

222. Letter signed "Momus," sarcastically treating a fancy dress ball recently held in Washington. *New York Whig*, April 6 (weekly edition, April 11). Paraphed by Webster on a clipping in The New York Public Library.

223. "To Gentlemen of the Medical Profession," signed, telling of confirmation of his views on cholera by a Baltimore physician and saying that he will publish a new edition of his *History of Epidemic and Pestilential Diseases* if the profession will underwrite the cost. *Connecticut Herald*, May 8.

224. A letter from Webster to Lemuel Shattuck, dated New Haven, November 18, 1829, is incorporated in an unsigned article, "History of Elementary School Books," in the *New England Magazine*, June (Vol. II, pp. 474–476). The letter was reprinted in the *Hampshire Gazette*, September 26.

225. Letter, signed "Verus," criticizing the President's views and remarks, especially on foreign capital and copyright. *Commercial Advertiser*, July 18 (*Spectator*, July 23). Paraphed by Webster in the New York Public Library file.

226. Signed article, "To the Friends of Literature," discussing the faults of Lindley Murray's grammar. *New York Evangelist*, December 1. Reprinted in the *Vermont Chronicle*, December 21.

1833

227. Signed recommendation for Aaron Ely's *School Dictionary*, as part of an advertisement. *Commercial Advertiser*, May 15.

228. Signed letter to the editor of the *Daily Troy Press*, dated New Haven, May 22, denying their assertion that Webster's forthcoming edition of the Bible was actuated by sectarian or party spirit. *Boston Courier*, June 8. Apparently first published in the paper addressed, of which the compiler has not found a file of the appropriate period. Reprinted in an unidentified paper, June 11 (clipping in The New York Public Library), the *Commercial Advertiser*, June 17 (*Spectator*, June 20), and the *Connecticut Herald*, June 18. James Fenimore Cooper refers to the *Commercial Advertiser* reprint of this letter in his *Letters to his Countrymen* (New York, 1834), pp. 49–50.

The compiler believes that the letter signed "Prudens" in the Commercial Advertiser *of June 17* (Spectator, *June 20*), *about Webster's proposed edition of the Bible, was based on material provided by Webster but is not by him. She thinks the author may have been his son, William, or one of his sons-in-law, Chauncey A. Goodrich.*

229. Letter to the editor, signed "A Citizen," on the education and treatment of colored people in New Haven, claiming their status to be as good as that of the white laboring class. *Connecticut Herald*, September 10. Paraphed by Webster in the New York Public Library file.

230. Signed letter "To the Citizens of the United States," dated New Haven, October, 1833, on Webster's edition of the Bible. *Religious Intelligencer*, October 5. Reprinted in the *Commercial Advertiser*, October 11, the *Connecticut Courant*, October 14, and the *Boston Recorder*, October 30.

231. Letter to the editor signed "Solon," on the definition of "citizen" as involved in the trial of a Miss Crandall for instructing colored persons "not natives of the state." *Connecticut Journal*, October 22. Paraphed by Webster in the New York Public Library file. (In his charge to the jury, printed in the *Connecticut Herald* of October 15, Chief Justice Daggett cites Webster's dictionary for a definition.)

1834

232. "The Times," signed "A Whig of '76," on the evils of constant change of administration in an elective republic. *Commercial Advertiser*, February 14 (*Spectator*, February 20). Paraphed by Webster in the New York Public Library file.

233. Signed letter to the editors, in reply to criticisms of Webster's dictionaries by "Senex" in the issue of February 1. *New York Mirror*, March 8.

234. Letter to the editor, signed "an Inquirer or an Enquirer," about certain incorrect spellings. *Spectator*, April 3. Paraphed by Webster in the New York Public Library file. Although the letter is addressed to the editor of the *Commercial Advertiser*, it has not been found in that paper.

235. Signed letter to the editor on the derivation of "manna." *Religious Intelligencer*, May 3.

236. Unsigned letter on the tyranny of pretended friends of the people. *Commercial Advertiser*, May 5 (*Spectator*, May 8). Paraphed by Webster in the New York Public Library file.

237. Resolution of condolence on the death of Lafayette, probably written at least in part by Webster. *Connecticut Herald*, August 12. See Appendix A, No. 22.

238. Signed letter to the editor on fanciful etymologies in a forthcoming Hebrew dictionary. *New York Observer*, September 13.

239. Unsigned letter attacking the Democratic party, in the guise of satiric chapter heads for a history of the party. *Commercial Advertiser*, November 24 (*Spectator*, November 27). Paraphed by Webster in the New York Public Library file. Reprinted in the *Connecticut Journal*, December 2.

240. Review of John Orville Taylor, *The District School* (New York, 1834) in the form of a letter from "Mentor." *Commercial Advertiser*, November 25. Paraphed by Webster in the New York Public Library file of the first reprint. Reprinted in the *Free Elector*, February 10, 1835, and the *New England Advocate*, February 11.

In the Worcester Palladium, *November 26, is an unsigned article, "Webster's Dictionary," accusing Joseph E. Worcester's dictionary of substantial borrowings from Webster's. This initiated a controversy in which Webster took part, summarized in Part Four below, rubric K.*

1835

241. Signed letter transmitting an unsigned article, "Winters of uncommon severity," drawn partly from Webster's *History of Epidemic and Pestilential Diseases*, 1799. *Connecticut Journal*, January 13. Reprinted in the *American Journal of Science and Art*, April (Vol. XXVIII, pp. 183–187), and in part in the *Baltimore Gazette and Daily Advertiser*, April 16, *Niles' Weekly Register*, May 16, and the *New Hampshire Patriot*, Febru-

ary 15, 1836. Also reprinted in the *Hartford Daily Courant*, March 1, 1934.

242. Letter headed "What is the matter?" signed "Solon," asserting fallacies in the concept that all men are created equal. *Commercial Advertiser*, January 20 (*Spectator*, January 22). Autographed by Webster in the New York Public Library file.

243. Unsigned article beginning, "It has been stated...," on the Mayflower Compact and the Connecticut constitution. *Commercial Advertiser*, January 20 (*Spectator*, January 22). Autographed by Webster in the New York Public Library file.

244. Letter to the editor, signed "Wilberforce," protesting against illustrated Bibles and too many pictures in school books. *Free Elector*, January 27. Paraphed by Webster in the New York Public Library file

245. Signed letter to the editor of the *New Haven Palladium*, protesting his having compared the Jacksonian party to the old Federalists. New Haven *Daily Herald*, January 28. Reprinted in the *New Haven Palladium*, January 31, and the *Connecticut Herald*, February 3.

246. Signed "Notice," dated February 2, warning against reprinting Webster's old *American Spelling Book*, saying that now only the *Elementary* is authorized. *New Hampshire Patriot*, February 9.

247. Signed letter to the editor of the *New Haven Palladium*, continuing the discussion in No. 245 above. *Connecticut Herald*, February 10. Reprinted in the *Boston Courier*, February 12, and the *New Haven Palladium*, February 14, with the editor's answer.

In Ford's Notes *(Vol. II, pp. 517–518) and Warfel's* Letters of Noah Webster *(pp. 446–448) is printed a letter from Webster to the editor of "the Palladium" (Worcester? New Haven?), dated February 17, but the compiler has been unable to find it in a contemporary newspaper. The MS is found in the Webster Papers; the letter may never have been sent to the editor addressed. It defends his having changed his opinions during the course of his life.*

248. Letter to the editor, signed "Justus," attacking Freemasonry. *Free Elector*, February 24. Paraphed by Webster in the New York Public Library file.

249. Resolutions against abolitionists, signed by Webster among others. New Haven *Daily Herald*, September 11. See Appendix A, No. 23.

250. "To Citizens of All Classes," signed "All-together," asking the public to abandon the use of the term "shilling." *New Haven Palladium*, October 3. Paraphed by Webster in the New York Public Library file.

251. Signed letter to the editor, declaring that abolitionists take harmful advantage of Daniel Webster's views on freedom of discussion. *Religious Intelligencer*, October 17.

252. "Reminiscences for Critics," unsigned, discussing the widespread use of Webster's dictionary and text books. *Commercial Advertiser*, October 19. Attributed to Webster by the compiler.

253. Signed letter to the editor replying to "An Abolitionist." *Religious Intelligencer*, October 31. The gentleman had, in the issue of October 21, countered No. 251 above.

254. Letter to the editor, signed "Sober Sense," suggesting that abolitionists should agitate in the South rather than in the North. New Haven *Daily Herald*, November 2. Paraphed by Webster in the New York Public Library file of the *Connecticut Herald*, in which the article was reprinted, November 3.

255. Letter to the editor, signed "Cato," on mobs and lynch law, blaming the Jackson administration for current difficulties. *Connecticut Herald*, November 10. Paraphed by Webster in the New York Public Library file.

1836

256. Series of three signed articles entitled "Philology," on theories of orthography, pronunciation, definition, grammar, etc. *The Knickerbocker*, February, March, and April (Vol. VII, pp. 163–168, 234–246, 347–357). An extract of the portion regarding corruption in the King James version of the Bible was published in the *New-Yorker*, April 9, and reprinted in the *New Haven Palladium*, April 30. Another extract, consisting of the remarks on grammar and textbooks thereof, was printed in the *St. Louis Commercial Bulletin*, May 9 and 11.

257. Initialled article, "Observations on the severe winters of 1740–41. . . ." New Haven *Daily Herald*, March 9. Reprinted in the *Connecticut Herald*, March 15.

258. Letter to the editor, signed "Spectator," on depreciation of money from too large issues of bank notes. New Haven *Daily Herald*, March 23. Paraphed by Webster in the New York Public Library file of the *Connecticut Herald*, in which it was reprinted, March 29.

259. Signed letter to the editor replying to criticisms of Webster's dictionaries which had been made in a prospectus for a dictionary by Charles Richardson, printed in the March issue of the magazine. *American Historical Magazine*, April (Vol. I, pp. [159]–160).

260. Letter to the editor, signed "Common Sense," opposing trade

unions. *Commercial Advertiser*, April 1 (*Spectator*, April 4). Paraphed by Webster in the New York Public Library file.

261. Letter headed "Christianity the Support of Republican Institutions," signed " '76," lamenting the failure of the principles on which the United States was founded, and maintaining that the Bible is the remedy for political evils. *Connecticut Observer*, April 2. Paraphed by Webster in the New York Public Library file.

262. Unsigned "Brief Review" of a dictionary published in England by James Knowles. *New Haven Palladium and Republican*, May 14. Attributed to Webster by the compiler. Reprinted in the *Boston Courier*, June 1, the *Connecticut Courant*, July 18, and the *Spectator*, September 15.

263. Signed article, "Etymologies and Criticism," on the imperfect knowledge of etymology shown in some recent publications. *Quarterly Christian Spectator*, June (Vol. VIII, pp. 311–319).

In the Commercial Advertiser, *August 26* (Spectator, *August 29*), *appeared an editorial on the London police which moved Webster to write the proprietors. An undated letter from him to Francis Hall and Co., signed "Sidney," is found in the Webster Papers, New York Public Library; the compiler has not discovered it printed in the paper addressed. It is printed in Warfel's* Letters of Noah Webster, *pp. 504–506, with the date August 29, 1837, added. Not only is this date incorrect, but the letter is annotated (p. 534) as if it were the "Sidney" letter which stirred up such a political storm late in 1837 (No. 289 below and Part Four of this section, rubric L).*

264. Signed notice headed "Caution," warning the public against continuing editions of Webster's superseded *American Spelling Book*. *Commercial Advertiser*, September 10. Reprinted in the New Haven *Daily Herald*, September 14, with adverse comment.

265. Unsigned letter to the editor, objecting to their remarks in reprinting No. 264. New Haven *Daily Herald*, September 16. The letter is certainly Webster's, though not acknowledged.

266. Signed letter to the editor, on misrepresentations of character and motive in the press (evoked by some sarcastic remarks on his explanation of cold winters, published in the *Newburyport Herald*, September 9, and reprinted in the New Haven *Daily Herald*, October 1, and the *Connecticut Herald*, October 4). New Haven *Daily Herald*, October 14. An extract was published in the *Daily National Intelligencer*, October 25 (weekly edition, October 26).

267. Signed letter addressed to the editor of the *Commercial Advertiser*, comment on an article about careless speech which had appeared in the

paper on September 7. *New Haven Palladium*, October 22. Reprinted in the *Boston Courier*, November 1 (semi-weekly edition, November 3).

268. Signed letter to David McClure, dated October 25, analyzing, with considerable reservations, the prospectus of Girard College. *National Intelligencer*, November 2. Reprinted in the *Lexington* (*Ky.*) *Observer*, November 23, the *Religious Intelligencer*, December 3, the *New Haven Palladium*, December 3, the *Western Presbyterian Herald*, December 29, the *Christian Advocate and Journal*, January 13, 1837, in Webster's *Collection of Papers*, 1843, and in Warfel, *Letters of Noah Webster*, pp. 452–457.

269. Signed letter to the editor, discussing Webster's edition of the Bible and certain philological points, in response to a review of his Bible in the issue of December 1. *Boston Courier*, December 16. There were replies and further criticism of this Bible during 1837.

270. Signed letter to Mr. Salem Town, dated December 16, 1836, discussing Town's *Analysis of Derivative Words in the English Language* (New York, 1835, 1836, etc.). *New-Yorker*, December 31 (Vol. II, p. 237).

1837

271. Initialled letter to the editor, on King Alfred's attempts to find the Northwest passage. *New Haven Palladium*, January 28.

In the Philadelphia Mirror *of January 30 and the New Haven* Daily Herald *of February 22 are letters initialled "N.W.," but the former is certainly not by Webster and the latter probably not. The first is a description of Marietta, Ohio, possibly by Nahum Ward of that city, and the second is a description of some agricultural experiments in Maryland.*

272. Signed letter to the editor, dated March 1, replying to strictures on Webster's orthography published in the preceding issue. *Common School Advocate*, March (Vol. I, No. 3, p. 19). Reprinted in the *Indiana Democrat*, April 12.

273. "Influence of Names," signed "Monitor," on pretentious names for humble occupations, opposing employment of women in factories, etc. New Haven *Daily Herald*, May 2. Paraphed by Webster in the New York Public Library file of the *Connecticut Herald*, in which it was reprinted May 9.

274. Extract from a letter, unsigned, beginning, "You have read history . . . ," on the tyranny of so-called friends of the people. *Commercial Advertiser*, May 12 (*Spectator*, May 15). Marked by Webster in the New

York Public Library file of the latter in a manner to suggest his authorship. It is certainly in line with his views; cf. No. 236 above.

275. Letter to the editor signed "A Farmer's Son," on high prices of food, neglect of agricultural training, land speculation, etc. *Connecticut Observer*, July 15. Paraphed by Webster in the New York Public Library file.

276. Letter signed "Probus," on suitable material for presidential candidates. *Commercial Advertiser*, July 21 (*Spectator*, July 24). Paraphed by Webster in the New York Public Library file.

277. Letter to the editor signed "W——," on a point of grammar. *Commercial Advertiser*, July 21 (*Spectator*, July 24). Not acknowledged by Webster, though checked by him in the New York Public Library file, and probably his; referred to as his in the Boston *Daily Evening Transcript*, July 31.

278. Letter to the editor signed "W.,"on certain misused words. New Haven *Daily Herald*, July 26. Not acknowledged by Webster, but felt by the compiler to be his without question; one of the words castigated is "comptroller," a particular *bête-noire* of his.

279. Series of "Critical Notices," unsigned, mostly on word usage. *New Havener*, intermittently from July 29, 1837, to June 9, 1838. It is likely that Webster wrote these; he is especially likely to have written an article in the issue of August 5 about the adoption of his orthography by William H. McGuffey and others; this was reprinted in the Cincinnati *Daily Herald and Gazette*, August 16, and in Webster's 1839 circular "To the Friends of Literature" (Title 763).

280. Signed letter on the misuse of certain words. *Spectator*, July 30. Reprinted in part in the Boston *Daily Evening Transcript*, July 31.

281. Signed letter to the editor, dated August 10, about publishing problems in the United States, outlining Webster's experiences with various of his own works. *Boston Recorder*, August 18. Reprinted in the *Connecticut Observer*, September 2, the *New Haven Journal*, September 16, and the *New York Evangelist*, November 11.

282. Signed letter to the editor, on word usages. *Vermont Telegraph*, August 30.

283. Signed letter to the editor pointing out certain philological errors in an article in the March issue. *Quarterly Christian Spectator*, September (Vol. IX, pp. 431–433).

284. "Address to the People of the United States," signed "Aurelius," on the Constitution, demagoguery, etc. *Worcester Palladium*, September 20. Marked by Webster in the New York Public Library file in a way to suggest his authorship, and felt by the compiler to be his without doubt.

285. Signed letter to Charles Richardson, in two installments, setting forth errors in the latter's dictionary. *New Havener*, September 30 and October 7.

286. Article, "Education," signed "M.," on physical exercises, manual labor, etc., as worthless educational projects. *Connecticut Observer*, October 21. Paraphed by Webster in the New York Public Library file.

287. Signed article, "Propagation of Errors," on errors in grammatical rules repeated from author to author. *Connecticut Observer*, November 4.

288. Letter to the editor, signed "Baxter," attributing contemporary evils to Jeffersonian principles, and declaring education useless without the Bible. *Connecticut Observer*, November 11. Paraphed by Webster in the New York Public Library file.

289. Article, signed "Sidney," and titled by the editor "A Voice of Wisdom," discussing the condition of the United States. *Commercial Advertiser*, November 20 (*Spectator*, November 23). Among more specific complaints, the writer asserts that the Constitution needs revision; that universal suffrage is unwise "without adequate control"; that intelligent, experienced, and propertied citizens are the best leaders; and that "the *form* of a free government remains, but the *spirit* of it is lost." Reprinted in the *Montreal Herald*, November 25, the *Albany Evening Journal*, December 1, and the *Columbia Republican* some time before December 8 (no copy located). Reprinted in part in the *Montreal Gazette*, November 25, the *Albany Argus*, November 30, the New York *Morning Courier* and the New York *Evening Star*, December 11, the *Boston Daily Advocate*, before December 18 (no copy located), the Washington *Globe* and the *New York Evening Post*, December 18, the *Columbian Register*, December 23, and the *Wayne* (N.Y.) *Sentinel*, before December 27 (no copy located).

Webster's authorship, conjectured at the time, is shown in his correspondence and papers. The article had wide repercussions, reaching the floor of the New York state legislature; for these see Part Four below, rubric L. Because of a statement in the article that "men have found that the chance of having a good chief magistrate by *birth* are about equal to the chances of obtaining one by popular election," the writer was accused of being a monarchist, and the enemies of the Whig party tried to pin this label on it. In The New York Public Library is a clipping of the article marked up by Webster. Against this remark he wrote, "When the article first appeared in print, the declaration in this sentence threw the whigs in the state of New York into convulsions. They interpreted it, as favoring the introduction of Monarchy. It so happens that the writer, in giving his opinion, had not the least reference to a monarchical form of government.

The opinion refers merely to the manner of constituting or obtaining a chief magistrate." In the resultant newspaper furore there are various references to the article's being reprinted in pamphlet form; the compiler has found one pamphlet edition (Title 736), but this seems to precede the newspaper references.

1838

290. Article signed "Detector," comparing the principles of Fanny Wright and Robert Dale Owen with those of Jefferson. *Connecticut Herald*, January 16. Paraphed by Webster in the New York Public Library file.

291. "To the Abolitionists," signed "Monitor," deploring their lack of discretion. *Connecticut Observer*, January 27. Paraphed by Webster in the New York Public Library file.

292. Signed letter to the editor, a tribute to Dr. Nathan Perkins, Webster's language tutor. *Connecticut Observer*, February 3. Reprinted in the *Boston Recorder*, March 2.

293. Two articles, "Remarks on Parties and Popular Deception," signed "Trumbull," condemning faction and demagoguery, and defending the Hartford Convention. *Hampshire Gazette*, February 14 and 21. Paraphed and autographed by Webster on clippings in The New York Public Library.

294. Two unsigned articles, "Gems of Politics," consisting of sayings on various topics, mostly quotations from Jefferson. *New-Yorker*, February 24 and March 10. Marked by Webster on clippings in The New York Public Library in a manner to suggest his authorship; referred to as being by "N.W." by the editor (March 3).

295. Signed letter to Horace Greeley, explaining reasons for some of his orthography, as requested in a letter from Greeley in the same issue. *New-Yorker*, March 3.

296. Letter to the editor signed "Seneca," continuing the ideas in the "Trumbull" articles (No. 293 above), attributing ignorance of the history, principles, and theory of government on the part of modern youth to too much fiction and juvenile literature. *Hampshire Gazette*, March 14. Paraphed by Webster on a clipping in The New York Public Library.

297. "Instability of Laws," signed "A Lover of Stability," lamenting the course of recent United States history. *Hampshire Gazette*, March 21. Paraphed by Webster on a clipping in The New York Public Library.

298. "To the Members of the Woodbury Convention," signed "Alpha," asserting that Jefferson's ideas undermine religion, morals, and

republican institutions. *Connecticut Herald*, March 27. Paraphed by Webster on a clipping in The New York Public Library.

299. Series of eight numbered articles, "Thoughts on Political Affairs," all but the first signed "Hampden," on defects of the Constitution, advocating limited suffrage in electing senators, ridiculing puerility of congressmen, and lamenting party spirit. *Hampshire Gazette*, April 4, 11, 18, and 25 and May 2, 9, 16, and 23. Paraphed by Webster on clippings in The New York Public Library. In the Webster Papers there is a draft of the fifth article in his hand.

300. Unsigned letter to the editor, blaming the sad condition of the United States on following the ideas of Jefferson and Paine. *Middletown Constitution*, April 18. Paraphed by Webster in the New York Public Library file.

301. Signed letter to the editor, explaining his spelling of "traveler," and remarking on the use of the subjunctive mood. *New-Yorker*, April 28.

302. Letter signed "Boleus," suggesting that the societies for the promotion of the Gospel might work among Americans "who bid defiance to the constitution" to better purpose than among the Indians. *New Haven Palladium and Republican*, April 7(?). Seen only as a clipping in The New York Public Library, paraphed by Webster; 1838 seems the most likely year. Evoked by the situation in Georgia regarding seizure of Indian lands.

303. Letter to the editor, initialled "N.W.," crediting John Fitch as the real pioneer of the steamboat. *New-Yorker*, June 2. This is quite likely Webster; he was interested in Fitch's work.

304. Letter to the editor, signed "Verax," showing that Jefferson rather than Jackson first claimed that government officials may interpret the Constitution without appeal. *Hampshire Gazette*, September 19. Paraphed by Webster on a clipping in The New York Public Library.

305. "Hurry, Hurry, Hurry!" signed "Howard," condemning the passion for speed in American life, particularly in education. *Connecticut Observer*, September 29. Paraphed by Webster in the New York Public Library file. A manuscript of this, differing somewhat from the printed version, is in the Pierpont Morgan Library.

306. Letter to the editor, signed "M.," countering a favorable review of Sanders' speller by protesting against the use of synonyms as definitions. *Worcester Palladium*, October 10. The compiler believes this is probably by Webster.

307. Letter to the editor, signed "Mather," again attacking Sanders' speller and praising Webster's, in reply to "A Teacher," who had replied to No. 306. *Worcester Palladium*, October 17. Also probably by Webster.

"Green," in the issue of October 31, suggested that "M." and "Mather" had an interest in Webster's book.

308. Unsigned article beginning, "As the subject of educating the children...," about the principles of the English language, discussing various spelling books and dictionaries, to the advantage of Webster's series. *Connecticut Observer*, October 27. Marked by Webster in the New York Public Library file in a manner to suggest his authorship.

In the Hampshire Gazette, *November 7, appears a letter to the editor, signed "Hampshire," opposing the political views of Timothy J. Gridley, and referring to an election in Amherst in 1816. Webster marked this on a copy of the paper in The New York Public Library, but it seems unlikely that he wrote it, because of the glowing terms in which it refers to him. He may have provided the information on which it is based. Gridley's reply appeared in the same paper, December 5.*

309. "Common School Convention" report, signed by Webster as president. New Haven *Daily Herald*, November 15. See Appendix A, No. 24.

310. Signed article on efforts towards world peace and the decline of monarchies because of the spread of commerce and manufactures. *Connecticut Observer*, November 17. Reprinted, with editorial comment, in the *New-Yorker*, December 15. Although these comments were intended to be favorable, Webster thought they reflected on him, and wrote a long letter to Horace Greeley, the editor;[7] as far as the compiler can ascertain, the letter was not published.

311. Letter to the editor, signed "Candor," discussing various current problems and their treatment in this newspaper. *Worcester Palladium*, November 28. Paraphed by Webster in the New York Public Library file.

312. Article signed "Probus," analyzing Pond's edition of Lindley Murray's grammar. *Hampshire Gazette*, December 5. Attributed to Webster by the compiler. In the New York Public Library file the article has MS corrections by him.

313. Article signed "Octogenarian," regretting the failure of the United States to found and maintain a true republic. *Middletown Constitution*, December 5. Attributed to Webster by the compiler. The article has MS corrections by him in the New York Public Library file.

314. Letter "To the Professor of Hebrew in the Theological Institution in Andover" (Moses Stuart), signed "W.,"asking about a disputed

[7]Ca. December 20, 1838. Seen by the compiler when in the possession of an autograph dealer; present whereabouts unknown (transcript in Webster Papers, New York Public Library).

translation in Psalm 77. *Boston Recorder*, December 14. Noted by Webster in the New York Public Library file in a manner to suggest his authorship. A reply, signed "E.,"appeared in the issue of December 28.

315. Editorial note quoting two or three paragraphs from Webster on English philology. *New Haven Palladium*, December 15. The quotation is credited to "a communication to the National Intelligencer," but the compiler has not found such a letter published therein.

316. Article signed "Undeniable Truth," seeking to show, by quotation from Jefferson, that many of President Jackson's measures were based on Jeffersonian precedents. *Middletown Constitution*, December 19. Autographed by Webster in the New York Public Library file. This was part of a debate which filled the columns of several papers, beginning with an article "What is Democracy?" in the *Commercial Advertiser*, September 22.

1839

317. Signed letter to the Reverend William Buckland of Oxford, England, dated November 16, 1838, about his recent book on geology, offering suggestions about certain Hebrew words. *American Journal of Science and Arts*, January (Vol. XXXV, pp. 375–376).

318. Signed letter to the editor, commenting on the opposition to Webster's edition of the Bible. *Connecticut Observer*, January 5.

319. Letter to the editor, signed "Querist," on the use of the Bible and prayer in schools. *Connecticut Observer*, January 12. Paraphed by Webster in the New York Public Library file.

320. Signed letter to the editor, disputing an assertion in an earlier issue that the Persians were ancestors of the Chaldeans. *Connecticut Observer*, February 2.

321. Series of five articles, "Philological Miscellany," signed "Z." and "X." *New York Evangelist*, February 9, May 4, September 7, and September 14, 1839, and January 18, 1840. Probably by Webster.

322. Signed letter to the editor, citing statistics gathered by Webster in 1785–86 on the population of various states. *New Haven Record*, March 16. Reprinted in the *National Intelligencer*, April 9.

323. Unsigned letter to the editor beginning, "It is surprising to observe. . . ," about errors in current popular views of American political history. *United States Gazette*, April 6. Autographed by Webster on a clipping in The New York Public Library.

324. Letter to the editor, signed "A Parent," criticizing Town's and Sanders' spellers. New Haven *Daily Herald*, April 30. Attributed to Webster by the compiler.

325. Letter to the editor, headed "Spelling Books" and signed "A.M.," attacking Sanders' speller in reply to favorable notices it had received in the paper. *Boston Recorder*, June 21. Felt by the compiler to be almost certainly by Webster.

326. Article beginning, "Among the Reports on Common Schools . . . ," signed "Senex," about erroneous procedures followed in schools. *Connecticut Courant*, July 6. Paraphed by Webster on a clipping in The New York Public Library.

327. Unsigned article headed "Donations," listing books which Webster had presented to Yale, Middlebury College, Amherst, the Hartford Young Men's Institute, and the town of West Hartford. *Republican Farmer*, July 17. Reprinted in the *Litchfield Enquirer*, August 29, the New Haven *Daily Herald*, August 31, the *New Haven Palladium*, September 14, the *Connecticut Courant*, September 21, the *New Haven Record*, October 5, the *Boston Recorder*, October 25, and the *Connecticut Common School Journal*, January [1], 1840 (Vol. II, p. 100).

328. Signed letter to the editor, describing a recent tornado in Connecticut and an earlier one, and asking for eye-witness reports. New Haven *Daily Herald*, August 2. Reprinted in the *Connecticut Courant*, August 10.

329. Signed letter to the editor, in reply to a request in the issue of October 12 that Webster publish a recent lecture, declining to do so. *New Haven Record*, October 19.

330. Signed letter to the editor, discussing the use of the Bible in schools, Webster's edition, etc. New Haven *Daily Herald*, November 23.

331. Signed letter to the editor, further discussing the use of the Bible in schools, arising from an exchange of letters in the issues from November 21 to 26. New Haven *Daily Herald*, November 27.

332. Signed letter to the editor, dated November 22, in reply to his assertion, in the issue of November 6, that Webster's work "has long been supplanted." *Baltimore American*, November 27. Reprinted in the *Sentinel of Freedom*, December 3.

333. Signed letter to the editor, still further commenting on the Bible in schools. New Haven *Daily Herald*, November 30.

334. Signed letter to the editor, commenting on a legal decision that copyright may be taken on a compilation as well as on original work, and complaining of plagiarisms of his works. New Haven *Daily Herald*, December 31. Reprinted in the *Connecticut Herald*, January 4, 1840.

1840

In the New Haven Record *of January 4 Webster's name appears in a group of signers of a testimonial to the paper.*

335. Signed letter opposing "creating capital" by banks and speculation, as disruptive of stable government. *New Haven Record*, January 18.

336. Article headed "American History," signed "Americus," pointing out errors in several United States history texts and praising Webster's as correct. *Connecticut Observer*, February 1. Autographed by Webster on a clipping in The New York Public Library; a draft is in the Webster Papers.

337. Letter headed "Mistakes in Education," signed "Senex," on teaching children things which he regards as of no use in later life. *Vermont Chronicle*, April 8. Paraphed by Webster on a clipping in The New York Public Library.

338. Letter to the editor, headed "Spiritual Existence," signed "Watts," discussing the existence of God and the meaning of "spirit." *Connecticut Observer*, April 18. Corrected and paraphed by Webster on a clipping in The New York Public Library.

339. Letter headed "Education of Females," signed "Senex," urging education for girls in domestic economy rather than in the sciences. *Vermont Chronicle*, April 22. Marked by Webster on a clipping in The New York Public Library as if to suggest authorship.

340. Signed letter to the state legislature objecting to the spelling "comptroller," which had officially been changed to "controller" at Webster's instance, thirty years before. New Haven *Daily Herald*, May 19. Reprinted in the New Haven *Evening Palladium*, May 20.

341. Signed letter making certain corrections and expansions in the excerpt from a talk by Webster on July 4, printed in the July 21 issue. New Haven *Daily Herald*, July 22. See Appendix B.

342. "To the Young of Both Sexes," signed "Franklin," advising them on education and careers, objecting to teaching girls geometry, algebra, rhetoric, zoology, and higher mathematics. *National Aegis*, August 5. Not acknowledged by Webster, but the MS in his hand is in the Pierpont Morgan Library, and the content is very similar to "Advice to the Young," Chapter XIX of his *History of the United States*. Reprinted in the New Haven *Daily Herald*, August 20.

343. Signed letter drawing attention to Webster's works. *Vermont Chronicle*, October 28. Reprinted in the New Haven *Daily Herald*, December 2.

344. Signed article, "A Brief History of Spelling Books," dated November 25, discussing Webster's and other spellers. *Congregational Observer*, December 5. A partial draft is in the Webster Papers, and a full draft in the Pierpont Morgan Library.

345. Signed letter to the editor of the *American Eclectic*, commenting

adversely on the orthography in its first number. New Haven *Daily Herald*, December 19. Not found in the magazine itself.

346. Series of ten signed articles (Nos. 4 to 10 misnumbered 5 to 11), "Observations on Orthography." *Congregational Observer*, December 19 and 26, 1840, January 9, 16, 23, and 30, February 13 and 27, and March 20 and 27, 1841. Reprinted in part in the New Haven *Daily Herald*, December 21 and 26 and January 7, the New Haven *Evening Palladium*, December 24 and January 1, and the *Hampshire Gazette*, January 20.

347. Signed letter to the editor about John Fitch and the invention of the steamboat. New Haven *Daily Herald*, December 23. Reprinted in the New Haven *Evening Palladium*, December 24, and in part in the *Commercial Advertiser*, December 31 (*Spectator*, January 2).

1841

348. Signed letter to the editor, stating where in Webster's works explanations of foreign words and phrases may be found. New Haven *Daily Herald*, January 30.

349. Initialled letter to the editor, commenting on various words, and suggesting "heliography" or "photography" instead of "daguerreotypy" for the art of fixing images on metal plates by means of light. New Haven *Daily Herald*, February 3.

350. Signed letter "To the Country School Master," defending the form of presentation in Webster's speller, in reply to some objections published in the issue of February 24. New Haven *Daily Herald*, February 25.

351. Signed letter to the editor about spring colds and premature changing to thinner clothing. New Haven *Daily Herald*, April 14. Ironically, two years later Webster caught a fatal cold from this same rash act (Ford's *Notes*, Vol. II, p. 361).

352. Signed article, "Question in Philosophy," expressing the belief that water flows faster at night than by day, and asking millers for their experience. New Haven *Daily Herald*, April 15.

353. "On Philology, by Noah Webster," discussing pronunciation and certain school books. *Northern Light*, June (Vol. I, p. 43).

354. Signed letter, dated June 1, "To Charles Anthon," questioning the etymology in his classical dictionary. *Commercial Advertiser*, June 4 (*Spectator*, June 9). Anthon's reply was published in the issue of June 7 (June 9); its date, April 5, is probably a misprint for June 5.

355. Signed letter in reply to Dr. Anthon. *Commercial Advertiser*, June 15 (*Spectator*, June 19). Reprinted in the *Boston Courier*, June 17.

356. Signed letter to the editor, regarding a point of history raised by a reference in the issue of June 22 to a proposal to erect a Wyoming massacre monument. New Haven *Daily Herald*, June 24.

357. Signed letter to the editor, on the sorry state of English philology. *Commercial Advertiser*, July 2.

358. Signed letter to the editor, on various misusages of words. *Commercial Advertiser*, July 24 (*Spectator*, July 28).

359. Signed letter concerning discrepancies in Webster's works and his constant efforts to improve them. *Northern Light*, October (Vol. I, p. 109).

360. Signed letter "To the Citizens of the United States," on the state of English philology and certain incorrect usages. New Haven *Daily Herald*, October 2.

361. Signed letter replying to criticisms by Mr. Salem Town. *Northern Light*, November (Vol. I, p. 125). Reprinted in part in *To the Friends of American Education* (New Haven, 1842), a leaflet by "Americanus" (see Part Four below, rubric M).

362. Signed letter in appreciation of praise accorded Webster's dictionary, and discussing certain misused words. *Boston Courier*, November 5 (semi-weekly edition, November 8; weekly edition, November 11).

363. "The Age of Spelling Books," signed "A Teacher," on Webster's and other spellers. *Hampshire Gazette*, November 30. See Part Four below, rubric J.

364. Signed letter to the editor, giving Webster's adverse evaluation of Alonzo B. Chapin's *English Spelling Book*, and commenting on errors in contemporary grammars. New Haven *Daily Herald*, December 20. This letter was a by-product of a long debate in the press between "C." (Chapin) and "Americanus," who was Webster's son, William; see Part Four below, rubric M.

1842

365. Signed letter to the editor, using a notice of a lecture by Professor Silliman as an excuse for drawing attention to his own *Manual of Useful Studies*. *New Haven Palladium*, January 8.

366. Signed letter to the editor, dated January 5, on pronunciation and etymology. *Hampshire Gazette*, January 11.

367. Signed letter to the editor, headed "Lexicography," in response to a review of the dictionary which had appeared in the issue of December 8. *Christian Advocate and Journal*, January 12 (Vol. XVI, p. 88).

368. Signed letter to the editor, following up the preceding. *Christian Advocate and Journal*, February 9 (Vol. XVI, p. 104).

369. Signed "Letter to a Gentleman in Andover," dated February 23, discussing Webster's views and writings on etymology, errors in the Bible, etc. *New England Puritan,* March 3.

370. Signed letter to the editor, declining to follow his suggestion that Webster's Fourth of July speech in Amherst be published. New Haven *Daily Herald,* July 25.

371. Signed article, "Philology," dated September 20. *Daily National Intelligencer,* September 30. Reprinted in two installments in an unidentified paper (clipping, Webster Papers).

372. Signed letter "To the Gentlemen of the Law," on the origin of feuds and the meaning of "fee." *Daily National Intelligencer,* October 14.

373. Essay introductory to an advertisement for Webster's octavo dictionary. *Commercial Advertiser,* November 15 and later. Attributed to Webster by the compiler. Reprinted in the *New York Observer,* December 31 and later, and April 1 and 8, 1843.

374. Letter "To William Miller & Co.," signed "Monitor," regarding Miller's millenial prophecies. New Haven *Daily Herald,* November 25. Webster's authorship is shown by the MS in his hand in the New Haven Colony Historical Society. Reprinted in Warfel, *Letters of Noah Webster,* pp. 525–526.

375. Signed letter to the editor, discussing Webster's *Improved Grammar* and other grammars, declining to publish further works, since they would only become objects of plagiarism. *Boston Courier,* December 20.

376. Signed letter about unusual atmospheric phenomena and their effect on the ignorant. New Haven *Daily Herald,* December 31. Reprinted in the *American Laborer,* February, 1843 (Vol. I, pp. 351–352), and in part in the *New York Observer,* February 4, 1843.

1843

377. Signed letter to the editor, expressing the wish that critics who talk about what Webster has *not* done would pay some attention to what he *has* done, and challenging them to compile a better dictionary. New Haven *Daily Herald,* January 13.

378. Signed letter to Henry Jones, further commenting on atmospheric phenomena. New Haven *Daily Herald,* February 18. Cf. No. 376.

379. Signed letter to the editor, with still further remarks on atmospheric phenomena. New Haven *Daily Herald,* February 22.

380. Letter to the editor, signed "W.,"on comets. New Haven *Daily Herald,* March 11. Probably by Webster because of his interest in the subject and a reference to having been a child in 1769.

381. Signed letter, headed "Orthography," dated March 22, in reply to "Old Dilworth," who had criticized the paper for following Webster's orthography. *New York Tribune*, March 24.

Webster died on May 28. Obituaries began appearing the following day; for a summary of these, see Appendix J.

PART FOUR: NEWSPAPER CONTROVERSIES INVOLVING WEBSTER

It is easy to comprehend the sharp differences of opinion and exchanges of letters, newspaper articles, and pamphlets involved in the political give-and-take of the late eighteenth and early nineteenth centuries, but Noah Webster's dictionary has become such an institution and his speller and other school books have dropped so far out of remembrance that it is difficult today to conceive the bitterness—and wordiness—of the attacks and counterattacks between Webster and persons of varying degrees of importance and competence in lexicography and pedagogy.

Some of the attempts to ridicule and deprecate Webster's textbooks and his educational theories were made by persons who had a financial interest in rival works, but others were merely the outcries of those whose sense of tradition was offended—for Webster fostered many innovations and was outspoken in his condemnation of the spellers and dictionaries which were standard when he first challenged their positions.

The present section summarizes the principal disputes in which Webster engaged, chiefly in the press. The following categories of newspaper items have been omitted: acknowledgments by editors of the receipt of material; letters from disputants promising later replies; and editorial notes merely correcting typographical errors.

A. *"Dilworth's Ghost" Controversy, 1784–1785*

1. Letter to "Mr. N—— W———, A.M. alias Esq.," signed "Dilworth's Ghost," in the *Freeman's Chronicle*, June 24, 1784, reprinted in the *Connecticut Herald*, June 30, and the *New York Journal*, July 15. An attack by a person purporting to be the ghost of Thomas Dilworth, author of the spelling book which was standard when Webster's was published, criticizing Webster's ideas and his books. The writer appears to have been a former New York City school teacher named Hughes, at this time living in Dutchess County.

2. Signed letter from Webster to the editor, dated Hartford, July 5, in the *Freeman's Chronicle*, July 8, 1784, reprinted in Warfel, *Letters of Noah Webster*, pp. 9–11. Discussing the attack and refusing to notice further communications unless signed (a resolution to which he did not adhere).

3. Letter to the editor, signed "Thomas Dilworth," in the *Connecticut Journal*, July 14, 1784. Ridiculing and replying to "Dilworth's Ghost."

4. Signed letter from Webster to the editor, dated Hartford, July 22, and another dated September 13, in the *New York Journal*, September 23, 1784, reprinted in the *Connecticut Journal*, December 15. The first is a reply to No. 1, as reprinted in the former paper, in the same terms as No. 2, and the second is a protest that the first had not been published. The first is reprinted in Warfel, *Letters of Noah Webster*, pp. 11–19.

5. Letter from Tapping Reeve of Litchfield, Connecticut, to John Canfield of Sharon, Connecticut, published in the *American Mercury*, October 11, 1784. Commending Webster's *Grammatical Institute*.

6. Note to the editor, signed "Entity," requesting publication of an article signed "A Learner of English Grammar," dated "State of Connecticut, Nov. 1, 1784," both in the Litchfield, Conn., *Weekly Monitor*, December 21, 1784. The latter replies to No. 5, pointing out errors in Webster's work.

7. [Article or letter, signed "A.B.," in the *Weekly Monitor*, December 28, 1784. Replying to No. 6. No copy located; known only from the reply, No. 8.]

8. Letter to the editor, signed "A L. of E.G.," dated January 6, in the *Weekly Monitor*, January 11, 1785. Replying to No. 7.

9. Letter "To Noah Webster, A.M. alias Noah Webster, jun. Esq.," signed "D.—— G.——," dated November 10, 1784, in the *Weekly Monitor*, January 4 and 11, 1785, reprinted in the *Connecticut Journal*, January 12. Attacking Webster's works. This seems to be a different person from the "Dilworth's Ghost" of Nos. 1 to 4 (cf. No. 11).

10. Signed letter from Webster to the editor, in the *Weekly Monitor*, January 18, 1785, reprinted in the *Connecticut Journal*, February 9. Replying to "A Learner of English Grammar," "Entity," and the new "Dilworth's Ghost," with the assumption that the latter two are the same person.

11. Letter, signed "D—— G——," dated January 6, in the *Weekly Monitor*, January 25, 1785. Further attacking Webster. In this the writer denies any knowledge of "Dilworth's Ghost" of the *Freeman's Chronicle* in July, 1784.

12. Signed letter from Webster "To Dilworth's Ghost, alias Entity,

alias A Learner of English Grammar," in the *Weekly Monitor*, February 1, 1785, reprinted in Warfel, *Letters of Noah Webster*, pp. 19–24. Further replying to various attacks.

13. Letter to the editor, signed "A.B.," dated January 17, in the *Weekly Monitor*, February 8, 1785. Counterattacking the same three pseudonymous writers, and assuming them all to be the same person.

14. Signed letter from Webster to the editor, in the *Weekly Monitor*, February 8, 1785. Further denying the various charges.

15. Signed letter from Webster "To Dilworth's Ghost, &c.," in the *Weekly Monitor*, February 15, 1785, reprinted in Warfel, *Letters of Noah Webster*, pp. 25–31. Rebutting criticisms in detail.

16. [Article or letter by "Dilworth's Ghost," in the *Weekly Monitor*, February 22, 1785. Not found, but known by announcement of its receipt and by a list of errata, in the issues of February 8 and March 1, respectively.]

17. Verse, signed "Philodilworth," in the *Weekly Monitor*, March 1, 1785. Satirizing "Dilworth's Ghost." On a clipping in the Webster Papers Webster has written that he suspects the author to be Joel Barlow.

18. Letter, signed "Dilworth's Ghost," dated February 25, in the *Weekly Monitor*, March 8, 1785. Continuing the attacks on Webster's work. In the same issue is a short note from the same writer regarding an erroneous quotation in one of his previous articles.

19. Anonymous verse beginning "Here Dilworth's Ghost comes piping hot...," in the *Weekly Monitor*, March 8, 1785. Ridiculing "Dilworth's Ghost," "Entity," and "A Learner of English Grammar."

B. *Philadelphia Controversies, 1787*

The day after Christmas, 1786, Webster settled in Philadelphia, and on April 10, 1787, recorded in his diary: "Wait on the Trustees of the Epis[l] Academy. Accept of a place there 6 months—@ 200 £ a year—Currency." Various later authorities, including one of Webster's sons-in-law, have referred to his being in charge of the Academy, which was not the case. William Cobbett, in a later controversy, used an unkind anecdote about Webster and this appointment, to the effect that when someone congratulated him upon it, Webster replied that it was the institution which was to be congratulated (*Porcupine's Gazette*, July 28, 1798).

In March, 1787, Webster had written a newspaper article which stirred up considerable controversy; the appointment to the Academy brought forth another exchange of letters; and the publication of the third edition of his grammar at about the same time stirred up a third battle. Because the three became intertwined to a certain extent, they are summarized as a group, though the separate threads have been kept apart as far as possible.

The "Domestic Debt" Controversy

1. "Thoughts on the Domestic Debt of the United States and the present state of affairs in Massachusetts, Addressed to the Governor of that Commonwealth. By a Citizen of Philadelphia," an article opposing the proposed funding of the public debt, in the *Pennsylvania Gazette*, March 21, 1787, reprinted in the *Boston Gazette*, April 9, the *New Haven Gazette*, April 12 (extracts only, and attributed to Peletiah Webster), the *Essex Journal*, April 18, and the *New Hampshire Mercury*, April 25. The general idea, sometimes in the same words, was used in No. XXVIII of Webster's *Essays*, 1790. The fact that Webster was the author eventually came out in the resultant newspaper debate (see below); it is further shown by an entry in his diary for March 16, 1787, "Write a Letter Govr Bowdoin." (When the Pennsylvania funding act was repealed in 1789, Webster noted in his diary, April 1, "I predicted this two years ago, & was abused in the paper for my opinions.") This article and its successors were preceded and accompanied in the Philadelphia papers by an extensive debate on paper money, in which Webster was not involved.

2. Anonymous attack on the funding plan, in the *Pennsylvania Gazette*, April 18, 1787, reprinted in the *Independent Gazetteer*, May 1, and in the *Boston Gazette*, May 7.

3. Letter from "A Pennsylvanian," in the *Pennsylvania Gazette*, *Freeman's Journal*, and *Independent Gazetteer*, April 25, reprinted in the *Boston Gazette*, May 28, and in part in the *Massachusetts Centinel*, May 9. Attacking Nos. 1 and 2 and supporting the funding system.

4. Letter from "A Friend to Public Credit," in the *Pennsylvania Packet*, May 1, 1787. Attacking Nos. 1 and 2 and objecting to discussion by outsiders, such as "our newly adopted literary speculators."

5. Attack on No. 3 by "Another Pennsylvanian," in the *Pennsylvania Gazette*, May 2, 1787.

6. Article signed "Justice," in the *Pennsylvania Gazette*, May 2, 1787. Accusing Dr. Ewing, provost of the University of Pennsylvania, of being

"A Pennsylvanian," and hostile to the Episcopal Academy; this article also accuses Ewing of being "Seth" in that controversy (see below).

7. Anonymous "Extract of a letter from a Gentleman in the country," in the *Pennsylvania Packet*, May 4, 1787. Supporting the funding system and particularly attacking No. 4.

8. Signed letter from John Ewing in the *Pennsylvania Packet*, May 4, 1787, reprinted in the *Pennsylvania Gazette*, May 9. Replying to No. 6, denying authorship of No. 3, and stating that Noah Webster had, in his presence, denied authorship of the initial article.

9. Unsigned note in the third person, in the *Pennsylvania Packet*, May 5, 1787. Promising a statement refuting the aspersions which had been cast on Webster.

10. Signed letter from Webster to the editor, in the *Pennsylvania Packet*, May 8, 1787, reprinted in the *Pennsylvania Gazette*, May 9. Acknowledging his responsibility for the initial article, and explaining away his previous denial on the basis that he was the writer of it as a letter, but not the author of it as a newspaper article.

11. Signed letter from Webster "To the Public," in the *Pennsylvania Gazette*, May 9, 1787, reprinted in the *Independent Gazetteer*, May 10, and in Warfel, *Letters of Noah Webster*, pp. 62–68. Discussing the funding system and replying to No. 3. In the course of this Webster referred to his having "crushed, almost with my single pen, a state combination" against the Revolution and Confederation, a boast which later brought down ridicule upon him. On May 10, Andrew Ellicott wrote to his wife from Philadelphia, "The people of this State continue much divided on the subject of Government; and Politics run high—Mr Webster the Lecturer. . . has been here but a short time; but in that time has had the fortune to enter into the spirit of the contending parties, and has already got his hands full."[8]

12. Signed letter from Webster, in the *Independent Gazetteer*, May 10, 1787. Claiming that he has not published any recent remarks on the funding system, and will not do so except over his own name.

13. Letter signed "A New-England Man," in the *Independent Gazetteer*, May 12, 1787. Picking a flaw in a statement in No. 11.

14. Anonymous article in the *Independent Gazetteer*, May 15, 1787. Poking fun at some of Webster's statements in No. 11.

15. Attack on Dr. Ewing by "A Friend to Liberality," in the *Independent Gazetteer*, May 15, 1787, reprinted in part in the *Newport Mercury*, June 18. Replying to No. 8, supporting "Justice" (No. 6).

[8]Catharine Van C. Mathews, *Andrew Ellicott, his Life and Letters* (New York, [1908]), p. 61.

16. Attack on Dr. Ewing by "Justice," in the *Pennsylvania Gazette*, May 16, 1787. Replying to No. 8, calling it "a collection of quibbles."

17. Letter signed "Cid Hamet Benengelli," in the *Independent Gazetteer*, May 18, 1787. Supporting No. 14, suggesting that Webster and Dr. Andrews of the Episcopal Academy were "Justice."

18. Letter signed "Truth," in the *Independent Gazetteer*, May 18, 1787. Supporting Webster, saying he is not meddling in the affairs of Pennsylvania, but dealing with problems of the whole nation.

19. Letter signed "A.B.," in the *Independent Gazetteer*, May 21, 1787. Hitting at outsiders who meddle in local affairs.

20. Attack on Dr. Ewing by "Another Friend to Liberality," in the *Independent Gazetteer*, May 23, 1787. Praising "Justice," and accusing Dr. Ewing of being "Seth" (see below).

The "Seth" Controversy

1. Notice that Webster "has accepted of the place of Master of [the English] language in the [Episcopal] Academy," in the *Independent Gazetteer*, April 14, 1787, reprinted in the *Maryland Journal*, April 20.

2. Article signed "Seth," in the *Freeman's Journal*, April 18, 1787. Satirically sympathizing with Webster for having to accept an underpaid teaching job after having published textbooks. "Seth" was Thomas Freeman, a former teacher at the Episcopal Academy (see No. 8 below).

3. Article signed "Lamech," in the *Freeman's Journal*, April 25, 1787. Seconding "Seth."

4. Letter to the editor, signed "Adam," in the *Freeman's Journal*, April 25, 1787, reprinted in Warfel, *Letters of Noah Webster*, pp. 59–62. Defending Webster against "Seth." "Adam" is generally considered to have been Webster, and probably was. In the New York Public Library file of the paper he has written, "N W I suppose," perhaps with the uncertain memory of later years.

5. Three letters signed "Seth," in the *Freeman's Journal*, May 2, 9, and 23, 1787. Further ridiculing Webster, assuming him to be "Adam." More contributions were promised but apparently never appeared.

6. Article signed "R.," in the *Independent Gazetteer*, May 26, 1787. Accusing Dr. Ewing of the University of Pennsylvania of being "Seth." This accusation had already been twice made in the course of the "Domestic Debt" controversy (above).

7. Article signed "A Friend to Harmony among Citizens," in the *Independent Gazetteer*, May 28, 1787. Also accusing Dr. Ewing of being "Seth."

8. Signed letter by Thomas Freeman, in the *Freeman's Journal* and the *Independent Gazetteer*, May 30, 1787. Admitting his identity as "Seth," to save Dr. Ewing embarrassment. In this letter Freeman indicated that he suspects Webster of being "Justice" in the "Domestic Debt" controversy (above).

9. Letter signed "An enemy to falsehood," in the *Independent Gazetteer*, May 31, 1787. Replying to No. 7, defending Dr. Ewing from the accusation therein.

Criticisms of the Third Edition of the Grammar

1. Series of articles criticizing Webster's grammar, signed "A Country Schoolmaster," in the *Independent Gazetteer*, May 9 and 31 and June 26 and 30, 1787.

2. Series of articles criticizing Webster's grammar, signed by James Kidd, in the *Freeman's Journal*, May 9, 16, and 30, June 13, 20, and 27, and August 1 and 8, 1787, reprinted in part in the *Maryland Gazette*, May 25 and June 8, 22, and 29, and (one only) in the *Independent Gazetteer*, May 30.

3. Signed letter from Webster to Kidd, in the *Freeman's Journal*, May 23, 1787. Replying to the first two articles of No. 2.

4. Letter to the editor signed "Lutius," in the *Independent Gazetteer*, May 26, 1787. Quarreling with a point in Webster's grammar.

5. Letter to the editor signed "Nestor," in the *Independent Gazetteer*, May 29, 1787. Replying to No. 4.

6. Signed letter from Kidd to Webster in the *Freeman's Journal*, May 30, 1787. Replying to No. 3, and adding further criticisms.

7. Letter signed "Y," in the *Independent Gazetteer*, June 1, 1787. Belittling Kidd's criticisms and that of "Lutius."

8. Letter from "Lutius" to "Nestor," in the *Independent Gazetteer*, June 2, 1787. Replying to No. 5.

9. Letter to the editor signed "Blunt," in the *Independent Gazetteer*, June 4, 1787. Counter attacking "Y," with personal abuse of him and Webster.

10. Letter to the editor from "Nestor," in the *Independent Gazetteer*, June 5, 1787. Counter-reply to No. 8.

11. Letter to the editor from "W.X.," in the *Independent Gazetteer*, June 6, 1787. Replying to "Y," suggesting that he has an interest, as printer or vendor, in Webster's book.

12. Signed letter from Webster to Kidd, in the *Freeman's Journal*,

June 6, 1787. Replying to No. 6, denying that he has written any of the anonymous newspaper articles.

13. Mock recommendation for the *Grammatical Institute*, signed by James Kidd, in the *Independent Gazetteer*, June 7, 1787. Repeating many of Kidd's criticisms; it is not clear whether he wrote this himself or if someone used his name.

14. Letter to Kidd from "Corn-stalk," in the *Independent Gazetteer*, June 8, 1787. Ridiculing No. 13.

15. Mock letter from Webster in the *Independent Gazetteer*, June 11, 1787. Satirically discussing the compilation of and profits from the *Grammatical Institute.*

16. Signed letter from Kidd to Webster in the *Freeman's Journal*, June 13, 1787. Replying to No. 12, and accusing Webster of writing scurrilous anonymous articles in the other controversies raging at the time.

17. Letter to the editor signed "Senex," in the *Independent Gazetteer*, June 18, 1787. Censuring both Kidd and "A Country Schoolmaster" for being abusive rather than scholarly in their criticisms, and mildly supporting Webster, though twitting him for vanity.

18. On June 22 in the *Independent Gazetteer* the editor reported that he had received a contribution in this controversy signed "A Retired Citizen," but that he declined to print it as too scurrilous.

19. Letter to the editor signed "Germanus," in the *Independent Gazetteer*, July 12, 1787. Suggesting, in view of the discussion of grammar then going on, that someone prepare rules for spelling in a form to help foreigners learn English.

20. Letter to the editor signed "Y," in the *Independent Gazetteer*, August 8, 1787. Satirically berating all grammarians.

21. Two signed letters from Webster to Kidd, in the *Freeman's Journal*, October 17 and 24, 1787, reprinted in part in the *Massachusetts Centinel*, November 17. Temperately answering the criticisms in No. 2.

22. Two signed letters from Kidd to Webster, in the *Freeman's Journal*, November 7 and 14, 1787. Replying to No. 21, though more temperately than before. The issue of November 21, 1787, promises "James Kidd to Noah Webster in our next," but the compiler has found no further rounds in this battle.

c. *"Argus"-Thomas Greenleaf Controversy, 1794*

1. Letter to Thomas Greenleaf and John Fellows (editors of the *New York Journal*) signed "Argus," in the *American Minerva*, October 23,

1794, reprinted in the *Herald*, October 27 and 30, and the *Gazette of the United States*, October 28. Attacking their republication of the second volume of Rabaut's *History of the Revolution in France* as garbled and abridged to suppress instances of Jacobin abuses. Webster was the editor of the *American Minerva*, and the compiler believes he was "Argus."

2. Signed letter to the editor from Greenleaf and Fellows, in the *American Minerva*, October 25 and 27, reprinted in the *Herald*, October 27 and 30, and the *Gazette of the United States*, October 29 and 30. Denying the accusations in No. 1.

3. Letter to Greenleaf and Fellows signed "Argus," in the *American Minerva*, October 29, 1794, reprinted in the *Herald*, October 30, and the *Gazette of the United States*, October 31. Repeating the charge that the work reprinted has been altered to make it pro-Jacobin.

4. Signed letter to "Argus" from Greenleaf and Fellows, in the *American Minerva*, November 1, 1794, reprinted in the *Herald*, November 3. Further denying the charges.

5. Letter "To the Public" signed "Argus," in the *American Minerva*, November 5, 1794, reprinted in the *Herald*, November 6. Closing—on his part—the controversy by saying that since his opponents misconstrued his criticism they did not make adequate reply.

6. Letter to the editor signed "Civis," in the *American Minerva*, November 5, 1794. Supporting "Argus" and his views.

7. Signed letter to "Civis" from Greenleaf and Fellows, in the *American Minerva*, November 7, 1794. Counterattacking, and accusing Webster of being "Civis."

8. Letter to "Argus" signed "Adieu," in the *American Minerva*, November 7, 1794, reprinted in the *Herald*, November 10. Asserting that his criticism of the work has not damaged it, and has in fact increased its sale.

9. Unsigned note in the *American Minerva*, November 7, 1794: "The Editor informs Messrs. Greenleaf and Fellows that Argus and Civis are different persons, and as he believes, unconnected with each other."

D. *Controversies over the Jay Treaty, 1794–1795*

In the autumn of 1794 the American press began to devote a large amount of space to Jay's Treaty with Great Britain—the negotiations preceding it, its contents and ratification, and such closely related concerns as resolutions by various bodies for and against the treaty, the evacuation of Western posts by the British under its terms, the impressment of American seamen, and the question of treaties with other countries, particularly France and Spain. Webster was among the most vigorous supporters of the treaty, and as editor of the *American Minerva* and its country edition, the *Herald*, took an active part in the discussions. Scores of unsigned editorial references to the treaty in his two papers well into the year 1796 can safely be attributed to him. The present summary confines itself to two specific exchanges of opinions and abuse.

"A," "Curtius," and Others, 1794

1. Article signed "A," in the *New York Journal*, October 25 and 29, 1794. Scathingly criticizing John Jay for his conduct of diplomatic negotiations with England.

2. Letter to the editor signed "Curtius," in the *American Minerva*, October 28, reprinted in the *Herald*, October 30. Defending Jay and attributing criticism of him to a Jacobin desire for war with England. The compiler believes that Webster was "Curtius"; he used this pseudonym the following year (see below).

3. Letter to the editor signed "A.K.," in the *American Minerva*, October 28, 1794. Ridiculing "A's" claim that Jay did not speak for the people.

4. Reply to No. 2 signed "A," in the *New York Journal*, November 1, 1794. Calling Jay's mission to England unconstitutional.

5. Letter to Thomas Greenleaf (editor of the *New York Journal*) signed "Fair Play," in the *American Minerva*, November 4, 1794, reprinted in the *Herald*, November 6, the *Gazette of the United States*, November 7, and the *New York Journal*, November 8. Attacking "A" and defending Jay's conduct. The compiler believes that "Fair Play" was also Webster.

6. Letter to the editor signed "Regulator," in the *American Minerva*, November 5, 1794. Ironically dealing with "A's" objections to Jay's mission.

7. Letter to the editor signed "Curtius," in the *American Minerva*, November 6, 1794, reprinted in the *Herald*, November 10. Further attacking "A."

"Decius," "Curtius," and Others, 1795

1. Unsigned editorial in the *American Minerva*, July 3, 1795, reprinted in the *Herald*, July 4, the *Gazette of the United States*, July 8, the *Federal Orrery*, July 13, the *Columbian Centinel*, July 15, and the *Columbian Chronicle*, July 17. Remarking on the great interest in Jay's Treaty, the

text of which had just been published, censuring hasty condemnation of it, and expressing hope that a dispassionate analysis will soon appear. Probably intended to set the stage for No. 2.

2. Unsigned "Candid Remarks on the Treaty," in the *American Minerva*, July 4, 1795, reprinted in the *Gazette of the United States*, July 7, the *Herald*, July 8, the *Federal Orrery*, July 16, the Boston *Mercury*, July 17, the *Columbian Centinel*, July 18, the *Massachusetts Spy*, July 29 and August 5, and the *New Hampshire Journal*, July 28 and August 4. Favorably discussing the treaty in detail.

3. Series of five articles signed "Decius," in the *Argus*, July 10, 11, 13, 14, and 16, 1795, reprinted in the *American Minerva*, July 18–31, the *Herald*, July 22–August 1, and in part in the *Independent Chronicle*, July 20–27. Analyzing adversely the Jay Treaty; accusing Webster of misrepresentation in "Candid Remarks." "Decius" was possibly Henry B. Livingston (1757–1823), a New York lawyer who was a violent opponent of the treaty, though he was Jay's brother-in-law.

4. Article signed "A Calm Observer," in the *American Minerva*, July 14, 1795, reprinted in the *Herald*, July 16, the *Gazette of the United States*, July 17, and the *American Mercury*, July 27. Referring to No. 2, claiming the treaty would adversely affect United States trade. In an introductory note Editor Webster warns the reader that "Calm Observer" errs in his interpretation.

5. Unsigned editorial in the *American Minerva*, July 17, 1795, reprinted in the *Herald*, July 18, the *New Hampshire Journal*, August 4, and the *Augusta Chronicle*, August 29 (headed "A Tub to a Whale"). Pointing out that the treaty cannot be fairly judged without an exhaustive study of other treaties, commercial conditions, etc.

6. Series of twelve articles, "Vindication of the Treaty...," six signed "Curtius," in the *American Minerva*, July 18, 20, 21, 22, 23, 24, 27, 29, and 30 and August 1, 4, and 5, 1795, reprinted in the *Herald*, July 22–August 8, and in part in the *Baltimore Telegraphe*, July 24–August 15, the *Albany Register*, August 3, the *Federal Orrery*, August 2–24, the *Albany Gazette*, August 10–September 28, the *Hudson* (N.Y.) *Gazette*, August 20–September 10, the *New Hampshire Journal*, September 8–22; also in two or three contemporary books on the treaty (see below, Nos. 12, 14, and 15) and in Webster's *Collection of Papers*, 1843. Favorably analyzing the treaty, article by article, in reply to No. 3. On Webster's personal file of the *Herald*, now at Yale, he has recorded that he wrote all the series except Nos. VI and VII, which were by Chancellor James Kent.

7. Letter to the editor signed "A Citizen," in the *Independent Chronicle*, July 20, 1795. Commenting that No. 2 had been reprinted in three Boston

papers, and asking that "Decius" also be reprinted, which was done in part in the same paper, July 20–27.

On July 22, 1795, the Argus *began running "The Defence," a series signed "Camillus," supporting Jay's Treaty; when the series broke off in the* Argus *it was continued in the* American Minerva, *and was reprinted elsewhere. It was by Alexander Hamilton with some help from Rufus King, and is reprinted in various editions of Hamilton's writings. It evoked its own subsidiary series of replies and support; Hamilton's authorship was generally surmised at the time.*

8. Unsigned editorial note in the *Aurora*, July 28, 1795, reprinted in the *Independent Chronicle*, August 10. Asserting that "Curtius" and "Camillus" are the same person.

9. Unsigned editorial note in the *American Minerva*, July 29, reprinted in the *Herald*, August 1, and the *Baltimore Telegraphe*, August 4. Denying the assertion in No. 8.

10. Unsigned editorial note in the *Aurora*, August 5, 1795. Refusing to believe the denial in No. 9.

11. Letter to the editor signed "Squib," in the *Vermont Gazette*, August 7, 1795, reprinted in the *Boston Gazette*, September 7. Objecting to No. 5, saying the people are capable of judging for themselves, and calling for the guillotine to wipe out aristocratic sentiment in the United States.

12. On August 12, 1795, according to the title-page, appeared the first edition of a compilation on the treaty: *Treaty of Amity . . . Conditionally Ratified . . . at Philadelphia, June 24, 1795. To Which is Annexed, A Copious Appendix*. Philadelphia, Printed by Henry Tuckniss, for Mathew Carey . . ., 1795. (Evans 29752; iv, 283 pp., with irregularities.) The "Vindication" is reprinted on pp. 194–275. Webster's copy, with annotations, is in The New York Public Library, and Jefferson's copy is in the Library of Congress.

13. "Remarks" to a reprint of No. 5 signed "Nineteenth April Seventy-Six," in the *Augusta Chronicle*, August 29, 1795. Attacking the treaty and Webster's support of it.

14. On September 3, 1795, and later, there was advertised in the *Independent Chronicle*, as "this day published," a pamphlet on the treaty which Evans (29757) enters as *Treaties with France, Great Britain, and the United States, With a Copious Appendix, Pro and Con*. Printed at Boston, by Hall and Nancrede . . ., 1795. In his annotation Evans states that this work contains Webster's Vindication, but the compiler has been unable

to locate a copy to verify this assertion, and suspects that the entry is hypothetical, made up from newspaper advertising. The advertisements do not specify which vindication of the treaty is given.

15. On November 2, 1795, was published a second edition of No. 12. The title is the same, with "Second Edition" added, and the imprint is "Philadelphia, Printed by Lang & Ustick, for Mathew Carey. . . . Nov. 2, 1795." (Evans 29753; [192] pp.) In this printing the "Vindication" appears on pp. 58–108. Copies in The New York Public Library and elsewhere.

E. *Philadelphia vs. New York Controversy, 1795*

1. Unsigned editorial in the *Minerva,* September 3, 1795 (*Herald,* September 5), doubtless by Webster, protesting against a proclamation by the Governor of Pennsylvania prohibiting intercourse with New York because of yellow fever there. The writer contrasts this action unfavorably with New York's gift of $5,000 to Philadelphia when she was suffering from the fever in 1793. Reprinted in part in the *Federal Intelligencer,* September 9.

2. Unsigned letter in the *American Daily Advertiser,* September 10, justifying the Pennsylvania proclamation and saying that the *Minerva's* mention of the $5,000 gift is petty and negates the spirit of the gift. Reprinted in the *New York Gazette,* September 12.

3. Unsigned "Extract of a Letter from New-York, dated 14th October," in the *Aurora,* October 16. Praising Philadelphia for raising $7,000 to send to New York for fever relief, in contrast to New York, where many wealthy people would not contribute for their own city. The writer again brings up Webster's asserted lapse of taste. Reprinted in the New York *Daily Advertiser,* October 19 and 28, and the *Argus,* October 22.

4. Unsigned letter in the *Argus,* October 26, objecting to No. 3, but also referring to Webster's poor taste. Reprinted in the *Aurora,* October 27, with comment.

5. Unsigned "Extract of another letter from New York, dated 26th October," in the *Aurora,* October 28, replying to No. 4. Reprinted in the *Argus,* November 2.

6. Doggerel headed "Echo, Junior, No. I" and signed "Johnny Scrive," in the New York *Daily Advertiser,* October 28, burlesquing No. 3 and accusing its writer of trying to stir up bad feeling between the two cities. Perhaps by Webster (see below).

7. Letter to the editor signed "Candidus," in the *Argus,* November 2, attacking No. 6 and implying that Webster wrote it.

F. *"Calm Observer" Controversy, 1795*

1. Series of three letters, signed "A Calm Observer," in the *Aurora*, October 23, 26, and 28, 1795. Reprinted in the *Minerva*, October 28 and 29. These are addressed to Oliver Wolcott, Secretary of the Treasury, and charge the President with having drawn advances on his salary.

2. Unsigned editorial in the *Minerva*, October 29 (*Herald*, October 31), defending the President. Reprinted in the *Aurora*, November 2, the *American Mercury*, November 9, the Charleston *City Gazette*, November 17, the *Vermont Gazette*, November 20, the *Farmer's Museum*, November 24, and in *Porcupine's Works*, Vol. IV, pp. 424–426. This was probably written by Webster, though on the reprint in *Porcupine's Works* there is a footnote suggesting Alexander Hamilton as the author. Hamilton certainly was interested in the affair, for on October 26 and 27 he wrote Wolcott, trying to ascertain the identity of "Calm Observer" and other pseudonymous writers.[9]

3. Unsigned "Remarks," in the *Aurora*, November 2, attacking No. 2. Reprinted in the Charleston *City Gazette*, November 17, the *Vermont Gazette*, November 20, and in *Porcupine's Works*, Vol. IV, pp. 426–428.

4. In Letter XIX of a series by "Pittachus," in the *Aurora*, November 21, the charge against the President is reiterated.

5. There was another unsigned editorial against "Calm Observer" in the *Minerva*, November 21 (*Herald*, November 25), probably by Webster. Reprinted in the *Aurora*, November 28, the *Federal Orrery*, December 7, and the *South Carolina State Gazette*, December 31.

6. With its reprint of No. 5 on November 28, the *Aurora* published an unsigned editorial supporting "Calm Observer" and criticizing Webster and Hamilton.

G. *"Harrington" Controversy, 1796*

1. Unsigned editorial in the *Minerva*, February 15, 1796 (*Herald*, February 17), probably by Webster, sharply criticizing Virginia for recent actions in regard to debts, the Jay Treaty, and proposed amendments to the Constitution. See No. 12 below.

2. Unsigned letter in the *Aurora*, February 16, defending Virginia and accusing the editor of the *Minerva* of anti-federalism.

[9] Wolcott Papers, Connecticut Historical Society; printed in Henry Cabot Lodge's edition of Hamilton's *Works*, Vol. X, pp. 125–126.

3. Unsigned editorial in the *Minerva*, March 17 (*Herald*, March 19), declaring that the Jay Treaty is not a proper subject for debate in the House of Representatives and concerns only the executive branch of the government. Probably written by Webster.

4. First eight of a series of essays signed "Harrington," in the *Gazette of the United States*, March 30 and 31 and April 2, 4, 6, 8, 11, and 13, the first four reprinted in the *Aurora*, April 4, 9, 23, and 25. These essays discuss the functions of the different parts of the government, opposing Webster's views.

5. Unsigned editorial in the *Minerva*, March 31 (*Herald*, April 2), expanding earlier remarks about the role of the House of Representatives.

6. Unsigned letter in the *Gazette of the United States*, April 13, stating that the House's uncertainty about the Jay Treaty is causing insurance underwriters to hesitate to issue policies, and urging the Southern states to make known their intentions. The writer suggests that if they oppose the Administration in Congress the Northern states might prefer to divide the Union.

7. No. IX of the "Harrington" series, *Gazette of the United States*, April 15. Replying to No. 5.

8. Unsigned editorial in the *Minerva*, April 15 (*Herald*, April 16), commenting on No. 6. The writer—probably Webster—takes the view that possible disruption of the Union is more serious than debate over a treaty; he claims that the Northern states bore the brunt of the Revolution and the establishment of the Republic, and that if the Southern states continue to oppose the Administration the North will consider it a challenge to the Union. Reprinted in the *Philadelphia Gazette*, April 18, the *Farmer's Museum*, April 26, the *Columbian Museum*, May 3, and the *South Carolina State Gazette*, May 4.

9. Unsigned editorial in the *Argus*, April 18, scoffing at the *Minerva's* fears of dissolution of the Union. Reprinted in the *Aurora*, April 20, and the *South Carolina State Gazette*, May 4.

10. Nos. XI and XII of the "Harrington" series, *Philadelphia Gazette*, April 19 and 22, reprinted in the *Minerva*, May 4 and 5, and the *Columbian Herald*, May 19 and 20. Citing the part played by different ethnic and regional groups in the Revolution, in reply to No. 8, and asserting that Webster is trying to disrupt the Union.

11. On April 20 Oliver Wolcott wrote Webster from Philadelphia, "I am told that Mr. Carey is *Harrington* but this *sub-rosa*—perhaps it is a mistake."[1]

[1]Webster Papers, New York Public Library.

12. Nos. XIII and XIV of the "Harrington" series, *Gazette of the United States*, April 22 and 27, the latter reprinted in part in the *Minerva*, May 18 (*Herald*, May 21). The first defends Virginia against her detractors, perhaps harking back to No. 1 as well as to No. 8. The second recites the role of the Southern states in the Revolution.

13. Two unsigned editorial notes in the *Minerva*, May 6 (*Herald*, May 7), discussing points raised by "Harrington" and asserting that Southern opposition to the Administration has damaged the North's business.

14. Unsigned editorial in the *Minerva*, May 18 (*Herald*, May 21), replying to No. 12. Reprinted in the *Gazette of the United States*, May 20, and the *Maryland Journal*, May 24; in editorial comment the latter asserts that Webster is recommending dissolution of the Union.

15. No. XV of the "Harrington" series, *Gazette of the United States*, May 27. General reply to various of Webster's articles about the South and its role in the Revolution.

16. James Thomson Callender in his *American Annual Register for . . . 1796* (pp. 86–87) reprints one paragraph of No. 8 and accuses Webster of being a British tool trying to disrupt the Union.

H. *Controversy about Joshua Coit, 1798*

1. Unsigned article in *Porcupine's Gazette*, June 9, 1798, attacking Representative Joshua Coit of Connecticut as vacillating and wasteful of Congress' time and money and advising him to take up farming.

2. Letter to the editor, signed "Amicus," in the *Commercial Advertiser*, June 15 (*Spectator*, June 16), reprinted in the *Time Piece*, June 20, with approving editorial comment. Accusing Peter Porcupine (William Cobbett) of baseness, indecency, slander, and scurrility, and calling for some restraint on the licentiousness of the press. Apparently written by Webster.

3. Letter to the editor, signed "Atticus," *New York Gazette*, June 21, defending Cobbett against No. 2. Reprinted in *Porcupine's Gazette*, June 23, with the editor's thanks to "Atticus" and a counterattack on Webster.

4. Series of anonymous editorial squibs in the *Time Piece*, June 26, calling the controversy a "tug of war" and ridiculing Porcupine and "Atticus" for their attacks on Webster.

5. Letter to the editor of the *New York Gazette*, signed "Amicus," in the *Commercial Advertiser*, June 26 (*Spectator*, June 27). Criticizing

the *Gazette* for printing No. 3 and accusing it of aping Porcupine scurrility.

6. Unsigned letter "To Noah Webster, newsmonger, Esquire, Pedagogue and Quack," *Porcupine's Gazette*, June 27, ridiculing him.

7. Unsigned letter to Webster, *Porcupine's Gazette*, July 7 (*Country Porcupine*, July 7 and 9). Abusing Webster, claiming his ire was aroused by Porcupine's circulation, and quoting praise of Porcupine's writings from others.

I. *Controversy over British Atrocities, 1798*

1. Unsigned editorial in the *Commercial Advertiser*, July 11, 1798, reprinted in the *Spectator*, July 14, the *South-Carolina State Gazette*, August 2, and in part in the *New York Gazette*, July 13, the New London *Bee*, July 25 (with approving comment), the *Independent Chronicle*, July 26, and in *Porcupine's Works*, Vol. IX, pp. 27–28. Using a Democratic Fourth of July celebration toast hoping for a French invasion of England as a text for a discussion of the spirit of revenge, citing British atrocities during the American Revolution. All those who replied to this took it to have been written by Webster, though it has not been found acknowledged by him.

2. Anonymous "Communication," in the *Argus*, July 13, 1798. Minimizing the importance of the toast mentioned, and calling for peace between America and France.

3. Article signed "Candidus," in the *New York Gazette*, July 13, 1798, reprinted in *Porcupine's Gazette*, July 17, and *Porcupine's Works*, Vol. IX, pp. 29–30. Denying that the asserted atrocities were British.

4. Anonymous "Communication," in the *Argus*, July 16. Poking fun at the imbroglio, especially since Webster—who was generally considered excessively Anglophile—was citing British misdeeds. (Two years earlier he had been accused of playing up French atrocities and overlooking those of the British during the American Revolution; anonymous writer and "Fishkill" in the *Argus*, April 27, 1796.)

5. Letter to the editors signed "A Real American," in the *New York Gazette*, July 18, 1798. Replying to No. 3 and affirming the authenticity of the atrocity incidents. "Candidus" considered the writer to be Noah Webster, but there is no evidence that he was.

6. Letter to the editors signed "Candidus," in the *New York Gazette*, July 19, 1798, reprinted in *Porcupine's Gazette*, July 21, and in *Porcupine's*

Works, Vol. IX, pp. 39–41. Replying to No. 5 and attacking Webster's position in the controversy.

7. Article by "A Farmer of West Chester," in *Porcupine's Gazette*, July 24, 1798, reprinted in the *New York Gazette*, July 26, *Russell's Gazette*, August 2, and in *Porcupine's Works*, Vol. IX, pp. 46–47. Assailing Webster for bringing up the atrocity story.

8. Apparently the final word was said by the editor of the *Time Piece*, July 27, 1798: "The attack of Porcupine and the Royal [i.e., New York] Gazette, on Noah, prove *he has* some *virtue* and *patriotism*."

J. *Controversies with Lyman Cobb, 1827–1841*

The person with whom Noah Webster tilted most often was Lyman Cobb, a school teacher and compiler of spelling books. In the latter capacity Cobb made great efforts to outstrip Webster, especially in the Old Northwest as education expanded rapidly there. Like Webster, Cobb was a Yankee, born in Lenox, Massachusetts, in 1800. Although Webster considered him a profligate illiterate, Cobb apparently had an elementary education in country schools and became a teacher at an early age.[2] About 1821 he issued the first edition of his speller; this and other texts of his continued to be published until the 1850's.[3]

"Examinator," 1827–1828

1. Series of thirteen articles entitled "Elementary Instruction," signed "Examinator," in the *Albany Argus*, July 6, 13, and 27, August 17, 21, and 24, November 16 and 23, December 21 and 25, 1827, January 4, and March 4 and 11, 1828, reprinted in pamphlet form (see below). Discussing the importance of the spelling book in education, analyzing Webster's and other spellers, attacking the discrepancies between Webster's spellers and dictionaries, objecting to Webster's innovations in spelling, and announcing that the purpose of the series is to create public

[2] *National Cyclopaedia of American Biography*, Vol. XXII, pp. 290–291; *Dictionary of American Biography*, Vol. IV, pp. 244–245.

[3] The sketch in the *National Cyclopaedia of American Biography* states that Cobb's speller was first published when he was nineteen (1819 or 1820), but the compiler has found no edition earlier than 1821.

interest in suitable textbooks. Lyman Cobb's authorship of the series is proved by its later appearance over his name. He claimed to have offered a prize for the best essay on spelling books, and to have written the essay himself when none was submitted; this may have been merely a fiction to justify his publication of criticism of Webster's works.

2. Signed letter from Webster to the editor, in the *Albany Argus*, December 14, 1827, reprinted in No. 4 and in Warfel, *Letters of Noah Webster*, pp. 420–423. Replying to the first eight installments of No. 1.

3. Letter to the editor signed "Examinator," in the *Albany Argus*, December 28, 1827, reprinted in No. 4. Replying to No. 2. No. XIII of the series also is in part a reply to No. 2.

4. In 1828 Cobb reprinted the series as a pamphlet: *A Critical Review of Noah Webster's Spelling-Book, first published in a Series of Numbers in the Albany Argus, in 1827 and 28, by Examinator. Printed in 1828.* (35 pp.) Pp. [3]–32 contain the series of articles, pp. 33–34 Webster's letter (No. 2), and pp. 34–35 Cobb's reply (No. 3). On p. [2], the verso of the title-page, is an "Advertisement" urging teachers and school committees to evaluate Webster's works more carefully. For a second edition of the *Critical Review*, incorporating material from other controversies, see below.

Attacks on the American Dictionary, *1829*

One of the spates of reviews and comments that followed the publication of the first edition of Webster's major dictionary in 1828 seems to involve Cobb.

1. Anonymous article headed "Webster's Dictionary," in the *New York Evening Post*, May 28, 1829, reprinted in the *Commercial Advertiser*, May 29, and the *Spectator* and the *Connecticut Courant*, June 2. Summarizing a favorable report on the dictionary by a committee of a meeting of teachers in New York and announcing that a version abridged by Joseph Worcester is to be published, as well as a new speller conformable to the dictionary in orthography. The introductory note in the *Commercial Advertiser* reprint suggests that this article was prepared by Webster.

2. Anonymous letter headed "Webster Dictionary and Spelling Book," in the *New York Evening Post*, June 27, 1829. Accusing Webster of unfair methods in securing approbation of his works from small and non-representative groups of teachers, and implying that Webster wrote the report under discussion; further insinuating dishonesty in Webster's

having engaged Daniel H. Barnes and Aaron Ely to compile books for him.[4] The compiler believes that the attack was written by Lyman Cobb.

3. Letter signed by Messrs. Borland, Mills, and Merchant (the teachers' committee concerned), in the *New York Evening Post*, July 1, 1829. Denying that Webster influenced the meetings, and declaring that the minutes are open for public inspection.

4. Letter from Mr. Merchant alone, in the *New York Evening Post*, July 3, 1829. Further replying to the charges in No. 2. References to the "Examinator" series suggest that he thought his antagonist was Cobb.

5. Letter headed "Dr. Webster and the Teachers," signed "A Schoolmaster," in the *New York Evening Post*, July 7, 1829. Attacking Webster and ridiculing Nos. 3 and 4.

6. Series of seventeen articles signed "Inquirer," in the New York *Morning Herald*, beginning about July 1, 1829, running to August 4. The series is preserved in clippings in the American Antiquarian Society, the first being from an unidentified paper, dated in MS July 4, 1829, crediting the *Morning Herald* as its source. Nos. VII, IX, and X of the series are to be found in surviving copies of the *Morning Herald* in the Library of Congress. Analyzing in detail Webster's *American Dictionary*, opposing its adoption as the standard. During the course of publication of the series the octavo abridgment of the dictionary was published, and No. XIV discusses it. Cobb was involved in the resultant discussion, and may have been "Inquirer."

7. Article signed "Candour," in the *New York Evening Post*, August 22, 1829. Commenting adversely on Webster's new *Elementary Spelling Book*, saying it was inconsistent with his dictionaries. "Candour" was probably not Cobb, since he says he is not the author of any textbooks.

8. Signed letter from Aaron Ely to the editor, in the *New York Evening Post*, August 26, 1829. Replying to No. 7, discussing the relations between Barnes, Webster, and himself.

9. Signed letter from Webster to the editors, in the *Commercial Advertiser*, August 26, 1829, reprinted in the *Spectator* and the *Boston Courier*, August 28. Defending his dictionaries against No. 6.

10. Note initialled "C" [Sherman Converse, publisher of the dictionaries], in the *Commercial Advertiser*, August 26, 1829, reprinted in the *Spectator*, August 28. Also defending the dictionaries against No. 6.

[4]Because of his absorption in the work of the major dictionary, Webster engaged Barnes to revise the spelling book and bring it into conformity with the dictionary. Barnes died before he had accomplished much, and Aaron Ely was hired in his place. As will be seen, Cobb and others claimed Ely was the real compiler of the *Elementary Spelling Book.*

Other persons answered "Inquirer," and the papers during August and September had frequent articles by "C.C.B.," "X.Y.Z.," "Longinus," and others. Many of these are now found only in unidentified clippings, and since none seems to have been written by Webster or Converse or Cobb, they are not separately described.

11. Signed letter from Converse to the editors, in the New York *Morning Herald*, August 27, 1829. Replying specifically to the charge in "Inquirer's" No. XIII that Daniel Barnes had written letters critical of Webster's work. Reprinted, with an anonymous letter charging Converse with prevarication, in an unidentified paper on September 5 (clipping, American Antiquarian Society).

12. Editorial note in the *New York Evening Post*, August 29, 1829. Acknowledging receipt of another contribution from "Candour," but refusing to print anything further on the controversy.

13. Article headed "Dr. Webster's New Publications," signed "Cicero," in the *Commercial Advertiser*, September 12, 1829, reprinted in the *Spectator*, September 18. Praising Webster's recent works, calling "Inquirer" and "Candour" unmanly, deprecating the dragging in of the name of the deceased Barnes, and doubting if Barnes ever wrote anything hostile to Webster.

14. Editorial note in the *Commercial Advertiser*, September 15, 1829, reprinted in the *Spectator*, September 18. Reporting that "Inquirer" had called and shown the editor Barnes' letter containing the passages referred to in No. 11.

15. Signed letter from Converse to the editor, in the *Commercial Advertiser*, September 18, 1829, headed "Cobb Vs. Barnes." Saying that since Barnes had changed his opinions, the date of the letters quoted should be indicated, and accusing Cobb of injuring the feelings of the Barnes family by violating the confidence of private correspondence. At this point another editor became weary, and announced that any further communications on the subject would have to be paid for as advertisements.

16. Signed letter from Converse to the editor, in the *Boston Courier*, September 28, 1829. Excoriating Cobb, who "has had the misfortune to have compiled a Spelling Book, and a small Dictionary."

17. Letter to the editor signed "Inquirer," in the *Boston Courier*, October 3, 1829. Taunting Converse for having fled to Boston to vent his spleen.

18. Signed letter from Converse to the editor, in the *Boston Courier*, October 3, 1829. Charging Cobb with using a disguise, and saying Converse has nothing to fear from a fair comparison of books.

Periodicals

The Critical Review, *1831*

1. *A Critical Review of the Orthography of Dr. Webster's Series of Books...including his former Spelling-Book, and the Elementary Spelling-Book, compiled by Aaron Ely, and published under the name of Noah Webster, LL.D. By Lyman Cobb....* New York: Published by Collins & Hannay.... 1831. (56 pp.) A second edition, containing an introduction signed by Cobb, new material on the quarto and octavo dictionaries, a slightly condensed reprint of the "Examinator" series, and new material on the Webster-Ely speller and Webster's orthography. From typographic evidence two printings can be distinguished, but they do not differ in content. This second edition was probably called forth by Webster's pamphlet *A Series of Books...*, 1830 and 1831 (Titles 755–757).

2. Unsigned favorable review of the pamphlet, in the *New York Evening Post*, November 4, 1831.

3. Unsigned letter to the editor, in the *New York Evening Post*, November 5, 1831. Objecting to No. 2, saying that Cobb is lambasting old errors which are constantly being corrected by Webster in new editions.

4. Letter signed "Candour," in the *New York Evening Post*, November 8, 1831. Counterattacking No. 3 and upholding Cobb's pamphlet.

5. Unsigned favorable review of the pamphlet in the *Louisville Focus*, November 15, 1831.

6. Broadside reply to the pamphlet, signed by Webster, dated November 15, 1831; see Title 758. Promising continued efforts to increase consistency in his works, "even at the *hazard of another pamphlet*, or *a new edition of the old one*," and claiming that all his works have been gone over by him and represent his labor and ideas.

7. Unsigned hostile review of the pamphlet in the New York *Daily Advertiser*, November 22, 1831, reprinted in No. 8. Saying that "Mr. Webster's reputation...cannot be materially affected by such small criticism as this."

8. Pamphlet reply to Cobb, *To the Friends of American Literature*; see Title 759. Undated, but after November 22, 1831; pseudonymous, but probably written, at least jointly, by Webster.

9. Unsigned favorable review of Cobb's pamphlet in the *New England Magazine*, December 1, 1831.

10. Unsigned generally unfavorable review of Cobb's pamphlet in the New York *Evangelist*, January 21, 1832.

11. Unsigned favorable review of Cobb's pamphlet in the *American Monthly Review*, February, 1832.

12. Unsigned generally unfavorable review of Cobb's pamphlet in the *Illinois Monthly Magazine*, February, 1832. Chiding him, as did some other reviewers, for trying to make his analysis seem brief by using small type.

On February 3, 1832, Webster wrote from New Haven to his son-in-law William C. Fowler, "Cobb's pamphlet has done me no harm here. One gentleman would not take it from the [post] office, another sent it back to him & a third came near to throw it in the fire. I learn that he was born in Lenox, Ms. & afterward lived with a man in Albany as a Kitchen boy, but was much addicted to lying, for which he was flogged & ran away, kept school & went to making school books & abusing mine. He is illiterate, but a most plodding fellow. . . ."[5] The matter of not taking a pamphlet from the post office refers to the fact that Cobb sent copies to many people without prepaying the postage, which was then possible. This tactless step brought upon him the ire of several persons who were not concerned with the pedagogic issues involved.

13. Letter to the editor signed "Postage Paid," in the *American Traveller*, February 7, 1832, reprinted in the *Connecticut Journal*, February 14 (with additional editorial remarks on the subject), and the *Middletown Sentinel*, February 29. Objecting to being sent a copy of Cobb's pamphlet without prepayment of postage.

14. Letter to the editor signed "Justice," in the *Connecticut Herald*, February 14, 1832. Attacking Cobb's pamphleteering activities.

15. Articles signed "T.," in the *Middlesex Gazette*, April 11 and 25, 1832. Attributing the lack of success of Cobb's pamphlet partly to small type and partly to the postage question, saying he has met no one who has read the pamphlet all the way through. "T." was very likely Thomas Miner. In the April 11 issue he quotes a letter from Webster referring to Cobb's "degree of persevering malevolence." "T." speaks of Cobb's "microscopic eye," and was not the first to intimate that he might find better use for his time and talents than going over Webster's books with a fine-toothed comb.

From October 24, 1833, to January 2, 1834, the Westfield *(N.Y.)* Courier *ran a series of articles signed "Aristides," critically evaluating Webster's spellers. A relative, in sending copies to Webster, attributed the series to a man engaged by Cobb to denigrate Webster's works. Apparently Webster did not reply to this attack.*

[5]In the possession of Mrs. Howard B. Field; transcript courtesy of Prof. Harry R. Warfel.

Webster's Counterattack, 1835

1. In February, 1835, Webster published some sort of attack on Cobb, as revealed in the correspondence with his New York bookseller-publishers, N. and J. White, quoted under Title 760.

2. An attack on Cobb, possibly the same one, seems to have been printed in Cincinnati in mid-year, 1835; see Title 761.

3. In July, 1835, Cobb issued a new preface to his speller, in an edition published in Watertown, New York, by Knowlton and Rice. In this he renews his attacks on Webster's inconsistencies, though he has been forced to retreat somewhat, for he adopted Webster's system of *indicating* pronunciation, although he continued to use Walker's orthography and pronunciation.

The War in the West, 1835–1837

As stated above, Cobb and his publishers had agents working in the West, especially in Ohio, attempting to introduce his textbooks into schools. Webster too had agents, of course, the principal one being his son, William, in Cincinnati. On September 29, 1835, William wrote his father, "We find that so little is affected [sic] by Cobb's agents in this quarter that we decided not immediately to insert the 'Statement of Facts' &c you sent...." In the same letter he remarks that "every newspaper communication in this place provokes a reply. And as your books are gaining ground, we feel it best that they should do so silently, for every new discussion brings up some new adversary to contend with."[6]

On November 7, 1835, N. and J. White wrote Webster, "Our agent in Ohio [a third White, probably a member of the family] informs us that he encountered Cobb's agent in Cleveland and effectually gave him a quietus,"[7] and the same or another triumph is reported by William Webster on December 20, telling his father that the Whites' agent "has come in contact with Cobb's agents once or twice, & in Cleaveland, he met one who was to deliver a lecture on 'discrepancies in Dr Websters books' that eve^g^. To *prepare him better* for the lecture, White put into his hands one of the *pamphlets*! In the Eve^g^ White went to the lecture, & then after Cobb's agent had sat half an hour in seeming uneasiness, he gave notice that he should defer the lecture on account of the paucity of

[6] Webster Papers, New York Public Library.
[7] Ellsworth Papers, Connecticut Historical Society.

numbers there. The next morn^{g}, he was off betimes for Detroit. The misrepresentations of Cobb's men are great & scandalous, & There is really no method to counteract him but through agents. Wherever men of intelligence are met with, he must lose ground; but his influence in the smaller towns and among the unlearned is sometimes felt."[8]

At about the same time the father was writing to the son, "I have sent you a copy of a Certificate or testimonial from the officers of Yale College, in favor of my books. This you will have published, wherever you may think it necessary or useful, to counteract the misrepresentations of L Cobb.... I know not to what an extent this may be necessary, but I suppose the misrepresentations have been made chiefly in Ohio, Kentucky & Indiana."[9]

N. and J. White wrote Webster on January 7, 1836, "We have rec^{d} several letters from our Agent[.] He is now in the southern counties of the State on the Ohio River. He says that Cobb has made the most extraordinary exertions, and that it was necessary to have something done to counteract him. He has great confidence in the benefits that will be derived from his exertions." And they wrote again on February 15, "Our Agent...has returned.... He has labored manfully and we trust successfully to counteract Cobb. He brought with him one of your Sp Books marked by Cobb himself...."[1]

On April 14, 1837, William Webster wrote his father from aboard the "Steam Boat Troy," "I saw Henry Ellsworth at Indianapolis. He sent you the paper of that place containing Cobb's attack & the reply. I have furnished him with additional armor & he will follow up the affair. But from all I can learn Cobb will do but little in that State...."[2]

Cobb-Griffen Pamphlets, 1836

1. *Review of the Elementary Spelling Book, Compiled by Aaron Ely, and published under the name of Noah Webster, LL.D. Extracted principally from Cobb's Critical Review*.... Sandy Hill, (N.Y.): Griffen, Mabbett, & Co. 1836. (28 pp.) Mainly a reprint of parts of the *Critical Review*, with a four-page introduction signed by Cobb. On the verso of the title is printed the statement of a group of teachers who met in New York in 1829 and rejected the use of the Webster speller.

[8]Webster Papers, New York Public Library.
[9]Pierpont Morgan Library.
[1]Ellsworth Papers, Connecticut Historical Society.
[2]Webster Papers, New York Public Library.

2. *A Summary of some of the Most Prominent Defects in Webster's Elementary Spelling Book, Compiled by Aaron Ely, and published under the name of Noah Webster, LL.D. Compiled from Cobb's Criticisms, by Joseph Griffen.* Sandy Hill, N.Y. Published by Griffen, Mabbett, & Co. 1836. (16 pp.) Consists mostly of lists of inconsistencies and "defects" in Webster's speller; includes the 1829 teachers' statement, as in No. 1, but not Cobb's preface.

3. Presumably one or the other of these pamphlets is referred to in a letter to the editor, signed "An American," published in the *Knickerbocker*, January, 1837 (Vol. IX, pp. 98–99), reprinted in the *Common School Adovcate*, March: "I have before me an examination of Dr. Webster's publications, by one of these spelling-book makers, the compilation of which must have cost the labor of several months. It fell, still-born, from the press; for it is disfigured with personal abuse and ignorance; but it serves to illustrate the zeal and true value of the opposition...."

4. Another edition of No. 1, with added material, was published in New York in 1844. Since Webster was dead and his heirs were busy with arrangements to continue publication of the dictionaries, no notice seems to have been taken of this attack.

Webster and McMinn's Counterattack, 1841–1842

An article, "The Age of Spelling Books," signed by "Teacher," appeared in the *Hampshire Gazette*, November 30, 1841, reprinted in part in the *Boston Courier*, December 3, and the New Haven *Daily Herald*, December 14. The compiler believes that this was written by Webster. It discusses at length the spellers on the market, comparing all others unfavorably with Webster's; those of Cobb are the most fully analyzed and condemned, and Cobb's life and activities and his use of agents are dealt with. "Teacher" asserts that "Cobb failed, and is now a baker in New York. But his booksellers laid one third of the towns in New York under contribution for many years. Last winter the teachers in one County revolted.... In consequence...the papers inform us that Cobb is making a new Spelling Book with Webster's orthography."

Cobb and his works were not entirely a lost cause, however. In 1842 the Superintendent of the Common Schools in Pennsylvania included Cobb's speller, reader, and dictionary in a list of recommended texts. John McMinn of Washington, Pennsylvania, wrote to Webster about this on October 25, 1842, adding that although Cobb's works were in general use, he himself considered Webster's far superior. He says, "I have been requested to give my views on the *books recommended*, through the newspapers of the County. I have just prepared a hasty article in defense of your Books, which are gradually being introduced, on account of their *superiority* alone, even in spite of the exertions of Cobb, and his Agents, and bribed Newspaper editors...."[3]

McMinn's article was published, according to his next letter, but the compiler has not located it. In this letter, November 29, McMinn says he has been censured for criticizing the recommendations of the Superintendent, but that opposition to them is strong in the state, and that Webster's works are gaining ground, though they are hard to procure except in the larger cities. He refers to another article he has written, pointing out the defects in Cobb's works, which has been handed to an editor, who will doubtless publish it.[4] The compiler has not found this article in print.

K. *Attack on Worcester's Dictionary, 1834–1835*

1. Unsigned article, "Webster's Dictionary," in the *Worcester Palladium*, November 26, 1834, accusing Joseph E. Worcester's dictionary of substantial borrowings from Webster's. Although Webster checked this in his copy of the paper (New York Public Library), there is no evidence that he wrote it. When, later in the dispute, Worcester accused him of being the author, Webster did not deny it, though the editor of the *Worcester Palladium* did so on his behalf (No. 9 below).

2. Signed letter from Worcester, December 3, in the *Worcester Palladium*, December 10. Denying the charges, and explaining the nature of his connection with the abridgment of Webster's *American Dictionary*.

3. Signed letter to the editor from Webster, December 11, in the *Worcester Palladium*, December 17, replying to No. 2 and repeating the charges.

4. Unsigned editorial, *Worcester Palladium*, December 24, analyzing Worcester's dictionary and comparing it unfavorably with Webster's.

5. Signed letter from Worcester, January 10, 1835, in the *Worcester Palladium*, January 21, with editorial remarks. Defending himself against Nos. 3 and 4.

6. Signed letter from Webster, January 25, in the *Worcester Palladium*, January 28, resuming the controversy.

[3] Ellsworth Papers, Connecticut Historical Society.
[4] Ibid.

7. Signed letter from Worcester, February 6, in the *Worcester Palladium*, February 11. Citing sources other than Webster from which his material was drawn, and suggesting that Webster was responsible for the initial article.

8. Unsigned editorials supporting Worcester's side of the argument appeared in the *Literary Gazette* (Concord, N.H.), January 30, February 6, and February 20.

9. Signed letter from Webster, February 13, in the *Worcester Palladium*, February 18. With an editorial note denying that Webster wrote or inspired thc initial article in the dispute.

10. Signed letter from Worcester, February 28, in the *Worcester Palladium*, March 11. Further denying the plagiarism charges and taxing Webster with evading the issue of responsibility for the initial article.

11. Signed letter from Webster, March 14, in the *Worcester Palladium*, March 25. After this the exchange of letters was carried on through the mails rather than through the press.

L. *Reactions to "A Voice of Wisdom,"* 1837–1838

1. On November 20, 1837, the *Commercial Advertiser* published an article by Webster, signed "Sidney," discussing the deplorable state of the country (see Part Three of this section, No. 289). It was widely reprinted and had extensive political repercussions, though Webster himself published no replies to its critics.

2. Editorial comment on the article, in the *Montreal Gazette*, November 25, 1837.

3. Editorial comment in the *Daily Albany Argus*, November 30, 1837, reprinted in its weekly edition, December 2. Denouncing the monarchical and Federalist views of the writer, suggesting that he is "an ancient jurist, now in advanced age"—i.e., Chancellor James Kent.

4. Editorial comment in the *Albany Evening Journal*, December 1, 1837, reprinted in the *New Haven Palladium*, December 16. Attacking the article, and asserting that its publication was injurious to the Whig cause; accusing the author of being a monarchist; and denying the implication in No. 3 that Kent was the author. Webster commented on this editorial in an unpublished letter to William L. Stone, editor of the *Commercial Advertiser*, on December 4, 1837.[5]

5. Editorial comment in the *Commercial Advertiser*, December 2, reprinted in the *Spectator*, December 7, and in part in the New York *Morn-*

[5]Fragment, Webster Papers, New York Public Library.

ing Courier, December 11. Defending the article against Nos. 3 and 4, and denying that Kent was the writer.

6. Editorial comment in the *Daily Albany Argus*, December 2, 1837, reprinted in its weekly edition, December 9. Commenting that the quotation of large portions of the article, with approval, by the *Montreal Gazette*, a high Tory paper, shows the "high-toned federal doctrines" of the writer. This gave rise to a subsidiary exchange about Canadian politics.

7. A pamphlet printing of the article (Title 736), probably issued in the first week of December. It contains, in an introductory note, a quotation from No. 5, so it does not antedate December 2; on December 8 Webster, in a letter to William C. Fowler, speaks as if it were in print.[6]

8. Resolution of the Albany Democratic Whig General Committee, in the *Albany Evening Journal*, December 5, 1837, reprinted in the *New York Daily Express*, December 7. Denouncing the principles in the article and objecting to their being foisted on the Whig party in New York state; with editorial comment approving the resolution. Probably also published in the *Albany Daily Advertiser* and the *Daily Albany Argus*, but no copies located; in the *New York Daily Express* reprint there is added editorial approval, condemning those who doubt the ability of the people to govern themselves.

9. Editorial comment in the *Daily Albany Argus*, December 8, 1837, reprinted in its weekly edition, December 16. Referring to a reprint of the article with approval, by the *Columbia Republican* (not located), and declaring that the attribution to Kent was made by a contributor and not by the editor, who does not accept it.

10. Editorial comment in the New York *Morning Courier*, December 11, 1837. Referring to the discussion raging in Albany, doubting Kent's authorship, attacking the article, and disclaiming attempts to foist its ideas on the Whig party.

11. Editorial comment in the New York *Evening Star*, December 11, 1837. Declaring that the editor had not previously taken notice of the article and its "antediluvian opinions," and replying to No. 10. From this point these two papers went off into their own dispute, only indirectly concerned with "Sidney."

12. Editorial, "Our Correspondent Sydney [sic]," in the *Commercial Advertiser*, December 13, 1837, reprinted in the *Spectator*, December 14. Replying to the Albany papers and the New York *Morning Courier*,

[6] In the possession of Mrs. Howard B. Field; transcript courtesy of Prof. Harry R. Warfel.

claiming that, when they opposed Jackson's administration, the latter and the *Albany Evening Journal* expressed the sentiments for which they now blame "Sidney."

13. Editorial comment in the *New York Daily Express*, December 14, 1837. Professing to see in No. 12 an apology for the article, and denying Kent's authorship.

14. Resolution of the Whig Young Men's Committee (New York), in the *Commercial Advertiser*, December 16, 1837, reprinted in the *Spectator*, December 18. Condemning the views expressed in the article; with two different editorial comments disagreeing with the resolution, one headed "Juvenile Indiscretion."

15. Editorial comment in the *New Haven Palladium*, December 16, 1837. Censuring the article and commending the resolution of the Albany Whigs (No. 8).

16. Editorial comment in the *Boston Daily Advocate*, date unknown, reprinted in the Washington *Globe*, December 18. Attacking the article.

17. Editorial comment in the *Albany Evening Journal*, December 18, 1837, reprinted in the *Journal of Commerce*, December 22. Accusing Webster of being the writer of the article. Another comment in the same issue repeats the charge, and says the article is to be reprinted in pamphlet form.

18. Editorial comment in the New York *Morning Courier*, December 18, reprinted in the *Commercial Advertiser*, December 19, and the *Spectator*, December 21. Attacking the editor's sneering comments in No. 14.

19. Editorial comment in the *New York Evening Post*, December 18, 1837. Commenting on the dissension among Whig editors over the article, approving the article as "the precise echo, in better language, of. . .political orthodoxy."

20. Resolution of the General Committee of the Whig Young Men, December 15, in the *New York Gazette*, December 18, 1837, reprinted in the *Commercial Advertiser*, December 19, and the *Spectator*, December 21. Disclaiming "Sidney's" views and their ascription to the Whig party; with approving editorial comment.

21. [Editorial comment in the *Albany Evening Journal*, December 18, 1837. Reviving the question of authorship of the article, pointing to Noah Webster. No copy located; deduced from reply, No. 22.]

22. Editorial comment in the *Daily Albany Argus*, December 19, 1837, reprinted in its weekly edition, December 23. Agreeing that Webster is the likely author. Another comment in the same issue speaks of the debate between Whig editors in New York.

23. Resolutions of the Whig General Committee, December 19, in

the *Commercial Advertiser*, December 20, 1837. Denying Whig party responsibility for sentiments of anonymous newspaper writers, no matter how important the individuals may be. With approving editorial comment, referring to the writer of the original article as the "Great American Unknown."

24. Editorial comment in the Washington *Globe*, December 20, 1837. Surmising that the article was a feeler from the Federalist Whigs, who were alarmed at its reception and now disavow it.

25. On December 21, 1837, Webster wrote two letters, on one sheet, to William L. Stone, editor of the *Commercial Advertiser*. The first is a defense, in the third person, of the article, and the second a personal letter to Stone, signed "The Unknown," telling him to use the defense or not, as he sees fit; apparently Stone did not print it. A postscript adds, "You will be careful not to use any phrase, which will show that I do not live in N York—such as *we have received*. . . ."[7] Printed in Warfel, *Letters of Noah Webster*, pp. 511–512.

26. Although it is undated and so cannot be placed exactly in the sequence, another letter by Webster, probably related to No. 25, is addressed to "Messrs. Editors" and signed "Rutledge," endorsed by him "Sent to be published in N.Y. But returned."[8] This discusses the political situation in the United States, denies that there is any monarchical sentiment, asserts that the United States has made "a wrong choice of three chief magistrates since the days of Washington," and defends "Sidney's" article.

27. Editorial comment in the *Journal of Commerce*, December 22, 1837. Claiming that the exchange of articles in New York has been unimportant; quoting the *Albany Evening Journal* on Webster's authorship (No. 17); and defying the "regency" to make all they can by pamphlet distribution of the article.

28. Editorial titled "Federalism Unmasked," in the *Columbian Register*, December 23, 1837. Summarizing the furor, asserting that the article shows the Whigs to be the old "high-toned federalists," accusing the Whigs of being tainted by association with the Hartford Convention, and attacking the Congressional record of William W. Ellsworth, Whig candidate for the governorship of Connecticut (and one of Webster's sons-in-law).

29. Editorial comment in the *Wayne* (N. Y.) *Sentinel*, date unknown, reprinted in the Washington *Globe*, December 27, 1837. Interpreting the article to call for election of a president for life.

[7] Webster Papers, New York Public Library. [8] Ibid.

30. Editorial comment in the *Globe*, December 26, 1837. Ridiculing No. 27 for suggesting Webster as the author of the article.

31. Editorial comment in the *Commercial Advertiser*, December 29, 1837, reprinted in the *Spectator*, January 1, 1838. Teasing the *Globe* about the authorship of the article.

32. Editorial comment in the *Ithaca Chronicle*, date unknown, reprinted in the *Albany Evening Journal*, December 30, 1837. Attacking Webster as the author of the article, threatening to abandon his orthography for Cobb's if he is "such an inveterate monarchist."

33. Editorial comment in the *Columbian Register*, December 30, 1837. Facetiously discussing the attribution of the article to Webster; based on a comment in the *Albany Advertiser*, not located.

34. Editorial comment in the *New Haven Palladium*, December 30, 1837. Justifying Stone for having printed the article, since he prefaced it with cautionary remarks, and saying the writer should publish under his own name, as being worth hearing.

35. Editorial comment in the *Globe*, January 1, 1838. Stating that 50,000 reprints had been ordered, and promising to try to uncover the true author.

36. Editorial comment in the New York *Evening Star*, January 2, 1838. Chiding the Loco Focos for reprinting the article.

37. Editorial comment in the *Oswego* (N.Y.) *Herald*, date unknown, reprinted in the *Globe*, January 5, 1838. Suggesting that the article was written to please Canadian loyalists, since the *Commercial Advertiser* had a large circulation in Canada.

38. Although not mentioning "Sidney" or his article by name, No. V of a series signed "Poplicola," in the *Commercial Advertiser*, January 9, 1838, reprinted in the *Spectator*, January 15, discusses factions and parties and the general validity of the reaction of the people, in opposition to the views of the article. "Poplicola" was Caleb Cushing, a Whig Representative from Massachusetts. On December 30, 1837, he had written to William L. Stone,"I have read 'Sidney' carefully (as well as 'Marcellus' [Title 735]) & am *disappointed*. Begging your pardon, I think it very shallow & very weak, & I do believe that but for the auspicious paper in which it was published, & above all the preface you gave to the article, it would have fallen stillborn from the press, for the mere want of any inherent vitality of its own. I shall send you two or three nos. upon it."[9]

39. Editorial comment in the *Albany Evening Journal*, January 22, 1838, reprinted in the *Daily Albany Argus*, January 23, and its weekly

[9] Ibid.

edition, January 27. Stating that General White, of the New York legislature, had repudiated the doctrines of the article for himself and his friends. In reprinting this the editor of the *Daily Albany Argus* added critical remarks about it.

40. Report of legislative debates, in the *Daily Albany Argus*, January 24, 1838, reprinted in its weekly edition, January 27. Reporting a debate on a bill regarding licensing of auctioneers, in the course of which the question of the definition of "Federal" and "Federalist" came up, leading to an exchange of remarks about the "Sidney" controversy. The same issues contain a summary of the debates, with editorial comment on this point.

41. Letter to the editor from "a Democrat of the school of '98," in the *Daily Albany Argus*, January 26, 1838, reprinted in its weekly edition, February 3. Attacking the monarchical sentiments of the article.

42. [Editorial comment in the New York *New Era*, date unknown. Stating that a Whig committee in New York had purchased 10,000 copies of a reprint of the article. Not located, and known only from denials in No. 43 and in the *Albany Evening Journal*, January 26, 1838.]

43. Editorial comment in the *Daily Albany Argus*, January 27, 1838, reprinted in its weekly edition, February 3. Stating that Willis Hall, chairman of the New York Whig Young Men's General Committee, denies the statement in No. 42.

44. Report of Mr. Hall's speech in the assembly, in the *Daily Albany Argus*, January 27, 1838, reprinted in the *Albany Evening Journal*, January 31. Part of the debate on the bill of auctioneers (see No. 40), in which Hall refers to "Sidney" and asserts that "the Van Buren party are at this time publishing an edition of Forty Thousand Copies...to be distributed...as coming *from the whigs* and containing whig principles!"

45. In a "Prospectus for the Extra Globe," in the *Globe*, March 7, 1838, proposing a new anti-Federalist newspaper, the editors quote liberally from the original article.

46. Unsigned article, "Whig Activity and Objects," in the *New Era*, June 14, 1838. Critically analyzing the Whig party and its views, citing "Sidney," and accusing Clay and Daniel Webster of monarchical ideas; the article also quotes from "Marcellus" (Title 735). Apparently the *New Era* reprinted "Sidney," but the issue containing the reprint has not been located.

47. In the *New-Yorker*, December 15, 1838, Editor Horace Greeley, in commenting on Webster's denial—in a signed letter in the *Connecticut Observer*, November 17, 1838 (q.v.)—that the propertied classes in America desire a monarchy, takes this to demonstrate that Webster cannot have been "Sidney."

48. From 1838 to 1840 various editors who opposed William L. Stone of the *Commercial Advertiser* used the fact that he had printed the "Sidney" article as a stick wherewith to belabor him; e.g., "A Party is known by the Character of its Leaders," in the *Daily Albany Argus*, September 21, 1840.

49. Editorial comment in the *Commercial Advertiser*, September 24, 1840, reprinted in the *Spectator*, September 26. Denying that Stone had ever endorsed the monarchical sentiments attributed to "Sidney."

M. *"Americanus"-Chapin Controversy, 1841–1842*

1. Series of articles, in the form of letters to the editor, signed "Americanus," in the New Haven *Daily Herald*, November 29, December 2, 9, 17, and 23, 1841 and January 18, 1842. Criticising in detail Alonzo B. Chapin's *English Spelling Book*. Since replies ran concurrently, some of the articles reply to points made in defense by Chapin. "Americanus" was William G. Webster, son of Noah Webster (see No. 13).

2. Series of letters to the editor signed "C," in the *Daily Herald*, November 30 and December 6, 15, and 21, 1841. Replying to No. 1. There seems no doubt that "C" was Chapin, author of the books attacked.

3. Signed letter to the editor from Noah Webster, in the *Daily Herald*, December 20, 1841. Reviewing unfavorably Chapin's book, apparently as an upshot of the exchange of opinions above.

4. Letter to the editor signed "S," in the *Hampshire Gazette*, December 28, 1841, reprinted in the *Daily Herald*, January 4, 1842, and the *New York Tribune*, February 2. Lamenting that after all his useful labors Webster should find his works attacked and plagiarized.

5. Unsigned editorial note in the *Daily Herald*, January 3, 1842. Declining to publish anything further in the dispute.

6. In the Webster Papers, New York Public Library, is an unpublished letter to Webster from "S," dated Northampton, January 24, 1842, expressing the hope that Webster will voluntarily give credit to Dr. William Allen (former president of Bowdoin College) for the words he contributed to recent editions of Webster's dictionaries. "S" states that a reply to No. 4 by "that literary coxcomb Hamersly [sic]"[1] had been sent to the *Hampshire Gazette* and the *Northampton Courier*, but declined by them both.

[1]William J. Hamersley, a partner in the Hartford bookstore of Belknap and Hamersley.

7. Article, "Review of Webster on Orthography," signed by A. B. Chapin, in the *Practical Christian and Church Chronicle*, January 14, 1842, reprinted in the *Daily Herald*, January 29. Attacking Webster's system of orthography and the inconsistencies between his various works. An editorial note (Chapin was the editor) calls attention to the article, saying it is published here because the *Daily Herald* refused it (see No. 11).

8. No. 7 was reprinted as an "Extra" of the newspaper, in the form of an eight-page pamphlet. Copy in The New York Public Library.

9. Signed letter from Webster to the editor, in the *Daily Herald*, January 17, 1842, reprinted in the *Practical Christian and Church Chronicle*, January 28. Replying to No. 7.

10. Signed letter from Webster "To the Public," in the *Practical Christian and Church Chronicle*, January 28, 1842. Defending his works. In an unsigned editorial note in the same issue, headed "Webster's Letter," Chapin comments on and replies to this and No. 9.

11. Unsigned editorial note in the *Daily Herald*, January 29, 1842. In reprinting No. 7, the editor denies that it was submitted to him for publication, saying he intended to ignore the dispute, which he did until No. 7 was published as a pamphlet.

12. *To the Friends of American Education*, signed "Americanus." A seven-page pamphlet dated January, 1842 (no wrappers; caption title). Summarizing the dispute, referring to Nos. 7 and 8. Copy in The New York Public Library.

13. Signed letter from William G. Webster to Chapin, in the *Practical Christian and Church Chronicle*, February 4, 1842. Ending the controversy by saying that the disputants are hopelessly at variance, and the public not interested; declaring that Noah Webster had no hand in the "Amercanus" articles, except insofar as the first was based on some of his notes, and that he did not read them until they were in print.

APPENDIXES

APPENDIX A – CORPORATE WRITINGS BY OR PROBABLY BY WEBSTER

Webster was frequently called upon to draw up pronouncements, constitutions, resolutions, and similar formal declarations for official and unofficial groups with which he was associated. In some instances he himself acknowledged his authorship; in others it can be inferred; and the identification of still other examples is now probably lost beyond recovery. The following corporate writings are those claimed by Webster or imputed to him by the compiler or others.

1

The constitution of the Philological Society in New-York. Instituted, April 7, 1788. New-York: Printed by Harrisson and Purdy.... M.DCC.LXXXVIII.

7 pp. 18 cm. P. [1], title-page. P. [2], blank. Pp. [3]–7, text.
DLC, NN (photostat).
Evans 21320, Sabin 54576.

Webster was the moving spirit of this organization, and its constitution is attributed to him by Professor Allen Walker Read,[2] who reprinted it in *American Speech*, February, 1941 (Vol. XVI, pp. 71–72), in a note supplementary to his article, "The Philological Society of New York, 1788," in the same journal, April, 1934 (Vol. IX, pp. 131–136).

The Society took part in the New York parade marking the adoption of the Federal Constitution. The *New York Daily Advertiser*, August 2, 1788, contains an article, "Federal Procession," describing the celebration. Although this is signed by Richard Platt as chairman, the Yale file of the paper has a marginal note by Webster, "N Webster assisted in drawing up this account," and in his diary for July 26 and 28 he wrote, "Employed in arranging a general account of the procession for the

[2]Letter to the compiler, January 4, 1943.

public" and "Writing an account of the procession." Webster cannot, however, have viewed the procession as a whole, since he marched in it. The article was reprinted in at least ten contemporary newspapers, and later in a pamphlet, *Interesting Documents*... (New York, 1819), pp. [5]–37.

2

[Charitable Society announcements, 1792.]

In the *Connecticut Courant*, November 19, 1792, there appeared a notice, signed by Webster as representative of the Charitable Society, concerning a law for registration of slaves to be freed. It is probable that he also wrote the invitation to the Society's meeting, in the same issue. Activity in the society is shown in his diary for 1793.

3

[Address of Hartford citizens to George Washington, 1793.]

An "Address from the Inhabitants of this city [Hartford], to the President of the United States," dated August 2, signed by Samuel Wyllys as chairman, congratulating Washington on his recent proclamation of neutrality, was published in the *Connecticut Courant*, August 19, 1793. In the Yale file of this paper Webster has written, "For drafting this Address—the Committee were John Trumbull, Chauncey Goodrich & N Webster," and in his diary for July 28 he records, "...drew up Resolutions respecting neutrality of U States." The address was reprinted in the *Middlesex Gazette* and *Dunlap's American Daily Advertiser*, August 24.

4

[New Haven remonstrance, 1801.]

On July 27, 1801, there appeared concurrently in the *Connecticut Courant* and five other newspapers, including Webster's *Commercial Advertiser*, a "Remonstrance of the Merchants of New-Haven on the appointment of Samuel Bishop, Esq. Collector of the Revenue of that port...," over the signatures of Jeremiah Atwater, Elias Shipman, and others. This document was widely reprinted in other papers and in pamphlet form, and evoked a flood of comment pro and con. Although there is no evidence beyond Webster's having noted the article and heavily marked up Jefferson's reply in his copy of the *Connecticut Courant* (now at Yale) and his having, in a manuscript list of pamphlets (New York Public Library), ticked this one with a mark usually indicating his own writings, the compiler believes that Webster wrote the "Remonstrance." He was frequently a ghost writer for civic meetings; he was an avowed opponent of the Bishop family (see his *Rod for the Fool's Back*, Title 723); he strongly disapproved of Jefferson's administration and its actions; and he wrote at length on this particular appointment and on the spoils system in general to James Madison (Ford's *Notes*, Vol. I, pp. 515–522, and Vol. II, pp. 60–63).

One of the pamphlets born of this dispute was *An Examination of the President's Reply to the New-Haven Remonstrance*, published in New York in 1801 under the pseudonym "Lucius Junius Brutus." This has sometimes been attributed to Webster, but his copy of it, now in the Watkinson Library, has his note ascribing it to William Cranch, a brother-in-law of his wife. There was a *Reply to Lucius Junius Brutus's Examination*, also New York, 1801, by "Leonidas." Various replies to "Leonidas" were made in the press, and Webster may have had a hand in these.

5

An act to incorporate the Bank of Connecticut.... [Hartford, 1803.]

2 pp. 20 x 33 cm.
CT.

NOTES

1. The compiler's notes record another copy (not now located), corrected and revised by Webster and endorsed by him, "This bill I drew before I went to Hartford May 1803. It was copied by Mr Judson Canfield & introduced into the House of Representatives—which measure ended in the Act of Assembly of that Session for vesting the moneys of the State in the banks." There are two drafts of the act in the Webster Papers.

2. The act as passed is published in the Connecticut *Acts and Laws Made and Passed in... May... 1803*, pp. 635–636.

6

An address, to the freemen of Connecticut. Hartford: Printed by Hudson & Goodwin. 1803.

6, (1) pp. 22 cm. P. [1], title-page. P. [2], note about a meeting of "the Federal Members" of the General Assembly which resulted in this address, "ordered to be published" by the committee. Pp. [3]–6, text, a discussion of the method of insuring the election of Federalists to the state legislature. P. [7], list of approved Federalist candidates for nomination.

CT, CTHT-W, CTHI, CTY, DLC, ICU, MB, MHI, MWA, NHI, NN.
Sabin 15644 and between 102333 and 102334.

NOTES

1. Reprinted in the New Haven *Visitor*, June 7 and September 13, the *Connecticut Courant*, June 8 and September 7, the *American Citizen*, June 10, the *Republican Watch Tower*, June 11, the *Middlesex Gazette*, June 13 and September 12, the *National Intelligencer*, June 15, the *Spectator*, June 22, the Hudson, N. Y., *Balance*, June 28, and the *Oracle of the Day*, July 2.

2. Although Webster's name nowhere appears in this pamphlet, which is signed (p. 6) by Jonathan Ingersoll and S. Sam Smith, the compiler believes that Webster wrote it. The New-York Historical Society copy has a manuscript note, "Noah Webster Esq. is the reputed author of this pamphlet." See Note 3 on No. 8 below.

7

[New Haven Chamber of Commerce to Thomas Jefferson, 1806.]

In the *Connecticut Herald*, February 11, 1806, is a "Memorial of the Chamber of Commerce in New-Haven" to the President and Congress, dated February 7, and signed by Henry Daggett, President, on British policy towards neutral trade, impressment of seamen, etc. The New York Public Library file of this paper contains a note by Webster suggesting his authorship. The article was reprinted in the *New England Palladium*, February 21.

8

An address, to the freemen of Connecticut. Hartford; printed by Hudson & Goodwin. 1806.

7 pp. 23 cm. P. [1], title-page. P. [2], blank. Pp. [3]–7, text, preceded by an introductory note signed by Elijah Hubbard, Hartford, May 24, 1806.

CSMH, CT, CTHT-W, CTHI, CTY, MAJ, MWA, NN, RPB, Merriam.
Sabin 15645 and 102334.

NOTES

1. Reprinted in the *Connecticut Courant*, August 27.

2. A satirical paraphrase was published in the *American Mercury*, June 5.

3. Believed by the compiler to have been written by Webster, though not acknowledged by him. A copy formerly in her possession was endorsed by him "N° 2," suggesting that No. 6 above was the first.

9

[Charitable Society notices, 1807.]

It is very likely that Webster wrote or helped write the constitution of the Charitable Society, published in the *Connecticut Herald*, February 10, 1807. He wrote the call to a meeting to organize the society, in the same paper on January 20 (paraphed on a clipping in The New York Public Library), and later an article about the society in the issue of February 17 (see Part Three of this section, No. 154).

10

[Citizens of New Haven to Thomas Jefferson, 1808.]

A "Memorial of the Inhabitants of the Town of New-Haven" to the President, against the embargo, was published in the *Connecticut Journal*, September 1, 1808. Webster was one of the signers, and one of the committee of five which prepared the document. A manuscript of it is in the Webster Papers. It was reprinted in the *Commercial Advertiser*, September 3, the *Connecticut Herald*, and the *New England Palladium*, September 6, the *Connecticut Courant*, September 7, the *Middlesex Gazette*, September 8, and the Hudson, N. Y., *Balance*, September 13.

11

[New Haven anti-embargo resolutions, 1809.]

In the *Connecticut Herald*, January 31, 1809, there appeared some resolutions by the residents of New Haven against the embargo, signed by Elisha Munson as town clerk. The MS, in the Webster Papers, is endorsed by Webster, "First draft. Jan^{y}, 1809. The resolutions as transcribed & altered I presented to the Committee of the town—& they were adopted without the smallest alteration. The resolutions adopted at the subsequent meeting, I drafted also, but as a member of a committee. They were adopted as I offered them." Reprinted in the *Connecticut Journal*, February 2, the *Commercial Advertiser*, February 3, and the *Middlesex Gazette*, February 9.

12

New Haven, May 1, 1811. The subscribers have been appointed. . . .

Two leaves, printed only on recto of first. 25 x 20 cm.
MiDeaEd, NN.

NOTES

1. A protest against the Non-Importation Act, inviting merchants and citizens of other commercial towns to unite with the New Haven Chamber of Commerce in memorializing the General Assembly and the President on the subject. The Henry Ford Museum copy bears the signatures of the seven members of the committee, Webster being one of them.

2. A draft and two manuscript copies are in the Webster Papers, one endorsed by Webster, "Letter from the Chamber of Commerce, N Haven May. 1811. drafted for the Committee by N Webster. . . ." There is also the draft of resolutions of a similar tenor adopted by the citizens. Both the invitation and the "Patriotic Resolutions," the latter dated May 4 and signed by Elisha Munson, town clerk, were published in the *Connecticut Herald*, May 7. Webster indicated his authorship of the latter on a clipping in The New York Public Library. The resolutions were reprinted in the *Connecticut Journal*, May 9, the *Connecticut Courant*, May 15, the *Middlesex Gazette*, May 23, and the *Columbian Museum*, May 30.

3. In the *Connecticut Herald* of May 28 appeared further resolutions of a like nature from East Haven, signed by Bela Farnham, town clerk. A clipping of these in The New York Public Library is annotated by Webster, "Written by N. Webster at the request of the committee of the town." A petition to the President, published in the *Connecticut Journal*, June 13, may also have been written by Webster.

13

Sir, the multiplied evils. . . . Joseph Lyman, chairman. [Northampton? 1814.]

Broadside, 33 x 21 cm.
NN.

NOTES

1. An analysis of the military and political situation in New England, with an invitation to towns in Hampshire, Franklin, and Hampden counties, Massachusetts, to petition the General Court to call a convention. Undated, but probably issued in late January or early February, 1814.

2. Webster's authorship is attested by his endorsement on the copy located: "At the meeting convened at Northampton, Jany 19, 1814.... After consultation, & a proposition made by N Webster that a Convention of Delegates...should be requested by the several towns, N Webster, Mr. Williams of Deerfield & Lewis Strong, were appointed a Committee to draft a Circular Letter to the towns—& this task fell upon N Webster, who made a draft, which, with a few alterations, appears as printed within...." He also endorsed the broadside, "This is the germ of the celebrated Hartford Convention. NW."

3. Reprinted in Webster's *Collection of Papers*, 1843, and in Ford's *Notes*, Vol. II, pp. 125–128, where it is erroneously dated January 5, which was the date of Judge Lyman's letter calling the January 19 meeting.

14

[Hampshire Bible Society constitution, 1816.]

Webster was one of the directors of the Hampshire Bible Society, and may well have had a hand in drawing up its constitution and a circular letter of July 24, 1816, appealing for contributions and memberships, of which he was one of six signers (copy in The New York Public Library).

15

To the Rev. [blank] Sir, the trustees of Amherst Academy have, for some time past, contemplated the establishment of a charitable institution, for the purpose of educating pious indigent young men for the gospel-ministry.... Amherst, Sept. 11, 1818.... [Northampton(?), 1818.]

Two leaves, printed only on recto of first. 25 x 19 cm.
NN.

NOTES

1. This invitation to a meeting to discuss the proposed "charitable institution" (now Amherst College) is signed by Webster as one of a committee of three. He may well have written it.

2. Reprinted: *Hampshire Gazette*, November 10, following an article, signed "Plain Dealing," opposing the plan; Webster's *Collection of Papers*, 1843, pp. 234–235; Frederick Tuckerman, *Amherst Academy* (Amherst, 1929), pp. 236–237.

3. The constitution and by-laws for the endowment fund are reprinted in the *Collection of Papers* (pp. 227–234), though they were not written by Webster, but by Colonel Rufus Graves. Webster does, however, seem to have written the memorandum of reasons for moving Williams College to Amherst, presented to a Williams College committee in May, 1819 (*Collection of Papers*, pp. 239–243).[3] For other writings by Webster on behalf of Amherst College, see Part Three of this section, Nos. 188–190, 192.

4. There was no press in Amherst at this time. Printing for Amherst Academy was probably done in Northampton.

16

[Massachusetts Legislature's reply to the Governor, 1819.]

Webster's authorship of an "answer to the Address of the Governor [of Massachusetts], May Session," in the *Columbian Centinel*, June 5, 1819, is shown by the manuscript draft in the Webster Papers and by his use of the item in his *Collection of Papers*, 1843. It was also reprinted in the *Hampshire Gazette*, June 15, 1819, and in Warfel, *Letters of Noah Webster*, pp. 396–399.

17

Commonwealth of Massachusetts. In the year of Our Lord eighteen hundred and twenty. An act to establish a permanent fund for the support of public schools.... [Boston, 1820?]

[3]Tuckerman (op. cit., pp. 237–239) prints a document headed "Reasons for Removing Williams College to Amherst," footnoting it with a reference to the *Collection of Papers*. The text he gives is only part of that found in Webster's book, however, and is less polished. Therefore it may be closer to the original manuscript, which the compiler has not located.

4 pp. 24 cm.
NN.

Apparently written by Webster. One copy is endorsed in his hand, "By N Webster. The plan did not suceed [sic]" and another, "NW proposed but not adopted" and "Introduced by N Webster but not adopted."

18

[Amherst Sunday School documents, 1820.]

Since the manuscript of it is in his hand, Webster was probably the author of the constitution or "Plan" for the Sunday School of the First Parish, Amherst, adopted April 12, 1820. On April 18 he was elected chairman of the Board of Managers of the school, and it is also likely that he wrote its regulations, which were adopted on July 3. The two documents and the minutes of the meetings of the three dates mentioned are found in an unidentified clipping (probably from an Amherst paper of the late nineteenth century) in the Webster Papers. This was the first Sunday School in Amherst.

19

[Amherst College material, 1821.]

A notice of the election of officers and the rules for admission to the newly-formed Amherst College, signed by Webster as president of the Board of Trustees, were published in the *Hampshire Gazette*, June 20, 1821. He probably wrote other material about Amherst in the newspapers in 1821 and 1822; see note on No. 15, above.

20

[Resolutions on Greek independence, 1823.]

In December, 1823, three items relating to Greek independence, signed by Webster as chairman of a meeting to consider the subject, appeared in the papers. The minutes of a preliminary meeting were in the *Connecticut Journal*, the *Connecticut Courant*, and the *Connecticut Herald* of December 23. The *Journal* and the *Herald* for December 30 contain resolutions supporting the cause of Greek independence and an "Address to the Citizens of New Haven...." The "Address," which was reprinted in the *Religious Intelligencer*, January 3, 1824, is annotated by Webster, "N Webster & C A Goodrich," on a clipping in The New York Public Library.

21

[Fayetteville fire committee address, 1831.]

Webster is one of the signers and the possible author of an "Address" of a committee seeking funds to relieve sufferers from a fire in Fayetteville, N.C., printed in the *Connecticut Journal* and *Connecticut Herald*, June 14, 1831.

22

[New Haven resolution on the death of Lafayette, 1834.]

Webster's name appears as one of a committee of five which drew up a resolution of condolence from the citizens of New Haven to the family of Lafayette upon the latter's death, published in the *Connecticut Herald*, August 12, 1834.

23

[New Haven anti-abolitionist resolutions, 1835.]

The New Haven *Daily Herald*, September 11, 1835, published the resolutions of a public meeting condemning abolitionist activities, Webster being one of the five vice-presidents and one of the signers of the resolutions. Reprinted in the *New Haven Palladium*, September 12, and the *Religious Intelligencer*, September 19.

24

[Common School Convention report, 1838.]

A report of a "Common School Convention" in New Haven, signed by Webster as president, appeared in the New Haven *Daily Herald*, November 15, 1838, reprinted in the *New Haven Palladium*, November 28.

APPENDIX B – WEBSTER'S LECTURES AND SPEECHES

When Webster was teaching in Baltimore in the latter part of 1785, he composed a series of five lectures on the English language. The inception and progress of the writing are noted in his diary between August 25 and October 6. He presented the series for the first time between October 19 and 26, the entry for the final date in his diary being: "Read my fifth & last Lecture & close my school. The Lectures have rec^{d} so much applause that I am induced to revise & continue reading them in other towns."[4]

This he did, addressing audiences up and down the Eastern seaboard for about fifteen months. The series was expanded and altered from time to time, and in smaller communities Webster sometimes gave only one or two of the lectures. He also delivered lectures on other subjects in the large cities. The series on language became the basis of his *Dissertations on the English Language*, 1789.

Teaching, politics, courtship, and other preoccupations in Philadelphia in 1787 caused Webster to give up lecturing, which had helped him gain income and repute, but he continued throughout his life to give occasional addresses, lectures, and speeches, particularly in his late years, when he had become something of a sage, and a survivor of the Revolutionary War period.

Only a fraction of Webster's lectures were printed; those that were have been listed in the main body of the present work. The following list records his known platform appearances and the accompanying newspaper or other references. Those listed under 1785, 1786, and 1787 represent all or part of the series on language, unless otherwise noted. Reference to all the dates in these years, sometimes with brief comment, is found in Webster's diary.

1785

October 19, 21, 22, 24, 25, and 26, Baltimore, in Dr. Allison's church. The next to last lecture was a repetition of the first. Price, one quarter

[4]Ford's *Notes*, Vol. I, p. 141.

dollar for single lectures, 7s. 6d. for the series. Advertised in the *Maryland Gazette* and *Maryland Journal*, October 18.

November 17, 18, 22, and 24, Richmond, in the Capitol. An unsigned letter headed Richmond, November 26, praising the series, was printed in the *Newport* (R.I.) *Mercury*, December 19. The compiler suspects that Webster wrote this himself.

It is not clear whether Webster lectured in Petersburg on November 29. His diary records his arrival there on November 26 and on November 28 says, "Procure Mason Hall to read a Lecture in tomorrow evening." The entry for the 29th is "Disappointed,"[5] which might mean either that the attendance was poor, or that the lecture was not held at all.

December 6, 7, 8, and 9, Williamsburg, in a room of the College of William and Mary.

December 21 and 23, Alexandria. The second lecture, scheduled for the 22nd, was postponed because of inadequate publicity.[6]

1786

January 5, 6, and 7, Annapolis, in the State House. A "Fragment of a letter from a gentleman in Annapolis to his friend in this town [Baltimore]," praising the series, appeared in the *Maryland Gazette*, January 10, reprinted in the *Pennsylvania Mercury*, January 20, and the *Connecticut Courant*, January 30.

January 14, 16, and 17, Frederick. At first "to a small company," but later "to a more numerous audience."

February 8, 10, 11, and 13, Wilmington, in the Academy. An unsigned letter headed Wilmington, February 8, praising the series, was printed in the *New Haven Gazette*, March 23. Webster's comment at the end of the series was "Read my last Lecture to a crouded audience, whose applause is flattering. More taste for science in these States than below."[7]

February 28, March 2, 4, 7, 9, and 11, Philadelphia, in a room at the University of Pennsylvania. Advertised in the *Pennsylvania Evening Herald*, February 22 and 25, the *Pennsylvania Packet*, February 26, March 10 and 11, and the *Independent Gazetteer*, March 11. A favorable review of the first lecture appeared in the *Pennsylvania Packet*, March 2, and a short news item that Webster was lecturing in Philadelphia in the *New Haven Gazette*, March 9.

[5]Ibid., p. 143.
[6]Ibid., p. 145.
[7]Ibid., p. 149 (February 13, 1786).

March 15, Philadelphia. A lecture "on the connection between property and power; the difference in the constitutions of government, the literary, agricultural, and commercial improvements of the united states, with remarks on slavery, climate, &c."[8] given for the benefit of the Pennsylvania Hospital. Advertised in the *Pennsylvania Evening Herald*, March 11 and 15, the *Independent Gazetteer*, March 11, and the *Pennsylvania Journal*, *Pennsylvania Gazette*, and *Freeman's Journal*, March 15.

A signed advertisement by Webster, dated March 13, appeared in the *Pennsylvania Packet*, March 14, 15, and 16 and in the *Freeman's Journal* and *Pennsylvania Evening Herald*, March 15, announcing a repetition of the lecture which dealt with education, if a sufficient number of persons subscribed. Apparently this never took place.

From March 21 to 24 Webster was in Princeton, but was unable to secure an adequate subscription for a lecture series, despite the encouragement of the college authorities. He wrote to Timothy Pickering that the students were preparing for examinations, and that they had no cash.[9]

April 6, 11, 13, 15, 18, 20, 25, and 27, New York, in the City Hall, the fourth lecture being a repetition of the first. Advertised in the New York *Daily Advertiser*, March 31–April 26 at intervals, the *New York Gazetteer*, March 31 and April 4, and the *New York Packet*, April 6, 10, 13, and 20. A note about the New York presentation of the series appeared in the *New Haven Gazette*, April 6. On April 11 the *Daily Advertiser* published a review of the first lecture, praising the intent and content, but critical of the delivery and certain ideas advanced. Webster replied with a signed letter dated April 12, published in the issue of April 13, to which the original "Correspondent" replied in the issue of April 18. Webster was supported by editorial comment in the issue of April 17, though Professor Warfel, in his biography of Webster, thinks that the initial criticism was written by the editor, Francis Childs.

April 29, New York. A lecture on the United States, not part of the series.

May 11, 12, 13, 16, 17, and 18, Albany. Webster complained of poor attendance, saying, "The Dutch have no taste for the English language."[1]

June 6, 7, 8, 9, 12, and 13, Hartford. The first lecture was held in the North Meeting House, but led to disturbances, Webster recording in his "Lesser Journal," "Begin my lectures . . . ; disturbed by a mob. Let it be remembered that in the year 1786, there are in Hartford people so

[8] *Pennsylvania Evening Herald*, March 11, 1786.

[9] March 24, 1786, Pickering Papers, Massachusetts Historical Society; Ford's *Notes*, Vol. I, p. 152, n 3.

[1] In his "Lesser Journal;" Ford's *Notes*, Vol. I, p. 156, n 1.

illiberal, that they will not permit Lectures to be read in a Church because they cannot be admitted without paying two shillings! The General Assembly to whom I presented Tickets, attended. They ought at least to have been secured from the insults of wealthy farmers."[2] Webster "obtained permission of the Govr & Upper House to read in the State House, but it was judged not prudent," so the rest of the series was delivered "at Mr Colliers dancing Room."[3] Advertised in the *Connecticut Courant*, June 5, though the advertisement describes a lecture on government, etc., rather than the series on language. For a further comment on the Hartford reception, see that on New Haven below.

June 19, 21, 22, 23, 26, 28, and 30, New Haven, in the State House, the third lecture being a repetition of the first. The series was favorably reviewed in the *New Haven Gazette*, June 29, reprinted in the *Massachusetts Gazette*, July 3, and the *Newport Mercury*, July 17. On June 30 Webster wrote to Timothy Pickering, "I read my Lectures to a few friends in Hartford, but most people paid no attention to them. I was at home. In New Haven I have about 70 hearers, consisting of the best families in town, and a few scholars; a greater number in proportion to the size of the town than I have had before; and they seem more pleased with the plan than any audience I have had."[4] In connection with the New Haven lecture series there was issued a broadside "Syllabus" of the series, dated June 15, already described (Title 737).

July 13, 17, 21, 24, 26, (28?), and 31, Boston, in "Mr. Hunt's School House." Price for the series, 12s. for gentlemen, 6s. for ladies. Advertised in the *Massachusetts Gazette*, July 10, 13, 17, and 31, the *Massachusetts Centinel*, July 12 and 26, and the *Boston Gazette*, July 17. The first lecture was favorably reviewed in the *Massachusetts Centinel*, July 15, reprinted in the *New Haven Gazette*, July 27. Delivery of a lecture on the 28th is recorded in Webster's "Lesser Journal," but not in his diary.[5]

July 29, Boston. An out-of-series lecture on politics.

August 4, 7, 9, 11, 14, and 16, Salem, in "Mr Noyes's school house."

August 21, 24, 25, 28, 29, and 30, Portsmouth, in "the Assembly room." Advertised in the *New Hampshire Mercury*, August 23 and 30.

September 1, 6, and 7, Newburyport, in "Mr. Long's School House." Advertised in the *Essex Journal*, September 6.

September 19, Boston, in Fanueil Hall. A repetition of the lecture on

[2]Ibid., p. 157, n 3.

[3]Ibid., p. 158 (sub June 7) and n 1.

[4]Pickering Papers, Massachusetts Historical Society; Ford's *Notes*, Vol. I, p. 159, n 3.

[5]Ford's *Notes*, Vol. I, p. 162.

education from the series given earlier. Advertised in the *Massachusetts Gazette*, September 15, and the *Massachusetts Centinel*, September 16.

September 25, 26, 27, 28, and 29, Providence. Advertised in the *United States Chronicle*, September 28.

October 4, 9, 10, and 11, Newport, in Mr. Roger's Academy. Price, 7s. 6d. Advertised in the *Newport Mercury*, October 2. The advertisement says that "A Syllabus will be delivered with the Tickets," which may mean that the New Haven syllabus (above, June 19) was still being used, or that similar broadsides were printed for other presentations of the series.

October 17, New London.

October 24 and 25, Norwich.

November 27, 29, and 30 and December 1 and 6, New Haven.

December 19, New York, in "Mr. Hulett's Dancing Room, in Little-Queen-Street." Price, 4s. A repetition of the lecture on education from the series. Advertised in the *Daily Advertiser*, December 16 and 18, as the beginning of a short series, but no later lecture is recorded in Webster's diary.

1787

Apparently with a new year Webster planned a new series of lectures, but it did not develop beyond its original presentation in Philadelphia, at the University of Pennsylvania. He records in his diary that on January 2 he published subscription papers for a course of lectures, and that on January 3 he received permission to use the University facilities.[6] If these were printed papers, no copy has been located by the compiler. A series on "Language, Education, & Government" was advertised in the *Pennsylvania Packet*, January 6 and later.

The first lecture, on "the repugnancy between our Manners and Government," was advertised in the *Pennsylvania Packet*, January 26 and 27, and the *Independent Gazetteer*, January 26, and was delivered on the 27th. A second lecture, on government, paper money, inflation, and speculation, was announced in the same papers of February 5th and 6th, and was delivered on the 6th. In the *Independent Gazetteer*, February 7, there was a letter signed "Juvenis," gibing at Webster for the number of subjects covered by his lectures. A reply in the third person, declining to be drawn into controversy, appeared in the issue of February 8. A final lecture, on the reform of the alphabet, was delivered on the 24th; it

[6]Ibid., p. [208].

had been announced in the *Pennsylvania Packet*, February 22, 23, and 24, and the *Pennsylvania Herald*, February 24. A series of four newspaper articles published initially in the *Pennsylvania Packet* between February 15 and 21 (q.v., Section Nine, Part Three, No. 52), was based on the lectures which Webster was delivering at this time.

1788

As noted in his diary, on April 28 Webster read a paper before the Philological Society of New York, of which he was one of the moving spirits.

1793

May 9, New Haven. Oration before the Society for Promotion of Freedom. This was published as a pamphlet, *Effects of Slavery*, 1793 (Title 720).

1798

July 4, New Haven. Webster's Fourth of July oration was published, and is described above as Title 738.

1799

June 10, Hartford. "A Dissertation on the supposed Change in the Temperature of Winter," read at the Connecticut Academy of Arts and Sciences. Published by the Academy in 1810 (Title 799).

1802

July 4, New Haven. Another Fourth of July oration which was published; Title 739.

1808

October 25, New Haven. A discourse on racial tolerance, given before the Connecticut Academy of Arts and Sciences. The manuscript is in the Webster Papers, New York Public Library.

1814

July 4, Amherst. A Fourth of July oration delivered before the Knox and Warren branches of the Washington Benevolent Society. This was published; see Title 740.

Lectures and Speeches

1818

October 14, Northampton. Address before the Hampshire, Franklin, and Hampden Agricultural Society's annual meeting, on agricultural topics. This was published; Title 741.

1820

August 9, Amherst. Address at the laying of the cornerstone of Amherst College. Published in a volume with the sermon on the same occasion by Daniel A. Clark; Title 742.

1821

September 18, Amherst. Webster made the "introductory remarks" at the ceremony of inauguration of Zephaniah S. Moore as first president of Amherst College.

1824

July 4, aboard the *Edward Quesnel.* William G. Webster notes in his journal of the trip to France and England that his father gave a short patriotic talk to his fellow passengers.

November 23, Cambridge (England). Impromptu remarks before the Cambridge Bible Society. Reported in the *Cambridge Chronicle and Journal and Huntingdonshire Gazette,* November 26.[7]

1830

November 10, Hartford. Lecture, on educational problems, in the City Hall before a "Literary Convention," of which Webster was the president. Reported in the *Connecticut Mirror,* November 13, the *New England Weekly Review,* November 15, the *Connecticut Courant,* November 16, and the *Boston Courier,* November 18.

1831

January 3, Washington. A lecture before the House of Representatives on the English language. Reported in the *Daily National Intelligencer,* January 8, and the *Connecticut Herald,* January 11; the latter

[7]Reference courtesy of the Cambridge University Library. See Webster's letter to his wife about the occasion, Ford's *Notes,* Vol. II, pp. 264–265.

quoted the *United States Gazette* to the effect that the House was an appropriate audience, for its members were those who abused the language most.

[July ?], Portland. A note in the *Connecticut Herald,* July 19, reprinted in *Niles' Weekly Register,* August 6, makes a brief quotation from "a public lecture lately delivered at Portland" by Noah Webster.

1835

The *New Haven Palladium* of September 12 mentions a speech by Webster at a public meeting to discuss the activities of the abolitionists.

1839

August 6, Litchfield. Lecture on "the inaccuracy of words in the English language," in the Court House. Reported in the *Litchfield Enquirer,* August 8, and the New Haven *Daily Herald,* August 12.

On August 29 the annual meeting of the American Institute of Instruction was held in Springfield, Massachusetts. Webster was present, and according to newspaper reports in the *Connecticut Courant,* August 31, and the *Boston Recorder,* September 6, he had been invited to speak; but there is no reference to the fact that he did.

October 2, New Haven. Two lectures (afternoon and evening) on language and textbooks, in the Free Church. Announced by Webster in a signed notice in the New Haven *Daily Herald,* September 12 and 14, and further announced in the same paper on October 1 and 2. Reported in the *New Haven Record,* October 5, reprinted in the New Haven *Daily Herald,* October 7. On October 12 the former paper published a letter signed "Cheever," urging that Webster publish the lectures; replied to by Webster in a signed article in the same paper on October 19, pointing out that his views were already in print in his books.

1840

April 21, Hartford. Historical account of Connecticut, given at the Center Church at a meeting of the Connecticut Historical Society to celebrate the bicentennial of the state constitution. Announced in the *Connecticut Courant* and the New Haven *Daily Herald,* October 26, 1839, *Hartford Daily Courant,* January 29, 1840, and again on April 21, *Connecticut Observer,* February 8, *Connecticut Courant,* April 18 (also in *Niles' Weekly Register,* April 25, though by that date the occasion had already taken place). Reported in the *Hartford Daily Courant,* April 22,

24, 25, 26, 28, 29, and 30 and May 1, 2, and 4; New Haven *Daily Herald*, April 22; *Connecticut Courant, Connecticut Observer*, and *New England Weekly Review*, April 25; New Haven *Evening Palladium*, April 29; *New Haven Record* and the *Log Cabin*, May 2; and *Niles' Weekly Register* and the *Hingham Patriot*, May 9. The *Hartford Daily Courant* on May 9 presented a supplement to describe the occasion. The manuscript of this address is in the Webster Papers (see Appendix D), and The New York Public Library also has a copy of the program.

July 4, New Haven. Talk to the children at a Sunday School Fourth of July celebration. Excerpt in the New Haven *Daily Herald*, July 21, reprinted in *Niles' Weekly Register*, August 22. A signed letter from Webster, making certain corrections, appeared in the former, July 22. The manuscript is in the Webster Papers.

1842

June 29, Hartford, in Gilman's saloon. Lecture "on the origin and history of political parties in the United States; on the defects of the Constitution; and on the permanent causes of our public Evils." Announced in the *Hartford Daily Courant*, June 29, and reported in the *Boston Courier*, July 1, the editor suggesting that the lecture would be well received in Boston.

July 4, Amherst. A "discourse . . . upon the history of Political Parties since the commencement of the Government." Reported in the New Haven *Daily Herald*, July 21, and the *Northampton Courier*, August 2. The former suggested that the remarks be printed, to which Webster replied in a signed letter, published in the issue of July 25, declining to allow publication.

APPENDIX C – PUBLISHED PERSONAL LETTERS OF WEBSTER

The following list is restricted to letters which were not written for publication; for letters so intended, see Section Nine. Letters from which excerpts are given in the course of a secondary study are not recorded—e.g., five sentences from Webster to Oliver Wolcott, September 17, 1800, in Richard J. Purcell, *Connecticut in Transition, 1775–1818* (Washington and London, 1918), p. 235, n. 18—because in most cases such quotations come from the published versions cited below. This exclusion extends even to Professor Warfel's biography of Webster, since all the letters from which he quotes extensively therein are given in his later collection of Webster letters.

The four works in which almost all published Webster letters are found have been given catch-references, as follows:

Notes, for Emily E. F. Ford, comp., *Notes on the Life of Noah Webster* (2 vols., New York, 1912).

Letters, for Harry R. Warfel, ed., *Letters of Noah Webster* (New York, [1954]).

Proceedings, for the Massachusetts Historical Society's *Proceedings*.

Collections, for the same Society's *Collections*.

Other books are cited by the author's surname or the first word or two of the title. They include:

Baldwin, Simeon E., ed., *Life and Letters of Simeon Baldwin* (New Haven, [1919]).

Beardsley, Eben E., *Life and Times of William Samuel Johnson*... (New York, 1876).

Bradsher, Earl L., *Mathew Carey*... (New York, 1912).

Connor, Eva G., comp., *Letters to Children* (New York, 1938).

Felt, Joseph B., *Memorials of William Smith Shaw* (Boston, 1852).

First Century of National Existence... (Hartford and San Francisco, 1872).

King, Charles R., ed., *Life and Correspondence of Rufus King*... (6 vols., New York, 1894–1900).

Report of the Committee of the House of Representatives... appointed to prepare... articles of impeachment against William Blount... [Philadelphia, 1797].

Sparks, Jared, ed., *Correspondence of the American Revolution...* (4 vols., Boston, 1853).

Stokes, Anson B., *Memorials of Eminent Yale Men...* (2 vols., New Haven, 1914).

Thomas, Ebenezer S., *Reminiscences...* (2 vols., Hartford, 1840).

Todd, Charles B., *Life and Letters of Joel Barlow...* (New York and London, 1886).

Tuckerman, Frederick, *Amherst Academy... 1814–1861* (Amherst, 1929).

Webster, Noah, *Collection of Papers...* (New York, etc., 1843).

Wells, William V., *Life and Public Services of Samuel Adams...* (3 vols., Boston, 1865).

Wolcott, Samuel, *Memorial of Henry Wolcott... and... Descendants* (New York, 1881).

York Town... (Brooklyn, 1881). (Title 765 of the present work.)

Names of magazines and other serials are written out or abbreviated in forms which should be readily intelligible.

DATE	ADDRESSEE	PRINTED
	1783	
January 6	John Canfield	*Notes*, I: 57–58 (part) *Letters*, 3–4
	1784	
March 24	Samuel Adams	*Notes*, II: 450–451 *Letters*, 7–8 Wells, III: 207–208
July 5	James Madison	*Letters*, 8–9
	1785	
July 18	George Washington	*Notes*, I: 92–93 *Letters*, 36–37 Sparks, IV: 111–112
August 22	Hudson and Goodwin	*Letters*, 37–38

October 28	Timothy Pickering	*Notes*, I: 99–101 (part) *Letters*, 38–39 *Proceedings*, 43: 123–124 (misdated 1786)
December 16	George Washington	*Letters*, 39–41
December 18	George Washington	*Notes*, I: 107–108 *Letters*, 41–43

1786

January 20	Timothy Pickering	*Notes*, I: 147–148n *Letters*, 43–44 *Proceedings*, 43: 124–125
March 22	Hudson and Goodwin	*Letters*, 45–46
March 24	Timothy Pickering	*Notes*, I: 152–153n *Proceedings*, 43: 125
March 31	George Washington	*Notes*, I: 110 *Letters*, 46
April 9	Timothy Pickering	*Proceedings*, 43: 126
April 14	Mary Coxe	*Notes*, I: 114 (part)
April 25	Timothy Pickering	*Notes*, I: 101 *Proceedings*, 43: 126–127
May 12	Timothy Pickering	*Proceedings*, 43: 127–128
May 21	Timothy Pickering	*Proceedings*, 43: 128
May 24	Benjamin Franklin	*Notes*, II: 455–456 *Letters*, 49–51 *Hist. Mag.*, III (1859): 119
May 25	Timothy Pickering	*Notes*, I: 156–157n *Letters*, 51–52 *Proceedings*, 43: 128–129
June 23	Benjamin Franklin	*Notes*, II: 457–458 *Letters*, 52–53 *Hist. Mag.*, III (1859): 119–120
June 30	Timothy Pickering	*Notes*, I: 159n *Proceedings*, 43: 129–130

August 10	Timothy Pickering	*Notes*, I: 117–118, 163n (part) *Letters*, 53–55 *Proceedings*, 43: 130–131
September 13	Timothy Pickering	*Proceedings*, 43: 132
October 28	Benjamin Franklin	*Notes*, II: 405–406 *Letters*, 55–56

1787

[January 5?][8]	Benjamin Franklin	*Notes*, II: 454 *Letters*, 44–45 (under 1786)
March 15	James Bowdoin	*Collections*, Ser. 7, Vol. 6: 173–183[9]
June 20	Rebecca Greenleaf	*Letters*, 68–69
August 28	Rebecca Greenleaf	*Letters*, 69–70
September 15	Rebecca Greenleaf	*Letters*, 70–71
October 11	Rebecca Greenleaf	*Letters*, 71–73
December 19	William Young	*Notes*, II: 406–407

1788

January 27	Rebecca Greenleaf	*Letters*, 73–74
February 9	Jeremy Belknap	*Letters*, 74–76 *Collections*, Ser. 6, Vol. 4: 385–387
February 10	Benjamin Rush	*Notes*, I: 176–177 (part)
February 10	Rebecca Greenleaf	*Letters*, 76–78
February 24	Benjamin Rush	*Notes*, I: 177–178
June 24	[Hudson and Goodwin?]	*Amer. Hist. Record*, I (1872): 374

[8] Although Webster was in Philadelphia in 1786, the compiler believes that this undated letter belongs early in 1787, on the basis of his movements and references in the letter to the forthcoming *American Selection*.

[9] Although this letter was not intended for publication, it was printed in the *Pennsylvania Herald* and the *Pennsylvania Packet*, May 16, 1787.

July 14	George Washington	*Notes*, I: 180–181 *Letters*, 78–79 Webster, 166–167 *York Town*
July 31	William Young[1]	
August 31	Elisha Babcock	Stokes, I: 321
September 4	Hudson and Goodwin	*Letters*, 79–80
November 24	William Young	Yale U. Lib. *Gazette*, IX (1935): 99–100 (part)[2]
	1789	
January 31	Mason F. Cogswell	*Letters*, 80–81
February 1	James Greenleaf	*Notes*, II: 407–409 *Letters*, 81–83
February 15	James Greenleaf	*Notes*, I: 197–198 *Letters*, 83–85
May 7	Jeremy Belknap	*Collections*, Ser. 6, Vol. 4: 430
May 16	James Greenleaf	*Notes*, II: 409–410
May 20	Benjamin Franklin	*Notes*, II: 458
June 6	James Greenleaf	*Notes*, II: 411–412
August 12	James Greenleaf	*Notes*, I: 203–204
September 19	Jeremy Belknap	*Notes*, I: 205–206 *Proceedings*, 43: 133
September 20	James Greenleaf	*Notes*, I: 206–207
October 12	James Greenleaf	*Notes*, II: 412–415
December 4	James Greenleaf (incomplete)	*Notes*, II: 415–417
December 25	James Greenleaf	*Notes*, II: 417–418
	1790	
September 2	George Washington	*Notes*, I: 288–289 *Letters*, 85–86
October 14	Thomas Jefferson	*Letters*, 86–87
December 12	Thomas Jefferson	*Letters*, 87–90
	1791	
April 17	James Greenleaf	*Notes*, II: 419–420

[1]Not intended for publication, but a quotation from it was given in a letter from Nathaniel Patten to "the public," in the *American Mercury*, May 31, 1790.

[2]The article also contains short excerpts from Webster to Young, [May 3] and [July 3], 1788.

August 14	Mathew Carey	Bradsher, 127–128
October 10	Timothy Pickering	*Notes*, I: 304–306 *Proceedings*, 43: 133–134
October 13	James Greenleaf	*Notes*, II: 420–422 *Letters*, 103–105
December 18	Timothy Pickering	*Notes*, I: 308–309 (part) *Proceedings*, 43: 134–135
	1792	
March 10	Timothy Pickering	*Notes*, I: 309–310 *Proceedings*, 43: 135–136
March 31	Timothy Pickering	*Notes*, I: 311–312 *Proceedings*, 43: 136
August 26	Timothy Pickering	*Notes*, I: 312 *Proceedings*, 43: 136–137
November 11	Timothy Pickering	*Notes*, I: 314–315 *Proceedings*, 43: 137
	1793	
April 10	Timothy Pickering	*Notes*, I: 322 *Letters*, 108–110 *Proceedings*, 43: 137–138
April 22	Timothy Pickering	*Notes*, I: 324–325 *Proceedings*, 43: 138
May 4	James Greenleaf	*Notes*, II: 422–423
May 25	Oliver Wolcott	*Notes*, I: 326–327 *Letters*, 110–111
June 24	James Greenleaf	*Notes*, II: 423–425 *Letters*, 111–114
July 8	James Greenleaf	*Notes*, II: 426–427
September 2	James Greenleaf	*Notes*, II: 428
September 26	Oliver Wolcott	*Notes*, I: 373
October 10	Oliver Wolcott	*Notes*, I: 373–375 (part) *Letters*, 114–116

October 16	James Greenleaf	*Notes*, II: 429–430
October 23	James Greenleaf	*Notes*, II: 428–429
October 31	James Greenleaf	*Notes*, II: 430
December 7	Jedidiah Morse	*Letters*, 116–117

1794

January 8	Timothy Pickering	*Notes*, I: 381 (part) *Proceedings*, 43: 138 (part)
March 2	James Greenleaf	*Notes*, II: 430–432
April 20	George Washington	*Letters*, 117–118
June 28	[to certain associates][3]	*Letters*, 123–124
October 11	James Greenleaf	*Notes*, II: 432

1795

January 2	Theodore Sedgwick	*Letters*, 124–126
March 8	Oliver Wolcott	*Letters*, 126–127
March 24	Samuel Williams	*Letters*, 128
July 30	Oliver Wolcott	*Notes*, I: 392–393 *Letters*, 128–130

1796

July 10	Constantin Volney[4]	*Letters*, 136–137
September 2	Hudson and Goodwin	*Vineland Hist. Mag.*, 14 (1929): 102–103
September 30	Joseph Dennie	*Letters*, 141–142
November 24	Timothy Pickering	*Notes*, I: 408–409 *Letters*, 142–143 *Proceedings*, 43: 139
December 8	Timothy Pickering	*Notes*, I: 409–410 *Letters*, 143–144 *Proceedings*, 43: 139–140
December 24	Alexander J. Dallas	
December [26]	Alexander J. Dallas[5]	

[3]Headed "To the Friends of the Minerva" by Warfel; not for publication in that paper, but a private report to its backers.

[4]See *Notes*, I: 407 for an endorsement to Timothy Pickering on this letter.

[5]Presumably not intended for publication, but printed in the New York *Argus* and the New York *Diary*, December 31, 1796.

1797

May 15	Jedidiah Morse	*Letters*, 147–148
May 22	Timothy Pickering	*Notes*, I: 420–421 *Proceedings*, 43: 140–141
May 30	Timothy Pickering	*Notes*, I: 421 *Proceedings*, 43: 141
May 30	Rufus King	*Notes*, I: 420 (part) *Letters*, 149–150
June 1	Rufus King	*Letters*, 150–159
July 2	Timothy Pickering	*Notes*, I: 421–422 (part) *Proceedings*, 43: 141
July 7	Timothy Pickering	*Notes*, I: 422 *Proceedings*, 43: 142
July 11	Timothy Pickering	*Report*, cxlvi–cxlvii[6]
August 25	Thomas Bradford	*Notes*, II: 433
September 20	Timothy Pickering	*Notes*, I: 424–425 *Proceedings*, 43: 142
September 23	Timothy Pickering	*Notes*, I: 425–427 *Proceedings*, 43: 142–143
October 31	Timothy Pickering	*Notes*, I: 427–428 *Proceedings*, 43: 144
November 2	Timothy Pickering	*Notes*, I: 430–431 *Proceedings*, 43: 146–147
November 3	Timothy Pickering	*Notes*, I: 432 *Proceedings*, 43: 147
December 2	Benjamin Rush	*Letters*, 171–172
December 15	Benjamin Rush	*Notes*, I: 456 (part)

1798

January 4	Jeremy Belknap	*Notes*, I: 457 *Proceedings*, 43: 147–148

[6] Also printed in the *Philadelphia Gazette*, December 17, 1797, and the *Merchant's Daily Advertiser*, December 21, though it was not intended for publication.

April 6	Benjamin Rush	*Notes*, I: 458–459 (part)
April 13	Timothy Pickering	*Notes*, I: 433–434 *Proceedings*, 43: 148–149
May 12	Timothy Pickering	*Notes*, I: 462–463 *Letters*, 180–181 *Proceedings*, 43: 149–150
July 9	E Waddington[7]	*Letters*, 181–182 (as July 6)
July 17	Timothy Pickering	*Notes*, I: 464–465 *Letters*, 182–184 *Proceedings*, 43: 150–151
July 17	Benjamin Rush	*Notes*, I: 466 (part)
November 1	Rufus King	*Notes*, I: 454 (part) *Letters*, 184–187 King, II: 455–456 (part)
November 1	Benjamin Rush	*Notes*, I: 468–469 (part)
November 25	John Eliot	*Collections*, Ser. 1, Vol. 6: 76–77 (part)
December 4	Benjamin Rush	*Notes*, I: 470 (part) *Letters*, 194–196

1799

February 15	Benjamin Rush	*Notes*, I: 471 (part) *Letters*, 196–198
February 27	Benjamin Rush	*Notes*, I: 471–472 (part)
July 10	Rufus King	*Letters*, 201–203
October 20	Timothy Pickering	*Notes*, I: 473–475 *Proceedings*, 43: 151–152

[7] Although this was intended as a personal letter, the recipient sent it to William Cobbett, who published it in his *Porcupine's Gazette*, July 28, 1798 (later reprinted in Cobbett's *Works*). This letter is dated July 9 in the former and July 6 in the latter. July 9 seems the more likely date, since the letter to which it is a reply is dated July 6, and had to travel from New York to New Haven.

November 26	Benjamin Rush	*Notes*, I: 475 (part) *Letters*, 203–204

1800

February 18	Benjamin Rush	*Notes*, I: 475–476 (part)
February 26	Benjamin Rush	*Notes*, I: 476
March 3	Timothy Pickering	*Notes*, I: 476–477 *Letters*, 215–216 *Proceedings*, 43: 152–153
April 12	Rufus King	*Letters*, 216–217
June 23	Oliver Wolcott	*Notes*, I: 477–478 *Letters*, 217–218
August 22	Rufus King	*Letters*, 218–220
September 17	Oliver Wolcott	*Notes*, I: 504–506 *Letters*, 220–222
December 15	Benjamin Rush	*Notes*, I: 478–479 (part) *Letters*, 227–228

1801

June 12	Rufus King	*Letters*, 231
July 18	James Madison	*Notes*, I: 515–522 *Letters*, 232–235
September 11	Benjamin Rush	*Notes*, I: 479–480 (part) *Letters*, 235–237
October 1	Oliver Wolcott	*Notes*, I: 481–482 *Letters*, 237–239
October 13	Oliver Wolcott	*Notes*, I: 522–523 *Letters*, 239–240

1802

January 22	Stephen Twining	*Notes*, I: 524–525 *Letters*, 248–249
March 2	Samuel Bayard	*Letters*, 249–250
March 12	Durrie and Peck	*Letters*, 250–251

	1803	
April 13	Oliver Wolcott	*Notes*, I: 530 Wolcott, 290–291 (part, although printed as if a complete letter)
October 3	Stephen Jacob	*Letters*, 253
[December]	Simeon Baldwin	*Letters*, 253–254 Baldwin, 333–334
	1804	
January 23	Benjamin Silliman	*Notes*, I: 539 (part)
August 20	James Madison	*Letters*, 255–257 Webster, 168–169 *Old South Leaflet* No. 197, 18–20
October 20	James Kent	*Letters*, 257–262
	1805	
June 14	Mathew Carey	*Letters*, 262–263
August 18	John West	*Letters*, 263–264
	1806	
February 20	Thomas Jefferson	*Letters*, 265
March 6	Jedidiah Morse	*Letters*, 265–266
May 5	Rufus King	*Letters*, 266–268
July 30	Jedidiah Morse	*Letters*, 268–269
August 18	Mathew Carey	*Notes*, II: 433–434
December 24	Albert Gallatin	*Notes*, II: 12–13, 14 (part) *Letters*, 269–271
	1807	
February 28	Rufus King	*Letters*, 275 King, V: 11–12 (part)
April 20	William S. Johnson	Beardsley, 165–166
June 15	Samuel L. Mitchill	*Letters*, 275–276
July 6	Rufus King	*Letters*, 277–278 King, V: 37–38

August 18	John West	*Letters*, 281–282
September 27	Jonas Platt	*Notes*, II: 87n *Letters*, 278–279
October 19	Joel Barlow	*Notes*, II: 30 (part) *Letters*, 292–294 Todd, 244–246
November 12	Joel Barlow	*Notes*, II: 31–32 (part) *Letters*, 294–300 Todd, 247–252
	1808	
May 13	Oliver Wolcott	*Notes*, II: 36–37 *Letters*, 300–301
October 13	Joel Barlow	*Notes*, II: 39 *Letters*, 308–309 Todd, 220–221
December 17	Timothy Pickering	*Notes*, II: 56–57 *Proceedings*, 43: 153–154
December 20	Thomas Dawes	*Notes*, II: 42–48 (part) *Letters*, 309–315 (part)
	1809	
February 20	James Madison	*Notes*, II: 60–63 *Letters*, 315–318
July 25	Thomas Dawes[8]	*Notes*, II: 65–71 *Letters*, 318–324
	1810	
September 26	Oliver Wolcott	*Letters*, 332–333
	1811	
February 12	Josiah Quincy	*Notes*, II: 101–102
	1813	
May 19	John Jay	*Notes*, II: 118–119 *Letters*, 334–335

[8]Although addressed to an individual, this letter was obviously intended for publication; it appeared in the *Columbian Centinel*, August 2, 1809.

June 9	John Jay	*Notes*, II: 120–121
December 15	David Daggett	*Letters*, 335–336

1815

November 6	Edward H. Cobb	*Letters*, 336–337
November 20	George Goodwin and Sons	*Letters*, 337–339

1816

July 20	Harriet Webster Cobb	*Letters*, 339–341

1817

	William S. Shaw	Felt, 322–326 (part)

1818

February 25	Harriet Webster Cobb	*Letters*, 395–396

1820

March 30	Solomon Smead	*Notes*, II: 156–157 (part)
		Letters, 399–400
June 27	Jeremiah Evarts	*Letters*, 401–402
September 27	William Leffingwell	*Letters*, 402–403

1821

January 22	DeWitt Clinton	*Letters*, 403–404
September 19	Board of Trustees, Amherst Academy	*Letters*, 404–405 Tuckerman, 55
November 5	Stephen Van Rensselaer	*Letters*, 405–407
November 8	John Jay	*Notes*, II: 160
November	John Jay	*Notes*, II: 160–163

1822

January 2	Stephen Van Rensselaer	*Letters*, 407–408
March 19	Harriet Webster Cobb	*Letters*, 408–409

1823

September 24	Charles Webster	*Boston Post*, September 14, 1924; *New York Herald Tribune*, November 2, 1924; and in other newspapers
December 12	Samuel L. Mitchill	*Letters*, 410–412

1824

June–July[9]	Rebecca Greenleaf Webster	*Notes*, II: 199–202
July 10	Rebecca Greenleaf Webster	*Notes*, II: 205–207
July 12	Harriet Webster Cobb	*Notes*, II: 207–209
July 13	Rebecca Greenleaf Webster	*Notes*, II: 209–210
July 21	Rebecca Greenleaf Webster	*Notes*, II: 210–216
August 1	Rebecca Greenleaf Webster	*Notes*, II: 220–223
August 19	Eliza Steele Webster	*Notes*, II: 224–227
August 20	Rebecca Greenleaf Webster	*Notes*, II: 227–228
August 27	Rebecca Greenleaf Webster	*Notes*, II: 228–230
September 8	Rebecca Greenleaf Webster	*Notes*, II: 239–240
September 19	Rebecca Greenleaf Webster	*Notes*, II: 244–245
September 24	Rebecca Greenleaf Webster	*Notes*, II: 246–247
October 16	Rebecca Greenleaf Webster	*Notes*, II: 248–251
November 27	Rebecca Greenleaf Webster	*Notes*, II: 264–265
December 6	Rebecca Greenleaf Webster	*Notes*, II: 266–268
December 20	Samuel Lee	*Notes*, II: 271–273 *Letters*, 412–414 Webster, 289–290 *New England Mag.*, I (1831): [369]–370 *Chr. Sci. Monitor*, June 19, 1956
December 26	Rebecca Greenleaf Webster	*Notes*, II: 273–275 (part)

1825

January 27	Rebecca Greenleaf Webster	*Notes*, II: 275–276
February 15	Rebecca Greenleaf Webster	*Notes*, II: 283–284

[9] Written in several installments while at sea.

1826

March 17	James Madison	*Notes,* II: 294–295
August 28	DeWitt Clinton	*Letters,* 414–417
September 30	Daniel Webster	*Notes,* II: 297–300 *Letters,* 417–420

1827

January 29	Daniel Webster	*Notes,* II: 301
April 7	E[liakim] Phelps	*Pellet,* No. 6 (April 23, 1872), pp. [3]–4

1829

November 18	Lemuel Shattuck	*New England Mag.,* II (1832): 474–476 *Hampshire Gazette,* September 26, 1832

1830

February 9	Emily Ellsworth Fowler	*Notes,* II: 315–316n Connor, 87
December 14	Rebecca Greenleaf Webster	*Notes,* II: 319
December 17	Rebecca Greenleaf Webster	*Notes,* II: 320
December 29	Harriet Webster Cobb Fowler	*Letters,* 423–424

1831

January 7	Rebecca Greenleaf Webster	*Notes,* II: 322
January 26	Rebecca Greenleaf Webster	*Notes,* II: 322–324
January 29	William C. Fowler	*Letters,* 424–425
February 3	Rebecca Greenleaf Webster	*Notes,* II: 324–326
February 7	Rebecca Greenleaf Webster	*Notes,* II: 326–327 (misdated 1832)
February 16	Rebecca Greenleaf Webster	*Letters,* 426–427[1]
September 10	[Addressee unknown]	*Letters,* 427–428

[1] A facsimile of this letter has been printed, but the compiler has been unable to determine when, where, or by whom.

1832

	Thomas Miner (?)[2]	
July 24	William C. Fowler	*Letters*, 431–432
August 17	William G. Webster	*Notes*, II: 333 (part)
August 24	William G. Webster	*Notes*, II: 333–334

1833

November 28	Elizabeth Webster Perry	*Conn. Mag.*, VII (1901): 157–158
November 28	William J. Thompson	Rutgers U. Lib. *Journal*, II (1939): 45

1834

February 24	[Sidney and Richard] Morse	*Letters*, 433
September 6	Daniel Webster	*Notes*, II: 338–350 *Letters*, 433–445 *Amer. Hist. Rev.*, IX (1903): 96–104

1835

January 7	Harriet Webster Cobb Fowler	*Letters*, 445–446
April 6	Harriet Webster Cobb Fowler	*Letters*, 448–450

1836

January 3	Harriet Webster Cobb Fowler	*Letters*, 450–452
January 23	William G. Webster	*Notes*, II: 351
May 3	William G. Webster	*Notes*, II: 327n (part)
October 25	David McClure	*Letters*, 452–457 Webster, 291–294
November 21	Thomas Miner	*New Englander*, I (1843): 567–568 *Literature*, II (1889): 350 (part)

[2]Probably intended as a personal letter, but published in part in the *Middlesex Gazette*, April 11, 1832.

1837

January 14	William C. Fowler	*Letters*, 457–458
January 30	Edward D. Ingraham	*Letters*, 458–459
March 30	Daniel Webster	*Letters*, 459–460
May 6	William D. Williamson	*Notes*, II: 448 (part)
July 24	George Gibbs	*Proceedings*, 43: 154–155
October 30	William C. Fowler	*Letters*, 506–509
November 15	William C. Fowler	*Letters*, 509–511
November 30	William G. Webster	*Notes*, II: 353–354 (part)
December 26	Horace Greeley	*Amer. Speech*, 25 (1950): [101]–104

1838

April 8	William G. Webster	*Notes*, II: 354–355 (part)
May 1	William G. Webster	*Notes*, II: 355 (part)
November 15	Lewis G. Clark	*Letters*, 515–517 *Lippincott's Mag.*, V (1870): 448–452

1840

March 10	Henry Barnard, Jr.	*Amer. Jour. of Educ.*, 13 (1863): 123–124, and 26 (1876): [195]–196 *First Century*, 355; 1873 ed., 367; 1874 ed., 355[3]
June 13	Reuben Langdon	*Letters*, 517–518
July 29	Ebenezer S. Thomas	*Notes*, II: 356–357 *Proceedings*, 43: 155–156 Thomas, II: 169–170

[3]Also quoted in extenso in Sec. XVI of Vol. I of James Hammond Trumbull, ed., *Memorial History of Hartford County*... (2 vols., Boston, [1886]).

1841

February 27	William C. Fowler	*Letters*, 518–520
May 3	J[ohn] W. Webster	*Conn. Mag.*, VII (1901): 157, with facsimile facing; facsimile also in *Jour. Amer. Hist.*, III (1909): 132

1842

July 10	Rebecca Greenleaf Webster	*Notes*, II: 357–358

APPENDIX D – UNFINISHED AND UNPUBLISHED WORKS

Because each involves an imprint, two of Webster's projects which were never finished have already been described (Titles 746–747); certain others are described below, even though one or two of them apparently did not get past the planning stage. The following list also includes a few manuscripts which were completed but never published. These are selected as being the most important of a fairly large number of unpublished Webster MSS, some completed and some not, to be found in various repositories, chiefly the Pierpont Morgan Library and The New York Public Library.

1

[Joseph Ingraham's journal of a voyage to the Northwest Coast, 1790.]

In 1790 Joseph Ingraham, a nephew of Mrs. Webster, returned from a voyage to the Northwest Coast, whither he had sailed as first mate of the *Columbia* under Captain John Kendrick. On August 11 William Greenleaf, Webster's father-in-law and Ingraham's grandfather, wrote Webster from Boston,[4] "... I found the Ship Columbia arriv'd from Canton, on which I mentioned to Son Daniel the conversation I had with you, relative to Capt Ingrahams Journal of the Voyage. I desir'd Daniel to sound the Capt on the subject, which he has done, & is commissioned to make proposals, to you upon it & which he will do by the fryday's Mail, I am informed his observations have been large & very accurate, his drafts numerous in curiositys, besides general drafts of the countrys visited, that he has found Capt Cook eroneous in many points, & made many discoverys, not mentioned by him, that his Journal consists of unadorned facts, which he ment to embellish as well as he could in order to

[4]Rather than have this quotation bristle with insertions of "sic," it is given litteratim without them.

publish it some future time, but now inclines to have it completed by your Masterly pen. Capt Ingraham has promised to keep the Journal in his own hands, 'till he hears from you...."[5] Daniel Greenleaf also wrote to Webster on the same subject on the following day,[6] but the replies are not to be found, and nothing came of the proposition.

2

[A biography of George Washington, 1800.]

In 1800 Webster expressed interest in obtaining access to Washington's papers and writing a biography, but this project was never more than a suggestion. See Webster to Timothy Pickering, March 3, 1800 (the published versions of which are listed in Appendix C).

3

"A Word to an Old-Fashioned Churchman," ca. 1810.

Webster wrote but never published an article or pamphlet with this title, in reply to John Bowden's answer to his *Peculiar Doctrines of the Gospel*, 1809. The MS is in the Webster Papers; a short extract appears in Ford's *Notes*, Vol. II, p. 79.

4

[An analysis of the government of the United States, 1815.]

An untitled document which begins, "Report, That as all civil government is intended to protect the rights, & promote the interest of the people who are to be governed...," endorsed by Webster "February, 1815," is in the Webster Papers. It analyzes the theory and practice of the government of the United States, and appears to have been prepared for presentation to the legislature of Massachusetts, in connection with the Hartford Convention.

5

"A Synopsis of Radical Words in more than Twenty Languages," 1821.

[5]Webster Papers, New York Public Library; Ford's *Notes*, Vol. I, pp. 286–287.

[6]Ibid., 287. The footnote locating the papers of the voyage in the Massachusetts Historical Society is in error; the Ingraham MS in that Society's collections relates to a later voyage to the South Pacific.

Late in 1821 Webster had "complete or nearly so" a manuscript of this work, prepared in conjunction with the compilation of his large dictionary. It was intended to be an appendix to one of his dictionaries, but was never used. The surviving portions of the MS are in the Webster Papers. It is described in a letter from Webster to John Jay, November, 1821, printed in Ford's *Notes*, Vol. II, pp. 160–163. See also Charlton Laird,"Etymology, Anglo-Saxon, and Noah Webster," *American Speech*, February, 1946 (Vol. XXI, pp. 3–15), and pp. 349–350 of Warfel's biography.

6

[An anthology of sermons, 1822.]

A project, which came to nothing, for "a collection of original sermons, adapted to the use of families & private religious meetings" is outlined by Webster in a manuscript circular letter of September 20, 1822. The draft and a copy are in the Webster Papers; the letter sent to Edward D. Griffin, president of Williams College, is in the Connecticut State Library.

7

[An anthology of expurgated English poetry, 1823.]

That Webster had such a project in mind, and that it was abandoned because a similar work had already been published in Philadelphia, is shown by comments in a letter from Thomas Dawes to Webster, March 20, 1823, printed in Ford's *Notes*, Vol. II, pp. 187–190.

8

[A circular about the spelling book, 1828–1832?]

A manuscript, believed by the compiler to fall within the above years, endorsed in two hands (neither Webster's) "Communication from Mr Webster concerning his Sp Book" and "Circular from N. Webster for publication," is to be found in the Webster Papers. It discusses, in the third person, various spellers on the market and recommends Webster's; it also recommends his dictionaries.

9

[A religious tract, 1832.]

Using a printed form letter, the American Tract Society addressed Webster on October 15, 1832, asking him to write a tract for their use. Nothing seems to have come of this.

10

[Historical sketch of Connecticut, 1840.]

Webster's lengthy speech on the history of Connecticut delivered April 21, 1840 (see Appendix B), was never published, though it would make a substantial work. The manuscript is in the Webster Papers; the Connecticut Historical Society has a copy in another hand, with corrections by Webster.

11

[Prayers, various dates.]

In the Webster Papers there is a volume of twenty-seven pages of manuscript prayers composed by Webster for various occasions. One of them, written on the eve of sailing for Europe, is printed in Ford's *Notes*, Vol. II, pp. 198–199.

APPENDIX E – DUBIOUS AND ERRONEOUS ASCRIPTIONS TO WEBSTER

Because of the difficulty of identifying anonymous and pseudonymous material in general, from confusion of Noah Webster with Noah Worcester[7] or with Peletiah Webster (who both wrote on some of the same subjects as Noah), or from errors of one sort or another, various articles, pamphlets, and books have been incorrectly credited to Noah Webster in bibliographies, library catalogues, sales catalogues, etc. When the compiler began her researches on Webster, about 1910, such mistaken ascriptions were especially common in library catalogues, but in the intervening years the better identification of early nineteenth-century pamphlets and careful attention to the differences between the various Websters and Worcesters have reduced such errors to a minimum. The following list, therefore, concentrates on erroneous references in published works which a researcher is apt to encounter.

1. The compiler does not agree with Professor Warfel's attribution to Webster of the rhymed tribute to Timothy Dwight, 1777, quoted on p. 31 of his biography of Webster.

2. *Remarks on a Pamphlet, Entituled "A Dissertation on the Political Union..." By a Connecticut Farmer*, ([New Haven], 1784), Evans 18782 and Sabin 80405, sub Roger Sherman (also attributed to Benjamin Gale), is entered under Webster in the catalogue of the James H. Trumbull sale, American Art Association, March 22, 1921, lot 1078.

3. The advertisement by Joseph Crukshank of "Webster's Political Essays" in *Dunlap's American Daily Advertiser*, March 19, 1791, is probably a reference to Peletiah Webster, not Noah.

4. In listing children's books, the *Cambridge History of American Literature* (4 vols., New York, 1917–1921) records, Vol. II, p. 637, a "History of the Little Boy found under a Haycock" and "The Political Balance," both 1792, as works of Noah Webster. Neither has been found by the compiler, and the second hardly sounds like a juvenile. These

[7]It is confusion with Noah Worcester which has led to the assertion, sometimes made in books and articles on shoemaking, that Noah Webster was once a cobbler.

ascriptions do not appear in the 1954 edition. Note also that the citation of p. 354 under Noah Webster's name in the index of Vol. I (both editions) is in error, the reference being to Daniel Webster.

5. *The Political Progress of Britain* (Philadelphia, 1795), Sabin 10066, which is really by James T. Callender, is erroneously ascribed to Noah Webster on p. 207 of Herbert S. Stone, *First Editions of American Authors* (Cambridge, Mass., 1893).

6. *Three Letters to Abraham Bishop... By Connecticutensis* (Hartford, 1800), Sabin 5591, 15875, and 95742, probably by David Daggett, is mistakenly attributed to Noah Webster in lot 1078 of the Trumbull sale catalogue, cited above.

7. On p. 335 of Vol. VII of Justin Winsor's *Narrative and Critical History of the United States* (8 vols., Boston and New York, [1884–1889]) there is a garbled reference crediting to Noah Webster a "Vindication of the Vice President of the United States," which is really *An Examination of the Various Charges* (Philadelphia, 1803, and later), Sabin 98530, by William P. Van Ness.

8. The *Compendious Dictionary* of 1806 is erroneously referred to as the "Columbian Dictionary" in certain secondary works.

9. On p. 374 of Vol. V of the revised edition of Samuel Halkett and John Laing's *Dictionary of Anonymous and Pseudonymous English Literature* (7 vols., Edinburgh and London, 1926–1934), Noah Webster is credited with *The Stranger's Monitor...by Elias Monitor* (New York, 1812). This is probably a bibliographical ghost as well as a mal-ascription, for it appears to be a garbled reference to *Stranger's Apology...by Elias Monitor* [Noah Worcester?]... (Boston, 1812), Sabin 49984.

10. In his *Life and Writings of Jared Sparks* (2 vols., Boston and New York, 1893), Vol. I, p. 224, Herbert B. Adams mistakes Noah Webster for Noah Worcester in calling the former the editor of the *Christian Disciple* (Boston, 1813–1823). See also the following entry.

11. "Capital Punishments," by "A.B.," in the *Christian Disciple*, March, 1817 (Vol. V, pp. 74–79), is erroneously attributed to Noah Webster in Ford's *Notes*, Vol. II, p. 536, where both the title and page references are garbled. It is by Noah Worcester.

12. *A Letter to the Secretary of the Treasury, on the Commerce and Currency of the United States, by Aristides* (New York, 1819), Sabin 1977 and 102364, is ascribed to Noah Webster in Franklin B. Dexter, *Biographical Sketches of the Graduates of Yale* (6 vols., New York, 1885–1912), Vol. IV, p. 75, No. 32, probably because occasionally Webster used the pseudonym "Aristides" and wrote on similar topics. On Dexter's authority the compiler listed this work in her list of Webster's writings in

Ford's *Notes*, but she does not now accept this ascription, having found no support for it in her later researches in Noah Webster's books and papers.

APPENDIX F – WORKS RELATED TO THE SPELLER, PLAGIARISMS, ETC.

The compiler made notes on scores of spellers, readers, grammars, and dictionaries which were in use when Webster entered the textbook field, were used concurrently and so were rivals, or superseded his works. Particularly in his later years Webster tended to regard almost any book on the English language as a plagiarism of his work. It is true that similarities in arrangement and presentation were bound to occur, and that many compilers did not exercise enough initiative to choose different examples and selections from his. However, there is only one instance (No. 9 below) in which an out-and-out appropriation of material seems to have been made.

Because the bibliographical recording of American textbooks has broadened since the compiler began her work,[8] the following listing has been confined to plagiarisms and books specifically designed to simplify, "improve,"or accompany Webster's speller, which was the only one of his works to receive this compliment.

Kneeland's American Definition Spelling Book

1802

1. The American definition spelling book: in which the words are not only rationally divided into syllables, accurately accented, the various sounds of the vowels, represented by figures, and their parts of speech properly distinguished, but the definition or signification affixed to each word; upon a plan agreeable to Mr. Noah

[8]See especially Arthur G. Kennedy, *Bibliography of Writings on the English Language* (Cambridge and New Haven, 1927).

Webster's easy standard. Designed for the use of schools. By Abner Kneeland, school-master. The first edition. Published according to act of Congress. Keene, Newhampshire, printed by John Prentiss, for the author. 1802.

179, (1) pp. 19 cm. P. [i], title-page. P. [ii], recommendations. P. [iii], dedication, "To the American Academies and Schools. . . ." Pp. [iv]–vi, preface. Pp. [7]–165, text. Pp. [166]–179, appendix, including material on earthquakes, "youthful excesses," advice to apprentices, etc. P. [180], errata, advertisements.
DLC, British Museum.

1804

2. ——— Kingsbery & Blake's first edition, with many corrections and improvements, by the author. Published according to act of Congress. Windsor, (Vermont,) Printed by Nahum Mower, 1804.

249, (3) pp. 16 cm.
CSmH, DLC, MWA, VtHi, VtU.
This edition does not have the appendix, but otherwise is substantially the same as the preceding. The three unnumbered pages are errata.

1809

3. ——— Hough's edition—revised copy. Concord: Printed and published by George Hough. . . . 1809.

211 pp. 17 cm.
MWA, PU.

Hough's second, third, and fourth editions of this work (1814, 1820, 1826) omit Webster's name from the title-page, though he is still discussed in the preface.

After Webster's death there appeared another work with a title similar to this: Robert McK. Ormsby's The American Definition Spelling Book, on an Improved Plan; in which the Spelling and Pronunciation are Generally according to the Principles of Noah Webster, *of which two editions were published in Bradford, Vermont, in 1844 (copies of both in the Library of Congress).*

Scofield's "Dictionary to the American Spelling Book"

1818

4. *On February* 10, 1818, *there was deposited with the copyright office in Washington the title-page of* "*A* Dictionary, *to the American Spelling Book, Designed for the Use of Schools. By P. Scofield,*" *but the work apparently never materialized.*

Marshall's "Webster Improved"

1819

5. *On November 12, 1819, Elihu F. Marshall of Rochester, New York, entered for copyright the title "Webster Improved: being a Spelling Book of the English Language; or the American Tutor's Assistant...." Before publication, however, he seems to have changed the title, for the compiler has found no printed version with this wording, but Marshall did publish* A Spelling Book of the English Language; or, The American Tutor's Assistant, *of which there were editions in Saratoga Springs, N. Y., 1820 and 1821; Concord, N.H., 1823; Plymouth, Mass., 1826; Bellows Falls, Vt., 1830; etc. The contents are similar to those of Webster's speller, though Marshall followed Walker's orthography.*

Ellis' Mirror

1820

6. A mirror to Noah Webster's spelling book; containing, a concise definition of the words, as arranged in the different tables in Noah Webster's spelling book, from the 4th to the 47th tables:

together, with a just pronunciation of the same, agreeable to Webster's pronouncing dictionary and the most approved modern authors. By William R. Ellis, M.D. Lebanon. Printed by A. Van Vleet. 1820.

173, (1) pp. 17 cm. P. [i], title-page. P. [ii], copyright notice, to Ellis, District of Ohio, May 24, 1820. P. [iii], preface. Pp. iv–v, directions, abbreviations, and a recommendation. P. [vi], blank. Pp. 7–173, text, consisting of Webster's tables mentioned on the title-page. P. [174], errata.

NNC-T (imperfect).

Ohio Imprints, 546.

Guilford's versions of the spelling book

1831

7. The American spelling book; containing the rudiments of the English language, for the use of schools in the United States. By Noah Webster, Esq. Revised and improved by Nathan Guilford. Cincinnati: Published by N. & G. Guilford, Morgan and Sanxay, and O. Farnsworth. Stereotyped at the Cincinnati Stereotype Foundry. 1831.

144 pp., illus. 18 cm. P. [1], title-page. P. [2], blank. Pp. [3]–144, text (see below).

NN.

NOTES

1. The copy located has MS annotations by Webster.

2. The contents are much altered and rearranged from the then current version of Webster's speller, and material is added, including four fables. The cuts resemble those of the 1804 editions, and eight more—of animals—have been added. There is no copyright notice.

8. The Western spelling book; being an improvement of The American spelling book, by Noah Webster. Designed for the use

of common schools. By Nathan Guilford. Published by N. & G. Guilford, Cincinnati, W. W. Worsley, Louisville, J. Fisher & Son, Wheeling, and O. Farnsworth, Yellow Springs. Stereotyped at the Cincinnati Type Foundery. 1831.

144 pp., incl. frontis., illus. 16 cm. P. [1], blank. P. [2], frontispiece, unsigned, a schoolmaster and his pupils, with the legend, "Well may tyrants tremble; for the schoolmaster is abroad!" P. [3], title-page. P. [4], copyright notice to Guilford, Ohio District, April 30, 1831. Pp. [5]–144, text, based on the preceding entry, but with changes in the words given as examples, etc.

DLC, NN.

9. The Western spelling book; containing easy lessons in spelling and reading. Designed for the use of common schools. By Nathan Guilford. Published by N. & G. Guilford, Cincinnati, W. W. Worsley, Louisville, J. Fisher & Son, Wheeling, and O. Farnsworth, Yellow Springs. Stereotyped at the Cincinnati Type Foundry. 1831.

144 pp., incl. frontis., illus. 16 cm.

CtY.

NOTES

1. The contents of this issue are the same as those of the preceding, the title-page being the only difference. This marks the fourth step in the transition from the authorized speller to a plagiarism: (1) authorized edition, published by the Guilfords (e.g., Title 222); (2) edition retaining Webster's title and name, but adding Guilford's; (3) edition with a new title but with Webster's name as well as Guilford's; (4) edition with new title and Guilford's name alone, and no indication of the Websterian origin.

2. An entirely different *Western Spelling Book*, by Hall J. Kelley, was published in Cincinnati in 1832.

1835

10. *That there was another edition of Guilford's version in* 1835 *is suggested by an advertisement of James Morrow of South Hanover*

(Hanover, Indiana) in the Cincinnati Standard *of June* 11 *and* 18, 1835*: "The subscriber has recently published...at this place and at Madison...Western Spelling Book (Guilford's)."*

Evans' "Keys"

1831

11 & 12. *On October* 24, 1831, *"A Key to Dr. Noah Webster's American Spelling Book, or Dr. Webster Explained," was entered for copyright in Kentucky by Hickman S. Evans, and on December* 16, 1834, *Evans entered "A Key to the Meaning of Dr. Webster's Elementary Spelling Book, Defined and Pronounced, for the Use of Schools." American Imprints Inventory, No.* 38, Supplemental Check List of Kentucky Imprints *(Louisville,* 1942*), Nos.* 1037 *and* 1062. *Apparently neither book was actually published.*

The Western Primer

1833

13. The Western primer, or Introduction to Webster's spelling book. Illustrated with seventy-seven wood cuts. Cincinnati: Published by Corey & Fairbank. 1833.

35 pp., incl. frontis., illus. 14 cm. P. [1], blank. P. [2], frontispiece, unsigned, three elaborately dressed ladies surrounded by exotic birds. P. [3], title-page. P. [4], publisher's notice; copyright notice, District of Ohio, 1833, without name of claimant; and stereotype notice of J. A. James, Cincinnati. Pp. 5–35, text, including the alphabet and numbers, simple lessons, moral tales, the Ten Commandments, the Lord's Prayer, etc.

IHi.

NOTES

1. Advertised in the Cincinnati *Standard*, November 15, 1833; advertised by Corey and Fairbank on the flyleaves of their edition of the *Elementary Spelling Book*, 1834.

2. Some of the woodcuts are based on Anderson's.

1835

14. —— Cincinnati, Corey, Fairbank, and Webster, 1835.

35 pp. [incl. frontis.], illus. 16 cm.
OC (imperfect).

NOTES

1. Advertised by Corey, Fairbank and Webster and later by Corey and Webster, *Cincinnati Daily Gazette*, July 20 and October 10, 1835, and elsewhere.

2. The copy located lacks a frontispiece, but appears to have had one.

1837

15. —— Columbus: Published by I. N. Whiting. [1837.]

35 pp., incl. frontis., illus. 15 cm.
Greenwood.
The cover title adds the year 1837 to the imprint.

The Elementary Reader

1833

16. *In the Cincinnati* Standard, *November* 15, 1833, *the firm of Corey and Fairbank advertised "The Elementary Reader; to accompany Webster's Spelling Book," as if they were the publishers. They also advertised it in their* 1834 *edition of the speller. The compiler has not, however, found a copy earlier than the following.*

1835

17. The elementary reader; to accompany Webster's spelling book. An introduction to the Western reader. By an experienced teacher. Last edition. Cincinnati: Corey, Fairbank & Webster. 1835.

180 pp., incl. frontis., illus. 10 cm. P. [i], publisher's advertisements. P. [ii], frontispiece, consisting of two cuts. P. [iii], title-page. P. [iv], recommendation; copyright notice, 1833, without name of holder; and imprint,"Stereotyped by J. A. James, No. 1, Baker Street, Cincinnati," and "Lane Seminary, Printed by the Students' Typographical Association." Pp. [v]–vi, "Advertisement," dated Cincinnati, September 26, 1833. Pp. vii–viii, table of contents. Pp. 9–80, text, not taken from any of Webster's works.

DLC.

NOTES

1. The advertising on p. [i] includes: "Corey and Fairbank's Series of School Books. 1. The Western Primer, or Introduction to Webster's Spelling Book: with 77 cuts. 2. Webster's Elementary Spelling Book. 3. The Primary Reader: embellished with cuts. 4. The Elementary Reader: with 130 cuts. 5. Hall's Western Reader. 6. Murray's Grammar.... 7. Miss Beecher's Geography.... 8. Webster's Dictionary...."

2. In the *Cincinnati Daily Gazette*, February 15, 1836, and later, the firm advertised several of these works, including the *Elementary Reader*, saying that they "are all stereotype works, and have passed through editions amounting to 100,000 copies within two years."

3. The *Primary Reader* mentioned in the above list was advertised by Corey and Webster in the *Cincinnati Whig*, October 23, 1835, and later, and in other Cincinnati papers. The compiler has not been able to locate a copy, and so cannot tell its relationship, if any, to Webster's works.

1837

18. ——— Cincinnati. Burgess and Crane 1837.

180 pp., incl. frontis., illus. 16 cm.

Not seen by the compiler. A copy was formerly in the possession of Mr. Harlow Lindley, who provided a description. The present location of this copy is unknown.

1841

19. *George Conclin of Cincinnati advertised the* Elementary Reader *as one of his publications on the rear flyleaf of* Cincinnati in 1841 *(Cincinnati,* 1841*), but the compiler has found no other indication of such an edition.*

The Illustrated Webster Spelling Book

1856

20. The illustrated Webster spelling book with two hundred and fifty engravings. London Ward & Lock. 158 Fleet St. [1856?]

(3), 128, (3) pp., incl. frontis., illus. 21 cm. Three unnumbered pages of publisher's advertisements. P. [i], blank. P. [ii], frontispiece, by Dalziel. P. [iii], title-page. P. [iv], publisher's note, stating that the book "has been most carefully compiled by an eminent English scholar," with newspaper notices, and imprint, "Printed by Petter and Galpin, Playhouse Yard, adjoining the 'Times' Office." Pp. [v]–vi, preface, praising Webster's speller and William G. Webster's improvement thereon, mentioning the artists whose work is used (Gilbert, Harvey, Berket Foster, Portch, and Dalziel), and dedicating the work to "All English children," with a footnote referring to the *Illustrated Webster Reader* (q.v.) as "in preparation." Pp. [vii]–viii, explanation of method. Pp. [9]–128, text, much reworked from Webster, and with illustrations on almost every page. Three unnumbered pages of publisher's advertisements.

British Museum.

Ascribed to 1856 by the British Museum.

20a. Same, with "Twentieth Thousand" at head of title.

MWA, NN, Merriam.

NOTES

1. The imprint is on p. 128 instead of p. [iv] and the footnote in the preface refers to the companion work as "now ready."

2. A "fortieth thousand" is advertised in *The Athenaeum*, July 30, 1859, p. 160, at 1/- in cloth gilt, 2/- colored, in extra cloth, gilt edges.

1878

21. —— London Ward, Lock, & Co. . . . [1878?]

128 pp., incl. frontis., illus. 20 cm.
British Museum.

NOTES

1. Similar in content to the preceding, except that the publisher's note on p. [iv] has been replaced by an ornament.
2. Ascribed to 1878 by the British Museum.

In 1858 Dean & Son, 11 Ludgate Hill, London, published Noah Webster's British & American Illustrated Spelling & Reading Book, *96 unnumbered pages, illustrated, of which there is a copy in The New York Public Library. The text and illustrations differ completely from Webster's works, and this seems to be merely a case of trading on the value of the name, which carried weight even in England.*

APPENDIX G – WEBSTER'S PUBLIC SERVICE

Webster's membership in charitable societies, chambers of commerce, educational institutions, etc. has been covered in Appendix A, which also includes such of his service as an elected or appointed public official as resulted in imprints. The compiler kept a list of other references to his public service, which is summarized below. No attempt has been made to assemble additional material or to document her notes more fully.

Manuscript sources for this appendix include the archives of the state of Connecticut and the cities of Hartford and New Haven; these are located respectively in the State Library, the Hartford City Clerk's Office, and the New Haven City Clerk's Office.

1784

On January 6, 1784, in a Hartford town meeting, Webster was appointed one of a committee "to consider and fix the Limits of that part or the whole of this Town which is proposed to be incorporated into a City. . . ." (Connecticut Archives, Towns and Lands, Ser. 1, Vol. X, No. 9.)

1791–1792

Webster's name appears as one of the signers of a petition to the Connecticut legislature for permission to operate a lottery to raise funds for a new Court House in Hartford, dated May 2, 1791. (Connecticut Archives, Civil Officers, Ser. 2, Vol. IX, No. 38.) Apparently this proposal failed, and another approach was tried, for Webster's diary for October 10–11, 1791, says, "Set on foot subscription for Court House." On May 17, 1792, he and others signed another petition, offering the fund they had raised and requesting a state grant to complete the cost. (Connecticut Archives, Civil Officers, Ser. 2, Vol. III, No. 122.) Webster's diary on May 23–25 records that the petition was heard and on May 28 that it was rejected.

1792–1793

On March 26, 1792, at a Hartford town meeting, Webster was elected to the Common Council. (Hartford Archives, Record of City Meetings, 1784–1845, pp. 41–42, 44; *Connecticut Courant*, April 2, 1792.)

On March 31, 1792, Webster was appointed by the Hartford council to a committee to select the site for a public dock. His diary from July to September has occasional references to this work. On September 3 a preliminary report was submitted and accepted. On September 15 a second report was submitted and approved. (Hartford Archives, Court of Common Council, Vol. A, pp. 55–56, 59–68.) On September 17 a new committee, of which Webster was a member, was appointed to carry on the project. Their report was submitted to and approved by a town meeting on December 31 and a new committee (again including Webster) named to complete the establishment of a site. This report and an accompanying map were accepted at a town meeting on April 8, 1793. (Hartford Archives, Town Votes, No. 2, pp. 341–345.)

On March 31, 1792, the council also appointed Webster to a committee on gutters and sidewalks. A report was accepted on April 1, 1793, and a further report on July 29, 1793. (Hartford Archives, Court of Common Council, Vol. A, pp. 57–58, 70–71, 73–74.)

On May 14, 1792, Webster was one of the signers of a petition to the Connecticut legislature asking that a bank be chartered in Hartford. (Connecticut Archives, Finance and Currency, Ser. 2, Vol. I, Nos. 59 [petition] and 60 [proposed act]; the petition is printed in James Hammond Trumbull, *Memorial History of Hartford*, pp. 330–331.) Apparently he also helped draft the proposed act, for in the manuscript two sections of it seem to be in his hand. His diary records the hearing of the petition on May 18 and the passage of the act in the entry for May 23–25. The act as passed is printed in the Connecticut *Acts and Laws, Made and passed . . . May . . . 1792*, pp. 416–419. Webster's interest in banks had been evidenced in newspaper writings before this time (see, e.g., Part Nine, Section Three, No. 80), and his part in the inception of this particular project is shown in his diary for February 6, 1792.

On September 15, 1792, the council added Webster to a committee to place merestones (boundary markers) in the city; a report was submitted April 1, 1793. (Hartford Archives, Court of Common Council, Vol. A, pp. 68–70.) He records this activity in his diary, and on September 22, 1792, his account book lists a bill to the city for four days' work, totalling £1/4.

On September 17, 1792, at a Hartford town meeting Webster was appointed to a committee "to enquire into the true state of the Town Property, and Accounts." (Hartford Archives, Town Votes, No. 2, p. [340].)

1793

On March 25, 1793, Webster was re-elected to the Hartford Common Council. (Hartford Archives, Record of City Meetings, 1784–1785, pp. 45–47.)

On April 3, 1793, Webster recorded in his diary, "School District meeting; vote to set up public schools. . . ; choose me Clerk and Committee Man."

Early in 1793 robberies were occurring in the mails between New York and Hartford. On April 17 Postmaster General Timothy Pickering commissioned Webster an agent to attempt to correct the situation. Webster was unable to find the culprit since, as it was later discovered, the thief was a postal employee and was aware of the measures that were being taken to trap him. Webster's commission is in the Webster Papers, New York Public Library, endorsed by him with pertinent information; it is printed in Ford's *Notes*, Vol. I, p. 323.

1794

On March 20, 1794, Webster recorded in his diary his presence, in New York, at a meeting "of the Citizens to petition Legislature to grant money to fortify this port."

1799

At the annual City Meeting in New Haven, June 4, 1799, Webster was elected to the Common Council. (*Connecticut Journal*, June 12, 1799.)

Webster was one of five signers of a petition to the Connecticut legislature, September 3, 1799, asking incorporation of the Connecticut Academy of Arts and Sciences. He probably had a hand in the writing of the act which effected the incorporation (Connecticut Archives, Corporations, Vol. II, Nos. 57–59; the act is published in the Connecticut *Acts and Laws, Made and passed. . . October. . . 1799*, pp. 515–516; in the Academy's *Memoirs*, Vol. I (1810), pp. [v]–vi; and elsewhere.)

On December 23, 1799, a New Haven town meeting appointed Webster to a committee "to make a general Inquiry into ye State of ye poor in this Town." The committee's report was accepted by a town meeting on September 15, 1800, and a new committee, including Webster, was appointed to sell the poorhouse and establish another. On December 8, 1800, a town meeting appointed a further committee of inquiry, which also included Webster. (New Haven Archives, Town Meetings, Vol. 5, pp. 283–284, 289.)

Appendix G

1800

Webster was elected to the May, 1800, session of the Connecticut House of Representatives. (*Connecticut Courant*, May 12; New Haven *Messenger*, May 13; *Connecticut Journal*, May 14.)

Webster was defeated for election to the national House of Representatives in May, 1800. (New Haven *Messenger*, May 20, 1800.)

At the New Haven annual City Meeting, June 3, 1800, Webster was re-elected to the Common Council. (*Connecticut Journal*, June 4, 1800.)

At the July 7, 1800, meeting of the New Haven council, Webster was appointed a juror of the City Court. (New Haven Archives, Court of Common Council, Vol. 1, p. 134.)

1801

Under a date line of "New Haven, Mar. 28," the Charleston, S.C., *City Gazette* of April 24, 1801, carried a story reporting that on March 11, at a town meeting in New Haven called to discuss fire prevention, about twenty Federalists stayed after the rest had left and passed a resolution addressed to John Adams, complimenting him for having left the country in a state of prosperity, and regretting his having failed of re-election. On March 13, the story continues, a committee of this "rump," including Webster, waited on Adams as he passed through the city, but he declined to receive an address. According to the story, the resolution was entered as part of the city records.

In the Yale University Library is a manuscript "account of the number of Children in the several schools in the town and city of New Haven in the winter of 1801, taken by Noah Webster, one of the Visitors. . . ," endorsed April 8, 1801.

[Webster was re-elected to the council at the June, 1801, New Haven annual city meeting.]

1802

At a New Haven town meeting on April 12, 1802, Webster was named to a committee to prepare a petition to the legislature about determining the boundary between New Haven and East Haven. The committee's report was received at a town meeting on January 10, 1803. (New Haven Archives, Town Meetings, Vol. 5, pp. 300, 305.)

At a city council meeting on April 29, 1802, Webster was appointed to a committee to consider realigning Union Street. Their report was accepted on May 4 and a new committee, including Webster, appointed to make the survey; this report was accepted on June 1. (New Haven Archives, Court of Common Council, Vol. 1, pp. 165–170.)

Webster served in the May, 1802, session of the Connecticut House of Representatives. Apparently he served on a committee to consider a petition from religious bodies outside the established church objecting to paying taxes to that church, for there is in the Webster Papers, New York Public Library, a document in his hand, "Remarks intended as a Report on the Petition of Darrow and others. Baptists and Methodists, Legislature of Connecticut, May, 1802." See also 1803.

[Webster was re-elected to the council at the June, 1802, New Haven annual city meeting.]

At a council meeting on July 13, 1802, Webster was appointed to the Health Committee. (New Haven Archives, Court of Common Council, Vol. 2, p. 1.)

Webster served in the October, 1802, session of the Connecticut House of Representatives. On November 4 he spoke in opposition to a bill removing property qualifications for voters; in the course of his remarks he told an anecdote about porpoises which stirred up bad feeling, and the Democrats turned the phrase against him by dubbing themselves "the porpoises of Connecticut." The debate is reported in the *American Mercury*, December 2, 1802, and there appeared in the same paper from December 9, 1802, to April 28, 1803, a series of twelve numbered articles by "Gracchus" attacking Webster and the opposition to the bill.

On November 30, 1802, the New Haven city council appointed Webster to a committee to report on existing and recommended roads in the newer part of the city. Their report was accepted on April 2, 1803, and a further report called for; this was accepted (with changes) on August 22, and a new committee, including Webster, was appointed to survey certain new roads. (New Haven Archives, Court of Common Council, Vol. 2, pp. 3–5, 30.)

At a town meeting on December 13, 1802, Webster was named to a committee to prepare a record of the town's fiscal affairs. Reports were submitted at town meetings on December 27, 1802, and January 24, 1803. (New Haven Archives, Town Meetings, Vol. 5, pp. 302, 307.)

1803

On January 10, 1803, a New Haven town meeting named Webster to a committee to report on the city's rights and claims in certain fisheries and oyster and clam beds. (New Haven Archives, Town Meetings, Vol. 5, p. 305.)

Webster served in the May, 1803, session of the Connecticut House of Representatives. He was a member of a committee that reported adversely on a petition of the state's Baptists for adoption of the principle of separation of church and state. (*Connecticut Courant*, June 1, 1803; copy of the petition, endorsed by Webster, in the Webster Papers, New York Public Library.) He also wrote an act to incorporate the Bank of Connecticut; see Appendix A, No. 5. At this session an unofficial committee of Federalist members of the legislature met and prepared and published *An Address to the Freemen of Connecticut*, which Webster probably wrote; see Appendix A, No. 6.

At a New Haven city meeting on June 7, 1803, Webster was re-elected to the city council. (*New Haven Visitor*, June 14, 1803.)

At a council meeting on June 30, 1803, Webster was named to a committee to survey and lay out Olive Street. (New Haven Archives, Court of Common Council, Vol. 2, p. 8.)

At a council meeting on October 18, 1803, Webster was appointed to a committee to confer with the fire wardens on the city's fire regulations. Their report was accepted and the regulations were amended at a meeting on October 25. (New Haven Archives, Court of Common Council, Vol. 2, pp. 40–42. Cf. January 4, 1805.)

1804

Webster served in the May, 1804, session of the Connecticut House of Representatives. (*New Haven Visitor*, April 12; *Connecticut Courant*, April 18.)

Webster's name appears in the May, 1804, list of Justices of the Peace in Connecticut. (Connecticut Archives, Civil Officers, Ser. 2, Vol. 24, No. 12.) He also served in this capacity in later years.

At a council meeting on May 9, 1804, Webster was appointed to a committee to draw up a petition to the legislature for the incorporation of a municipal aqueduct company. (New Haven Archives, Court of Common Council, Vol. 2, pp. 53–54.)

[Webster was re-elected to the council at the June, 1804, New Haven annual city meeting.]

On November 5, 1804, the council named Webster to a committee to consider planting trees along the streets. (New Haven Archives, Court of Common Council, Vol. 2, p. 61.)

1805

The New Haven council on January 4, 1805, appointed Webster to a committee to revise the city's fire laws. (New Haven Archives, Court of Common Council, Vol. 2, p. 61.)

Webster's name appears in the May, 1805, list of Justices of the Peace for Connecticut. (Connecticut Archives, Civil Officers, Ser. 2, Vol. 24, No. 104.)

[Webster was re-elected to the council at the June, 1805, New Haven annual city meeting.]

Webster served in the October, 1805, session of the Connecticut House of Representatives, acting as second clerk. (*Connecticut Herald*, September 24 and October 15, 1805.)

At a meeting of "the Friends of the Constitution and Government in the State of Connecticut" on October 29, 1805, Webster was recommended for nomination for the national House of Representatives, and in May, 1806, he was nominated by the legislature. (*Connecticut Herald*, March 25, 1806; *Connecticut Journal*, May 22; *American Mercury*, May 29.)

1806

On January 3, 1806, the council appointed Webster to a committee to survey and lay out certain streets. The committee's report was accepted February 26, 1807. (New Haven Archives, Court of Common Council, Vol. 2, pp. 78, 110.)

Webster was elected to the May, 1806, session of the Connecticut House of Representatives; he was named one of the clerks of the session, but declined to serve. (*Connecticut Herald*, April 8 and May 20, 1806; *Connecticut Courant*, May 14.) In the Webster Papers, New York Public Library, is his draft of a resolution prepared for submission to this session, calling for the appointment of a committee to revise the statutes of the state. In this session, as in that of May, 1803, a caucus of Federalist members drew up an *Address to the Freemen of Connecticut*, possibly written by Webster; see Appendix A, No. 8.

On June 3, 1806, the New Haven annual City Meeting elected Webster an alderman. (*Connecticut Journal*, June 5; *Connecticut Herald*, June 10.)

On July 7, 1806, the council named Webster to a committee to devise rules for the public market and to choose a clerk for it. Their report was accepted on August 6, and Webster and one other member were named to complete the appointment. (New Haven Archives, Court of Common Council, Vol. 2, pp. 98, 103–104.)

The New Haven council on September 24, 1806, appointed Webster to a committee to consider "the subject of running Horses in the Streets." (New Haven Archives, Court of Common Council, Vol. 2, p. 105.)

Appendix G

Webster was elected to the October, 1806, session of the Connecticut House of Representatives. (*Connecticut Herald*, September 16, 1806; *American Mercury*, September 25.) In the Webster Papers, New York Public Library, is a draft by Webster of a resolution against making appropriations in closed sessions. Although intended for this session, it is endorsed by him "not offered."

1807

On April 30, 1807, the New Haven council named Webster as a replacement on a committee to survey Crown Street. A report was accepted May 5, 1809. (New Haven Archives, Court of Common Council, Vol. 2, pp. 113, 141.)

[Webster was re-elected Alderman at the June, 1807, New Haven annual city meeting.]

On June 30, 1807, the council appointed Webster to a committee to confer with a property owner regarding land to be taken for the widening of an intersection. (New Haven Archives, Court of Common Council, Vol. 2, p. 118.)

Webster was elected to the October, 1807, session of the Connecticut House of Representatives. (*Connecticut Courant*, September 30, 1807.) In the Webster Papers, New York Public Library, is a draft by Webster of a resolution intended for this session, recommending changes in the manner of nomination of the President and Vice-President of the United States; it is endorsed by him "Not proposed."

At a New Haven town meeting on December 28, 1807, Webster was chosen Moderator. (New Haven Archives, Town Journal, Vol. 6, p. 1.)

1808

In April, 1808, Webster was recommended for nomination for the national House of Representatives. (*Connecticut Herald*, April 5 and 12, 1808.)

[Webster was re-elected Alderman at the June, 1808, New Haven annual city meeting.]

At a New Haven city meeting on August 23, 1808, Webster was appointed one of a committee to draw up a protest to President Jefferson against the embargo. (New Haven Archives, Town Journal, Vol. 6, pp. 5–9.) For the publication of this document, see Appendix A, No. 10. Further resolutions on the same subject are recorded in the minutes of a meeting on January 28, 1809 (ibid., pp. 13–17; Appendix A, No. 11); Webster claimed authorship of these.

1809

On May 5, 1809, the New Haven council appointed Webster to a committee to survey the widening of Water Street. (New Haven Archives, Court of Common Council, Vol. 2, p. 141.)

1810

Webster was nominated for the national House of Representatives in the 1810 election, but was defeated. (*Connecticut Mirror*, March 12, 1810; *Connecticut Herald*, March 20; *Connecticut Mirror*, October 22.)

1811

On May 4, 1811, a New Haven city meeting named Webster one of a committee to draw up a petition to the President for repeal of the Non-Importation Act. (New Haven Archives, Town Journal, Vol. 6, pp. 26–31; see Appendix A, No. 12.)

1812

In March, 1812, Webster's name was proposed for the national House of Representatives by the Federalists, and in May he won the nomination. (*Connecticut Mirror*, March 30 and May 25, 1812.)

1814–1815

At a town meeting in Amherst, Massachusetts, on January 3, 1814, Webster was chosen Moderator; the meeting adopted resolutions protesting against the embargo. These were printed in the *Hampshire Gazette*, January 19, 1815, and the *New England Palladium*, February 1.

On February 1, 1814, Webster was appointed Justice of the Peace in Hampshire County, Massachusetts, but he endorsed his commission,"I never took the oath." (Webster Papers, New York Public Library.)

On May 2, 1814, Webster was elected to the Massachusetts House of Representatives for the 1814–1815 session; he served on the standing committee "on bills in the third reading" and on special committees to arrange the printing of the proceedings of the Hartford Convention; to consider measures to counteract the fluctuating value of bank notes; to adopt suitable measures on the news of peace with England; and to report election returns. (*Rules and Orders...House of Representatives...Massachusetts, 1814; Columbian Centinel*, October 22, 1814, January 21 and February 1 and 15, 1815.) His speech of October 13 approving the calling of the Hartford Convention was published in the Boston *Weekly Messenger* and the *Dedham Gazette*, November 4, 1814.

Appendix G

1815–1816

On May 8, 1815, Webster was elected to the 1815–1816 session of the Massachusetts House of Representatives. In this session he served on the joint standing committee on banks and banking and on a special committee to report on the advisability of regularizing surveying practices in the state. (*Rules and Orders... House of Representatives... Massachusetts, 1815; Columbian Centinel*, June 3, 1815, and January 31, 1816.)

On February 13, 1816, the Massachusetts General Court passed an act incorporating Webster and four other persons as trustees of the ministerial fund of the First Parish of Amherst. (Calvin D. Cowles, comp., *Genealogy of the Cowles Families in America* [New Haven, 1929], Vol. I, p. 345.) A manuscript copy of the act in the Webster Papers, New York Public Library, is endorsed by Webster, "Fund never raised."

In the fall of 1816 Webster was nominated for the national House of Representatives."Seventy Six" in the *Franklin Herald*, October 22, 1816, and "A Friend to Native Citizens" in the *Hampshire Gazette*, October 30, objected to his nomination on the basis of his brief residence in the state; but he was supported by "A Farmer" in the former issue and by "Hancock" in the latter, as well as by "An Elector" in the *Hampshire Gazette* of September 25.

1819–1820

On May 6, 1819, Webster was elected to the 1819–1820 session of the Massachusetts House of Representatives. (*Hampshire Gazette*, May 11, 1819; *Columbian Centinel*, May 15.) He served on the joint standing committee on the incorporation of parishes and other religious societies, and special committees as follows: to consider the expediency of revising the election laws, of providing a permanent fund for supporting common schools, and of providing a permanent bridge-building fund; to consider subscribing to Gales and Seaton's edition of the state constitutions; to estimate the expenses involved in the separation of Maine; further to consider the school fund; to consider the request of the Massachusetts General Hospital for a legislative grant; to consider a bill relieving towns of the expense of supporting paupers imprisoned for debt; to consider levying a tax on an English insurance company's Boston office; and to consider measures to prevent the circulation of purported Bank of Canada notes. (*Rules and Orders... House of Representatives... Massachusetts, 1819*; *Columbian Centinel*, June 5 and 23, 1819, and January 15, 19, and 29, and February 9 and 16, 1820; Boston *Yankee*, June 10, 1819; *Boston Gazette*, January 20, 1820; draft of report on Maine question in Webster Papers, New York Public Library.) A report of a committee of both houses on the expenses and resources of the Commonwealth was published in 1820; a copy in the Watkinson Library (Trinity College, Hartford) has been endorsed by Webster, "This report was in consequence of my Motion." At this session Webster wrote the "Answer to the Address of the Governor, May Session" and a proposed public school bill; see Title 753 (Section XII) and Appendix A, Nos. 16, 17.

1823, 1831, 1834, 1835

For Webster's participation in and writing of documents for civic meetings in these years, see Appendix A, Nos. 20–23.

1839

Webster is listed as one of the eloquent proponents of a resolution, adopted at a meeting of citizens on October 23, 1839, calling for improvement and protection of the New Haven cemetery. (New Haven *Daily Herald*, October 24, 1839.)

APPENDIX H – ANNE ROYALL AND NOAH WEBSTER

During one of her extensive trips Mrs. Anne Royall, an eccentric woman journalist of the early nineteenth century[9], visited New Haven and called on various notables. She gives the following account of a visit to Webster on pages 387–388 of her anonymous *Sketches of History, Life and Manners, in the United States, by a Traveller* (New Haven, 1826):

"New-Haven is a very hot-bed of literary men.... Nothing could equal the pleasure I felt at the prospect of seeing...men with whose names and celebrity I had long been acquainted.... After Mr. M. [Jedidiah Morse], the next man I called on was the celebrated Mr. W. I knocked at the door with more than common enthusiasm; for though we back-woods folks are not learned ourselves, we have a warm liking for learned people. In a few minutes, a low chubby man, with a haughty air, stepped into the room; his face was round and red, and by no means literary looking. He was dressed in black broadcloth, in dandy style; in short, he comes nearer the description of a London cockney, than any character I can think of; he eyed me with ineffable scorn, and scarcely deigned to speak at all. I am sorry for his sake I ever saw the man, as it gave me infinite pain to rescind an opinion I had long entertained of him."

Mrs. Royall's book was reviewed in the *Connecticut Mirror* of June 12, 1826. The review was a moderate one, emphasizing what she had to say about Hartford. There is not the slightest suggestion that Webster wrote it or had anything to do with it; but Mrs. Royall considered the review an attack, and felt Webster was behind it, as shown in this verbatim excerpt from a letter she wrote from Hartford, June 11, 1826, to a Troy, New York, editor, O. L. Holley:[1]

[9]There are biographies of Mrs. Royall by Sarah H. Porter (Cedar Rapids, 1909) and George S. Stuyvesant (Boston, [1937]). In this appendix quotations are litteratim, without the use of "sic."

[1]Original in Yale University Library. Either the newspaper appeared slightly ahead of its date or Mrs. Royall misdated her letter. Holley endorsed the letter "From Mrs. Royall—a sort [of] literary Wild-Cat from the Backwoods."

"The work you no doubt by this time have seen, but my motives in this address is to inlist your humanity & tallents against a bitter though not a very formidable rival a specimen of whose envy & unblushing malignity you will find in the Con. Mirror herewith forwarded. The enemy alluded to, & whom I believe to be at the bottom [of] if not the writer of the piece you will find, is a Mr. W. mentioned in the description of New Haven in 'sketches by a traveller.' The piece it is true is almost too low for the notice of a gentleman were it not incumbent on those generous friends of humanity who have lifted me from suffering indigenc[e] to a state of ease & independence.... But this wretch calling himself a christian would snatch the bread from my lips which is stretched out by a generous country. I have no positive prooff (nor do I seek any) that Mr. W. is the instigator of the piece, but his snaky looks and underhanded machinations abundantly confirms suspicion. This affair in the sketches he thinks will play ruin with his *big* Dictionary particularly as I am so ably patronized & he is afraid to come out openly, as the moment he does that he is done with the good & respectable. I was told by a friend in New Haven that he took a copy in his hand & ran to every man of distinction in town pointing out the gramatical & other errors, it is quite laughable to see his spindle-shanks almost in a run proceeding through the streets of N.H. in a state of distraction to the great amusement of the citizens but particularly the students of Y[ale] C[ollege], but the more he says against the work the faster it sells & this doubles his ire."

Two weeks later, however, in writing to Jared Sparks (Boston, June 30, 1826), Mrs. Royall was inclined to shift the blame somewhat: "Of all my enemies Mr. W. of New Haven mentioned under the head of literary men is the most dangerous because the most deep and malignant[.] I do not mean W. himself who with deference is just the pompouse blockhead I have described him. But that deep designing puritanical [Sherman] Converse who has taken upon him the responsibility of the mighty Dictionary is working against me underhandedly...."[2]

[2]Original in Harvard University Library.

APPENDIX I - PORTRAITS AND STATUES OF NOAH WEBSTER

1. *Verstille miniature, 1788.* In his diary for February 12, 1788, Webster recorded that he sat for a miniature by William Verstille, in New York. Extensive search by the compiler has failed to discover this miniature or any further information about it.

2. *Anonymous engraving, 1789.* In 1789, in their first edition of the speller, the firm of Thomas and Andrews began to use as a frontispiece a crude engraved portait of Webster by an unknown artist. George E. Littlefield, in his *Early Schools and School-Books of New England* (Boston, 1904), p. 156, suggests that Paul Revere was the engraver, but there seems to be no support for this view; the work is not listed as Revere's by the leading authority, Clarence S. Brigham, in his *Paul Revere's Engravings* (Worcester, Mass., 1954). Because of the spiky appearance of the hair someone dubbed this "the porcupine portrait," and it was much ridiculed. In *Porcupine's Political Censor* for March, 1797, in a mock "Will and Testament," p. 110, William Cobbett wrote, "To my dear fellow labourer Noah Webster...I will and bequeath...six Spanish milled dollars, to be expended on a new plate of his portrait at the head of the spelling-book, that which graces it at present being so ugly that it scares the children from their lessons...," and "Observer" in the *New-York Gazette*, June 18, 1800, in ridiculing Webster's projected dictionary, added, "the portrait of Mr. W. will hereafter be hung up *in terrorem* in our seminaries of learning, as it now frowns in that far-famed spelling book." This engraving was used as a frontispiece in Thomas and Andrews' editions of the speller, 1789–1803, the grammar, 1790–1803, and the reader, 1790–1803. It is reproduced as Plate I, in Warfel's biography (facing p. 188), and in Littlefield (op. cit., p. 134). As poor as this engraving was, an even cruder copy of it was made about 1802 and used in editions published in Wilmington, Delaware, in that year (Titles 69–70; Plate VIII).

3. *Sharples pastels, 1793–1801.* In Independence Hall, Philadelphia, and the Metropolitan Museum of Art, New York, are pastel portraits iden-

tified as Noah Webster, attributed to James Sharples. Sharples and members of his family were making and duplicating portraits in the United States from about 1793 to 1801; these pictures must therefore date from that period. The Philadelphia copy is reproduced in color in Elroy M. Avery, *History of the United States* (7 vols., Cleveland, 1904–1910), Vol. VI, p. 414, and in *Journal of American History*, January, 1910 (Vol. IV, p. [58]). For the work of the Sharples family and the difficulty of identifying subjects and the work of different individuals, see Katharine McC. Knox, *The Sharples, Their Portraits of George Washington and his Contemporaries* (New Haven, 1930). The Sharples pastel recorded by Theodore Bolton (*Early American Portrait Draughtsmen in Crayons* [New York, 1923], p. 80) as being in the possession of Charles A. Munn in 1922 is the one now in the Metropolitan Museum.

4. *Morse oil portrait, 1823.* The American artist-scientist Samuel F. B. Morse, who was a son of Webster's old friend Jedidiah Morse, painted a half-length portrait of Webster in 1823. This has become the most widely reproduced likeness of Webster. The original oil is in the possession of a Webster descendant, Mr. Waldo Hutchins, Jr., of New York. It is reproduced as the frontispiece of Warfel's biography and in the *American Collector*, May, 1941 (Vol. X, p. 10). Various institutions and Webster descendants possess copies in oil made at various dates, some of them possibly by Morse himself.

Occasionally the Morse portrait is reproduced with an attribution to Jared Flagg, as in an engraved version by Frederick W. Halpin in Volume II of the Philadelphia, 1872, edition of James Herring's *National Portrait Gallery of Distinguished Americans* (the earlier editions of which had used Herring's own portrait of Webster). Either this is a case of misattribution, or Flagg's portrait is a copy of Morse. (Flagg did an original portrait of Mrs. Webster, reproduced in Warfel's biography, facing p. 418.)

Numerous woodcuts and engravings have been made from the Morse portrait, some of them with minor changes, some utilizing only a portion of the original. The following are the principal versions up to the mid-1880s, by which time the photographic half-tone had taken over:

A. Engravings substantially reproducing the original.

(1) Asher B. Durand. Used in the 1828, 1841, 1844, and 1845 unabridged dictionary (Titles 583, 586–588). No. 664 of David McN. Stauffer, *American Engravers upon Copper and Steel* (New York, 1907).

(2) D. C. Hinman. Frontispiece to Volume II of the *American Literary Magazine*, 1848.

(3) Joseph Andrews and Stephen A. Schoff. Used in Merriam Company unabridged dictionaries from about 1849 to 1854.

(4) John C. Buttre. Used in Merriam Company unabridged dictionaries about 1855–1856.

(5) [J. G.?] Kellogg. Used in Merriam Company unabridged dictionaries from about 1859 to 1861, and as the frontispiece to Volume VII of the *Congregational Quarterly*, 1865.

(6) Henry B. Hall. Used in Merriam Company unabridged dictionaries from about 1864 to 1868.

(7) Unidentified engraver. Used in Merriam Company unabridged dictionaries from about 1870 to 1872.

(8) H. B. Hall and Sons, with modifications in detail, such as the chair back and the paper in Webster's hand. Used in Merriam Company unabridged dictionaries from about 1878 into the '90s.

(9) Asaph Willard, reduced to a bust. Used in a Merriam Company quarto dictionary of 1881, and in James Hammond Trumbull, ed., *Memorial History of Hartford County, Connecticut* (2 vols., Boston, 1886), Vol. I, facing p. 172. Stauffer, op. cit., No. 3393.

(10) A. W. Elson and Company, with modifications in detail. Frontispiece to Scudder's biography, 1882 and later.

B. Engraving considerably altered.

About 1867 (in which year it was copyrighted) Alonzo Chappel executed a steel engraving from the Morse portrait, in which the figure is extended to full-length and furniture, books, bookshelves, and draperies are added. This was used facing p. 489 of Volume I of the 1868 edition of Alonzo Chappel and Evert A. Duyckinck's *National Portrait Gallery of Eminent Americans*; it does not appear in the [1861–1862] or 1874 editions of the same work.

C. Woodcuts, reduced to a bust.

(1) S[amuel] Wallin. Engraved by "B & E" (probably Bobbett and Edmonds), this was used in the *International Magazine*, August, 1851 (Vol. IV, p. 12); engraved by "L-B" (probably Lossing-Barritt), it appears in Abner D. Jones, *Illustrated American Biography* (3 vols., New York, 1853–1855), Vol. I, p. 251 (also on p. 133 of the 1858 and 1869 editions, which appeared under the title of *American Portrait Gallery*), and in the *United States Magazine*, August, 1855 (Vol. II, p. 81).

(2) W[illiam?] Roberts, reversed. On p. 474 of Volume I of Evert A. and George L. Duyckinck's *Cyclopaedia of American Literature* (2 vols., New York, [1855]), and in later editions.

(3) E. Sears, *Phrenological Journal*, March, 1871 (Vol. LII, p. 153).

5. *Herring oil portrait, 1833.* On September 21, 1833, Webster added as a postscript to a letter to his daughter Harriet, "I ought perhaps to add that Mr Herring of N York is publishing memoirs of distinguished me[n] in this country, with engravings of their portraits done in elegant style. He has seen fit to request my portrait, & is now engaged in painting it himself. The picture is not finished. When it is, you will have the opinions of your friends here as to the likeness."[3] This portrait, engraved by George Parker, was used in the first three editions of James Herring's *National Portrait Gallery of Distinguished Americans* (4 vols., New York, etc., 1834–1839; 5 vols., Philadelphia, etc., 1852–1867; 4 vols., Philadelphia, 1853–1854). According to a note by the compiler, "the family never considered it a faithful likeness." The original is in the possession of a descendant, Mrs. William A. Ellis.

6. *Ives plaster bust, 1840.* In 1840 Chauncey B. Ives executed in New York a bust of Webster in plaster. A letter, signed "Leo," puffing Ives' work appeared in the *Commercial Advertiser* of November 18, 1840, mentioning Webster among those whose busts Ives had executed, and stressing the fact that Ives' busts were not merely life masks of the subject. Ives showed this and other busts at the National Academy of Design in 1841.

On July 9, 1840, Webster wrote to his son-in-law William C. Fowler, "William [Webster] engaged Mr Ives to procure 6 copies of my bust in plaster, & they have arrived. The likeness is said to be very exact.... William has sent one for you.... If the Faculty of Amherst College will permit a copy of it to be set in the library or other apartment, I will present one.... Considering what interest I took in founding the institution, it seems to be, if not proper, at least not improper, to place my bust in one of the public rooms. But on this subject, I am not anxious...."[4]

The copy sent to the Fowlers is in the possession of their granddaughter, Mrs. Howard B. Field. The Amherst copy was accepted by the college but cannot now be found there.[5] In later years copies were given by descendants to the Long Island Historical Society and the Massachusetts Historical Society, but neither of these copies is still in

[3]In the possession of Mrs. Howard B. Field; transcript courtesy of Prof. Harry R. Warfel.

[4]In the possession of Mrs. Howard B. Field, transcript courtesy of Prof. Harry R. Warfel. Fowler's reply is printed in part as Appendix XXXVI of Ford's *Notes*.

[5]Newton F. McKeon, Director of the Amherst College Library, to the editor, November 19, 1954. The college more recently acquired a modern bronze cast from the plaster.

the hands of the original recipient.[6] A copy is in the Princeton University Library, and one which has been bronzed is in the possession of the G. & C. Merriam Company. A photograph of the bust appears on the cover of the *Amherst Graduates' Quarterly*, August, 1933 (Vol. XXII, No. 4).

A mediocre engraving of this bust was made by an unidentified person about 1845 and used in dictionaries published by Huntington and Savage in New York (e.g., Title 648).

NOTE A: *Other portraits from life*

In Ye Olde Tavern in West Brookfield, Massachusetts, located in a building once occupied by the Merriams' publishing concern, is a pair of portraits labeled Noah and Rebecca Webster, on loan from the West Brookfield Historical Society. The portraits were damaged in a fire in 1937 and have been much restored. The identifications are tenuous, and the portraits do not resemble others of Mr. and Mrs. Webster. The subjects appear to be in their late twenties, which would place the pictures, if they are the Websters, in the 1780s, but the costumes and technique appear to be much later than that. It is not likely that these are the Websters.

Various silhouettes of the Websters exist. In a letter to his daughter Harriet, October 23, 1832, Webster wrote,"I send you a profile—I suppose you will own & love it. It is certainly a good likeness. It is taken by a Mr Seager—& in about half an hour's time, and I send a copy to all your sisters. . . ."[7] In writing Webster on September 19, 1837, his niece Jerusha Parker acknowledged receipt of "the portrait," very likely another silhouette.[8]

NOTE B: *Posthumous portraits and statues*

In 1933 the G. and C. Merriam Company, wishing to avoid further use of reworked versions of the Morse portrait, commissioned Edwin B. Child of Dorset, Vermont, to execute a new portrait of Noah Webster. In gathering material, Mr. Child studied earlier portraits, and drew most heavily on the Ives bust and the Morse portrait. The portrait was

[6]Gift to the former mentioned in its *Second Annual Report* (1865), p. 24; not in inventory and not found by search and examination of unidentified busts by Miss Edna Huntington, Librarian, and the editor, December 16, 1954. Gift to the latter mentioned in its *Proceedings*, Ser. 3, Vol. 45 (1913), p. 303; Stephen T. Riley, Librarian, to the editor, December 16, 1954: ". . . the plaster bust of Noah Webster was given to one of the Boston Schools many years ago. . . ."

[7]In the possession of Mrs. Howard B. Field; transcript provided by Prof. Harry R. Warfel.

[8]Webster Papers, New York Public Library.

exhibited at the Century of Progress exposition in Chicago, and now hangs in the offices of the company. It is reproduced in various Merriam-Webster dictionaries subsequent to 1933. Some account of the genesis of the painting will be found in "The Librarian" in the *Boston Transcript*, November 6, 1935.

Of late 19th and early 20th century statues of Webster, one at least was done by an artist who had seen him and portrayed him from life. About 1880 Chauncey B. Ives, then in Rome, made a model for a full-length statue, probably intended for use on the Connecticut state house, but a bas-relief portrait by Carl H. Conrads was used instead. Mr. Ives kept the trial piece in his studio, where it was seen by the compiler's mother in 1892, and at her instance two or three bronzes were cast. One is now owned by Mrs. Richmond Mayosmith and another by Mrs. Theodore L. Bailey, both Webster relatives. The maquette is reproduced in Ford's *Notes* (Vol. II, facing p. 229; see also Vol. I, p. 13, n. 1, for Mrs. Ford's visit to Ives' studio).

A statue of Webster by Lee Lawrie is on one of the buttresses of Harkness Tower at Yale University, built in 1937. In 1942 a monumental statue by Korczak Ziolkowski was unveiled in West Hartford, Connecticut, Webster's birthplace. The figure on the Noah Webster memorial at Amherst College, executed by W. D. Paddock and dedicated in 1914, is allegorical and is not intended as a literal likeness.[9]

[9] *Amherst Graduates' Quarterly*, Vol. 4, pp. 124–129 (January, 1915) and Vol. 29, pp. 350–351 (August, 1940).

APPENDIX J – SELECTED REFERENCES ON THE LIFE AND WRITINGS OF WEBSTER

Over the long period during which she did research on Noah Webster, the compiler used hundreds of books and articles, many of which contained no direct reference to Webster but helped to give background on the times and milieu in which he lived and worked. Categories in which the compiler used the major secondary works include literary and journalistic history, educational history, linguistic and lexicographical history, history of the regions and institutions with which Webster was identified, local and national political history, history of printing in various localities, and reminiscences of Webster's friends, enemies, and contemporaries. She also consulted hundreds of book sale catalogues. It has not seemed necessary to swell the bulk of the present work by listing these sources, which are easily available and are known to students in the fields concerned. Those from which specific information has been drawn have been cited in the footnotes.

The following list, therefore, confines itself to biographies and sketches of Webster (including obituaries and eulogies), checklists of his writings, and articles and monographs on special aspects of the man and his work.

During Webster's lifetime hundreds of articles about him and his works appeared in newspapers and magazines—some of them listed above in Section Nine—but there was only one organized biographical sketch (see below, Section 2).

1. *Obituary notices and eulogies*

The New Haven newspapers were, of course, the first to announce Webster's death, which occurred there May 28, 1843. News stories and obituaries appeared in the *Daily Herald* and *Daily Palladium* of May 29. Announcements of the funeral appeared in the same papers on May 30, with accounts of resolutions passed by a group of gentlemen of the city, the Association of Congregational Ministers of the Eastern District of

New Haven County, and (*Daily Palladium*, May 31) the members of the bar. Accounts of the funeral appeared in the same papers for June 1 and in the *Daily Morning Courant* for June 3.

No attempt is made here to record notices which appeared outside of New Haven, except for the following sampling from the three major cities: *New York Tribune*, May 30, *New York Morning Express*, May 31, *New York Observer*, June 3; Boston *Daily Evening Transcript*, May 31, *Boston Recorder*, June 1; *Pennsylvania Inquirer*, May 31.

Obituaries also appeared in magazines in 1843, of which examples are the *Church Chronicle and Record*, June 2 (Vol. VII, p. 172), *The New Englander*, October (Vol. I, pp. 565–568), and, in England, *The Gentleman's Magazine*, August (n.s., Vol. XX, pp. 208–209).

The sermon preached at Webster's funeral by Nathaniel W. Taylor was later published in William C. Fowler's *Essays* (Hartford, 1876), pp. 62–71. A poem by Lydia Sigourney "On the Death of Dr. Webster" —which, however, could serve as a lament for any Christian—appeared in *The New World*, June 24 (Vol. VI, p. [731]). A memorial service was held in the chapel of Amherst College on July 4, 1843. The eulogy on that occasion, by Horatio M. Spofford, was not published; the manuscript is in the possession of Mrs. Howard B. Field. A later eulogy, an "Address delivered at the grave of Noah Webster..., New Haven, June fifteenth, 1902," by George H. Ford, was published in *Revolutionary Characters of New Haven* (New Haven, 1911), pp. [53]–58.

2. *Biographical sketches and biographies*

1834

James Herring and James B. Longacre, *National Portrait Gallery of Distinguished Americans* (4 vols., New York, etc., 1834–1839), ten unnumbered pages in Volume II, with a portrait by Herring, engraved by Parker. This sketch was extended to twelve pages in later editions (5 vols., Philadelphia, 1852–1867; 4 vols., Philadelphia, 1853–1854; 3 vols., Philadelphia, 1872), all printed from the same plates, though in the last-named the portrait is by Flagg, engraved by Halpin.

1844

In the Hartford Journal, *March 12, 1844, and other papers, it was announced that the Reverend Leonard Bacon had agreed to write a biography of Webster, but the plan was not carried out. In the Webster Papers is Bacon's draft, about a hundred pages, covering Webster's life up to about 1800.*

1845

Anonymous "Memoir," pp. v–x of the "University Edition" of the abridged *American Dictionary*. Also in later printings. Probably by William C. Fowler.

1847

Chauncey A. Goodrich,"Memoir of the Author," pp. [xiv]–xxii of the first posthumous revision of the unabridged *American Dictionary*.[1] Also in later printings. Shows derivation from the preceding.

1848

Chauncey A. Goodrich,"Life and Writings of Noah Webster. . .," *American Literary Magazine*, January, 1848 (Vol. II, pp. [5]–32). Nearly a third of this article is taken verbatim from the preceding entry.

1849

John W. Barber, in his *Connecticut Historical Collections. . ., Improved Edition* (New Haven, [1849]), pp. 566–568. There had been a few lines about Webster on pp. 49–50 of the original edition (1836), repeated in two later editions. In the 1849 edition, the first after Webster's death, this fuller sketch appeared, and continued to be used in later editions.

1850

[Abigail G. Whittelsey?], "Noah Webster," *Mrs. Whittelsey's Magazine for Mothers and Daughters*, October, 1850 (Vol. I, pp. 309–312). Includes an account of a personal meeting with Webster.

1851

Anonymous, "Noah Webster," *International Magazine*, August, 1851 (Vol. IV, pp. 12–16).

1853

Abner D. Jones, in his *Illustrated American Biography* (3 vols., New York, 1853–1855), Vol. I, pp. 251–252. Repeated in the same compiler's *American Portrait Gallery*. . . (New York, 1858 and 1869), pp. 133–134.

[1] This was published in September, 1847, but no copy has been located with a title-page dated earlier than 1848. G. & C. Merriam to the editor, May 9, 1956.

1855

Evert A. and George L. Duyckinck, in their *Cyclopaedia of American Literature* (2 vols., New York, 1855–1856), Vol. I, pp. 474–479. Also in later printings.

Anonymous,"Noah Webster, LL.D.," *United States Magazine*, August and September, 1855 (Vol. II, pp. 81–82, 103).

1857

Benson J. Lossing, in his *Eminent Americans* (New York, 1857), pp. 224–225.

1860

Webster first appeared as an entry in the *Encyclopaedia Britannica* with the eighth edition, 1853–1860. A short sketch of him is in Volume XXI, published in 1860; it was expanded in later editions.

1865

Increase N. Tarbox, "Noah Webster," *The Congregational Quarterly*, January, 1865 (Vol. VII, pp. [1]–16).

1870

L[ewis] Gaylord Clark,"Noah Webster," *Lippincott's Magazine*, April, 1870 (Vol. V, pp. 448–452).

1871

Anonymous,"Noah Webster, the Eminent Lexicographer," *The Phrenological Journal*, March, 1871 (Vol. 52, pp. 153–158).

1875

Horace E. Scudder, "A Patriotic School-Master," *Atlantic Monthly*, September, 1875 (Vol. 36, pp. 330–339).

1882

Horace E. Scudder, *Noah Webster* (Boston, n.d. [copyright 1881]), in the American Men of Letters series. Later printings in 1883, 1890, 1897, and 1899. In addition to the *Atlantic Monthly* article in 1875, Scudder, as background for this work, had delivered a lecture on Webster at the New England Historical and Genealogical Society, May 1, 1878. The work was reviewed by Francis A. March in the *Nation*, May 25, 1882 (Vol. 34, pp. 449–450); by Emily Fowler

Ford in the *Brooklyn Daily Eagle* and the *Commercial Advertiser*, May 30; anonymously in the *Century Illustrated Monthly Magazine*, June (Vol. XXIV [n.s. Vol. II], pp. 306–307); and elsewhere.

A book-length biography having appeared, the listing of periodical articles from this point on is highly selective.

1883

Joel Benton, "An Unwritten Chapter in Noah Webster's Life. . . ," *Magazine of American History*, July, 1883 (Vol. X, pp. [52]–56). Describes Webster's romantic interest in Rebecca Pardee of Sharon, Connecticut.

1892

[Frederick G. Harrison], in his *Biographical Sketches of Preeminent Amercans* (Boston, 1892, etc.) (Unpaged.)

1894

[P. J. O'Byrne], "Celebrated Shoemakers. Noah Webster. . . ," *Shoe and Leather Record* (London), February 23, 1894. The point of this article is based on an error (see introductory note to Appendix E).

1907

Franklin B. Dexter, in his *Biographical Sketches of the Graduates of Yale* (6 vols., New York, 1885–1912), Vol. IV (1907), pp. 66–79.

1912

Emily Ellsworth Fowler Ford, comp., *Notes on the Life of Noah Webster*. Described above as Title 766.

1914

Anson P. Stokes, in his *Memorials of Eminent Yale Men* (2 vols., New Haven, 1914), Vol. I, pp. 312–322.

1929

Edward Wagenknecht, "The Man behind the Dictionary," *Virginia Quarterly Review*, April, 1929 (Vol. V, pp. 246–258).

1936

Ervin C. Shoemaker, *Noah Webster, Pioneer of Learning*. New York, 1936. 347 pp.

Selected References

Harry R. Warfel, *Noah Webster, Schoolmaster to America.* New York, 1936. 460 pp.

1942
Isabel Proudfit, *Noah Webster, Father of the Dictionary,* New York, [1942]. For young people.

3. *Checklists of Webster's writings*

The first systematic attempt at a complete record of Noah Webster's writings, the germ of the present work, was made in 1882 by the compiler and her brother Paul Leicester Ford. Previously there had been partial checklists in general reference works, such as Henry C. Bohn's revision of William T. Lowndes' *Bibliographer's Manual of English Literature* (6 vols., London, 1857–1864; London and New York, 1869), Vol. V, pp. 2864–2865, and S. Austin Allibone's *Critical Dictionary of English Literature* (3 vols., Philadelphia, 1871), Vol. III, pp. 2627–2629.

In 1882 the two young Fords compiled, as a Christmas present for their father, Gordon L. Ford, a list based on his collection, part of which consisted of Webster's own copies of his works. Only six copies of the list were printed, as *Websteriana, A Catalogue of Books by Noah Webster, Collated from the Library of Gordon L. Ford* (Brooklyn, 1882), consisting of twenty leaves, printed on the rectos only. Copy No. 1 is at Yale, copies No. 4 and 5 are in The New York Public Library, copy No. 6 is in the Boston Public Library, and copies No. 2 and 3 are in private hands. Copy No. 1 has the title-page printed in red and black, and the large initials in gold. It has been heavily extra-illustrated (presumably by Gordon Ford) with engravings, title-pages, and manuscript matter, including a fourteen-leaf MS list of Webster's writings in his own hand.

Short checklists of varying degrees of fullness and accuracy appeared in later reference works, among them Herbert S. Stone, *First Editions of American Authors* (Cambridge, Mass., 1893), pp. 206–208, and Franklin B. Dexter, *Biographical Sketches of the Graduates of Yale* (6 vols., New York, 1885–1912), Vol. IV, pp. 69–79.

When the compiler edited her mother's *Notes* in 1912, she included (Vol. II, pp. [521]–540) a checklist of Webster's writings, though it did not attempt to list all the editions of the speller, grammar, or reader. The compiler also assisted in preparing the Webster listing in Joseph Sabin's *Dictionary of Books Relating to America*; this list was published in 1936, in Volume 27, pp. 541–558 (Nos. 102332 to 102401 inclusive).

Appendix J

4. *Special aspects of Noah Webster*

Allen, Frederic S., *Noah Webster's Place among English Lexicographers*... (Springfield, Mass., [1909]).

Laird, Charlton, "Etymology, Anglo-Saxon, and Noah Webster," *American Speech*, February, 1946 (Vol. XXI, pp. [3]–15).

Logan, Conrad T., "Noah Webster's Influence on American Spelling," *Elementary English Review*, January, 1937 (Vol. XIV, pp. 18–21).

Malone, Kemp, "A Linguistic Patriot," *American Speech*, October, 1925 (Vol. I, pp. 26–31).

Neumann, Joshua H., "American Pronunciation According to Noah Webster (1873)," a mimeographed excerpt from an unpublished doctoral dissertation, Columbia University, 1924. (Copies in the Columbia, New York Public, University of North Carolina, and Yale libraries, and the American Antiquarian Society.)

Read, Allen W., "Noah Webster as a Euphemist," *Dialect Notes*, July, 1934 (Vol. VI, pp. [385]–391).

Read, Allen W., "Noah Webster's Project in 1801 for a History of American Newspapers," *Journalism Quarterly*, September, 1934 (Vol. XI, pp. 258–275).

Skeel, Emily Ellsworth Ford, "Salesmanship of an Early American Best Seller," *Papers* of the Bibliographical Society of America, 1938 (Vol. 32, pp. 38–46).

Smith, G. Hubert, "Noah Webster, the Archaeologist," *American Anthropologist*, October–December, 1931 (Vol. 33, pp. 620–624).

Smith, Gerald A., "Noah Webster's Conservatism," *American Speech*, May, 1950 (Vol. 25, pp. [101]–104).

Thompson, Everett E., "Noah Webster and Amherst College," *Amherst Graduates' Quarterly*, August, 1933 (Vol. 22, pp. [289]–299).

Warthin, Aldred S., "Noah Webster as Epidemiologist," *Journal* of the American Medical Association, March 17, 1923 (Vol. 80, pp. 755–764).

Winslow, Charles-Edward A., "The Epidemiology of Noah Webster," *Transactions* of the Connecticut Academy of Arts and Sciences, January, 1934 (Vol. 32, pp. [23]–109).

Zunder, Theodore A., "Noah Webster and *The Conquest of Canaan*," *American Literature*, May, 1929 (Vol. I, pp. [200]–202).

APPENDIX K – GEOGRAPHICAL DIRECTORY OF PRINTERS, PUBLISHERS, BOOKSELLERS, STEREOTYPERS, ETC.

Which items in the bibliography bear the names of these firms or individuals may be determined from the index. The date given is for the earliest appearance of the name in a Webster or related book. Names in parentheses are mentioned only, and do not appear in any located Webster edition.

The businesses have been described by what seems to have been their major function, but because some of these trades overlapped, especially in the eighteenth century, the identifying word may not be the only one applicable. In most cases firm names in the same community containing the same surnames represent a continuation of a firm with changes in partnerships. No research has been done here to establish the history of the firms, though a note has been made when it is known that identical surnames do not represent the same individual. No entries have been made for Webster as his own publisher. Engravers are not listed; they may be found in Appendix I.

THE UNITED STATES

Connecticut

Hartford

1783 Hudson and Goodwin, publishers
1785 Barlow and Babcock, publishers
1790 Elisha Babcock, publisher
1797 (John Babcock, publisher)
1806 Oliver D. Cooke, publisher
1807 Lincoln and Gleason, booksellers
1817 George Goodwin and Sons, printers
1818 Hudson and Co., publishers[2]
1823 W. Hudson and L. Skinner, printers
1825 H. Hudson, bookseller

[2]This is Henry Hudson, son of Barzillai of the 1783 firm of Hudson and Goodwin.

1831 D. F. Robinson and Co., booksellers
1837 (Francis J. Huntington and Co., publishers)—see also New York
1838 Martinson and Co., printers
1841 Brown and Parsons, publishers
(Case, Tiffany and Co., printers)
1842 (Belknap and Hamersley, booksellers)
1845 Richard H. Hobbs, stereotyper

Litchfield
1835 (Sylvester Galpin, bookseller)

Middletown
1809 T. Dunning, printer
1827 William H. Niles, publisher

New Haven
1788 I. Beers (and Co.), booksellers and publishers
1798 T. and S. Green, printers
1800 Read and Morse, printers
1802 William W. Morse, printer
1803 Joel Walter, printer
1804 Increase Cook and Co., publishers
Sidney's Press
1806 Bronson, Walter and Co., publishers
Oliver Steele and Co., printers—see also Albany, Buffalo
1812 Howe and DeForest, publishers
Walter and Steele, publishers
1822 Sherman Converse, printer—see also New York
Howe and Spalding, publishers
1828 Hezekiah Howe, publisher
1831 Sidney Babcock, publisher
Baldwin and Treadway, printers
Durrie and Peck, publishers
A. H. Maltby, bookseller
S. Wadsworth, bookseller
1832 L. H. Young, bookseller
?1833 Whitmore and Minor, printers
1835 J. Peck, printer
1837 B. L. Hamlen, printer

New London
1792 (Timothy Green and Son, booksellers)
1807 Ebenezer P. Cady, printer

Delaware

Wilmington

1797 Peter Brynberg, bookseller
1802 Bonsal and Niles, publishers
1804 James Wilson, publisher
1816 Robert Porter, bookseller

Georgia

Atlanta

1863 Franklin Steam Printing House; J. J. Toon and Co., publishers

Macon

1863 Burke, Boykin and Co., publishers
1865 J. W. Burke and Co., publishers

Savannah

1809 (Collier and Hill, publishers)

Indiana

Hanover

1835 (James Morrow, publisher)

Lawrenceburgh

1839 James A. Morgan and Co., publishers[3]—see also Cincinnati

Madison

1835 (James Morrow, publisher)

Kentucky

Lexington

1806 (Joseph Charless, publisher)—see also Philadelphia
1812 Maccoun, Tilford and Co., publishers
Thomas T. Skillman, printer
1820 James W. Palmer, publisher; Sign of the Bible
1823 W. W. Worsley, publisher

Louisville

1823 Worsley and Collins, booksellers
1826 (John P. Morton, bookseller)
1831 Morton and Smith, booksellers
W. W. Worsley, publisher
1832 Wilcox, Dickerman and Co., publishers
?1845 Morton and Griswold, booksellers

[3]Called Morgan and Anthony in Webster's accounts.

Maine

Brunswick

1821 J. Griffin, printer

Hallowell

1821 W. F. Lane, bookseller

Portland

1811 A. Lyman and Co., publishers
J. McKown, printer

1821 William Hyde, bookseller

1839 O. L. Sanborn, publisher

1841 Sanborn, Sherburne and Co., publishers
Sherburne and Co., publishers—see also Boston and Philadelphia

1842 Sanborn and Carter, publishers

Maryland

Baltimore

1796 Thomas, Andrews, and Butler, booksellers

1825 Cushing and Jewett, publishers

1829 Joseph Jewett, publisher

1831 Cushing and Sons, publishers
McDowell and Son, booksellers
Plaskitt and Co., booksellers

?1838 Cushing and Brother(s), publishers
Jno. Cushing and Co., publishers

Massachusetts

Amherst

1844 J. S. and C. Adams, publishers

Boston

?1786 Peter Edes, printer—see also Newport, R.I.

1788 S. Hall, bookseller
J. Hastings, bookseller

1789 Thomas and Andrews, publishers
Isaiah Thomas and Co., publishers

1790 (Benjamin Guild, bookseller?)

1794 John W. Folsom, printer

1795 Hall and Nancrede, publishers

1804 David Carlisle, printer
Ebenezer Larkin, bookseller
John West (and Co.), publisher
West and Greenleaf, publishers

1807 David West, bookseller and publisher
1808 E. G. House, printer
1810 O. C. Greenleaf, bookseller
West and Blake, booksellers
1814 West and Richardson, publishers
1815 Bradford and Read, publishers
1816 Thomas W. White, printer
1819 J. H. A. Frost, printer
West, Richardson, and Lord, publishers
1820 Ezra Lincoln, printer
1821 C. Ewer, bookseller
1824 Richardson and Lord, publishers
1829 Boston Type and Stereotype Foundry
1830 Richardson, Lord, and Holbrook, publishers
1831 Carter and Hendee, publishers
1839 George A. and J. Curtis, stereotypers; New England Type and Stereotype Foundry
1841 Crocker and Brewster, booksellers
1843 R. H. Sherburne, bookseller—see also Philadelphia and Portland, Me.
Tappan and Dennett, booksellers
1845 Little and Brown, booksellers
B. B. Mussey, bookseller

Brookfield
1804 (E. Merriam and Co., publishers)
1835 E. and L. Merriam, publishers

Haverhill
1821 N. Burrill, bookseller

Leominster
1796 Charles Prentiss, printer

Newburyport
1805 Thomas and Whipple, booksellers
1809 Edward Little and Co., booksellers
William Sawyer and Co., booksellers

Northampton
1791 William Butler, printer
1818 Thomas W. Shepard and Co., printers

Salem
1805 Cushing and Appleton, publishers
Joshua Cushing, publisher

Springfield
1845 G. and C. Merriam, publishers
Worcester
1789 Isaiah Thomas, bookseller
1796 Thomas, Son, and Thomas, booksellers

Michigan
Detroit
1838 (J. S. and S. A. Bagg, printers)
(Bagg, Barnes and Co., printers)

New Hampshire
Claremont
1833 John Wilcox, publisher
1842 (Claremont Manufacturing Co., publishers)—see also Simeon Ide, Windsor, Vt.
Concord
1809 George Hough, publisher
1827 Manahan, Hoag and Co., publishers
1828 Horatio Hill and Co., publishers
?1831 Chase and Dunlap, stereotypers
1832 Moses G. Atwood, publisher
Atwood and Sanborn, publishers
Jacob Perkins, stereotyper
1833 Cofnin and Roby, stereotypers
D. D. Fiske, printer
1836 Atwood and Brown, publishers
1837 Brown's, publishers
Roby, Kimball, and Merrill, publishers
1839 (Hoag and Atwood, publishers)
1841 John F. Brown, publisher
1842 Luther Roby, publisher
1843 Rufus Merrill, publisher
Exeter
1809 Charles Norris and Co., printers
Franklin
1842 Peabody and Daniell, publishers
Keene
1802 John Prentiss, printer
Newport
1834 John Wilcox, publisher

Portsmouth
1805 Charles Pierce, bookseller
1809 Charles Tappan, bookseller
1816 J. F. Shores, bookseller
Tappan and Foster, booksellers
1821 H. Gray, bookseller
Sanbornton
?1833 Charles Lane, publisher
1835 Samuel Gerrish Hayes, publisher; Sandbornton Power Press
Walpole
1807 Thomas and Thomas, booksellers

New Jersey

Burlington
1792 Isaac Neale, printer
Elizabeth
1802 John Woods, printer
1836 E. Sanderson, printer
Newark
1793 John Woods, printer
New Brunswick
1797 Abraham Blauvelt, printer
1828 Terhune and Letson, publishers
1840 John Terhune, publisher
Trenton
1810 George Sherman, printer

New York

Albany
1788 W. Falconer and Co., booksellers
1796 Charles R. and George Webster, publishers
Thomas, Andrews, and Penniman, booksellers
1806 Webster(s) and Skinner(s), publishers
1831 Little and Cummings, booksellers
O. Steele, bookseller—see also Buffalo and New Haven
Brooklyn
1802 Thomas Kirk, printer
Buffalo
1832 Steele and Faxon, publishers
1833 Oliver G. Steele, publisher—see also Albany, New Haven

Canaan
  1795 (Elihu Phinney, publisher)
Canandaigua
  1820 Bemis and Ward, publishers
  1825 J. D. Bemis and Co., publishers
  1827 Bemis, Morse, and Ward, publishers
  1835 Morse and Harvey, publishers
  1839 (Clarendon Morse, publisher)[4]
Cazenovia
  1834 S. H. Henry and Co., publishers
  1841 Henry, Hitchcock and Co., publishers
Cooperstown
  1815 H. and E. Phinney, booksellers
Fredonia
  1832 (H. C. Frisbee, publisher)
Hudson
  1788 Ashbel Stoddard, printer and bookseller
  1805 William E. Norman, publisher
New York city (see also Brooklyn)
  1787 Samuel Loudon, printer
  1788 T. Allen, bookseller
    Berry and Rogers, booksellers
    Samuel Campbell, publisher
    S. and R. Campbell, booksellers
    Francis Childs, printer and bookseller
    T. Greenleaf, printer
    Harrisson and Purdy, printers
    R. Hodge, bookseller
    S. and J. Loudon, printers
    J. Reid, bookseller
  1789 J. Patterson, printer
  1793 George Bunce and Co., publishers
  1796 Hopkins, Webb and Co., publishers
  1797 (W. A. Davis, printer)
    (D. Dunham, bookseller)
    George F. Hopkins, publisher
    Evert A. Duyckinck and Co., booksellers
    Robert Wilson, printer

[4]This is not the Morse represented in the two preceding entries; his name was Chauncey.

1799 Ebenezer Belden and Co., publishers
C. Davis, publisher
Benjamin Gomez, bookseller
J. Harrisson, bookseller
N. Judah, bookseller
R. Magill, bookseller
P. A. Mesier, bookseller
1800 G. and R. Waite, publishers
1801 G. Jansen and Co., publishers
T. B. Jansen and Co., publishers
L. Nichols, printer
1803 I. Collins, publisher
(Zachariah Lewis, publisher)
(Joseph Mills, printer)
T. and J. Swords, publishers
William W. Vermilye, printer
1807 Brisban and Brannan, booksellers
1809 Jonathan Seymour, printer
Williams and Whiting, publishers
1811 Isaac Riley, publisher
1815 G. Long, printer
1820 E. and J. White, stereotypers
1821 Elihu White, stereotyper
1822 G. Bruce, stereotyper
1823 C. N. Baldwin, stereotyper
1827 A. Chandler, stereotyper
1828 Sherman Converse, publisher—see also New Haven
1829 J. P. Haven, bookseller
R. Lockwood, bookseller
1830 E. White's Type and Stereotype Foundery
White, Gallaher, and White, publishers
1831 E. Bliss, bookseller
Collins and Hannay, booksellers
L. D. Dewey, publisher
McElrath and Bangs, publishers
John T. West and Co., printers
1832 (American Tract Society, publishers)
N. and J. White, publishers
1834 James Van Norden, printer
1835 (R. and G. Wood, publishers)
1836 Redfield and Lindsay, stereotypers

1837 F. J. Huntington and Co., publishers—see also New Haven
1838 J. S. Redfield, stereotyper
1839 Collins, Keese and Co., publishers
1840 George F. Cooledge (and Brother), publishers
1841 White and Sheffield, publishers
?1842 Applegate's Steam Presses
Redfield and Savage, stereotypers
1843 Harper and Brothers, publishers
Huntington and Savage, publishers
Webster and Clark, publishers
1845 C. A. Alvord, printer
Mark H. Newman, bookseller
1849 (Charles C. Savage, stereotyper)
1857 D. Appleton and Co., publishers
1890 American Book Company, publishers

Poughkeepsie
1809 Joseph Nelson, printer
Chester Parsons and Co., publishers

Pulaski
1840 C. D. Loomis and Co., publishers[5]

Rochester
1831 Hoyt, Porter and Co., publishers
1834 Marshall and Dean, printers

Sandy Hill
1836 Griffen, Mabbett and Co., printers

Troy
1804 (T. Collier, publisher)
1807 Rensselaer Book Store; Wright, Goodenow, and Stockwell, printers—see also Bennington, Vt.

Utica
1805 Merrell and Seward, publishers
1806 Asahel Seward, publisher
1808 Seward and Williams, publisher
1817 William Williams, publisher
1842 Bennett, Backus, and Hawley, publishers

Watertown
1833 Knowlton and Rice, publishers

[5]This firm appears in some of Webster's records as Loomis and Brayton.

North Carolina

Edenton

?1809 [Henry or James Wills?]

Newbern

1803 Martin and Ogden, publishers

1804 (Franklin and Garrow, publishers)

Raleigh

1863 Biblical Recorder Print
Bronson, Farrar and Co., publishers

Ohio

Cincinnati

1821 B. and I. Collins, stereotypers
John P. Foote, publisher

1822 Morgan (and) Lodge (and Co.), publishers

1825 Anson(?) N. Deming, printer
N. and G. Guilford, publishers

1827 W. M. and O. Farnsworth, Jr., printers
Morgan, Fisher, and L'Hommedieu, publishers

1828 Morgan and Sanxay, publishers

1831 Cincinnati Type Foundry
Cincinnati Stereotype Foundry
O. Farnsworth, publisher

1833 Corey and Fairbank, publishers
J. A. James, stereotyper

1834 Students' Typographical Association of Lane Seminary

1835 Corey, Fairbank, and Webster, publishers

1836 Burgess and Morgan, publishers
Corey and Webster, publishers
(Webster, Burgess, and Morgan, publishers)

1837 Burgess and Crane, publishers

1841 (George Conclin, publisher)

1842 J. A. Morgan, publisher—see also Lawrenceburgh, Ind.

?1843 E. Morgan and Co., publishers

Cleveland

1830 David B. McLain, printer
R. Pew and Co., publishers

1832 (Madison Kelley, publisher)

1836 Sanford and Lott, printers and booksellers

1841 M. C. Younglove, publisher

Columbus
1833 Jenkins and Glover, publishers
1837 I. N. Whiting (and Huntington), publishers
Dayton
1849 B. F. Ells, publisher
Lebanon
1820 A. Van Vleet, printer
Medina
1841 O. W. McKinney, printer
Portsmouth
1839 (Elisha Glover, publisher)
Yellow Springs
1831 O. Farnsworth, publisher

Oregon

Oregon City
1847 Oregon Printing Association, publishers

Pennsylvania

Chambersburg
1798 Robert Harper, printer
Erie
1839 Henry L. Harvey, publisher
1841 Oliver Spafford, publisher
Philadelphia
1786 (Thomas Dobson, bookseller)
1787 (Joseph Crukshank, printer)
Prichard and Hall, publishers
Young and M'Culloch, publishers
1788 (William Spotswood, publisher)
W. Young, publisher
1792 (Charles Cist, printer)
1795 Mathew Carey, publisher
Lang and Ustick, printers
Henry Tuckniss, printer
1800 (William Duane, publisher)
1802 Joseph Charless, printer—see also Lexington, Ky.
1804 (Benjamin Johnson, printer)
Jacob Johnson and Co., publishers
1805 David Hogan, publisher
Thomas Irwin, printer

?1809 (Binny and Ronaldson, typefounders)
1810 L. Dobelbower, printer
T. Stiles, printer
1811 Jane Aitken, printer
Johnson and Warner, publishers
B. and T. Kite, publishers
1813 William Greer, printer
1824 J. Howe, stereotyper
Kimber and Sharpless, publishers
1828 Robert H. Sherburne, publisher—see also Boston and Portland, Me.
1830 John P. Ayres, publisher
L. Johnson, stereotyper
1831 John Grigg, bookseller
U. Hunt, bookseller
Key and Mielke, booksellers
Tower and Hogan, booksellers
1837 J. Crissy, printer
1839 (Thomas, Cowperthwait and Co., publishers)
1843 Smith and Peck, publishers
1845 Carey and Hart, booksellers
1846 Jesper Harding, publisher

Pittsburgh
1814 Cramer, Spear, and Eichbaum, printers
1830 Hogan and Co., booksellers
1835 Johnston and Stockton, publishers
1839 (Patterson, publisher)

Wellsboro
1836 (Josiah Emery, publisher)

Rhode Island

Providence
1789 John Carter, printer
Peter Edes, printer—see also Boston

South Carolina

Charleston
1788 Mrs. A. Timothy, bookseller
1815 P. W. Johnston, printer
1831 O. A. Roorbach, bookseller

Tennessee

Knoxville

1841 (James Williams, printer)

Place unknown

1841 (Pryor and Whiteman, publishers)

Vermont

Bennington

1788 (Haswell and Russell, publishers)

?1790 Anthony Haswell, publisher

?1800 William Stockwell, printer

1807 Wright, Goodenow, and Stockwell, printers[6]—see also Troy, N.Y.

Bradford

1844 A. Low, publisher

Brattleboro

1809 Fessenden, Holbrook, and Porter, publishers[7]
William Fessenden, publisher

1816 John Holbrook, publisher

1819 Abijah Burbank, publisher

1820 Holbrook and Fessenden, publishers[8]

1832 Brattleboro' Power Press

1841 Brattleboro' Typographic Company

Burlington

1831 Chauncey A. Goodrich, publisher

1835 Smith and Harrington, publishers

Montpelier

1839 E. P. Walton and Son(s), publishers

Wells River

1831 White and Wilcox, publishers

1833 White and Homan, publishers

1835 Ira White, publisher

Windsor

?1802 Nahum Mower, publisher

1804 Kingsbery and Blake, publishers

1827 Simeon Ide, publisher—see also Claremont Manufacturing Co., Claremont, N. H.

[6]This is Henry Stockwell, not the William Stockwell of the preceding entry.

[7]This firm appears in Webster's accounts as Holbrook, Fessenden, and Porter.

[8]This is not the same Fessenden as in the earlier Brattleboro entries; this represents Joseph, William's brother.

Virginia-West Virginia

Alexandria

1800 J. and J. D. Westcott, printers and booksellers

Wheeling

1831 J. Fisher and Son, publishers
1839 A. and R. Fisher, publishers
1840 (Stephens and Garwood, publishers)
?1841 (Robb and Stephenson, publishers)

Hawaii

Lahainaluna

1845 [Press of the Mission Seminary]

CANADA

Ontario

Hamilton

1843 A. H. Armour and Co., booksellers
1845 Ramsay and McKendrick, booksellers

Kingston

1843 Ramsay, Armour and Co., booksellers

Quebec

Montreal

1836 H. H. Cunningham, publisher
1843 Armour and Ramsay, publishers

ENGLAND

Bristol

?1816 T. Long, bookseller

Coventry

1808 Pratt, Smith, and Lesson, printers

Croydon

1799 West, circulating library

London

1797 (Charles Dilly, bookseller)
1798 J. and A. Arch, publishers
Knight and Triphook, publishers
H. D. Symonds, publisher
1799 E. Harding, publisher
W. West, publisher

1800 G. G. and J. Robinson, publishers
G. Woodfall, printer
1808 Craddock and Joy, booksellers
Longman, Hurst, Rees, and Orme, booksellers
R. Scholey, bookseller
1818 R. Edwards, printer and bookseller
T. Hamilton, bookseller
W. Kent, bookseller
Sherwood, Neely, and Jones, booksellers
1830 Black, Young, and Young, publishers
1832 Richard Taylor, printer
1840 Henry G. Bohn, publisher
?1856 Petter and Galpin, printers
Ward and Lock, publishers
1858 Dean and Son, publishers

Ripley
1799 Crowder, circulating library

Tewkesbury
1799 W. Dyde, printer

JAPAN

Osaka
1887 Masajiro Kashiwabara, publisher

Tokyo
1871 Bensei Kyosho, publisher
1887 Jironosuke Kansaki, publisher
Shoundo Kappan-sho, printers

ILLUSTRATIONS

PLATE I.
The "porcupine portrait" (Title 16 and later)
American Antiquarian Society

FABLE I. *Of the Boy that ſtole Apples.*

FABLE II. *The Country Maid and her Milk-pail.*

FABLE III. *The Fox and the Swallow.*

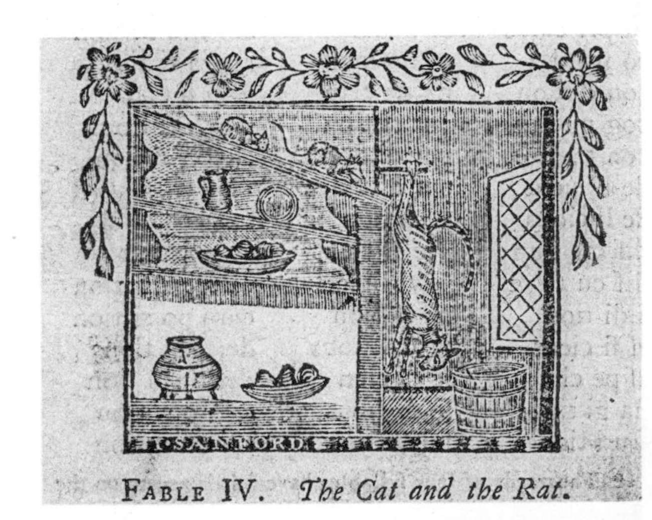

FABLE IV. *The Cat and the Rat.*

FABLE V. *The Fox and the Bramble.*

FABLE VI. *The Bear and the two Friends.*

FABLE VII. *The two Dogs.*

FABLE VIII. *The partial Judge.*

PLATE II.
Young and M'Culloch's set (Title 7 and later). *John Carter Brown Library*

Fable I.—*Of the* Boy *that ſtole* Apples.

Fable II.—*The* Country Maid *and her* Milk Pail.

Fable III.—*The* Fox *and the* Swallcw.

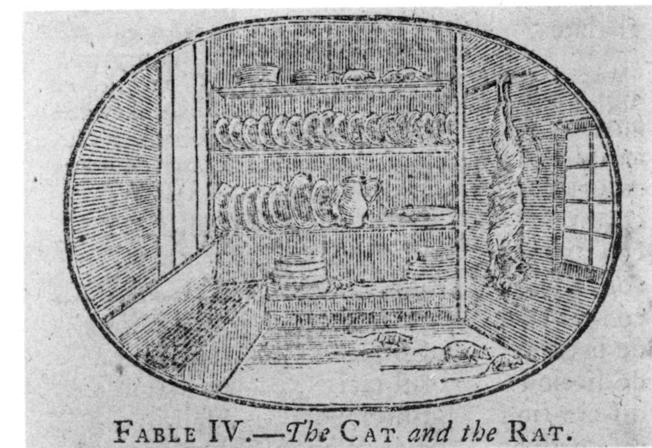

Fable IV.—*The* Cat *and the* Rat.

Fable V.—*The* Fox *and the* Bramble.

Fable VI.—*The* Bear *and the* Two Friends.

Fable VII.—*The* Two Dogs.

Fable VIII.—*The* Partial Judge.

PLATE III.

Thomas and Andrews' set (Title 16 and later). *American Antiquarian Society*

FABLE I. *Of the Boy that ſtole Apples.*

FABLE II. *The Country Maid and her Milk-pail.*

FABLE III. *The Fox and the Swallow.*

FABLE IV. *The Cat and the Rat.*

FABLE V. *The Fox and the Bramble.*

FABLE VI. *The Bear and the two Friends.*

FABLE VII. *The two Dogs.*

FABLE VIII. *The partial Judge.*

PLATE IV.

Hudson and Goodwin's first set (Title 17 and later). *The New York Public Library*

Fable I. *Of the Boy that stole Apples.*

Fable II. *The Country Maid and her Milk pail.*

Fable III. *The Fox and the Swallow.*

Fable IV. *The Cat and the Rat.*

FABLE V. *The Fox and the Bramble.*

FABLE VI. *The Bear and the two Friends.*

FABLE VII. *The two Dogs.*

FABLE VIII. *The partial Judge.*

PLATE V.

Hudson and Goodwin's second set, by Asa W. Lay (Title 26 and later). *Connecticut State Library*

FABLE I. *Of the Boy that Stole Apples.*

FABLE II. *The Country Maid and her Milk-pail.*

FABLE III. *The Fox and the Swallow.*

FABLE IV. *The Cat and the Old Rat.*

FABLE V. *The Fox and the Bramble.*

FABLE VI. *The Bear and the two Friends.*

FABLE VII. *The Two Dogs.*

FABLE VIII. *The partial Judge.*

PLATE VI.

Samuel Campbell's set, by Isaac Sanford (Title 28). *Connecticut State Library*

PLATE VII.

Samuel Campbell's frontispiece, by Alexander Anderson (Title 28)

Connecticut State Library

PLATE VIII.
Bonsal and Niles' frontispiece (Title 69 and later)
The New York Public Library

FABLE I. *Of the Boy that ſtole Apples.*

FABLE II. *The Country Maid and her Milk Pail.*

FABLE III. *The Fox and the Swallow.*

FABLE IV. *The Cat and the Rat.*

FABLE V. *The Fox and the Bramble.*

FABLE VI. *The Bear and the two Friends.*

FABLE VII. *The two Dogs.*

FABLE VIII. *The partial Judge.*

PLATE IX.

Hudson and Goodwin's third set, by Zadoc Howe and William Wadsworth (Title 55 and later).

The New York Public Library

Fable I. *Of the Boy that ſtole Apples.*

Fable II. *The Country Maid and her Milk Pail.*

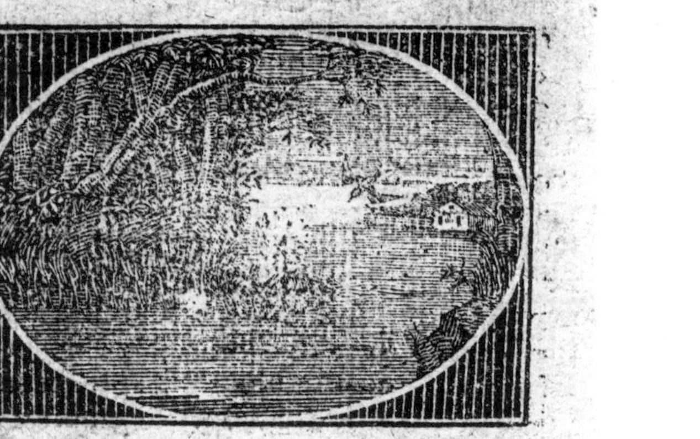

Fable III. *The Fox and the Swallow.*

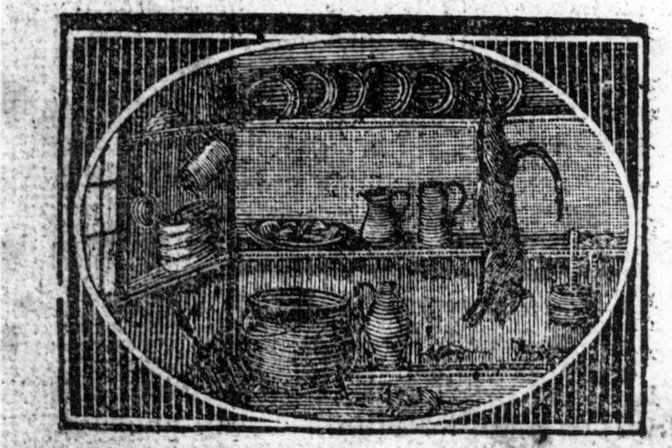

Fable IV. *The Cat and the Rat.*

FABLE V. *The Fox and the Bramble.*

FABLE VI. *The Bear and the Two Friends.*

FABLE VII. *The two Dogs.*

FABLE VIII. *The partial Judge.*

PLATE X.

Hudson and Goodwin's fourth set, by Abner Reed (Title 62 and later). *The New York Public Library*

Fable I. *Of the* Boy *that ſtole Apples.*

Fable II. *The* Country Maid *and her* Milk Pai

Fable III. *The* Fox *and the* Swallow.

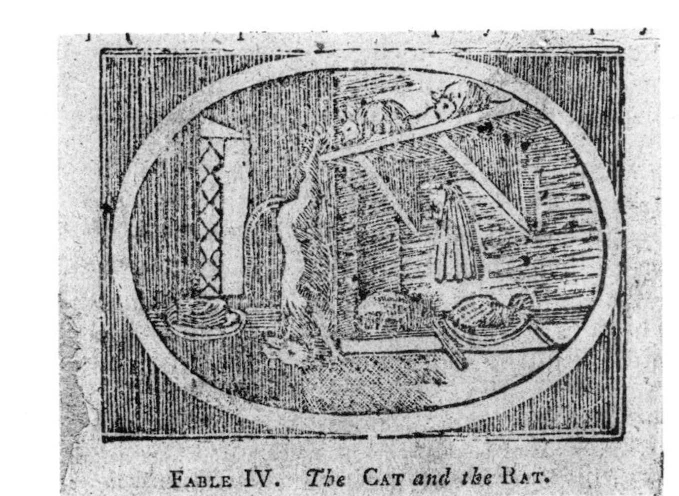

Fable IV. *The* Cat *and the* Rat.

PLATE XI.

Bonsal and Niles' set (Title 69 and later). *The New York Public Library*

FABLE I. *Of the boy that ſtole Apples.*

FABLE II. *The country Maid and her Milk Pail.*

FABLE III. *The Fox and the ſwallow.*

li quor an ti quity

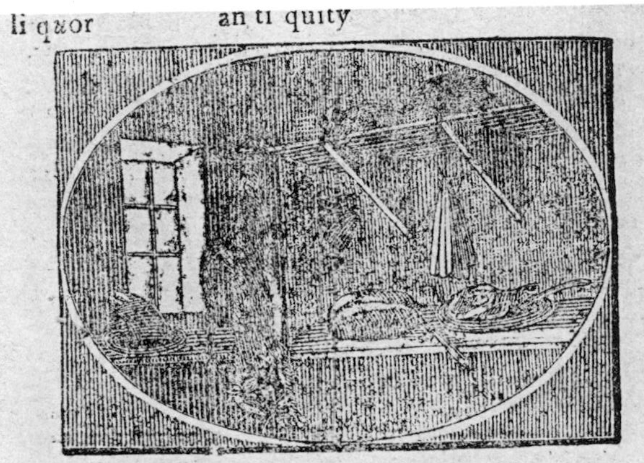

FABLE IV. *The Cat and the Rat.*

• pin ion ver mil ion

FABLE V. *The Fox and the Bramble.*

The derivatives follow the same rule.

FABLE VI. *The Bear and the Two Friends.*

an ti bac chus

FABLE VII, *The Two Dogs.*

FABLE VIII. *The partial judge.*

A Farmer came to a neigbouring Lawyer, ex-

PLATE XII.

Martin and Ogden's set (Title 79). *New-York Historical Society*

FABLE I.

Of the Boy that stole Apples.

FABLE II.

The Country Maid and her Milk Pail.

FABLE III.

The Fox and the Swallow.

FABLE IV.

The Cat and the Rat.

FABLE V.

The Fox and the Bramble.

FABLE VI.

The Bear and the Two Friends.

FABLE VII.

The Two Dogs.

FABLE VIII.

The Partial Judge.

PLATE XIII.

First set by Alexander Anderson (Title 89 and later). *American Antiquarian Society*

FABLE I.

Of the Boy that stole Apples.

FABLE II.

The Country Maid and her Milk Pail.

FABLE III.

The Fox and the Swallow.

FABLE IV.

The Cat and the Rat.

FABLE V.

The Fox and the Bramble.

FABLE VI.

The Bear and the Two Friends.

FABLE VII.

The Two Dogs.

FABLE VIII.

The Partial Judge.

PLATE XIV.

Fessenden, Holbrook, and Porter's set (Title 119 and later). *G. and C. Merriam Company*

FABLE I.
Of the Boy that stole Apples.

FABLE II.
The Country Maid and her Milk pail.

FABLE III.
The Fox and the Swallow.

FABLE IV.
The Cat and the Rat.

FABLE V.

The Fox and the Bramble.

FABLE VI.
The Bear and the two Friends.

FABLE VII.
The Two Dogs.

FABLE VIII.
The Partial Judge.

PLATE XV.
Second set by Alexander Anderson (Title 178 and later). *The New York Public Library*

FABLE I.
Of the Boy that stole Apples.

FABLE II.
The Country Maid and her Milk pail.

FABLE III.
The Fox and the Swallow.

FABLE IV.
The Cat and the Rat.

FABLE V.

The Fox and the Bramble.

FABLE VI.

The Bear and the two Friends.

FABLE VII.

The Two Dogs.

FABLE VIII.

The Partial Judge.

PLATE XVI.

Hudson and Company's set, by John W. Barber (Title 200 and later). *The New York Public Library*

FABLE I.

Of the Boy that stole Apples.

FABLE II.

The Country Maid and her Milk pail.

FABLE III.

The Two [illegible]ogs.

FABLE IV.

The partial Judge.

PLATE XVII.

Cuts for the *Elementary Spelling Book* (Title 273 and later). *Watkinson Library*

PLATE XVIII.
First frontispiece by Alexander Anderson (Title 178 and later)
The New York Public Library

A

Grammatical Institute,

OF THE

ENGLISH LANGUAGE,

COMPRISING,

An easy, concise, and systematic Method of

EDUCATION,

Designed for the Use of *English* Schools

In *AMERICA*.

IN THREE PARTS.

PART I.

CONTAINING,

A new and accurate Standard of Pronunciation.

BY NOAH WEBSTER, A. M.

Usus est Norma Loquendi. CICERO.

HARTFORD:

PRINTED BY HUDSON & GOODWIN,

FOR THE AUTHOR.

PLATE XIX.

First edition of the speller, 1783 (Title 1)

The New York Public Library

THE

AMERICAN

SPELLING BOOK:

CONTAINING,

An eaſy ſtandard of Pronunciation.

Being the FIRST PART of a

Grammatical Inſtitute

OF THE

Engliſh Language.

IN THREE PARTS.

BY NOAH WEBSTER, Jun'r. ESQUIRE.

The ELEVENTH Edition.

HARTFORD:

PRINTED BY HUDSON AND GOODWIN.

PLATE XX.

First known edition entitled *American Spelling Book*, 1788

(Title 11)

John Carter Brown Library

THE

AMERICAN

SPELLING BOOK;

CONTAINING,

THE RUDIMENTS

OF THE

ENGLISH LANGUAGE,

FOR THE

USE OF SCHOOLS

IN THE

UNITED STATES.

By NOAH WEBSTER, Esq.

Johnson's ~~Fort~~ FIRST REVISED IMPRESSION.

1803

1804

PLATE XXI.
The model copy of the *American Spelling Book*, revised, 1804 (Title 89)
American Antiquarian Society

THE

ELEMENTARY

SPELLING BOOK;

BEING

AN IMPROVEMENT

ON THE

AMERICAN SPELLING BOOK.

BY NOAH WEBSTER, LL. D.

NEW-YORK.

PUBLISHED BY J. P. HAVEN AND R. LOCKWOOD.

Stereotyped by A. Chandler.

1829.

PLATE XXII.
First edition of the *Elementary Spelling Book*, 1829 (Title 261)
Watkinson Library

AN AMERICAN

SELECTION

OF

Leſſons in Reading and Speaking.

CALCULATED

To improve the MINDS and refine the TASTE of YOUTH.

AND ALSO

To inſtruct them in the GEOGRAPHY, HISTORY, and POLITICS of the UNITED STATES.

To which is prefixed,

RULES in ELOCUTION, and DIRECTIONS for expreſſing the principal PASSIONS of the Mind.

BEING

The THIRD PART of a Grammatical Inſtitute of the Engliſh Language.

BY NOAH WEBSTER, jun. ESQ.

THE THIRD EDITION,
GREATLY ENLARGED.

Begin with the Infant in his Cradle: Let the firſt Word he liſps be Waſhington.
MIRABEAU.

PHILADELPHIA:
Printed and ſold by YOUNG and M'CULLOCH, at the Corner of *Second* and *Cheſnut-ſtreets.*

M.DCC.LXXXVII.

PLATE XXIII.
First edition of the reader entitled *American Selection*, 1787
(Title 452)
The New York Public Library

A

Compendious Dictionary

OF THE

English Language.

In which FIVE THOUSAND Words are added
to the number found in the BEST ENGLISH COMPENDS;

The ORTHOGRAPHY is, in some instances, corrected;

The PRONUNCIATION marked by an Accent or other suitable Direction;

And the DEFINITIONS of many Words amended and improved.

TO WHICH ARE ADDED FOR THE BENEFIT OF THE

MERCHANT, the STUDENT and the TRAVELLER,

I.—TABLES of the MONEYS of most of the commercial Nations in the world, with the value expressed in Sterling and Cents.

II.—TABLES of WEIGHTS and MEASURES, ancient and modern, with the proportion between the several weights used in the principal cities of Europe.

III.—The DIVISIONS of TIME among the Jews, Greeks and Romans, with a Table exhibiting the Roman manner of dating.

IV.—An official List of the POST-OFFICES in the UNITED STATES, with the States and Counties in which they are respectively situated, and the distance of each from the seat of Government.

V.—The NUMBER of INHABITANTS in the United States, with the amount of EXPORTS.

IV.—New and Interesting CHRONOLOGICAL TABLES of remarkable Events and Discoveries.

BY NOAH WEBSTER, ESQ.

From Sidney's Press.

FOR HUDSON & GOODWIN, BOOK-SELLERS, HARTFORD, AND INCREASE COOKE & CO.

BOOK-SELLERS, NEW-HAVEN.

1806.

PLATE XXIV.
Webster's first dictionary, 1806 (Title 577)
The New York Public Library

1782 2394

AN

AMERICAN DICTIONARY

OF THE

ENGLISH LANGUAGE:

INTENDED TO EXHIBIT,

I. The origin, affinities and primary signification of English words, as far as they have been ascertained.
II. The genuine orthography and pronunciation of words, according to general usage, or to just principles of analogy.
III. Accurate and discriminating definitions, with numerous authorities and illustrations.

TO WHICH ARE PREFIXED,

AN INTRODUCTORY DISSERTATION

ON THE

ORIGIN, HISTORY AND CONNECTION OF THE

LANGUAGES OF WESTERN ASIA AND OF EUROPE,

AND A CONCISE GRAMMAR

OF THE

ENGLISH LANGUAGE.

BY NOAH WEBSTER, LL. D.

IN TWO VOLUMES.

VOL. I.

He that wishes to be counted among the benefactors of posterity, must add, by his own toil, to the acquisitions of his ancestors.—*Rambler.*

NEW YORK:
PUBLISHED BY S. CONVERSE.
PRINTED BY HEZEKIAH HOWE—NEW HAVEN.
1828.

PLATE XXV.
First edition of the unabridged dictionary, 1828 (Title 583)
The New York Public Library

The AMERICAN MINERVA,

Patroneſs of Peace, Commerce, and the Liberal Arts.

Publiſhed (Daily) *by* GEORGE BUNCE, & Co. *No.* 37, *Wall-ſtreet, nearly oppoſite the Tontine Coffee-houſe, at Six Dollars per annum.*

VOL. I.] *NEW-YORK,* MONDAY, December 9, 1793. [NUMB. 1.

THE HERALD; A GAZETTE FOR THE COUNTRY.

Publiſh WEDNESDAYS *and* SATURDAYS, *by* GEORGE BUNCE & Co. *No.* 12, *Wall-ſtreet, near the City-hall, at* THREE DOLLARS *per annum.*

NUMB. 1.] *NEW-YORK, WEDNESDAY,* JUNE 4, 1794. [VOL. I.

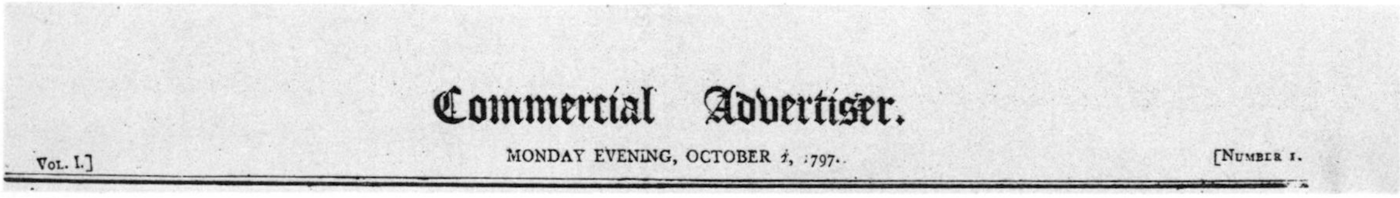

Commercial Advertiser.

VOL. I.] MONDAY EVENING, OCTOBER 2, 1797. [NUMBER 1.

The Spectator.

VOL. I.] NEW-YORK, WEDNESDAY, OCTOBER 4, 1797. [NUMBER 1.

PLATE XXVI.

Mastheads of newspapers edited by Webster

(Titles 789, 791–793)

The New York Public Library

INDEX

INDEX

A (pseudonym, not Webster), 492
A. B. (pseudonym, Webster), 447
A. B. (pseudonym, not Webster), 484, 485, 488, 563
A. C. (pseudonym, probably not Webster), 454
A. K. (pseudonym, not Webster), 492
A. M. (pseudonym, probably Webster), 477
A. Z. (pseudonym, Webster), 436, 437
Abolition/abolitionists, 310, 468, 473, 530, 538
Abolition Society, *see* Connecticut Society for the Promotion of Freedom
Abolitionist, an (pseudonym, not Webster), 468
"Abolitionists, so called, To the" (Webster), 363
"Abraham Bishop unmask'd," *see Rod for the fool's back*
Accentuation, 218
Account of the epidemic yellow fever (Seaman), 374
"Account of the most remarkable battles" (Webster), 164
Academicus (pseudonym, Webster), 460
Academus (pseudonym, not Webster), 460
Act to establish a permanent fund, an, 528
Act to incorporate the Bank of Connecticut, 523
Adam (pseudonym, Webster), 488
Adams, J. S. and C., 238, 239
Adams, John, 316, 337, 417, 427, 451, 578; administration of, 318
Adams, John Quincy, 228
Adams, Samuel, 541
Adams power press, 113
Addison, Joseph, 162, 171, 219
"Additional observations on the nature of fever" (Webster), 453
"Address delivered at the grave of Noah Webster" (Ford), 595
Address, delivered at the laying of the cornerstone . . . Amherst (Webster), 331
Address, delivered before the Hampshire, Franklin and Hampden Agricultural Society (Webster), 330
"Address from the inhabitants of [Hartford]" (Webster et al.), 522
"Address of Congress to the inhabitants of the province of Quebec," 162
"Address of Congress to the people of Great Britain . . . 1774," 162
"Address" on Fayetteville fire (Webster), 530
Address to the citizens of Connecticut (Webster), 321
"Address to the citizens of New Haven" (Webster), 529
Address to the freemen of Connecticut, 1803 (Webster), 523–524
Address to the freemen of Connecticut, 1806 (Webster), 524–525
"Address to the ladies" (Webster), 168, 169, 339, 391
"Address to the people of Connecticut" (projected publication, Webster), 435
Address to the people of the state of New-York, on the subject of the Constitution (Jay), reviewed, 392
Address to the people of the state of New-York, shewing the necessity of making amendments (anon.), reviewed, 392

Index

"Address to the President of the U.S. on the subject of his address" (Webster?), 320
"Address to the President of the U.S. on the subject of his administration" (Webster), 319
"Address to y[o]ung gentlemen" (Webster), 168, 169, 339, 444
"Address to yung ladies," *see* "Address to the ladies"
Adieu (pseudonym, not Webster), 491
"Advertisement" (to unabridged dictionary), 233, 234, 241
Advertisement. A new edition of the Bible, 357
"Advice to a young tradesman" (Franklin), 164
"Advice to Connecticut folks, a bit of" (Webster), 338, 440
"Advice to masons" (Webster), 388
"Advice to the young" (Webster), 211, 478
Aesop, 11
"Affinity between the languages of Europe and Asia, On the" (Webster), 455
"After the Norman conquest" (Webster), 210
"Agathocles and Calista" (anon.), 162
Agriculture, 203, 211, 219, 311, 412, 445, 453, 454, 459, 463, 471, 533, 537; *see also* Ergot; Forestry; Manure; Potatoes; Theory of vegetation
"Agriculture" (illustration), 191, 218
Aitken, Jane, 284
Albany, N.Y., W. lectures in, 533
Albany Democratic Whig General Committee, 511, 512
Alexandria, Va., W. lectures in, 532
All-together (pseudonym, Webster), 467
"Allegiance, on" (Webster), 339
Allegory of printing press (illustration), 95, 110
Allen, Thomas, 26, 387
Allen, William, 516
Alpha (pseudonym, Webster), 473
Alphabet, rhymed (New England primer), 368, 369
Alphabet, special, 267
Alphonzo (pseudonym, Webster), 391, 392
Alvord, C. A., 262, 263
"America" (Webster), 210
American, an (pseudonym, Webster), 311, 389, 393, 449
American, an (pseudonym, not Webster), 270, 508
American Academy of Arts and Sciences, 430, 431
American Book Company, 128, 129
"American crisis" (Paine), 162
American definition spelling book (Kneeland), 565–566
American definition spelling book (Ormsby), 566
American Dictionary (unabridged), 74, 85, 153, 225, 229, 231–243, 245, 249, 356, 468, 480, 481, 587; plans and progress, 225–226, 229, 355, 451, 452, 453, 457, 461, 462, 463; English edition, 240–243, 462; Cobb's attack on, 501–503
American dictionary, abridged by Webster, 244–248, 463
American dictionary, abridged by Worcester, 238, 242, 249–255, 462, 501, 509
American eclectic (magazine), 478–479
American geography (Morse), 164, 341
American Indians, 338, 389, 393, 474; mounds, 389; wars, 199, 210
American Institute of Instruction, W. attends, 538
"American instructor" (proposed title), 6
"American lessons in reading and speaking" (variant title), 182
American magazine, 158, 168, 387–397, 398, 442
American Mercury (newspaper), carrier's address, 335
American Minerva (newspaper), 398–413; principles and policies, 399, 405, 406, 408, 409, 411, 412; labor troubles, 400; improvements, 401, 405; delivery, 407, 410
American preceptor (Bingham), 176

Index

American Revolution, 203, 210, 338, 434, 436; *see also* Harrington
American selection (Webster), 163–190, 191, 192, 338, 339, 341
American spelling book (Webster), 10–85, 95, 106, 174, 461, 467, 469; as title, 11
"American states" (Webster), 305
American Tract Society, 561
Americanus (pseudonym, not Webster), 516–517
Americus (pseudonym, Webster), 455, 478
Ames, Fisher, 176
Amherst Academy/College, 263, 331, 353, 354, 460, 477, 527, 528, 529, 537, 552, 591, 593, 595
Amherst, Mass., W. moderator of town meeting, 583; First Parish, 529, 584
Amicus (pseudonym, probably Webster), 498
Analysis of the government of the United States (unpublished work, Webster), 559
Anderson, Alexander, 19, 24, 37, 42, 58, 59, 85, 86, 95, 109, 138, 209, 210, 214, 571
Andrews, Ebenezer (as individual), 35, 171, 275; *see also* Thomas and Andrews
Andrews, John, 163, 165, 488
Andrews, Joseph, 590
"Animals" (Webster), 203, 220
"Animals of the United States" (Webster), 211
Annapolis, Md., W. lectures in, 532
Anonymity, Webster's use of, 153, 273, 275, 280
Another Friend to Liberality (pseudonym, not Webster), 488
Another Pennsylvanian (pseudonym, not Webster), 486
"Answer to His Exc. John Brooks"/ "Answer to the address of the Governor" (Webster), 353, 528
Anthology of English poetry, expurgated (projected work, Webster), 560
Anthology of sermons (projected work, Webster), 560
Anthology Society, 228
Anthon, Charles: classical dictionary, 479
Anthony, *see* Morgan and Anthony
"Antiquity" (Webster), 389, 393
"Any other time will do as well" (Webster), 272
Appeal to Americans (Webster), 323; *see also* Voice of Wisdom
Apple: cider, 453; trees, 446
Applegate's steam presses, 123, 124
Appleton, D. and Co., 128, 129, 132, 134, 195
Appleton, Nathaniel W., 158, 168, 340
Appleton, *see* Cushing and Appleton
Arch, J. and A., 280
Architecture, 218, 221
Argus (pseudonym, probably Webster), 490–491
Aristarchus (pseudonym, not Webster), 452
Aristides (pseudonym, Webster), 318, 461
Aristides (pseudonym, not Webster), 443, 505, 563
Aristocratic tendencies / aristocracy (U.S.), 400, 407, 408, 447, 494; *see also* Monarchical doctrines; Voice of Wisdom
Armour, A. H. and Co., 126
Armour and Ramsay, 126, 127
Army, United States, 420, 451; militia, 419, 420
Arnold, Benedict: "To the inhabitants of America," 434
"Art of pushing into business" (Webster), 390
"Art of speaking" (variant title), 167
Ascham, Roger: *Schoolmaster*, 434
Ash, John, 142
"Atmosphere, the" (Webster), 220
Atmospheric phenomena, *see* Climate
Atonement, 207, 208
Atrocity stories, 406, 499–500
Attention! or new thoughts (Webster), 309
Atticus (pseudonym, not Webster), 498
Atwater, Jeremiah, 522
Atwood, Moses G., 79, 92, 94, 95, 97, 98, 100

Index

Atwood and Brown, 103
Atwood and Sanborn, 94
Auctioneers, licensing of, 515
Auctions of Webster's books, *see* Trade sales
Aurelius (pseudonym, Webster), 471
"Author of the Conquest of Canaan, To the" (Webster), 392
Authorized title-page, 126
"Authors of the London Review, To the" (Webster), 393
Ayres, John P. 250

B (pseudonym, Webster), 459
B, E. L., *see* Barber, Edmund L.
B, J. W., *see* Barber, John W.
B & E., *see* Bobbett and Edmonds
Babcock, Elisha, 158, 192, 193, 194, 367, 368, 369, 371, 544
Babcock, John, 369
Babcock, Sidney, 78, 105, 107, 108, 114, 137, 138, 154, 155, 156, 190, 195, 214, 215, 216, 218, 219, 220, 290, 302, 360, 380
Bache, Benjamin F., 406, 407
Backus, *see* Bennett, Backus, and Hawley
Bacon, Leonard, 378, 595
"Bad habits easily acquired" (anon.), 287
Bagg, J. S. and S. A., 105
Bagg, Barnes and Co., 105
Baldwin, Abraham, 405, 421
Baldwin, Charles N., 65, 67, 69, 70, 74, 75
Baldwin, Simeon, 550
Baldwin and Treadway, 160, 210
Baltimore, Md.: schools, 438; W. copyrights in, 162; W. lectures in, 531; W's school of music in, 438, 531
Bangs, *see* M'Elrath and Bangs
Bank of Connecticut, 523
Bank of Pennsylvania, 448
Bank of the United States, 401, 426
"Banking institutions" (Webster), 221
Banks and banking, 218, 221, 319, 320, 352, 445, 446, 478, 576, 584; *see also* Finance
Baptists, 579
Barber, Edmund L., 210
Barber, John W., 65, 191, 210, 218
Barker, E. H., 240, 241
Barlow, Joel, 6, 152, 162, 164, 165, 229, 421, 450, 485, 551; *Two letters to the citizens of the United States*, 421
Barlow and Babcock, 142, 161
Barnard, Henry, Jr., 556
Barnes, Daniel H., 235, 502, 503
Barnes, *see* Bagg, Barnes and Co.
Barratt, Joseph, 347
Barruel, Augustin de: History of Jacobinism, 423, 450
Bascome, Edward, 347
Baxter (pseudonym, Webster), 472
Bayard, Samuel, 427, 549
Bearcroft, William: *Red book*, 235
"Bee, the" (anon.), 274
Beecher, Lyman, 191
Beers, Isaac and Co., 185, 390
"Behold, how great a matter" -(Webster), 283
Belden, Ebenezer (and Co.), 40, 318, 319, 398, 422, 429
Belknap, Jeremy, 176, 388, 389, 390, 396, 397, 543, 544, 547
Belknap and Hamersley, 516
Bellamy, John, 459
"Bellows, a" (Webster), 272
Belzebub (pseudonym, Webster?), 390
Bemis, James D. and Co., 68
Bemis, Morse and Ward, 71, 72, 75
Bemis and Ward, 61, 75, 92, 93, 94
Bennett, Backus, and Hawley, 124
Bennington, Vt., Webster in, 13
Bensei kyosho, 134
Berry and Rogers, 387
Bible, 298, 314, 360; use of, 5, 6, 7, 161, 164, 476, 477; errors in, 299, 301, 378, 468, 475–476, 481; Webster's edition, 301, 357, 377–382, 459, 465, 470, 476, 477; illustrations, 467; as remedy for political evils, 469; fundamental to education, 472; *see also* Pentateuch
Biblical Recorder Print, 133
Bicameral legislature, 424
Bigotry, 413
"Bill of mortality" (Webster), 430
"Bills of credit" (Webster), 199, 210

Index

"Bills of rights" (Webster), 337
Bingham, Caleb, 168, 176
Binny and Ronaldson, 46
Biography for the use of schools (Webster), 209
Bishop, Abraham, 315, 452, (523), 563; *Connecticut Republicanism*, 314; *Oration delivered in Wallingford*, 328
Bishop, Samuel, 452, 522
Black, Young, and Young, 240, 241, 242, 243
Blake, *see* Kingsbery and Blake; West, David
Blauvelt, Abraham, 279
Bliss, E. 137
Blount, William, 449
Blunt (pseudonym, not Webster), 489
Bobbett and Edmonds, 590
Bohn, Henry G., 242
Boleus (pseudonym, Webster), 474
Boltwood, Lucius, 153
Bonsal and Niles, 31, 36
Book reviews, 388
Borland, John, 502
Boston, 391
Boston Type and Stereotype Foundry, 249, 250, 251, 381
Boucher, Jonathan: glossary, 242
Bowden, John, 294, 559
Bowdoin, James, 294, 486, 543
Bowdoin College, 516
"Boy who played truant" (Webster), 368
"Boy who was bit by a mouse" (Webster), 368
Boykin, *see* Burke, Boykin and Co.
Bradford, Samuel, 319, 320
Bradford, Thomas, 547
Bradford and Read, 53
Brannan, *see* Brisban and Brannan
Brattleboro' Power Press, 93
Brattleboro' Typographic Co., 116
Brayton, *see* Loomis, C. D., and Co.
Brewster, *see* Crocker and Brewster
Bridges, construction of, 456
"Brief account of the origin of [Amherst"] (Webster), 331
Brief history of epidemic . . . diseases (Webster), 345–349, 464, 466; reviewed, 425, 426
"Brief history of our ancestors" (Webster), 207
"Brief history of political parties" (Webster), 353
Brief view (Webster), 199, 299–300
Brisban and Brannan, 152, 229
Bristol patriot (pseudonym, not Webster), 287
Bronson, Farrar and Co., 133
Bronson, Walter and Co., 205
Brooks, John, 353, (528)
Brown, —— (John F.?), 104
Brown, Charles Brockden, 425
Brown, John F., 83
Brown and Parsons, 108, 112, 118, 123, 125
Bruce, G., 63
Brutus (pseudonym, Webster), 399
Brynberg, Peter, 46, 279, 284
Buchanan, James, 142
Buckland, William, 476
Buel, William, 374, 375
Bunce, George (and Co.), 23, 26, 173, 174, 201, 276, 277, 278, 311, 398, 402, 403, 404, 406, 408
Burbank, Abijah, 60
Burgess, ——, 105
Burgess and Crane, 104, 215, 216, 572
Burgess and Morgan, 102, 103, 108, 214, 215
Burgoyne, John, 176
Burke, Boykin and Co./Burke, J. W. and Co., 132, 133
Burney, Fanny, 171
Burnham genealogy, 351
Burrill, N., 288
Burton, James R., 233, 237
Butler, William, 193, 194, 329
Butler, *see* Thomas, Andrews, and Butler
Butter, Henry: *Scholar's companion*, 301
Buttre, John C., 590
"By agriculture we live. By commerce we thrive" (illustration), 45

C (pseudonym, not Webster), 227, 376, 378, 455, 502, 516
C. C. B. (pseudonym, not Webster), 503
Cady, Ebenezer P., 200
Callender, James T., 563; *American annual register*, 406, 498

Calm Observer (pseudonym, not Webster), 493, 496
Calvinist, a (pseudonym, Webster), 294
Cambridge, England, W. lectures to Bible Society, 537; W. finishes dictionary in, 234
Camillus (pseudonym, not Webster), 494
Campbell, S. and R., 390
Campbell, Samuel, 12, 16, 19, 20, 21, 278, 387, 447
Candidus (pseudonym, probably Webster), 456
Candidus (pseudonym, not Webster), 495, 499
Candor (pseudonym, Webster), 447, 475
Candour (pseudonym, not Webster), 502, 503, 504
Canfield, John, 484, 541
Canfield, Judson, 523
Cape Cod canal, 446
Capital punishment, 446
"Capital punishments" (Noah Worcester), 563
Carey, Mathew, 23, 151, 153, 277, 278, 280, 416, 494, 495, 497, 545, 550
Carey and Hart, 239
Carlisle, David, 39, 40, 42
" 'Carpe diem.' Horace. 'Take time by the forelock.' Plain English" (Webster), 272
Carrier of the American Mercury presents (Webster), 335
Carrier's address, 335–336
Carter, John, 16
Carter, Hendee and Co., 93, 126, 137
Case, Tiffany and Co., 258
Catarrh, 452
Cato (pseudonym, Webster), 468
Cecilia (Burney), 171
Census figures: 1800, 37, 50; 1810, 46, 49, 50, 70; 1820, 62, 64, 70
"Century sermons," proposed, 424
Chandler, Adoniram, 72, 73, 75, 78, 86, 87, 88, 89, 90, 91, 95, 97, 99, 100, 102, 103, 104, 106, 111, 256, 257
Channing, William Ellery, 191
Chapin, Alonzo B.: *English spelling book*, reviewed, 480; discussed, 516–517
Chapin, Calvin, 378
Chappel, Alonzo, 590
"Character of Juliana" (Webster), 162
Chardin, Sir John, 186
Charitable Society (Hartford), 455, 522, 525
"Charity and humanity" (Webster), 283
Charless, Joseph, 41, 44, 282
Charleston, S. C., 388; Webster in, 9, 162
Chase and Dunlap, 80
Chastellux, Marquis de, 176; *Travels in North America*, 441
Chatham (pseudonym, Webster), 321
Chauncey, ——, 80
Chauncey, Charles, 221
Cheever (pseudonym, not Webster), 538
Chesterfield, Lord, 164
Child, Edwin B., 592
Childs, Francis, 390, 396, 533
Chimneys, 388, 410
Cholera, 464; *see also* Epidemics
Christ, divinity of, 207, 208
Christian disciple (periodical), 563
"Chronological account (table)" (Webster), 5, 7, 200; *see also* Outline of American History
"Chronology" (Webster), 221
"Chronology of remarkable events" (anon.), 166
Cicero, 5, 8, 142
Cicero (pseudonym, not Webster), 503
Cid Hamet Benengalli (pseudonym, not Webster), 488
Cincinnati Stereotype/Type Foundry, 568, 569
Cincinnati, Society of the, 437
Circular. Titles which begin with this word are entered under the next major word
"Circular from N. Webster for publication," 560
Circuses, denounced, 330
Cist, Charles, 274, 275
"Citizen" (word), 465
Citizen, a (pseudonym, Webster), 454, 465

Index

Citizen, a (pseudonym, not Webster), 102, 451, 493
Citizen of America, a (pseudonym, Webster), 308
Citizen of Connecticut, a (pseudonym, Webster), 315
Civis (pseudonym, not Webster), 451, 491
Claremont Manufacturing Co., 122
Clark, Daniel A., 331
Clark, Erastus, 189
Clark, Lewis G., 556
Clark, *see* Webster and Clark
Clay, Henry, 41, 44, 285, 515
Clergymen or other well informed gentlemen . . . Circular. To the (Webster), 343
Climate, 203, 211, 220, 345, 424, 425, 431, 451, 459, 481, 533; *see also* Winter
Clinton, DeWitt, 552, 554
"Cliosophic oration" (Webster), 327, 444
Cobb, Edward H., 552
Cobb, Harriet W., *see* Fowler, Harriet W. Cobb
Cobb, Lyman, 98, 356, 357–359, 500–509; *Critical review*, 501, 504–505, 507; speller, 506
Cobbett, William, 346, 410, 417, 449, 450, 485, 498, 548, 588
Cofnin and Roby, 289
Cogswell, Mason F., 268, 544
Cogswell, William, 354
Coins, coinage, 218, 263; symbolism on, 446
Coit, Joshua, controversy about, 498–499
Colds, 479
Coleman, William, 427, 428, 455
Collection of essays (Webster), 164, 168, 225, 269, 337–342, 363, 378; reviewed, 445
Collection of essays on a variety of subjects (anon.), 276
"Collection of improper and vulgar expressions" (Webster), 158
Collection of papers on . . . bilious fevers (Webster), 373–376
Collection of papers on political . . . subjects (Webster), 352–354
"Collection of phenomena, relative to the connection between earthquakes, tempests, and epidemic distempers" (Webster), 451
Collier, Thomas, 36
Collier and Hill, 46, 47
Collins, B. and I., 62
Collins, I., 33
Collins, *see* Worsley and Collins
Collins and Hannay, 137, 504
Collins, Keese and Co., 83
Columbia (ship), 558
"Columbian dictionary" (erroneous title), 563
Columbian magazine, 388, 397
"Come, we'll take the t'other sip" (Webster), 272
Comets, 481
Commendations of . . . Webster's books, 360–361
Commerce and industry, 199, 302, 311, 337, 388, 399, 400, 410, 417, 422, 427, 437, 445, 446, 447, 470, 475, 533; *see also* Shipping
"Commerce and manufacturers" (illustration), 191, 218
Commercial advertiser (newspaper), 413–429; policies, 414
"Common School Convention," 530
Common school dictionary (Webster), 229–230, 244
Common Sense (pseudonym, Webster), 468
Common Version, *see* Bible
"Communication from Mr. Webster concerning his Sp Book," 560
Commutation question, 435, 436, 437
Compendious dictionary (Webster), 200, 206, 227–228, 229, 231; reviewed, 455, 456
Compensation, workmen's, 447
"Complete dictionary," 229
"Comprehensive system of education," 7
"Comptroller" (word), 471, 478
Conclin, George, 573
Concord, N.H., Webster in, 80
Confederate spellers, 130–133

Congress, 399, 405, 418, 497, 498; puerility in, 474; W. lectures before, 537
"Conjectures and theories in philosophy, on" (Webster), 207
Connecticut, 5, 7, 343; census, 1774, 6; constitution, 467, 538
Connecticut Academy of Arts and Sciences, 343, 355, 431, 432, 450, 536, 577
Connecticut courant (newspaper), carrier's address, 335–336
Connecticut Farmer (pseudonym, not Webster), 562
Connecticut Historical Society, 353, 538
Connecticut legislature, 438, 439, 478, 523, 524; W.'s service in, see Appendix G
Connecticut Republicanism, an oration (Bishop), 314; *see also Oration "On the extent"*
Connecticut Society for the Promotion of Freedom, 310, 536
Connecticutensis (pseudonym, not Webster), 563
"Connection of earthquakes with epidemic diseases, on the" (Webster), 451
Conquest of Canaan (Dwight), 162, 392, 393
Conrads, Carl H., 593
Constantia (pseudonym, Webster), 393
Constitution of the Philological Society, 521
Constitution of the United States, celebration of adoption, 394, 521; discussion of, 158, 192, 203, 210, 307, 308, 353, 389, 390, 426, 442, 471, 472, 474, 496, 539; pamphlets on, reviewed, 392; text, 166
Contented freeman, a (pseudonym, Webster), 437
"Continuation of the history of the United States" (Webster), 212, 213, 214, 216
"Controversies and their effects" (Webster), 199
Convention-man, a (pseudonym, not Webster), 436, 437
Conventions, extra-legal, 439; *see also* Hartford; Middletown
Converse, Sherman, 153, 207, 232, 233, 234, 235, 249, 250, 251, 502, 503, 587
Cook, James, 568
Cooke, Increase and Co., 185, 203, 204, 227, 229
Cooke, Oliver D., 200, 229
Cooledge, George F. (and Brothers), 84, 112, 114, 119, 122, 123, 124, 126, 128, 129, 131, 133, 260, 261
Cooper, James Fenimore: *Letters to his countrymen*, 465
Cooper, Thomas, 425
Copyright, 17, 18, 36, 37, 58, 74, 78, 353, 441, 463, 464
Corey, Abijah W., 98
Corey and Fairbank, 92, 95, 96, 97, 98, 99, 570, 571, 572
Corey, Fairbank, and Webster, 212, 213, 571, 572
Corey and Webster, 98, 99, 155, 213, 571, 572
Corn-stalk (pseudonym, not Webster), 490
Corporate writings (Webster), 521–530
"Correspondence with . . . Madison on the . . . Constitution" (Webster), 353
Correspondent (pseudonym, Webster), 435
Correspondent (pseudonym, not Webster), 533
"Counsels of old men despised" (Webster), 283
Country Schoolmaster, a (pseudonym, not Webster), 489, 490
Courtship, 393
Cowper, William, 395
Cowperthwait, *see* Thomas, Cowperthwait and Co.
Coxe, Mary, 542
Coxe, William, 186
Craddock and Joy, 284
Cramer, Spear and Eichbaum, 286
Cranch, William, 523
Crandall, Prudence, 465
Crane, *see* Burgess and Crane; Morgan, Lodge and Co.
Crissy, J., 322
"Critical remarks on . . . Darwin's theory of fever" (Webster), 453

Index

Critical review of . . . Webster's Series of Books (Cobb), 356, 358
Crocker, Zebulon, 378
Crocker and Brewster, 237
Crowder, ——, 281
Cruckshank, Joseph, 367, 562
Cummings, *see* Little and Cummings
Cunningham, H. H., 81
Currency, *see* Coins and coinage; Finance
Currie, William, 363, 415, 416; *Sketch of . . . yellow fever*, 347
Curtis, George A. and J., 83
Curtius (pseudonym, Webster and Kent), 492–494
Curtius (pseudonym, probably Webster), 492
Curtius (pseudonym, probably not Webster), 441
Curto (pseudonym, not Webster), 451
Cushing, Caleb, 514
Cushing, Jno. and Co., 106
Cushing, Joshua, 186, 318
Cushing and Appleton, 182, 186, 187
Cushing and Brother(s), 106, 108, 112, 116, 237
Cushing and Jewett, 67, 70, 74
Cushing and Sons, 67, 78, 79, 81, 87, 90, 93, 95, 96, 99, 102, 104, 106, 137, 245

D—— G——, *see* Dilworth's Ghost
Daboll, Nathan: *Schoolmaster's assistant*, Webster recommends, 450
Daggett, David, 465, 552, 563
Daggett, Henry, 524
"Daguerreotypy" (word), 479
Dallas, Alexander J., 448, 449, 546
Dalziel brothers, 573
Dana, Francis, 312
Dartmouth, 231
Darwin, Erasmus, 453
Davis, Cornelius, 180, 182
Davis, William A., 26
Dawes, Thomas, 176, 201, 208, 293, 312, 329, 457, 551, 560
Day, Jeremiah, 356
Day, Thomas, 162
Dean, *see* Marshall and Dean
Dean and Son, 574
"Death of Dr. Webster, On the" (Sigourney), 595
Debt, 311, 338, 339; public, 400, 401, 440, 441, 443, 486–487
Decency (pseudonym, Webster), 436
Decius (pseudonym, not Webster), 492, 493
"Decomposition of white lead paint, on the" (Webster), 432
Definition, 221, 299, 468, 474
DeForest, *see* Howe and DeForest
Demagoguery, 412, 466, 470, 471, 473; *see also* Mobs
Deming, Anson N., 68
Democrat (pseudonym, Webster), 401
Democrat of the School of '98, a (pseudonym, not Webster), 515
Democratic party/administration, 456, 466, 467, 468; Connecticut, 579; Kentucky, 400
"Demoralize" (word), 311
Dennett, *see* Tappan and Dennett
Dennie, Joseph, 546
"Description of the city of New-York" (Webster), 391
DeSoto, Ferdinand, 389
"Desultory thoughts" (Webster), 338, 440
Detector (pseudonym, Webster), 473
Detester of all envious productions, a (pseudonym, Webster?), 435
"Devil is in you, the" (Webster,) 338, 439
Dew, 431
Dewey, Loring D., 136
Dickerman, *see* Wilcox, Dickerman and Co.
Dictionaries: Unless definitely applying to another title, references to plans for a dictionary are indexed under *American dictionary*, unabridged
Dictionary for primary schools (Webster), 247, 256–259
Dictionary of the English language (Webster), *see Common School dictionary; American dictionary*, unabridged, English edition; *American dictionary*, abridged by Webster
"Dictionary to the American spelling book" (Scofield), 567

Dilly, Charles, 276
Dilworth, Thomas, *New guide to the English tongue*, 7; grammar, 141; as pseudonym, 483, 484
"Dilworth's Ghost (pseudonym, not Webster), 483–485
Directory, *see* France
Disciple of Washington, a (pseudonym, Webster), 459
"Discovery and settlement of North America" (Webster), 164, 199, 210
"Discovery of America" (Webster), 199, 210
"Discrepancies of English orthography" (Webster), 356, 357
"Discrimination between original holders, On a" (Webster), 339
Disease, 423, 425; *see also* Catarrh; Cholera; Colds; Epidemics; Fevers; Influenza; Yellow fever
"Diseases and remarkable events" (Webster), 199, 210
"Diseases of the United States" (Barratt), 347
"Dissenting members, To the" (Webster), 328
"Dissertation concerning the influence of language on opinions" (Webster), 338, 392
"Dissertation in English on the universal diffusion of literature" (Webster), 444
"Dissertation on the supposed change in the temperature of winter" (Webster), 431
Dissertations on the English language (Webster), 15, 158, 267–270, 327, 531
Diversions of Purley (Tooke), 152
"Divinity of Christ and the nature of the Atonement, On the" (Webster), 207
Dixie speller (Moore), 133
Dobelbower, L., 284
Dobson, Thomas, 135
Dodsley, Robert: *The Preceptor*, 60
"Domesday" (word), 339
Domestic debt, *see* Debt; Finance; Thoughts on . . .
Drake, Daniel, 191
"Drone, The" (anon.), 274
Drunkard's progress (illustration), 271, 288
Duane, William, 317
Duelling, 444
Dunham, Dunham, 26
Dunlap, *see* Chase and Dunlap
Dunning, T., 204
Durand, Asher B., 233, 589
Durrie and Peck, 78, 89, 91, 95, 137, 154, 160, 190, 210, 211, 212, 213, 215, 256, 298, 377, 549
Duyckinck, Evert (and Co.), 26, 33, 149, 150, 151, 180, 181, 183, 185, 201, 286
Dwight, Timothy, 162, 165, 392, 393, 458, 562; *Theology explained and defended*, reviewed, 459; *Triumph of infidelity*, reviewed, 394, 442; *see also Conquest of Canaan*
Dyde, W., 281

Eagle, illustration, 85; as symbol, 446
Eames, Wilberforce, 317
Earthquakes, 451, 458, 566
East Haven, Conn., resolutions of citizens, 526
Edes, Peter, 9, 168
Edmonds, *see* Bobbett and Edmonds
Education and educational theories, 158, 199, 216, 219, 220, 337, 353, 391, 393, 394, 400, 434, 443, 451, 452, 454, 462, 465, 467, 472, 474, 476, 477, 478, 528, 533, 535, 537; *see also* Women, education of
"Education" (Webster), 389, 390, 434
"Education of youth in America, On the" (Webster), 337
Education of youth in the United States (Webster), 231, 355
Edward Quesnel (ship), 551
Edwards, Jonathan: *Observations on the . . . Mohegan Indians*, reviewed, 394
Edwards, R., 287
"Effects of evergreens on climate, On the" (Webster), 431
Effects of slavery (Webster), 310, 403
Eichbaum, *see* Cramer, Spear, and Eichbaum

Index

Elector, an (pseudonym, not Webster), 584
Elementary dictionary (W. G. Webster), 260–261
Elementary grammar (Fowler), 263
Elementary primer (Webster), 136–139
Elementary reader (anon.), 195, 571–573
Elementary spelling book (Webster), 59, 74, 78, 79, 82, 84, 85–129, 136, 218, 260, 467, 479, 571, 572
Elements of English grammar (anon.), 157
Elements of history (Worcester), 199
Elements of useful knowledge (Webster), 7, 164, 199–206, 207, 210, 231, 299
Eliot, John, 548
Ellicott, Andrew, 176, 487
Ellis, William R., 567–568
Ells, B. F., 290
Ellsworth, Henry, 507
Ellsworth, Oliver, 381
Ellsworth, William W., 239, 262, 263, 380, 513
Elson, A. W. and Co., 590
Ely, Aaron, 85, 502; *School dictionary*, 465
Embargo, 456, 525, 526, 583
Emerson, John S., 262
Emery, Josiah, 102
"Emilia, or the happiness of retirement" (Webster), 162
"Emilius, or domestic happiness" (Webster), 162
Enemy to Falsehood, an (pseudonym, not Webster), 489
Enemy to Innovation, an (pseudonym, not Webster), 226
English ship of war righting herself (Webster), 286
"Enquiry into the origin of epidemic diseases" (projected title, Webster), 346
"Enquiry into the origin of words" (Webster), 339
Entity (pseudonym, not Webster), 484, 485
"Envy and deception" (Webster), 283
"Envy and malice" (Webster), 283
"Envy, hatred and revenge punished" (Webster), 283
Epidemics, 345, 415, 421, 423, 424, 425, 450, 451, 453; *see also* Cholera; Fevers; Influenza; Yellow fever; *Brief history of epidemic . . . diseases* and the doctors thereunder named; William Currie; *Collection of papers on . . . bilious fevers* and the doctors thereunder named
Episcopal Academy, Philadelphia, 163, 165–166, 441, 485, 487, 488
Equivocal generation, 451, 452
Ergot, 459
"Errors and defects in class-books" (Webster), 299
"Errors and obscurities in the Common Version of the Scriptures" (Webster), 299
"Errors in Butter's Scholar's Companion" (Webster), 301
"Errors in English grammars" (Webster), 301
"Errors in Richardson's dictionary" (Webster), 301
Esquire, use of, 7, 8, 10; *see also* Honorific terms
"Essay on punctuation" (anon.), 157
"Essay on the dets of the United States" (Webster), 339
Essay on the epidemics of . . . Maryland (Martin), 347
"Essay on the necessity . . . of reforming" (Webster), 267
"Essay on the rights of neutral nations" (Webster), 319, 352
Essays (Webster), *see Collection of essays*
"Etymologies and criticism" (Webster), 469
Etymology, 218, 469, 479, 480, 481
Evans, Hickman S., 570
Evans, *see* Bradbury and Evans
Evarts, Jeremiah, 152, 552
Evening advertiser, variant sub-title of *American Minerva*, q.v.
Evergreens, 431
"Every one to his notion" (Webster), 272
Ewer, C., 288

Ewing, John, 486–489
Examination into the leading principles (Webster), 308
Examination of the President's reply (Cranch?), 523
Examination of the various charges (Van Ness), 563
Examinator (pseudonym, not Webster), 500–501, 502, 504
Excise laws, *see* Taxes
Exercise, 444, 472; *see also* Sports
Exit (pseudonym, not Webster), 435
Experienced teacher, an (pseudonym, not Webster), 572
"Experiments respecting dew" (Webster), 431
"Explanation of prefixes, affixes or suffixes, and terminations" (Webster), 221
"Explanation of the reezons why marriage iz prohibited between natural relations" (Webster), 339
"Explanations of prepositions" (Webster), 301
Explanatory treatise on the subjunctive mode (H.J.H.), 270
"Extent and power of political delusion," *see Oration "On the extent . . ."*
Extravagance, 439, 440

Fables, 11, 86, 90, 91, 131, 132, 290
Fact (pseudonym, Webster), 388
Fair Play (pseudonym, probably Webster), 492
Fair Play (pseudonym, not Webster), 460
Fairbank, Daniel W., *see* Corey and Fairbank
Falconer, W. and Co., 390
"Family disagreements" (anon.), 164
Fanaticism, 409
Farmer, a (pseudonym, not Webster), 464, 584
Farmer of West Chester, a (pseudonym, not Webster), 500
"Farmer's catechizm" (Webster), 159, 192, 193, 194
Farmer's Son, a (pseudonym, Webster), 470
Farnham, Bela, 526
Farnsworth, O., 568, 569
Farnsworth, W. M. and O., Jr., 71
Farrar, *see* Bronson, Farrar and Co.
Faxon, *see* Steele and Faxon
Fayetteville, N.C., relief for sufferers from fire at, 530
"Federal(ist)" (word), 515
"Federal catechism" (Webster), 21, 22, 158, 159, 191, 192; *see also Little reader's assistant*
"Federal catechism" (not Webster), 158
Federal government, 305, 426, 439; preservation of union, 305, 444, 496–498
Federalist, a (pseudonym, Webster), 316
Federalist, The, reviewed, 392
Federalist party, 467; Connecticut, 329, 524; New York, 398; *see also* Voice of Wisdom
"Fee" (word), 481
Fellow of the College of Physicians, a (pseudonym, not Webster), 373
Fellows, John, 490, 491
Females, *see* Laws; Sexes; Women
Fenning, Daniel: *Universal spelling book*, 7, 11
Fenno, John, 406
Ferula (pseudonym, not Webster), 412
Fessenden, Joseph, 55, 92, 96
Fessenden, William, 45, 48, 49, 50, 52, 53, 54, 55
Fessenden, Holbrook, and Porter, 45
Feuds, origin of, 481
Fevers, 452, 453; *see also* Epidemics; Yellow fever
"Few plagiarisms, a" (Webster), 299
Fiction, deleterious effect of, 473
"Fidgets, The" (Webster), 272, 289, 290
Finance, 330, 410, 464, 478; *see also* Banks and banking; Coins; Debt; Inflation; Paper Money
First lessons for children (Webster), 136
Fisher, A. and R., 111, 116
Fisher, J. and Son, 95, 96, 108, 569
Fishkill (pseudonym, not Webster), 499

Fiske, D. D., 83
Fitch, ——, 143
Fitch, John, 474, 479
Fitzsimmons, Thomas, 308
Flagg, Jared, 589, 595
Fleming, Robert, 130, 131
Fletcher, Samuel, 82, 111
Following is a specimen, the (Webster), 232
Folsom, John W., 14, 16, 277
Food, high price of, 471
Foote, John P., 62, 64, 66
Fops, 401
For subscription. In February next (Webster), 236
Ford, Emily Ellsworth Fowler (Mrs. Gordon L.), 362, 554, 593
Ford, George H., 595
Ford, Gordon L., 350, 351, 362
Ford, Paul Leicester, 350
Foreign words and phrases, 246, 264
Forestry, 418, 459
"Form of association for young men" (Webster), 353
Foster, *see* Tappan and Foster
Fourth of July orations, Barlow, 165; Webster, 328–329, 481, 537, 539
Fowler, Emily E., *see* Ford, Emily
Fowler, Harriet W. Cobb (Mrs. William C.), 379, 552, 553, 554, 556, 591, 592
Fowler, William C., 85, 98, 154, 155, 221, 263, 354, 356, 357, 378, 379, 505, 511, 554, 555, 556, 557, 591, 595
France, current affairs in, 311, 313, 403, 404, 405, 407, 409, 411, 412, 413, 415, 416, 417, 418, 419, 420, 423, 424, 447, 450, 491
Franklin (pseudonym, Webster), 455, 478
Franklin, Benjamin, 6, 144, 165, 176, 267, 268, 269, 286, 287, 289, 308, 443, 542, 543, 544; portrait of, 195, 209; Advice to Young Tradesman, 164; Letters of Advice, 284; Parable against Persecution, 19; Poor Richard, 271; Way to Wealth, 164, 284, 286, 287; The Whistle, 189, 195, 273, 274
Franklin and Garrow, 35
Franklin steam printing house, 130, 131
Frederick, Md., W. lectures in, 532
Freeling, Francis, 286, 287
Freeman, Thomas, 488, 489
Freeman, a (pseudonym, Webster), 399, 442
Freemasonry, 423, 467
French Revolution, *see* France
Freneau, Philip, 165
Friend to American literature, a (pseudonym, probably Webster), 358
Friend to Harmony among Citizens (pseudonym, not Webster), 488
Friend to Liberality, a (pseudonym, not Webster), 487
Friend to Native Citizens, a (pseudonym, not Webster), 584
Friend to Public Credit, a (pseudonym, not Webster), 486
Friends of American literature, To the. Lyman Cobb has been . . . (Webster), 358–359
"Friends of Literature, To the" (Webster), 232
Friends of literature, To the (Webster), 359
Friends of literature in the United States. Circular. To the (Webster), 231
Friends of literature in the United States, To the (Webster), 232
Frisbee, H. C., 92
Frost, John H. A., 59, 60, 62, 63, 64, 66
Fuel, conservation of, 459
Funding, *see* Debt, public

Gale, Benjamin, 562
Gallaher, William, 89
Gallatin, Albert, 550
Galpin, Sylvester, 137
Galpin, *see* Petter and Galpin
Gambado, Geoffrey (pseudonym, not Webster), 391
Gambling, denounced, 330
Garcilaso de la Vega, 186
Gardiner, John S. J., 452
Garrow, *see* Franklin and Garrow
Garwood, *see* Stephens and Garwood
Genealogy (Webster), 350–351

"General description of Philadelphia" (Webster), 390
"General description of the city of New York" (Webster), 391
"General description of the United States" (Webster), 203
"General principles of government" (Webster), *see* "Principles of government and commerce"
"General view of the character . . . of our ancestors" (Webster), 207
"General views of the inhabitants of the U.S." (Webster), 203
"General Washington's circular letter," 164
"General Washington's farewel orders," 164
Genesee country, 412
Genet, Edmond, 400
Geographical data, 5, 6, 10; *see also Elements of useful knowledge*
"Geography" (Webster), 164, 199
"Geology" (Webster), 220
George, Daniel, 225
Georgia, 474; University of, 203
German, a (pseudonym, not Webster), 406
Germanus (pseudonym, not Webster), 490
Germany, 417
"Gesenius" (Webster), 360
Gesenius, Friedrich: Hebrew lexicon, 301
Ghost writer, Webster as, 521-530
Gibbon, Edward, 270, 393
Gibbs, George, 556
Gibbs, Josiah W.: Hebrew lexicon, 235
Gifts by Webster: books, 477; newspaper files, 422
"Gillotin, a" (Webster), 283
Girard College, 353, 470
Girl picking roses/men mowing (illustration), 92, 96
Glossary of archaic . . . words (Boucher-Hunter), 242
Glover, ——, 108
Glover, *see* Jenkins and Glover
God, 206; existence of, 478
Goliath (illustration), 209
Gomez, Benjamin, 26, 180
Goodenow, *see* Wright, Goodenow, and Stockwell
Goodrich, Chauncey, 522
Goodrich, Chauncey [A.], 77, 90, 91, 92, 93, 94, 225, 235, 238, 465, 530
Goodwin, George, and Sons, 230, 552
"Gospel vindicated, the," caption title of *Peculiar doctrines*, q.v.
"Government" (Webster), 389
"Government, on" (Webster), 337, 338
"Government and laws" (Webster), 210
"Governments on the eastern continent" (Webster), 305
Gracchus (pseudonym, not Webster), 579
"Grace of God in dollars, the" (Webster), 272, 283, 287, 289, 290
Grammar, 468, 471, 472, 480; errors in grammars, 291, 299, 301; neglect of subject, 5; teaching of, 142, 267, 435, 436
Grammar (textbook, Webster), evaluated, 456; lack of success, 151, 153, 154
"Grammatical errors in the Common Version" (Webster), 360
Grammatical institute (Webster), Part I and derivatives, 5–139 (*see also* Appendix F); Part II and derivatives, 141–160; Part III and derivatives, 161–195
Grammaticaster (pseudonym, not Webster), 158
Graves, Rufus, 528
Gray, H., 288
"Great-grandfather's books and pictures" (Scudder), 350
Greek independence, 529
Greeley, Horace, 473, 475, 515, 556
Green, Timothy and Son, 274, 328
"Green wood will last longer than dry" (Webster), 272
Greenleaf, Daniel, 335, 558, 559
Greenleaf, James, 268, 269, 341, 397, 544, 545, 546
Greenleaf, Oliver C., 47
Greenleaf, Rebecca, *see* Webster, Rebecca G.

Greenleaf, Thomas, 387, 406, 490–491, 492
Greenleaf, William, 558
Greer, William, 285
Gridley, Timothy J., 475
Griffen, Joseph, 507-508
Griffen, Mabbett, and Co., 507, 508
Griffin, Edward D., 560
Griffin, J., 287
Grigg, John, 137
Griswold, *see* Morton and Griswold
Grosvenor [Horace C.?], 290
Guild, Benjamin, 159
Guilford, N. and G., 68, 71, 568, 569
Guilford, Nathan, 77, 568, 569

H——, H—— J., 270
Hall, ——, 167, 393
Hall, Francis, and Co., 469
Hall, Henry B. (and Sons), 242, 351, 590
Hall, John H., 95
Hall, Willis, 515
Hall, *see* Prichard and Hall
Hall and Nancrede, 494
Halpin, Frederick W., 589, 595
Hamersley, William J., 516
Hamilton, Alexander, 316–318, 398, 408, 427, 451, 494, 496
Hamilton, T., 287
Hamlen, B. L., 156, 237, 301, 352
Hampden (pseudonym, Webster), 474
Hampshire (pseudonym, probably not Webster), 475
Hampshire Bible Society, 527
Hampshire, Franklin, and Hampden Agricultural Society, 330, 353, 537
Hancock (pseudonym, not Webster), 584
Hannay, *see* Collins and Hannay
Hansford, ——, 375
"Hard money" (anon.), 323
Hardie, James, 424
Harding, E., 281
Harding, Jesper, 222
Harper, Robert, 280
Harper and Brothers, 255, 347
Harrington (pseudonym, not Webster), 496–498
Harrington, *see* Smith and Harrington
Harris, ——, 114
Harrisson, John, 180
Harrisson and Purdy, 521
Hartford, Conn., courthouse lottery, 575; memorials from inhabitants, 522; "Topographical description" (Webster), 430; W.'s public service in, *see* Appendix G
Hartford Convention, 353, 473, 513, 527, 559, 583
Harvey, Asahel, 108
Harvey, Henry L., 109
Hastings, J., 390, 393
Haswell, Anthony, 17, 21, 24, 315
Haswell and Russell, 13, 14
Haven, John P., 86
Hawaiian dictionary, 261–262
Hawley, *see* Bennett, Backus, and Hawley
Hayes, Samuel Gerrish, 81, 82, 83
Haygarth, John, 375
Hayman, Francis, 59
Hazard, Ebenezer, 389, 390, 396–397
"He does not work it right" (Webster), 272, 274
"He has come out at the little end of the horn" (Webster), 272
He hoakakaolelo, 261–262
"He is sowing his wild oats" (Webster), 272
"He would have his own way" (Webster), 272, 287, 290
Heartman, Charles F., 369
Hebrew language, 235, 301, 458, 466, 475, 476
"Held" (word), 310
"Heliography" (word), 479
Hendee, *see* Carter, Hendee and Co.
Henry, S. H. (and Co.), 95, 97, 98, 102, 106, 107, 112
Henry, Hitchcock and Co., 112, 116
Herald (newspaper), 402–413; delivery of, 404, 405, 410
Herring, James, 589, 591, 595
Hickory, Giles (pseudonym, Webster), 389
Hill, Horatio, and Co., 73, 76, 80
Hill, *see* Collier and Hill
Hillhouse, James, 456

Hinman, David C., 589
Hint for Free-Masons (anon.), reviewed, 423
"Historical sketch of Connecticut" (Webster; unpublished), 561
"History; concise account of the war," *see* "Sketches of the rise, progress . . ."
History of animals (Webster), 205–206
"History of Columbus" (Barlow), 164
History of epidemic pestilences (Bascome), 347
"History of pestilential diseases" (projected title, Webster), 346
"History of the little boy found under a haycock" (probably not Webster), 562
"History of the revolution in America" (Webster), 203
"History of the United States" (Webster), 164
History of the United States (Webster), 164, 209, 210–217, 299, 353, 478
Hitchcock, *see* Henry, Hitchcock and Co.
Hoag, C., and Atwood, M. G., 72
Hoan Strewbe (pseudonym, not Webster), 231
Hobbs, Richard H., 262, 263
Hodge, R., 387
Hogan, David, 186, 187, 188, 189, 190, 284
Hogan, *see* Towar and Hogan
Hogan and Co., 245
Holbrook, John, 55, 57, 59, 60, 61
Holbrook and Co., 98
Holbrook and Fessenden, 55, 61, 62, 63, 64, 66, 67, 69, 70, 71, 87, 90, 245
Holbrook, Fessenden, and Porter, 42, 43, 47; *see also* Fessenden, Holbrook, and Porter
Holland, William M., 218, 221
Holley, O. L., 586
Holmes, Abiel, 397, 455; *American Annals*, reviewed, 455
Homan(s), ——, 101; *see also* White and Homan
Home, Henry, 164
Honorific terms, 7, 401; pretentious names for humble work, 470
Honorius (pseudonym, Webster), 435
Hooker, Nathaniel, 164
Hopkins, George F., 291, 411, 412, 413, 414, 415, 420, 422; *see also* Hopkins, Webb and Co.; Hopkins and Co.
Hopkins, Stephen, 306
Hopkins and Co., 411; *see also* George F. Hopkins; Hopkins, Webb and Co.
Hopkins, Webb and Co., 374, 398, 408, 411
Horace, 142
Horse raising, 330
Horwitz, [Jonathan H.?], 301
Hosack, Alexander: *Inaugural essay*, reviewed, 410
Hosack, David: *Essays on various subjects of medical science*, 454
Hotchkiss, Sarah, 462
Hough, George, 566
House, Eleazer G., 43, 44, 47, 48, 49, 51
"How should I work it?" (Webster), 272
Howard (pseudonym, Webster), 474
Howe, Hezekiah (and Co.), 154, 209, 231, 233, 244, 298, 356, 377
Howe, J., 67, 69, 71, 73, 74, 76, 77, 83
Howe, Zadoc, 27
Howe and DeForest, 205, 206
Howe and Spalding, 153, 207
Howells, William Cooper, 96
Howells, William Dean, 96
Hoyt, ——, 115
Hoyt, Porter and Co., 92, 94, 98, 115, 137
Hudson, Henry, 65, 67, 68, 69, 85
Hudson, W., 69
Hudson, W., and Skinner, L., 65, 66, 68
Hudson and Co., 55, 57, 58, 60, 61, 63, 64, 65, 66
Hudson and Goodwin, 5, 6, 7, 8, 9, 10, 11, 12, 13, 14, 15, 16, 18, 19, 21, 22, 24, 25, 27, 28, 29, 30, 31, 32, 33, 36, 39, 40, 42, 44, 45, 47, 48, 49, 51, 52, 53, 135, 141, 143, 144, 145, 146, 147, 148, 149, 150, 163, 165, 167, 168, 170, 171, 172, 173, 174, 176, 179, 181, 182, 183, 199, 200, 201, 202, 204, 205, 227, 271, 305, 309, 310, 335, 345, 346, 390, 523, 524, 541, 542, 543, 544, 546

Hughes, [Thomas?], 483
"Human ignorance" (Webster), 219
Humboldt, Baron von, 191
Humphrey, Heman, 354
Humphreys, David, 176; *Essay on . . . General Israel Putnam*, reviewed, 395
Humphreys, James, 320
Hunt, U., 137
Hunter, Joseph, 242
Huntington, Francis J. (and Co.), 237, 247, 248, 257, 258
Huntington, *see* Whiting, I. N.
Huntington and Savage, 248, 258, 259, 262–264, 592
Hurst, *see* Longman, Hurst, Rees, and Orme
Hyde, William, 288
"Hymn to gratitude" (Addison), 219

"I have seen and I have not seen" (Livingston), 273
"I told you so" (Webster), 272, 280
Ide, Simeon, 122, 288
"If I was (were) he" (Webster), 272, 280, 290
Illustrated Webster reader, 195, 573
Illustrated Webster spelling book, 573–574
"Illustrations of grammar" (Webster), 221
Impressment, 491, 524
"Improprieties and errors in the Common Version" (Webster), 301
Improved grammar (Webster), 154–156, 481
In the press, and in February . . . (Webster), 236
"Inconstancy of the populace" (Webster), 283
"Indian wars" (Webster), 199, 210
Industrious man, an (pesudonym, Webster), 439
Inflation, 535
Influenza, 443
Ingersoll, Charles, 78
Ingersoll, Jonathan, 524
Ingraham, Edward D., 556
Ingraham, Joseph, journal of, 558, 559
"Injustice, absurdity, and bad policy of laws against usury" (Webster), 339
Inquirer (pseudonym, not Webster), 502, 503
Inquirer, or an Enquirer, an (pseudonym, Webster), 466
Inspector (pseudonym, Webster), 454
"Instructions respecting moral and political conduct" (Webster), 207
Instructive and entertaining lessons (Webster), 190–191, 218, 219, 222
Insurance and insurance companies, 319, 410, 458; *see also* Workmen's compensation
Interesting documents, 522
Introduction to English grammar (Webster), 156
"Introduction to grammar" (Webster), 11
Introduction to the history of America (anon.), 166
Ireland, 400
Irwin, Thomas, 186
"It is better to borrow than to buy" (Webster), 272
"It is just as the fit takes him" (Webster), 272, 289, 290
"It will do for the present" (Webster), 272
Ives, Chauncey, 262, 591, 592, 593

Jackson, Andrew, 464, 474; administration, 468, 476, 512
Jackson, Thomas J., 131
Jacob, Stephen, 183, 550
Jacobins, American, 417, 423, 425; French, see France
James, J. A., 109, 118, 121, 123, 570, 572
Jansen, George, and Co., 182
Jansen, Thomas B., and Co., 182
Japanese editions of the speller, 134–135
Jay, John, 392, 551, 552, 560; *see also* Jay Treaty
Jay Treaty, 353, 420; controversies over, 491–495, 496–498; printed text, 494–495
Jefferson, Thomas, 18, 176, 192, 272, 319, 321, 340, 341, 426, 445, 462, 473, 474, 494, 523, 524, 525, 526, 544, 550; letter to Mazzei, 329, 411; *Notes on Virginia*, 176, 340; Jeffersonian principles, 472, 473, 474, 476

Jenkins and Glover, 95
Jewett, Joseph, 75; *see also* Cushing and Jewett
"Jewish story concerning Abraham" (Franklin) 19, 20
Jocosus (pseudonym, not Webster), 443
Johnson, Arthur and Helen-May, 181
Johnson, Benjamin, 38
Johnson, Gordon: *Introduction to arithmetic*, 446
Johnson, Jacob (and Co.), 34, 36, 37, 38, 40, 41, 42, 44, 46
Johnson, L., 76
Johnson, Samuel, 162, 435; dictionary, 241, 292, 456
Johnson, William S., 550
Johnson and Warner, 46, 47, 48, 50, 51, 52, 54, 55, 57, 285
Johnston, P. W., 53
Johnston and Stockton, 100
Jones, Henry, 481
Journal of the transactions and occurrences (Winthrop; ed. Webster), 371–372
Joy, *see* Craddock and Joy
Judah, Naphthali, 26, 180, 183
Judd, William, 438
Judges, appointment of, 437, 438
Judson, Roswell, 235
Juliana (ship), 413
Junior, use of, 8, 37
Jury system, origin of, 445
Justice (pseudonym, not Webster), 486, 487, 488, 489, 505
Justice of the Peace, Webster's service as, Appendix G
Justitius (pseudonym, not Webster), 401
Justus (pseudonym, Webster), 467
Juvenis (pseudonym, not Webster), 440, 535
"Juventutem bene actam..." (Webster), 327, 362

Kansaki, Jironosuke, 135
Kashiwabara, Masajiro, 134
Keese, *see* Collins, Keese and Co.
Kelley, Hall J., 569
Kelley, Madison, 92
Kellogg, [Jarvis G.?], 590
Kendrick, John, 558
Kent, James, 493, 510, 511, 512, 550
Kent, W., 287
Key and Mielke, 137
"Key to Dr. Noah Webster's American spelling book" (Evans), 570
Key to the classical pronunciation (Walker), 249–255
"Key to the meaning of Dr. Webster's elementary spelling book" (Evans), 570
Kidd, James, controversy with, 489–490
Killingworth, Conn., 435
Kimball, *see* Roby, Kimball, and Merrill
Kimber and Sharpless, 67, 69, 72, 76, 77, 88, 92, 100, 102, 108, 112, 119, 245
King, Rufus, 348, 398, 427, 494, 547, 548, 549, 550
Kingsbery and Blake, 566
Kingsley, James L., 234
Kirk, Thomas, 30
Kite, B. and T., 284
Kneeland, Abner, 565–566
Knight and Triphook, 280
Knowles, James: dictionary reviewed, 469
Knowlton and Rice, 95, 96, 98, 107, 110, 112, 115, 120, 124, 506

L-B, *see* Lossing-Barritt
L. of E. G., a, *see* "Learner of English grammar"
Lafayette, Marquis de, death, 530
LaFontaine, Jean de, 11
Lahainaluna Seminary, 262
"Lamb, the" (Webster), 37
Lamech (pseudonym, not Webster), 488
Land: public, sale of, 440; speculation in, 471; western, 400, 437
Lane, Charles, 82, 83
Lane, W. F., 288
Lane Seminary, 97, 572
Lang and Ustick, 495
Langdon, Reuben, 556
Language(s), 302, 338, 392, 443, 455, 457; Webster's study of, 473; Webster's lectures on, Appendix B; *see also* Honorific terms; Orthography; Philology

Index

"Language, Education, and Government" (Webster), 535
Larkin, Ebenezer, 39, 45
"Last revised edition", 128
Latin oration, *see* "Juventutem bene actam"
Law, study of, 443
Lawrie, Lee, 593
"Laws respecting females" (Webster et al.), 221
Laws, colonial, 390, 391
Lawyers, 439, 440; Webster as, 444, 445, 446
Lay, Asa W., 19
Learner of English Grammar (pseudonym, not Webster), 484, 485
Lectures by Webster, 327–331, 438, 439, 440, 441, 477, 478, Appendix B; *see also* Appendix H for legislative speeches
Lee, Samuel, 353, 464, 553
Leffingwell, William, 552
Leo (pseudonym, not Webster), 591
Leonidas (pseudonym, not Webster), 523
Lesson, *see* Pratt, Smith, and Lesson
"Lessons for youth" (Webster), *see Instructive and entertaining lessons*
"Lessons in speaking" (Webster), 165
"Let sage discretion the gay world despise" (Webster?), 392
Letson, J., 108
"Letter from a lady, a" (Webster), 339, 393
"Letter from General Washington", 352
"Letter from Noah Webster to George Washington", *see 1781*
"Letter from Noah Webster, Esq. . . . to a friend", cover title of *Peculiar doctrines*, q.v.
"Letter . . . on the operation of manure" (Mitchill), 413
"Letter on the value and importance of the American commerce to Great-Britain" (Webster), 319
"Letter to a young gentleman commencing his education" (Webster), *see* "Instructions respecting moral . . . conduct"
Letter to Dr. David Ramsay (Webster), 292, 456
Letter to General Hamilton (Webster), 316–318
"Letter to the author. . . ." (Webster), 339
Letter to the governors (Webster), 291
Letter to the Hon. Daniel Webster (Webster), 322, 353
Letter to the Hon. John Pickering (Webster), 297
"Letter to the Rev. Samuel Lee" (Webster), 353
Letter to the Secretary of the Treasury (anon.), 563
"Letters critical and practical. . . ." (proposed title, Webster), 267
"Letters of advice" (Franklin), 284
Letters of Noah Webster, 363
Letters on yellow fever (Webster), 363
Letters to a young gentleman (Webster), 207–208, 299
Letters to Dr. Joseph Priestley, *see Ten letters . . .*
Lewis, Zachariah, 398, 429
Lexiphanes (pseudonym, Webster?), 435
L'Hommedieu, *see* Morgan, Fisher, and L'Hommedieu
"Liberty and equality" (Webster), 283, 428
Licenses to print Webster's speller, 26, 36–37, 74, 85, 86, 89, 102, 111; *see also* introductory notes to various years in Section One, Part One
Lincoln, Abraham, 256
Lincoln, Ezra, 331
Lincoln and Gleason, 229
Lindsay, *see* Redfield and Lindsay
"Lines written by a youth" (Webster?), 391
Linn, William: *Serious considerations on the election of a president*, reviewed, 425
Liquor, 439; *see also* Drunkard's progress
Litchfield, Conn., W. lectures in, 538
Literary Convention (Hartford, 1830), 537
Little, Edward, and Co., 47, 188, 189

Little and Brown, 239
Little and Cummings, 137
Little Franklin (Webster), 195
Little reader's assistant (Webster), 159, 176, 191–194, 270
Livingston, ——, 165
Livingston, Henry B., 493
Livingston, William, 273
LL.D. degree, 461, 463
Lockwood, Roe, 86
Loco Focos, 514
Lodge, *see* Morgan, Lodge and Co.
"Logan's speech," 176, 189, 192
Logic, 221
Long, G., 286
Long, T., 286
Longinus (pseudonym, not Webster), 503
Longman, Hurst, Rees, and Orme, 284
Loomis, C. D. and Co./Loomis and Brayton, 112, 115, 120
Lord, Melville, 93, 94, 126
"Lord, I thank thee . . ." (Webster), 283
Lossing-Barritt, 590
Lott, *see* Sanford and Lott
Loudon, John, 391
Loudon, Samuel, 387, 391
Loveleap, Jemima (pseudonym, Webster?), 390
Lover of Good Cider, a (pseudonym, Webster?), 453
Lover of his Country, a (pseudonym, Webster), 464
Lover of Stability, a (pseudonym, Webster), 473
Lower classes, 408, 412, 448; *see also* Mobs
Lowth, Robert, 141, 142
Lucius Junius Brutus (pseudonym, not Webster), 523
Lutheran, a (pseudonym, not Webster), 406
Lutius (pseudonym, not Webster), 489
Lyman, A. and Co., 295
Lyman, Joseph, 363, 526, 527
Lynch law, 468

M (pseudonym, Webster), 472, 474–475
M., T., *see* Miner, Thomas
M. D. Esquire (pseudonym, not Webster), 270
Mabbett, *see* Griffen, Mabbett, and Co.
McClure, David, 353, 470, 555
Maccoun, Tilford and Co., 44, 285
M'Culloch, John, 157, 158, 166, 167
M'Dowell and Son, 137
M'Elrath and Bangs, 136, 137
"M'Fingal" (Trumbull), 162
McGuffey, William Holmes, 101, 191, 471
McKendrick, *see* Ramsay and McKendrick
McKenzie, Henry, 162
McKinney, O. W., 118, 119, 122
M'Kown, J., 295
McLain, David B., 288
McMinn, John, 508–509
Madison, James, 306, 353, 523, 541, 549, 550, 551, 554
Magill, R[obert?], 180
Mails, *see* Post office
Mallet, Paul H.: *Northern antiquities*, 270
Maltby, A. H., 154, 377
Manahan, Hoag and Co., 71, 72, 73
"Manna" (word), 466
Manual of useful studies (Webster), 220–222, 480
Manure, 330, 431, 454
Maps, 205, 342, 394, 396
Marcellus (pseudonym, Webster), 322, 514, 515
Marcus Aurelius (pseudonym, Webster), 451
Markoe, Peter: *The times*, reviewed, 394
Marriage, 339
Marshall, Elihu F., 567
Marshall and Dean, 289
Martin, Ennalls, 347
Martin and Ogden, 33, 34
Martinson and Co., 257
Massachusetts Historical Society: formation of, 404; Webster's membership in, 404; paper by Webster presented at, 430
Massachusetts legislature, 439, 528, 559; W.'s service in, see Appendix G

Index

Massachusetts magazine, 397
Master of Arts degree: use of "A.M.," 7, 8; thesis, 444
"Materials of clothing, Of the" (Webster), 191, 219
Mather (pseudonym, Webster), 474–475
Mather, Allen, Webster's elegy on death of, 438
Mayflower Compact, 467
Mazzei, Philip, 329, 411
Meigs, Josiah, 203, 330, 450
Mellen, John, Jr., 430
"Memorial of the Chamber of Commerce," 524
"Memorial of the inhabitants of the town of New Haven," 525
Mentor (pseudonym, Webster), 466
Mercantile evening advertiser, sub-title of *American Minerva*, q.v.
Mercantile Library Association, New York, 302
Merchant, Aaron M., 502
Merrell and Seward, 40, 185
Merriam, E. and L./E. and Co., 35, 96, 98, 99, 109, 138
Merriam, G. and C., 122, 129, 225, 239
Merrill, Rufus, 138; *see also* Roby, Kimball, and Merrill
Mesier, P. A., 26, 33, 180
Meteors, 395
Methodists, 579
Metric system, 272, 445
Michigan, University of, 60, 155
Middlebury College, 231, 463, 477
Middlesex County [Conn.] Medical Society, 347
Middletown Convention, 436, 437
Mielke, *see* Key and Mielke
"Military events" (Webster), 199, 210
Miller, ——, 184
Miller, Edward, 376, 451, 452, 453
Miller, William, 481
Million of True Republicans, a (pseudonym, Webster), 448
Mills, Abraham, 502
Mills, Joseph, 429
Milnor, James, 378
Miner, Thomas, 211, 221, 234, 505, 555
Minerva (newspaper), *see American Minerva*
"Mines, minerals, and mineral springs" (Webster), 203
Minor, *see* Whitmore and Minor
Minot, George R.: *History of the insurrection in Massachusetts*, reviewed, 394–395
Mirabeau, Honoré, 174
Mirror to Noah Webster's spelling book (Ellis), 567
Miscellaneous papers (Webster), 319–320; reviewed, 452
"Miscellaneous remarks on divizions of property (Webster), 339
Mistakes and corrections (Webster), 301, 361
"Mistakes in the Hebrew lexicon" (Webster), 301; *see also* "Gesenius"
Mitchill, Samuel Latham, 375, 376, 430, 431, 451, 550, 553
Mobs, 404, 468, 533
"Modes of teaching the English language" (Webster), 353
Momus (pseudonym, Webster), 464
Monarchical doctrines, 323, 472, 510–516
Monitor (pseudonym, Webster), 470, 473, 481
Monitor, Elias (pseudonym, not Webster), 563
Monroe, James, 418
Monson, Eneas, 375
Monson, Eneas, Jr., 375
Montefiore, Joshua: *Commercial dictionary*, 319, 320
Montgomery County, New York, yellow fever in, 375
Monthly magazine and review, 425
Moore, Mrs. M. B., 133
Moore, Zephaniah S., 537
"Moral catechism" (Webster), 22, 23, 86, 209, 218
"Moral sentiments" (Webster), 7
"Moral system" (Webster), 221
"Morality" (Webster), 339, 393
Mordell, Albert, 176
Morgan, Ephraim (and Co.), 108, 110, 112, 116, 117, 118, 121, 122, 127, 216, 237

Morgan, James A. (and Co.), 108, 109, 118, 121, 122, 123; *see also* Morgan and Anthony
Morgan, James T. (and Co.), 108
Morgan and Anthony, 108
Morgan, Fisher, and L'Hommedieu, 71, 108
Morgan and Lodge, 64, 66, 108
Morgan and Sanxay, 73, 108, 568
Morrow, James, 569
Morse, Clarendon, 108, 112, 115, 124
Morse, Jedidiah, 164, 228, 293, 306, 341, 342, 418, 449, 455, 546, 547, 550, 586, 589; *American geography*, 338, 341, 391, 394
Morse, Samuel F. B., 342; *see also* "Morse portrait"
Morse, Sidney and Richard, 555
Morse, William W., 283, 328
Morse and Harvey, 98, 99
Morse portrait, 134, 195, 233, 237,242, 342, 351, 589–590, 592
Mortality statistics, 345, 376
Morton, John P., 70
Morton and Griswold, 261
Morton and Smith, 105, 136
Moseley, Finnie, and Pryor, 121
Moses, 207
Mower, Nahum, 31, 34, 184, 187, 566
Multiplied evils . . . , Sir, the (Webster), 526–527
Munson, Elisha, 525, 526
Murray, Lindley, 152, 189, 299, 456, 464, 475
"Museum of natural history," 139
Music, 339, 393, 433, 438, 441
Mussey, B. B., 105, 239
Mythology, 432

N., A., 302
N. W. Secundus (pseudonym, not Webster), 9
National Academy of Design, 591
National bank, *see* Bank of the United States
"National language" (W. G. Webster?), 260
National pictorial primer, 128
Navy, British, mutiny, 412
Navy, United States, 399, 420
Neale, Isaac, 274
Negroes, education of, 465; *see also* Slavery
"Negroes complaint, the" (Webster?), 395
Nelson, Joseph, 295
Nestor (pseudonym, not Webster), 489
Neutrality/rights of neutrals, 319, 428, 452, 522, 524
New American spelling book (Webster), 78
New-England Man, a (pseudonym, not Webster), 487
New England primer (Webster, ed.), 367–370
New England Type and Stereotype foundry, 83
New Haven, 586; cemetry, 585; Chamber of Commerce, 524, 526; memorials from inhabitants, 522, 525, 526, 529, 530; school statistics, 578; yellow fever, 375, 428, 454; W.'s public service in, see Appendix G
New London, Conn., W. lectures in, 535
New Testament, *see* Bible
"New thoughts . . ." (Webster), *see Attention . . .*
New Township Academy, New Haven, 458
New York city, description of (Webster), 341, 391, 418; fortification, 577; statistics, 451; street names, 401; yellow fever, 374, 376
New York city directory, first, 391
New-York Commercial Advertiser, *see Commercial Advertiser*
New-York (*Evening*) *Advertiser*, Subtitle of *American Minerva*, q.v.
New York Evening Post, 427
New York Gazette, 423
New York legislature, 472
New York Lyceum, 302
New York Mercantile Advertiser, 423
New-York Prices-Current, 415
New-York Spectator, *see Spectator*
Newburyport, Mass., W. lectures in, 534
Newman, Mark H., 239

Newport, R.I., W. lectures in, 535
News-boy's address to his customers (Webster), 335
Newspapers, history of, 343; value of, 399; tax on, 399; Webster's comments on, 408, 419; abuse of press, 424, 469
Nichols, Lewis, 150, 151
Niles, William H., 72, 73, 75, 77, 88, 91, 92, 97, 103
Niles, *see* Bonsal and Niles
Nineteenth April Seventy-Six (pseudonym, not Webster), 494
Noah Webster on youth and old age, 364
Noah Webster's British and American illustrated spelling and reading book, 574
Non-Importation Act, *see* Embargo
Norfolk, Va., yellow fever in, 375
Norman, William O., 370
Norris, Charles, and Co., 188, 189
Northampton, Mass., W. lectures in, 330, 353, 536
Northwest passage, 470
Norwich, Conn., W. lectures in, 535
"Nose, a" (Webster), 272
Notary public, Webster as, 445, 446
"Notes, historical and critical" (Webster), 267, 270
Notes on the life of Noah Webster (Ford), 362
Notes on Virginia (Jefferson), 176, 340
"Number of deaths . . . in New-York" (Webster), 431

Oaths of allegiance, *see* Test laws
Observations on a letter from Noah Webster (Bowden), 294
"Observations on commerce" (Webster), 302
Observations on language (Webster), 302
Observations on the . . . American Revolution (Price), 305
"Observations on the travels . . . of Ferdinand De Soto" (Belknap), 389
Observator (pseudonym, Webster), 460
Observer (pseudonym, Webster), 418
Observer (pseudonym, not Webster), 309, 588
Octogenarian (pseudonym, Webster), 475
"Ode to spring" (Webster?), 392
"Of government, laws, crimes, trespasses, contracts, and courts of justice" (Webster), 219, 221
"Of man" (Webster), 221
"Of numbers," 5, 37, 62
Of the, Titles beginning with these words are inverted to the first major word
Ogasawara, Chojiro, 134
Ogden, *see* Martin and Ogden
Old age, 364, 394
Old Dilworth (pseudonym, not Webster), 482
Old-fashioned Churchman (pseudonym, not Webster), 294, 363
"Old maid in the fidgets, an" (illustration), 284
Old South leaflets, 164, 270, 306, 354
Old spelling book, Webster's (Webster), 82
On a, on the, Titles beginning with these words are inverted to the first major word
Oram, James, 415
Oration, "On the extent . . ." (Bishop), 315
Oration pronounced before the citizens of New Haven . . . July 4th 1798 (Webster), 328
Oration pronounced before the citizens of New Haven . . . July, 1802 (Webster), 328–329
Oration pronounced before the Knox and Warren branches . . ., 329
"Orders of architecture" (Webster), 221
Oregon Printing Association, 129, 130
"Origin of Amherst College" (Webster), 353, 354
"Origin of mythology" (Webster), 432
"Origin of the copy-right laws" (Webster), 353
"Origin of the first bank in the U.S." (Webster), 352
"Origin of the Hartford convention" (Webster), 353
"Origin of the human race" (Webster), 210

"Origins of man, and of the Americans" (Webster), 199
Orme, *see* Longman, Hurst, Rees, and Orme
Ormsby, Robert McK., *566*
Orpheus (pseudonym, Webster), 393, 441
Orthography, 205, 221, 299, 337, 356, 360, 435, 457, 461, 462, 464, 468, 470, 471, 473, 479, 482, 567
Orthography, reformed, 201, 225, 267, 268, 312, 340, *535*; *see also* Alphabet, special; -our spelling
Osgood, David: *Wonderful works of God*, 312
Osler, Sir William, 347
Otway, Thomas, 162, 164
-our spelling, 142, 162, 165, 167, 457
"Outline of American history" (Webster), 7
Owen, Robert Dale, 473

P (pseudonym, probably Webster), 461
P.Q. (pseudonym, Webster), *446*
P., F. B., 380
Paddock, Willard D., *593*
Paine, Thomas, 162, 474; *Age of Reason*, 403
Paint, 432
Palmer, James W., *61*
Panoplist and Missionary Magazine, 293
Paper, 97, 115, 117, 166, 169, 268, 269, 275, 387, 396, 397, 410, 428; special, 60, 235; paper mill, 113
Paper money, 438, 439, 468, 535, 583
"Paper money, on" (Webster), 338
Parent, a (pseudonym, probably Webster), *476*
"Parental indulgence" (Webster), 283
"Parish" (word), 339
Parker, George, *591*, *595*
Parker, Jerusha (Mrs. Samuel), *592*
Parker, Samuel, 221
"Parliament" (word), 339
Parsons, Chester, and Co., 295
Parsons, *see* Brown and Parsons
Partch, Clarence E.: "Noah Webster," *363*
Party spirit/party government, 306, 399, 408, 424, 440, 461, 462, 465, 473, 474
Passive mood, 142
"Patriot, the" (Webster), 445, *446*
Patriotic association, 457
Patten, Nathaniel, *544*
Patterson, ——, 108
Patterson, J., *368*
Peabody and Daniell, 84
Peace and Justice (pseudonym, Webster), 458
Peck, J., 191
Peck, *see* Durrie and Peck; Smith and Peck
Peculiar doctrines of the gospel (Webster), 293–296, 457, *559*
"Peer" (word), 445
"Pendulum without a bob, a" (Webster), 272
Penniman, *see* Thomas, Andrews, and Penniman
Pennsylvania, Hospital, 533; Superintendent of Common Schools, 508, 509; University of, 8, 532, *535*
Pennsylvanian, a (pseudonym, not Webster), 486, 487
Pentateuch, 207
Percival, James G., 234, 235
Percival, Thomas, 375
Percy, Thomas, 270
Perkins, Benjamin D., 457
Perkins, Jacob, 81
Perkins, Nathan, 473
Perry, Elizabeth Webster, *555*
Perry, William: *Royal standard English dictionary*, 7
Personal abuse/scurrilous language, 399, 412, 424, 448, 449, 490, 498, 499, 573, 593
Petersburg, Va., W. lectures in (?), *532*
Petter and Galpin, 573
Pew, R., and Co., 288
Phelps, Eliakim, *554*
Philadelphia, 338, 390, 495; Academy of Medicine, 416
Phillips, Ambrose, 164
Phillips, William, 108
Philo-Barruel (pseudonym, Webster?), 450
Philodilworth (pseudonym, not Webster), 485

Philo Prompter (pseudonym, not Webster), 288
Philological Society (New York), 392, 521–522, 536
Philology, 353, 360, 461, 476, 479, 480, 481
"Philology" (Webster), 463, 468
Philomathes (pseudonym, not Webster), 142, 438
Philosophical and practical grammar (Webster), 141, 151–153, 154, 159, 221, 233, 234, 235, 240, 242
Phinney, Elihu, 194
Phinney, Henry and Elihu, 56
"Photography" (word), 479
Physicians of Philadelphia. . . . Circular, To the (Webster), 373, 407, 448
Pickering, John: *Vocabulary*, 297
Pickering, Timothy, 22, 23, 135, 136, 268, 269, 274, 297, 340, 449, 533, 534, 542, 543, 545, 546, 547, 548, 549, 551, 559, 577
Picket, Albert and John W., 101
Pickpenny, Peter (pseudonym, Webster), 390
"Pictorial edition," 128, 260
Pierce, Charles, 39, 45
Pierpont, John: reader, 261
Pike, Nicholas: *New and complete system of arithmetic*, reviewed, 392
Pinckney, Charles, 418
Pindar, Roger (pseudonym, not Webster), 274
"Piracy" (Webster), 199, 210
Pirates, 399
Pirates, The (anon.), 285–286
Pittachus (pseudonym, not Webster), 496
Place names, correct orthography of, 11
Plagiarism, 7, 299, 390, 399, 418, 477, 565
Plague, *see* Epidemics
"Plague of wealth" (anon.), 286, 287
Plain and comprehensive grammar (Webster), 145, 157
Plain Dealing (pseudonym, not Webster), 528
Plain Man, a (pseudonym, not Webster), 314
Plain, Timothy (pseudonym, not Webster), 313
"Plan, addressed to Francis Freeling" (anon.), 286, 287
"Plan of policy" (Webster), 305
Plaskitt and Co., 137
Platt, Jonas, 551
Platt, Richard, 521
Plea for a miserable world, 331
Pocket dictionary (W. G. Webster), 262, 263
Poems by Noah Webster, 363
Poetry by Webster, 37, 335–336, 363, 368, 390, 391, 392, 395, 436, 438, 440 (not Webster's, 285, 577)
Poland, partition of, 403
"Political and ecclesiastical affairs, commerce, arts, customs, education" (Webster), 199
"Political balance, the" (anon.), 562
"Political economy" (Webster), 283
"Political events" (Webster), 210
Political parties, 353, 539; *see also* Party spirit
Political progress of Britain (Callender), 563
Polok, Moses, 285
Pond, E., 475
Pope, Alexander, 164, 165
Poplicola (pseudonym, Webster), 439
Poplicola (pseudonym, not Webster), 514
"Popular delusion" (Webster), 283
"Popular discontent" (Webster), 283
Population of the United States, 427, 476
Porcupine, Peter (pseudonym), *see* William Cobbett
"Porcupine portrait," 15, 32, 146, 179, 185, 588
Porcupine's Gazette, 421
"Porpoises of Connecticut," 579
Porter, Robert, 55
Porter, *see* Holbrook, Fessenden, and Porter; Hoyt, Porter and Co.
Portius (pseudonym, Webster), 401
Portland, Me., W. lectures in, 538
Portraits of Webster, Appendix I; *see also* Morse Portrait, "porcupine portrait"

Portsmouth, N.H., W. lectures in, 534
Post office, mails, 410, 419; W. as special agent, 577
Postage Paid (pseudonym, not Webster), 505
Potatoes, 330, 430, 453
Power, 532; abuse of, 409, 413
"Practicability of well amusing the latter years of life" (Webster?), 394
"Practical and philosophical grammar," *see Philosophical and practical grammar*
Practice of putting into the hands . . . (Webster), 219
Pratt, Smith, and Lesson, 284
"Prayer before sailing to Europe" (Webster), 363, 561
Prayers composed by Webster, 561
"Precepts concerning the social relations" (Webster), 37
Prefixes and affixes, 218, 221
"Prejudice" (Webster), 283
Prentiss, Charles, 278, 279
Prentiss, John, 566
"Present condition of the several states" (Webster), 203
President of United States, method of nomination, 582; *see also* names of individual presidents
Press, *see* Newspapers
Price, Richard: *Observations*, 305
"Price" (Webster), 283
Prichard and Hall, 308
Priestley, Joseph, 313, 346; *Letters to the inhabitants of Northumberland*, 313
Primary reader, 572
Primers, 135–139; *see also* New England primer
Princeton, 8, 152, 231, 533
"Principles of government and commerce" (Webster), 158, 192, 337, 389
Private Citizen (pseudonym, Webster), 309, 443
Prizes, Webster's books as, 169, 459
Probus (pseudonym, Webster), 471, 475
Prompter, The (Webster), 271–290, 414, 444, 445
Prompter, a series of essays (anon.), 288
Pronunciation, 299, 360, 463, 468, 480; teaching of, 360, 436
"Property" (Webster), 221
Proposal for publishing . . . (Webster?), 348–349
"Proposals for . . . *American Minerva*" (Webster), 398, 399
"Prosody" (Trumbull), 141, 144, 152, 221
Providence, R.I., W. lectures in, 535
Prudens (pseudonym, probably not Webster), 347, 465
Pryor and Whiteman, 121
"Public, To the. A request" (Webster), 346
Public, To the. It is a subject (Webster), 402
Public, To the. Lyman Cobb has lately . . . (Webster), 357–358
"Public good is direct common sense" (anon.), 287
Public Spirit (pseudonym, Webster), 456
Publisher, Webster as own, 23, 26, 142, 149, 167, 208, 269, 275, 277, 340, 346, 372, 379, 381, 471
Punctilio, Peter (pseudonym, Webster), 393
"Punctuation" (Lowth), 141
"Punctuation" (Webster), 221
Purdy, *see* Harrisson and Purdy
Puzzle, Peter (pseudonym, Webster), 446

Quarantine, *see* Epidemics; Yellow fever
"Queen Mab" (Shakespeare), 162
Querist (pseudonym, Webster), 476
"Question whether Moses was the writer . . ." (Webster), 207
Quincy, Josiah, 551

R (pseudonym, not Webster), 488
Rabaut Saint-Etienne, Jean Paul: *History of the Revolution in France*, 491
"Rags! rags!" (Webster), 276, 279, 446
"Raising potatoes, on" (Webster), 430
Ramsay, ——, 375
Ramsay, David, 292
Ramsay, Armour and Co., 126, 127

Ramsay and M'Kendrick, 127
Read, *see* Bradford and Read
Read and Morse, 313, 315
Real American, a (pseudonym, perhaps Webster), 499
Real Friend to Republicanism (pseudonym, Webster), 401
"Reasons for removing Williams College to Amherst" (Webster?), 528
Recommendations, 5, 6, 225, 232, 355; W.'s recommendations: for books by others, 446, 450, 465; for schools, 458, 462; for other things, 460, 477
Red book: practical orthography (Bearcroft), 235
Redfield, J.S., 106, 110, 113, 114, 115, 116, 117, 118, 119, 120, 124, 125, 221, 380
Redfield and Lindsay, 103, 104, 214, 215, 216, 219
Redfield and Savage, 123, 124, 125, 128, 221, 260
"Redress of grievances, on" (Webster), 338
Reed, Abner, 29
Rees, *see* Longman, Hurst, Rees, and Orme
Reeve, Tapping, 484
"Reflections on closing the author's literary labors" (Webster), 221
"Reform of spelling, on a" (Webster), 158
"Register" (of state papers), 396, 404
"Register of the times" (proposed publication, Webster), 404
"Regularity of the city of Philadelphia, on the" (Webster), 338
Regulator (pseudonym, not Webster), 492
Reich, Gottfried C., 376
Reid, J., 390
Relief, 446
Religion/theology, 390, 443
Remarks on a pamphlet entituled "A dissertation" (Sherman?), 562
"Remarks on certain causes of disease in large cities" (Webster), 375
"Remarks on cleanliness and ventilation," *see* "Remarks on certain causes of diseases"
"Remarks on Gibbon's style" (Webster), 393
"Remarks on government, manners, and debt" (Webster), 164, 388, 441
"Remarks on Mr. Webster's calculations" (Mellen), 430
"Remarks on the connection between catarrh and malignant fevers" (Webster), 452
"Remarks on the history of . . . Hartford" (Webster), 430
"Remarks on the late meteor" (Webster), 395
"Remarks on the manners, government, laws, and domestic debt" (Webster), *see* "Remarks on government"
"Remarks on the method of burying the dead" (Webster), 338
"Remonstrance of the merchants of New Haven" (Webster?), 522
Rensselaer Book Store, 42
Renunciation of Unitarianism (anon.), 294
"Reply to a letter of David McClure" (Webster), 353
Reply to Lucius Junius Brutus (anon.), 523
"Reply to Mr. Mellen's remarks" (Webster), 430
Republican clubs/societies, 321, 406; rallies, 452; "Republican" as party name, 462
"Respecting accuracy in speaking and writing" (Webster), 207
Respondent (pseudonym, not Webster), 435
Retired Citizen, a (pseudonym, not Webster), 490
Revere, Paul, 15, 588
Reviewer, the (pseudonym, Webster?), 442
"Revolt and division of empire," *see* "Counsels of old men despised"
Revolution in France considered (Webster), 311–312, 352, 402, 403, 404, 409
Reynolds, ——, 375
Reynolds, Sackett, 108
"Rhapsody" (trans. Webster?), 391

"Rhetoric, composition, style" (Webster), 221
Rice, C., 95
Richardson, Charles: dictionary, 301, 468, 472
Richardson and Lord, 66, 86, 87, 93, 126; *see also* West and Richardson; West, Richardson, and Lord
Richardson, Lord, and Holbrook, 88, 90, 245
Richmond, Va., W. lectures in, 532
"Rights of neutrals," *see* "Essay on the rights . . ."
Riley, Isaac, 159
Ritter's patent metallic paste and strap, 460
"Rivers of the United States" (Webster), 199
Roads, 419, 446
Robb and Stephenson, 121
Robbins, Asher, 306
Robbins, Thomas, 216, 220
Roberts, William, 590
Robinson, D. F., and Co., 137, 245
Robinson, G. G. and J., 348
Roby, Luther, 122, 125
Roby and Co., 112
Roby, Kimball, and Merrill, 104, 107, 108, 110, 113, 118
Roby, *see also* Cofnin and Roby
Rod for the fool's back (Webster), 314–315
Rod for the fool's back, or an examination (anon.), 314
Rogers, John, martyrdom of, 368
Roorbach, O. A., 137
"Rose, the" (Webster), 37
Rosenbach, A. S. W., 285
Rousseau, Jean Jacques: *Social contract*, 306
Rowe, Nicholas, 164
Royall, Anne, 586–587
Rudiments of English grammar (Webster), 22, 158–160, 191, 192, 193, 270; *see also Little reader's assistant*
"Rules for behavior" (Chesterfield), 164
"Rules for genteel behavior" (Webster), 393
"Rules of logic" (Webster), 221
"Rules of orthography" (Webster), 221
Rules of punctuation from Webster's dictionary, 235
Rush, Benjamin, 328, 346, 348, 373, 374, 388, 416, 543, 547, 548, 549; *Account of the bilious fever*, reviewed, 404
Russell, John, 450
Russell, *see* Haswell and Russell
Rutledge (pseudonym, Webster), 513

S (pseudonym, not Webster), 516
S., I., *see* Sanford, Isaac
S. Converse proposes to publish . . ., 249
Salem, Mass., W. lectures in, 534
Sanborn, O. L., 108, 110, 112
Sanborn and Carter, 112, 124, 126
Sanborn, Sherburne and Co., 119
Sanctius, 157
Sandbornton Power Press, 81, 82
Sanders, Charles W.: speller, 474, 476, 477
Sanderson, E., 252, 253, 254, 255, 257
Sands, Robert C., 358, 359
Sanford, Isaac, 11, 14, 16, 20
Sanford and Co./Sanford and Lott, 103, 106, 112, 113, 117, 119, 122
Sanxay, *see* Morgan and Sanxay
Savage, Charles C., 128; *see also* Huntington and Savage; Redfield and Savage
Savage, James, 152, 228
Sawyer, William, and Co., 45, 47
"Saxons" (Webster), 210
Saybrook, Conn., information about, 343
Schoff, Stephen A., 590
Scholey, R., 284
Schoolmaster, a (pseudonym, not Webster), 502
Schoolmaster and pupils (illustration), 569
Schools, Webster's: Sharon, Conn., 434, 435; Hartford, 436, 437; Baltimore, 438; *see also* Episcopal Academy, Philadelphia; New Township Academy; Union School
Scipio (pseudonym, Webster), 400
Scofield, P., 567

Scott, Joseph, 418
Scrive, Johnny (pseudonym, perhaps Webster), 495
Scudder, Horace, 350
Scurrilous language, *see* Personal abuse
Seager, ——, 592
Seaman, Valentine, 374
Sears, E., 590
Sedgwick, Theodore, 546
Seduction, 444
"Self-tormenting" (Hooker), 164
Seneca (pseudonym, Webster), 473
Senex (pseudonym, Webster), 460, 477, 478
Senex (pseudonym, not Webster), 101, 466, 490
Sentimental and humorous essays (Webster), 280, 281
Sequel to . . . Elementary spelling book, 128, 135, 261
"Series of books," 244, 245
Series of books for systematic instruction (Webster), 356–357
Serious considerations on the election of a president (Linn), reviewed, 425
Sermon delivered [at the laying of the corner stone of . . . Amherst] (Clark), 331
Seth (pseudonym, not Webster), 487, 488, 489
1781. *Yorktown. Letter from Noah Webster to George Washington*, 362
'76 (pseudonym, Webster), 469
Seventy-Six (pseudonym, not Webster), 584
Seward, Asahel, 40, 41, 43, 49, 50, 51, 52, 187, 188
Seward and Williams, 44, 46, 54, 56, 188, 189, 190
Sexes, relations between, 391
Seymour, J., 293, 294
Shakers, 235
Shakespeare, 162, 164, 165, 310
Sharon, Conn., 391, 434, 435
Sharples, James, 588–589
Sharpless, *see* Kimber and Sharpless
Shattuck, Lemuel, 153, 162, 206, 464, 554
Shaw, William S., 552
"She carries the bell" (Webster), 272
Sheffield, *see* White and Sheffield
Sheffield, Mass., yellow fever in, 374–375
Shepard, Thomas W., and Co., 330
Sherburne, Robert H./Sherburne and Co., 74, 84, 85, 112, 120, 125
Sheridan, Thomas: dictionary, 7
Sherman, George, 295
Sherman, Roger, 562
Sherwood, Neely and Jones, 287
"Shilling" (word), 467
Shipman, Elias, 522
Shipping, 399, 413, 456
Shisui, Yoyu, 134
Shores, J. F., 54
"Short view of the origin and progress of . . . natural philosophy" (Webster), 444
Shorter Catechism, 368
Shoundo Kappan-sho, 135
Sidney (pseudonym, Webster), 323, 456, 469, 472, 510–516
Sidney's Press, 185, 202, 203, 204, 227, 229
"Sign of the Bible," 61
Sigourney, Lydia, 595
Silliman, Benjamin, 153, 249, 480, 550; *Journal of Science*, 461
Sir: Titles beginning with this word are entered under the first major word
Skeel, Emily Ellsworth Ford, 362
' Sketch of the history of banks" (Webster), 319
"Sketch of the history of the late war" (Webster), 164
Sketch of the rise and progress of the yellow fever (Currie), 347
Sketches of American policy (Webster), 305–307
Sketches of history, life and manners (Royall), 586
"Sketches of the history and progress of commerce" (Webster), 399
"Sketches of the rise, progress and consequences of the late revolution" (Webster), 338
Skillman, Thomas T., 285
Skin, fever remedies, 453

Skinner, E. W. and C., 80
Skinner, *see* Hudson and Skinner; Webster(s) and Skinner(s)
Slander, *see* Personal abuse
Slaves and slavery/slave labor, 162, 310, 395, 403, 522, 533; *see also* Abolition
Smead, Solomon, 552
Smith, Cotton M., 391
Smith, Elihu H., 374, 376
Smith, John: *History of Virginia*, 389
Smith, Juliana, 434
Smith, S. Sam, 524
Smith, Samuel S. (president of Princeton), 154
Smith, *see also* Morton and Smith; Pratt, Smith, and Lesson
Smith and Harrington, 94, 98, 99
Smith and Peck, 352
Sober sense (pseudonym, Webster), 468
Society for the promotion of agriculture, arts, and manufactures (Albany), 430, 431
"Solar system" (Webster), 199, 218, 220; illustration of, 218, 220
Solon (pseudonym, Webster), 465, 467
Southgate, ——, 463
Soyaku Tsuzuriji-sho, 134
Spafford, Oliver, 112, 118
Spalding, *see* Howe and Spalding
Sparks, Jared, 587
Spear, *see* Cramer, Spear, and Eichbaum
"Specimen of definition, a" (Webster), 221
"Specimens of emendations of language in this edition of the New Testament" (Webster), 380
"Spectator" (Addison), 171
Spectator (pseudonym, Webster), 468
Spectator (newspaper), 414–429; policies, 415
Spector, Benjamin, 363
Speculation, 471, 478, 535
Speed, American passion for, 474
Spellers, discussed, 438, 461, 475, 476, 478, 479, 500–509, 560
Spelling, *see* Orthography
Spelling book of the English language (Marshall), 567
Spiers, Alexander: dictionary, 262
Spofford, Horatio M., 595
Sports, brutal, denounced, 330; *see also* Exercise
Spotswood, William, 388
Springfield, Mass., W. attends meeting at, 538
Squib (pseudonym, not Webster), 494
Stable Republican, a (pseudonym, Webster), 399
Stag (illustration), 85
"Stanzas from Addison's Hymn to gratitude," 219
Stark (pseudonym, Webster), 461
State governments, abolition of, 426
"State of English philology" (Webster), 353, 360
Statistics, 343, 345, 346, 418, 423, 424, 425, 427, 430, 431, 450, 476, 578
"Staves" (word), 463
Steady habits (pseudonym, not Webster), 457
Steamboat, invention of, 474, 479
Steele, Oliver (and Co.), 152, 205, 411
Steele, Oliver G., 92, 96, 137, 245
Steele and Faxon, 93, 137, 245
Stephens and Garwood, 115–116
Stephenson, *see* Robb and Stephenson
Stereotyping/stereotype plates, 53, 70, 74, 78, 82, 83, 87, 89, 93, 96, 98, 99, 100, 104, 105, 114, 117, 119, 120, 121, 122, 126, 135, 137, 138, 212, 213, 215, 216, 221
Stiles, Ezra, 6, 7, 19, 340, 389, 393, 396
Stiles, Thomas T., 189, 190
"Stitch in time saves nine, a" (Webster), 272, 290
Stock, J. E., 294
Stockton, *see* Johnston and Stockton
Stockwell, William, and Co., 315
Stockwell, *see* Wright, Goodenow, and Stockwell
Stoddard, Ashbel, 369, 370, 390
"Stolen waters are sweet" (Webster), 276, 280, 281, 283, 287, 289, 447
Stone, William L., 510, 513, 514, 516
"Story and speech of Logan, a Mingo chief," *see* "Logan's speech"
"Story of La Roche" (McKenzie?), 162

"Story of Sir Edward and Louisa" (McKenzie?), 162
Stranger's apology (N. Worcester?), 563
Stranger's monitor (ghost), 563
Street names, change of monarchical, 401
Stricken (pseudonym, Webster), 400
"Stricken"/"struck" (word), 400
"Strictures on an article in the Christian Observer" (Webster), 458
Strong, Lewis, 527
Stuart, Moses, 235, 293, 378, 475
Students' Typographical Association of Lane Seminary, 97, 572
Study, excessive, 444
Subjunctive mood, 270, 280, 291, 474
Subscriber (pseudonym, possibly Webster), 394
Subscribers have been appointed, the, 526
Suffrage, 472, 474, 579
Sun, 452
Sunday school, 529, 539
"Supplement to an American dictionary," 239
"Supplement to the Elementary spelling book," *see Teacher*
"Supposed change in the temperature of winter, on the" (Webster), 352
Swift, Jonathan, 162
Swords, T. and J., 33
Syllabification, 7, 8
Syllabus of Mr. Webster's lectures, 327
Symonds, H. D., 280
Synonyms, dictionary of, 454
"Synopsis of radical words" (Webster; unpublished), 559

T (pseudonym, not Webster), 505
Tacitus, 267
"Take time by the forelock," *see* " 'Carpe diem' . . ."
Tappan, Charles, 45
Tappan and Dennett, 352
Tappan and Foster, 54
Taxes, 309, 399, 418, 437, 439; tax riots, 404; single tax, 445
Taylor, ——, 375
Taylor, John O.: *The district school*, reviewed, 466
Taylor, Nathaniel W., 595
Taylor, Richard, 241, 242, 243
Teacher (pseudonym, probably Webster), 508
Teacher, The (Webster), 135, 191, 218–219, 220, 221
Teacher and pupils in classical garb (illustration), 103
"Tell me a story" (Webster), 283, 289
Temperature, *see* Climate; Winter
Ten letters to Dr. Joseph Priestly (Webster), 313, 425
Terhune, John, 108, 112, 114, 123
Terhune and Letson, 74, 75, 77, 88, 91, 92, 98, 103, 108
Terry, Nathaniel, 329
Test laws, 338, 439
"Test laws, oaths of allegiance and abjuration, and partial exclusion from office, on" (Webster), 338
Testimonials, *see* Recommendations
"Teutonic and Gothic nations" (Webster), 210
Thayer, John: *Account of the conversion of*, reviewed, 394
Theater, denounced, 330
"Theological remarks" (Webster), 390
"Theory of government" (Webster), 305
"Theory of vegetation, on the" (Webster), 430
"This day published," 14–15
Thomas, Ebenezer S., 556
Thomas, Isaiah (as individual), 35, 142, 171, 268, 269, 275, 371, 397
Thomas [Isaiah, bookstore in Worcester], 25, 34, 145, 170, 175, 178, 369
Thomas, Isaiah, and Co., 267
Thomas and Andrews, 8, 11, 15, 17, 18, 20, 21, 22, 23, 24, 25, 26, 27, 28, 29, 30, 31, 32, 34, 35, 39, 45, 145, 146, 147, 148, 149, 150, 151, 166, 169, 170, 171, 172, 174, 175, 177, 178, 179, 180, 181, 183, 184, 185, 187, 271, 273, 275, 277, 279, 337, 588
Thomas, Andrews, and Butler, 25, 148, 175, 178
Thomas, Andrews, and Penniman, 25, 32, 148, 175, 178
Thomas, Cowperthwait and Co., 108, 237

Thomas, Son, and Thomas, 175, 178
Thomas and Thomas, 42
Thomas and Whipple, 39, 45
Thompson, William J., 555
Thomson, James, 164
Thoughtful, Tom (pseudonym, Webster), 439
"Thoughts on the domestic debt . . ." (Webster), 486
Thoughts on the political situation (anon.), reviewed, 395
Three letters to Abraham Bishop (Dagget?), 563
"Tickler, the" (Webster), 414
Tilford, *see* Maccoun, Tilford and Co.
Timothy, Ann, 390, 395
"Titus Manlius," Hamilton called, 451
To the: Titles which begin with these words are inverted to the next word
"To those who write, and those who teach, the English language" (Webster), 299
Tobacco, 400
Tom the Tinker (pseudonym, not Webster), 232
Tooke, John Horne: *Diversions of Purley*, 152
Toon, J. J., and Co., 130, 131
"Topographical description of Hartford" (Webster), 430
Tornado, 477
Towar and Hogan, 137, 245
Town, Salem, 476, 480; *Analysis*, 301, 470
Trade, *see* Commerce and industry; Shipping
Trade sales and auctions, 78, 80, 278
Trade unions, 468
Translation/translator, 391, 402, 403, 405; *see also* Bible, errors in
"Traveler" (word), 474
Treadway, *see* Baldwin and Treadway
Treaties with France, Great Britain, 494
Treaty of amity . . . 1795, *see* Jay treaty
Triphook, *see* Knight and Triphook
Triumph of Infidelity, *see* Dwight, Timothy
Trumbull (pseudonym, Webster), 473
Trumbull, Benjamin: *History of Connecticut*, 350
Trumbull, John, 6, 141, 144, 152, 162, 309, 522
Trumbull, Jonathan, 437
Trustees of Amherst Academy, Sir, the (Webster), 527
Truth (pseudonym, not Webster), 488
Tuckniss, Henry, 494
Twining, Stephen, 549
Two epistles of free stricture (Judson), 235
"Two industrious girls in Poughkeepsie, of the" (Webster), 368
Type, 37, 41, 275, 405; standing, 12, 15, 151; special, 235
Tytler, James, 346

Undeniable Truth (pseudonym, Webster), 476
"Underlip, the" (Webster), 272
Union, preservation of, *see* Federal government
Union school (New Haven), 458
United States history, textbooks, 478; *see also History of the United States*
Unknown, the (pseudonym, Webster), 513
Unpublished writings, Appendix D
Usury, 339, 406, 422; interest, 418

Vail, Robert W. G., 26
Value of the Bible (Webster), 298
Van Buren, Martin, 306, 515
Van Ness, William P., 563
Van Norden, James, 256
Van Rensselaer, Stephen, 552
Van Vleet, A., 568
"Vegetable productions" (Webster), 203, 211
Verax (pseudonym, Webster), 474
Verity (pseudonym, Webster), 463
Vermilye, William W., Jr., 33, 185
"Verses on the new year" (Webster), 390
Verstille, William, 588
Verus (pseudonym, Webster), 464
Viator (pseudonym, Webster), 446
"View of the U(nited) S(tates) capitol" (illustration), 209, 210, 211
"Vindication of the treaty of amity," 353

Vindication of the Vice President (Van Ness), 563
Virginia, *see* Harrington
"Virtuous, the" (anon.), 172
"Vision of Columbus" (Barlow), 162, 164
Vocabulary, or collection of words and phrases (Pickering), 297
"Vocal music, on" (Webster), 339, 441
Voice of Wisdom (Webster), 323, 472–473, 510–516
Volney, Constantin, 546
Vox Populi Americani (pseudonym, not Webster), 412
"Vulgar error, a" (anon.), 274

W (initial or pseudonym, Webster), 409, 410, 442, 455, 458, 462, 463, 471, 475, 481
W. X. (pseudonym, not Webster), 489
W., C. C., 157
Waddington, E., 449, 548
Wadsworth, S., 154
Wadsworth, William, 27
Waite, G. and R., 36, 181, 182, 183
Walker, John, 249–255
Wallin, Samuel, 590
Wallingford, Conn., 328
Walpole, N. H., data on newspapers in, 344
Walter, Joel, 282, 321
Walter and Steele, 205, 206
Walton, E. P. and Son(s), 110, 112, 113, 119, 122, 127
Walton and Co., 108
War, denounced, 330
War of 1812, 458; *see also* Embargo
"War of the dictionaries," 225
"War of the Revolution" (Webster), 210
Ward, Nahum, 470
Ward, *see* Bemis and Ward
Ward and Lock/Ward, Lock and Co., 195, 573, 574
Warfel, Harry R., 214, 263, 269, 306, 335, 363, 427
Warfel, Ruth Farquhar, 363
Warner, *see* Johnson and Warner
Washington, George, 6, 269, 305, 306, 307, 308, 337, 338, 341, 352, 362, 496, 522, 541, 544, 546; death, 424, 426; Farewell Address, 203, 211; projected biography, 559
Washington, George, portrait, 11, 12, 16, 19, 131, 165, 209
Washington, D.C., 419, 445; W. lectures in, 537
Washington Benevolent Society, 329
Water, flow of, 479
Waterbury, Conn., 438
Watson, James, 398
Watts (pseudonym, Webster), 478
"Way to wealth" (Franklin), 164, 284, 286, 287, 289
Webb, Joseph D., 411, 412, 413; *see also* Hopkins, Webb and Co.
Webster, Charles, 553
Webster, Charles R. and George, 21, 28, 32, 36, 38, 39, 47, 48, 49, 148, 149, 150, 159, 167, 169, 172, 173, 174, 177, 180, 182, 184, 187, 273, 281
Webster, Daniel, 322, 353, 379, 468, 515, 554, 555, 556, 563
Webster, Eliza S., 553
Webster, Harriet, *see* Fowler, Harriet W. Cobb
Webster, John W., 557
Webster, Louisa, 381
Webster, Noah, Sr., 388
Webster, Peletiah, 486, 562
Webster, Rebecca Greenleaf, 543, 553, 554, 557; marriage, 442; portrait, 589, 592
Webster, William G., 80, 89, 95, 98, 101, 102, 103, 104, 105, 106, 111, 213, 214, 215, 216, 235, 238, 248, 260, 263, 289, 347, 350, 359, 361, 465, 506–507, 516–517, 537, 555, 556, 573, 591
Webster, Burgess, and Morgan, 102, 214
Webster and Clark, 156, 352
Webster(s) and Skinner(s), 41, 43, 50, 54, 59, 60, 62, 63, 87, 92, 96, 151, 203, 245
Webster elementary reader, 195
Webster genealogy (Webster), 350–351
"Webster improved" (Marshall), 567

Index

"Webster's Donation," 169
"Webster's first book," 139
Webster's old spelling book, 82
"Webster's political essays," 562
Weights and measures, 218, 263; *see also* Metric system
West, David, 45, 47, 229
West, John (and Co.), 35, 36, 39, 40, 42, 43, 44, 45, 47, 48, 49, 50, 53, 229, 550, 551
West, John T., and Co., 136
West, W., 281
West (firm), 281
West and Blake, 47
West and Greenleaf, 39
West and Richardson, 51, 54, 56, 57, 297
West, Richardson, and Lord, 59, 60, 62, 63, 64
West Hartford, Conn., 477
West Indies, 447
Westcott, J. and J. D., 282
Western primer (anon.), 570–571, 572
Western spelling book (Kelley), 569
Western spelling book (Webster-Guilford), 568–570
"West's edition," *see* John West and Co.; West and Richardson
"What is everybody's business is nobody's business" (Webster), 272
"When a man is going downhill, every one gives him a kick" (Webster), 272, 286
"When a man's name is up, he may lay (lie) abed till noon" (Webster), 272
"Whether the universal diffusion . . ." (Webster), *see* "Dissertation in English . . ."
Whig of '76, a (pseudonym, Webster), 465
Whig party, 472; *see also* Voice of wisdom
Whig Young Men's Committee (New York), 512, 515
Whipple, *see* Thomas and Whipple
"Whistle, the" (Franklin), 189, 195, 273, 274
White, E. and J., 61, 63, 64, 65, 66, 67, 68, 71, 72, 75
White, Elihu, 62, 63, 64, 66, 67, 68, 69, 70, 89
White, [Fortune C.?], 515
White, Henry, 239, 262, 263
White, Ira, 84, 100, 101, 107, 108, 110, 111, 112, 115, 120
White, N. and J. (firm), 77, 79, 80, 92, 94, 95, 96, 97, 98, 99, 100–101, 102, 104, 110, 111, 113, 211, 246, 247, 248, 252, 253, 254, 256, 257, 358, 377, 379, 506, 507
White, Norman (individual), 89, 111, 379
White, Roswell N., 214
White, T. M., 54, 57, 297
White, Gallaher, and White, 89, 91, 92, 137, 154, 245, 246, 251
White and Homan, 95, 101
White and Sheffield, 253, 254, 255
White and Wilcox, 92, 98
Whiteman, *see* Pryor and Whiteman
White's, E., Type and Stereotype Found(e)ry, 245, 246, 247, 248
Whiting, I.N./Whiting and Huntington, 106, 112, 117, 125, 217, 245, 571
Whiting, Samuel, 294; *see also* Williams and Whiting
Whitmore and Minor, 79
Whitridge, ——, 290
Wilberforce (pseudonym, Webster), 467
Wilcox, ——, 92
Wilcox, John, 137, 138, 288, 289, 290
Wilcox, William, 401
Wilcox, Dickerman and Co., 95, 100, 211, 212
Willard, Asaph, 590
Willard, Emma, 460
Willard, Sidney, 297
Williams, —— 527
Williams, Henry B.: *Academy for grown horsemen*, reviewed, 391
Williams, James, 121
Williams, Samuel, 546
Williams, Thomas S.: German-English dictionary, 262
Williams, William, 57, 188
Williams and Whiting, 294
Williams College, 231, 460, 528, 560

Williamsburg, Va., W. lectures in, 532
Williamson, William D., 556
Wilmington, Del., W. lectures in, 532
Wilson, James, 36
Wilson, Robert, 149
Wimble, William (pseudonym, Webster?), 440
Winter, 352, 431, 454, 462, 466, 468, 469
Winthrop, John, 340, 371–372, 396, 442
Wirt, William, 191, 464
"Wisdom and benevolence of God" (Webster), 218
With a view to collect authentic facts . . . (Webster), 343–344
"With the latest corrections," 58
Wolcott, Oliver, 402, 427, 496, 497, 540, 545, 546, 549, 550, 551
Women, education of, 389, 394, 435, 443, 460, 478; in factories, 470
Wonderful works of God (Osgood), 312
Wood, R. and G., 98
Woodbury convention, 473
Woodfall, G., 348
Woods, John, 183, 275, 276
Wool, 330
Worcester, Joseph E., 199, 249, 299; dictionary, 509–510; *see also American dictionary*, abridged by Worcester
Worcester, Noah, 562, 563
Worcester, Samuel: *Christian psalmody*, reviewed, 459
Worcester Palladium (newspaper), 475
"Word to an old fashioned churchman" (Webster), 294, 363, 559
Word usage, 471, 480, 538
Workmen's compensation, 410, 447
Worsley, W. W., 65, 67, 68, 69, 70, 76, 569
Worsley and Collins, 65
Wounds of a Friend, the (pseudonym, not Webster), 292
Wright, Fanny, 473
Wright, Goodenow, and Stockwell, 42, 45
Wyllys, Samuel, 522
Wyncoop (Wynkoop), Benjamin, 416, 418
Wyoming valley, 438, 480

X (pseudonym, probably Webster), 476
X. Y. Z. (pseudonym, not Webster), 503
Xenophon, 308

Y (pseudonym, not Webster), 489, 490
Yale College/University, 6, 145, 231, 269, 327, 356, 364, 433, 434, 444, 461, 477, 507, 587, 593
"Yankee" (word), 458
Yellow fever, 345, 373–376, 408, 410, 415, 416, 418, 422, 423, 428, 451, 454, 495; *see also* Epidemics; Fever
Yorktown, Battle of, 341, 362
Young, Arthur: *Tour of Ireland*, 400
Young, L. H., 348–349
Young, William, 11, 12, 13, 16, 144, 145, 156, 157, 166, 388, 442, 543, 544
Young, *see* Black, Young, and Young
Young and M'Culloch, 10, 143, 163, 166, 367, 390
Young Bachelor, a (pseudonym, Webster), 394
Young Men's Institute, Hartford, 477
Younglove, Moses C., 117, 119, 122, 125
Youth and old age, Noah Webster on, 364
Youth of nineteen (pseudonym, Webster), 392

Z (pseudonym, Webster), 438
Z (pseudonym, probably Webster), 476
Z (pseudonym, not Webster), 443
Zimmermann, Johann Georg von: *Essay on national pride*, 417
Ziolkowski, Korczak, 593
Zoology, 203, 206, 211, 220

This book, A BIBLIOGRAPHY OF THE WRITINGS OF NOAH WEBSTER, *was completed in March, 1958. It was composed in Monotype Bell and printed by Clarke & Way, Inc. at The Thistle Press in New York. The collotype illustrations are by the Meriden Gravure Company; the paper specially made by the Worthy Paper Company; the binding executed by the Russell-Rutter Company. Designed by Bert Clarke.*

The edition is limited to 500 copies, of which this is No. 464 .

RENEWALS 691-4574
DATE DUE